One Hundred Major Modern Writers

ESSAYS FOR COMPOSITION

Robert Atwan
William Vesterman
Rutgers University

Bobbs-Merrill Educational Publishing
Indianapolis

Copyright © 1984 by The Bobbs-Merrill Company, Inc.

Printed in the United States of America

All rights reserved. No part of this book shall be reproduced or transmitted in any form or by any means, electronic or mechanical, including photocopying, recording, or by any information or retrieval system, without written permission from the Publisher:

The Bobbs-Merrill Company, Inc.
4300 West 62nd Street
Indianapolis, Indiana 46268

First Edition 1984
First Printing 1984
Acquisitions: James B. Smith
Developmental: Paul O'Connell
Copy Editing and Production: Vicki Pryor
Graphic Arts Coordination: Bob Reed
Cover Design: Gregg Butler
   Illustration by Jemerson
Design: L. Daniel Kirklin
Composition: Rogers Typesetting
Printing: R. R. Donnelley & Sons Company

Library of Congress Cataloging in Publication Data

Atwan, Robert.
   100 major modern writers.

   1. College readers. I. Vesterman, William, 1942–   . II. Title. III. Title: One hundred major modern writers.
PE1122.A82   1984   808'.0427   83-11775
ISBN 0-672-61602-5

Acknowledgments

Three photographs in "The Boston Photographs," reproduced by permission of Stanley Forman, Boston *Herald*, Pulitzer Prize, 1976.

Three illustrations in "A Biographical Homage to Mickey Mouse," reproduced here by permission of Walt Disney Productions. © Walt Disney Productions.

Two illustrations in "A Biographical Homage to Mickey Mouse," from *Studies in Animal and Human Behavior*, 1971, by Konrad Lorenz, reproduced here by permission of Konrad Lorenz.

(The Acknowledgments are continued after the "Disciplines and Themes" section.)

Contents

Rhetorical Tables of Contents   vii

Preface   xvii

James Agee	*Knoxville: Summer 1915*	1
Frederick Lewis Allen	*Main Street America–1900*	7
Roger Angell	*On the Ball*	11
Hannah Arendt	*Denmark and the Jews*	14
Michael Arlen	*Ode to Thanksgiving*	21
Isaac Asimov	*Pure and Impure: The Interplay of Science and Technology*	26
Russell Baker	*Little Red Riding Hood Revisited*	34
James Baldwin	*If Black English Isn't a Language, Then Tell Me, What Is?*	38
Jacques Barzun	*The Wasteland of American Education*	43
Simone de Beauvoir	*Knowing New York*	52
Bruno Bettelheim	*Joey, A Mechanical Boy*	56
Daniel Boorstin	*The Rhetoric of Democracy*	66
Jorge Luis Borges	*The Disinterested Killer Bill Harrigan*	78
Jacob Bronowski	*Likenesses*	84
Gwendolyn Brooks	*Dreams of a Black Christmas*	87
Nigel Calder	*The Comet Is Coming*	96
Rachel Carson	*The Changing Year*	101
Willa Cather	*Small-Town Life*	110
G. K. Chesterton	*On Sightseeing*	114
Robert Coles	*Children of Affluence*	119
Aaron Copland	*How We Listen to Music*	131
Guy Davenport	*Finding*	138

CONTENTS

Joan Didion	On the Mall	149
	On Keeping a Notebook	156
Annie Dillard	Mirages	164
W. E. B. DuBois	Jacob and Esau	169
René Dubos	Territoriality and Dominance	181
Ralph Ellison	Hidden Name and Complex Fate	188
Nora Ephron	The Boston Photographs	199
M. F. K. Fisher	Young Hunger	208
E. M. Forster	Racial Exercise	213
Sigmund Freud	The Relation of the Poet to Day-Dreaming	218
Erich Fromm	The Nature of Symbolic Language	228
Robert Frost	Education By Poetry	238
Northrup Frye	The Keys to Dreamland	250
Paul Fussell	The Boy Scout Handbook	261
Martin Gardner	The Harvard Man Who Put the Ease in Casey's Manner	268
William Golding	Thinking as a Hobby	277
Stephen Jay Gould	A Biographical Homage to Mickey Mouse	286
Graham Greene	The Revolver in the Corner Cupboard	298
S. I. Hayakawa	How Dictionaries Are Made	304
Lillian Hellman	The Fig Tree	308
Ernest Hemingway	The Clark's Fork Valley, Wyoming	312
Edward Hoagland	The Courage of Turtles	316
Langston Hughes	Salvation	324
Aldous Huxley	Selected Snobberies	328
Ada Louise Huxtable	Houston	333
William James	Habit	340
Elizabeth Janeway	Water	348
Randall Jarrell	The Taste of the Age	354
Sir James Jeans	Why the Sky Looks Blue	362
C. G. Jung	A Vision of Life After Death	365
Pauline Kael	Movies on Television	370
Rudyard Kipling	A Snake Farm	382
D. H. Lawrence	Rex	389
Helen Lawrenson	The Bulls of Pamplona vs. the Ivy League	398
C. S. Lewis	The Trouble with "X"...	407
Wyndham Lewis	The Secret of the Success of Charlie Chaplin	413

CONTENTS

Basil Liddell Hart	*William Tecumseh Sherman: The First Modern General*	417
Walter Lippmann	*The Indispensable Opposition*	425
Jack London	*The Carter and the Carpenter*	434
Norman Mailer	*Marilyn Monroe*	444
William Manchester	*How I Slew My First Man*	449
Mary McCarthy	*Catholic Education*	455
Marshall McLuhan	*Classroom Without Walls*	459
John McPhee	*The Search for Marvin Gardens*	463
Margaret Mead	*New Superstitions for Old*	476
H. L. Mencken	*Criminology*	482
Jessica Mitford	*On Embalming*	487
Ashley Montague	*Social Change and Human Change*	494
Samuel Eliot Morison	*History as a Literary Art*	501
John Muir	*Digging a Well*	512
Lewis Mumford	*Sport and the "Bitch-Goddess"*	516
Vladimir Nabokov	*Colored Hearing*	522
V. S. Naipaul	*The New Tehran*	527
José Ortega y Gasset	*Emotional Reality*	535
George Orwell	*Shooting an Elephant*	540
	A Hanging	548
	Politics and the English Language	553
Dorothy Parker	*Mrs. Post Enlarges on Etiquette*	566
S. J. Perelman	*Dental or Mental, I Say It's Spinach*	571
J. H. Plumb	*The Stars in Their Day*	576
Katherine Anne Porter	*The Future Is Now*	581
J. B. Priestly	*Block Thinking*	588
Lillian Ross	*The Vinyl Santa*	594
Bertrand Russell	*Education and Discipline*	598
Logan Pearsall Smith	*Words from the Sea*	605
Susan Sontag	*Science Fiction Films: The Imagination of Disaster*	609
Gay Talese	*Punks and Pushers*	614
Lewis Thomas	*Notes on Punctuation*	621
James Thurber	*University Days*	626
Barbara Tuchman	*This is the End of the World: The Black Death*	635
John Updike	*Crush Vs. Whip*	646
Evelyn Waugh	*Half in Love With Easeful Death*	650
H. G. Wells	*Ellis Island*	659
Eudora Welty	*A Sweet Devouring*	663
Paul West	*The VAB Beside the Sea*	670

Edith Wharton	*Henry James Asks Directions*	676
E. B. White	*Death of a Pig*	680
	The Essayist	690
Edmund Wilson	*The Problem of English*	693
Tom Wolfe	*The Right Stuff*	701
Virginia Woolf	*The Death of the Moth*	710
Richard Wright	*Innocence*	715

Disciplines and Themes 721

Rhetorical Tables of Contents

I. Illustration and Exemplification

Frederick Lewis Allen	Main Street America–1900	7
Michael Arlen	Ode to Thanksgiving	21
Isaac Asimov	Pure and Impure: The Interplay of Science and Technology	26
Simone de Beauvoir	Knowing New York	52
Daniel Boorstin	The Rhetoric of Democracy	66
Robert Coles	Children of Affluence	119
Joan Didion	On Keeping a Notebook	156
W. E. B. DuBois	Jacob and Esau	169
Nora Ephron	The Boston Photographs	199
M. F. K. Fisher	Young Hunger	208
E. M. Forster	Racial Exercise	213
Sigmund Freud	The Relation of the Poet to Day-Dreaming	218
Erich Fromm	The Nature of Symbolic Language	228
Robert Frost	Education By Poetry	238
Paul Fussell	The Boy Scout Handbook	261
William Golding	Thinking as a Hobby	277
S. I. Hayakawa	How Dictionaries Are Made	304
Aldous Huxley	Selected Snobberies	328
William James	Habit	340
Randall Jarrell	The Taste of the Age	354
Pauline Kael	Movies on Television	370
Norman Mailer	Marilyn Monroe	444
Mary McCarthy	Catholic Education	455
Jessica Mitford	On Embalming	487
Samuel Eliot Morison	History as a Literary Art	501
Lewis Mumford	Sport and the "Bitch-Goddess"	516

José Ortega y Gasset	*Emotional Reality*	535
George Orwell	*Politics and the English Language*	553
Dorothy Parker	*Mrs. Post Enlarges on Etiquette*	566
J. H. Plumb	*The Stars in Their Day*	576
J. B. Priestly	*Block Thinking*	588
Lillian Ross	*The Vinyl Santa*	594
Logan Pearsall Smith	*Words from the Sea*	605
Lewis Thomas	*Notes on Punctuation*	621
John Updike	*Crush Vs. Whip*	646
Evelyn Waugh	*Half in Love with Easeful Death*	650
Eudora Welty	*A Sweet Devouring*	663
Edmund Wilson	*The Problem of English*	693

II. Classification

Isaac Asimov	*Pure and Impure: The Interplay of Science and Technology*	26
Daniel Boorstin	*The Rhetoric of Democracy*	66
G. K. Chesterton	*On Sightseeing*	114
Aaron Copland	*How We Listen to Music*	131
Joan Didion	*On the Mall*	149
W. E. B. DuBois	*Jacob and Esau*	169
René Dubos	*Territoriality and Dominance*	181
Erich Fromm	*The Nature of Symbolic Language*	228
Robert Frost	*Education By Poetry*	238
Northrup Frye	*The Keys to Dreamland*	250
Paul Fussell	*The Boy Scout Handbook*	261
William Golding	*Thinking as a Hobby*	277
Aldous Huxley	*Selected Snobberies*	328
Ada Louise Huxtable	*Houston*	333
D. H. Lawrence	*Rex*	389
Wyndham Lewis	*The Secret of the Success of Charlie Chaplin*	413
Basil Liddell Hart	*William Tecumseh Sherman: The First Modern General*	417
Margaret Mead	*New Superstitions for Old*	476
Ashley Montague	*Social Change and Human Change*	494
Lewis Mumford	*Sport and the "Bitch-Goddess"*	516
José Ortega y Gasset	*Emotional Reality*	535
George Orwell	*Politics and the English Language*	553
Dorothy Parker	*Mrs. Post Enlarges on Etiquette*	566
J. B. Priestly	*Block Thinking*	588
Lillian Ross	*The Vinyl Santa*	594

ix RHETORICAL TABLES OF CONTENTS

Bertrand Russell	Education and Discipline	598
Logan Pearsall Smith	Words from the Sea	605
Susan Sontag	Science Fiction Films: The Imagination of Disaster	609
Lewis Thomas	Notes on Punctuation	621
Barbara Tuchman	This is the End of the World: The Black Death	635
Evelyn Waugh	Half in Love with Easeful Death	650
E. B. White	The Essayist	690
Tom Wolfe	The Right Stuff	701

III. Comparison and Contrast

Frederick Lewis Allen	Main Street America–1900	7
Isaac Asimov	Pure and Impure: The Interplay of Science and Technology	26
Jacques Barzun	The Wasteland of American Education	43
Gwendolyn Brooks	Dreams of a Black Christmas	87
W. E. B. DuBois	Jacob and Esau	169
René Dubos	Territoriality and Dominance	181
M. F. K. Fisher	Young Hunger	208
Sigmund Freud	The Relation of the Poet to Day-Dreaming	218
Northrup Frye	The Keys to Dreamland	250
Randall Jarrell	The Taste of the Age	354
Pauline Kael	Movies on Television	370
Marshall McLuhan	Classroom Without Walls	459
Margaret Mead	New Superstitions for Old	476
H. L. Mencken	Criminology	482
Bertrand Russell	Education and Discipline	598
Barbara Tuchman	This is the End of the World: The Black Death	635
John Updike	Crush Vs. Whip	646
Eudora Welty	A Sweet Devouring	663

IV. Analogy and Metaphor

Jacob Bronowski	Likenesses	84
Nigel Calder	The Comet Is Coming	96
Rachel Carson	The Changing Year	101
Annie Dillard	Mirages	164
René Dubos	Territoriality and Dominance	181
Robert Frost	Education By Poetry	238

Sir James Jeans	*Why the Sky Looks Blue*	362
C. S. Lewis	*The Trouble with "X" . . .*	407
Wyndham Lewis	*The Secret of the Success of Charlie Chaplin*	413
George Orwell	*Politics and the English Language*	553
J. B. Priestly	*Block Thinking*	588
Logan Pearsall Smith	*Words from the Sea*	605
Eudora Welty	*A Sweet Devouring*	663
Paul West	*The VAB Beside the Sea*	670
Tom Wolfe	*The Right Stuff*	701

V. PROCESS ANALYSIS

Jacob Bronowski	*Likenesses*	84
Rachel Carson	*The Changing Year*	101
Aaron Copland	*How We Listen to Music*	131
Guy Davenport	*Finding*	138
Joan Didion	*On Keeping a Notebook*	156
W. E. B. DuBois	*Jacob and Esau*	169
Nora Ephron	*The Boston Photographs*	199
Sigmund Freud	*The Relation of the Poet to Day-Dreaming*	218
Robert Frost	*Education By Poetry*	238
Stephen Jay Gould	*A Biographical Homage to Mickey Mouse*	286
S. I. Hayakawa	*How Dictionaries Are Made*	304
William James	*Habit*	340
Sir James H. Jeans	*Why the Sky Looks Blue*	362
C. G. Jung	*A Vision of Life After Death*	365
Rudyard Kipling	*A Snake Farm*	382
D. H. Lawrence	*Rex*	389
Wyndham Lewis	*The Secret of the Success of Charlie Chaplin*	413
Mary McCarthy	*Catholic Education*	455
H. L. Mencken	*Criminology*	482
Jessica Mitford	*On Embalming*	487
Ashley Montague	*Social Change and Human Change*	494
Samuel Eliot Morison	*History as a Literary Art*	501
Lewis Mumford	*Sport and the "Bitch-Goddess"*	516
J. H. Plumb	*The Stars in Their Day*	576
Gay Talese	*Punks and Pushers*	614
H. G. Wells	*Ellis Island*	659
E. B. White	*Death of a Pig*	680
	The Essayist	690

RHETORICAL TABLES OF CONTENTS

VI. Cause and Effect

Hannah Arendt	Denmark and the Jews	14
Isaac Asimov	Pure and Impure: The Interplay of Science and Technology	26
Jacques Barzun	The Wasteland of American Education	43
Bruno Bettelheim	Joey, A Mechanical Boy	56
Willa Cather	Small-Town Life	110
Robert Coles	Children of Affluence	119
W. E. B. DuBois	Jacob and Esau	169
René Dubos	Territoriality and Dominance	181
Ralph Ellison	Hidden Name and Complex Fate	188
Paul Fussell	The Boy Scout Handbook	261
Martin Gardner	The Harvard Man Who Put the Ease in Casey's Manner	268
Stephen Jay Gould	A Biographical Homage to Mickey Mouse	286
Graham Greene	The Revolver in the Corner Cupboard	298
William James	Habit	340
Sir James Jeans	Why the Sky Looks Blue	362
Pauline Kael	Movies on Television	370
D. H. Lawrence	Rex	389
Wyndham Lewis	The Secret of the Success of Charlie Chaplin	413
Walter Lippmann	The Indispensable Opposition	425
Ashley Montague	Social Change and Human Change	494
George Orwell	Shooting an Elephant	540
	Politics and the English Language	553
J. H. Plumb	The Stars in Their Day	576
Katherine Anne Porter	The Future Is Now	581
Barbara Tuchman	This is the End of the World: The Black Death	635
Richard Wright	Innocence	715

VII. Definition

Isaac Asimov	Pure and Impure: The Interplay of Science and Technology	26
James Baldwin	If Black English Isn't a Language, Then Tell Me, What Is?	38
Bruno Bettelheim	Joey, A Mechanical Boy	56
Nigel Calder	The Comet Is Coming	96

Robert Coles	Children of Affluence	119
René Dubos	Territoriality and Dominance	181
Ralph Ellison	Hidden Name and Complex Fate	188
Erich Fromm	The Nature of Symbolic Language	228
Robert Frost	Education By Poetry	238
Paul Fussell	The Boy Scout Handbook	261
Aldous Huxley	Selected Snobberies	328
William James	Habit	340
Elizabeth Janeway	Water	348
Walter Lippmann	The Indispensable Opposition	425
Margaret Mead	New Superstitions for Old	476
Samuel Eliot Morison	History as a Literary Art	501
Lewis Mumford	Sport and the "Bitch-Goddess"	516
Vladimir Nabokov	Colored Hearing	522
J. B. Priestly	Block Thinking	588
E. B. White	The Essayist	690

VIII. DESCRIPTION

James Agee	Knoxville: Summer 1915	1
Frederick Lewis Allen	Main Street America–1900	7
Roger Angell	On the Ball	11
Michael Arlen	Ode to Thanksgiving	21
Simone de Beauvoir	Knowing New York	52
Jorge Luis Borges	The Disinterested Killer Bill Harrigan	78
Gwendolyn Brooks	Dreams of a Black Christmas	87
Joan Didion	On the Mall	149
Annie Dillard	Mirages	164
M. F. K. Fisher	Young Hunger	208
Stephen Jay Gould	A Biographical Homage to Mickey Mouse	286
Graham Greene	The Revolver in the Corner Cupboard	298
Lillian Hellman	The Fig Tree	308
Ernest Hemingway	The Clark's Fork Valley, Wyoming	312
Edward Hoagland	The Courage of Turtles	316
Langston Hughes	Salvation	324
Ada Louise Huxtable	Houston	333
Rudyard Kipling	A Snake Farm	382
D. H. Lawrence	Rex	389
Helen Lawrenson	The Bulls of Pamplona vs. the Ivy League	398

Basil Liddell Hart	William Tecumseh Sherman:	
	The First Modern General	417
Jack London	The Carter and the Carpenter	434
William Manchester	How I Slew My First Man	449
Mary McCarthy	Catholic Education	455
John McPhee	The Search for Marvin Gardens	463
Jessica Mitford	On Embalming	487
John Muir	Digging a Well	512
Vladmir Nabokov	Colored Hearing	522
V. S. Naipaul	The New Tehran	527
George Orwell	A Hanging	548
Lillian Ross	The Vinyl Santa	594
Gay Talese	Punks and Pushers	614
Evelyn Waugh	Half in Love With Easeful Death	650
H. G. Wells	Ellis Island	659
Paul West	The VAB Beside the Sea	670
E. B. White	Death of a Pig	680
Tom Wolfe	The Right Stuff	701
Virginia Woolf	The Death of the Moth	710

IX. NARRATION

James Agee	Knoxville: Summer 1915	1
Russell Baker	Little Red Riding Hood Revisited	34
Simone de Beauvoir	Knowing New York	52
Jorge Luis Borges	The Disinterested Killer Bill Harrigan	78
Guy Davenport	Finding	138
W. E. B. DuBois	Jacob and Esau	169
M. F. K. Fisher	Young Hunger	208
Martin Gardner	The Harvard Man Who Put the Ease in Casey's Manner	268
Graham Greene	The Revolver in the Corner Cupboard	298
Lillian Hellman	The Fig Tree	308
Langston Hughes	Salvation	324
C. G. Jung	A Vision of Life After Death	365
Rudyard Kipling	A Snake Farm	382
Helen Lawrenson	The Bulls of Pamplona vs. the Ivy League	398
Jack London	The Carter and the Carpenter	434
William Manchester	How I Slew My First Man	449
John McPhee	The Search for Marvin Gardens	463
John Muir	Digging a Well	512
George Orwell	Shooting an Elephant	540

xiv RHETORICAL TABLES OF CONTENTS

S. J. Perelman	*Dental or Mental, I Say It's Spinach*	571
Susan Sontag	*Science Fiction Films: The Imagination of Disaster*	609
Gay Talese	*Punks and Pushers*	614
James Thurber	*University Days*	626
Barbara Tuchman	*This is the End of the World: The Black Death*	635
Edith Wharton	*Henry James Asks Directions*	676
E. B. White	*Death of a Pig*	680
Tom Wolfe	*The Right Stuff*	701
Virginia Woolf	*The Death of the Moth*	710
Richard Wright	*Innocence*	715

X. ARGUMENT AND PERSUASION

Hannah Arendt	*Denmark and the Jews*	14
Isaac Asimov	*Pure and Impure: The Interplay of Science and Technology*	26
James Baldwin	*If Black English Isn't a Language, Then Tell Me, What Is?*	38
Jacques Barzun	*The Wasteland of American Education*	43
Gwendolyn Brooks	*Dreams of a Black Christmas*	87
Willa Cather	*Small-Town Life*	110
G. K. Chesterton	*On Sightseeing*	114
Aaron Copland	*How We Listen to Music*	131
W. E. B. DuBois	*Jacob and Esau*	169
Nora Ephron	*The Boston Photographs*	199
E. M. Forster	*Racial Exercise*	213
Sigmund Freud	*The Relation of the Poet to Day-Dreaming*	218
Northrup Frye	*The Keys to Dreamland*	250
Paul Fussell	*The Boy Scout Handbook*	261
S. I. Hayakawa	*How Dictionaries Are Made*	304
Aldous Huxley	*Selected Snobberies*	328
Randall Jarrell	*The Taste of the Age*	354
Pauline Kael	*Movies on Television*	370
C. S. Lewis	*The Trouble with "X" . . .*	407
Basil Liddell Hart	*William Tecumseh Sherman: The First Modern General*	417
Walter Lippmann	*The Indispensable Opposition*	425
Mary McCarthy	*Catholic Education*	455
Marshall McLuhan	*Classroom Without Walls*	459

H. L. Mencken	*Criminology*	482
Ashley Montague	*Social Change and Human Change*	494
Samuel Eliot Morison	*History as a Literary Art*	501
George Orwell	*Politics and the English Language*	553
J. H. Plumb	*The Stars in Their Day*	576
Katherine Anne Porter	*The Future Is Now*	581
J. B. Priestly	*Block Thinking*	588
Edmund Wilson	*The Problem of English*	593

PREFACE

This comprehensive collection of outstanding twentieth-century writers and thinkers should present students at the introductory level with some highly encouraging educational facts about writing: that distinguished authors often write on topics well within the range of a student writer's experience, judgment, and interests; that writing of high quality can be lively and need not be intimidating for readers; that accomplished authors often write in forms short enough to provide useful models for the kinds of essays students themselves really write; and that good writing is practiced and valued in a wide range of disciplines.

The book is designed to work in many different composition courses. Taken together, the selections have the benefits of comprehensiveness and modernity. Since the concerns of the essays continue to be part of twentieth-century life and thought, these essays are not only interesting to read, but should be more directly useful in learning to write than would be those by equally distinguished writers of the past. In our experience, it is generally from modern essays that techniques of skillful writing can become more readily learned and brought to the many compositional tasks within higher education and beyond it. Moreover, given an increasing curricular specialization, a collection focusing on the twentieth century may best reflect the kinds of writing used in and across today's disciplines, many of which scarcely existed a century ago.

Perhaps because the essay itself is such an open form, courses that work mainly with the essay employ a variety of instructional approaches, and any useful book must be flexible enough to accommodate them. For this reason the collection offers an abundance of material usable within several frameworks. The essays can be organized in at least four ways:

1. For those courses that arrange their material around the rhetorical categories of description, narration, exposition, and argumentation;
2. For those courses that organize their work around the examination and comparison of topics associated with various disciplines;
3. For those courses that move from short, informal essays on personal subjects toward formal writing used in research papers;
4. For courses that focus on the essay as a vigorous and continually evolving literary form.

By including more than one essay by some notable essayists, this collection also allows for the examination of an individual writer's particular techniques in some depth.

Each selection is introduced by a biographical note that briefly describes the author's achievements and claims to distinction. Questions intended as aids for reading, writing, and class discussion follow each selection. The questions address the issues of the essay's content, examine its rhetorical and stylistic techniques, investigate matters of tone and audience, point to comparisons with other essays in the book, and suggest topics for student writing.

From Stephen Jay Gould's description of Mickey Mouse's biological evolution to Carl Jung's vision of life after death; from Gwendolyn Brooks' memories of childhood Christmas to Michael Arlen's ironical look at a typical Thanksgiving; from John McPhee's search for the real Marvin Gardens and Ada Louise Huxtable's search for the real Houston to Isaac Asimov's search for the true relation of science to technology—this highly diverse collection of distinguished writing shows students how accomplished authors achieve independent and interesting points of view and express them with clarity and force.

We wish to thank Professors John Clifford, University of North Carolina; Franklin Court, Northern Illinois University; Don Richard Cox, The University of Tennessee; Judith Fishman, Queens College of the City University of New York; Rosanna Grassi, Syracuse University; James Kirkland, East Carolina University; William Lutz, Rutgers University; George Miller, University of Delaware; and Charles Schuster, University of Washington. Their comments and suggestions were invaluable in the preparation of the manuscript. For help in assembling that manuscript, we also wish to thank Patricia Perrine, Anne Sherber, and Errol Somay.

R.A.
W.V.

JAMES AGEE

James Agee (1909–1955) was born in Knoxville, Tennessee, and was educated at Phillips Exeter Academy and Harvard University. As a staff writer for Fortune magazine during the Depression, he wrote an impassioned account of Alabama sharecroppers, Let Us Now Praise Famous Men (1941). Between 1943 and 1948 he served as movie reviewer for The Nation; Agee on Film, a collection of his reviews, was published posthumously in 1958.

"Knoxville: Summer 1915" was printed as the prologue to Agee's Pulitzer Prize-winning novel, A Death in the Family (1955). This lyrical, autobiographical essay clearly demonstrates what Agee called his "amphibious style-prose," a prose style "that would run into poetry when the occasion demanded."

Knoxville: Summer 1915

We are talking now of summer evenings in Knoxville, Tennessee in the time that I lived there so successfully disguised to myself as a child. It was a little bit mixed sort of block, fairly solidly lower middle class, with one or two juts apiece on either side of that. The houses corresponded: middle-sized gracefully fretted wood houses built in the late nineties and early nineteen hundreds, with small front and side and more spacious back yards, and trees in the yards, and porches. These were soft-wooded trees, poplars, tulip trees, cottonwoods. There were fences around one or two of the houses, but mainly the yards ran into each other with only now and then a low hedge that wasn't doing very well. There were few good friends among the grown people, and they were not poor enough for the other sort of intimate acquaintance, but everyone nodded and spoke, and even might talk short times, trivially, and at the two extremes of the general or the particular, and ordinarily next door neighbors talked quite a bit when they happened to run into each other, and never paid calls. The men were mostly small businessmen, one or two very modestly executives, one or two worked with their hands, most of them clerical, and most of them between thirty and forty-five.

But it is of these evenings, I speak.

Supper was at six and was over by half past. There was still daylight, shining softly and with a tarnish, like the lining of a shell; and the carbon lamps lifted at the corners were on in the light, and the locusts were started, and the fire flies were out, and a few frogs were flopping in the dewy grass, by the time the fathers and the children came out. The children ran out first hell bent and yelling those names by which they were known; then the fathers sank out leisurely in crossed suspenders, their collars removed and their necks looking tall and shy. The mothers stayed back in the kitchen washing and drying, putting things away, re-crossing their traceless footsteps like the lifetime journeys of bees, measuring out the dry cocoa for breakfast. When they came out they had taken off their aprons and their skirts were dampened and they sat in rockers on their porches quietly.

It is not of the games children play in the evening that I want to speak now, it is of a contemporaneous atmosphere that has little to do with them; that of the fathers of families, each in his space of lawn, his shirt fishlike pale in the unnatural light and his face nearly anonymous, hosing their lawns. The hoses were attached at spigots that stood out of the brick foundations of the houses. The nozzles were variously set but usually so there was a long sweet stream of spray, the nozzle wet in the hand, the water trickling the right forearm and the peeled-back cuff, and the water whishing out a long loose and low-curved cone, and so gentle a sound. First an insane noise of violence in the nozzle, then the still irregular sound of adjustment, then the smoothing into steadiness and a pitch as accurately tuned to the size and style of stream as any violin. So many qualities of sound out of one hose: so many choral differences out of those several hoses that were in earshot. Out of any one hose, the almost dead silence of the release, and the short still arch of the separate big drops, silent as a held breath, and the only noise the flattering noise on leaves and the slapped grass at the fall of each big drop. That, and the intense hiss with the intense stream; that, and that same intensity not growing less but growing more quiet and delicate with the turn of the nozzle, up to that extreme tender whisper when the water was just a wide bell of film. Chiefly, though, the hoses were set much alike, in a compromise between distance and tenderness of spray, (and quite surely a sense of art behind this compromise, and a quiet deep joy, too real to recognize itself), and the sounds therefore were pitched much alike; pointed by the snorting start of a new hose; decorated by some man playful with the nozzle; left empty, like God by the sparrow's fall, when any single one of them desists; and all, though near alike, of various pitch; and in this unison. These sweet pale streamings in the light lift out their pallors and their voices all together, mothers hushing their children, the hushing unnaturally prolonged, the men gentle and silent and each snail-like withdrawn into the quietude of what he singly is doing, the urination of huge children stood loosely military against an invisible wall, and gently happy and peaceful, tasting the mean goodness of their living like the last of their suppers in their mouths; while the locusts carry on this noise of hoses on their much higher and sharper key. The noise of the locust is dry, and it seems not to be rasped or vibrated but urged from him as if through a small orifice by a breath that can never give out. Also there is never one locust but an illusion of at least a thousand. The noise of each locust is pitched in some classic locust range out of which none of them varies more than two full tones: and yet you seem to hear each locust discrete from all the rest, and there is a long, slow, pulse in their noise, like the scarcely defined arch of a long and high set bridge. They are all around in every tree, so that the noise seems to come from nowhere and everywhere at once, from the whole shell heaven, shivering in your flesh and teasing your eardrums, the boldest of all the sounds of night. And yet it is habitual to summer nights, and is of the great order of noises, like the noises of the sea and of the blood her precocious grandchild, which you realize you are hearing only when you catch yourself listening. Meantime from low in the dark, just outside the swaying horizons of the hoses, conveying always grass in the damp of dew and its strong green-back smear of smell, the regular yet spaced noises of the crickets, each a sweet cold silver noise three-noted, like the slipping each time of three matched links of a small chain.

But the men by now, one by one, have silenced their hoses and drained and coiled them. Now only two, and now only one, is left, and you see only ghostlike shirt with the sleeve garters, and sober mystery of his mild face like the lifted face of large cattle enquiring of your presence in a pitchdark pool of meadow; and now he too is gone; and it has become that time of evening when people sit on their porches, rocking gently and talking gently and watching the street and the standing up into their sphere of possession of the trees, of birds hung havens, hangars. People go by; things go by. A horse, drawing a buggy, breaking his hollow iron music on the asphalt; a loud auto; a quiet auto; people in pairs, not in a hurry, scuffling, switching their weight of aestival body, talking casually, the taste hovering over them of vanilla, strawberry, pasteboard and starched milk, the image upon them of lovers and horsemen, squared with clowns in hueless amber. A street car raising its iron moan; stopping; belling and starting, stertorous; rousing and raising again its iron increasing moan and swimming its gold windows and straw seats on past and past and past, the bleak spark crackling and cursing above it like a small malignant spirit set to dog its tracks; the iron whine rises on rising speed; still risen, faints; halts; the faint stinging bell; rises again, still fainter; fainting, lifting, lifts, faints forgone: forgotten. Now is the night one blue dew.

>   Now is the night one blue dew, my father has drained, he has coiled the hose.
>   Low on the length of lawns, a frailing of fire who breathes.

Content, silver, like peeps of light, each cricket makes his comment over and over in the drowned grass.
A cold toad thumpily flounders.
Within the edges of damp shadows of side yards are hovering children nearly sick with joy of fear, who watch the unguarding of a telephone pole. Around white carbon corner lamps bugs of all sizes are lifted elliptic, solar systems. Big hardshells bruise themselves, assailant: he is fallen on his back, legs squiggling.
Parents on porches: rock and rock: From damp strings morning glories: hang their ancient faces.
The dry and exalted noise of the locusts from all the air at once enchants my eardrums.

On the rough wet grass of the back yard my father and mother have spread quilts. We all lie there, my mother, my father, my uncle, my aunt, and I too am lying there. First we were sitting up, then one of us lay down, and then we all lay down, on our stomachs, or on our sides, or on our backs, and they have kept on talking. They are not talking much, and the talk is quiet, of nothing in particular, of nothing at all in particular, of nothing at all. The stars are wide and alive, they seem each like a smile of great sweetness, and they seem very near. All my people are larger bodies than mine, quiet, with voices gentle and meaningless like the voices of sleeping birds. One is an artist, he is living at home. One is a musician, she is living at home. One is my mother who is good to me. One is my father who is good to me. By some chance, here they are, all on this earth; and who shall ever tell the sorrow of being on this earth, lying, on quilts, on the grass, in a summer evening, among the sounds of the night. May God bless my people, my uncle, my aunt, my mother, my good father, oh, remember them kindly in their time of trouble; and in the hour of their taking away.

After a little I am taken and put to bed. Sleep, soft smiling, draws me unto her: and those receive me, who quietly treat me, as one familiar and well-beloved in that home: but will not, oh, will not, not now, not ever; but will not ever tell me who I am.

Discussion Questions

1. How would you describe Agee's feelings about his childhood? How do the first and last sentences affect your impression of the essay as a whole?

2. What does Agee mean by a "contemporaneous atmosphere"? How is that atmosphere reflected in the details of the childhood summer nights that Agee recalls? How does the recurrent use of sounds contribute to that atmosphere?

3. Both Agee and Frederick Lewis Allen attempt to render an image of early twentieth-century America. How do their methods differ? Which paragraph of Agee's essay comes closest to containing the kind of information Allen is most interested in?

4. In Agee's account of his childhood summer evenings, one night seems exactly like another. Why does it seem this way? Select a period of your childhood and in a brief essay describe that period as though it existed in both a particular and general way.

Frederick Lewis Allen

One of the most widely known "informal" historians of American society, Frederick Lewis Allen (1890–1954), was born in Boston and educated at Harvard University. A long-time editor of Harper's Magazine *and an astute observer of social change, Allen, in a series of highly readable books, reported optimistically on the dynamics of capitalism and democracy in twentieth-century America. His books include a famous study of the 1920's,* Only Yesterday *(1931), a similar study of the 1930's,* Since Yesterday *(1940), and a survey of the entire first half of the twentieth century,* The Big Change: America Transforms Itself 1900–1950, *from which the following selection is drawn.*

Main Street America—1900

If a neatly adjusted time machine could take you back to the Main Street of an American town in 1900, to look about you with your present-day eyes, your first exclamation would probably be, "But look at all those horses!"

For in that year 1900 there were registered in the whole United States only 13,824 automobiles (as compared with over 44 million in 1950). And they were really few and far between except in the larger cities and the well-to-do resorts. For in 1900 everybody thought of automobiles as playthings of the rich—and not merely of the rich, but of the somewhat adventurous and sporting rich: people who enjoyed taking their chances with an unpredictable machine that might at any moment wreck them. There were almost no paved highways outside the cities, and of course there were no roadside garages or filling stations; every automobilist must be his own desperate mechanic. Probably half the men and women of America had never seen a car. When William Allen White organized a street fair in Emporia, Kansas, in 1899, the automobile which was brought there for the occasion—and proved to be the most exciting exhibit of the fair—came from Chicago by rail; it was the first automobile ever to have crossed the Missouri River.

But horses were everywhere, pulling surreys, democrats, buggies, cabs, delivery wagons of every sort on Main Street, and pulling harvesters on the tractorless farms out in the countryside.

The sights and sounds and sensations of horse-and-carriage life were part of the universal American experience: the clop-clop of the horses' hoofs; the stiff jolting of an iron-tired carriage on a stony road; the grinding noise of the brake being applied to ease the horse on a downhill stretch; the necessity of holding one's breath when the horse sneezed; the sight of sand, carried up on the tires and wooden spokes of a carriage wheel, spilling off in little cascades as the wheel revolved; the look of a country road overgrown by grass, with three tracks in it instead of two, the middle one made by horses' hoofs; the special male ordeal of getting out of the carriage and walking up the steeper hills to lighten the load; and the more severe ordeal, for the unpracticed, of harnessing a horse which could recognize inexperience at one scornful glance. During a Northern winter the jingle of sleigh bells was everywhere. On summer evenings, along the tree-lined streets of innumerable American towns, families sitting on their front porches would watch the fine carriages of the town as they drove past for a proud evening's jaunt, and the cognoscenti would wait eagerly for a glimpse of the banker's trotting pair or the sporting lawyer's 2:40 pacer. And one of the magnificent sights of urban life was that of a fire engine, pulled by three galloping horses, careening down a city street with its bell clanging.

It is hard for us today to realize how very widely communities were separated from one another when they depended for transportation wholly on the railroad and the horse and wagon—and when telephones were still scarce, and radios nonexistent. A town which was not situated on a railroad was really remote. A farmer who lived five miles outside the county seat made something of an event of hitching up and taking the family to town for a Saturday afternoon's shopping. (His grandchildren make the run in a casual ten minutes, and think nothing of it.) A trip to see friends ten miles away was likely to be an all-day expedition, for the horse had to be given a chance to rest and be fed. No wonder that each region, each town, each farm was far more dependent upon its own resources—its own produce, social contacts, amusements—than in later years. For in terms of travel and communication the United States was a very big country indeed.

No wonder, furthermore, that the majority of Americans were less likely than their descendants to be dogged by that frightening sense of insecurity which comes from being jostled by forces—economic, political, international—beyond one's personal ken. Their horizons were close to them. They lived among familiar people and familiar things—individuals and families and fellow townsmen much of their own sort, with ideas intelligible to them. A man's success or failure seemed more likely than in later years to depend upon forces and events within his own range of vision. Less often than his sons and grandsons did he feel that his fortune, indeed his life, might hang upon some decision made in Washington or Berlin or Moscow, for reasons utterly strange to his experience. The world at which he looked over the dashboard of the family carriage might not be friendly, but at least most of it looked understandable.

Discussion Questions

1. What general impression of American life in 1900 does Frederick Lewis Allen want to convey in this essay? How does his final paragraph use that impression and expand upon it?
2. Describe the differences in method between Allen's depiction of a world with only a few automobiles and his depiction of a world wholly dependent upon the horse.
3. Compare Allen's account of Main Street in 1900 to James Agee's recollection of Knoxville in 1915. Isolate one instance of similarity. Are the effects of each passage equally similar?
4. Using Allen's essay as a model, write a brief essay of your own in which you project an American Main Street in the year 2000. Imagine a common phenomenon today that may no longer be part of the American scene.

ROGER ANGELL

A senior fiction editor with The New Yorker, Roger Angell regularly contributes humor, verse, and sportswriting to that magazine. Born in New York City in 1920, Angell graduated from Harvard University in 1942 and afterward served with the United States Army Air Force in the Pacific. After the war, Angell became a senior editor of Holiday magazine and in 1956 joined the staff of The New Yorker.

Angell is the author of The Stone Arbor and Other Stories (1966), A Day in the Life of Roger Angell (1970), The Summer Game (1972), Five Seasons (1977), and Late Innings (1982). In 1980, Angell won the George Polk Award for commentary. His finely detailed and perceptive books and essays on baseball (he also covers tennis, horse racing, rowing, hockey, and football) have made him one of the preeminent writers on current American sports.

On the Ball

It weighs just over five ounces and measures between 2.86 and 2.94 inches in diameter. It is made of a composition-cork nucleus encased in two thin layers of rubber, one black and one red, surrounded by 121 yards of tightly wrapped blue-gray wool yarn, 45 yards of white wool yarn, 53 more yards of blue-gray wool yarn, 150 yards of fine cotton yarn, a coat of rubber cement, and a cowhide (formerly horsehide) exterior, which is held together with 216 slightly raised red cotton stitches. Printed certifications, endorsements, and outdoor advertising spherically attest to its authenticity. Like most institutions, it is considered inferior in its present form to its ancient archetypes, and in this case the complaint is probably justified; on occasion in recent years it has actually been known to come apart under the demands of its brief but rigorous active career. Baseballs are assembled and hand-stitched in Taiwan (before this year the work was done in Haiti, and before 1973 in Chicopee, Massachusetts), and contemporary pitchers claim that there is a tangible variation in the size and feel of the balls that now come into play in a single game; a true peewee is treasured by hurlers, and its departure from the premises, by fair means or foul, is secretly mourned. But never mind: any baseball is beautiful. No other small package comes as close to the ideal in design and utility. It is a perfect object for a man's hand. Pick it up and it instantly suggests its purpose; it is meant to be thrown a considerable distance—thrown hard and with precision. Its feel and heft are the beginning of the sport's critical dimensions; if it were a fraction of an inch larger or smaller, a few centigrams heavier or lighter, the game of baseball would be utterly different. Hold a baseball in your hand. As it happens, this one is not brand-new. Here, just to one side of the curved surgical welt of stitches, there is a pale-green grass smudge, darkening on one edge almost to black—the mark of an old infield play, a tough grounder now lost in memory. Feel the ball, turn it over in your hand; hold it across the seam or the other way, with the seam just to the side of your middle finger. Speculation stirs. You want to get outdoors and throw this spare and sensual object to somebody or, at the very least, watch somebody else throw it. The game has begun.

Discussion Questions

1. At what point in the essay does Angell specifically say that he is speaking about baseballs? Why doesn't he use the word "baseball" in his opening sentence?

2. Locate the point at which Angell shifts from talking about the baseball in general to a particular baseball. What is the effect of this shift on the reader?

3. Compare Angell's techniques of description to Ernest Hemingway's. How do these writers use similar techniques to establish a sense of immediacy?

4. In what sense is a baseball an "institution"? How does the term allow Angell to enlarge the scope of his topic?

5. Using Angell's descriptive methods of specificity and immediacy, write a brief account of another such "institution"—a football, bowling ball, hockey puck, and so forth.

Hannah Arendt

Hannah Arendt (1906–1975), the distinguished political theorist and historian, was born and educated in Germany, where she studied classics and philosophy. Two of her mentors, Martin Heidegger and Karl Jaspers, were among the leading continental philosophers of the period. She was an outstanding student and apparently destined for academic life, but her career was destroyed by Hitler's laws against the Jews in the professions. She fled to France and became active in Jewish refugee work. Escaping once more after the Nazi invasion of France, she came to the United States, where she held a variety of part-time jobs connected with publishing while she learned English and planned her most famous book, The Origins of Totalitarianism (1951). With her new success in a new country and in a new language, she resumed the academic career Hitler had interrupted. She went on to write many books on politics and philosophy and was at work on an examination of basic philosophical concepts like the meaning of "thinking" when she died. The following essay, which appears in Eichmann in Jerusalem (1963), shows her skill in organizing and integrating narration and argument.

Denmark and the Jews

At the Wannsee Conference, Martin Luther, of the Foreign Office, warned of great difficulties in the Scandinavian countries, notably in Norway and Denmark. (Sweden was never occupied, and Finland, though in the war on the side of the Axis, was the one country the Nazis never even approached on the Jewish question. This surprising exception of Finland, with some two thousand Jews, may have been due to Hitler's great esteem for the Finns, whom perhaps he did not want to subject to threats and humiliating blackmail.) Luther proposed postponing evacuations from Scandinavia for the time being, and as far as Denmark was concerned, this really went without saying, since the country retained its independent government, and was respected as a neutral state, until the fall of 1943, although it, along with Norway, had been invaded by the German Army in April, 1940. There existed no Fascist or Nazi movement in Denmark worth mentioning, and therefore no collaborators. In Norway, however, the Germans had been able to find enthusiastic supporters; indeed, Vidkun Quisling, leader of the pro-Nazi and anti-Semitic Norwegian party, gave his name to what later became known as a "quisling government." The bulk of Norway's seventeen hundred Jews were stateless, refugees from Germany; they were seized and interned in a few lightning operations in October and November, 1942. When Eichmann's office ordered their deportation to Auschwitz, some of Quisling's own men resigned their government posts. This may not have come as a surprise to Mr. Luther and the Foreign Office, but what was much more serious, and certainly totally unexpected, was that Sweden immediately offered asylum, and even Swedish nationality, to all who were persecuted. Dr. Ernst von Weizsäcker, Undersecretary of State of the Foreign Office, who received the proposal, refused to discuss it, but the offer helped nevertheless. It is always relatively easy to get out of a country illegally, whereas it is nearly impossible to enter the place of refuge without permission and to dodge the immigration authorities. Hence, about nine hundred people, slightly more than half of the small Norwegian community, could be smuggled into Sweden.

It was in Denmark, however, that the Germans found out how fully justified the Foreign Office's apprehensions had been. The story of the Danish Jews is *sui generis*, and the behavior of the Danish people and their government was unique among all the countries of Europe—whether occupied, or a partner of the Axis, or neutral and truly independent. One is tempted to recommend the story as required reading in political science for all students who wish to learn something about the enormous power potential inherent in non-violent action and in resistance to an opponent possessing vastly superior means of violence. To be sure, a few other countries in Europe lacked proper "understanding of the Jewish question," and actually a majority of them were opposed to "radical" and "final" solutions. Like Denmark, Sweden, Italy, and Bulgaria proved to be nearly immune to anti-Semitism, but of the three that were in the German sphere of influence, only the Danes dared speak out on the subject to their German masters. Italy and Bulgaria sabotaged German orders and indulged in a complicated game of double-dealing and double-crossing, saving their Jews by a tour de force of sheer ingenuity, but they never contested the policy as such. That was totally different from what the Danes did. When the Germans approached them rather cautiously about introducing the yellow badge, they were simply told that the King would be the first to wear it, and the Danish government officials were careful to point out that anti-Jewish measures of any sort would cause their own immediate resignation. It was decisive in this whole matter that the Germans did not even succeed in introducing the vitally important distinction between native Danes of Jewish origin, of whom there were about sixty-four hundred, and the fourteen hundred German Jewish refugees who had found asylum in the country prior to the war and who now had been declared stateless by the German government. This refusal must have surprised the Germans no end, since it appeared so "illogical" for government to protect people to whom it had categorically denied naturalization and even permission to work. (Legally, the prewar situation of refugees in Denmark was not unlike that in France, except that the general corruption in the Third Republic's civil services enabled a few of them to obtain naturalization papers, through bribes or "connections," and most refugees in France could work illegally, without a permit. But Denmark, like Switzerland, was no country *pour se débrouiller*.) The Danes, however, explained to the German officials that because the stateless refugees were no longer German citizens, the Nazis could not claim them without Danish assent. This was one of the few cases in which statelessness turned out to be an asset, although it was of course not statelessness per se that saved the Jews but, on the contrary, the fact that the Danish government had decided to protect them. Thus, none of the preparatory moves, so important for the bureaucracy of murder, could be carried out, and operations were postponed until the fall of 1943.

What happened then was truly amazing; compared with what took place in other European countries, everything went topsy-turvey. In August, 1943—after the German offensive in Russia had failed, the Afrika Korps had surrendered in Tunisia, and the Allies had invaded Italy—the Swedish government canceled its 1940 agreement with Germany which had permitted German troops the right to pass through the country. Thereupon, the Danish workers decided that they could help a bit in hurrying things up; riots broke out in Danish shipyards, where the dock workers refused to repair German ships and then went on strike. The German military commander proclaimed a state of emergency and imposed martial law, and Himmler thought this was the right moment to tackle the Jewish question, whose "solution" was long overdue. What he did not reckon with was that—quite apart from Danish resistance—the German officials who had been living in the country for years were no longer the same. Not only did General von Hannecken, the military commander, refuse to put troops at the disposal of the Reich plenipotentiary, Dr. Werner Best; the special S.S. units (*Einsatzkommandos*) employed in Denmark very frequently objected to "the measures they were ordered to carry out by the central agencies"—according to Best's testimony at Nuremberg. And Best himself, an old Gestapo man and former legal adviser to Heydrich, author of a then famous book on the police, who had worked for the military government in Paris to the entire satisfaction of his superiors, could no longer be trusted, although it is doubtful that Berlin ever learned the extent of his unreliability. Still, it was clear from the beginning that things were not going well, and Eichmann's office sent one of its best men to Denmark—Rolf Günther, whom no one had ever accused of not possessing the required "ruthless toughness." Günther made no impression on his colleagues in Copenhagen, and now von Hannecken refused even to issue a decree requiring all Jews to report for work.

Best went to Berlin and obtained a promise that all Jews from

Denmark would be sent to Theresienstadt regardless of their category—a very important concession, from the Nazis' point of view. The night of October 1 was set for their seizure and immediate departure—ships were ready in the harbor—and since neither the Danes nor the Jews nor the German troops stationed in Denmark could be relied on to help, police units arrived from Germany for a door to door search. At the last moment, Best told them that they were not permitted to break into apartments, because the Danish police might then interfere, and they were not supposed to fight it out with the Danes. Hence they could seize only those Jews who voluntarily opened their doors. They found exactly 477 people, out of a total of more than 7,800, at home and willing to let them in. A few days before the date of doom, a German shipping agent, Georg F. Duckwitz, having probably been tipped by Best himself, had revealed the whole plan to Danish government officials, who in turn, had hurriedly informed the heads of the Jewish community. They, in marked contrast to Jewish leaders in other countries, had then communicated the news openly in the synagogues on the occasion of the New Year services. The Jews had just time enough to leave their apartments and go into hiding, which was very easy in Denmark, because, in the words of the judgment, "all sections of the Danish people, from the King down to simple citizens," stood ready to receive them.

They might have remained in hiding until the end of the war if the Danes had not been blessed with Sweden as a neighbor. It seemed reasonable to ship the Jews to Sweden, and this was done with the help of the Danish fishing fleet. The cost of transportation for people without means—about a hundred dollars per person—was paid largely by wealthy Danish citizens, and that was perhaps the most astounding feat of all, since this was a time when Jews were paying for their own deportation, when the rich among them were paying fortunes for exit permits (in Holland, Slovakia, and, later, in Hungary) either by bribing the local authorities or by negotiating "legally" with the S.S., who accepted only hard currency and sold exit permits, in Holland, to the tune of five or ten thousand dollars per person. Even in places where Jews met with genuine sympathy and a sincere willingness to help, they had to pay for it, and the chances poor people had of escaping were nil.

It took the better part of October to ferry all the Jews across the five to fifteen miles of water that separates Denmark from Sweden. The Swedes received 5,919 refugees, of whom at least 1,000 were of German origin, 1,310 were half-Jews, and 686 were non-Jews married to Jews. (Almost half the Danish Jews seem to have remained in the country and survived the war in hiding.) The non-Danish Jews were better off than ever before, they all received permission to work. The few hundred Jews whom the German police had been able to arrest were shipped to Theresienstadt. They were old or poor people, who either had not received the news in time or had not been able to comprehend its meaning. In the ghetto, they enjoyed greater privileges than any other group because of the never-ending "fuss" made about them by Danish institutions and private persons. Forty-eight persons died, a figure that was not particularly high, in view of the average age of the group. When everything was over, it was the considered opinion of Eichmann that "for various reasons the action against the Jews in Denmark has been a failure," whereas the curious Dr. Best declared that "the objective of the operation was not to seize a great number of Jews but to clean Denmark of Jews, and this objective has now been achieved."

Politically and psychologically, the most interesting aspect of this incident is perhaps the role played by the German authorities in Denmark, their obvious sabotage of orders from Berlin. It is the only case we know of in which the Nazis met with *open* native resistance, and the result seems to have been that those exposed to it changed their minds. They themselves apparently no longer looked upon the extermination of a whole people as a matter of course. They had met resistance based on principle, and their "toughness" had melted like butter in the sun, they had even been able to show a few timid beginnings of genuine courage. That the ideal of "toughness," except, perhaps, for a few half-demented brutes, was nothing but a myth of self-deception, concealing a ruthless desire for conformity at any price, was clearly revealed at the Nuremberg Trials, where the defendants accused and betrayed each other and assured the world that they "had always been against it" or claimed, as Eichmann was to do, that their best qualities had been "abused" by their superiors. (In Jerusalem, he accused "those in power" of having abused his "obedience." "The subject of a good government is lucky, the subject of a bad government is unlucky. I had no luck.") The atmosphere had changed, and although most of them must have known that they were doomed, not a single one of them had the guts to defend the Nazi ideology. Werner Best claimed at Nuremberg that he had played a complicated double role and that it was thanks to him that the Danish officials had been warned of the impending catastrophe; documentary evidence showed, on the contrary, that he himself had proposed the Danish operation in Berlin, but he explained that this was all part of the game. He was extradited to

Denmark and there condemned to death, but he appealed the sentence, with surprising results; because of "new evidence," his sentence was commuted to five years in prison, from which he was released soon afterward. He must have been able to prove to the satisfaction of the Danish court that he really had done his best.

Discussion Questions

1. What are the various attitudes toward Dr. Best implied in Hannah Arendt's use of the word, "curious"?

2. Is Arendt being ironic at the end of the essay? What would her view of the Danish people finally be, were she writing ironically? What would it be, were she not?

3. Both Hannah Arendt and Walter Lippman see the need for political "opposition." But are they concerned with the same thing? In an essay, define what each means by "political opposition."

4. Arendt scorns the "toughness" of the Nazi officials. How does her style define her own relation to courage and "toughness"? What sentences would you point to as expressive of courage in their author?

MICHAEL ARLEN

Born in London in 1930, Michael J. Arlen came to the U.S. in 1940. After graduating from Harvard University, Arlen worked as a reporter for Life magazine and in 1966 became a regular contributer to The New Yorker. He is the author of Exiles (1970), An American Verdict (1973), and an account of his quest for his Armenian roots, Passage to Ararat (1975), which won a National Book Award for contemporary affairs. His insightful essays on television have been collected in three volumes: The Living Room Wars (1969), The View from Highway 1 (1976), and The Camera Age (1981). His Thirty Seconds (1980) is a highly entertaining and informative report of how an advertising agency designs and produces a television commercial.

In "Ode to Thanksgiving," Arlen, by taking an irreverent look at a favorite American holiday, shows how family traditions can degenerate into mere conventions.

Ode to Thanksgiving

It is time, at last, to speak the truth about Thanksgiving, and the truth is this. Thanksgiving is really not such a terrific holiday. Consider the traditional symbols of the event: Dried cornhusks hanging on the door! Terrible wine! Cranberry jelly in little bowls of extremely doubtful provenance which everyone is required to handle with the greatest of care! Consider the participants, the merrymakers: men and women (also children) who have survived passably well throughout the years, mainly as a result of living at considerable distances from their dear parents and beloved siblings, who on this feast of feasts must apparently forgather (as if beckoned by an aberrant Fairy Godmother), usually by circuitous routes, through heavy traffic, at a common meeting place, where the very moods, distempers, and obtrusive personal habits that have kept them all happily apart since adulthood are then and there encouraged to slowly ferment beneath the cornhusks, and gradually rise with the aid of the terrible wine, and finally burst forth out of control under the stimulus of the cranberry jelly! No, it is a mockery of a holiday. For instance: *Thank you, O Lord, for what we are about to receive.* This is surely not a gala concept. There are no presents, unless one counts Aunt Bertha's sweet rolls a present, which no one does. There is precious little in the way of costumery: miniature plastic turkeys and those witless Pilgrim hats. There is no sex. Indeed, Thanksgiving is the one day of the year (a fact known to everybody) when all thoughts of sex completely vanish, evaporating from apartments, houses, condominiums, and mobile homes like steam from a bathroom mirror.

Consider also the nowhereness of the time of year: the last week or so in November. It is obviously not yet winter: winter, with its death-dealing blizzards and its girls in tiny skirts pirouetting on the ice. On the other hand, it is certainly not much use to anyone as fall: no golden leaves or Oktoberfests, and so forth. Instead, it is a no-man's-land between the seasons. In the cold and sobersides northern half of the country, it is a vaguely unsettling interregnum of long, mournful walks beneath leafless trees: the long, mournful walks following the midday repast with the dread inevitability of pie following turkey, and the leafless trees looming or standing about like eyesores, and the ground either as hard as iron or slightly mushy, and the light snow always beginning to fall when one is halfway to the old green gate—flecks of cold, watery stuff plopping between neck and collar, for the reason that, it being not yet winter, one has forgotten or not chosen to bring along a muffler. It is a corollary to the long, mournful Thanksgiving walk that the absence of this muffler is quickly noticed and that four weeks or so later, at Christmastime, instead of the Sony Betamax one had secretly hoped the children might have chipped in to purchase, one receives another muffler: by then the thirty-third. Thirty-three mufflers! Some walk! Of course, things are more fun in the warm and loony southern part of the country. No snow there of any kind. No need of mufflers. Also, no long, mournful walks, because in the warm and loony southern part of the country everybody drives. So everybody drives over to Uncle Jasper's house to watch the Cougars play the Gators, a not entirely unimportant conflict which will determine whether the Gators get a Bowl bid or must take another post-season exhibition tour of North Korea. But no sooner do the Cougars kick off (an astonishing end-over-end squiggly thing that floats lazily above the arena before plummeting down toward K. C. McCoy and catching him on the helmet) than Auntie Em starts hustling turkey. Soon Cousin May is slamming around the bowls and platters, and Cousin Bernice is oohing and ahing about "all the fixin's," and Uncle Bob is making low, insincere sounds of appreciation: "Yummy, yummy, Auntie Em, I'll have me some more of these delicious yams!" Delicious yams? Uncle Bob's eyes roll wildly in his head. Billy Joe Quaglino throws his long bomb in the middle of Grandpa Morris saying grace, Grandpa Morris speaking so low nobody can hear him, which is just as well, since he is reciting what he can remember of his last union contract. And then, just as J. B. (Speedy) Snood begins his ninety-two-yard punt return, Auntie Em starts dealing everyone second helpings of her famous stuffing, as if she were pushing a controlled substance, which it well might be, since there are no easily recognizable ingredients visible to the naked eye.

Consider for a moment the Thanksgiving meal itself. It has become a sort of refuge for endangered species of starch: cauliflower, turnips, pumpkin, mince (whatever "mince" is), those blessed yams. Bowls of luridly colored yams, with no taste at all, lying torpid under a lava flow of marshmallow! And then the sacred turkey. One might as well try to construct a holiday repast around a fish—say, a nice piece of haddock. After all, turkey tastes very similar to haddock: same consistency, same quite remarkable absence of flavor. But then, if the Thanksgiving *pièce de résistance* were a nice piece of boiled haddock instead of turkey, there wouldn't be all that fun for Dad when Mom hands him the sterling-silver, bone-handled carving set (a wedding present from her parents and not sharpened since) and then everyone sits around pretending not to watch while he saws and tears away at the bird as if he were trying to burrow his way into or out of some grotesque, fowl-like prison.

What of the good side to Thanksgiving, you ask. There is always a good side to everything. Not to Thanksgiving. There is only a bad side and then a worse side. For instance, Grandmother's best linen tablecloth is a bad side: the fact that it is produced each year, in the manner of a red flag being produced before a bull, and then is always spilled upon by whichever child is doing poorest at school that term and so is in need of greatest reassurance. Thus: "Oh, my God, *Veronica*, you just spilled grape juice [or plum wine or tar] on Grandmother's best linen tablecloth!" But now comes worse. For at this point Cousin Bill, the one who lost all Cousin Edwina's money on the car dealership three years ago and has apparently been drinking steadily since Halloween, bizarrely chooses to say: "Seems to me those old glasses are always falling over." To which Auntie Meg is heard to add: "Somehow I don't remember receivin' any of those old glasses." To which Uncle Fred replies: "That's because you and George decided to go on vacation to Hawaii the summer Grandpa Sam was dying." Now Grandmother is sobbing, though not so uncontrollably that she can refrain from murmuring: "I think that volcano painting I threw away by mistake got sent me from Hawaii, heaven knows why." But the gods are merciful, even the Pilgrim-hatted god of cornhusks and soggy stuffing, and there is an end to everything, even to Thanksgiving. Indeed, there is a grandeur to the feelings of finality and doom which usually settle on a house after the Thanksgiving celebration is over, for with the completion of Thanksgiving Day the year itself has been properly terminated: shot through the cranium with a high-velocity candied yam. At this calendrical nadir, all energy on the planet has gone, all fun has fled, all the terrible wine has been drunk.

But then, overnight, life once again begins to stir, emerging, even by the next morning, in the form of Japanese window displays and Taiwanese Christmas lighting, from the primeval ooze of the nation's department stores. Thus, a new year dawns, bringing with it immediate and cheering possibilities of extended consumer debt, office-party flirtations, good—or, at least, mediocre—wine, and visions of Supersaver excursion fares to Montego Bay. It is worth noting, perhaps, that this true new year always starts with the same mute, powerful mythic ceremony: the surreptitious tossing out, in the early morning, of all those horrid aluminum-foil packages of yams and cauliflower and stuffing and red, gummy cranberry substance which have been squeezed into the refrigerator as if a reenactment of the siege of Paris were shortly expected. Soon afterward, the phoenix of Christmas can be observed as it slowly rises, beating its drumsticks, once again goggle-eyed with hope and unrealistic expectations.

Discussion Questions

1. Arlen begins his essay "It is time, at last, to speak the truth about Thanksgiving." What assumptions is he making right off about the reader's attitude toward the topic? What sort of writing about Thanksgiving does Arlen assume most people are familiar with? How does his humor depend upon those assumptions?

2. Arlen's address to the reader shifts from "me" to "you." What effect do these pronoun shifts have on the reader's involvement? Suppose Arlen had used "I" or "we" instead; what difference would that have made?

3. Make a list of the main props of a typical Thanksgiving. How does Arlen work these props into his essay? What precisely doesn't he like about them?

4. How does Arlen's sense of holiday traditions compare with Gwendolyn Brooks's?

5. Who are the characters appearing in this essay? Whose family do they belong to? What does Arlen find amusing about their behavior? Do the family members find each other amusing? Explain.

6. If you agree with Arlen's view of a Thanksgiving celebration, try writing a similar account of another American holiday (for example, Christmas, the Fourth of July, New Year's Eve, and so forth). If you disagree with Arlen's view, try writing an alternative description of a Thanksgiving holiday. Can you offer a positive account of Thanksgiving without relying on the conventional responses that Arlen makes fun of in his essay?

Isaac Asimov

The author of over two hundred books, Isaac Asimov was born in Russia in 1920 and grew up in Brooklyn, New York. He received a doctorate in biochemistry from Columbia in 1948, but eventually gave up a teaching career to write full time. Many of his science fiction novels, especially I, Robot *(1950) and* The Foundation Trilogy *(1974), are considered classics of the genre. An obsessive writer who claims that writing is his "only interest," Asimov is equally well known for his nonfiction books on science, which include, besides his numerous volumes of collected essays,* The Chemicals of Life *(1954),* Inside the Atom *(1956; 1966),* The Realm of Numbers *(1959),* The Wellsprings of Life *(1960), and* The Intelligent Man's Guide to Science *(1960). He has recently written a scientific study of the Bible.*

In the following essay, which originally appeared in Saturday Review, *Asimov brings his characteristic lucidity to bear on a modern problem that has serious humanistic as well as scientific implications.*

Pure and Impure: The Interplay of Science and Technology

It is easy to divide a human being into mind and body and to attach far greater importance and reverence to the mind. Similarly, the products of the human mind can be divided into two classes: those that serve to elevate the mind and those that serve to comfort the body. The former are the "liberal arts," the latter, the "mechanical arts."

The liberal arts are those suitable for free men who are in a position to profit from the labors of others in such a way that they are not compelled to work themselves. The liberal arts deal with "pure knowledge" and are highly thought of, as all things pure must be.

The mechanical arts, which serve agriculture, commerce, and industry, are necessary, too; but as long as slaves, serfs, peasants, and others of low degree know such things, educated gentlemen of leisure can do without them.

Among the liberal arts are some aspects of science. Surely the kinds of studies that have always characterized science—the complex influences that govern the motions of the heavenly bodies, for instance, and that control the properties of mathematical figures and even of the universe itself—are pure enough. As history progressed, though, science developed a low habit of becoming applicable to the work of the world and, as a result, those whose field of mental endeavor lies in the liberal arts (minus science) tend to look down on scientists today as being in altogether too great a danger of dirtying their hands.

Scientists, in response, tend to ape this Greek-inherited snobbishness. They divide science into two parts; one deals only with the difficult, the abstruse, the elegant, the fundamental—in other words, "pure science," a truly liberal art. The other type of science is any branch that goes slumming and becomes associated with such mechanical arts as medicine, agriculture, and industry—clearly a form of impure science. "Impure" is a rather pejorative adjective. It is more common to talk of "basic science" and "applied science." On the other hand, differentiation by adjective alone may not seem enough. The same noun applied to both makes the higher suspect and lends the lower too much credit. There has thus been a tendency to call applied science "technology."

We can therefore speak of "science" and "technology" and we know very well which is the loftier, nobler, more aristocratic, and (in a whisper) the purer of the two. Yet the division is man-made and arbitrary and has no meaning in reality. The advance of knowledge of the physical universe rests on science *and* technology; neither can flourish without the other.

Technology is, indeed, the older of the two. Long before any human being could possibly have become interested in vague speculations about the universe, the hominid precursors of modern human beings were chipping rocks in order to get a sharp edge, and technology was born. Further advances, by hit and miss, trial and error, and even by hard thought, were slow, of course, in the absence of some understanding of basic principles that would guide the technologists in the direction of the possible and inspire them with a grasp of the potential.

Science, as distinct from technology, can be traced back as far as the ancient Greeks who advanced beautiful and intricate speculations. The speculations perhaps tended to become more beautiful, certainly more intricate, but there was no way in which they could have become more in accord with reality. The Greeks, alas, spun their speculations out of deductions based on what they guessed to be principles, and they sharply limited any temptation to indulge in a comparison of their conclusions with the world about them.

It was only when scientists began to observe the real world and to manipulate it that "experimental science" arose. This was in the 16th century, and the most able practitioner was the Italian scientist, Galileo Galilei, who began work toward the end of that century. Thus began the Scientific Revolution.

In the 18th century, when enough scientists recognized their responsibility toward the mechanical arts, we had the Industrial Revolution; it reshaped human life.

Such is the psychological set of our minds toward a separation of science into pure and impure, basic and applied, useless and useful, intellectual and industrial, that even today it is difficult for people to grasp the frequent and necessary interplay between them.

Consider the first great technologist of the modern era, the Scottish engineer, James Watt. Though he did not invent the steam engine, he developed the first one with a condensing chamber and was the first to devise attachments that converted the back-and-forth motion of a piston into the turning of a wheel. He also invented the first automatic feedback devices that controlled the engine's output of steam. In short, beginning in 1769, he developed the first truly practical and versatile mechanism for turning inanimate heat into work and thus started the Industrial Revolution. But was Watt a mere tinkerer? Was he a technologist and nothing more?

At the time there lived a Scottish chemist, Joseph Black, who, in his scientific studies of heat in 1764, measured the quantity of heat it takes to boil water. As heat energy pours into water, he found, its temperature goes up rapidly. As water begins to boil, however, vast quantities of heat are absorbed without further rise in temperature. The heat goes entirely into the conversion of liquid to vapor, a phenomenon known as "the latent heat of evaporation." The result is that steam contains far more energy than does hot water at exactly the same temperature.

Watt, who knew Black, learned of this latent heat and familiarized himself with the principle involved. That principle guided him in his improvements of the already existing steam engines. Black, in turn, impressed with the exciting application of his discovery, lent Watt a large sum of money to support him in his work. The Industrial Revolution, then, was the product of a fusion of science and technology.

Nor is the flow of knowledge entirely in the direction from science toward technology. While many people (even nonscientists) can now recognize that scientific research and discovery, however pure and abstract they may seem, may turn out to have some impure and practical application, few (even among scientists) seem to recognize that, if anything, the flow is stronger in the other direction. Science would stop dead without an input from technology.

In 1581, Galileo, then 17 years old, discovered the principle of the pendulum. In the 1590s, he went on to study the behavior of falling bodies and was greatly hampered by his lack of any device to measure small intervals of time accurately. The first good timepiece was not developed until 1656, when the Dutch scientist, Christiaan Huygens, applied Galileo's principle of the pendulum to construct what we would today call a "grandfather's clock." The principle of the pendulum, by itself, would have done little to advance science. The application of the pendulum principle and the technological development of timepieces made it possible for scientists to make the kind of observations they could never have made before.

In similar fashion, astronomy could not possibly have progressed much past Copernicus without technology. The crucial key to astronomical advance began with spectacle-makers, mere artisans who ground lenses, and with an idle apprentice boy, who, in 1608, played with those lenses—and discovered the principle of the telescope. Galileo built such a telescope and turned it on the heavens. No greater revolution in knowledge has ever occurred in so short a time as the second it took him to turn his telescope on the moon and discover mountains there. In brief, the history of modern science is the history of the development, through technology, of the instruments that are its tools.

Yet tools do not represent the only influence of technology. The products of technology offer a field for renewed speculation. For instance, although Watt had greatly increased the efficiency of the steam engine, it still remained very inefficient. Up to 95 percent of the heat energy of the burning fuel was wasted and was not converted into useful work. A French physicist, Nicolas Carnot, applied himself to this problem. Involving himself with something as technological as the steam engine, he began to consider the flow of heat from a hot body to a cold body and ended up founding the science of thermodynamics (from the Greek for "heat-movement").

Nor is it true that science and technology interacted only in the past. The year 1979 is, by coincidence, a significant year for two great men who seem to typify the very epitome of the purest of science on the one hand and the most practical of technology on the other—Albert Einstein, the greatest scientist since Newton, and Thomas Alva Edison, the greatest inventor since anybody. This year marks the centennial of Einstein's birth. It is also the centennial of Edison's greatest invention, the electric light. How did the work of each man invade the field of the other?

Surely, the theory of relativity, which Einstein originated, is as pure an example of science as one can imagine. The very word "practical" seems a blasphemy when applied to it. Yet the theory of relativity describes the behavior of objects moving at sizable fractions of the speed of light as nothing else can. Subatomic particles move at such speeds, and they cannot be studied properly without a consideration of their "relativistic motions." This means that modern particle accelerators can't exist without taking into account Einstein's theory, and all our present uses of the products of these accelerators would go by the board. We would not have radioisotopes, for instance, for use in medicine, in industry, in chemical analysis—and, of course, we would not have them as tools in advancing research into pure science, either.

Out of the theory of relativity, moreover, came deductions that interrelated matter and energy in a definite way (the famous $E = mc^2$). Until Einstein gave us this equation, matter and energy had been thought to be independent and unconnected entities. Guided by the theory, we came to see more meaning in energy aspects of research in subatomic particles, and in the end, the nuclear bomb was invented and nuclear-power stations were made possible.

Einstein worked outside the field of relativity, too. In 1917, he pointed out that if a molecule is at a high-energy level (a concept made possible by the purely scientific quantum theory, which had its origin in 1900) and if it is struck by a photon (a unit of radiation energy) of just the proper frequency, the molecule drops to lower energy. It does this because it gives up some of its energy in the form of a photon of the precise frequency and moving in the precise direction as the original photon.

Thirty-six years later, in 1953, Charles Hard Townes made use of Einstein's theoretical reasoning to invent the "maser" that could amplify a short-wave radio ("micro-wave") beam of photons into a much stronger beam. In 1960, Theodore Harold Maiman extended the principle to the still shorter-wave photons of visible light and devised the first "laser." The laser has infinite applications, from eye surgery to possible use as a war weapon.

And Edison?

The net result of his inventions was to spread the use of electricity the world over; to increase greatly the facilities for the generation and transmission of electricity; to make more important any device that would make that generation and transmission more efficient and economical. In short, Edison made the pure-science study of the flow and behavior of the electric current an important field of study.

Charles Proteus Steinmetz was certainly a technologist. He worked for General Electric and had two hundred patents in his name. Yet he also worked out, in complete mathematical detail, the intricacies of alternating-current circuitry, a towering achievement in pure science. Similar work was done by Oliver Heaviside.

As for Edison himself, his own work on the electric light unwittingly led him in the direction of purity. After he had developed the electric light, he labored for years to improve its efficiency and, in particular, to make the glowing filament last longer before breaking. As was usual for him, he tried everything he could think of. One of his hit-and-miss efforts was to seal a metal wire into the evacuated electric light bulb near, but not touching, the filament. The two were separated by a small gap of vacuum.

Edison then turned on the electric current to see if the presence of the metal wire would somehow preserve the life of the glowing filament. It didn't, and Edison abandoned the approach. However, he noticed that an electric current flowed from the filament to the wire across that vacuum gap. Nothing in Edison's vast practical knowledge of electricity explained this flow of current, but he observed it, wrote it up in his notebooks, and patented it. The phenomenon was called the "Edison effect," and it was Edison's only discovery in pure science—but it arose directly out of his technology.

Did this seemingly casual observation lead to anything? Well, it indicated that an electric current has, associated with it, a flow of matter of a particularly subtle sort—matter that was eventually shown to be electrons, the first subatomic particles to be recognized. Once this was discovered, methods were found to modify and amplify the electron flow in vacuum and, in this way, to control the behavior of an electric current with far greater delicacy than the flipping of switches could. Out of the Edison effect came the huge field of electronics.

There are other examples. A technological search for methods to eliminate static in radiotelephony served as the basis for the development of radio astronomy and the discovery of such phenomena as quasars, pulsars, and the big bang.

The technological development of the transistor brought on an improved way of manipulating and controlling electric currents, and has led to the computerization and automation of society. Computers have become essential tools in both technology and science. A computer was even necessary for the solution of one of the most famous problems in pure mathematics—the four-color problem.

The technological development of a liquid-fuel rocket has led to something as purely astronomical as the mapping, in detail, of Mars and of experiments with its soil.

The fact is that science and technology are one.

Just as there is only one species of human being on earth, and all divisions into races, cultures, and nations are but man-made ways of obscuring that fundamental truth, so there is only one scientific endeavor on earth—the pursuit of knowledge and understanding—and all divisions into disciplines and levels of purity are but man-made ways of obscuring *that* fundamental truth.

PURE AND IMPURE

Discussion Questions

1. Why, according to Asimov, does the word "technology" have pejorative meanings? In what sense does it differ from "science"?

2. According to the essay, in what ways does technology help advance science? What specifically does technology provide that scientific research requires?

3. How do the references to Einstein and Edison support Asimov's argument?

4. How does Asimov's view of science compare to Bronowski's view? Would Asimov mainly agree or disagree with Bronowski's view?

5. Asimov leads his readers to the conclusion that two areas of thought they had customarily regarded as different are in fact the same: "science and technology are one." How has he prepared us for this conclusion? Do you find it convincing? Can you offer counter examples that would argue for the more customary separation of the two areas?

6. Using Asimov's method, write an essay in which you argue by means of example how two areas of endeavor that people frequently contrast are actually closely interrelated; for example, criticism and creativity, work and play.

Russell Baker

A widely syndicated essayist and humorist, Russell Baker was born in Loudoun County, Virginia, in 1925. After the Second World War, Baker completed his B.A. at Johns Hopkins University and in 1947 started as a cub reporter on the police beat for the Baltimore *Sun. A skillful journalist, Baker quickly moved up the news ladder and in 1954 became a member of the* New York Times's *Washington Bureau. As a columnist for the* Times *since 1962, he has specialized in political satire and witty critiques of assorted American absurdities.*

Baker won the Pulitzer Prize for Commentary in 1979. His newspaper columns have been collected in An American in Washington *(1961),* No Cause for Panic *(1964),* All Things Considered *(1965), and* Poor Russell's Almanac *(1972). In 1979, he wrote a musical comedy,* Home Again. *The following essay shows him having fun with one of his favorite amusements—the "modern American language."*

Little Red Riding Hood Revisited

In an effort to make the classics accessible to contemporary readers, I am translating them into the modern American language. Here is the translation of "Little Red Riding Hood":

Once upon a point in time, a small person named Little Red Riding Hood initiated plans for the preparation, delivery and transportation of foodstuffs to her grandmother, a senior citizen residing at a place of residence in a forest of indeterminate dimension.

In the process of implementing this program, her incursion into the forest was in midtransportation process when it attained interface with an alleged perpetrator. This individual, a wolf, made inquiry as to the whereabouts of Little Red Riding Hood's goal as well as inferring that he was desirous of ascertaining the contents of Little Red Riding Hood's foodstuffs basket, and all that.

"It would be inappropriate to lie to me," the wolf said, displaying his huge jaw capability. Sensing that he was a mass of repressed hostility intertwined with acute alienation, she indicated.

"I see you indicating," the wolf said, "but what I don't see is whatever it is you're indicating at, you dig?"

Little Red Riding Hood indicated more fully, making one thing perfectly clear—to wit, that it was to her grandmother's residence and with a consignment of foodstuffs that her mission consisted of taking her to and with.

At this point in time the wolf moderated his rhetoric and proceeded to grandmother's residence. The elderly person was then subjected to the disadvantages of total consumption and transferred to residence in the perpetrator's stomach.

"That will raise the old woman's consciousness," the wolf

said to himself. He was not a bad wolf, but only a victim of an oppressive society, a society that not only denied wolves' rights, but actually boasted of its capacity for keeping the wolf from the door. An interior malaise made itself manifest inside the wolf.

"Is that the national malaise I sense within my digestive tract?" wondered the wolf. "Or is it the old person seeking to retaliate for her consumption by telling wolf jokes to my duodenum?" It was time to make a judgment. The time was now, the hour had struck, the body lupine cried out for decision. The wolf was up to the challenge. He took two stomach powders right away and got into bed.

The wolf had adopted the abdominal-distress recovery posture when Little Red Riding Hood achieved his presence.

"Grandmother," she said, "your ocular implements are of an extraordinary order of magnitude."

"The purpose of this enlarged viewing capability," said the wolf, "is to enable your image to register a more precise impression upon my sight systems."

"In reference to your ears," said Little Red Riding Hood, "it is noted with the deepest respect that far from being underprivileged, their elongation and enlargement appear to qualify you for unparalleled distinction."

"I hear you loud and clear, kid," said the wolf, "but what about these new choppers?"

"If it is not inappropriate," said Little Red Riding Hood, "it might be observed that with your new miracle masticating products you may even be able to chew taffy again."

This observation was followed by the adoption of an aggressive posture on the part of the wolf and the assertion that it was also possible for him, due to the high efficiency ratio of his jaw, to consume little persons, plus, as he stated, his firm determination to do so at once without delay and with all due process and propriety, notwithstanding the fact that the ingestion of one entire grandmother had already provided twice his daily recommended cholesterol intake.

There ensued flight by Little Red Riding Hood accompanied by pursuit in respect to the wolf and a subsequent intervention on the part of a third party, heretofore unnoted in the record.

Due to the firmness of the intervention, the wolf's stomach underwent ax-assisted aperture with the result that Red Riding Hood's grandmother was enabled to be removed with only minor discomfort.

The wolf's indigestion was immediately alleviated with such effectiveness that he signed a contract with the intervening third party to perform with grandmother in a television commercial demonstrating the swiftness of this dramatic relief for stomach discontent.

"I'm going to be on television," cried grandmother.

And they all joined her happily in crying, "What a phenomena!"

Discussion Questions

1. How would you describe the central joke of the essay? What do we need to know in order to understand Baker's humor? Jokes are often "on" someone—whom is this joke on?

2. Go through the essay underlining all the words and phrases that comprise what Baker calls the "modern American language." Where have you heard language like this before? How would you classify the types of expressions Baker uses?

3. Which fairy tale is grimmer—Baker's or the original "Little Red Riding Hood"? Why does Baker change the story?

4. In what way is Baker's response to language similar to that of George Orwell in "Politics and the English Language"? How does Orwell describe what Baker pokes fun at? Is there a serious side to Baker's tale?

5. Choose another classic tale and write another version of it by "translating" it into a different style and idiom. Imagine, for example, the story of Cinderella reported on the six o'clock news.

JAMES BALDWIN

The son of a minister, James Baldwin was born in 1924 in Harlem, where he began preaching at the age of fourteen. After graduating high school, he took jobs as a maintenance worker, factory worker, and waiter. He received a fellowship in 1948 and moved to France, where he wrote his first two novels, Go Tell It on the Mountain *(1953) and* Giovanni's Room *(1956), along with a series of autobiographical essays,* Notes of a Native Son *(1955).*

In 1957, Baldwin returned to the United States and took an active role in the civil rights movement. Out of his first-hand experiences with racism he wrote the essays collected in Nobody Knows My Name *(1961) and* The Fire Next Time *(1963). After the assassinations of Martin Luther King and Malcolm X, he moved back to France, disillusioned with the prospects for racial equality in his native land. His most recent books include three novels,* Tell Me How Long the Train's Been Gone *(1968),* If Beale Street Could Talk *(1974), and* Just Above My Head *(1979), as well as two nonfiction works,* No Name in the Street *(1972) and* The Devil Finds Work *(1976).*

If Black English Isn't a Language, Then Tell Me, What Is?

The argument concerning the use, or the status, or the reality, of black English is rooted in American history and has absolutely nothing to do with the question the argument supposes itself to be posing. The argument has nothing to do with language itself but with the *role* of language. Language, incontestably, reveals the speaker. Language, also, far more dubiously, is meant to define the other—and, in this case, the other is refusing to be defined by a language that has never been able to recognize him.

People evolve a language in order to describe and thus control their circumstances, or in order not to be submerged by a reality that they cannot articulate. (And, if they cannot articulate it, they *are* submerged.) A Frenchman living in Paris speaks a subtly and crucially different language from that of the man living in Marseilles; neither sounds very much like a man living in Quebec; and they would all have great difficulty in apprehending what the man from Guadeloupe, or Martinique, is saying, to say nothing of the man from Senegal—although the "common" language of all these areas is French. But each has paid, and is paying, a different price for this "common" language, in which, as it turns out, they are not saying, and cannot be saying, the same things: They each have very different realities to articulate or control.

What joins all languages, and all men, is the necessity to confront life, in order, not inconceivably, to outwit death: The price for this is the acceptance, and achievement, of one's temporal identity. So that, for example, though it is not taught in the schools (and this has the potential of becoming a political issue) the south of France still clings to its ancient and musical Provençal, which resists being described as a "dialect." And much of the tension in the Basque countries, and in Wales, is due to the Basque and

Welsh determination not to allow their languages to be destroyed. This determination also feeds the flames in Ireland for among the many indignities the Irish have been forced to undergo at English hands is the English contempt for their language.

It goes without saying, then, that language is also a political instrument, means, and proof of power. It is the most vivid and crucial key to identity: It reveals the private identity, and connects one with, or divorces one from, the larger public, or communal identity. There have been, and are, times, and places, when to speak a certain language could be dangerous, even fatal. Or, one may speak the same language, but in such a way that one's antecedents are revealed, or (one hopes) hidden. This is true in France, and is absolutely true in England: The range (and reign) of accents on that damp little island make England coherent for the English and totally incomprehensible for everyone else. To open your mouth in England is (if I may use black English) to "put your business in the street": You have confessed your parents, your youth, your school, your salary, your self-esteem, and, alas, your future.

Now, I do not know what white American would sound like if there had never been any black people in the United States, but they would not sound the way they sound. *Jazz*, for example, is a very specific sexual term, as in *jazz me, baby*, but white people purified it into the Jazz Age. *Sock it to me*, which means, roughly, the same thing, has been adopted by Nathaniel Hawthorne's descendants with no qualms or hesitations at all, along with *let it all hang out* and *right on! Beat to his socks*, which was once the black's most total and despairing image of poverty, was transformed into a thing called the Beat Generation, which phenomenon was, largely, composed of *uptight*, middle-class white people, imitating poverty, trying to *get down*, to get *with it*, doing their *thing*, doing their despairing best to be *funky*, which we, the blacks, never dreamed of doing—we *were* funky, baby, like *funk* was going out of style.

Now, no one can eat his cake, and have it, too, and it is late in the day to attempt to penalize black people for having created a language that permits the nation its only glimpse of reality, a language without which the nation would be even more *whipped* than it is.

I say that this present skirmish is rooted in American history, and it is. Black English is the creation of the black diaspora. Blacks came to the United States chained to each other, but from different tribes: Neither could speak the other's language. If two black people, at that bitter hour of the world's history, had been able to speak to each other, the institution of chattel slavery could never have lasted as long as it did. Subsequently, the slave was given, under the eye, and the gun, of his master, Congo Square, and the Bible—or, in other words, and under these conditions, the slave began the formation of the black church, and it is within this unprecedented tabernacle that black English began to be formed. This was not, merely, as in the European example, the adoption of a foreign tongue, but an alchemy that transformed ancient elements into new language: *A language comes into existence by means of brutal necessity, and the rules of the language are dictated by what the language must convey.*

There was a moment, in time, and in this place, when my brother, or my mother, or my father, or my sister, had to convey to me, for example, the danger in which I was standing from the white man standing just behind me, and to convey this with a speed, and in a language, that the white man could not possibly understand, and that, indeed, he cannot understand, until today. He cannot afford to understand it. This understanding would reveal to him too much about himself, and smash that mirror before which he has been frozen for so long.

Now, if this passion, this skill, this (to quote Toni Morrison) "sheer intelligence," this incredible music, the mighty achievement of having brought a people utterly unknown to, or despised by "history"—to have brought this people to their present, troubled, troubling, and unassailable and unanswerable place—if this absolutely unprecedented journey does not indicate that black English is a language, I am curious to know what definition of language is to be trusted.

A people at the center of the Western world, and in the midst of so hostile a population, has not endured and transcended by means of what is patronizingly called a "dialect." We, the blacks, are in trouble, certainly, but we are not doomed, and we are not inarticulate because we are not compelled to defend a morality that we know to be a lie.

The brutal truth is that the bulk of the white people in America never had any interest in educating black people, except as this could serve white purposes. It is not the black child's language that is in question, it is not his language that is despised: It is his experience. A child cannot be taught by anyone who despises him, and a child cannot afford to be fooled. A child cannot be taught by anyone whose demand, essentially, is that the child repudiate his experience, and all that gives him sustenance, and enter a limbo in which he will no longer be black, and in which he knows that he can never become white. Black people have lost too many black children that way.

And, after all, finally, in a country with standards so untrustworthy, a country that makes heroes of so many criminal mediocrities, a country unable to face why so many of the nonwhite are in prison, or on the needle, or standing, futureless, in the streets—it may very well be that both the child, and his elder, have concluded that they have nothing whatever to learn from the people of a country that has managed to learn so little.

Discussion Questions

1. Why does Baldwin think that "dialect" is a patronizing and inaccurate term for Black English? What does he think will be gained by having Black English considered as a "language" in its own right?

2. Why didn't Baldwin write his entire essay in Black English? Do you think that it weakens his argument that he is able to present an articulate and passionately reasoned plea for Black English in the "common" language, which he implies is less capable of dealing with reality? Can you sense any internal conflict between both "languages" in the essay itself?

3. In what sense is Baldwin's essay about something other than language? What, to Baldwin's thinking, is more important than language?

4. Nearly all groups—such as teenagers, for example—develop special languages to express what they feel are distinctive beliefs, thoughts, and emotions. Think of an example of such a language and discuss how it fits Baldwin's definition of what a language is and how it evolves.

5. How do Baldwin's senses of the meaning and function of language and style differ from those of Edmund Wilson? Make a list of particular differences. Do you find any similarities? Again, make a list.

JACQUES BARZUN

Jacques Barzun was born in France in 1907. On coming to the United States, he found in Columbia University a part of America that was to become a life-long professional home. He received his B.A., M.A., and Ph.D. degrees all at Columbia. Even before he had completed his studies, he was teaching history at Columbia, and he worked as a teacher and administrator of that university for the rest of his academic life.

In addition to the essays published in leading periodicals for four decades, the books that Barzun has written, translated, or edited take up well over a column of small type in professional directories, and the list continues to grow. He has addressed history, music, education, language, and contemporary social issues, not to mention crime fiction. In addition to volume and breadth, Barzun's writing has often proved so enduring that his books become reissued years after their initial date of publication. Such a book is Teacher in America (1945). The essay that follows appears in a slightly altered form as the preface to that book in its 1981 edition.

The Wasteland of American Education

To those who follow the news about education, the present state of American schools and colleges must seem vastly different from that which I described in my book *Teacher in America* when it first appeared. Thirty-six years have passed, true; but the normal drift of things will not account for the great chasm. The once proud and efficient public school system of the United States—especially its unique free high school for all—has turned into a wasteland where violence and vice share the time with ignorance and idleness, besides serving as battleground for vested interest, social, political, and economic.

The new product of that debased system, the functional illiterate, is numbered in millions, while various forms of deceit have become accepted as inevitable—"social promotion" or passing incompetents to the next grade to save face; "graduating" from "high school" with eighth-grade reading ability; "equivalence of credits" or photography as good as physics; "certificates of achievement" for those who fail the "minimum competency" test; and most lately, "bilingual education," by which the rudiments are supposedly taught in over ninety languages other than English. The old plan and purpose of teaching the young what they truly need to know survives only in the private sector, itself hard-pressed and shrinking in size.

Meantime, colleges and universities have undergone a comparable devastation. The great postwar rush to college for a share in upward mobility and professional success was soon encouraged and enlarged by public money under the GI bills and the National Defense Education Act. Under this pressure higher education changed in quality and tone. The flood of students caused many once modest local colleges and deplorable teachers' colleges to suddenly dub themselves universities and attempt what they were not fit for. State university systems threw out branches in cities already well provided with private, municipal, or denominational institutions; and new creations—junior colleges and community colleges—entered the competition for the student moneys and other grants coming out of the public purse. The purpose and manner of higher education were left behind.

No doubt some of the novelties were beneficial. The junior and community colleges, with their self-regarding concern for good teaching, often awakened talent in students overlooked in the scramble for admission to better-known places. But at all institutions, old and new, the increase in numbers requiring expansion—wholesale building, increase of staff, proliferation of courses, complex administration, year-round instruction—brought on a state of mind unsuited to teaching and learning. In their place, the bustle became a processing and a being processed.

This deep alteration went unnoticed in the excitement of change and growth. But other influences soon made it clear that the idea of college and university as seats of learning was being lost. Because of its evident social usefulness in war and peace, the academic profession after 1945 enjoyed two decades of high repute. The public no longer regarded "the professor" with distant respect for remote activities, but gave cordial admiration as between men of the world.

The result was the introduction on the campus of a new standard of judgment. Scholars and scientists who had done something acknowledged by the outside world were a source of renown to the institution; they were the men who could bring home notable research projects, with money from government or private foundations; they were valuable properties like top baseball players. And since every college and university was "expanding to meet social needs," these men were haggled over by rival places like artworks at an auction. The terms offered showed in dollars their value as bringers of prestige and in "free time for research" the new conception of what an academic man was for. In the upward bidding between alma mater and the raiding institution it was not unusual to reach an offer guaranteeing "no obligation to teach" or (the next best thing) "leave of absence every other term."

Thus was the "flight from teaching" made explicit and official and nationwide. It had begun well before the war, during the Roosevelt years, when Washington drew on academic experts for help in administering the New Deal. But in those early days a scholar so drafted was expected to resign his university post after a one- or two-year leave. During the war this requirement would have seemed unfair, and so the custom grew of using the university as a permanent base for far-flung excursions. The large private foundations encouraged the practice and were not resisted: how could these prize men be retained on the faculty if they were denied the opportunities of high research? A large foundation can subsidize work in ten, twelve, twenty departments simultaneously, and protest would come from them all if the policy were established of chaining the professor to the classroom. The leave of absence—the absence itelf—became the sign of the really able.

This new behavior forced on the academy could be called a species of colonialism on the part of the foundations and the government. Bringing money, they obtained spheres of influence and exerted control without rights; their favor was sought and cherished; and they obviously diverted the professional allegiance from the university to the outside power. With a dispersed, revolving faculty, the institution ceased to have a recognizable individual face. At the same time, the federal or foundation rules under which grants were made introduced a new bureaucratic element into the customary ways of academic self-governance. And this too changed the academic atmosphere for the worse. Under the double strain of expansionism inside and colonialism outside, the university lost its wholeness (not to say its integrity) and prepared the way for its own debacle in 1965—1968.

The unresisted student and faculty riots of those years were the logical counterpart of unfulfilled promises. Brought up in the progressive mode of the lower schools, young people eager for higher learning—and others indifferent but caught in the rush—found themselves on campuses where teaching was regarded as a disagreeable chore: students were an obstacle to serious work. Teaching was left to those few who, having seen it, still believed in it, and to those others who could not "get an offer" from elsewhere or a grant from Croesus public and private. Since such derelicts were not directing teams of research associates in studies of current social questions, or traveling on missions to settle the problems of Appalachian poverty or Venezuelan finance, there was nothing for them to do but teach. And much of this teaching was excellent, as is shown by the gratitude of many who took their degrees in those years.

But the prevailing mode was that of neglect and it bore hard on students, at a time when every kind of desirable occupation was becoming the subject of an academic course leading to a certificate. The "credentials society" was in full development and the need for high marks and glowing recommendations was imperative. When so-called teachers left in mid-semester or steadily missed office hours or showed their lack of interest in class or conference, they bred emotions likely to explode in future. Quite apart from the threat of the draft for the war in Vietnam, student feeling by the mid-Sixties was one of open disaffection from the university and its faculty and from the society and its culture.

These last two objects of resentment were bound to fill students' minds when their mentors were so loudly diagnosing and dosing the ills of society. As for the hatred of high bourgeois culture, it was communicated by nearly every contemporary novel, play, painting, or artist's biography that found a place in the popular part of the curriculum. So the age was past when "freshman year" in a good college came as a revelation of wonders undreamed of, as the first mature interplay of minds.

Moreover, in the new ambulant university, what might have been fresh and engrossing was presented in its least engaging form, that of the specialist: not anthropology as a distinctive way of looking at peoples and nations, with examples of general import, but accumulated detail about a tribe the instructor had lived with—and apparently could not get away from. At best, the announced "introductory course" did not introduce the subject but tried to make recruits for advanced work in the field. This attitude no doubt showed dedication of a sort. It was easier to bear, perhaps, than the indifference of others who, in the name of the discussion method, let the students "exchange ideas" without guidance or correction—each class hour a rap session. But in none of these forms could the exercise be called undergraduate teaching; and its parallel in graduate school was equally stultifying to the many who in those years went on, hoping against hope to obtain true learning from institutions claiming the title.

The violent rebels against boredom and neglect, make-believe and the hunt for credentials never made clear their best reasons, nor did they bring the university back to its senses; the uprising did not abate specialism or restore competence and respect to teaching. The "great teacher awards" given here and there only meant tokenism and lip service and provided an ironic commentary on the reality. The flight from the campus did cease, but that was owing to the drying up of federal money and the foundations' abandonment of world salvation by academic means. What the upheaval left was disarray shot through with the adversary spirit. It expressed itself in written rules arrived at by struggle and compromise, through committees and representative bodies set up as the arena of divergent needs and claims. Students, faculties, and administrators tried to rebuild in their own special interest the institution they had wrecked cooperatively. But, alas, the duty to teach well cannot be legislated.

The result, fostered by a fresh wave of government regulation and supervision in favor of women and subnationalities, was predictable. Colleges and universities have become bureaucracies like business and government. To defend its life against its envious neighbors, against City Hall, the state, and Washington, as well as against militant groups and individuals within the academy obviously needs officials of the bureaucratic type; and their attitude inevitably spreads throughout the campus by contagion. In these conditions the old idea of *membership* in the university is virtually impossible to maintain. It is not compatible with corralling groups for contentious action or the jealous vindication of stipulated rights.

Nor are these sentiments sweetened by the present state of perpetual penury. Inflation makes balancing the budget a heroic annual act, which can only be done at the cost of some scholarly or educational need. Often bankruptcy is averted only by acrobatic bookkeeping. And while the cost of tuition goes up, student enrollments go down—partly because of the population decline, partly because there are too many colleges, partly because industry and other unadvertised agencies have come to provide in many fields a training parallel to the schools'.

In this matter of enrollments, the colleges and universities were badly misled by statistics public and private. In the Sixties, state and federal departments predicted a great surge of students by 1975. Many institutions responded by still more building, still more courses to prepare the future teachers of these expected hordes. Today, it is estimated that there are 125,000 Ph.D.s without a post—and many others, long on tenure, but with few or none to teach.

A great opportunity was missed after the time of troubles. Chaos and the will to reform gave the chance to recast the American college and university into simpler ways, intellectually sounder and more in keeping with its new material conditions. Simplicity would have meant not just giving up grants and foundation playthings such as "institutes" and "centers" for immediate social action, but also many ornamental activities, including public sports. Some of us who urged the move at the time were ridiculed as "scholastic-monastic," but I accept the phrase as tersely descriptive of a still desirable direction. "Monastic" here has of course nothing to do with religion or asceticism or the muddle of coeducation and cohabitation now part of campus life. It betokens merely the mind concentrated on study in a setting without frills. To rediscover its true purpose is always in order for an institution or any other being, and doing so entails scraping away all pointless accretions. It is always a painful act, but it is least painful after a catastrophe such as happened in 1965 – 1968.

The new direction would have had to be taken by several institutions in concert. They would have been criticized and misrepresented and denounced in the ordinary heedless way. They might even have suffered a few lean years; but with reduced tuitions and a shorter, clearer, and solider curriculum; with enhanced teaching and voluntary scholarship (as opposed to the publish-or-perish genre); with increased accessibility to the gifted poor, they would soon have earned respect and a following—a following of the best, by natural self-selection; after which, public support in money would have flowed to them by sheer economic preference.

Instead of that transformation we have but ruins barely concealed by ivy. For students, not the monastic life, but a shabby degradation of the former luxury; not the scholastic life, either, but a tacitly lowered standard, by means of which instructors maintain their rating on the annual student evaluation and the students themselves ensure the needed grades in the credentials game. For the faculty, salaries dropping fast under the inflation that also raises the cost of operation and tuition. For the administration, nothing but the harried life among demands, protests, and regulations. To expect "educational leadership" from men and women so circumstanced would be a cruel joke.

The manifest decline is heartbreakingly sad, but it is what we have chosen to make it, in higher learning as well as in our public schools. There, instead of trying to develop native intelligence and give it good techniques in the basic arts of man, we professed to make ideal citizens, supertolerant neighbors, agents of world peace and happy family folk, at once sexually adept and flawless drivers of cars. In the upshot, a working system has been brought to a state of impotence. Good teachers are cramped or stymied in their efforts, while the public pays more and more for less and less. The failure to be sober in action and purpose, to do well what can actually be done, has turned a scene of fruitful activity into a spectacle of defeat, shame, and despair.

If both halves of the American educational structure have fallen into such confusion during the years since the appearance of *Teacher in America* in 1945, what is the use of reading it now?—a legitimate question, which I asked myself when the reissuing of the book was proposed to me. I can only think that the book is read because it deals with the difficulties of schooling, which do not change. Please note: the difficulties, not the problems. Problems are solved or disappear with the revolving times. Difficulties remain. It will always be difficult to teach well, to learn accurately; to read, write, and count readily and competently; to acquire a sense of history and develop a taste for literature and the arts—in short, to instruct and start one's education or another's.

For this purpose no school or college or university is ever just right; it is only by the constant effort of its teachers that it can even be called satisfactory. For a school is the junior form of a government and a government is never good, though one may be better than the rest. The reason is the same in both cases: the system must create—not by force and not by bribes—some measure of common understanding and common action in the teeth of endless diversity. A government deals mainly with divergent wills, a school with divergent minds. Both try to generate motive power by proposing desirable goals. But all these elements are fluid, shifting, barely conscious, mixed with distracting, irrelevant forces and interests. And just as there are few statesmen or good politicians who can govern, so there are few true teachers and no multitude of passable ones.

If *Teacher in America* serves in any degree to make these generalities concrete and intelligible, then it has value in the present, when they seem so largely ignored or forgotten. I have been told a good many times by different persons that reading the book helped to determine their choice of teaching as a career. On hearing this I always express regret—not because I believe the life of teaching a misfortune, but because it is an unnatural life. Again like governing, teaching is telling somebody else how to think and behave; it is an imposition, an invasion of privacy. That it is presumably for another's good does not change the unhappy fact of going against another's desire—to play, whistle, or talk instead of listening and learning: teaching is a blessing thoroughly disguised.

And yet we cannot do without teaching—or governing. We see right now all around us the menace of the untaught—the menace to themselves and to us, which amounts to saying that they are unself-governed and therefore ungovernable. There is unfortunately no method or gimmick that will replace teaching. We have seen the failure of one method after another—"look and say" in reading has been a national disaster; and technology in the form of the teaching machine has been no less fallacious and absurd: it takes superior teaching and learning ability to profit from the device. And so it is with film and tape and television. Teaching will not change; it is a hand-to-hand, face-to-face encounter. There is no help for it—we must teach and we must learn, each for himself and herself, using words and working at the perennial Difficulties.

That is the condition of living and surviving at least tolerably well: let us say, as well as the beasts of the field, which have instruction from within—and no need of any book.

Discussion Questions

1. What does Barzun see as some inevitable limitations to the state of affairs he would *wish* to see in American education?
2. What issues and themes in the essay are collected by the metaphor "disarray shot through with the adversary spirit"?
3. Compare Barzun's account of educational difficulties to those of Robert Frost and Bertrand Russell.
4. Write a brief history of your own education in which you locate your own relation to the goals Barzun favors as well as to those he opposes.

SIMONE DE BEAUVOIR

Simone de Beauvoir was born in Paris in 1908 and educated at the Sorbonne. One of the leading figures of the French Existentialist Movement, she taught philosophy until 1943, when she devoted herself to an independent career as a writer. The author of many philosophical novels, she has also written a study of the Marquis de Sade and a highly acclaimed examination of aging, The Coming of Age (1972). Her most celebrated work is The Second Sex (1949), a comprehensive analysis of the sexual, social, biological, and historical development of women.

The following account of the human and inhuman aspects of New York City is from her travel-book, America Day by Day (1953).

Knowing New York

Suddenly, in the dead of night and in deepest slumber, a voice spoke wordlessly: "Something has happened to me." I was asleep, and I did not know whether it was joy or catastrophe that had overtaken me. Perhaps, as so often happens in my dreams, I was dead . . . perhaps I would awake on the other side of the grave. Opening my eyes, I felt frightened. Then I remembered. This was not quite the beyond. This was New York.

This was no mirage. New York was here, everything was real.

The truth burst from the blue sky, the soft damp air, more triumphant than the dubious enchantment of the night before. It was nine o'clock on a Sunday morning, the streets were deserted, light still lingered in the neon signs. There was not a person in sight, nor a car in the street—nothing to break the rectilinear course of Eighth Avenue. The streets were all cubes, prisms and parallelograms—concrete abstract designs, their surfaces abstract intersections made by two books. The building materials had neither density nor structure; space itself had been poured into molds. I did not stir, but I looked. I was here, and New York would be mine. I felt again that joy I had known fifteen years ago when, leaving the station, from the top of the monumental stairway I saw all the roofs of Marseilles spread out below me; I had a year, two years, to pass alone in an unknown city. I did not stir, but I looked down, thinking, "This strange town is my own future, and it will be my past. Between these houses that have existed for years and centuries without me are streets laid out for thousands of people who are not me and never will be." But now I was walking, going down Broadway. It was me, all right. I was walking in streets not built for me, and in which my life had not yet left tracks, streets with no scent of the past. No one knew of my presence; I was still a ghost, and I glided through the city without disturbing anyone. And yet, henceforth, my life would conform to the layout of the streets and houses; New York would belong to me, and I to it.

    I drank orange juice at a counter and sat down in a chair in a shoeshine booth; little by little I came to life and the city grew more familiar. The surfaces had become façades; the solids, houses. In the roadway, dust and old newspapers were raised by the wind. After Washington Square all mathematics went by the board. Right angles were broken; streets were no longer numbered but named; lines became curved and confused. I was lost as though in some European town. The houses had only three or four floors and deep colors varying between red, ochre and black; washing was hung out to dry on fire escapes that zigzagged up the façades. The washing that promised sun, the shoeshine men posted on street corners, the terraced roofs vaguely recalled some southern town; the faded red of the houses reminded me of London fogs. Actually, this neighborhood was unlike any I knew, but I felt I should like it.

    The landscape changed. The word "landscape" suited this city abandoned by men and invaded by the sky—a sky that soared over the skyscrapers, plunged down into the straight streets, as if too vast for the city to annex—a mountain sky.
I was walking in the depths of a canyon, between high cliffs that never saw the sun. There was the tang of salt in the air. Man's history is not inscribed on these poised and knowingly-calculated buildings; they are nearer to prehistoric caverns than the houses of Paris or Rome. In Paris, in Rome, history has filtered to the very roots of the soil; Paris stretches down to the center of the earth. New York's Battery does not have such deep roots. Beneath the subways, the drains and heating plants, the rock is virgin and inhuman. This morning, between this rock and the open sky, Wall Street and Broadway, deep in the shadows of their gigantic buildings, belonged to nature. The little russet church, with its cemetery of flat tombstones, was as unexpected and as moving in the middle of Broadway as some Calvary on the wild seashore.

    The sun was so beautiful, the waters of the Hudson so green, that I got on the boat which takes the visiting sightseers from the Middle West to the Statue of Liberty. But I did not get off at the fort-like little island. I wanted only to see the Battery as I had so often seen it in the movies. I saw it. Its towers looked fragile from a distance. They rest so exactly on their vertical edges that the slightest tremor would make them collapse like card houses. As the boat drew nearer, their foundations looked firmer. But the steepness of their lines was fascinatingly persistent. What a field day they would provide for bombardiers!

There are hundreds of restaurants in these streets, but on Sunday all are closed. The one I eventually found was crowded; I ate hastily, hurried by the waitress. There was no place to rest. Nature was kinder. New York became human again in this harshness: Pearl Street with its elevated railway, Chatham Square, Chinatown, the Bowery. I was getting tired. Slogans ran through my head: "City of Contrasts." The little streets, smelling of groceries and wrapping paper, lie beneath thousand-windowed façades making a contrast. I found one at every turn, each different from the other. "A city erect," "Fascinating geometry," "Delirious geometry," that precisely is what these skyscrapers were, these splendid façades, these avenues: I was seeing them. I had, also, often read "New York is its cathedrals." I could have invented the expression; all the old clichés had sounded hollow. And yet, in the freshness of my discovery, the words "contrasts" and "cathedrals" came to my lips, and I was astonished to find them so stale, whereas the realities they tried to grasp did not change. I had been told, more precisely, that, on Sundays, in the Bowery, drunks sleep on the pavement. Here was the Bowery, and here were the drunks sleeping on the pavement. That was just what the words meant, and I was shocked by their accuracy; why were they so empty and yet so true? It was not through mere words that I was going to catch on to New York. I no longer hoped to catch on while going through a state of change. Words, images, knowledge, effort would serve no purpose; to say they were true or untrue was meaningless. It was no good comparing things here with anything else; they existed in another way here. And I looked and looked, with the astonishment of a blind man who had just got back his sight.

Discussion Questions

1. What is de Beauvoir's first impression of New York City? Where is she when she forms that impression? Where does her impression begin to change?

2. To what details of the city does de Beauvoir devote most of her attention? How does this choice affect her response to New York?

3. In this passage, de Beauvoir is essentially a sightseer. How does her attitude toward sightseeing differ from or resemble G. K. Chesterton's in "On Sightseeing"?

4. In the final paragraph, how does New York City correspond to the clichés about it? Write an essay that describes an experience of travel in which your expectations were shaped by clichés.

BRUNO BETTELHEIM

A Distinguished Professor of Psychology and Psychiatry at the University of Chicago and the author of numerous books on childhood and education, Bruno Bettelheim was born in Vienna in 1903. After Austria fell to the Nazis, Bettelheim spent a year in concentration camps and then escaped to the United States, where he specialized in treating severely disturbed and schizophrenic children. Among his most recent books are The Uses of Enchantment: The Meaning and Importance of Fairy Tales *(1976), which won both the National Book Award and the National Book Critics' Circle Award,* Surviving and Other Essays *(1979), and* On Learning to Read: The Child's Fascination With Meaning *(1982).*

"Joey, A Mechanical Boy" first appeared in Scientific American *in 1959. Though recent studies of autism have found some of Bettelheim's views questionable, a more compelling, compassionate case study of childhood schizophrenia would be hard to find.*

Joey, A Mechanical Boy

Joey, when we began our work with him, was a mechanical boy. He functioned as if by remote control, run by machines of his own powerfully creative fantasy. Not only did he himself believe that he was a machine but, more remarkably, he created this impression in others. Even while he performed actions that are intrinsically human, they never appeared to be other than machine-started and executed. On the other hand, when the machine was not working we had to concentrate on recollecting his presence, for he seemed not to exist. A human body that functions as if it were a machine and a machine that duplicates human functions are equally fascinating and frightening. Perhaps they are so uncanny because they remind us that the human body can operate without a human spirit, that body can exist without soul. And Joey was a child who had been robbed of his humanity.

Not every child who possesses a fantasy world is possessed by it. Normal children may retreat into realms of imaginary glory or magic powers, but they are easily recalled from these excursions. Disturbed children are not always able to make the return trip; they remain withdrawn, prisoners of the inner world of delusion and fantasy. In many ways Joey presented a classic example of this state of infantile autism. In any age, when the individual has escaped into a delusional world, he has usually fashioned it from bits and pieces of the world at hand. Joey, in his time and world, chose the machine and froze himself in its image. His story has a general relevance to the understanding of emotional development in a machine age.

Joey's delusion is not uncommon among schizophrenic children today. He wanted to be rid of his unbearable humanity, to become completely automatic. He so nearly succeeded in attaining this goal that he could almost convince others, as well as himself, of his mechanical character. The descriptions of autistic children in the literature take for their point of departure and comparison the normal or abnormal human being. To do justice to Joey I would have to compare him simultaneously to a most inept infant and a highly complex piece of machinery. Often we had to force ourselves by a conscious act of will to realize that Joey was a child. Again and again his acting-out of his delusions froze our own ability to respond as human beings.

During Joey's first weeks with us we would watch absorbedly as this at once fragile-looking and imperious nine-year-old went about his mechanical existence. Entering the dining room, for example, he would string an imaginary wire from his "energy source"—an imaginary electric outlet—to the table. There he "insulated" himself with paper napkins and finally plugged himself in. Only then could Joey eat, for he firmly believed that the "current" ran his ingestive apparatus. So skillful was the pantomime that one had to look twice to be sure there was neither wire nor outlet plug. Children and members of our staff spontaneously avoided stepping on the "wires" for fear of interrupting what seemed the source of his very life.

For long periods of time, when his "machinery" was idle, he would sit so quietly that he would disappear from the focus of the most conscientious observation. Yet in the next moment he might be "working" and the center of our captivated attention. Many times a day he would turn himself on and shift noisily through a sequence of higher and higher gears until he "exploded," screaming "Crash, crash!" and hurling items from his ever present apparatus—radio tubes, light bulbs, even motors or, lacking these, any handy breakable object. (Joey had an astonishing knack for snatching bulbs and tubes unobserved.) As soon as the object thrown had shattered, he would cease his screaming and wild jumping and retire to mute, motionless nonexistence.

Our maids, inured to difficult children, were exceptionally attentive to Joey; they were apparently moved by his extreme infantile fragility, so strangely coupled with megalomaniacal superiority. Occasionally some of the apparatus he fixed to his bed to "live him" during his sleep would fall down in disarray. This machinery he contrived from masking tape, cardboard, wire and other paraphernalia. Usually the maids would pick up such things and leave them on a table for the children to find, or disregard them entirely. But Joey's machine they carefully restored: "Joey must have the carburetor so he can breathe." Similarly they were on the alert to pick up and preserve the motors that ran during the day and the exhaust pipes through which he exhaled.

How had Joey become a human machine? From intensive interviews with his parents we learned that the process had begun even before birth. Schizophrenia often results from parental rejection, sometimes combined ambivalently with love. Joey, on the other hand, had been completely ignored.

"I never knew I was pregnant," his mother said, meaning that she had already excluded Joey from her consciousness. His birth, she said, "did not make any difference." Joey's father, a rootless draftee in the wartime civilian army, was equally unready for parenthood. So, of course, are many young couples. Fortunately most such parents lose their indifference upon the baby's birth. But not Joey's parents. "I did not want to see or nurse him," his mother declared. "I had no feeling of actual dislike—I simply didn't want to take care of him." For the first three months of his life Joey "cried most of the time." A colicky baby, he was kept on a rigid four-hour feeding schedule, was not touched unless necessary and was never cuddled or played with. The mother, preoccupied with herself, usually left Joey alone in the crib or playpen during the day. The father discharged his frustrations by punishing Joey when the child cried at night.

Soon the father left for overseas duty, and the mother took Joey, now a year and a half old, to live at her parents' home. On his arrival the grandparents noticed that ominous changes had occurred in the child. Strong and healthy at birth, he had become frail and irritable; a responsive baby, he had become remote and inaccessible. When he began to master speech, he talked only to himself. At an early date he became preoccupied with machinery, including an old electric fan which he could take apart and put together again with surprising deftness.

Joey's mother impressed us with a fey quality that expressed her insecurity, her detachment from the world and her low physical vitality. We were struck especially by her total indifference as she talked about Joey. This seemed much more remarkable than the actual mistakes she made in handling him. Certainly he was left to cry for hours when hungry, because she fed him on a rigid schedule; he was toilet-trained with great rigidity so that he would give no trouble. These things happen to many children. But Joey's existence never registered with his mother. In her recollections he was fused at one moment with one event or person; at another, with something or somebody else. When she told us about his birth and infancy, it was as if she were talking about some vague acquaintance, and soon her thoughts would wander off to another person or to herself.

When Joey was not yet four, his nursery school suggested

that he enter a special school for disturbed children. At the new school his autism was immediately recognized. During his three years there he experienced a slow improvement. Unfortunately a subsequent two years in a parochial school destroyed his progress. He began to develop compulsive defenses, which he called his "preventions." He could not drink, for example, except through elaborate piping systems built of straws. Liquids had to be "pumped" into him, in his fantasy, or he could not suck. Eventually his behavior became so upsetting that he could not be kept in the parochial school. At home things did not improve. Three months before entering the Orthogenic School he made a serious attempt at suicide.

To us Joey's pathological behavior seemed the external expression of an overwhelming effort to remain almost nonexistent as a person. For weeks Joey's only reply when addressed was "Bam." Unless he thus neutralized whatever we said, there would be an explosion, for Joey plainly wished to close off every form of contact not mediated by machinery. Even when he was bathed he rocked back and forth with mute, engine-like regularity, flooding the bathroom. If he stopped rocking, he did this like a machine too; suddenly he went completely rigid. Only once, after months of being lifted from his bath and carried to bed, did a small expression of puzzled pleasure appear on his face as he said very softly: "They even carry you to your bed here."

For a long time after he began to talk he would never refer to anyone by name, but only as "that person" or "the little person" or "the big person." He was unable to designate by its true name anything to which he attached feelings. Nor could he name his anxieties except through neologisms of word contaminations. For a long time he spoke about "master paintings" and "a master painting room" (i.e., masturbating and masturbating room). One of his machines, the "criticizer," prevented him from "saying words which have unpleasant feelings." Yet he gave personal names to the tubes and motors in his collection of machinery. Moreover, these dead things had feelings; the tubes bled when hurt and sometimes got sick. He consistently maintained this reversal between animate and inanimate objects.

In Joey's machine world everything, on pain of instant destruction, obeyed inhibitory laws much more stringent than those of physics. When we came to know him better, it was plain that in his moments of silent withdrawal, with his machine switched off, Joey was absorbed in pondering the compulsive laws of his private universe. His preoccupation with machinery made it difficult to establish even practical contacts with him. If he wanted to do something with a counselor, such as play with a toy that has caught his vague attention, he could not do so: "I'd like this very much, but first I have to turn off the machine." But by the time he had fulfilled all the requirements of his preventions, he had lost interest. When a toy was offered to him, he could not touch it because his motors and his tubes did not leave him a hand free. Even certain colors were dangerous and had to be strictly avoided in toys and clothing, because "some colors turn off the current, and I can't touch them because I can't live without the current."

Joey was convinced that machines were better than people. Once when he bumped into one of the pipes on our jungle gym he kicked it so violently that his teacher had to restrain him to keep him from injuring himself. When she explained that the pipe was much harder than his foot, Joey replied: "That proves it. Machines are better than the body. They don't break, they're much harder and stronger." If he lost or forgot something, it merely proved that his brain ought to be thrown away and replaced by machinery. If he spilled something his arm should be broken and twisted off because it did not work properly. When his head or arm failed to work as it should, he tried to punish it by hitting it. Even Joey's feelings were mechanical. Much later in his therapy, when he had formed a timid attachment to another child and had been rebuffed, Joey cried: "He broke my feelings."

Gradually we began to understand what had seemed to be contradictory in Joey's behavior—why he held on to the motors and tubes, then suddenly destroyed them in a fury, then set out immediately and urgently to equip himself with new and larger tubes. Joey had created these machines to run his body and mind because it was too painful to be human. But again and again he became dissatisfied with their failure to meet his need and rebellious at the way they frustrated his will. In a recurrent frenzy he "exploded" his light bulbs and tubes, and for a moment became a human being—for one crowning instant he came alive. But as soon as he had asserted his dominance through the self-created explosion, he felt his life ebbing away. To keep on existing he had immediately to restore his machines and replenish the electricity that supplied his life energy.

What deep-seated fears and needs underlay Joey's delusional system? We were long in finding out, for Joey's preventions effectively concealed the secret of his autistic behavior. In the meantime we dealt with his peripheral problems one by one.

During his first year with us Joey's most trying problem was toilet behavior. This surprised us, for Joey's personality was not "anal" in the Freudian sense; his original personality damage had antedated the period of his toilet-training. Rigid and early toilet-taining, however, had certainly contributed to his anxieties. It was our effort to help Joey with this problem that led to his first recognition of us as human beings.

Going to the toilet, like everything else in Joey's life, was surrounded by elaborate preventions. We had to accompany him; he had to take off all his clothes; he could only squat, not sit, on the toilet seat; he had to touch the wall with one hand, in which he also clutched frantically the vacuum tubes that powered his elimination. He was terrified lest his whole body be sucked down.

To counteract this fear we gave him a metal wastebasket in lieu of a toilet. Eventually, when eliminating into the wastebasket, he no longer needed to take off all his clothes, nor to hold on to the wall. He still needed the tubes and motor which, he believed, moved his bowels for him. But here again the all-important machinery was itself a source of new terrors. In Joey's world the gadgets had to move their bowels, too. He was terribly concerned that they should, but since they were so much more powerful than men, he was also terrified that if his tubes moved their bowels, their feces would fill all of space and leave him no room to live. He was thus caught in some fearful contradiction.

Our readiness to accept his toilet habits, which obviously entailed some hardship for his counselors, gave Joey the confidence to express his obsessions in drawings. Drawing these fantasies was a first step toward letting us in, however distantly, to what concerned him most deeply. It was the first step in a year-long process of externalizing his anal preoccupations. As a result he began seeing feces everywhere; the whole world became to him a mire of excrement. At the same time he began to eliminate freely wherever he happened to be. But with this release from his infantile imprisonment in compulsive rules, the toilet and the whole process of elimination became less dangerous. Thus far it had been beyond Joey's comprehension that anybody could possibly move his bowels without mechanical aid. Now Joey took a further step forward; defecation became the first physiological process he could perform without the help of vacuum tubes. It must not be thought that he was proud of this ability. Taking pride in an achievement presupposes that one accomplishes it of one's own free will. He still did not feel himself an autonomous person who could do things on his own. To Joey defecation still seemed enslaved to some incomprehensible but utterly binding cosmic law, perhaps the law his parents had imposed on him when he was being toilet-trained.

It was not simply that his parents had subjected him to rigid, early training. Many children are so trained. But in most cases the parents have a deep emotional investment in the child's performance. The child's response in turn makes training an occasion for interaction between them and for the building of genuine relationships. Joey's parents had no emotional investment in him. His obedience gave them no satisfaction and won him no affection or approval. As a toilet-trained child he saved his mother labor, just as household machines saved her labor. As a machine he was not loved for his performance, nor could he love himself.

So it had been with all other aspects of Joey's existence with his parents. Their reactions to his eating or noneating, sleeping or wakening, urinating or defecating, being dressed or undressed, washed or bathed did not flow from any unitary interest in him, deeply embedded in their personalities. By treating him mechanically his parents made him a machine. The various functions of life—even the parts of his body—bore no integrating relationship to one another or to any sense of self that was acknowledged and confirmed by others. Though he had acquired mastery over some functions, such as toilet-training and speech, he had acquired them separately and kept them isolated from each other. Toilet-training had thus not gained him a pleasant feeling of body mastery; speech had not led to communication of thought or feeling. On the contrary, each achievement only steered him away from self-mastery and integration. Toilet-training had enslaved him. Speech left him talking in neologisms that obstructed his and our ability to relate to each other. In Joey's development the normal process of growth had been made to run backward. Whatever he had learned put him not at the end of his infantile development toward integration but, on the contrary, farther behind than he was at its beginning. Had we understood this sooner, his first year with us would have been less baffling.

It is unlikely that Joey's calamity could befall a child in any time and culture but our own. He suffered no physical deprivation; he starved for human contact. Just to be taken care of is not enough for relating. It is a necessary but not a sufficient condition. At the extreme where utter scarcity reigns, the forming of relationships is certainly hampered. But our society of mechanized plenty often makes for equal difficulties in a child's learning to relate. Where parents can provide the simple creature-comforts for their children only at the cost of significant effort, it is likely that they will feel pleasure in being able to provide for them; it is this, the parents' pleasure, that gives children a sense of personal worth and sets the process of relating in motion. But if comfort is so readily available that the parents feel no particular pleasure in winning it for their children, then the children cannot develop the feeling of being worthwhile around the satisfaction of their basic needs. Of course parents and children can and do develop relationships around other situations. But matters are then no longer so simple and direct. The child must be on the receiving end of care and concern given with pleasure and without the exaction of return if he is to feel loved and worthy of respect and consideration. This feeling gives him the ability to trust; he can entrust his well-being to persons to whom he is so important. Out of such trust the child learns to form close and stable relationships.

For Joey, relationship with his parents was empty of pleasure in comfort-giving as in all other situations. His was an extreme instance of a plight that sends many schizophrenic children to our clinics and hospitals. Many months passed before he could relate to us; his despair that anybody could like him made contact impossible.

When Joey could finally trust us enough to let himself become more infantile, he began to play at being a papoose. There was a corresponding change in his fantasies. He drew endless pictures of himself as an electrical papoose. Totally enclosed, suspended in empty space, he is run by unknown, unseen powers through wireless electricity.

As we eventually came to understand, the heart of Joey's delusional system was the artificial, mechanical womb he had created and into which he had locked himself. In his papoose fantasies lay the wish to be entirely reborn in a womb. His new experiences in the school suggested that life, after all, might be worth living. Now he was searching for a way to be reborn in a better way. Since machines were better than men, what was more natural than to try rebirth through them? This was the deeper meaning of his electrical papoose.

As Joey made progress, his pictures of himself became more dominant in his drawings. Though still machine-operated, he has grown in self-importance. Another great step forward is represented in a picture in which he has acquired hands that do something, and he has had the courage to make a picture of the machine that runs him. Later still the papoose became a person, rather than a robot encased in glass.

Eventually Joey began to create an imaginary family at the school: the "Carr" family. Why the Carr family? In the car he was enclosed as he had been in his papoose, but at least the car was not stationary; it could move. More important, in a car one was not only driven but also could drive. The Carr family was Joey's way of exploring the possibility of leaving the school, of living with a good family in a safe, protecting car.

Joey at last broke through his prison. In this brief account it has not been possible to trace the painfully slow process of his first true relations with other human beings. Suffice it to say that he ceased to be a mechanical boy and became a human child. This newborn child was, however, nearly 12 years old. To recover the lost time is a tremendous task. That work has occupied Joey and us ever since. Sometimes he sets to it with a will; at other times the difficulty of real life makes him regret that he ever came out of his shell. But he has never wanted to return to his mechanical life.

One last detail and this fragment of Joey's story has been told. When Joey was 12, he made a float for our Memorial Day parade. It carried the slogan: "Feelings are more important than anything under the sun." Feelings, Joey had learned, are what make for humanity; their absence, for a mechanical existence. With this knowledge Joey entered the human condition.

Discussion Questions

1. What are the main features of Joey's imaginary world? In what ways does his world differ from a normal child's? Can you also find ways in which it is similar?

2. What does Bettelheim believe caused Joey's condition? Is there a single cause or several causes? Point out examples from the text to show how Bettelheim uses causation to help organize his essay.

3. Find three or four examples of Joey's speech that differ from ordinary speech. What do your examples have in common? How do they conform to what Bettelheim calls "word contamination"? How does Joey's language conform to Erich Fromm's views on symbolism?

4. How does Bettelheim enlarge the scope of his essay so that it goes beyond that of a single case study? How is Joey's condition symptomatic of our culture? Do you agree or disagree with Bettelheim's analysis? Explain why or why not.

DANIEL BOORSTIN

One of America's most prominent historians, Daniel J. Boorstin was born in Atlanta, Georgia, in 1914. He graduated from Harvard College and received his doctorate from Yale University. As a Rhodes Scholar at Oxford he took highest honors and was admitted as a barrister-at-law of the Inner Temple, London. He has served as Director of the National Museum of History and Technology, as Senior Historian of the Smithsonian Institution, and is currently Librarian of Congress. A former Professor of American History at the University of Chicago, he is the author of the Pulitzer Prize-winning, three-volume reinterpretation of American history, The Americans (1958–1973). Among his other books are The Genius of American Politics (1953), The Image: A Guide to Pseudo-Events in America (1962), The Decline of Radicalism: Reflections on America Today (1969), and The Sociology of the Absurd (1970). He has written numerous articles on a wide variety of topics for periodicals ranging from professional journals to TV Guide.

    The following historical view of advertising's cultural role is reprinted from Boorstin's Democracy and Its Discontents (1974).

The Rhetoric of Democracy

Advertising, of course, has been part of the mainstream of American civilization, although you might not know it if you read the most respectable surveys of American history. It has been one of the enticements to the settlement of this New World, it has been a producer of the peopling of the United States, and in its modern form, in its world-wide reach, it has been one of our most characteristic products.

Never was there a more outrageous or more unscrupulous or more ill-informed advertising campaign than that by which the promoters for the American colonies brought settlers here. Brochures published in England in the seventeenth century, some even earlier, were full of hopeful overstatements, half-truths, and downright lies, along with some facts which nowadays surely would be the basis for a restraining order from the Federal Trade Commission. Gold and silver, fountains of youth, plenty of fish, venison without limit, all these were promised, and of course some of them were found. It would be interesting to speculate on how long it might have taken to settle this continent if there had not been such promotion by enterprising advertisers. How has American civilization been shaped by the fact that there was a kind of natural selection here of those people who were willing to believe advertising?

Advertising has taken the lead in promising and exploiting the new. This was a new world, and one of the advertisements for it appears on the dollar bill on the Great Seal of the United States, which reads *novus ordo seclorum*, one of the most effective advertising slogans to come out of this country. "A new order of the centuries"—belief in novelty and in the desirability of opening novelty to everybody has been important in our lives throughout our history and especially in this century. Again and again advertising has been an agency for inducing Americans to try anything and everything—from the continent itself to a new brand of soap. As one of the more literate and poetic of the advertising copywriters, James Kenneth Frazier, a Cornell graduate, wrote in 1900 in "The Doctor's Lament":

> *This lean M.D. is Dr. Brown*
> *Who fares but ill in Spotless Town.*
> *The town is so confounded clean,*
> *It is no wonder he is lean,*
> *He's lost all patients now, you know,*
> *Because they use Sapolio.*

The same literary talent that once was used to retail Sapolio was later used to induce people to try the Edsel or the Mustang, to experiment with Lifebuoy or Body-All, to drink Pepsi-Cola or Royal Crown Cola, or to shave with a Trac II razor.

And as expansion and novelty have become essential to our economy, advertising has played an ever-larger role: in the settling of the continent, in the expansion of the economy, and in the building of an American standard of living. Advertising has expressed the optimism, the hyperbole, and the sense of community, the sense of reaching which has been so important a feature of our civilization.

Here I wish to explore the significance of advertising, not as a force in the economy or in shaping an American standard of living, but rather as a touchstone of the ways in which we Americans have learned about all sorts of things.

The problems of advertising are of course not peculiar to advertising, for they are just one aspect of the problems of democracy. They reflect the rise of what I have called Consumption Communities and Statistical Communities, and many of the special problems of advertising have arisen from our continuously energetic effort to give everybody everything.

If we consider democracy not just as a political system, but as a set of institutions which do aim to make everything available to everybody, it would not be an overstatement to describe advertising as the characteristic rhetoric of democracy. One of the tendencies of democracy, which Plato and other antidemocrats warned against a long time ago, was the danger that rhetoric would displace or at least overshadow epistemology, that is, *the temptation to allow the problem of persuasion to overshadow the problem of knowledge.* Democratic societies tend to become more concerned with what people believe than with what is true, to become more concerned with credibility than with truth. All these problems become accentuated in a large-scale democracy like ours, which possesses all the apparatus of modern industry. And the problems are accentuated still further by universal literacy, by instantaneous communication, and by the daily plague of words and images.

In the early days it was common for advertising men to define advertisements as a kind of news. The best admen, like the best journalists, were supposed to be those who were able to make their news the most interesting and readable. This was natural enough, since the verb to "advertise" originally meant, intransitively, to take note or to consider. For a person to "advertise" meant originally, in the fourteenth and fifteenth centuries, to reflect on something, to think about something. Then it came to mean, transitively, to call the attention of another to do something, to give him notice, to notify, admonish, warn or inform in a formal or impressive manner. And then, by the sixteenth century, it came to mean: to give notice of anything, to make generally known. It was not until the late eighteenth century that the word "advertising" in English came to have a specifically "advertising" connotation as we might say today, and not until the late nineteenth century that it began to have a specifically commercial connotation. By 1879 someone was saying, "Don't advertise unless you have something worth advertising." But even into the present century, newspapers continue to call themselves by the title "Advertiser"—for example, the Boston *Daily Advertiser*, which was a newspaper of long tradition and one of the most dignified papers in Boston until William Randolph Hearst took it over in 1917. Newspapers carried "Advertiser" on their mastheads, not because they sold advertisements but because they brought news.

Now, the main role of advertising in American civilization came increasingly to be that of persuading and appealing rather than that of educating and informing. By 1921, for instance, one of the more popular textbooks, Blanchard's *Essentials of Advertising*, began: "Anything employed to influence people favorably is advertising. The mission of advertising is to persuade men and women to act in a way that will be of advantage to the advertiser." This development—in a country where a shared, a rising, and a democratized standard of living was the national pride and the national hallmark—meant that advertising had become the rhetoric of democracy.

What, then, were some of the main features of modern American advertising—if we consider it as a form of rhetoric? First, and perhaps most obvious, is *repetition*. It is hard for us to realize that the use of repetition in advertising is not an ancient device but a modern one, which actually did not come into common use in American journalism until just past the middle of the nineteenth century.

The development of what came to be called "iteration copy" was a result of a struggle by a courageous man of letters and advertising pioneer, Robert Bonner, who bought the old New York *Merchant's Ledger* in 1851 and turned it into a popular journal. He then had the temerity to try to change the ways of James Gordon Bennett, who of course was one of the most successful of the American newspaper pioneers, and who was both a sensationalist and at the same time an extremely stuffy man when it came to things that he did not consider to be news. Bonner was determined to use advertisements in Bennett's wide-circulating New York *Herald* to sell his own literary product, but he found it difficult to persuade Bennett to allow him to use any but agate type in his advertising. (Agate was the smallest type used by newspapers in that day, only barely legible to the naked eye.) Bennett would not allow advertisers to use larger type, nor would he allow them to use illustrations except stock cuts, because he thought it was undignified. He said, too, that to allow a variation in the format of ads would be undemocratic. He insisted that all advertisers use the same size type so that no one would be allowed to prevail over another simply by presenting his message in a larger, more clever, or more attention-getting form.

Finally, Bonner managed to overcome Bennett's rigidity by leasing whole pages of the paper and using the tiny agate type to form larger letters across the top of the page. In this way he produced a message such as "Bring home the New York Ledger tonight." His were unimaginative messages, and when repeated all across the page they technically did not violate Bennett's agate rule. But they opened a new era and presaged a new freedom for advertisers in their use of the newspaper page. Iteration copy—the practice of presenting prosaic content in ingenious, repetitive form—became common, and nowadays of course is commonplace.

A second characteristic of American advertising which is not unrelated to this is the development of *an advertising style*. We have histories of most other kinds of style—including the style of many unread writers who are remembered today only because they have been forgotten—but we have very few accounts of the history of advertising style, which of course is one of the most important forms of our language and one of the most widely influential.

The development of advertising style was the convergence of

several very respectable American traditions. One of these was the tradition of the "plain style," which the Puritans made so much of and which accounts for so much of the strength of the Puritan literature. The "plain style" was of course much influenced by the Bible and found its way into the rhetoric of American writers and speakers of great power like Abraham Lincoln. When advertising began to be self-conscious in the early years of this century, the pioneers urged copywriters not to be too clever, and especially not to be fancy. One of the pioneers of the advertising copywriters, John Powers, said, for example, "The commonplace is the proper level for writing in business; where the first virtue is plainness, 'fine writing' is not only intellectual, it is offensive." George P. Rowell, another advertising pioneer, said, "You must write your advertisement to catch damned fools—not college professors." He was a very tactful person. And he added, "And you'll catch just as many college professors as you will of any other sort." In the 1920's, when advertising was beginning to come into its own, Claude Hopkins, whose name is known to all in the trade, said, "Brilliant writing has no place in advertising. A unique style takes attention from the subject. Any apparent effort to sell creates corresponding resistance. . . . One should be natural and simple. His language should not be conspicuous. In fishing for buyers, as in fishing for bass, one should not reveal the hook." So there developed a characteristic advertising style in which plainness, the phrase that anyone could understand, was a distinguishing mark.

At the same time, the American advertising style drew on another, and what might seem an antithetic, tradition—the tradition of hyperbole and tall talk, the language of Davy Crockett and Mike Fink. While advertising could think of itself as 99.44 percent pure, it used the language of "Toronado" and "Cutlass." As I listen to the radio in Washington, I hear a celebration of heroic qualities which would make the characteristics of Mike Fink and Davy Crockett pale, only to discover at the end of the paean that what I have been hearing is a description of the Ford dealers in the District of Columbia neighborhood. And along with the folk tradition of hyperbole and tall talk comes the rhythm of folk music. We hear that Pepsi-Cola hits the spot, that it's for the young generation— and we hear other products celebrated in music which we cannot forget and sometimes don't want to remember.

There grew somehow out of all these contradictory tendencies—combining the commonsense language of the "plain style," and the fantasy language of "tall talk"—an advertising style. This characteristic way of talking about things was especially designed to reach and catch the millions. It created a whole new world of myth. A myth, the dictionary tells us, is a notion based more on tradition or convenience than on facts; it is a received idea. Myth is not just fantasy and not just fact but exists in a limbo, in the world of the "Will to Believe," which William James has written about so eloquently and so perceptively. This is the world of the neither true nor false—of the statement that 60 percent of the physicians who expressed a choice said that our brand of aspirin would be more effective in curing a simple headache than any other leading brand.

That kind of statement exists in a penumbra. I would call this the "advertising penumbra." It is not untrue, and yet, in its connotation it is not exactly true.

Now, there is still another characteristic of advertising so obvious that we are inclined perhaps to overlook it. I call that *ubiquity*. Advertising abhors a vacuum and we discover new vacuums every day. The parable, of course, is the story of the man who thought of putting the advertisement on the other side of the cigarette package. Until then, that was wasted space and a society which aims at a democratic standard of living, at extending the benefits of consumption and all sorts of things and services to everybody, must miss no chances to reach people. The highway billboard and other outdoor advertising, bus and streetcar and subway advertising, and skywriting, radio and TV commercials— all these are of course obvious evidence that advertising abhors a vacuum.

We might reverse the old mousetrap slogan and say that anyone who can devise another place to put another mousetrap to catch a consumer will find people beating a path to his door. "Avoiding advertising will become a little harder next January," the *Wall Street Journal* reported on May 17, 1973, "when a Studio City, California, company launches a venture called Store Vision. Its product is a system of billboards that move on a track across supermarket ceilings. Some 650 supermarkets so far are set to have the system." All of which helps us understand the observation attributed to a French man of letters during his recent visit to Times Square. "What a beautiful place, if only one could not read!" Everywhere is a place to be filled, as we discover in a recent *Publishers Weekly* description of one advertising program: "The $1.95 paperback edition of Dr. Thomas A. Harris' million-copy best seller 'I'm O.K, You're O.K.' is in for full-scale promotion in July by its publisher, Avon Books. Plans range from bumper stickers to airplane streamers, from planes flying above Fire Island, the Hamptons and Malibu. In addition, the $100,000 promotion budget calls for 200,000 bookmarks, plus brochures, buttons, lip-cards, floor and counter displays, and advertising in magazines and TV."

The ubiquity of advertising is of course just another effect of our uninhibited efforts to use all the media to get all sorts of information to everybody everywhere. Since the places to be filled are everywhere, the amount of advertising is not determined by the *needs* of advertising, but by the *opportunities* for advertising which become unlimited.

But the most effective advertising, in an energetic, novelty-ridden society like ours, tends to be "self-liquidating." To create a cliché you must offer something which everybody accepts. The most successful advertising therefore self-destructs because it becomes cliché. Examples of this are found in the tendency for copyrighted names of trademarks to enter the vernacular—for the proper names of products which have been made familiar by costly advertising to become common nouns, and so to apply to anybody's products. Kodak becomes a synonym for camera. Kleenex a synonym for facial tissue, when both begin with a small k, and Xerox (now, too, with a small x) is used to describe all processes of copying, and so on. These are prototypes of the problem. If you are successful enough, then you will defeat your purpose in the long run—by making the name and the message so familiar that people won't notice them, and then people will cease to distinguish your product from everybody else's.

In a sense, of course, as we will see, the whole of American civilization is an example. When this was a "new" world, if people succeeded in building a civilization here, the New World would survive and would reach the time—in our age—when it would cease to be new. And now we have the oldest written Constitution in use in the world. This is only a parable of which there are many more examples.

The advertising man who is successful in marketing any particular product, then—in our high-technology, well-to-do democratic society, which aims to get everything to everybody—is apt to be diluting the demand for his particular product in the very act of satisfying it. But luckily for him, he is at the very same time creating a fresh demand for his services as advertiser.

And as a consequence, there is yet another role which is assigned to American advertising. This is what I call "erasure." Insofar as advertising is competitive or innovation is widespread, erasure is required in order to persuade consumers that this year's model is superior to last year's. In fact, we consumers learn that we might be risking our lives if we go out on the highway with those very devices that were last year's lifesavers but without whatever special kinds of brakes or wipers or seat belt is on this year's model. This is what I mean by "erasure"—and we see it on our advertising pages or our television screen every day. We read in the *New York Times* (May 20, 1973), for example, that "For the price of something small and ugly, you can drive something small and beautiful"—an advertisement for the Fiat 250 Spider. Or another, perhaps more subtle example is the advertisement for shirts under a picture of Oliver Drab: "Oliver Drab. A name to remember in fine designer shirts? No kidding. . . . Because you pay extra money for Oliver Drab. And for all the other superstars of the fashion world. Golden Vee [the name of the brand that is advertised] does not have a designer's label. But we do have designers. . . . By keeping their names *off* our label and simply saying Golden Vee, we can afford to sell our $7 to $12 shirts for just $7 to $12, which should make Golden Vee a name to remember. Golden Vee, you only pay for the shirt."

Having mentioned two special characteristics—the self-liquidating tendency and the need for erasure—which arise from the dynamism of the American economy, I would like to try to place advertising in a larger perspective. The special role of advertising in our life gives a clue to a pervasive oddity in American civilization. A leading feature of past cultures, as anthropologists have explained, is the tendency to distinguish between "high" culture and "low" culture—between the culture of the literate and the learned on the one hand and that of the populace on the other. In other words, between the language of literature and the language of the vernacular. Some of the most useful statements of this distinction have been made by social scientists at the University of Chicago—first by the late Robert Redfield in his several pioneering books on peasant society, and then by Milton Singer in his remarkable study of Indian civilization, *When a Great Tradition Modernizes* (1972). This distinction between the great tradition and the little tradition, between the high culture and the folk culture, has begun to become a commonplace of modern anthropology.

Some of the obvious features of advertising in modern America offer us an opportunity to note the significance or insignificance of that distinction for us. Elsewhere I have tried to point out some of the peculiarities of the American attitude toward the *high* culture. There is something distinctive about the place of thought in American life, which I think is not quite what it has been in certain Old World cultures.

THE RHETORIC OF DEMOCRACY

But what about distinctive American attitudes to *popular* culture? What is our analogue to the folk culture of other peoples? Advertising gives us some clues—to a characteristically American democratic folk culture. Folk culture is a name for the culture which ordinary people everywhere lean on. It is not the writings of Dante and Chaucer and Shakespeare and Milton, the teachings of Machiavelli and Descartes, Locke or Marx. It is, rather, the pattern of slogans, local traditions, tales, songs, dances, and ditties. And of course holiday observances. Popular culture in other civilizations has been for the most part both an area of continuity with the past, a way in which people reach back into the past and out to their community, and at the same time an area of local variations. An area of individual and amateur expression in which a person has his own way of saying, or notes his mother's way of saying or singing, or his own way of dancing, his own view of folk wisdom and the cliché.

And here is an interesting point of contrast. In other societies outside the United States, it is the *high* culture that has generally been an area of centralized, organized control. In Western Europe, for example, universities and churches have tended to be closely allied to the government. The institutions of higher learning have had a relatively limited access to the people as a whole. This was inevitable, of course, in most parts of the world, because there were so few universities. In England, for example, there were only two universities until the early nineteenth century. And there was central control over the printed matter that was used in universities or in the liturgy. The government tended to be close to the high culture, and that was easy because the high culture itself was so centralized and because literacy was relatively limited.

In our society, however, we seem to have turned all of this around. Our high culture is one of the least centralized areas of our culture. And our universities express the atomistic, diffused, chaotic, and individualistic aspect of our life. We have in this country more than twenty-five hundred colleges and universities, institutions of so-called higher learning. We have a vast population in these institutions, somewhere over seven million students.

But when we turn to our popular culture, what do we find? We find that in our nation of Consumption Communities and emphasis on Gross National Product (GNP) and growth rates, advertising has become the heart of the folk culture and even its very prototype. And as we have seen, American advertising shows many characteristics of the folk culture of other societies: repetition, a plain style, hyperbole and tall talk, folk verse, and folk music. Folk culture, wherever it has flourished, has tended to thrive in a limbo between fact and fantasy, and of course, depending on the spoken word and the oral tradition, it spreads easily and tends to be ubiquitous. These are all familiar characteristics of folk culture and they are ways of describing our folk culture, but how do the expressions of our peculiar folk culture come to us?

They no longer sprout from the earth, from the village, from the farm, or even from the neighborhood or the city. They come to us primarily from enormous centralized self-consciously *creative* (an overused word, for the overuse of which advertising agencies are in no small part responsible) organizations. They come from advertising agencies, from networks of newspapers, radio, and television, from outdoor-advertising agencies, from the copywriters for ads in the largest-circulation magazines, and so on. These "creators" of folk culture—or pseudo-folk culture—aim at the widest intelligibility and charm appeal.

But in the United States, we must recall, the advertising folk culture (like all advertising) is also confronted with the problems of self-liquidation and erasure. These are by-products of the expansive, energetic character of our economy. And they, too, distinguish American folk culture from folk cultures elsewhere.

Our folk culture is distinguished from others by being discontinuous, ephemeral, and self-destructive. Where does this leave the common citizen? All of us are qualified to answer.

In our society, then, those who cannot lean on the world of learning, on the high culture of the classics, on the elaborated wisdom of the books, have a new problem. The University of Chicago, for example, in the 1930's and 1940's was the center of a quest for a "common discourse." The champions of that quest, which became a kind of crusade, believed that such a discourse could be found through familiarity with the classics of great literature—and especially of Western European literature. I think they were misled; such works were not, nor are they apt to become, the common discourse of our society. Most people, even in a democracy, and a rich democracy like ours, live in a world of popular culture, our special kind of popular culture.

The characteristic folk culture of our society is a creature of advertising, and in a sense it *is* advertising. But advertising, our own popular culture, is harder to make into a source of continuity than the received wisdom and commonsense slogans and catchy songs of the vivid vernacular. The popular culture of advertising attenuates and is always dissolving before our very eyes. Among the charms, challenges, and tribulations of modern life, we must count this peculiar fluidity, this ephemeral character of that very kind of culture on which other peoples have been able to lean, the kind of culture to which they have looked for the continuity of their traditions, for their ties with the past and with the future.

We are perhaps the first people in history to have a centrally organized mass-produced folk culture. Our kind of popular culture is here today and gone tomorrow—or the day after tomorrow. Or whenever the next semi-annual model appears. And insofar as folk culture becomes advertising, and advertising becomes centralized, it becomes a way of depriving people of their opportunities for individual and small-community expression. Our technology and our economy and our democratic ideals have all helped make that possible. Here we have a new test of the problem that is at least as old as Heraclitus—an everyday test of man's ability to find continuity in his experience. And here democratic man has a new opportunity to accommodate himself, if he can, to the unknown.

Discussion Questions

1. According to Boorstin, what traditions of American democracy led to the development of modern advertising? Do you think that associating these traditions with something as commonplace as advertising has a debunking effect? Does Boorstin think so?

2. What rhetorical devices does Boorstin think are essential to advertising technique? How does Boorstin connect these verbal devices to some of the main characteristics of American culture and democracy?

3. What distinction does Boorstin draw between high and low culture? Can you think of additional examples of this distinction in your everyday life? How is his distinction crucial to his conclusion that advertising is the characteristic folk culture of our society? Can you think of some examples of folk culture that have nothing to do with advertising? Could these examples be used to make a case against Boorstin's claim?

4. Compare Boorstin's attitudes in this essay to Edmund Wilson's attitudes toward language and education. How might Wilson respond to Boorstin's consideration of advertising? Would Wilson find any cultural value in advertising?

5. Select an advertisement or commercial that you find particularly interesting and show how its message and rhetorical method conform to Boorstin's analysis.

JORGE LUIS BORGES

The great Argentine master of short prose forms, Jorge Luis Borges was born in Buenos Aires in 1899. In the 1930's, long before the growth of his present international reputation, Borges conceived of and wrote a collection of essays called A Universal History of Infamy *from which the following (in many ways fictionalized) account of Billy the Kid is taken.* Borges calls his own manner in the book "baroque," which he defines as "that style which exhausts (or tries to exhaust) all its possibilities and which borders on its own parody." As a reader who knows or who looks up the facts of the outlaw's life will see, one of the elements bordering on parody is the end, where the tendencies of authors to mythologize criminals and of readers to venerate them (from a safe distance) are playfully handled.

The Disinterested Killer Bill Harrigan

An image of the desert wilds of Arizona, first and foremost, an image of the desert wilds of Arizona and New Mexico—a country famous for its silver and gold camps, a country of breathtaking open spaces, a country of monumental mesas and soft colors, a country of bleached skeletons picked clean by buzzards. Over this whole country, another image—that of Billy the Kid, the hard rider firm on his horse, the young man with the relentless six-shooters, sending out invisible bullets which (like magic) kill at a distance.

The desert veined with precious metals, arid and blinding-bright. The near child who on dying at the age of twenty-one owed to the justice of grown men twenty-one deaths—"not counting Mexicans."

The Larval Stage

Along about 1859, the man who would become known to terror and glory as Billy the Kid was born in a cellar room of a New York City tenement. It is said that he was spawned by a tired-out Irish womb but was brought up among Negroes. In this tumult of lowly smells and woolly heads, he enjoyed a superiority that stemmed from having freckles and a mop of red hair. He took pride in being white; he was also scrawny, wild, and coarse. At the age of twelve, he fought in the gang of the Swamp Angels, that branch of divinities who operated among the neighborhood sewers. On nights redolent of burnt fog, they would clamber out of that foul-smelling labyrinth, trail some German sailor, do him in with a knock on the head, strip him to his underwear, and afterward sneak back to the filth of their starting place. Their leader was a gray-haired Negro, Gas House Jonas, who was also celebrated as a poisoner of horses.

Sometimes, from the upper window of a waterfront dive, a woman would dump a bucket of ashes upon the head of a prospective victim. As he gasped and choked, Swamp Angels would swarm him, rush him into a cellar, and plunder him.

Such were the apprentice years of Billy Harrigan, the future Billy the Kid. Nor did he scorn the offerings of Bowery playhouses, enjoying in particular (perhaps without an inkling that they were signs and symbols of his destiny) cowboy melodramas.

Go West!

If the jammed Bowery theaters (whose top-gallery riffraff shouted "Hoist that rag!" when the curtain failed to rise promptly on schedule) abounded in these blood and thunder productions, the simple explanation is that America was then experiencing the lure of the Far West. Beyond the sunset lay the goldfields of Nevada and California. Beyond the sunset were the redwoods, going down before the ax; the buffalo's huge Babylonian face; Brigham Young's beaver hat and plural bed; the red man's ceremonies and his rampages; the clear air of the deserts; endless-stretching range land; and the earth itself, whose nearness quickens the heart like the nearness of the sea. The West beckoned. A slow, steady rumor populated those years—that of thousands of Americans taking possession of the West. On that march, around 1872, was Bill Harrigan, treacherous as a bull rattler, in flight from a rectangular cell.

The Demolition of a Mexican

History (which, like certain film directors, proceeds by a series of abrupt images) now puts forward the image of a danger-filled saloon, located—as if on the high seas—out in the heart of the all-powerful desert. The time, a blustery night of the year 1873; the place, the Staked Plains of New Mexico. All around, the land is almost uncannily flat and bare, but the sky, with its storm-piled clouds and moon, is full of fissured cavities and mountains. There are a cow's skull, the howl and the eyes of coyotes in the shadows, trim horses, and from the saloon an elongated patch of light. Inside, leaning over the bar, a group of strapping but tired men drink a liquor that warms them for a fight; at the same time, they make a great show of large silver coins bearing a serpent and an eagle. A drunk croons to himself, poker-faced. Among the men are several who speak a language with many s's, which must be Spanish, for those who speak it are looked down on. Bill Harrigan, the red-topped tenement rat, stands among the drinkers. He has downed a couple of *aguardientes* and thinks of asking for one more, maybe because he hasn't a cent left. He is somewhat overwhelmed by these men of the desert. He sees them as imposing, boisterous, happy, and hatefully wise in the handling of wild cattle and big horses. All at once there is dead silence, ignored only by the voice of the drunk, singing out of tune. Someone has come in—a big, burly Mexican, with the face of an old Indian squaw. He is endowed with an immense sombrero and with a pair of six-guns at his side. In awkward English, he wishes a good evening to all the gringo sons of bitches who are drinking. Nobody takes up the challenge. Bill asks who he is, and they whisper to him, in fear, that the Dago—that is, the Diego—is Belisario Villagrán, from Chihuahua. At once, there is a resounding blast. Sheltered by that wall of tall men, Bill has fired at the intruder. The glass drops from Villagrán's hand; then the man himself drops. He does not need another bullet. Without deigning to glance at the showy dead man, Bill picks up his end of the conversation. "Is that so?" he drawled. "Well, I'm Billy the Kid, from New York." The drunk goes on singing, unheeded.

One may easily guess the apotheosis. Bill gives out handshakes all around and accepts praises, cheers, and whiskeys. Someone notices that there are no notches on the handle of his revolver and offers to cut one to stand for Villagrán's death. Billy the Kid keeps this someone's razor, though he says that "It's hardly worthwhile noting down Mexicans." This, perhaps, is not quite enough. That night, Bill lays out his blanket beside the corpse and—with great show—sleeps till daybreak.

Deaths for Deaths' Sake

Out of that lucky blast (at the age of fourteen), Billy the Kid the hero was born, and the furtive Bill Harrigan died. The boy of the sewer and the knock on the head rose to become a man of the frontier. He made a horseman of himself, learning to ride straight in the saddle—Wyoming- or Texas-style—and not with his body thrown back, the way they rode in Oregon and California. He never completely matched his legend, but he kept getting closer and closer to it. Something of the New York hoodlum lived on in the cowboy; he transferred to Mexicans the hate that had previously been inspired in him by Negroes, but the last words he ever spoke were (swear) words in Spanish. He learned the art of the cowpuncher's maverick life. He learned another, more difficult art—how to lead men. Both helped to make him a good cattle rustler. From time to time, Old Mexico's guitars and whorehouses pulled on him.

With the haunting lucidity of insomnia, he organized populous orgies that often lasted four days and four nights. In the end, glutted, he settled accounts with bullets. While his trigger finger was unfailing, he was the most feared man (and perhaps the most anonymous and most lonely) of that whole frontier. Pat Garrett, his friend, the sheriff who later killed him, once told him, "I've had a lot of practice with the rifle shooting buffalo."

"I've had plenty with the six-shooter," Billy replied modestly. "Shooting tin cans and men."

The details can never be recovered, but it is known that he was credited with up to twenty-one killings—"not counting Mexicans." For seven desperate years, he practiced the extravagance of utter recklessness.

The night of the twenty-fifth of July, 1880, Billy the Kid came galloping on his piebald down the main, or only, street of Fort Sumner. The heat was oppressive and the lamps had not been lighted; Sheriff Garrett, seated on a porch in a rocking chair, drew his revolver and sent a bullet through the Kid's belly. The horse kept on; the rider tumbled into the dust of the road. Garrett got off a second shot. The townspeople (knowing the wounded man was Billy the Kid) locked their window shutters tight. The agony was long and blasphemous. In the morning, the sun by then high overhead, they began drawing near, and they disarmed him. The man was gone. They could see in his face the used-up look of the dead.

He was shaved, sheathed in ready-made clothes, and displayed to awe and ridicule in the window of Fort Sumner's biggest store. Men on horseback and in buckboards gathered for miles and miles around. On the third day, they had to use make-up on him. On the fourth day, he was buried with rejoicing.

Discussion Questions

1. What effects are created for you by Borges's insistence on cinematic language in the essay? Does he seem less serious in his purpose? More aware of other biographies? What does cinematic language allow him to do that more ordinary biographies avoid?

2. How does this meaning of "disinterested" differ from that of "uninterested"? What point about the word in the title does the essay as a whole emphasize?

83 DISINTERESTED KILLER BILL HARRIGAN

3. Compare Borges's brief summary of a life to Basil Liddell Hart's summary of the life of General Sherman. What organizational principles does each writer employ in order to present a complex figure in a brief time? Borges, for example, at times employs a chronological organization. In what ways does he depart from it and for what purposes? What devices does Borges use that are like Liddell Hart's paradoxes?

4. Pick a historical figure about whom you know some basic facts. Were you to use Borges's techniques as a model in writing a short life, what facts would you choose to fictionalize and why?

Jacob Bronowski

Born in Poland in 1908, Jacob Bronowski went to England in 1920 and has lived there ever since. A distinguished theoretical mathematician, he left university teaching in 1942 to concentrate on wartime research involving statistical methods. After the war, his interests–though still largely mathematical–came to include the history and philosophy of science, which he has taught both in England and the United States.

    His difficulties as a boy of twelve in learning English had the somewhat paradoxical effect of giving him an abiding love for the literature of England and America, as well as for the English language itself. That love has become manifest in numerous essays and books along with a very well received television series. In all these media, Bronowski seeks to articulate in English the elegance and wonder of scientific investigation to those who do not know it firsthand. The mainstay of his effort–and, as he claims in the essay that follows, the mainstay of science itself–is the finding of analogies through which the unknown becomes "explained" in terms of the known, and the complex in terms of the simple.

Likenesses

Man has only one means to discovery, and that is to find *likenesses* between things. To him, two trees are like two shouts and like two parents, and on this likeness he has built all mathematics. A lizard is like a bat and like a man, and on such likenesses he has built the theory of evolution and all biology. A gas behaves like a jostle of billiard balls, and on this and kindred likenesses rests much of our atomic picture of matter.

In looking for intelligibility in the world, we look for unity; and we find this (in the arts as well as in science) in its unexpected likenesses. This indeed is man's creative gift, to find or make a likeness where none was seen before—a likeness between mass and energy, a link between time and space, an echo of all our fears in the passion of Othello.

So, when we say that we can explain a process, we mean that we have mapped it in the likeness of another process which we know to work. We say that a metal crystal stretches because its layers slide over one another like cards in a pack, and then that some polyester yarns stretch and harden like a metal crystal. That is, we take from the world round us a few models of structure and process (the particle, the wave, and so on), and when we research into nature, we try to fit her with these models.

Yet one powerful procedure in research, we know, is to break down complex events into simpler parts. Are we not looking for the understanding of nature in these? When we probe below the surface of things, are we not trying, step by step, to reach her ultimate and fundamental constituents?

We do indeed find it helpful to work piecemeal. We take a sequence of events or an assembly to pieces: we look for the steps in a chemical reaction, we carve up the study of an animal into organs and cells and smaller units within a cell. This is our atomic approach, which tries always to see in the variety of nature different assemblies from a few basic units. Our search is for simplicity, in that the distinct units shall be few, and all units of one kind identical.

And what distinguishes one assembly of these units from another? the elephant from the giraffe, or the right-handed molecule of sugar from the left-handed? The difference is in the organization of the units into the whole; the difference is in the structure. And the likenesses for which we look are also likenesses of structure.

This is the true purpose of the analytic method in science: to shift our gaze from the thing or event to its structure. We understand a process, we explain it, when we lay bare in it a structure which is like one we have met elsewhere.

Discussion Questions

1. What "likenesses" or analogies does Bronowski employ (for example, "building," "picture") and how do they contribute to his explanation?

2. What effects does Bronowski create for his reader by his strategic use of rhetorical questions?

3. Compare Bronowski's views of "likenesses" to those of Robert Frost on the same subject.

4. Write an essay based on Bronowski's definition of analysis, in which you shift your "gaze from the thing itself to its structure." Your subject need not be scientific. A sonnet will do as well as a cyclone.

Gwendolyn Brooks

The first black author to win the Pulitzer Prize, Gwendolyn Brooks has ranked as a leading voice in American poetry since the 1940's. Born in Topeka, Kansas, in 1917, she grew up in Chicago, where she graduated from Wilson Junior College in 1936. A member of the American Academy of Arts and Letters, Gwendolyn Brooks has taught poetry at numerous colleges and universities, and has received many literary awards, including a Guggenheim Fellowship in 1946. In 1945, Mademoiselle magazine voted her one of the ten women of the year, and in 1968, she was named Poet Laureate of Illinois.

  Throughout her writing, Gwendolyn Brooks remains close to what Langston Hughes called "the ordinary aspects of black life." Her early volumes of poetry, A Street in Bronzeville (1945), Annie Allen (1949), and Bronzeville Boys and Girls (1956) are characterized by their integration of traditional lyric diction and black urban dialect. Since the Second Black Writers' Conference in 1967, however, her writing has grown more politically responsive to racial and feminist issues. In the Mecca (1968) deals tough-mindedly with violence and ghetto misery. The personal tension between Gwendolyn Brooks's love for tradition and ritual and her awareness of the cultural condition of black people today can be clearly observed in the following autobiographical essay.

Dreams of a Black Christmas

When I was a child, it did not occur to me, even once, that the black in which I was encased (I called it brown in those days) would be considered, one day, beautiful. Considered beautiful and called beautiful by great groups.

I had always considered it beautiful. I would stick out my arm, examine it, and smile. Charming! And convenient, for mud on my leg was not as annunciatory as was mud on the leg of light Rose Hurd.

Charm—and efficiency.

This delight in my pigmentation was hardly a feature of my world. One of the first "world"-truths revealed to me when I at last became a member of SCHOOL was that, to be socially successful, a little girl must be Bright (of skin). It was better if your hair was curly, too—or at least Good Grade (Good Grade implied, usually, no involvement with the Hot Comb)—but Bright you marvelously *needed* to be. Exceptions? A few. Wealth was an escape passport. If a dusky maiden's father was a doctor, lawyer, City Hall employee, or Post Office man, or if her mother was a Schoolteacher, there was some hope: because that girl would often have lovelier clothes, and more of them, than her Bright competitors; and her hair was often long, at *least*, and straight—oh so Hot Comb straight! Such a damsel, if she had virtually nothing to do with the *ordinary* black women of the class, might be favored, might be Accepted.

My father was a janitor. My mother had been a schoolteacher in Topeka before her marriage, but that did not count. Who knew it, anyhow? Of course, not many knew of my father's lowly calling. Still, there was something about me—even though in the early years I wore decent dresses because my Aunt Beulah, a sewing teacher at the Booker Washington High School in Tulsa, was making them for me, sending, on occasion, five at a time—SOMETHING—that stamped me "beyond the pale." And thereby doubly.

All I could hope for was achievement of reverence among the Lesser Blacks. Alas. Requisites for eminence among these I had not. I had not brass or sass. I did not fight brilliantly, or at all, on the playground. I was not ingenious in gym, carrying my team single-handedly to glory. I could not play jacks. I could not ride a bicycle. I did not whisper excitedly about my Boyfriends. For the best of reasons. I did not have any. Among the Lesser Blacks my decent dresses were hinderers to my advance. The girls who did not have them loathed me for having them. When they bothered to remember that I was alive, that is. When they bothered to remember that I was alive, they called me "ol' stuck-up heifer"; and they informed me that they wanted "nothin' t' do with no rich people's sp'iled chirren." Doubtless, this decision amazed the Bright and the *truly* rich, whom the critics openly adored.

As for the Men in the world of School—the little Bright ones looked through me as if I happened to inconvenience their vision, and those of my own hue rechristened me Ol' Black Gal.

These facts of my eight-year membership in school served to sully the truly nice delights of crayon and chalk and watercolor, of story time, and textbooks with cheery pictures of neat, gay-colored life-among-the-white-folks.

Home, however, always warmly awaited me. Welcoming, enveloping. Home meant a quick-walking, careful, Duty-Loving mother, who played the piano, made fudge, made cocoa and prune whip and apricot pie, drew tidy cows and trees and expert houses with chimneys and chimney smoke, who helped her children with arithmetic homework, and who sang in a high soprano:

"Brighten the corner where you are!–
Br-rrr-righten the corner where you are!–
Some one far from harbor you may guide
   across the bar–
Brigh-TEN the cor-nerr–
   where
      you
         are."

Home meant my father, with kind eyes, songs, and tense recitations for my brother and myself. A favorite of his, a wonderful poem about a pie-making lady. Along had come a man, weary, worn, to beg of the lady a pie. Those already baked, she informed him, were too large for the likes of him. She said she would bake another. It, too, was "large." And the next was large. And the next, and the next. Finally the traveler, completely out of patience, berated her and exclaimed that henceforth she should draw her own sustenance from the bark of trees. And she became, *mirabile dictu*, a woodpecker and flew off. We never tired of that. My father seemed to Gwendolyn and Raymond a figure of power. He had those rich Artistic Abilities, but he had more. He could fix anything that broke or stopped. He could build long-lasting fires in the ancient furnace below. He could paint the house, inside and out, and could whitewash the basement. He could spread the American Flag in wide loud magic across the front of our house on the Fourth of July and Decoration Day. He could chuckle. No one has ever had, no one will ever have, a chuckle exactly like my father's. It was gentle, it was warmly happy, it was heavyish but not hard. It was secure, and seemed to us an assistant to the Power that registered with his children. My father, too, was almost our family doctor. We had Dr. Carter, of course, precise and semi-twinkly and effective—but it was not always necessary to call him. My father had wanted to be a doctor. Thwarted, he read every "doctor book" (and he remembered much from a black tradition) he could reach, learning fine secrets and curing us with steams, and fruit compotes, and dexterous rubs, and, above all, with bedside compassion. "Well, there, young lady! How's that throat now?" "Well, let's see now. This salve will take care of that bruise! Now, we're going to be all right." In illness there was an advantage: the invalid was royalty for the run of the seizure.

And of course my father furnished All the Money. The "all" was inadequate, felt Keziah Wims Brooks: could he not leave the McKinley Music Publishing Company, which was paying him about twenty-five dollars a week (from thirty to thirty-five when he worked overtime)? Uncle Paul, her sister Gertrude's husband, worked at City Hall—had a "snap" job—made *fifty* dollars a week. . . True, during the bad times, during the Depression, when McKinley, itself stricken, could pay my father only in part—sometimes eighteen dollars, sometimes ten dollars—my family ate beans. But children dread, often above all else, dissension in the house, and we would have been quite content to entertain a beany diet every day, if necessary, and not live in Lilydale as did bungalow-owning Aunt Gertrude and Uncle Paul, if only there could be, continuously, the almost musical Peace that we had most of the time.

Home. Checker games. Dominoes. Radio (Jack Benny, Ben Bernie, and Kate Smith; "Amos and Andy"; Major Bowes' "Amateur Hour"; Wayne King, the Waltz King; and "Ladies and

Gentlemen: Ea-sy Aces"). Christmases. I shall stop right here to tell about those. They were important.

The world of Christmas was firm. Certain things were done. Certain things were not done.

We did not put Christmas trees outdoors.

We did not open Christmas presents on Christmas Eve.

And we had *not* made fruitcakes two or three months ahead of time.

A Christmas tree, we felt—my mother, my father, my brother, and I—belonged in the living room. Green, never silver or gold or pink. Full-branched and aspiring to the ceiling.

Christmas presents were wrapped and hidden on Christmas Eve. Oh, the sly winks and grins. The furtive rustle of tissue, the whip of ribbon off the spool, semiheard. The trippings here and there in search of secure hiding places. Our house had nooks and crannies, a closet, a pantry, alcoves, "the little room," an extensive basement: There were hiding places aplenty.

Fruitcakes were made about a week before Christmas. We didn't care what the recipe books said. We liked having all the Christmas joy as close together as possible. Mama went downtown, as a rule, for the very freshest supplies, for then, as now, distributors sent their *worst* materials to "the colored neighborhood." Candied cherries and pineapple but no citron. Mama didn't like citron (*I* did and do), so that was out. Candied orange and lemon, however. Figs galore. Dates galore. Raisins, raisins, raisins.

We children had the bake-eve fun of cutting up the candied fruit, shelling and chopping the nuts, and mixing everything together. Our fingers got tired, our teeth and tongues never. We tasted and tasted and took gay tummy aches to bed. Next day, the house was rich with the aroma of brandied fruit and spice. How wonderful. How happy I was.

It was the baking of the fruitcakes that opened our Christmas season. After that, there was the merriest playing of Christmas carols on the piano by my mother and me, with everybody singing: mysterious shopping jaunts; the lingering, careful purchase of Christmas cards: the visit to Santa Claus: the desperately scrupulous housecleaning: for my mother and myself, the calls at the beauty shop for Christmas hairdos (you had to look your very best on Christmas Day): the Christmas hunt, undertaken by all, with the marvelous pungent symbol *found* and borne back triumphantly through the dusk of the third or fourth day before Christmas.

All this. So much more that fades, and fades. I almost forgot the high, high angel-food cake, made a day or two before Christmas. We were, somehow, not great Christmas-cookie advocates, but there would be a few frosted cookies about. We had Christmas candy. And filled candies and Christmas mints. Some of those dates, too, were stuffed with nuts and sugared over, to make another sort of confection.

On Christmas Eve we decorated the Christmas tree. So much silver tinsel. And ropes of fringed gold, and red, silver, blue, and gold balls, and a star on top. We children hung our stockings on the mantel—in the morning they would ache with apples, oranges, nuts, and tiny toys—over our, yes, *real* fireplace! That night we were allowed to "sample the sample"—that is, "test" fruitcake that my mother always made in a shallow pan, along with the proper proud giants—and with it we had eggnog with nutmeg on top.

With what excited pleasure my brother and I went to bed, trying to stay awake to hear Santa Claus come down our chimney, but always failing, for Santa was a sly old soul. We went to sleep with radio carols in our ears, or to the sweet sound of Mama playing and singing "Silent Night," or "Hark! The Herald Angels Sing," or "O Little Town of Bethlehem."

Next day it was so hard to wait for the sky to turn on its light. As soon as it did, out of bed we children threw ourselves and rushed into the living room. There we found, always, that Papa had turned on the Christmas-tree lights, and under the tree shone *just about* everything we had asked of Santa Claus. (Of course, Mama *always* "helped" us with our letters to Santa Claus.) My brother remembers trains and tracks, baseball equipment, wagons, skates, games. Various Christmases brought me dishes, a rocking chair, a doll house, paper dolls which I liked better than hard dolls because so much more could be done with the paper ones. My most delicate and exquisite Christmas-gift memory is of a little glass deer, dainty-antlered, slender-legged, and filled with perfume.

Of course, there were clothes—"secondary" gifts.

And BOOKS.

About books. My "book Christmas" had already begun, on Christmas Eve, soon after the Christmas tree was strung with lights. It was for long my own personal tradition to sit behind the tree and read a paper book I still own: *The Cherry Orchard*, by Marie Battelle Schilling, and published by the David C. Cook Publishing Company. It had been given me by Kayola Moore, my Sunday school teacher. I don't know why I enjoyed reading that book, Christmas Eve after Christmas Eve, to the tune of black-walnut candy crunching.

And back I went—to the back of the Christmas tree—with my

new books. Late, late. After the relatives, after the Christmas turkey, after the cranberries—fresh!—none of your canned cranberries for us—and the mashed potatoes and gravy and baked macaroni and celery and candied sweet potatoes and peas-and-carrots, and the fruitcake and angel cake and eggnog. Back, while the rest of the family forgot it all in bed, to the else-dark room. The silence. The black-walnut candy. And the books that began the giving again.

It did not trouble me, then, that Santa was white and Christ and Christmas were offered as white, except for That One of the "wise men," with role ever slurred, ever understated.

Today, *my* house has not yet escaped the green-tree-fruitcake-eggnog-gifts-on-Christmas-morning "esthetic," even in this our time of black decision and ascent. The human heart delights in "celebration." Human beings delight in the Day set apart for singing and feasting and dancing and fancy dress—or "best" apparel—and the special giving of gifts and twenty-four-hour formalized love. An urgent need is a holiday for blacks, to be enjoyed by blacks everywhere. Worldwide. . . .

In those old days we honored Easter, too. Easter, heralded by hot cross buns on Good Friday, was a time for true newness. On Easter Sunday we did not put on our winter heaviness even if the snow fell and the temperature plunged. No more the long underwear. My brother had white sleeveless undershirts and white shorts, new "oxfords." He had a new suit, a new coat, a new cap. I had patent leather shoes, white socks, girls' b.v.d.'s, light petticoats, a new dress, a new coat, a hat made of straw and ribbons. My self-sacrificing mother rarely had more than a new hat; my father had nothing. We—my mother, my brother, and I, *never* my father—trotted off to Sunday School. Carter Temple Colored Methodist Episcopal Church was at the northwest corner of our block. After Sunday School we went home, returning in the afternoon to take part in the Easter Program. Before coming back we had found our hidden Easter eggs, and had received our Easter baskets full of chocolate rabbits and cotton rabbits and jelly beans and bright marshmallow eggs and lots of green straw.

Birthdays. Large frosted cakes, strawberry and vanilla ice cream (sometimes little ice cream fruit and flower or animal forms found at Frozen Arts, just off 43rd and Cottage Grove); presents, beautifully ribboned; the half-hysterical little guests squeakily singing "Happy Birthday to you!" in honor of the half-hysterical little host or hostess; the wee pink or white candles doomed to be quickly lit, blown out, and forgotten.

Another loved special was Halloween. Pumpkin lanterns.

Sheets for ghost costumes. Polished red apples. Trick-or-treating. Angry neighbors.

The Thanksgiving Day menu was exactly the same as the Christmas menu, except that there were mince, pumpkin, and apple pies instead of cakes. Every Thanksgiving Day, as a prelude to the feast, I read Palmer Cox's "The Brownies' Thanksgiving."

Are you aware of a fact-that-should-be-startling about the High Days of my youth? All were Europe-rooted or America-rooted. Not one celebration in my black household or in any black household that I knew featured any black glory or greatness or grandeur.

A capricious bunch of entries and responses has brought me to my present understanding of fertile facts. Know-nows: I know now that I am essentially an essential African, in occupancy here because of an indeed "peculiar" institution. I know now that the Indian is the authentic American, unless *he* did some forcible country-taking, too. I know that I am in that company of thousands now believing that black tragedy is contrived. I know now that black fellow-feeling must be the black man's encyclopedic Primer. I know that the black-and-white integration concept, which in the mind of some beaming early saint was a dainty spinning dream, has wound down to farce, to unsavory and mumbling farce, and that Don L. Lee, a major and muscular black voice of this day, is correct in "The New Integrationist":

"I
seek
integration
of
negroes
with
black
people."

I know that the black emphasis must be, not *against white*, but *FOR black*. I know that a substantial manner of communication and transaction with whites will be, eventually, arrived at, arranged—*if* blacks remain in this country; but the old order shall not prevail; the day of head pats for nice little niggers, bummy kicks for bad bad Biggers, and apparent black acceptance of both, is done. In the Conference-That-Counts, whose date may be 1980 or 2080 (woe betide the Fabric of Man if it is 2080), there will be no looking up nor looking down.

It frightens me to realize that, if I had died before the age of fifty, I would have died a "Negro" fraction. . . .

Yes, needed is a holiday for blacks everywhere, a Black

World Day, with black excitement and black trimmings in honor of the astounding strength and achievement of black people. A yearly Black People's Day—akin, perhaps, to the black concept Kwanza, which, based on a traditional African holiday, is considered by many black people an alternative to commercial Christmas; for the week beginning December twenty-sixth, homes are decorated in red and black and green, the black representing the black nation, the red representing our shed blood, the green featured as a symbol of land for nation-establishment and a symbol, too, for live faith in our young.

I see, feel, and hear a potential celebration as Africa colors—thorough, direct. A thing of shout but of African quietness, too, because in Africa these tonals can almost coincide. A clean-throated singing. Drums; and perhaps guitars. Flags or a flag. Costumery, wholesomely gaudy; costumery which, for the African, is not affectation but merely a right richness that the body deserves. Foods; not pate de foie gras or creamed lobster de bon bon, but figs and oranges, and vegetables. . . . AND the profound and frequent shaking of hands, which in Africa is so important. The shaking of hands in warmth and strength and union.

Discussion Questions

1. Who are the "Bright Girls" that Gwendolyn Brooks refers to in her opening paragraphs? How is her opening account of School reinforced by the Don L. Lee lines she cites later on?

2. What contrast does Gwendolyn Brooks make between School and Home? What elements of home life does she recall most vividly?

3. Gwendolyn Brooks recalls "the almost musical Peace that we had most of the time." How do her recollections support this image?

4. Contrast Gwendolyn Brooks' memories of Christmas to Lillian Ross's account of that holiday. What emotional attitudes separate these two views of Christmas? How are those attitudes portrayed through each writer's use of detail?

5. Why does Gwendolyn Brooks introduce other holidays into her essay? What main concern do these lead to?

6. What is a "Know-now"? What does this expression imply about her earlier memories? Has knowing-now interfered with the joys of celebration that Gwendolyn Brooks writes about here? Explain.

7. Holidays, Gwendolyn Brooks reminds us, are important to people for many reasons. Using her criteria for why holidays are important, write an essay proposing a new holiday you think would be valuable to either a particular group or to the nation as a whole.

NIGEL CALDER

Nigel Calder, who has been called "one of the finest interpreters of scientific subjects for general readers," received the UNESCO Kalinga Prize for the Popularization of Science in 1972. Born in London, England, in 1931, and educated at Cambridge University, Calder has been the editor-in-chief of the New Scientist and science correspondent for The New Statesman. He has also created a number of science documentaries for the British Broadcasting Corporation.

Calder has written on a variety of scientific topics, including meteorology, geology, the brain, genetics, and the future of technology. His most recent books are Spaceships of the Mind (1978), Einstein's Universe (1979), and Nuclear Nightmares (1980). The following selection on Halley's Comet appeared as the prefatory essay to The Comet Is Coming! (1981).

The Comet Is Coming

Soothsayers and fiction-writers have a case: one day the Earth will collide with a bright comet or its dark corpse and the result will be world-wide mayhem. It has happened before. But the odds against a repetition in anyone's lifetime are very long indeed, so worry sooner about the effects of comets on mental health. Smudges of light move against the background of stars in what the comet lovers in our midst might say was a stately fashion (I would call it slovenly) and they infect the imagination of laymen and astronomers alike.

A comet travels faster than a spaceship, at many kilometres per second, but because it is far off it spends weeks inching its way across the sky. With a bright, roughly round head and a hairlike tail, a typical comet looks like a hurtling missile with streak-marks in its wake; you have to make a mental effort to realize that the object may be moving in any direction and the tail is never trailing straight behind it. Comets are sometimes confused with their impetuous kin, the meteors and meteorites that dash into the Earth's upper air from outer space and either burn up as 'shooting stars' or reach the ground as incandescent lumps of iron, stone and tar. The astronomers' term for the advent of a comet is an 'apparition', and its connotation with wraiths is wholly appropriate.

The most provocative apparition of all is now upon us, because the comet we call *Halley* is slanting in towards the Sun. It began its relentless countdown in 1948, when it faltered at the top of its trajectory, at thirty-five times the Earth–Sun distance. Since then it has been falling back, gathering speed, and in the 1970s it drew nearer than Neptune, the most remote of the great planets of the Sun. In 1977 the first of the large telescopes looked out for it, in the constellation of Canis Minor, but there was little hope of spotting the comet, small, faint and tail-less, as early as that. After further unsuccessful attempts, astronomers resigned themselves to not recovering *Halley* until the end of 1980. During 1981-4 the comet's path passes in front of the Milky Way, making it hard to see. In 1985, it will swoop into the heart of the Solar System and deploy its wanton tail. It will swing around the Sun early in 1986, being at its most visible in the first few months of that year. Then it will climb away and few of us will see it coming back, yet again, in 2061.

Every seventy-six years or so, *Halley* punctuates history like an exclamation mark in the sky. On its last return in 1910 the more spectacular 'Great January Comet' upstaged it but, as the brightest comet that reappears frequently, *Halley* exerts a special grip on the human mind. Although the present apparition will be a meager one, to say so will only boost the sales of binoculars and amateurs' telescopes. Professional astronomers know perfectly well that comets are a swindle: small, lightweight objects that look awesome because they generate voluminous heads and tails. They are striking astronomical sights and deserve an explanation, yet even when their tenuous nature has been fully disclosed they continue to cause astonishment and excitement out of all proportion to their substance. The coming of *Halley* means that we are due for a bout of comet fever.

Comets drive people dotty. Like the emperors and priests who used to tremble when they appeared, some members of the public are still eager to be duped by charlatans selling protection against the evil influence of comets, or pamphlets proclaiming the end of the world. But the eminent scientists, too, are vulnerable to the fever and concoct their most bizarre theories around comets. At one time Noah's Flood was blamed on the impact of a comet, and in the 1980s there is a solemn assertion that *Halley* causes influenza. While I shall not skimp Sir Fred Hoyle's speculations about such fevers afflicting the body, the psychiatry of comets seems less debatable.

A few prophylactic statements about where they and we operate in the cosmic scheme may be appropriate at the outset. The universe is large and violent, but we survive because our wagon (the Earth) is hitched to a bright but humdrum star (the Sun), far from the tumultuous centre of our Galaxy (the Milky Way). Other stars in our neighborhood scurry about, but only two interstellar matters are relevant to our parochial story: passing stars occasionally encounter comets wandering far from the Sun, and the Sun sometimes conducts all its family through dark, diffuse clouds of interstellar dust.

That family, the Solar System, consists of two significant

planets, Jupiter and Saturn, which resemble small, cool stars. In addition there are two fairly large icy planets, orbiting around the Sun far beyond Saturn: Uranus and Neptune. Reading inwards from Jupiter, there are four other planets, stony and much smaller: Mars, Earth, Venus and sweltering Mercury, closest to the Sun. After those, you can fill in further small planets like Pluto, Chiron, and the asteroids that circle between Jupiter and Mars; assorted moons that in some cases rival the stony planets in size; the rings that encircle Saturn, Jupiter and Uranus. Comets come close to the bottom of the list, but they obtrude because they jaywalk across the paths of the planets.

Few professional astronomers devote themselves full-time to the study of comets. The capital of their small kingdom is at an astrophysical observatory in Cambridge, Massachusetts, where a handful of experts record the sightings and orbits of all comets and lead the scientific efforts to understand them. In the theory now prevalent in Cometsville, a comet is a cosmic sorbet: a dirty snowball that comes tumbling out of the freezer of twilight space, far from the Sun. In commending this description as an anchor in the storm of other strange hypotheses I do not mean that you can be quite sure of it, at least not until a spaceborne robot or an astronaut lands on the supposed snowball in the heart of a comet.

In the warmth of the inner Solar System a comet releases clouds of vapour and dust that form the glowing head and then leak into the tail, which is the cosmic equivalent of an oil slick. Pieces of the dust later hit the Earth, as meteors. A few survivors among the comets evolve into menacing lumps of dirt in tight orbits around the Sun. For these reasons comets are, in my opinion, best regarded as a conspicuous form of sky pollution.

A description of comets by Maurice Dubin of the US National Aeronautics and Space Administration is candid:

> As the source of meteor streams and meteors in general they are presently viewed as a third-rate cosmic population lacking any influence on the goings-on of this world. . . . Perhaps their study may lead to unexpected discoveries despite the insignificance of these bodies.

To hold their own at scientific gatherings, Dubin and other students of the 'third-rate' objects like to say that comets will shed light on the primordial chemistry of the Solar System which gave Earth and the other planets their present character; they may also help in understanding the origin of life. Those are quite reasonable hopes. But as a contamination of the Solar System, from which meteors are the least objectionable end product, comets continue to influence 'this world' less benevolently than that.

They violate the elegant order of the heavens, and the response of nations without telescopes has often been astrological and pessimistic. This is the primitive form of comet fever. When you have established their true paths through space, a secondary affliction develops: an urge to see as many comets as possible. Finally comes the knowledge that cometary dust enters our atmosphere, and that comets themselves must sometimes strike the Earth's surface. These direct contacts with comets give rise to feverish theory-spinning, which has to be coolly assessed in order to diagnose any real dangers and formulate countermeasures.

Our generation may be better informed than previous ones but it is not immune to error. Indeed there is, at first sight, little to choose between some present-day propositions about comets and those that conceited folk mock as naïveties of their forefathers. Because *Halley* and its like are ostentatious and elusive, they create a no-man's-land of speculation where crazy ideas may be fantasies or brilliant insights. The interplay of imagination and evidence in this annex of astronomy says a good deal about the nature of science, and describing it may help to inoculate the more reasonable sections of the public against the predictable nonsense of *Halley's* return.

Discussion Questions

1. At the outset, Calder asks his readers to worry about the "effects of comets on mental health." What does he mean by that remark? How does Calder pick up on that statement throughout the selection?

2. List the metaphors that Calder uses to describe comets. How do these metaphors affect your sense of the significance of Halley's Comet?

3. There has been much discussion recently as to whether or not the United States should spend the money to launch a space vehicle to rendezvous with Halley's Comet and study it scientifically. From this selection, how would you infer Calder stands on this issue?

4. Do Calder's views on astrology support those of J. H. Plumb? Explain.

5. Calder cites an astronomer who says that comets are at present viewed as lacking "influence on the goings-on of this world," but then Calder goes on to say that comets do have an "influence" on this world. Explain in what sense Calder thinks that comets *do* have an influence. How does his sense of that influence differ from both popular and professional opinions about comets?

RACHEL CARSON

A zoologist and marine biologist, Rachel Carson (1907–1964) was one of the earliest scientific writers to be concerned with contemporary ecological hazards. Her most controversial book, The Silent Spring *(1962), a landmark study of the irresponsible use of insecticides, led to the formation of a presidential commission to study environmental dangers.*

In her scientific writings, as the following essay demonstrates, she manages eloquently to blend two capacities that, unfortunately, do not always appear together: rigorous observation and poetic sensitivity. "The Changing Year" originally appeared in The Sea Around Us *(1951), a study that won her the National Book Award.*

The Changing Year

Thus with the year seasons return.
Milton

For the sea as a whole, the alternation of day and night, the passage of the seasons, the procession of the years, are lost in its vastness, obliterated in its own changeless eternity. But the surface waters are different. The face of the sea is always changing. Crossed by colors, lights, and moving shadows, sparkling in the sun, mysterious in the twilight, its aspects and its moods vary hour by hour. The surface waters move with the tides, stir to the breath of the winds, and rise and fall to the endless, hurrying forms of the waves. Most of all, they change with the advance of the seasons. Spring moves over the temperate lands of our Northern Hemisphere in a tide of new life, of pushing green shoots and unfolding buds, all its mysteries and meanings symbolized in the northward migration of the birds, the awakening of sluggish amphibian life as the chorus of frogs rises again from the wet lands, the different sound of the wind which stirs the young leaves where a month ago it rattled the bare branches. These things we associate with the land, and it is easy to suppose that at sea there could be no such feeling of advancing spring. But the signs are there, and seen with understanding eye, they bring the same magical sense of awakening.

In the sea, as on land, spring is a time for the renewal of life. During the long months of winter in the temperate zones the surface waters have been absorbing the cold. Now the heavy water begins to sink, slipping down and displacing the warmer layers below. Rich stores of minerals have been accumulating on the floor of the continental shelf—some freighted down the rivers from the lands; some derived from sea creatures that have died and whose remains have drifted down to the bottom; some from the shells that once encased a diatom, the streaming protoplasm of a radiolarian, or the transparent tissues of a pteropod. Nothing is wasted in the sea; every particle of material is used over and over again, first by one creature, then by another. And when in spring the waters are deeply stirred, the warm bottom water brings to the surface a rich supply of minerals, ready for use by new forms of life.

Just as land plants depend on minerals in the soil for their growth, every marine plant, even the smallest, is dependent upon the nutrient salts or minerals in the sea water. Diatoms must have silica, the element of which their fragile shells are fashioned. For these and all other microplants, phosphorus is an indispensable mineral. Some of these elements are in short supply and in winter may be reduced below the minimum necessary for growth. The diatom population must tide itself over this season as best it can. It faces a stark problem of survival, with no opportunity to increase, a problem of keeping alive the spark of life by forming tough protective spores against the stringency of winter, a matter of existing in a dormant state in which no demands shall be made on an environment that already withholds all but the most meager necessities of life. So the diatoms hold their place in the winter sea, like seeds of wheat in a field under snow and ice, the seeds from which the spring growth will come.

These, then, are the elements of the vernal blooming of the sea: the 'seeds' of the dormant plants, the fertilizing chemicals, the warmth of the spring sun.

In a sudden awakening, incredible in its swiftness, the simplest plants of the sea begin to multiply. Their increase is of astronomical proportions. The spring sea belongs at first to the diatoms and to all the other microscopic plant life of the plankton. In the fierce intensity of their growth they cover vast areas of ocean with a living blanket of their cells. Mile after mile of water may appear red or brown or green, the whole surface taking on the color of the infinitesimal grains of pigment contained in each of the plant cells.

The plants have undisputed sway in the sea for only a short time. Almost at once their own burst of multiplication is matched by a similar increase in the small animals of the plankton. It is the spawning time of the copepod and the glassworm, the pelagic shrimp and the winged snail. Hungry swarms of these little beasts of the plankton roam through the waters, feeding on the abundant plants and themselves falling prey to larger creatures. Now in the spring the surface waters become a vast nursery. From the hills and valleys of the continent's edge lying far below, and from the scattered shoals and banks, the eggs or young of many of the bottom animals rise to the surface of the sea. Even those which, in their maturity, will sink down to a sedentary life on the bottom, spend the first weeks of life as freely swimming hunters of the plankton. So as spring progresses new batches of larvae rise into the surface each day, the young of fishes and crabs and mussels and tube worms, mingling for a time with the regular members of the plankton.

Under the steady and voracious grazing, the grasslands of the surface are soon depleted. The diatoms become more and more scarce, and with them the other simple plants. Still there are brief explosions of one or another form, when in a sudden orgy of cell division it comes to claim whole areas of the sea for its own. So, for a time each spring, the waters may become blotched with brown, jellylike masses, and the fishermen's nets come up dripping a brown slime and containing no fish, for the herring have turned away from these waters as though in loathing of the viscid, foul-smelling algae. But in less time than passes between the full moon and the new, the spring flowering of Phaeocystis is past and the waters have cleared again.

In the spring the sea is filled with migrating fishes, some of them bound for the mouths of great rivers, which they will ascend to deposit their spawn. Such are the spring-run chinooks coming in from the deep Pacific feeding grounds to breast the rolling flood of the Columbia, the shad moving in to the Chesapeake and the Hudson and the Connecticut, the alewives seeking a hundred coastal streams of New England, the salmon feeling their way to the Penobscot and the Kennebec. For months or years these fish have known only the vast spaces of the ocean. Now the spring sea and the maturing of their own bodies lead them back to the rivers of their birth.

Other mysterious comings and goings are linked with the advance of the year. Capelin gather in the deep, cold water of the Barents Sea, their shoals followed and preyed upon by flocks of auks, fulmars, and kittiwakes. Cod approach the banks of Lofoten, and gather off the shores of Iceland. Birds whose winter feeding territory may have encompassed the whole Atlantic or the whole Pacific converge upon some small island, the entire breeding population arriving within the space of a few days. Whales suddenly appear off the slopes of the coastal banks where the swarms of shrimplike krill are spawning, the whales having come from no one knows where, by no one knows what route.

With the subsiding of the diatoms and the completed spawning of many of the plankton animals and most of the fish, life in the surface waters slackens to the slower pace of midsummer. Along the meeting places of the currents the pale moon jelly Aurelia gathers in thousands, forming sinuous lines or windrows across miles of sea, and the birds see their pale forms shimmering deep down in the green water. By midsummer the large red jellyfish Cyanea may have grown from the size of a thimble to that of an umbrella. The great jellyfish moves through the sea with rhythmic pulsations, trailing long tentacles and as likely as not shepherding a little group of young cod or haddock, which find shelter under its bell and travel with it.

A hard, brilliant, coruscating phosphorescence often illuminates the summer sea. In waters where the protozoa Noctiluca is abundant it is the chief source of this summer luminescence, causing fishes, squids, or dolphins to fill the water with racing flames and to clothe themselves in a ghostly radiance. Or again the summer sea may glitter with a thousand thousand moving pinpricks of light, like an immense swarm of fireflies moving through a dark wood. Such an effect is produced by a shoal of the brilliantly phosphorescent shrimp Meganyctiphanes, a creature of cold and darkness and of the places where icy water rolls upward from the depths and bubbles with white ripplings at the surface.

Out over the plankton meadows of the North Atlantic the dry twitter of the phalaropes, small brown birds, wheeling and turning, dipping and rising, is heard for the first time since early spring. The phalaropes have nested on the arctic tundras, reared their young, and now the first of them are returning to the sea. Most of them will continue south over the open water far from land, crossing the equator into the South Atlantic. Here they will follow where the great whales lead, for where the whales are, there also are the swarms of plankton on which these strange little birds grow fat.

As the fall advances, there are other movements, some in the surface, some hidden in the green depths, that betoken the end of summer. In the fog-covered waters of Bering Sea, down through the treacherous passes between the islands of the Aleutian chain and southward into the open Pacific, the herds of fur seals are moving. Left behind are two small islands, treeless bits of volcanic soil thrust up into the waters of Bering Sea. The islands are silent now, but for the several months of summer they resounded with the roar of millions of seals come ashore to bear and rear their young—all the fur seals of the eastern Pacific crowded into a few square miles of bare rock and crumbling soil. Now once more the seals turn south, to roam down along the sheer underwater cliffs of the continent's edge, where the rocky foundations fall away steeply into the deep sea. Here, in a blackness more absolute than that of arctic winter, the seals will find rich feeding as they swim down to prey on the fishes of this region of darkness.

Autumn comes to the sea with a fresh blaze of phosphorescence, when every wave crest is aflame. Here and there the whole surface may glow with sheets of cold fire, while below schools of fish pour through the water like molten metal. Often the autumnal phosphorescence is caused by a fall flowering of the dinoflagellates, multiplying furiously in a short-lived repetition of their vernal blooming.

Sometimes the meaning of the glowing water is ominous. Off the Pacific coast of North America, it may mean that the sea is filled with the dinoflagellate Gonyaulax, a minute plant that contains a poison of strange and terrible virulence. About four days after Gonyaulax comes to dominate the coastal plankton, some of the fishes and shellfish in the vicinity become toxic. This is because, in their normal feeding, they have strained the poisonous plankton out of the water. Mussels accumulate the Gonyaulax toxins in their livers, and the toxins react on the human nervous system with an effect similar to that of strychnine. Because of these facts, it is generally understood along the Pacific coast that it is unwise to eat shellfish taken from coasts exposed to the open sea where Gonyaulax may be abundant, in summer or early fall. For generations before the white men came, the Indians knew this. As soon as the red streaks appeared in the sea and the waves began to flicker at night with the mysterious blue-green fires, the tribal leaders forbade the taking of mussels until these warning signals should have passed. They even set guards at intervals along the beaches to warn inlanders who might come down for shellfish and be unable to read the language of the sea.

But usually the blaze and glitter of the sea, whatever its meaning for those who produce it, implies no menace to man. Seen from the deck of a vessel in open ocean, a tiny, man-made observation point in the vast world of sea and sky, it has an eerie and unearthly quality. Man, in his vanity, subconsciously attributes a human origin to any light not of moon or stars or sun. Lights on the shore, lights moving over the water, mean lights kindled and controlled by other men, serving purposes understandable to the human mind. Yet here are lights that flash and fade away, lights that come and go for reasons meaningless to man, lights that have been doing this very thing over the eons of time in which there were no men to stir in vague disquiet.

On such a night of phosphorescent display Charles Darwin stood on the deck of the *Beagle* as she plowed southward through the Atlantic off the coast of Brazil.

> The sea from its extreme luminousness presented a wonderful and most beautiful appearance [he wrote in his diary]. Every part of the water which by day is seen as foam, glowed with a pale light.

> The vessel drove before her bows two billows of liquid phosphorus, and in her wake was a milky train. As far as the eye reached the crest of every wave was bright; and from the reflected light, the sky just above the horizon was not so utterly dark as the rest of the Heavens. It was impossible to behold this plain of matter, as if it were melted and consumed by heat, without being reminded of Milton's description of the regions of Chaos and Anarchy.[1]

Like the blazing colors of the autumn leaves before they wither and fall, the autumnal phosphorescence betokens the approach of winter. After their brief renewal of life the flagellates and the other minute algae dwindle away to a scattered few; so do the shrimps and the copepods, the glassworms and the comb jellies. The larvae of the bottom fauna have long since completed their development and drifted away to take up whatever existence is their lot. Even the roving fish schools have deserted the surface waters and have migrated into warmer latitudes or have found equivalent warmth in the deep, quiet waters along the edge of the continental shelf. There the torpor of semi-hibernation descends upon them and will possess them during the months of winter.

The surface waters now become the plaything of the winter gales. As the winds build up the giant storm waves and roar along their crests, lashing the water into foam and flying spray, it seems that life must forever have deserted this place.

For the mood of the winter sea, read Joseph Conrad's description:

> The greyness of the whole immense surface, the wind furrows upon the faces of the waves, the great masses of foam, tossed about and waving, like matted white locks, give to the sea in a gale an appearance of hoary age, lustreless, dull, without gleams, as though it had been created before light itself.[2]

But the symbols of hope are not lacking even in the grayness and bleakness of the winter sea. On land we know that the apparent lifelessness of winter is an illusion. Look closely at the bare branches of a tree, on which not the palest gleam of green can be discerned. Yet, spaced along each branch are the leaf buds, all the spring's magic of swelling green concealed and safely preserved under the insulating, overlapping layers. Pick off a piece of the rough bark of the trunk; there you will find hibernating insects. Dig down through the snow into the earth. There are the eggs of next summer's grasshoppers; there are the dormant seeds from which will come the grass, the herb, the oak tree.

---

[1] From *Charles Darwin's Diary of the Voyage of H. M. S. Beagle*, edited by Nora Barlow, 1934, Cambridge University Press, p. 107.

[2] From *The Mirror of the Sea*, Kent edition, 1925, Doubleday-Page, p. 71.

So, too, the lifelessness, the hopelessness, the despair of the winter sea are an illusion. Everywhere are the assurances that the cycle has come to the full, containing the means of its own renewal. There is the promise of a new spring in the very iciness of the winter sea, in the chilling of the water, which must, before many weeks, become so heavy that it will plunge downward, precipitating the overturn that is the first act in the drama of spring. There is the promise of new life in the small plantlike things that cling to the rocks of the underlying bottom, the almost formless polyps from which, in spring, a new generation of jellyfish will bud off and rise to the surface waters. There is unconscious purpose in the sluggish forms of the copepods hibernating on the bottom, safe from the surface storms, life sustained in their tiny bodies by the extra store of fat with which they went into this winter sleep.

Already, from the gray shapes of cod that have moved, unseen by man, through the cold sea to their spawning places, the glassy globules of eggs are rising into the surface waters. Even in the harsh world of the winter sea, these eggs will begin the swift divisions by which a granule of protoplasm becomes a living fishlet.

Most of all, perhaps, there is assurance in the fine dust of life that remains in the surface waters, the invisible spores of the diatoms, needing only the touch of warming sun and fertilizing chemicals to repeat the magic of spring.

Discussion Questions

1. What main idea about the sea does Rachel Carson want her readers to appreciate? How does this leading idea determine her choice of details?

2. What central analogy does Carson develop in this essay? Go through the essay and underline all the words and expressions that depend upon this analogy.

3. How does Carson's analogy help you understand the sea? What kind of picture do you get of it? Can you see any limitations in using the analogy? Would Jacob Bronowski find her analogy a sueful one scientifically?

4. What particular stylistic devices, such as images and metaphors, give Carson's essay its scientific dimension and what devices give it its poetic flavor? Find specific examples. Then, using Carson's essay as a model, choose a particular natural object (a tree, a meadow, a

mountain, and so forth), research it sufficiently to become familiar with its technical vocabulary, and finally work that vocabulary into an essay that makes your reader appreciate the beauty and "magic" of the natural world.

WILLA CATHER

Willa Cather (1873–1947) began her celebrated literary career contributing articles, sketches, and reviews of literature, music, drama, and art to the Nebraska State Journal while she was still an undergraduate at the University of Nebraska. Upon graduation in 1895, she worked as a journalist for several periodicals and between 1905 and 1912 served very successfully as managing editor of McClure's, the famous New York "muckraking" magazine.

    When her first novel appeared in 1912, Willa Cather left magazine editing to write full time. In 1913 she published O Pioneers! and then five years later My Antonia, two of the best-loved novels of the American frontier. Though she won a Pulitzer prize in 1922 for One of Ours, a novel about a young midwesterner's experience of European culture via the First World War, that book never achieved the popularity of The Professor's House (1925), Death Comes for the Archbishop (1927), or Shadows on the Rock (1931). Willa Cather called her talent for portraying the daily lives of ordinary men and women a "gift of sympathy." It is a gift she often found sadly lacking—as the following sketch shows—in the small-town world that meant so much to her.

Small-Town Life

It may be said the funerals make up the social life of many small towns. Social endeavors become discouraged in little western towns, like the crops in the south wind.

It has been argued before now that if the people in the villages all over the western states took more interest in each other, and could manufacture a smile when their neighbors had a stroke of good luck, or could find a sympathetic word to say when they were in trouble, that the corn itself would take heart o' grace and see some use in growing.

The privations that people suffer in our little western towns are of their own making, and are not brought upon them by God or the railroads or the weather.

Within the memory of all of us there was plenty of life and enthusiasm in every Nebraska town, as there is in Cheyenne or Deadwood today. The smallest village had its euchre clubs and whist clubs and dancing clubs, and nearly everybody spent money beyond their means. Then hard times and small crops came along for awhile, and everybody got remorseful and discouraged and more or less bitter.

People who met with financial reverses turned about and said spiteful things about their friends who had been more fortunate, and these friends, being human, withdrew within a wall of haughtiness and answered back with scorn.

As the phrase goes, people "got out of the habit of going" to see their friends, and soon enough they got out of the habit of caring about them at all. Now some of them are pessimistic and lay it on the weather or the corn. It would be no great wonder if the corn did get tired of growing to feed selfish and grouchy people.

In little eastern towns factions and indifference are to be expected. There are old blood feuds that have been handed down for generations and there are caste lines that everybody regards. But in a western town everybody has a second chance and begins again with no past behind him and a clean slate. He doesn't have to be mean because of tradition; because his father sanded sugar or watered his hay before he sold it.

Everybody has an opportunity to help in making a social side to life that will benefit him and his children, but he won't do it because he doesn't like this fellow or that fellow doesn't like him.

There is one thing the small-town man and woman will not do, and that is show courtesy to people whom they do not like; they hold such conduct to be bare deception. The fallacy of their theory is that nine times out of ten if they sat down beside these same distasteful people for an hour and did their part to sustain conversation, their hatred would vanish and their action would cease to be a deception.

William James, the psychologist, has so admirably explained that so often the act precedes the feeling in matters of courtesy and kindness. If it were necessary to feel a strong affection for people in order to conscientiously dine at their house or invite them to your own, there would be few dinner parties in the world.

Most of us don't try to love our friends after we are eighteen, unless we are fools or geniuses. We take them for what they are worth and let it go at that, knowing perfectly well that we ourselves are in need of reciprocal charity.

The small town lets its social arrears go and go until people are buried beneath an ashamed sense of their own remissness, and then they try to make it all up at funerals. When anyone dies whom they haven't broken bread with or called on for years, his fellow townsmen put on their black clothes and go to see him, and the women ravage their gardens to send him flowers. If a college student comes back to his native town and wants to see all his old friends together, he has to go to a funeral to do it. It's a futile and inexpensive sort of remorse and it's a dishonest way of paying social obligations.

Surely it is better to ask a man to dinner once during his lifetime than to go to his funeral, and surely it is pleasanter. It's a better plan to tell him that he's a good fellow and that he has deserved all the luck he's ever had, and more too, than to tell his widow about it someday. How many people have ever told the best lawyer in their town that they appreciate the fact that he is clever, or the best student in their schools that they take an interest in him?

Why is it that the common courtesies in life that make it easy sailing and compensate somewhat for the larger disappointments of life, come harder than blood in the small towns?

Discussion Questions

1. According to Willa Cather, what human obstacles stand in the way of improving small-town life? How does she think these obstacles can be overcome?

2. Why does Willa Cather use William James's comment that "so often the act precedes the feeling in matters of courtesy and kindness"? Explain what this means. How is it contrary to our customary notion of human behavior?

3. Cather's sketch was written in 1901. Compare her description of small-town life to Frederick Lewis Allen's description of a typical Main Street of 1900. Which writer paints a more attractive picture of life in that era? How does each writer's approach differ?

4. Cather ends her essay with a question. Do you think it is one she has answered or is it still in search of an answer? Explain.

5. Many people today would argue that what Cather says about small-town life should really be said about modern cities. Which do you think is *less* friendly to live in, a small town or a big city? Write an essay of about the same length as Cather's in which you discuss the respective social amenities of small towns and big cities. Try, like Cather, to focus on a single social phenomenon that allows you to make larger observations.

G. K. Chesterton

Gilbert Keith Chesterton (1874–1936) was one of the most prolific and most versatile men of letters in the early twentieth century. He wrote poetry, plays, novels, and essays, along with social and literary criticism and polemic. In the early days of radio, he conducted a weekly literary program for the British Broadcasting Company. Of all his work, his Father Brown detective stories continue to be perhaps most widely read.

While the following selection shows Chesterton in a more whimsical humor, it also shows his refusal, in sightseeing as in any other part of his life, to think the conventional thoughts of his day and to feel its conventional feelings.

On Sightseeing

I have often done my best to consider, in various aspects, what is really the matter with Sightseeing. Or rather, I hope, I have done my best to consider what is the matter with me, when I find myself faintly fatigued by Sightseeing. For it is always wiser to consider not so much why a thing is not enjoyable, as why we ourselves do not enjoy it. In the case of Sightseeing, I have only got so far as to be quite certain that the fault is not in the Sights and is not in the Sightseers. This would seem to drive the speculative philosopher back upon the dreadful and shocking conclusion that the fault is entirely in me. But, before accepting so destructive a deduction, I think there are some further modifications to be made and some further distinctions to be drawn.

The mere fact that a mob is going to see a monument ought not in itself to depress any imaginative and sympathetic mind. On the contrary, such a mind ought to perceive that there is something of the same mystery or majesty in the mob as in the monument. It is a weakness to fail in feeling that a statue standing on a pedestal above a street, the statue of a hero, carved by an artist, for the honour and glory of a city, is, so far as it goes, a marvellous and impressive work of man. But it is far more of a weakness to fail in feeling that a hundred statues walking about the street, alive with the miracle of a mysterious vitality, are a marvellous and impressive work of God. In so far as that ultimate argument affects the matter, the sightseer might almost as well travel to see the sightseers as to see the sights. There are, of course, vulgar and repulsive sightseers. There are, for that matter, vulgar and repulsive statues. But this cannot be a complete excuse for my own lamentable coldness; for I have felt it creeping over me in the presence of the most earnest and refined sightseers, engaged in inspecting the most classical and correct statues. Indeed (if I must make the disgraceful confession in the interests of intellectual discovery), I will own that I have felt this mysterious wave of weariness pass over me rather *more* often when the elegant and distinguished Archdeacon was explaining the tombs to the Guild of Golden Thoughts than when an ordinary shouting showman was showing them to a jolly rabble of trippers with beer bottles and concertinas. I am very much troubled with this unnatural insensibility of mind; and I have made many attempts, none of them quite successful, to trace my mental malady to its origin. But I am not sure that some hint of the truth may not be found in the first popular example that I gave—the example of a statue standing in a street.

Now, men have stuck up statues in streets as part of the general and ancient instinct of popular monumental art, which they exhibited in erecting pillars, building pyramids, making monoliths and obelisks, and such things, from the beginning of the world. And the conception may be broadly stated thus—that this sort of sight was meant for two different kinds of sightseers. First, the monument was meant to be seen accidentally; it was actually set up purposely in order to be seen accidentally. In other words, a striking tower on a hill, an arresting statue on a pedestal, a remarkable relief over an archway, or any other piece of public art, was intended for the traveller, and even especially for the chance traveller. It was meant for the passer-by, perhaps in the hope that he would not merely pass by; perhaps in the hope that he would pause, and possibly even meditate. But he would be meditating not only on something that he had never seen before, but on something that he had never expected to see. The statue would almost spring out upon him like a stage brigand. The archway would arrest him and almost bar his path like a barricade. He would suddenly see the high tower like a sort of signal; like a rocket suddenly sent up to convey a message, and almost a warning. This is the way in which many popular monuments have been seen; and this, some may agree with me in thinking, is pretty much the best way to see them. No man will ever forget the sights he really saw when he was not a sightseer. Every man remembers the thing that struck him like the thunderbolt of an instant, though it had stood there waiting for him as the memorial of an aeon. But, whether or no this be the best way of treating popular memorials, it is not the only way, and certainly has not been the only popular way. Historic relics, as a whole, have been treated differently in history as a whole. But, in history as a whole, the other way of seeing such sights was not what we commonly call sightseeing.

We might put the point this way: that the two ways of visiting the statue or the shrine were the way of the Traveller and the way of the Pilgrim. But the way of the Pilgrim almost always involved the way of the Pilgrimage. It was a ritual or ceremonial way: the way of a procession which had indeed come to see that shrine, but had not come to see anything else. The pilgrim does not feel, as the tourist does often quite naturally feel, that he has had his tour interrupted by something that does not happen to interest him. The pilgrimage must interest him, or he would never have been a pilgrim. He knows exactly what he wants to do; and, what is perhaps even more valuable, he knows for certain when he has done it. He cannot be dragged on from one thing to another; from one thing that interests him mildly to another thing that bores him stiff. He has undertaken a certain expedition with a certain logical end: an end both in the sense of a purpose and in the sense of termination. For a certain mystical reason of his own he wanted to visit a certain monument or shrine; and, now he has visited it, he is free to visit the nearest public-house or any other place he pleases.

But all this is altered, because we have passed from the age of monuments to the age of museums. We have been afflicted with the modern idea of collecting all sorts of totally different things, with totally different types of interest, including a good many of no apparent interest at all, and stuffing them all into one building, that the stranger may stray among a hundred distracting monuments or the pilgrim be lost among a hundred hostile shrines. When the traveller saw the statue of the hero, he did not see written on the pedestal: "This way to the Collection of Tropical Fungi," in which he possibly felt no interest at all. When the pilgrim found his way to the shrine, he did not find that the priest was eagerly waving him on to a glass case filled with the specimens of the local earthworms. Fungi and earthworms may be, and indeed are, exceedingly interesting things in themselves; but they are not things which men seek in the same mood which sends them to look at the statues of heroes or the shrines of saints. With the establishment of that entirely modern thing, the Museum, we have a new conception, which, like so many modern conceptions, is based on a blunder in psychology and a blindness to the true interests of culture. The Museum is not meant either for the wanderer to see by accident or for the pilgrim to see with awe. It is meant for the mere slave of a routine of self-education to stuff himself with every sort of incongruous intellectual food in one indigestible meal. It is meant for the mere Sightseer, the man who must see all the sights.

Of course, I am only speaking of this kind of sight as it affects this kind of sightseer. I do not deny that museums and galleries and other collections serve a more serious purpose for specialists who can select special things. But the modern popular practice of which I complain is bad, not because it is popular, but because it is modern. It was not made by any of the ancestral instincts of mankind; either the instinct that erected the crucifix by the wayside to arrest the wayfarer, or the instinct that erected the crucifix in the cathedral to be the goal of the worshipper. It is not a product of popular imagination, but of what is called popular education; the cold and compulsory culture which is not, and never will be, popular.

Discussion Questions

1. Is the distinction Chesterton makes in his first paragraph between himself and the activity he describes maintained throughout his essay? Describe the ways in which the distinction creates a relation between Chesterton and his reader.

2. How does Chesterton's choice of the general example of "statues" work to support his argument? Would other examples have worked as well for him?

3. Compare the relation Chesterton creates between himself and his fellow sightseers to that which Helen Lawrenson creates between herself and her fellow tourists.

4. Describe your own experience of seeing a famous sight or site. How does Chesterton's notion of what the role of a sightseer should be compare to that implicitly expressed by the style of Paul West?

ROBERT COLES

A *professor of psychiatry at the Harvard Medical School, Robert Coles has played a leading role in contemporary social reform since the 1960's. Volumes II and III of his five-volume study of the effects of poverty and stress on the young,* Children of Crisis *(1967–1978), a landmark of compassionate sociological scholarship, won the Pulitzer prize in 1973. In this series, Coles skillfully interweaves—as he does in the following essay—the real voices of young people with his own interpretive commentary. Coles believes that a proper understanding of human problems can take place only within the context of the actual language people use to talk about their problems, not through the smoke screen of professional jargon.*

Born in Boston in 1929, Robert Coles graduated from Harvard and took his M.D. from Columbia in 1954. He has received numerous awards for humanitarianism, including the Anisfield-Wolf Award in Race Relations and the Four Freedoms Award from B'nai B'rith. Besides his many publications in child psychology and civil rights, Coles has written extensively on literature. His literary studies include William Carlos Williams: The Knack of Survival in America *(1975),* Walker Percy: An American Search *(1978), and* Flannery O'Conner's South *(1980).*

Children of Affluence

It won't do to talk of *the* affluent in America. It won't do to say that in our upper-middle-class suburbs, or among our wealthy, one observes clear-cut, consistent psychological or cultural characteristics. Even in relatively homogeneous places there are substantial differences in homelife, in values taught, hobbies encouraged, beliefs advocated or sometimes virtually instilled. But it is the obligation of a psychological observer like me, who wants to know how children make sense of a certain kind of life, to document as faithfully as possible the way a common heritage of money and power affects the assumptions of particular boys and girls.

I started my work with affluent children by seeing troubled boys and girls; they were the ones I saw as a child psychiatrist *before* I began my years of "field work" in the South, then Appalachia, then the North, then the West. There are only a few hundred child psychiatrists in the United States, and often their time is claimed by those who have money. After a while, if one is not careful, the well-off and the rich come to be seen exclusively through a clinician's eye: homes full of bitterness, deceit, snobbishness, neuroses, psychoses; homes with young children in mental pain, and with older children, adolescents and young adults, who use drugs, drink, run away, rebel constantly and disruptively, become truants, delinquents, addicts, alcoholics, become compulsively promiscuous, go crazy, go wild, go to ruin.

We blame the alcoholism, insanity, meanness, apathy, drug usage, despondency, and, not least, cruelty to children we see or are told exists in the ghetto or among the rural poor upon various "socioeconomic factors." All of those signs of psychological deterioration can be found among quite privileged families, too—and so we remind ourselves, perhaps, that wealth corrupts.

No—it is not that simple. Wealth does not corrupt nor does it ennoble. But wealth does govern the minds of privileged children, gives them a peculiar kind of identity which they never lose, whether they grow up to be stockbrokers or communards, and whether they lead healthy or unstable lives. There is, I think, a message that virtually all quite well-off American families transmit to their children—an emotional expression of those familiar, classbound prerogatives, money and power. I use the word "entitlement" to describe that message.

The word was given to me by the rather rich parents of a child I began to talk with almost two decades ago, in 1959. I have watched those parents become grandparents, and have seen what they described as "the responsibilities of entitlement" handed down to a new generation. When the father, a lawyer and stockbroker from a prominent and quietly influential family, referred to the "entitlement" his children were growing up to know, he had in mind a social rather than a psychological phenomenon: the various juries or committees that select the Mardi Gras participants in New Orleans's annual parade and celebration. He knew that his daughter was "entitled" to be invited.

He wanted, however, to go beyond that social fact. He talked about what he had received from his parents and what he would give to his children, "automatically, without any thought," and what they too would pass on. The father was careful to distinguish between the social entitlement and "something else," a "something else" he couldn't quite define but knew he had to try to evoke if he was to be psychologically candid: "I mean they should be responsible, and try to live up to their ideals, and not just sit around wondering which island in the Caribbean to visit this year, and where to go next summer to get away from the heat and humidity here in New Orleans."

He was worried about what a lot of money can do to a personality. When his young daughter, during a Mardi Gras season, kept *assuming* she would one day become a Mardi Gras queen, he realized that his notion of "entitlement" was not quite hers. Noblesse oblige requires a gesture toward others.

He was not the only parent to express such a concern to me in the course of my work. In homes where mothers and fathers profess no explicit reformist persuasions, they nevertheless worry about what happens to children who grow up surrounded by just about everything they want, virtually on demand. "When they're like that, they've gone from spoiled to spoiled rotten—and beyond, to some state I don't know how to describe."

Obviously, it is possible for parents to have a lot of money yet avoid bringing up their children in such a way that they feel like members of a royal family. But even parents determined not to spoil their children often recognize what might be called the existential (as opposed to strictly psychological) aspects of their situation. A father may begin rather early on lecturing his children about the meaning of money; a mother may do her share by saying no, even when yes is so easy to say. And a child, by the age of five or six, has very definite notions of what is possible, even if it is not always permitted. That child, in conversation, and without embarrassment or the kind of reticence and secretiveness that come later, may reveal a substantial knowledge of economic affairs. A six-year-old girl I spoke to knew that she would, at twenty-one, inherit half a million dollars. She also knew that her father "only" gave her twenty-five cents a week, whereas some friends of hers received as much as a dollar. She was vexed; she asked her parents why they were so "strict." One friend had even used the word "stingy" for the parents. The father, in a matter-of-fact way, pointed out to the daughter that she did, after all, get "anything she really wants." Why, then, the need for an extravagant allowance? The girl was won over. But admonitions don't always modify the quite realistic appraisal children make of what they are heir to; and they don't diminish their sense of entitlement—a state of mind that pervades their view of the world.

In an Appalachian home, for instance, a boy of seven made the following comment in 1963, after a mine his father owned had suffered an explosion, killing two men and injuring seriously nine others: "I heard my mother saying she felt sorry for the families of the miners. I feel sorry for them, too. I hope the men who got hurt get better. I'm sure they will. My father has called in doctors from Lexington. He wants the best doctors in all Kentucky for those miners. Daddy says it was the miners' fault; they get careless, and the next thing you know, there's an explosion. It's too bad. I guess there are a lot of kids who are praying hard for their fathers. I wish God was nice to everyone. He's been very good to us. My daddy says it's been hard work, running the mine, and another one he has. It's just as hard to run a mine as it is to go down and dig the coal! I'm glad my father is the owner, though. I wouldn't want him to get killed or hurt bad down there, way underground. Daddy has given us a good life. We have a lot of fun coming up, he says, in the next few years. We're going on some trips. Daddy deserves his vacations. He says he's happy because he can keep us happy, and he does."

Abundance is this boy's destiny, he has every reason to believe, abundance and limitless possibility. He may even land on the stars. Certainly he has traveled widely in this country. He associates the seasons with travel. In winter, there is a trip south, to one or another Caribbean island. He worries, on these trips, about his two dogs, and the other animals—the guinea pigs, hamsters, rabbits, chickens. There is always someone in the house, a maid, a handyman. Still it is sad to say good-bye. Now if the family owned a plane, the animals could come along on those trips!

The boy doesn't really believe that his father will ever own a Lear jet; yet he can construct a fantasy: "I had this dream. In it I was walking through the woods with Daddy, and all of a sudden there was an open field, and I looked, and I saw a hawk, and it was circling and circling. I like going hunting with Daddy, and I thought we were hunting. But when I looked at him, he didn't have his gun. Then he pointed at the hawk, and it was coming down. It landed ahead of us, and it was real strange—because the hawk turned into an airplane! I couldn't believe it. We went toward the plane, and Daddy said we could get a ride anytime we wanted, because it was ours; he'd just bought it. That's when I woke up, I think."

Four years after the boy dreamed that his father owned a plane, the father got one. The boom of the 1970s in the coal fields made his father even richer. The boy was, of course, eager to go on flying trips; eager, also, to learn to fly. At thirteen, he dreamed (by day) of becoming an astronaut, or of going to the Air Force Academy and afterwards becoming a "supersonic pilot."

He would never become a commercial pilot, however; and his reasons were interesting. "I've gone on a lot of commercial flights, and there are a lot of people on board, and the pilot has to be nice to everyone, and he makes all these announcements about the seat belts, and stuff like that. My dad's pilot was in the Air Force, and then he flew commercial. He was glad to get out, though. He says you have to be like a waiter; you have to answer complaints from the customers, and apologize to them, just because the ride gets bumpy. It's best to work for yourself, or work for another person, if you trust him and like him. If you go commercial, like our pilot says, you're a servant."

Many of the children I have worked with are similarly disposed; they do not like large groups of people in public places—in fact, have been taught the value not only of privacy but of the quiet that goes with being relatively alone. Some of the children are afraid of those crowds, can't imagine how it would be possible to survive them. Of course, what is strange, unknown, or portrayed as unattractive, uncomfortable, or just to be avoided as a nuisance can for a given child become a source of curiosity, like an event to be experienced at all costs. An eight-year-old girl who lived on a farm well outside Boston wanted desperately to go to the city and see Santa Claus—not because she believed in him, but because she wanted to see "those crowds" she had seen on television. She got her wish, was excited at first, then became quite disappointed, and ultimately uncomfortable. She didn't like being jostled, shoved, and ignored when she protested.

A week after the girl had gone through her Boston "adventure" (as she had called the trip *before* she embarked upon it), each student in her third-grade class was asked to draw a picture in some way connected to the Christmas season, and the girl obliged eagerly. She drew Santa Claus standing beside a pile of packages, presents for the many children who stood near him. They blended into one another—a mob scene. Watching them but removed from them was one child, bigger and on a higher level—suspended in space, it seemed, and partially surrounded by a thin but visible line. The girl wrote on the bottom of the drawing, "I saw Santa Claus." She made it quite clear what she had intended to portray. "He was standing there, handing out these gifts. They were all the same, I think, and they were plastic squirt guns for the boys and little dolls for the girls. I felt sorry for the kids. I asked my mother why kids wanted to push each other, just to get that junk. My mother said a lot of people just don't know any better. I was going to force my way up to Santa Claus and tell him to stop being so dumb! My mother said he was probably a drunk, trying to make a few dollars so he could spend it in a bar that evening! I don't want to be in a store like that again. We went up to a balcony and watched, and then we got out of the place and came home. I told my mother that I didn't care if I ever went to Boston again. I have two friends, and they've never been to Boston, and they don't want to go there, except to ride through on the way to the airport."

She sounded at that moment more aloof, condescending, and snobbish than she ordinarily is. She spends her time with two or three girls who live on nearby estates. Those girls don't see each other regularly, and each of them is quite able to be alone—in fact, rather anxious for those times of solitude. Sometimes a day or two goes by with no formal arrangement to play. They meet in school, and that seems to be enough. Each girl has obligations—a horse to groom, a stall to work on. They are quite "self-sufficient," a word they have heard used repeatedly by their parents. Even with one's own social circle there is no point surrendering to excessive gregariousness!

Once up on her own horse, she is (by her own description) in her "own world." She has heard her mother use that expression. The mother is not boasting, or dismissing others who live in other worlds. The mother is describing, as does the child, a state of progressive withdrawal from people, and the familiar routines or objects of the environment, in favor of a mixture of reverie and disciplined activity.

Nothing seems impossible, burdensome, difficult. There are no distractions, petty or boring details to attend to. And one is closer to one's "self." The mother talks about the "self," and the child does, too. "It is strange," the girl comments, "because you forget yourself riding or skiing, but you also remember yourself the way you don't when you're just sitting around watching television or reading or playing in your room."

None of the other American children I have worked with have placed such a continuous and strong emphasis on the "self"—its display, its possibilities, its cultivation and development, even the repeated use of the word *self*. A ten-year-old boy who lived in Westchester County made this very clear. I met him originally because his parents were lawyers, and active in the civil rights movement. His father, a patrician Yankee, very much endorsed the students who went south in the early 1960s, and worked on behalf of integrated schools up north. The boy, however, attended private schools—a source of anguish to both father and son, who do not lend themselves to a description that suggests hypocrisy.

The boy knew that he, also, *would* be (as opposed to *wanted* to be) a lawyer. He was quick to perceive and acknowledge his situation, and as he did so, he brought his "self" right into the discussion: "I don't want to tell other kids what to do. I told my father I should be going to the public schools myself. Then I could say anything. Then I could ask why we don't have black kids with us in school. But you have to try to do what's best for your own life, even if you can't speak up for the black people. When I'm grown up I'll be like my father; I'll help the black people all I can. It's this way: first you build *yourself* up. You learn all you can. Later, you can *give of yourself*. That's what Dad says: you can't help others until you've learned to help yourself. It's not that you're being selfish, if you're going to a private school and your parents have a lot of money. We had a maid here, and she wasn't right in the head. She lost her temper and told Daddy that he's a phony, and he's out for himself and no one else, and the same goes for my sister and me. Then she quit. Daddy tried to get her to talk with us, but she wouldn't. She said that's all we ever do—talk,

talk. I told Daddy she was contradicting herself, because she told me a few weeks ago that I'm always doing something, and I should sit down and talk with her. But I don't know what to say to her! I think she got angry with me, because I was putting on my skis, for cross-country skiing, and she said I had too much, that was my problem. I asked her where the regular skis were, and she said she wouldn't tell me, even if she knew! It's too bad, what happened to her.

"I feel sorry for her, though. It's not fun to be a maid. The poor woman doesn't look very good. She weighs too much. She's only forty, my mother thinks, but she looks as if she's sixty, and is sick. She should take better care of herself. Now she's thrown away this job, and she told my mother last year that it was the best one she'd ever had, so she's her own worst enemy. I wonder what she'll think when she looks at herself in the mirror."

This boy was no budding egotist. If anything, he was less self-centered at ten than many other children of his community and others like it. He was willing to think about those less fortunate than himself—the maid, and black people in general. True, he would often repeat uncritically his father's words, or a version of them. But he was trying to respond to his father's wishes and beliefs as well as his words. It was impossible for him, no matter how compassionate his nature, to conceive of life as others live it—the maid and, yes, millions of children his age, who don't look in the mirror very often, and may not even own one; who don't worry about how one looks, and what is said, and how one sounds, and how one smells.

It is important that a child's sense of entitlement be distinguished not only from the psychiatric dangers of narcissism but from the less pathological and not all that uncommon phenomenon known as being "spoiled." It is a matter of degree; "spoiled" children are self-centered all right, petulant and demanding—but not as grandiose or, alas, saddled with illusions (or delusions) as the children clinicians have in mind when using the phrase "narcissistic entitlement." The rich or quite well-to-do are all too commonly charged with producing spoiled children. Yet one sees spoiled children everywhere, among the very poor as well as the inordinately rich.

In one of the first wealthy families I came to know there was a girl who was described by both parents as "spoiled." At the time, I fear, I was ready to pronounce every child in New Orleans's Garden District spoiled. Were they not all living comfortable, indeed luxurious, lives, as compared to the lives of the black or working-class white children I was getting to know in other sections of that city?

Nevertheless, I soon began to realize that it wouldn't do to characterize without qualification one set of children as spoiled, by virtue of their social and economic background, as against another set of children who were obviously less fortunate in many respects. One meets, among the rich, restrained, disciplined, and by no means indulged children; sometimes, even, boys and girls who have learned to be remarkably self-critical, even ascetic—anything but "spoiled" in the conventional sense of the word. True, one can find a touch and more of arrogance, or at least sustained self-assurance, in those apparently spartan boys and girls who seem quite anxious to deny themselves all sorts of presumably accessible privileges if not luxuries. But one also finds in these children a consistent willingness to place serious and not always pleasant burdens on themselves—to the point where they often struck me, when I came to their homes fresh from visits with much poorer age-mates, as remarkably *less* spoiled: not so much whining or crying; fewer demands for candy or other sweets; even, sometimes, a relative indifference to toys, however near at hand and expensive they may have been; a disregard of television—so often demanded by the children that I was seeing.

A New Orleans black woman said to me in 1961: "I don't know how to figure out these rich white kids. They're something! I used to think, before I took a job with this family, that the only difference between a rich kid and a poor kid is that the rich kid knows he has a lot of money and he grows up and becomes spoiled rotten. That's what my mother told me; she took care of a white girl, and the girl was an only child, and her father owned a department store in McComb, Mississippi, and that girl thought she was God's special creature. My mother used to come home and tell us about the 'little princess'; but she turned out to be no good. She was so pampered, she couldn't do a thing for herself. All she knew how to do was order people around.

"It's different with these two children. I've never seen such a boy and such a girl. They think they're the best ones who ever lived—like that girl in McComb—but they don't behave like her. They're never asking me to do much of anything. They even ask if they can help me! They tell me that they want to know how to do everything. The girl says she wants to learn how to run the washing machine and the dishwasher. She says she wants to learn all my secret recipes. She says she'd like to give the best parties in the Garden District when she grows up, and she'd like to be able to give them without anyone's help. She says I could serve the food, but she would like to make it. The boy says he's going to be a lawyer and a banker, so he wants to know how much everything costs. He doesn't want to waste anything. He'll see me throw something away, and he wants to know why. I only wish that my own kids were like him!

"But these children here are special, and don't they know it! That's what being rich is: you know you're different from most people. These two kids act as if they're going to be tops in everything, and they're pleased as can be with themselves, because there is nothing they can't do, and there's nothing they can't get, and there's nothing they can't win, and they're always showing off what they can do, and then before you can tell them how good they are, they're telling the same thing to themselves. It's confusing! They're not spoiled one bit, but oh, they have a high opinion of themselves!"

Actually, children like the ones she speaks of don't allow themselves quite the unqualified confidence she describes, though she certainly has correctly conveyed the appearance they give. Boys and girls may seem without anxiety or self-doubt; they have been brought up, as the maid suggests, to feel important, superior, destined for a satisfying, rewarding life—and at, say, eight or nine they already appear to know all that. Yet there are moments of hesitation, if not apprehension. An eleven-year-old boy from a prominent and quite brilliant Massachusetts family told his teachers, in an autobiographical composition about the vicissitudes of "entitlement": "I don't always do everything right. I'd like to be able to say I don't make any mistakes, but I do, and when I do, I feel bad. My father and mother say that if you train yourself, you can be right *almost* 100 percent of the time. Even they make mistakes, though. I like to be first in sports. I like to beat my brothers at skiing. But I don't always go down the slopes as fast as I could and I sometimes fall down. Last year I broke my leg. When I get a bad cold, I feel disappointed in myself. I don't think it's right to be easy on yourself. If you are, then you slip back, and you don't get a lot of the rewards in life. If you really work for the rewards, you'll get them."

A platitude—the kind of assurance his teachers, as a matter of fact, have rather often given him. In the fourth grade, for instance, the teacher had this written on the blackboard (and kept it there for weeks): "Those who want something badly enough get it, provided they are willing to wait and work." The boy considers that assertion neither banal nor unrealistic. He has been brought up to believe that such is and will be (for him) the case. He knows that others are not so lucky, but he hasn't really met those "others," and they don't cross his mind at all. What does occur to him sometimes is the need for constant exertion, lest he fail to "measure up." One "measures up" when one tries hard and succeeds. If one slackens or stumbles, one ought to be firm with oneself—but not in any self-pitying or self-excusing or self-paralyzing way. The emphasis is on a quick and efficient moment of scrutiny followed by "a fast pick-up."

Such counsel is not as callous as it may sound—or, ironically, as it may well have been intended to sound. The child who hears it gets, briefly, upset; but unless he or she stops heeding what has been said, quite often "a fast pick-up" does indeed take place—an effort to redeem what has been missed or lost, or only somewhat accomplished. Again, it is a matter of feeling entitled. A child who has been told repeatedly that all he or she needs to do is try hard does not feel inclined to allow himself or herself long stretches of time for skeptical self-examination. The point is to feel *entitled*—then act upon that feeling. The boy whose composition was just quoted from used the word "entitled" in another essay he wrote, this one meant to be a description of his younger (age five) brother. The writing was not, however, without an autobiographical strain to it: "I was watching my brother from my bedroom window. He was climbing up the fence we built for our corral. He got to the top, and then he just stood there and waved and shouted. No one was there. He was talking to himself. He was very happy. Then he would fall. He would be upset for a few seconds, but he would climb right back up again. Then he would be even happier! He was entitled to be happy. It is his fence, and he has learned to climb it, and stay up, and balance himself."

Discussion Questions

1. What does Coles mean by "entitlement"? Why does he give his source for the term? Are there any other sources? How does the term govern the course of his essay?

2. Examine the speech of the Appalachian mine owner's son. In what ways does Coles comment on it? What interests Coles about the boy's speech? Why, for example, doesn't the boy, who loves flying, want to become a commercial pilot? In what ways is he similar to the eight-year-old girl who visits Santa Claus?

3. Where do most of the children's expressions come from? Why is pinpointing that source so important to Coles's analysis?

4. What distinction does Coles make between entitlement and the dangers of narcissism? What does it mean in Coles's analysis to be "spoiled"? How does Coles use the New Orleans black woman to comment on this distinction?

5. Use Coles's notion of "entitlement" to comment on Richard Wright's "Innocence". How would Coles—as a child psychiatrist—respond to Wright's dilemma? Would he regard Wright as a "spoiled" child? Explain.

6. Coles lets the final quotation speak for itself. But what does it mean exactly? In a brief essay, write an analysis of the eleven-year-old boy's description of his younger brother. How does the boy's anecdote about his brother support Coles's larger view of "entitlement"? Do you think poor youngsters would express themselves in the same way, with the same meaning?

AARON COPLAND

The noted American composer Aaron Copland was born in Brooklyn, New York, in 1900 and studied orchestration in Paris. A former director of the League of Composers, Copland taught musical composition at Harvard and traveled widely as a lecturer and conductor throughout the United States and Europe. His score for the ballet Appalachian Spring *(1944) won the Pulitzer prize and the New York Music Critics' Award. His works, which make use of classical structures, asymmetric rhythms, folk music, cowboy tunes, and jazz idioms, include:* Concerto *(1926),* Short Symphony *(1933),* Billy the Kid *(1938),* Rodeo *(1942), and* Third Symphony *(1946). Copland also wrote the scores for such distinguished films as* Of Mice and Men *(1939),* Our Town *(1940), and* The Heiress *(1949).*

Copland's books include: What to Listen for in Music *(1939; 1957), in which the essay that follows originally appeared;* Our New Music *(1941),* Music and Imagination *(1952), and* Copland on Music *(1960).*

How We Listen to Music

We all listen to music according to our separate capacities. But, for the sake of analysis, the whole listening process may become clearer if we break it up into its component parts, so to speak. In a certain sense we all listen to music on three separate planes. For lack of a better terminology, one might name these: (1) the sensuous plane, (2) the expressive plane, (3) the sheerly musical plane. The only advantage to be gained from mechanically splitting up the listening process into these hypothetical planes is the clearer view to be had of the way in which we listen.

The simplest way of listening to music is to listen for the sheer pleasure of the musical sound itself. That is the sensuous plane. It is the plane on which we hear music without thinking, without considering it in any way. One turns on the radio while doing something else and absent-mindedly bathes in the sound. A kind of brainless but attractive state of mind is engendered by the mere sound appeal of the music.

You may be sitting in a room reading this book. Imagine one note struck on the piano. Immediately that one note is enough to change the atmosphere of the room—proving that the sound element in music is a powerful and mysterious agent, which it would be foolish to deride or belittle.

The surprising thing is that many people who consider themselves qualified music lovers abuse that plane in listening. They go to concerts in order to lose themselves. They use music as a consolation or an escape. They enter an ideal world where one doesn't have to think of the realities of everyday life. Of course they aren't thinking about the music either. Music allows them to leave it, and they go off to a place to dream, dreaming because of and apropos of the music yet never quite listening to it.

Yes, the sound appeal of music is a potent and primitive

force, but you must not allow it to usurp a disproportionate share of your interest. The sensuous plane is an important one in music, a very important one, but it does not constitute the whole story.

There is no need to digress further on the sensuous plane. Its appeal to every normal human being is self-evident. There is, however, such a thing as becoming more sensitive to the different kinds of sound stuff as used by various composers. For all composers do not use that sound stuff in the same way. Don't get the idea that the value of music is commensurate with its sensuous appeal or that the loveliest sounding music is made by the greatest composer. If that were so, Ravel would be a greater creator than Beethoven. The point is that the sound element varies with each composer, that his usage of sound forms an integral part of his style and must be taken into account when listening. The reader can see, therefore, that a more conscious approach is valuable even on this primary plane of music listening.

The second plane on which music exists is what I have called the expressive one. Here, immediately, we tread on controversial ground. Composers have a way of shying away from any discussion of music's expressive side. Did not Stravinsky himself proclaim that his music was an "object," a "thing," with a life of its own, and with no other meaning than its own purely musical existence? This intransigent attitude of Stravinsky's may be due to the fact that so many people have tried to read different meanings into so many pieces. Heaven knows it is difficult enough to say precisely what it is that a piece of music means, to say it definitely, to say it finally so that everyone is satisfied with your explanation. But that should not lead one to the other extreme of denying to music the right to be "expressive."

My own belief is that all music has an expressive power, some more and some less, but that all music has a certain meaning behind the notes and that that meaning behind the notes constitutes, after all, what the piece is saying, what the piece is about. This whole problem can be stated quite simply by asking, "Is there a meaning to music?" My answer to that would be, "Yes." And "Can you state in so many words what the meaning is?" My answer to that would be, "No." Therein lies the difficulty.

Simple-minded souls will never be satisfied with the answer to the second of these questions. They always want music to have a meaning, and the more concrete it is the better they like it. The more the music reminds them of a train, a storm, a funeral, or any other familiar conception the more expressive it appears to be to them. This popular idea of music's meaning—stimulated and abetted by the usual run of musical commentator—should be discouraged wherever and whenever it is met. One timid lady once confessed to me that she suspected something seriously lacking in her appreciation of music because of her inability to connect it with anything definite. That is getting the whole thing backward, of course.

Still, the question remains, How close should the intelligent music lover wish to come to pinning a definite meaning to any particular work? No closer than a general concept, I should say. Music expresses, at different moments, serenity or exuberance, regret or triumph, fury or delight. It expresses each of these moods, and many others, in a numberless variety of subtle shadings and differences. It may even express a state of meaning for which there exists no adequate word in any language. In that case, musicians often like to say that it has only a purely musical meaning. They sometimes go farther and say that *all* music has only a purely musical meaning. What they really mean is that no appropriate word can be found to express the music's meaning and that, even if it could, they do not feel the need of finding it.

But whatever the professional musician may hold, most musical novices still search for specific words with which to pin down their musical reactions. That is why they always find Tschaikovsky easier to "understand" than Beethoven. In the first place, it is easier to pin a meaning-word on a Tschaikovsky piece than on a Beethoven one. Much easier. Moreover, with the Russian composer, every time you come back to a piece of his it almost always says the same thing to you, whereas with Beethoven it is often quite difficult to put your finger right on what he is saying. And any musician will tell you that that is why Beethoven is the greater composer. Because music which always says the same thing to you will necessarily soon become dull music, but music whose meaning is slightly different with each hearing has a greater chance of remaining alive.

Listen, if you can, to the forty-eight fugue themes of Bach's *Well Tempered Clavichord*. Listen to each theme, one after another. You will soon realize that each theme mirrors a different world of feeling. You will also soon realize that the more beautiful a theme seems to you the harder it is to find any word that will describe it to your complete satisfaction. Yes, you will certainly know whether it is a gay theme or a sad one. You will be able, in other words, in your own mind, to draw a frame of emotional feeling around your theme. Now study the sad one a little closer. Try to pin down the exact quality of its sadness. Is it pessimistically sad; is it fatefully sad or smilingly sad?

Let us suppose that you are fortunate and can describe to

your own satisfaction in so many words the exact meaning of your chosen theme. There is still no guarantee that anyone else will be satisfied. Nor need they be. The important thing is that each one feel for himself the specific expressive quality of a theme or, similarly, an entire piece of music. And if it is a great work of art, don't expect it to mean exactly the same thing to you each time you return to it.

Themes or pieces need not express only one emotion, of course. Take such a theme as the first main one of the *Ninth Symphony*, for example. It is clearly made up of different elements. It does not say only one thing. Yet anyone hearing it immediately gets a feeling of strength, a feeling of power. It isn't a power that comes simply because the theme is played loudly. It is a power inherent in the theme itself. The extraordinary strength and vigor of the theme results in the listener's receiving an impression that a forceful statement has been made. But one should never try to boil it down to "the fateful hammer of life," etc. That is where the trouble begins. The musician, in his exasperation, says it means nothing but the notes themselves, whereas the nonprofessional is only too anxious to hang on to any explanation that gives him the illusion of getting closer to the music's meaning.

Now, perhaps, the reader will know better what I mean when I say that music does have an expressive meaning but that we cannot say in so many words what that meaning is.

The third plane on which music exists is the sheerly musical plane. Besides the pleasurable sound of music and the expressive feeling that it gives off, music does exist in terms of the notes themselves and of their manipulation. Most listeners are not sufficiently conscious of this third plane. It will be largely the business of this book to make them more aware of music on this plane.

Professional musicians, on the other hand, are, if anything, too conscious of the mere notes themselves. They often fall into the error of becoming so engrossed with their arpeggios and staccatos that they forget the deeper aspects of the music they are performing. But from the layman's standpoint, it is not so much a matter of getting over bad habits on the sheerly musical plane as of increasing one's awareness of what is going on, in so far as the notes are concerned.

When the man in the street listens to the "notes themselves" with any degree of concentration, he is most likely to make some mention of the melody. Either he hears a pretty melody or he does not, and he generally lets it go at that. Rhythm is likely to gain his attention next, particularly if it seems exciting. But harmony and tone color are generally taken for granted, if they are thought of consciously at all. As for music's having a definite form of some kind, that idea seems never to have occurred to him.

It is very important for all of us to become more alive to music on its sheerly musical plane. After all, an actual musical material is being used. The intelligent listener must be prepared to increase his awareness of the musical material and what happens to it. He must hear the melodies, the rhythms, the harmonies, the tone colors in a more conscious fashion. But above all he must, in order to follow the line of the composer's thought, know something of the principles of musical form. Listening to all of these elements is listening on the sheerly musical plane.

Let me repeat that I have split up mechanically the three separate planes on which we listen merely for the sake of greater clarity. Actually, we never listen on one or the other of these planes. What we do is to correlate them—listening in all three ways at the same time. It takes no mental effort, for we do it instinctively.

Perhaps an analogy with what happens to us when we visit the theater will make this instinctive correlation clearer. In the theater, you are aware of the actors and actresses, costumes and sets, sounds and movement. All these give one the sense that the theater is a pleasant place to be in. They constitute the sensuous plane in our theatrical reactions.

The expressive plane in the theater would be derived from the feeling that you get from what is happening on the stage. You are moved to pity, excitement, or gayety. It is this general feeling, generated aside from the particular words being spoken, a certain emotional something which exists on the stage, that is analogous to the expressive quality in music.

The plot and plot development is equivalent to our sheerly musical plane. The playwright creates and develops a character in just the same way that a composer creates and develops a theme. According to the degree of your awareness of the way in which the artist in either field handles his material will you become a more intelligent listener.

It is easy enough to see that the theatergoer never is conscious of any of these elements separately. He is aware of them all at the same time. The same is true of music listening. We simultaneously and without thinking listen on all three planes.

In a sense, the ideal listener is both inside and outside the music at the same moment, judging it and enjoying it, wishing it would go one way and watching it go another—almost like the composer at the moment he composes it; because in order to write his music, the composer must also be inside and outside his music, carried away by it and yet coldly critical of it. A subjective and objective attitude is implied in both creating and listening to music.

What the reader should strive for, then, is a more *active* kind of listening. Whether you listen to Mozart or Duke Ellington, you can deepen your understanding of music only by being a more conscious and aware listener—not someone who is just listening, but someone who is listening *for* something.

Discussion Questions

1. Which plane of listening do you think Copland values most? Why? Think about your own responses to music: Do you concentrate more on one plane than on the others?

2. How does Copland organize his essay? What is it about his method of organization that worries him? How would that concern be similar to organizational concerns in writing about other phenomena—for example, telling someone how to serve in tennis or explaining how to look at a painting?

3. If, as Copland says, we correlate all three planes instinctively whenever we listen, then why do we need to *learn* to listen? Don't we already know how? How do you think Copland would respond to that question?

4. How do Copland's views on aesthetic appreciation compare to those of Ortega y Gasset's? In what ways do both writers rely on similar methods of classification? Are their conclusions about aesthetic experiences similar?

5. Do you think Copland's analysis of how to listen to music could be applied to contemporary rock or country music? Using his advice about listening, write a brief essay in which you discuss an aspect of contemporary popular music that you think most people don't properly listen to when they hear that music.

GUY DAVENPORT

Born in South Carolina in 1927, Guy Davenport graduated from Duke University, received an advanced degree at Oxford as a Rhodes Scholar, and took his Ph.D at Harvard University. A translator of the classics, a poet, short story writer, illustrator, librettist, and Professor of English at the University of Kentucky, Davenport has written numerous critical essays and reviews (occasionally under the pseudonym Max Montgomery) for a variety of publications, including Hudson Review, National Review, The Virginia Quarterly, Life, *and the* New York Times Book Review.

Davenport has recently published two collections of short stories, the highly acclaimed Da Vinci's Bicycle (1979) *and* Eclogues (1981). *The autobiographical essay, "Finding," appeared in a collection of essays,* The Geography of the Imagination (1981).

Finding

Every Sunday afternoon of my childhood, once the tediousness of Sunday school and the appalling boredom of church were over with, corrosions of the spirit easily salved by the roast beef, macaroni pie, and peach cobbler that followed them, my father loaded us all into the Essex, later the Packard, and headed out to look for Indian arrows. That was the phrase, "to look for Indian arrows." Children detect nothing different in their own families: I can't remember noticing anything extraordinary in our family being the only one I knew of that devoted every Sunday afternoon to amateur archaeology.

We took along, from time to time, those people who expressed an interest in finding Indian arrows. Most of them, I expect, wanted an excuse for an outing. We thought of all neighbors, friends, and business associates in terms of whether they were good company or utter nuisances on our expeditions. Surely all of my attitudes toward people were shaped here, all unknowing. I learned that there are people who see nothing, who would not have noticed the splendidest of tomahawks if they had stepped on it, who could not tell a worked stone from a shard of flint or quartz, people who did not feel the excitment of the whoop we all let out when we found an arrowhead or rim of pottery with painting or incised border on it, a pot leg, or those major discoveries which we remembered and could recite forever afterward, the finding of an intact pipe, perfect celt, or unbroken spearhead elegantly core-chipped, crenulated and notched as if finished yesterday. "I've found one!" the cry would go up from the slope of a knoll, from the reaches of a plowed field, a gully. One never ran over; that was bad form. One kept looking with feigned nonchalance, and if one's search drew nigh the finder, it was permissible to ask to see. Daddy never looked at what other people found until we were back at the car. "Nice." he would say, or "That's really something." Usually he grunted, for my sister and I would have a fistful of tacky quartz arrowheads, lumpish and halfheartedly worked. Or we would have a dubious pointed rock which we had made out to be an arrowhead and which Daddy would extract from our plunder and toss out the car window.

These excursions were around the upper Savannah valley, out from places like Heardmont, Georgia, a ghost town in the thirties; Ware Shoals, South Carolina; Coronaca (passing through which my grandmother Davenport always exclaimed, "Forty years come on Cornelia!" and to my knowledge no one ever asked her why, and now we shall never know), Calhoun Falls, Abbeville, and a network of crossroads (usually named for their cotton gins), pecan groves, and "wide places in the road" like Iva, Starr, and Good Hope Community. The best looking was in autumn, when crops were in and frost had splintered the fields. It was then that arrowheads sat up on tees of red earth, a present to us all. A stone that has worked its way to the surface will remain on a kind of pedestal, surrounding topsoil having been washed away. These finds were considered great good fortune. "Just sitting right up there!" was the phrase. But these were usually tiny bird arrowheads in blue flint. Things worth finding were embedded, a telltale serif only showing. It was Daddy who found these. My best find was a round stone the size of a quarter, thick as three quarters, with Brancusi-like depressions on each surface, as if for forefinger and thumb. I'd thought it was the stone on which Indians twirled a stick with a bowstring, to make fire, yet the depressions did not seem to have been designed for that, or caused by it.

Years later, at Harvard, I took the stone, at Daddy's suggestion, around to an Indianologist at the Peabody Museum. He looked at it and laughed. Then he pulled open a drawer full of similar stones. What were they for? "We don't know," sighed the Indianologist. My father's guess that they were counters for some gambling game was probably right. The Cherokee whose stone artifacts we collected from their hunting grounds and campsites were passionate gamblers, and would stake squaw and papoose on a throw of the dice if all else were lost.

These Sunday searches were things all to themselves, distinctly a ritual whose *sacrum* had tacit and inviolable boundaries. Other outings, long forays into the chinquapin and hickory forests of Abbeville County, were for the pleasure of the walk and the odd pineknot, rich in turpentine, that one might pick up for the fire. There were summer drives for finding hog plums, wild peaches, and blackberries on the most abandoned of back dirt roads, autumn drives in search of muscadines and scuppernongs, the finding of which, gnarled high in trees like lianas, wanted as sharp an eye as an arrowhead. We were a foraging family, completely unaware of our passion for getting at things hard to find. I collected stamps, buttons, the cards that came with chewing gum, and other detritus, but these were private affairs with nothing of the authority of looking for Indian arrowheads.

Childhood is spent without introspection, in unreflective innocence. Adolescence turns its back on childhood in contempt and sometimes shame. We find our childhood later, and what we find in it is full of astounding surprises. As Proust has shown us, and Freud, its moments come back to us according to strange and inexplicable laws. If there is a penny on the sidewalk, I find it; I normally pick up seven or eight cents a week (I walk everywhere, rejecting the internal combustion engine as an effete surrender to laziness and the ignoble advantage of convenience), together with perfectly good pencils, firewood, and the rare dime. At Fiesole, when I should have been admiring the view, I unearthed with my toe a Mussolini nickel.

It is now shocking to me that I realized so few connections between things as a child. I vividly remember reading a book about Leonardo, and remember the important detail of his finding seashells in the mountains, but I thought that wonderful, wholly beyond my scope, failing to see any similarity between my amateur archaeology and Leonardo's. What controlled this severe compartmentalization of ideas was my sense of place. Books were read by the fire or by the Franklin heater in the kitchen; in the summer, under the fig tree, and what one read in books remained in the place where one read them. It did not occur to me that any of my teachers at school had ever heard of Leonardo da Vinci any more than of Tarzan, Victor Hugo, Robert Louis Stevenson, or the Toonerville Trolley, all of which were lumped together in my head as privacies in which no one else could be in the least interested.

The schoolroom was its own place, our home another, the red fields of the Savannah valley another, the cow pasture another, uptown, the movies, other people's houses: all were as distinct as continents in disparate geological epochs. The sociology of the South has something to do with this, I think. All occasions had their own style and prerogatives, and these were insisted upon with savage authority. At Grannyport's (thus her accepted name after its invention by us children) one never mentioned the moving pictures that played so great a part in my life, for Grannyport denied that pictures could move. It was, she said, patently illogical (she was absolutely right, of course, but I didn't know it at the time), and no dime could ever be begged of her for admission to the Strand (Hopalong Cassidy, The Lone Ranger, Roy Rogers) or the Criterion (Flash Gordon, Tarzan), for these places were humbug, and people who went to them under the pitiful delusion that pictures can move were certainly not to be financed by a grandmother who knew her own mind.

Nor could the movies be mentioned at Grandmother Fant's, for attending them meant going into public, a low thing that the Fants have never done. The Fants were French Huguenots, from Bordeaux. They were a kind of Greek tragedy in the third of a great trilogy. Once they were rich, with two ships that bore South Carolina cotton from Charleston to France. The United States Navy sank them both in the time of the War: there was a tale we heard over and over of Grandfather Sassard going down with the *Edisto*, standing impassively on her bridge, a New Testament clutched to his breast, his right arm saluting the colors of the Confederacy, which were soon to follow him beneath the waves of the Atlantic. His brother wore a friendship ring given him by Fitzhugh Lee, and this sacred ornament would be got out of a kind of jewel casket and shown to us. I don't think I ever dared touch it.

After the War my grandmother, born and raised in Charleston (she never said "the Yankees," but "the stinking Yankees," the one unladylike locution she ever allowed herself), married a Fant, who took her to Florida to homestead. There my uncles Paul and Silas were born, with teeth it was always pointed out, two tiny pink teeth each, for this was the *signum* of their fate. As they lay in their cradle a catamount sprang through the window and ate them. Sometimes it was an alligator that crawled into the house and ate them. As Granny Fant reached a matriarchal age, her stories began to develop structural variants. She used to ask me never to forget that we are descended from Sir Isaac Davis, though I have never been able to discover who Sir Isaac Davis was. Through him we were related to Queen Anne. And the stinking Yankees stole her wedding ring and gave it to the Holmans' cook, who wore it a day of glory and then returned it to Miss Essy.

Nor could I sing "The Birmingham Jail" at Granny Fant's, as Uncle Jamie had once spent a night in that place. Nor could we (later on, in adolescence) mention new births in Uncle Jamie's presence, for at forty he still did not know the facts of life, and Granny Fant was determined to keep up the illusion that humanity is restocked by the stork. She was, as my father and I discovered to our amazement, wrong. It turned out that Jamie thought pregnancy came about by the passage of a testicle into some unthinkable orifice of the female. He remarked reflectively that if he'd married he could only have had two children. "And I don't think I could have stood the pain."

Nor could we mention looking for arrowheads—the thought that her daughter, son-in-law, and their children walked all over fields and meadows in public would have sent Granny Fant to her bed with a vinegar rag across her forehead. My point is that throughout my childhood place determined mood and tone. My schoolteachers knew nothing of our archaeology. Certainly the Misses Anna and Lillie Brown would somehow disapprove; they were genteel. I cannot remember any mention whatever of history in grammar school. All we learned of the Civil War is that our principal, Miss May Russell, was taken from her bed and kissed as an infant by the notorious renegade Manse Jolly, who had, to Miss May's great satisfaction, galloped his horse down the length of a banquet table at which Union officers were dining, collapsing it as he progressed, emptying two sixshooters into the Yankees and yodeling, "Root hog or die!" This was the rebel yell that Douglas Southall Freeman gave for a recording and dropped dead at the end of. This grotesque fact would not have fazed Miss May Russell; what finer way would a gentleman wish to die? We all had to learn it: the *root* is pitched on a drunken high note in the flattest of whining cotton-planter's pronunciation, the *hawg* is screamed in an awful way, and the *aw dah* is an hysterical crescendo recalling Herod's soldiery at work on male infants. We loved squawling it, and were told to remember how the day was saved at Bull Run, when Beauregard and Johnson were in a sweat until the Sixth South Carolina Volunteers under Wade Hampton rode up on the left flank (they had assembled, in red shirts, around our own court house and marched away to Virginia to "The Palmyra Schottische").

But school was school, as church was church and houses were houses. What went on in one never overflowed into any other. I was perfectly capable in Sunday school of believing all the vicious bilge they wallowed in, and at home studying with glee the murders in the old *Sunday American*, and then spending the afternoon hunting arrowheads. After which came Jack Benny, and a chapter or two of Sir Walter Scott. To have mentioned religion while hunting Indian arrows would have been a breach of manners beyond conception or belief, insanity itself.

The rule was: everything in its place. To this day I paint in one part of my house, write in another, read in another; read, in fact, in two others: frivolous and delicious reading such as Simenon and Erle Stanley Gardner in one room, scholarship in another. And when I am away from home, I am somebody else. This may seem suspicious to the simple mind of a psychiatrist, but it seems natural enough. My cat does not know me when we meet a block away from home, and I gather from his expression that I'm not supposed to know him, either.

Shaw has Joan of Arc say that if everybody stayed at home, they would be good people. It is being in France that makes the English soldiers such devils. She and Shaw have a real point. A dog is a Turk only in his own yard. I am a professor only when I arrive in the classroom; I can feel the Jekyll-Hyde syndrome flick into operation. I have suffered the damnation of a heretic in rooms uncongenial and threatening. It takes a while to make a place for oneself in unfamiliar surroundings. It can be done; man can do anything. I have read Mann's Joseph novels beside the world's loudest jukebox in the recreation room of the XVIII Airborne Corps. A colleague remembers reading Tolstoy behind the field guns on Guadalcanal; another finished reading all of Shakespeare at the Battle of Kohima. Scholars took their work with them to the trenches in the First World War; Appollinaire was reading a critical journal when the shrapnel sprayed into his head. He saw the page all red before he felt the wound. Napoleon took a carriage of books with him to Waterloo. Sir Walter Scott, out hunting and with some good lines suddenly in his head, brought down a crow, whittled a pen from a feather, and wrote the poem on his jacket in crow's blood.

How capable we are off our turf ("far afield," "lost," "no place for me," the phrases run) may be one of the real tests of our acumen. I am a bad traveller. Even away from home with my family I could suffer acute nostalgia as a child. I know of no desolation like that of being in an uncongenial place, and I associate all travel with the possibility of uncongeniality—the Greyhound bus terminal in Knoxville with its toilets awash with urine and vomit, its abominable food and worst coffee in the universe (and their rule is that the more unpalatable the food, the higher the price), its moronic dispatchers, and the hordes of vandals in tight pink trousers and sleeveless T-shirts who patrol the place with vicious aimlessness; all airports; all meetings of any sort without exception; cocktail parties; lawn parties; dinner parties; speeches.

Some slackness of ritual, we are told, that hurt the feelings of the *dii montes*, the gnomes of the hills, allowed Rome to fall to the barbarians. These gods of place were *genii*, spirits of a place. All folklore knows them, and when a hero died who had wound his fate with that of a place, he joined its *genii* and thereafter partook of its life. Our word "congeniality" means kinship with the soul of a place, and places have souls in a way very like creatures.

In hunting Indian arrowheads we were always, it seemed, on congenial territory, though we were usually on somebody's land. We could trust them to know we were there; country people have suspicious eyes. My father was raised in the country and knew what to do and what not to do. Rarely would a farmer stroll out, in the way of peering at the weather or the road, and find out what we were up to. Likely as not, he would have some arrowheads back at the house and would give them to us. Never sell, give. He would be poorer than poor, but he would not sell a piece of rock.

Here at these unpainted clapboard sharecropper houses we would be invited to have a dipper of water from the well, cold, clean and toothsome. Sometimes a sweet-potato biscuit would be served by the lady of the house, a tall woman in an apron and with the manners of an English lady from the counties. We children would ask to see the pigs. Country people were a different nation, both black and white, and they exhibited *mores* long remembered. There was once an elder daughter who retired to a corner and tied herself into a knot of anguish. We assumed idiocy, as country people do not send their demented off to an asylum. But the mother explained, with simplicity, "She has been lewd, and she thinks you can see it in her."

And once we found a black family with our name, and traded family histories, blacks being as talkative and open as poor whites are silent and reticent, until we discovered that their folk had belonged to ours. Whereupon we were treated as visiting royalty; a veritable party was made of it, and when we were leaving, an ancient black Davenport embraced my father with tears in his eyes. "O Lord, Marse Guy," he said, "don't you wish it was the good old slavery times again!"

What lives brightest in the memory of these outings is a Thoreauvian feeling of looking at things—earth, plants, rocks, textures, animal tracks, all the secret places of the out-of-doors that seem not ever to have been looked at before, a hidden patch of moss with a Dutchman's Breeches stoutly in its midst, aromatic stands of rabbit tobacco, beggar's lice, lizards, the inevitable mute snake, always just leaving as you come upon him, hawks, buzzards, abandoned orchards rich in apples, peaches or plums.

Thoreauvian, because these outings, I was to discover, were very like his daily walks, with a purpose that covered the whole enterprise but was not serious enough to make the walk a chore or a duty. Thoreau, too, was an Indian-arrowhead collector, if collector is the word. Once we had found our Indian things, we put them in a big box and rarely looked at them. Some men came from the Smithsonian and were given what they chose, and sometimes a scout troop borrowed some for a display at the county fair. Our understanding was that the search was the thing, the pleasure of looking.

When, in later years, I saw real archaeologists at work, I felt perfectly at home among them: diggers at Mycenae and at Lascaux, where I was shown a tray of hyena coprolites and wondered which my father would have kept and which thrown away, for petrified droppings from the Ice Age must have their range from good to bad, like arrowheads and stone axes.

And I learned from a whole childhood of looking in fields how the purpose of things ought perhaps to remain invisible, no more than half known. People who know exactly what they are doing seem to me to miss the vital part of any doing. My family, praises be unto the gods, never inspected anything that we enjoyed doing; criticism was strictly for adversities, and not very much for them. Consequently I spent my childhood drawing, building things, writing, reading, playing, dreaming out loud, without the least comment from anybody. I learned later that I was thought not quite bright, for the patterns I discovered for myself were not things with nearby models. When I went off to college it was with no purpose whatsoever: no calling in view, no profession, no ambition.

Ambition was scorned by the Fants and unknown to the Davenports. That my father worked with trains was a glory that I considered a windfall, for other fathers sold things or processed things. If I am grateful for the unintentional education of having been taught how to find things (all that I have ever done, I think, with texts and pictures), I am even more grateful, in an inconsequential way, for my father's most astounding gift of all: being put at the throttle of a locomotive one night and allowed to drive it down the track for a whole five minutes. I loved trains, and grew up with them. I had drawn locomotives with the passion of Hokusai drawing Fujiyama. My wagon had been an imaginary locomotive more than it had been a rocket ship or buckboard. And here we were meeting the Blue Ridge one summer evening, and my father must have seen the look in my eyes as I peered into the cab of the engine. Suddenly I was lifted onto the step, and helped by the engineer—I believe his name was Singbell—into the ineffably important seat. The engine was merely switching cars in the yard, but it was my ten-year-old hand on the throttle that shoved the drivers and turned the wheels and sent plumes of steam hissing outward. Life has been downhill ever since.

But this is not the meaning of looking for Indian arrowheads.

That will, I hope, elude me forever. Its importance has, in maturity, become more and more apparent—an education that shaped me with a surer and finer hand than any classroom, an experience that gave me a sense of the earth, of autumn afternoons, of all the seasons, a connoisseur's sense of things for their own sake. I was with grown-ups, so it wasn't play. There was no lecture, so it wasn't school. All effort was willing, so it wasn't work. No ideal compelled us, so it wasn't idealism or worship or philosophy.

Yet it was the seeding of all sorts of things, of scholarship, of a stoic sense of pleasure (I think we were all bored and ill at ease when we went on official vacations to the mountains or the shore, whereas out arrowhead-looking we were content and easy), and most of all of foraging, that prehistoric urge still not bred out of man. There was also the sense of going out together but with each of us acting alone. You never look for Indian arrows in pairs. You fan out. But you shout discoveries and comments ("No Indian was ever around *here!*") across fields. It was, come to think of it, a humanistic kind of hunt. My father never hunted animals, and I don't think he ever killed anything in his life. All his brothers were keen huntsmen; I don't know why he wasn't. And, conversely, none of my uncles would have been caught dead doing anything so silly as looking for hours and hours for an incised rim of pottery or a Cherokee pipe.

I know that my sense of place, of occasion, even of doing anything at all, was shaped by those afternoons. It took a while for me to realize that people can grow up without being taught to see, to search surfaces for all the details, to check out a whole landscape for what it has to offer. My father became so good at spotting arrowheads that on roads with likely gullies he would find them from the car. Or give a commentary on what we might pick up were we to stop: "A nice spearhead back there by a maypop, but with the tip broken off."

And it is all folded away in an irrevocable past. Most of our fields are now the bottom of a vast lake. Farmers now post their land and fence it with barbed wire. Arrowhead collecting has become something of a minor hobby, and shops for the tourist trade make them in a back room and sell them to people from New Jersey. Everything is like that nowadays. I cherish those afternoons, knowing that I will never understand all that they taught me. As we grew up, we began not to go on the expeditions. Not the last, but one of the last, afternoons found us toward sunset, findings in hand, ending up for the day with one of our rituals, a Coca-Cola from the icebox of a crossroads store. "They tell over the radio," the proprietor said, "that a bunch of Japanese airplanes have blowed up the whole island of Hawaii."

Discussion Questions

1. Why didn't Davenport entitle his essay "Finding Arrowheads"? Why did he prefer to allow his title to remain general?
2. Note some of the details in the essay that Davenport cannot explain, things that he doesn't know. Why does he include such information? How do these unexplained details contribute to the general sense of "finding"
3. Do you think Davenport's essay is loosely or tightly constructed? Are there moments in which he seems to digress? If so, do you find the digressions disjointing or relevant to his purpose? How does Guy Davenport's use of the details of personal experience compare to that of Joan Didion in "On Keeping a Notebook"?
4. Reread Davenport's essay, paying close attention to the way he selects details. Then, choose a particular childhood activity—a hobby, game, and so forth—rooted in a definite time and place and describe it in a way that shows how it helped shape your present personality.

JOAN DIDION

Joan Didion was born in Sacramento, California, in 1934. Before graduating with a B.A. in English from the University of California, Berkeley, she took a few years off to work on magazines in New York City. In 1956, she received Vogue's Prix de Paris and for the next seven years worked as an associate editor at Vogue. She has also been a contributing editor to National Review and The Saturday Evening Post. In 1963, she won a Bread Loaf fellowship for fiction.

    The author of several screenplays and three novels, Run River (1963), Play It as It Lays (1970), and A Book of Common Prayer (1978), Joan Didion frequently contributes essays on contemporary American culture to numerous magazines. Her reportorial articles have been collected in two highly acclaimed volumes, Slouching Towards Bethlehem (1968), from which "On Keeping a Notebook" is reprinted, and The White Album (1979), in which "On the Mall" appeared. Her most recent book is Salvador (1983).

On the Mall

They float on the landscape like pyramids to the boom years, all those Plazas and Malls and Esplanades. All those Squares and Fairs. All those Towns and Dales, all those Villages, all those Forests and Parks and Lands. Stonestown, Hillsdale. Valley Fair, Mayfair, Northgate, Southgate, Eastgate, Westgate, Gulfgate. They are toy garden cities in which no one lives but everyone consumes, profound equalizers, the perfect fusion of the profit motive and the egalitarian ideal, and to hear their names is to recall words and phrases no longer quite current. Baby Boom. Consumer Explosion. Leisure Revolution. Do-It-Yourself Revolution. Backyard Revolution. Suburbia. "The Shopping Center," the Urban Land Institute could pronounce in 1957, "is today's extraordinary retail business evolvement. . . . The automobile accounts for suburbia, and suburbia accounts for the shopping center."

It was a peculiar and visionary time, those years after World War II to which all the Malls and Towns and Dales stand as climate-controlled monuments. Even the word "automobile," as in "the automobile accounts for suburbia and suburbia accounts for the shopping center," no longer carries the particular freight it once did: as a child in the late Forties in California I recall reading and believing that the "freedom of movement" afforded by the automobile was "America's fifth freedom." The trend was up. The solution was in sight. The frontier had been reinvented, and its shape was the subdivision, that new free land on which all settlers could recast their lives *tabula rasa*. For one perishable moment there the American idea seemed about to achieve itself, via F.H.A. housing and the acquisition of major appliances, and a certain enigmatic glamour attached to the architects of this newfound land. They made something of nothing. They gambled and sometimes lost. They staked the past to seize the future. I have difficulty now imagining a childhood in which a man named Jere Strizek, the developer of Town and Country Village outside Sacramento (143,000 square feet gross floor area, 68 stores, 1000 parking spaces, the Urban Land Institute's "prototype for centers using heavy timber and tile construction for informality"), could materialize as a role model, but I had such a childhood, just after World War II, in Sacramento. I never met or even saw Jere Strizek, but at the age of 12 I imagined him a kind of frontiersman, a romantic and revolutionary spirit, and in the indigenous grain he was.

I suppose James B. Douglas and David D. Bohannon were too.

I first heard of James B. Douglas and David D. Bohannon not when I was 12 but a dozen years later, when I was living in New York, working for *Vogue*, and taking, by correspondence, a University of California Extension course in shopping-center theory. This did not seem to me eccentric at the time. I remember sitting on the cool floor in Irving Penn's studio and reading, in *The Community Builders Handbook*, advice from James B. Douglas on shopping-center financing. I recall staying late in my pale-blue office on the twentieth floor of the Graybar Building to memorize David D. Bohannon's parking ratios. My "real" life was to sit in this office and describe life as it was lived in Djakarta and Caneel Bay and in the great chateaux of the Loire Valley, but my dream life was to put together a Class-A regional shopping center with three full-line department stores as major tenants.

That I was perhaps the only person I knew in New York, let alone on the Condé Nast floors of the Graybar Building, to have memorized the distinctions among "A," "B," and "C" shopping centers did not occur to me (the defining distinction, as long as I have your attention, is that an "A," or "regional," center has as its major tenant a full-line department store which carries major appliances; a "B," or "community," center has as its major tenant a junior department store which does not carry major appliances; and a "C," or "neighborhead," center has as its major tenant only a supermarket): my interest in shopping centers was in no way casual. I did want to build them. I wanted to build them because I had fallen into the habit of writing fiction, and I had it in my head that a couple of good centers might support this habit less taxingly than a pale-blue office at *Vogue*. I had even devised an original scheme by which I planned to gain enough capital and credibility to enter the shopping-center game: I would lease warehouses in, say, Queens, and offer Manhattan delicatessens the opportunity to sell competitively by buying cooperatively, from my trucks. I see a few wrinkles in this scheme now (the words "concrete overcoat" come to mind), but I did not then. In fact I planned to run it out of the pale-blue office.

James B. Douglas and David D. Bohannon. In 1950 James B. Douglas had opened Northgate, in Seattle, the first regional center to combine a pedestrian mall with an underground truck tunnel. In 1954 David D. Bohannon had opened Hillsdale, a forty-acre regional center on the peninsula south of San Francisco. That is the only solid bio I have on James B. Douglas and David D. Bohannon to this day, but many of their opinions are engraved on my memory. David D. Bohannon believed in preserving the integrity of the shopping center by not cutting up the site with any dedicated roads. David D. Bohannon believed that architectural setbacks in a center looked "pretty on paper" but caused "customer resistance." James B. Douglas advised that a small-loan office could prosper in a center only if it were placed away from foot traffic, since people who want small loans do not want to be observed getting them. I do not recall whether it was James B. Douglas or David D. Bohannon or someone else altogether who passed along this hint on how to paint the lines around the parking spaces (actually this is called "striping the lot," and the spaces are "stalls"): make each space a foot wider than it need be—ten feet, say, instead of nine—when the center first opens and business is slow. By this single stroke the developer achieves a couple of important objectives, the appearance of a popular center and the illusion of easy parking, and no one will really notice when business picks up and the spaces shrink.

Nor do I recall who first solved what was once a crucial center dilemma: the placement of the major tenant vis-à-vis the parking lot. The dilemma was that the major tenant—the draw, the raison d'être for the financing, the Sears, the Macy's, the May Company—wanted its customer to walk directly from car to store. The smaller tenants, on the other hand, wanted that same customer to *pass their stores* on the way from the car to, say, Macy's. The solution to this conflict of interests was actually very simple: *two major tenants*, one at each end of a mall. This is called "anchoring the mall," and represents seminal work in shopping-center theory. One thing you will note about shopping-center theory is that you could have thought of it yourself, and a course in it will go a long way toward dispelling the notion that business proceeds from mysteries too recondite for you and me.

A few aspects of shopping-center theory do in fact remain impenetrable to me. I have no idea why the Community Builders'

Council ranks "Restaurant" as deserving a Number One (or "Hot Spot") location but exiles "Chinese Restaurant" to a Number Three, out there with "Power and Light Office" and "Christian Science Reading Room." Nor do I know why the Council approves of enlivening a mall with "small animals" but specifically, vehemently, and with no further explanation, excludes "monkeys." If I had a center I would have monkeys, and Chinese restaurants, and Mylar kites and bands of small girls playing tambourine.

A few years ago at a party I met a woman from Detroit who told me that the Joyce Carol Oates novel with which she identified most closely was *Wonderland*.
I asked her why.
"Because," she said, "my husband has a branch there."
I did not understand.
"In Wonderland the center," the woman said patiently. "My husband has a branch in Wonderland."
I have never visited Wonderland but imagine it to have bands of small girls playing tambourine.

A few facts about shopping centers.
The "biggest" center in the United States is generally agreed to be Woodfield, outside Chicago, a "super" regional or "leviathan" two-million-square-foot center with four major tenants.
The "first" shopping center in the United States is generally agreed to be Country Club Plaza in Kansas City, built in the twenties. There were some other early centers, notably Edward H. Bouton's 1907 Roland Park in Baltimore, Hugh Prather's 1931 Highland Park Shopping Village in Dallas, and Hugh Potter's 1937 River Oaks in Houston, but the developer of Country Club Plaza, the late J. C. Nichols, is referred to with ritual frequency in the literature of shopping centers, usually as "pioneering J. C. Nichols," "trailblazing J. C. Nichols," or "J. C. Nichols, father of the center as we know it."
Those are some facts I know about shopping centers because I still want to be Jere Strizek or James B. Douglas or David D. Bohannon. Here are some facts I know about shopping centers because I never will be Jere Strizek or James B. Douglas or David D. Bohannon: a good center in which to spend the day if you wake feeling low in Honolulu, Hawaii, is Ala Moana, major tenants Liberty House and Sears. A good center in which to spend the day if you wake feeling low in Oxnard, California, is The Esplanade, major tenants the May Company and Sears. A good center in

which to spend the day if you wake feeling low in Biloxi, Mississippi, is Edgewater Plaza, major tenant Godchaux's. Ala Moana in Honolulu is larger than The Esplanade in Oxnard, and The Esplanade in Oxnard is larger than Edgewater Plaza in Biloxi. Ala Moana has carp pools. The Esplanade and Edgewater Plaza do not.

These marginal distinctions to one side, Ala Moana, The Esplanade, and Edgewater Plaza are the same place, which is precisely their role not only as equalizers but in the sedation of anxiety. In each of them one moves for a while in an aqueous suspension not only of light but of judgment, not only of judgment but of "personality." One meets no acquaintances at The Esplanade. One gets no telephone calls at Edgewater Plaza. "It's a hard place to run in to for a pair of stockings," a friend complained to me recently of Ala Moana, and I knew that she was not yet ready to surrender her ego to the idea of the center. The last time I went to Ala Moana it was to buy *The New York Times*. Because *The New York Times* was not in, I sat on the mall for a while and ate carmel corn. In the end I bought not *The New York Times* at all but two straw hats at Liberty House, four bottles of nail enamel at Woolworth's, and a toaster, on sale in Sears. In the literature of shopping centers these would be described as impulse purchases, but the impulse here was obscure. I do not wear hats, nor do I like carmel corn. I do not use nail enamel. Yet flying back across the Pacific I regretted only the toaster.

Discussion Questions

1. Joan Didion claims to have once been seriously interested in entering the "shopping-center game." Is she still interested? How did she perceive shopping centers when she was younger; how does she perceive them now?

2. How does Joan Didion convey her familiarity with shopping malls? How does that familiarity go beyond her personal experience of malls?

3. Explain what makes Joan Didion's essay something other than a response to the sociological topic, "The Development of the Shopping Mall in America."

4. Compare Joan Didion's sense of place to Ada Louise Huxtable's in "Houston." Do the writers share similar convictions about American architecture?

5. Most people have visited the kind of shopping mall Joan Didion describes in this essay. How does your experience of malls compare to hers? On the basis of your personal experience, write a short essay in which you agree or disagree with the image of malls expressed in her last paragraph.

On Keeping a Notebook

"'That woman Estelle,'" the note reads, "'is partly the reason why George Sharp and I are separated today.' *Dirty crepe-de-Chine wrapper, hotel bar, Wilmington RR, 9:45 a.m. August Monday morning.*"

Since the note is in my notebook, it presumably has some meaning to me. I study it for a long while. At first I have only the most general notion of what I was doing on an August Monday morning in the bar of the hotel across from the Pennsylvania Railroad station in Wilmington, Delaware (waiting for a train? missing one? 1960? 1961? why Wilmington?), but I do remember being there. The woman in the dirty crepe-de-Chine wrapper had come down from her room for a beer, and the bartender had heard before the reason why George Sharp and she were separated today. "Sure," he said, and went on mopping the floor. "You told me." At the other end of the bar is a girl. She is talking, pointedly, not to the man beside her but to a cat lying in the triangle of sunlight cast through the open door. She is wearing a plaid silk dress from Peck & Peck, and the hem is coming down.

Here is what it is: the girl has been on the Eastern Shore, and now she is going back to the city, leaving the man beside her, and all she can see ahead are the viscous summer sidewalks and the 3 a.m. long-distance calls that will make her lie awake and then sleep drugged through all the steaming mornings left in August (1960? 1961?). Because she must go directly from the train to lunch in New York, she wishes that she had a safety pin for the hem of the plaid silk dress, and she also wishes that she could forget about the hem and the lunch and stay in the cool bar that smells of disinfectant and malt and make friends with the woman in the crepe-de-Chine wrapper. She is afflicted by a little self-pity, and she wants to compare Estelles. That is what that was all about.

Why did I write it down? In order to remember, of course, but exactly what was it I wanted to remember? How much of it actually happened? Did any of it? Why do I keep a notebook at all? It is easy to deceive oneself on all those scores. The impulse to write things down is a peculiarly compulsive one, inexplicable to those who do not share it, useful only accidentally, only secondarily, in the way that any compulsion tries to justify itself. I suppose that it begins or does not begin in the cradle. Although I have felt compelled to write things down since I was five years old, I doubt that my daughter ever will, for she is a singularly blessed and accepting child, delighted with life exactly as life presents itself to her, unafraid to go to sleep and unafraid to wake up. Keepers of private notebooks are a different breed altogether, lonely and resistant rearrangers of things, anxious malcontents, children afflicted apparently at birth with some presentiment of loss.

My first notebook was a Big Five tablet, given to me by my mother with the sensible suggestion that I stop whining and learn to amuse myself by writing down my thoughts. She returned the tablet to me a few years ago; the first entry is an account of a woman who believed herself to be freezing to death in the Arctic night, only to find, when day broke, that she had stumbled onto the Sahara Desert, where she would die of the heat before lunch. I have no idea what turn of a five-year-old's mind could have prompted so insistently "ironic" and exotic a story, but it does reveal a certain predilection for the extreme which has dogged me into adult life; perhaps if I were analytically inclined I would find it a truer story than any I might have told about Donald Johnson's birthday party or the day my cousin Brenda put Kitty Litter in the aquarium.

So the point of my keeping a notebook has never been, nor is it now, to have an accurate factual record of what I have been doing or thinking. That would be a different impulse entirely, an instinct for reality which I sometimes envy but do not possess. At no point have I ever been able successfully to keep a diary; my approach to daily life ranges from the grossly negligent to the merely absent, and on those few occasions when I have tried dutifully to record a day's events, boredom has so overcome me that the results are mysterious at best. What is this business about "shopping, typing piece, dinner with E, depressed"? Shopping for what? Typing what piece? Who is E? Was this "E" depressed, or was I depressed? Who cares?

In fact I have abandoned altogether that kind of pointless

entry; instead I tell what some would call lies. "That's simply not true," the members of my family frequently tell me when they come up against my memory of a shared event. "The party was *not* for you, the spider was *not* a black widow, *it wasn't that way at all.*" Very likely they are right, for not only have I always had trouble distinguishing between what happened and what merely might have happened, but I remain unconvinced that the distinction, for my purposes, matters. The cracked crab that I recall having for lunch the day my father came home from Detroit in 1945 must certainly be embroidery, worked into the day's pattern to lend verisimilitude; I was ten years old and would not now remember the cracked crab. The day's events did not turn on cracked crab. And yet it is precisely that fictitious crab that makes me see the afternoon all over again, a home movie run all too often, the father bearing gifts, the child weeping, an exercise in family love and guilt. Or that is what it was to me. Similarly, perhaps it never did snow that August in Vermont; perhaps there never were flurries in the night wind, and maybe no one else felt the ground hardening and summer already dead even as we pretended to bask in it, but that was how it felt to me, and it might as well have snowed, could have snowed, did snow.

How it felt to me: that is getting closer to the truth about a notebook. I sometimes delude myself about why I keep a notebook, imagine that some thrifty virtue derives from preserving everything observed. See enough and write it down, I tell myself, and then some morning when the world seems drained of wonder, some day when I am only going through the motions of doing what I am supposed to do, which is write—on that bankrupt morning I will simply open my notebook and there it will all be, a forgotten account with accumulated interest, paid passage back to the world out there: dialogue overheard in hotels and elevators and at the hatcheck counter in Pavillon (one middle-aged man shows his hat check to another and says, "That's my old football number"); impressions of Bettina Aptheker and Benjamin Sonnenberg and Teddy ("Mr. Acapulco") Stauffer; careful *aperçus* about tennis bums and failed fashion models and Greek shipping heiresses, one of whom taught me a significant lesson (a lesson I could have learned from F. Scott Fitzgerald, but perhaps we all must meet the very rich for ourselves) by asking, when I arrived to interview her in her orchid-filled sitting room on the second day of a paralyzing New York blizzard, whether it was snowing outside.

I imagine, in other words, that the notebook is about other people. But of course it is not. I have no real business with what one stranger said to another at the hatcheck counter in Pavillon; in fact I suspect that the line "That's my old football number" touched not my own imagination at all, but merely some memory of something once read, probably "The Eighty-Yard Run." Nor is my concern with a woman in a dirty crepe-de-Chine wrapper in a Wilmington bar. My stake is always, of course, in the unmentioned girl in the plaid silk dress. *Remember what it was to be me:* that is always the point.

It is a difficult point to admit. We are brought up in the ethic that others, any others, all others, are by definition more interesting than ourselves; taught to be diffident, just this side of self-effacing. ("You're the least important person in the room and don't forget it," Jessica Mitford's governess would hiss in her ear on the advent of any social occasion; I copied that into my notebook because it is only recently that I have been able to enter a room without hearing some such phrase in my inner ear.) Only the very young and the very old may recount their dreams at breakfast, dwell upon self, interrupt with memories of beach picnics and favorite Liberty lawn dresses and the rainbow trout in a creek near Colorado Springs. The rest of us are expected, rightly, to affect absorption in other people's favorite dresses, other people's trout.

And so we do. But our notebooks give us away, for however dutifully we record what we see around us, the common denominator of all we see is always, transparently, shamelessly, the implacable "I." We are not talking here about the kind of notebook that is patently for public consumption, a structural conceit for binding together a series of graceful *pensées;* we are talking about something private, about bits of the mind's string too short to use, an indiscriminate and erratic assemblage with meaning only for its maker.

And sometimes even the maker has difficulty with the meaning. There does not seem to be, for example, any point in my knowing for the rest of my life that, during 1964, 720 tons of soot fell on every square mile of New York City, yet there it is in my notebook, labeled "FACT." Nor do I really need to remember that Ambrose Bierce liked to spell Leland Stanford's name "£eland $tanford" or that "smart women almost always wear black in Cuba," a fashion hint without much potential for practical application. And does not the relevance of these notes seem marginal at best?:

> In the basement museum of the Inyo County Courthouse in Independence, California, sign pinned to a mandarin coat: "This MANDARIN COAT was often worn by Mrs. Minnie S. Brooks when giving lectures on her TEAPOT COLLECTION."

Redhead getting out of car in front of Beverly Wilshire Hotel, chinchilla stole, Vuitton bags with tags reading:

MRS LOU FOX
HOTEL SAHARA
VEGAS

Well, perhaps not entirely marginal. As a matter of fact, Mrs. Minnie S. Brooks and her MANDARIN COAT pull me back into my own childhood, for although I never knew Mrs. Brooks and did not visit Inyo County until I was thirty, I grew up in just such a world, in houses cluttered with Indian relics and bits of gold ore and ambergris and the souvenirs my Aunt Mercy Farnsworth brought back from the Orient. It is a long way from that world to Mrs. Lou Fox's world, where we all live now, and is it not just as well to remember that? Might not Mrs. Minnie S. Brooks help me to remember what I am? Might not Mrs. Lou Fox help me to remember what I am not?

But sometimes the point is harder to discern. What exactly did I have in mind when I noted down that it cost the father of someone I know $650 a month to light the place on the Hudson in which he lived before the Crash? What use was I planning to make of this line by Jimmy Hoffa: "I may have my faults, but being wrong ain't one of them"? And although I think interesting to know where the girls who travel with the Syndicate have their hair done when they find themselves on the West Coast, will I ever make suitable use of it? Might I not be better off just passing it on to John O'Hara? What is a recipe for sauerkraut doing in my notebook? What kind of magpie keeps this notebook? *"He was born the night the Titanic went down."* That seems a nice enough line, and I even recall who said it, but is it not really a better line in life than it could ever be in fiction?

But of course that is exactly it: not that I should ever use the line, but that I should remember the woman who said it and the afternoon I heard it. We were on her terrace by the sea, and we were finishing the wine left from lunch, trying to get what sun there was, a California winter sun. The woman whose husband was born the night the *Titanic* went down wanted to rent her house, wanted to go back to her children in Paris. I remember wishing that I could afford the house, which cost $1,000 a month. "Someday you will," she said lazily. "Someday it all comes." There in the sun on her terrace it seemed easy to believe in someday, but later I had a low-grade afternoon hangover and ran over a black snake on the way to the supermarket and was flooded with inexplicable fear when I heard the checkout clerk explaining to the man ahead of me why she was finally divorcing her husband. "He left me no choice," she said over and over as she punched the register. "He has a little seven-month-old baby by her, he left me no choice." I would like to believe that my dread then was for the human condition, but of course it was for me, because I wanted a baby and did not then have one and because I wanted to own the house that cost $1,000 a month to rent and because I had a hangover.

It all comes back. Perhaps it is difficult to see the value in having one's self back in that kind of mood, but I do see it; I think we are well advised to keep on nodding terms with the people we used to be, whether we find them attractive company or not. Otherwise they turn up unannounced and surprise us, come hammering on the mind's door at 4 a.m. of a bad night and demand to know who deserted them, who betrayed them, who is going to make amends. We forget all too soon the things we thought we could never forget. We forget the loves and the betrayals alike, forget what we whispered and what we screamed, forget who we were. I have already lost touch with a couple of people I used to be; one of them, a seventeen-year-old, presents little threat, although it would be of some interest to me to know again what it feels like to sit on a river levee drinking vodka-and-orange-juice and listening to Les Paul and Mary Ford and their echoes sing "How High the Moon" on the car radio. (You see I still have the scenes, but I no longer perceive myself among those present, no longer could even improvise the dialogue.) The other one, a twenty-three-year-old, bothers me more. She was always a good deal of trouble, and I suspect she will reappear when I least want to see her, skirts too long, shy to the point of aggravation, always the injured party, full of recriminations and little hurts and stories I do not want to hear again, at once saddening me and angering me with her vulnerability and ignorance, an apparition all the more insistent for being so long banished.

It is a good idea, then, to keep in touch, and I suppose that keeping in touch is what notebooks are all about. And we are all on our own when it comes to keeping those lines open to ourselves: your notebook will never help me, nor mine you. "*So what's new in the whiskey business?*" What could that possibly mean to you? To me it means a blonde in a Pucci bathing suit sitting with a couple of fat men by the pool at the Beverly Hills Hotel. Another man approaches, and they all regard one another in silence for a while. "So what's new in the whiskey business?" one of the fat men finally says by way of welcome, and the blonde stands up, arches one foot and dips it in the pool, looking all the while at the cabana where Baby Pignatari is talking on the telephone. That is all there is to that, except that several years later I saw the blonde coming out of Saks Fifth Avenue in New York with her California complexion and a voluminous mink coat. In the harsh wind that day she looked old and irrevocably tired to me, and even the skins in the mink coat were not worked the way they were doing them that year, not the way she would have wanted them done, and there is the point of the story. For a while after that I did not like to look in the mirror, and my eyes would skim the newspapers and pick out only the deaths, the cancer victims, the premature coronaries, the suicides, and I stopped riding the Lexington Avenue IRT because I noticed for the first time that all the strangers I had seen for years—the man with the seeing-eye dog, the spinster who read the classified pages every day, the fat girl who always got off with me at Grand Central—looked older than they once had.

It all comes back. Even that recipe for sauerkraut: even that brings it back. I was on Fire Island when I first made that sauerkraut, and it was raining, and we drank a lot of bourbon and ate the sauerkraut and went to bed at ten, and I listened to the rain and the Atlantic and felt safe. I made the sauerkraut again last night and it did not make me feel any safer, but that is, as they say, another story.

Discussion Questions

1. What distinction does Joan Didion make between a notebook and a diary? Why does she keep one and not the other?

2. What is the effect on the reader of starting the essay with a sample notebook entry? How else might Joan Didion have begun her essay? Why do you think she chose to start this way rather than, say, with the fifth paragraph?

3. "Our notebooks give us away," says Joan Didion. What impression of her life do you get from her sample notebook entries? Is this the impression she wants to convey? Go through the essay and underline her entries: Do the locations, details, and people have anything in common?

4. Compare this essay to Joan Didion's "On the Mall." How do her thoughts about keeping a notebook conform to her style and language in "On the Mall"?

5. If you don't keep a personal notebook, try doing so for one week. At

the end of a week, go over your entries as though you were reading someone else's notebook: What do the notes have in common? What do they disclose about the personality of the writer? Then write a short essay—using Joan Didion's as a model—discussing what you believe is the value of keeping a notebook.

ANNIE DILLARD

Annie Dillard describes herself as "a poet and a walker with a background in theology and a penchant for quirky facts." Though her essays often give the impression of being the result of a spontaneous communion with the natural world, she insists that her real work is above all writing—"hard, conscious, terribly frustrating work."

Born in Pittsburg, Pennsylvania, in 1945, she graduated from Hollins College, where she also received her M.A. in 1968. Her first collection of essays, Pilgrim at Tinker Creek, a meticulous record of her naturalist excursions into Virginia's Roanoke Valley, won the 1974 Pulitzer Prize for general nonfiction. A frequent contributor to Harper's, Atlantic Monthly, The Living Wilderness, Prose, and many other periodicals, Dillard has also written Holy the Firm (1978) and a book of literary theory, Living by Fiction (1982). The following selection, "Mirages," appeared in her recent collection of essays, Teaching a Stone to Talk (1982).

Mirages

All summer long mirages appear over Puget Sound, mirages appear and vanish. While they last they mince and maul the islands and waters, and put us in thrall to our senses.

It is as though summer itself were a mirage, a passive dream of pleasure, itself untrue. For in winter the beaches lie empty; the gulls languish; the air is a reasonable stuff, chilled and lidded by clouds. We light the lamps early; we fasten the doors. We live in the mind. The water everywhere is vacant; the tankers alone still pass, their low diesel vibrations and their powerful wakes adding to the wind's whine and waves only a moment's more commotion; then they are gone.

No one is about. Although our island cabin is right on the beach, so we can see many miles of shoreline, in winter we see only a single human light. At dusk, someone in Canada lights a lamp; it burns near the shore of Saturna, a Canadian island across Haro Strait, seven nautical miles away. We look at this lone light all winter, wondering if the people there are as cheered by our light as we are by theirs. We plan to visit them in the summer and introduce ourselves, but we never do. In winter there is nobody, nothing. If you see a human figure, or a boat on the water, you grab binoculars.

But in summer everything fills. The day itself widens and stretches almost around the clock; these are very high latitudes, higher than Labrador's. You want to run all night. Summer people move into the houses that had stood empty, unseen, and unnoticed all winter. The gulls scream all day and smash cockles; by August they are bringing the kids. Volleyball games resume on the sand flat; someone fires up the sauna; in the long dusk, at eleven o'clock, half a dozen beach fires people the shore. The bay fills up with moored boats and the waters beyond fill with pleasure craft, hundreds of cruisers and sailboats and speedboats. The wind dies and stays dead, and these fierce waters, which in winter feel the strongest windstorms in the country, become suddenly like a resort lake, some tamed dammed reservoir, the plaything of any man-jack with a motor and a hull. Surely this is mirage. The heat is on, and the light is on, and someone is pouring drinks. On the beach we dip freshly dug clams in hot butter, we eat raw oysters from their shells. We play catch or sail a dinghy or holler; we have sand in our hair, calluses on our feet, hot brown skin on our arms. This is the life of the senses, the life of pleasures. It is mirage on the half shell. It vanishes like any fun, and the empty winds resume.

So much for the moral. The story is even simpler, a matter of gross physics and the senses. It is just that mirages abound here.

When winter's cloud cover vanishes, the naked planet lies exposed to marvels. The heated summer air, ground under cold northern air, becomes lenticular, shaped like a lentil or a lens. When the very air is a lens, how the mind ignites! We live among high heaps of mirages, among pickets and pilings and stacks of waving light. We live in a hall of mirrors rimmed by a horizon holey and warped.

Even now as I write, a mirage is pulling Saturna Island like taffy. The island's far shores are starting to yawn and heave from the water. What had been a flat beach has become a high cliff. I wonder: are the people still there, the people whose lamp we could see in the winter? Have they been stretched too, and pulled out of shape? If we went to meet them now, would we find them teetering in their garden like giraffes, unable to reach the ground and tend to their peas?

Few others see the mirages. I certainly never saw them until an article in *Scientific American* alerted me. Mirages, like anything unusual, are hard to see. The mind expects the usual. If a tanker appears to be plying ten yards above the surface of the water, the mind will pour in enough water to float the tanker properly, and deceive the eyes, and hush them with their Chicken-Little message for the brain. Brain never knows. "What mirages?" everyone says.

There are two other unexpected things about mirages, both of which, incidentally, are true of rainbows as well. One is that they photograph very well; the *Scientific American* article included a print which showed people walking about in the middle of a sailing fleet. The other is that enlarging lenses—telescopes, telephoto lenses, binoculars—far from betraying the shabbiness of the illusions, instead confirm and clarify them. I always look at mirages through binoculars; the binoculars' magnification adds both detail and substance to the vision. Great shimmering patches of color appear over the water, expanding and contracting in slats like venetian blinds; the binoculars enlarge the sight. The elongate cliffs of Saturna Island, rearing enormously from where no cliffs have ever been—these high palisades have a certain translucent, faked look to the naked eye, as if their matter, being so pulled, had stretched thin; but through binoculars they are as opaque as other cliffs, cliffy, solid, true headlands, and doubly mysterious.

Yesterday I stood on the beach and watched two light shows at once. It was fair and calm and hot; I faced a string of islands to the west. To the south I saw, spanning a wide channel between islands, a long crescendo-shaped warp, into which innocent little sailboats would wander and be wholly transformed into things glorious. A twenty-foot sloop entered the narrow end of the mirage. Before my eyes the sloop began to expand. Its mast grew like a beanstalk; its sails rose up like waterspouts. Soon the reckless boat, running down the light air and down the warp's widening crescendo, was flying a 150-foot spinnaker! There was a fleet of such boats in the sound. They were gigantic, top-heavy dreamsailers, mythic big ships sailing solar wind and stringing their dwarfed hulls after them like sea anchors. Now there, into the crescendo, went a white cabin cruiser, sport fishing for salmon; and here, at the other end, emerged a wedding cake, a wedding cake leaving a wake and steered by God knows what elongate gibbon of a vacationer at the wheel.

While these boats to the south were blooming transfigured over calm water, to the north the water itself was apparently erupting and bending into hills and valleys. The water itself, I say, had grown absurd, sloping this way and that in long parallel ridges like those of a washboard. There were no waves; instead the smooth water itself lay seemingly jagged and rucked as Appalachians, as enormous stairways, pleated into long lines of sixty-foot ridges and valleys. In this mess of slopes a host of white cabin cruisers was struggling uphill and down. The boats crawled up and over the pitches like tanks over earthworks and trenches; or their bows aimed at heaven, their hulls churning directly up ridges so steep I thought they would all flip over backward like so many unicycles. It was flat calm. Only that one patch of water was berserk, as if it had wearied of the monotony of being a seascape year after year and was now seeking coarsely to emulate the ranged bumps of land.

Then the show pulled out. In the south the giant sails and the wedding cake cruisers emerged from the dazzle suddenly ordinary in proportion and humble. Nevertheless, from their masts and over their cabins hung some remembered radiance, some light-shot tatters of their recent glory. They continued across the horizon as creatures who had been touched, like the straggling and shining caravans of the wilderness generation as it quit Sinai. In the north the little cruisers I had watched now steered from the canyons and found regular waters, which looked mighty dull. Other boats still hazarded into the ridges, but the heights were no longer so fearsome; gradually, over the space of an hour, the mountains sank back to the water, and the water closed over them in the way that water has always closed over everything, in literature and in fact: as if they had never been.

Discussion Questions

1. On Puget Sound in winter, Annie Dillard says, "the air is a reasonable stuff." Why does she choose this expression? How does the air differ in summer?

2. Look up the word "mirage" in a good dictionary. What connotations does the word have? How does Annie Dillard use those connotations in her essay?

3. What does Annie Dillard mean by "so much for the moral. The story is even simpler. . . ."? What is the moral; and why does she reverse the order and have the moral precede the tale?

4. Why are mirages hard to see? How do binoculars help? What difference do they make to the viewer?

5. In the mirage that concludes the essay, what does the sea begin to resemble? Note the metaphors that the mirage suggests. What connections can you think of between mirages and metaphors?

6. Mirages are not the only phenomena that transform the world of our senses. Using Annie Dillard's essay as a model, discuss some other form of natural illusion—for example, echoes, camouflage, rapture of the deep (nitrogen narcosis), and so forth. It would help you—as it did Annie Dillard—to obtain some scientific information about the phenomenon before writing up a story about it.

W. E. B. DuBois

W. E. B. DuBois (1868–1963) was born in Great Barrington, Massachusetts. He said that he did not begin to comprehend the magnitude of the problems posed by racial discrimination until he attended Fisk University, from which he graduated in 1888. From that time he devoted the great energies of a long life to opposing discrimination and advancing the cause of his race. Successively a university professor of Latin and Greek, sociology, economics, and history and one of the founders of the NAACP, he was a tireless editor, novelist, poet, playwright, and public speaker. The following essay was originally presented as a commencement address to the class of 1944 at Talladega College.

Jacob and Esau

I remember very vividly the Sunday-school room where I spent the Sabbaths of my early years. It had been newly built after a disastrous fire; the room was large and full of sunlight; nice new chairs were grouped around where the classes met. My class was in the center, so that I could look out upon the elms of Main Street and see the passersby. But I was interested usually in the lessons and in my fellow students and the frail rather nervous teacher, who tried to make the Bible and its ethics clear to us. We were a trial to her, full of mischief, restless and even noisy; but perhaps more especially when we asked questions. And on the story of Jacob and Esau we did ask questions. My judgment then and my judgment now is very unfavorable to Jacob. I thought that he was a cad and a liar and I did not see how possibly he could be made the hero of a Sunday-school lesson.

Many days have passed since then and the world has gone through astonishing changes. But basically, my judgment of Jacob has not greatly changed and I have often promised myself the pleasure of talking about him publicly, and especially to young people. This is the first time that I have had the opportunity.

My subject then is "Jacob and Esau," and I want to examine these two men and the ideas which they represent; and the way in which those ideas have come to our day. Of course, our whole interpretation of this age-old story of Jewish mythology has greatly changed. We look upon these Old Testament stories today not as untrue and yet not as literally true. They are simple, they have their truths, and yet they are not by any means the expression of eternal verity. Here were brought forward for the education of Jewish children and for the interpretation of Jewish life to the world, two men: one small, lithe and quick-witted; the other tall, clumsy and impetuous; a hungry, hard-bitten man.

Historically, we know how these two types came to be set forth by the Bards of Israel. When the Jews marched north after escaping from slavery in Egypt, they penetrated and passed through the land of Edom; the land that lay between the Dead Sea and Egypt. It was an old center of hunters and nomads, and the Israelites, while they admired the strength and organization of the Edomites, looked down upon them as lesser men; as men who did not have the Great Plan. Now the Great Plan of the Israelites was the building of a strong, concentered state under its own God, Jehovah, devoted to agriculture and household manufacture and trade. It raised its own food by careful planning. It did not wander and depend upon chance wild beasts. It depended upon organization, strict ethics, absolute devotion to the nation through strongly integrated planned life. It looked upon all its neighbors, not simply with suspicion, but with the exclusiveness of a chosen people, who were going to be the leaders of earth.

This called for sacrifice, for obedience, for continued planning. The man whom we call Esau was from the land of Edom, or intermarried with it, for the legend has it that he was twin of Jacob the Jew but the chief fact is that, no matter what his blood relations were, his cultural allegiance lay among the Edomites. He was trained in the free out-of-doors; he chased and faced the wild beasts; he knew vast and imperative appetite after long self-denial, and even pain and suffering; he gloried in food, he traveled afar; he gathered wives and concubines and he represented continuous primitive strife.

The legacy of Esau has come down the ages to us. It has not been dominant, but it has always and continually expressed and re-expressed itself; the joy of human appetites, the quick resentment that leads to fighting, the belief in force, which is war.

As I look back upon my own conception of Esau, he is not nearly as clear and definite a personality as Jacob. There is something rather shadowy about him; and yet he is curiously human and easily conceived. One understands his contemptuous surrender of his birthright; he was hungry after long days of hunting; he wanted rest and food, the stew of meat and vegetables which Jacob had in his possession, and determined to keep unless Esau bargained. "And Esau said, Behold, I am at the point to die: and what profit shall this birthright be to me? And Jacob said, Swear to me this day; and he swore unto him: and he sold his birthright unto Jacob."

On the other hand, the legacy of Jacob which has come down through the years, not simply as a Jewish idea, but more especially as typical of modern Europe, is more complicated and expresses itself something like this: life must be planned for the Other Self, for that personification of the group, the nation, the empire, which has eternal life as contrasted with the ephemeral life of individuals. For this we must plan, and for this there must be timeless and unceasing work. Out of this, the Jews as chosen children of Jehovah would triumph over themselves, over all Edom and in time over the world.

Now it happens that so far as actual history is concerned, this dream and plan failed. The poor little Jewish nation was dispersed to the ends of the earth by the overwhelming power of the great nations that arose East, North, and South and eventually became united in the vast empire of Rome. This was the diaspora, the dispersion of the Jews. But the idea of the Plan with a personality of its own took hold of Europe with relentless grasp and this was the real legacy of Jacob, and of other men of other peoples, whom Jacob represents.

There came the attempt to weld the world into a great unity, first under the Roman Empire, then under the Catholic Church. When this attempt failed, and the empire fell apart, there arose the individual states of Europe and of some other parts of the world; and these states adapted the idea of individual effort to make each of them dominant. The state was *all*, the individual subordinate, but right here came the poison of the Jacobean idea. How could the state get this power? Who was to wield the power within the state? So long as power was achieved, what difference did it make how it was gotten? Here then was war—but not Esau's war of passion, hunger and revenge, but Jacob's war of cold acquisition and power.

Granting to Jacob, as we must, the great idea of the family, the clan, and the state as dominant and superior in its claims, nevertheless, there is the bitter danger in trying to seek these ends without reference to the great standards of right and wrong. When men begin to lie and steal, in order to make the nation to which they belong great, then comes not only disaster, but rational contradiction which in many respects is worse than disaster, because it ruins the leadership of the divine machine, the human reason, by which we chart and guide our actions.

It was thus in the middle age and increasingly in the seventeenth and eighteenth and more especially in the nineteenth century, there arose the astonishing contradiction: that is, the action of men like Jacob who were perfectly willing and eager to lie and steal so long as their action brought profit to themselves and power to their state. And soon identifying themselves and their class with the state they identified their own wealth and power as that of the state. They did not listen to any arguments of right or wrong; might was right; they came to despise and deplore the natural appetites of human beings and their very lives, so long as by their suppression, they themselves got rich and powerful. There arose a great, rich Italy; a fabulously wealthy Spain; a strong and cultured France and, eventually, a British Empire which came near to dominating the world. The Esaus of those centuries were curiously represented by various groups of people: by the slum-dwellers and the criminals who, giving up all hope of profiting by the organized state, sold their birthrights for miserable messes of pottage. But more than that, the great majority of mankind, the peoples who lived in Asia, Africa and America and the islands of the sea, became subordinate tools for the profit-making of the crafty planners of great things, who worked regardless of religion or ethics.

It is almost unbelievable to think what happened in those centuries, when it is put in cold narrative; from whole volumes of tales, let me select only a few examples. The peoples of whole islands and countries were murdered in cold blood for their gold and jewels. The mass of the laboring people of the world were put to work for wages which led them into starvation, ignorance and disease. The right of the majority of mankind to speak and to act; to play and to dance was denied, if it interfered with profit-making work for others, or was ridiculed if it could not be capitalized. Karl Marx writes of Scotland: "As an example of the method of obtaining wealth and power in nineteenth century; the story of the Duchess of Sutherland will suffice here. This Scottish noblewoman resolved, on entering upon the government of her clan of white Scottish people to turn the whole country, whose population had already been, by earlier processes, reduced to 15,000, into a sheep pasture. From 1814 to 1820 these 15,000 inhabitants were systematically hunted and rooted out. All their villages were destroyed and burnt, all their fields turned into pasture. Thus this lady appropriated 794,000 acres of land that had from time immemorial been the property of the people. She assigned to the expelled inhabitants about 6,000 acres on the seashore. The 6,000 acres had until this time lain waste, and brought in no income to their owners. The Duchess, in the nobility of her heart, actually went so far as to let these at an average rent of 50 cents per acre to the clansmen, who for centuries had shed their blood for her family. The whole of the stolen clan-land she divided into 29 great sheep farms, each inhabited by a single imported English family. In the year 1835 the 15,000 Scotsmen were already replaced by 131,000 sheep."

"The discovery of gold and silver in America, the extirpation, enslavement and entombment in mines of the Indian population, the beginning of the conquest and looting of the East Indies, the turning of Africa into a warren for the commercial hunting of black-skins, signalized the rosy dawn of power of those spiritual children of Jacob, who owned the birthright of the masses by fraud and murder. These idyllic proceedings are the chief momenta of primary accumulation of capital in private hands. On their heels tread the commercial wars of the European nations, with the globe for a theater. It begins with the revolt of the Netherlands from Spain, assumes giant dimensions in England's anti-jacobin war, and continues in the opium wars against China. . . .

"Of the Christian colonial system, Howitt says: 'The barbarities and desperate outrages of the so-called Christians, throughout every region of the world, and upon people they have been able to subdue, are not to be paralleled by those of any other race, in any age of the earth.' This history of the colonial administration of Holland—and Holland was the head capitalistic nation of the seventeenth century—'is one of the most extraordinary relations of treachery, bribery, massacre, and meanness.'

"Nothing was more characteristic than the Dutch system of stealing men, to get slaves for Java. The men-stealers were trained for this purpose. The thief, the interpreter, and the seller were the chief agents in this trade; the native princes, the chief sellers. The young people stolen, were thrown into the secret dungeons of Celebes, until they were ready for sending to the slave ships. . . .

"The English East India Company, in the seventeenth and eighteenth centuries, obtained, besides the political rule in India, the exclusive monopoly of the tea trade, as well as of the Chinese trade in general, and of the transport of goods to and from Europe. But the coasting trade of India was the monopoly of the higher employees of the company. The monopolies of salt, opium, betel nuts and other commodities, were inexhaustible mines of wealth. The employees themselves fixed the price and plundered at will the unhappy Hindus. The Governor General took part in this private traffic. His favorites received contracts under conditions whereby they, cleverer than the alchemists, made gold out of nothing. Great English fortunes sprang up like mushrooms in a day; investment profits went on without the advance of a shilling. The trial of Warren Hastings swarms with such cases. Here is an instance: a contract for opium was given to a certain Sullivan at the moment of his departure on an official mission. Sullivan sold his contract to one Binn for $200,000; Binn sold it the same day for $300,000 and the ultimate purchaser who carried out the contract declared that after all he realized an enormous gain. According to one of the lists laid before Parliament, the East India company and its employees from 1757 to 1766 got $30,000,000 from the Indians as gifts alone. . . .

"The treatment of the aborigines was, naturally, most frightful in plantation colonies destined for export trade only, such as the West Indies, and in rich and well-populated countries, such as Mexico and India, that were given over to plunder. But even in the colonies properly so called, the followers of Jacob outdid him. These sober Protestants, the Puritans of New England, in 1703, by decrees of their assembly set a premium of $200 on every Indian scalp and every captured redskin: in 1720 a premium of $500 on every scalp; in 1744, after Massachusetts Bay had proclaimed a certain tribe as rebels, the following prices prevailed: for a male scalp of 12 years upward, $500 (new currency); for a male prisoner, $525; for women and children prisoners, $250; for scalps of women and children, $250. Some decades later, the colonial system took its revenge on the descendants of the pious pilgrim fathers, who had grown seditious in the meantime. At English instigation and for English pay they were tomahawked by redskins. The British Parliament, proclaimed bloodhounds and scalping as 'means that God and Nature had given into its hands.'"

"With the development of national industry during the eighteenth century, the public opinion of Europe had lost the last remnant of shame and conscience. The nations bragged cynically of every infamy that served them as a means to accumulating private wealth. Read, e.g., the naive *Annals of Commerce* of Anderson. Here it is trumpeted forth as a triumph of English statecraft that at the Peace of Utrecht, England extorted from the Spaniards by the Asiento Treaty the privilege of being allowed to ply the slave trade, between Africa and Spanish America. England thereby acquired the right of supplying Spanish America until 1743 with 4,800 Negroes yearly. This threw, at the same time, an official cloak over British smuggling. Liverpool waxed fat on the slave trade. . . . Aiken (1795) quotes that spirit of bold adventure which has characterized the trade of Liverpool and rapidly carried it to its present state of prosperity; has occasioned vast employment for shipping and sailors, and greatly augmented the demand for the manufactures of the country; Liverpool employed in the slave trade, in 1730, 15 ships; in 1760, 74; in 1770, 96; and in 1792, 132."

Henry George wrote of *Progress and Poverty* in the 1890s. He says: "At the beginning of this marvelous era it was natural to expect, and it was expected, that labor-saving inventions would lighten the toil and improve the condition of the laborer; that the enormous increase in the power of producing wealth would make real poverty a thing of the past. Could a man of the last century [the eighteenth]—a Franklin or a Priestley—have seen, in a vision of the future, the steamship taking the place of the sailing vessel; the railroad train, of the wagon; the reaping machine, of the scythe; the threshing machine, of the flail; could he have heard the throb of the engines that in obedience to human will, and for the satisfaction of the human desire, exert a power greater than that of all the men and all the beasts of burden of the earth combined; could he have seen the forest tree transformed into finished lumber—into doors, sashes, blinds, boxes or barrels, with hardly the touch of a human hand; the great workshops where boots and shoes are turned out by the case with less labor than the old-fashioned cobbler could have put on a sole; the factories where, under the eye of one girl, cotton becomes cloth faster than hundreds of stalwart weavers could have turned it out with their hand-looms; could he have seen steam hammers shaping mammoth shafts and mighty anchors, and delicate machinery making tiny watches; the diamond drill cutting through the heart of the rocks, and coal oil sparing the whale; could he have realized the enormous saving of labor resulting from improved facilities of exchange and communication—sheep killed in Australia eaten fresh in England, and the order given by the London banker in the afternoon executed in San Francisco in the morning of the same day; could he have conceived of the hundred thousand improvements which these only suggest, what would he have inferred as to the social condition of mankind?

"It would not have seemed like an inference; further than the vision went it would have seemed as though he saw; and his heart would have leaped and his nerves would have thrilled, as one who from a height beholds just ahead of the thirst-stricken caravan the living gleam of rustling woods and the glint of laughing waters. Plainly, in the sight of the imagination, he would have beheld these new forces elevating society from its very foundations, lifting the very poorest above the possibility of want, exempting the very lowest from anxiety for the material needs of life; he would have seen these slaves of the lamp of knowledge taking on themselves the traditional curse, these muscles of iron and sinews of steel making the poorest laborer's life a holiday, in which every high quality and noble impulse could have scope to grow."

This was the promise of Jacob's life. This would establish the birthright which Esau despised. But, says George, "Now, however, we are coming into collision with facts which there can be no mistaking. From all parts of the civilized world," he says speaking fifty years ago, "come complaints of industrial depression; of labor condemned to involuntary idleness; of capital massed and wasting; of pecuniary distress among businessmen; of want and suffering and anxiety among the working classes. All the full, deadening pain, all the keen, maddening anguish, that to great masses of men are involved in the words 'hard times,' afflicts the world today." What would Henry George have said in 1933 after airplane and radio and mass production, turbine and electricity had come?

Science and art grew and expanded despite all this, but it was warped by the poverty of the artist and the continuous attempt to make science subservient to industry. The latter effort finally succeeded so widely that modern civilization became typified as industrial technique. Education became learning a trade. Men thought of civilization as primarily mechanical and the mechanical means by which they reduced wool and cotton to their purposes, also reduced and bent humankind to their will. Individual initiative remained but it was cramped and distorted and there spread the idea of patriotism to one's country as the highest virtue, by which it became established, that just as in the case of Jacob, a man not only could lie, steal, cheat and murder for his native land, but by doing so, he became a hero whether his cause was just or unjust.

One remembers that old scene between Esau who had thoughtlessly surrendered his birthright and the father who had blessed his lying son; "Jacob came unto his father, and said, My Father: and he said, Here am I; who art thou? And Jacob said unto his father, I am Esau thy firstborn; I have done according as thou badest me; arise, I pray thee, sit and eat of my venison, that thy soul may bless me." In vain did clumsy, careless Esau beg for a blessing—some little blessing. It was denied and Esau hated Jacob because of the blessing: and Esau said in his heart, "The days of mourning for my father are at hand; then I will slay my brother Jacob." So revolution entered—so revolt darkened a dark world.

The same motif was repeated in modern Europe and America in the nineteenth and twentieth centuries, when there grew the superstate called the Empire. The Plan had now regimented the organization of men covering vast territories, dominating immense force and immeasurable wealth and determined to reduce to subserviency as large a part as possible, not only of Europe's own internal world, but of the world at large. Colonial imperialism swept over the earth and initiated the First World War, in envious scramble for division of power and profit.

Hardly a moment of time passed after that war, a moment in

the eyes of the eternal forces looking down upon us when again the world, using all of that planning and all of that technical superiority for which its civilization was noted; and all of the accumulated and accumulating wealth which was available, proceeded to commit suicide on so vast a scale that it is almost impossible for us to realize the meaning of the catastrophe. Of course, this sweeps us far beyond anything that the peasant lad Jacob, with his petty lying and thievery had in mind. Whatever was begun there of ethical wrong among the Jews was surpassed in every particular by the white world of Europe and America and carried to such length of universal cheating, lying and killing that no comparisons remain.

We come therefore to the vast impasse of today: to the great question, what was the initial right and wrong of the original Jacobs and Esaus and of their spiritual descendants the world over? We stand convinced today, at least those who remain sane, that lying and cheating and killing will build no world organization worth the building. We have got to stop making income by unholy methods; out of stealing the pittances of the poor and calling it insurance; out of seizing and monopolizing the natural resources of the world and then making the world's poor pay exhorbitant prices for aluminum, copper and oil, iron and coal. Not only have we got to stop these practices, but we have got to stop lying about them and seeking to convince human beings that a civilization based upon the enslavement of the majority of men for the income of the smart minority is the highest aim of man.

But as is so usual in these cases, these transgressions of Jacob do not mean that the attitude of Esau was flawless. The conscienceless greed of capital does not excuse the careless sloth of labor. Life cannot be all aimless wandering and indulgence if we are going to constrain human beings to take advantage of their brain and make successive generations stronger and wiser than the previous. There must be reverence for the *birthright* of inherited *culture* and that birthright cannot be sold for a dinner course, a dress suit or a winter in Florida. It must be valued and conserved.

The method of conservation is work, endless and tireless and planned work and this is the legacy which the Esaus of today who condemn the Jacobs of yesterday have got to substitute as their path of life, not vengeful revolution, but building and rebuilding. Curiously enough, it will not be difficult to do this, because the great majority of men, the poverty-stricken and diseased are the *real workers* of the world. They are the ones who have made and are making the *wealth* of this universe, and their future path is clear. It is to accumulate such knowledge and balance of judgment that they can reform the world, so that the workers of the world receive just share of the wealth which they make and that all human beings who are capable of work shall work. Not national glory and empire for the few, but food, shelter and happiness for the many. With the disappearance of systematic lying and killing, we may come into that birthright which so long we have called Freedom: that is, the right to act in a manner that seems to us beautiful; which makes life worth living and joy the only possible end of life. This is the experience which is Art and planning for this is the highest satisfaction of civilized needs. So that looking back upon the allegory and the history, tragedy and promise, we may change our subject and speak in closing of Esau and Jacob, realizing that neither was perfect, but that of the two, Esau had the elements which lead more naturally and directly to the salvation of man; while Jacob with all his crafty planning and cold sacrifice, held in his soul the things that are about to ruin mankind: exaggerated national patriotism, individual profit, and despising of men who are not the darlings of our particular God and the consequent lying and stealing and killing to monopolize power.

May we not hope that in the world after this catastrophe of blood, sweat and fire, we may have a new Esau and Jacob; a new allegory of men who enjoy life for life's sake; who have the Freedom of Art and wish for all men of all sorts the same freedom and enjoyment that they seek themselves and who work for all this and work hard.

Gentlemen and ladies of the class of 1944: in the days of the years of my pilgrimage, I have greeted many thousands of young men and women at the commencement of their careers as citizens of the select commonwealth of culture. In no case have I welcomed them to such a world of darkness and distractions as that into which I usher you. I take joy only in the thought that if work to be done is measure of man's opportunity you inherit a mighty fortune. You have only to remember that the birthright which is today in symbol draped over your shoulders is a heritage which has been preserved all too often by the lying, stealing and murdering of the Jacobs of the world, and if these are the only means by which this birthright can be preserved in the future, it is not worth the price. I do not believe this, and I lay it upon your hearts to prove that this not only need not be true, but is eternally and forever false.

Discussion Questions

1. What would DuBois's historical argument have lost were it not to have begun with the story of Jacob and Esau? How does the story continue to affect his historical narrative? Where and why does the writer see the story breaking down as a means of historical explanation?

2. With what effects does DuBois alternate between narrating history himself and quoting other historians? What would be lost were one or the other method used alone?

3. In what ways does DuBois's essay measure up to the standards argued for by S. E. Morison in "History as a Literary Art"? How, for example, does his use of language fulfill the requirements of liveliness and readability? Pick some particular examples of sentences you find written in an especially artful way.

4. DuBois originally read the essay as a speech. What elements of organization does the author employ to meet some of the problems of listeners who cannot refer back to a text? How, for example, does DuBois make use of repetition as an organizational device?

5. Toward the end of his essay, DuBois urges his audience to "conserve" certain values. On this issue, in what ways would he agree with people called "conservative" today? In what ways would he disagree?

RENÉ DUBOS

Born in France, René Dubos (1901–1982) came to the United States in 1924, where he completed his education (Ph.D., Rutgers, 1927) and became a naturalized citizen (1938). Starting as a microbiologist, Dubos came to write about more and more aspects of biology and eventually about human conditions generally. His last essay, written shortly before his death at the age of eighty-one, concerned social conditions in Poland. His many books include Bacterial and Mycotic Infections of Man *(1948)*, Louis Pasteur, Free Lance of Science *(1950)*, The Mirage of Health: Utopias and Modern Science *(1960) and* Man Adapting *(1965)*. The following selection comes from a collection of his essays called Man, Medicine and Environment *(1968)*.

Territoriality and Dominance

Animal populations living in a given area develop complex social structures for the control of territory and hierarchical organization. The size of the group, the extent of its territory, and the type of hierarchical organization are characteristic for each species, as are the means by which the animals communicate with each other and thus develop their social structure. The croaking of frogs, the song of birds, the howling of monkeys, and even the language of dolphins certainly play a role in establishing territorial claims and social status. Many other physiological characteristics and behavioural traits have a definite social meaning. For instance, the deposition of secretions, excretions, or other odorous substances at selected spots serves to mark territorial boundaries. Certain physical attributes or forms of display also contribute to the establishment of dominance within a given territory and social group.

Irrespective of the nature of its determinants, social organization has several important beneficial effects. It generates mechanisms that regulate population size more or less automatically; it limits the severity of conflicts within the group; and in many cases it prevents destructive combat except in unusual or unnatural situations.

Whenever the population density of a group increases beyond a safe limit, many of the low-ranking animals in the social hierarchy are removed from the reproductive pool. Some are chased out and compelled to emigrate; others are tolerated on the fringes of the group but not allowed to engage in heterosexual activity, becoming, as it were, social castrates.

That only the most vigorous and otherwise most able males have access to the females probably has some eugenic value; it tends to favour reproduction of genes responsible for physical and behavioural vigour. Notwithstanding, the greatest importance of forced emigration and of social castration is to limit the number of males available for mating and thus to prevent excessive population growth. The population-limiting effect of this social mechanism supplements that exerted by food shortages and by other selective biological processes. The remarkable outcome of these automatic mechanisms is that, in the case of many animal species, animal populations in the wild remain on the average much more stable than would be expected from the maximum reproductive potential. Automatic regulatory mechanisms of population size, involving both biological and social factors, have been found to operate also among animal populations maintained in laboratory environments.

Since the patterns of behaviour based on territoriality and social hierarchy have emerged in the course of evolutionary development, it can be taken for granted that they possess some adaptive value, if not for each individual member at least for the group as a whole. Studies of animal behaviour have revealed that fighting and social tensions subside once the hierarchical order is established and accepted, and that competition for food and for mates is abated. The group thus enjoys a social stability beneficial not only to its dominant members but also to the subordinate animals. Admittedly, the latter must yield their places to dominant animals in the feeding areas and consequently do not grow as rapidly as they otherwise would. On the other hand, these behaviour patterns, along with the restrictions imposed by territoriality, limit the numbers of animals breeding in a given area and thereby maintain an equilibrium between the population and its food resources. Such biological checks on food consumption are consonant with the belief of conservationists that exploitation of natural resources should remain somewhat below maximum utilization.

The population regulatory mechanisms mentioned above operate effectively because many members of the group are deprived of a chance to reproduce and others are sacrificed altogether. At first sight, therefore, it seems paradoxical to assert that the behavioural patterns involved in territoriality and dominance have adaptive value. By defining Darwinian fitness with reference to the population as a whole rather than to the individual organism, we can explain the paradox. In contrast, civilized human societies, and probably most primitive human societies as well, tend to regard the individual person as the significant biological unit. This difference sharply separates mankind from the rest of the living world and explains why many social mechanisms effective among animals are ethically unacceptable in human societies. For this reason, the automatic regulatory processes that control numbers of animals in nature are of limited importance in controlling the human population.

The pecking order among chickens and other birds, as well as other forms of hierarchical arrangement in animal societies, depends upon the ability of some animals to establish dominance over subordinate members of the group. For a long time it was thought that dominance was achieved through fierce combat, in particular when males were in conflict for the available females during the rut season. Savage fights between stags, walrus bulls, or male seals have long been part of wildlife lore. However, destructive combat rarely occurs under natural conditions; it is rare also among laboratory animals if the colony is left undisturbed once it has become stabilized. When males fight, the combat rarely is to the death. The stronger combatant intimidates and threatens, the weaker turns aside and retreats. The victor lets the vanquished flee unmolested.

The losing animal in a struggle saves itself from destruction by an act of submission, an act usually recognized and accepted by the winner. In some cases, for instance, the loser presents to its rival a vulnerable part of its body such as the top of the head or the fleshy part of the neck. The central nervous system of the winner recognizes the "meaning" of the presentation, and the instinct to kill is inhibited. Typical of this natural pattern is the behaviour of two wolves in combat. As soon as one of the animals realizes it cannot win, it offers its vulnerable throat to the stronger wolf; instead of taking advantage of the opportunity, the victor relents, even though an instant earlier it had appeared frantic to reach the now proffered jugular vein. Many fish that "fight" do not actually strike each other; they merely beat their tails in a way that creates shock waves of water against the sensitive lateral line of the other. To the observer this performance resembles more closely a complex ritual than a real fight.

The view that destructive combat is rare among wild animals is so much at variance with the "Nature, red in tooth and claw" legend that it may be useful to quote here a statement by Professor Niko Tinbergen, a well-known student of ethology, or animal behaviour: "It is a very striking and important fact that 'fighting' in animals usually consists of threatening or bluff. Considering the fact that sexual fighting takes such an enormous amount of the time (in the breeding season) of so many species, it is certainly astonishing that real fighting, in the sense of a physical struggle, is so seldom observed."

In some respects, fighting among animals under natural

conditions thus presents some analogy to German student duels; some wounds are permissible, but most battles constitute in reality bluffing contests and a confrontation of wits. As far as is known, only one type of creature in addition to man engages in systematic destructive war against other groups of the same species. At times when food is scarce among harvester ants, colonies of these ants are prone to raid those other colonies of the same species that have stored away seeds; they kill the owners and carry away the crop. It need not be emphasized that among men also war has often been waged for a food supply.

An extensive symposium on the symbolic nature of fighting between animals of the same species was recently held in London under the title "The Ritualization of Behaviour." This symposium noted that animals repeatedly tend to ritualize their aggression by such conduct as rearing up, roaring, showing their teeth, or erecting their ruffs, hackles, or neck hair. Since ritualization of behaviour is widespread also among higher apes, it is surprising that man differs from them, as well as from most other animals, in having practised warfare extensively with the intent to kill. History and contemporary events unfortunately leave no doubt that man is a killer, but the reason for this propensity is not readily found in evolutionary development. A few facts having a possible relevance to this problem seem worth mentioning here because they may point to the nature of the social mechanisms that have made man the only creature among the higher animals who will systematically engage in destructive internecine warfare.

Although war is extremely rare among animals living in the wild, naturally one finds a few exceptions to the rule of "bluff rather than fight." For example, when an animal enters the home ground of another member of the same species, the latter attacks at once, apparently with the intent to kill the intruder. Such hostile attitudes apply chiefly or only to animals of the same species; other animals with slightly different habits or nutritional needs are usually not considered as competitors, and their presence is tolerated. Thus the concept of the stranger seems to have had its origins in the fear of losing one's place in the sun to potential competitors for the available food and mates. The concept of foreigners in human life—along with the undertones of mistrust and fear associated with the word in all languages—may well have its biological origin in the hostile reaction of animals to strangers of their own kind moving into their own territory.

Comparative observations of primates living undisturbed in their natural habitats or in zoos have thrown further light on the possible social mechanisms through which man became a killer.

When primates live under natural conditions, territory is held in common by each band and is respected by the neighbour bands. Each individual animal within the band has right of access to the common territory. Order is maintained by a hierarchy of ranks evolved as each generation grows up. This hierarchy is subject to rearrangement in accordance with the strength of the leaders and with their performance in guiding and protecting the rest of the band. The leader of a primate society settles quarrels within the band before they become violent and even gives evidence of a realistic respect for the rights of neighbouring bands. Furthermore, the bonds of comradeship holding the wild society together are far more prominent in day-to-day life than are occasional episodes of pulling rank.

Regulatory mechanisms of peaceful interplay within the band break down when animals find themselves in environments unlike those in which they have evolved. In zoos, for example, especially in old, poorly designed ones, where animals are crowded, they have little opportunity for exploring and for the individualistic enterprise they normally exercise in the wild. In such an environment the selection of the group leader is no longer dependent on his having the ability for real leadership, as it is in the wild. As no food shortage exists in the zoo, an ape community there may become comparable to an urban human society, crowded and without tradition, yet enjoying material abundance.

Whenever primates are under crowded conditions, rank becomes established through fighting, and the wrong animals are likely to come to the top. They do not have to meet the test of useful performance in solving the problems of the band, and they commonly try to maintain their authority by threats or actual acts of violence. Quarrels between individual animals may become endemic, and now and then the whole society collapses. Females and young may be indiscriminately slaughtered in such outbreaks of violence. In brief, primates under crowded conditions, as they sometimes are in zoos, commonly treat their fellow inmates with extreme cruelty, but animals of the same species give no evidence of vicious behaviour when they live in their natural environment.

The observations made on primates probably have some bearing on the human condition. When man emerged from his animal background, he created for himself an environment and ways of life in which the social restraints achieved during his evolutionary development were no longer effective or suitable. Biological adaptation had not prepared him for the competitive attitudes that characterized his new social relations. He became a killer of his own species when he began to create new competitive social structures without developing social restraints to substitute for the biological wisdom of animal life evolved under natural conditions. Even today, violence and internecine conflicts are most common in highly competitive societies, particularly during periods of rapid change. Man has not yet learned to live in the zoo he has created for himself.

One of the most urgent needs of human life is to invent new ways of ritualizing social conflicts. Fortunately, this may not be as impossible as it appears at first sight. After all, the jousts between medieval knights, and some of the later traditions of military behaviour were comparable to the sham fights so common among animal populations in the wild; no one doubts that these battles of bravado averted countless wider conflicts. Can contemporary society develop effective techniques for the ritualization of conflicts? Is it too naïve to assume that global games (like the Olympics) and political confrontations can substitute for war? Competition in education and technology—or even in social welfare—can perhaps serve to evoke national potentialities that have often found their greatest expression in war's demanding and often stirring call to heroism. The race to the moon, and other forms of space exploration, may be modern expressions of what William James called the moral equivalent for war. If these sublimations of aggression can substitute for war, is any expenditure too great?

Discussion Questions

1. What does Dubos suggest would be the result of the "ritualization" of human conflict, and how does he support his suggestion?
2. Describe the organizational techniques by which Dubos links his observations of animals to human behavior.
3. What areas of agreement and disagreement would Dubos find with Lewis Mumford in his description of the ritualized conflict of sport?
4. Describe a human social situation (for example, the manners people adopt upon entering an elevator) in which the concepts of "territoriality" and "dominance" seem to offer a functional explanation for the observed behavior.
5. Dubos distinguishes civilized society from animal groups by saying that the former assumes the individual as the basic unit. What evidence does he bring to support this argument? What crucial difference does the distinction make for the issue of violence?

RALPH ELLISON

Ralph Waldo Ellison, named after the great American essayist and poet, was born in Oklahoma in 1914. After studying music at Tuskegee Institute, he moved to New York City in 1936 to become a sculptor, but found his true identity when he met Richard Wright while working for the Federal Writers Project. During World War II, Ellison served with the Merchant Marine. His first novel, Invisible Man (1952), won the National Book Award and is often listed as one of the twentieth century's most significant works of fiction. Ellison has lectured widely and has taught creative writing at Rutgers, Yale, Bard, and the University of Chicago.

The following essay is the first half of "Hidden Name and Complex Fate." It was originally delivered as a speech and was later printed in the author's collection of nonfiction, Shadow and Act (1964).

Hidden Name
and Complex Fate

In *Green Hills of Africa*, Ernest Hemingway reminds us that both Tolstoy and Stendhal had seen war, that Flaubert had seen a revolution and the Commune, that Dostoievsky had been sent to Siberia and that such experiences were important in shaping the art of these great masters. And he goes on to observe that "writers are forged in injustice as a sword is forged." He declined to describe the many personal forms which injustice may take in this chaotic world—who would be so mad as to try?—nor does he go into the personal wounds which each of these writers sustained. Now, however, thanks to his brother and sister, we do know something of the injustice in which he himself was forged, and this knowledge has been added to what we have long known of Hemingway's artistic temper.

In the end, however, it is the quality of his art which is primary. It is the art which allows the wars and revolutions which he knew, and the personal and social injustice which he suffered, to lay claims upon our attention; for it was through his art that they achieved their most enduring meaning. It is a matter of outrageous irony, perhaps, but in literature the great social clashes of history no less than the painful experience of the individual are secondary to the meaning which they take on through the skill, the talent, the imagination and personal vision of the writer who transforms them into art. Here they are reduced to more manageable proportions; here they are imbued with humane values; here, injustice and catastrophe become less important in themselves than what the writer makes of them. This is *not* true, however, of the writer's struggle with that recalcitrant angel called Art; and it was through *this* specific struggle that Ernest Hemingway became *Hemingway* (now refined to a total body of transcendent work, after forty years of being endlessly dismembered and resurrected, as it continues to be, in the styles, the themes, the sense of life and literature of countless other writers). And it was through this struggle with form that he became the master, the culture hero, whom we have come to know and admire.

It was suggested that it might be of interest if I discussed here this evening some of my notions of the writer's experience in the United States, hence I have evoked the name of Hemingway, not by way of inviting far-fetched comparisons but in order to establish a perspective, a set of assumptions from which I may speak, and in an attempt to avoid boring you by emphasizing those details of racial hardship which for some forty years now have been evoked whenever writers of my own cultural background have essayed their experience in public.

I do this *not* by way of denying totally the validity of these by now stylized recitals, for I have shared and still share many of their detailed injustices—what Negro can escape them?—but by way of suggesting that they are, at least in a discussion of a writer's experience, as *writer*, as artist, somewhat beside the point.

For we select neither our parents, our race nor our nation; these occur to us out of the love, the hate, the circumstances, the fate, of others. But we *do* become writers out of an act of will, out of an act of choice; a dim, confused and ofttimes regrettable choice, perhaps, but choice nevertheless. And what happens thereafter causes all those experiences which occurred before we began to function as writers to take on a special quality of uniqueness. If this does not happen then as far as writing goes, the experiences have been misused. If we do not make of them a value, if we do not transform them into forms and images of meaning which they did not possess before, then we have failed as artists.

Thus for a writer to insist that his personal suffering is of special interest in itself, or simply because he belongs to a particular racial or religious group, is to advance a claim for special privileges which members of his group who are not writers would be ashamed to demand. The kindest judgment one can make of this point of view is that it reveals a sad misunderstanding of the relationship between suffering and art. Thomas Mann and André Gide have told us much of this and there are critics, like Edmund Wilson, who have told of the connection between the wound and the bow.

As I see it, it is through the process of making artistic forms—plays, poems, novels—out of one's experience that one becomes a writer, and it is through this process, this struggle, that the writer helps give meaning to the experience of the group. And it is the process of mastering the discipline, the techniques, the fortitude, the culture, through which this is made possible that constitutes the writer's real experience as *writer*, as artist. If this sounds like an argument for the artist's withdrawal from social struggles, I would recall to you W. H. Auden's comment to the effect that:

> In our age, the mere making of a work of art is itself a political act. So long as artists exist, making what they please, and think they ought to make, even if it is not terribly good, even if it appeals to only a handful of people, they remind the Management of something managers need to be reminded of, namely, that the managed are people with faces, not anonymous members, that *Homo Laborans* is also *Homo Ludens*. . . .

Without doubt, even the most *engagé* writer—and I refer to true artists, not to artists *manqués*—begin their careers in play and puzzlement, in dreaming over the details of the world in which they become conscious of themselves.

Let Tar Baby, that enigmatic figure from Negro folklore, stand for the world. He leans, black and gleaming, against the wall of life utterly noncommittal under our scrutiny, our questioning, starkly unmoving before our naïve attempts at intimidation. Then we touch him playfully and before we can say *Sonny Liston!* we find ourselves stuck. Our playful investigations become a labor, a fearful struggle, an *agon*. Slowly we perceive that our task is to learn the proper way of freeing ourselves to develop, in other words, technique.

Sensing this, we give him our sharpest attention, we question him carefully, we struggle with more subtlety; while he, in his silent way, holds on, demanding that we perceive the necessity of calling him by his true name as the price of our freedom. It is unfortunate that he has so many, many "true names"—all spelling chaos; and in order to discover even one of these we must first come into the possession of our own names. For it is through our names that we first place ourselves in the world. Our names, being the gift of others, must be made our own.

Once while listening to the play of a two-year-old girl who did not know she was under observation, I heard her saying over and over again, at first with questioning and then with sounds of growing satisfaction, "I am Mimi Livisay? . . . *I* am Mimi Livisay . . . I *am* Mimi Livisay . . . I am *Mimi* Li-vi-say! I am Mimi . . ."

And in deed and in fact she was—or became so soon thereafter, by working playfully to establish the unity between herself and her name.

For many of us this is far from easy. We must learn to wear our names within all the noise and confusion of the environment in which we find ourselves; make them the center of all of our associations with the world, with man and with nature. We must charge them with all our emotions, our hopes, hates, loves, aspirations. They must become our masks and our shields and the containers of all those values and traditions which we learn and/or imagine as being the meaning of our familial past.

And when we are reminded so constantly that we bear, as Negroes, names originally possessed by those who owned our enslaved grandparents, we are apt, especially if we are potential writers, to be more than ordinarily concerned with the veiled and mysterious events, the fusions of blood, the furtive couplings, the business transactions, the violations of faith and loyalty, the assaults; yes, and the unrecognized and unrecognizable loves through which our names were handed down unto us.

So charged with emotion does this concern become for some of us, that we have, earlier, the example of the followers of Father Divine and, now, the Black Muslims, discarding their original names in rejection of the bloodstained, the brutal, the sinful images of the past. Thus they would declare new identities, would clarify a new program of intention and destroy the verbal evidence of a willed and ritualized discontinuity of blood and human intercourse.

Not all of us, actually only a few, seek to deal with our names in this manner. We take what we have and make of them what we can. And there are even those who know where the old broken connections lie, who recognize their relatives across the chasm of historical denial and the artificial barriers of society, and who see themselves as bearers of many of the qualities which were admirable in the original sources of their common line (Faulkner has made much of this); and I speak here not of mere forgiveness, nor of obsequious insensitivity to the outrages symbolized by the denial and the division, but of the conscious acceptance of the harsh realities of the human condition, of the ambiguities and hypocrisies of human history as they have played themselves out in the United States.

Perhaps, taken in aggregate, these European names which (sometimes with irony, sometimes with pride, but always with personal investment) represent a certain triumph of the spirit, speaking to us of those who rallied, reassembled and transformed themselves and who under dismembering pressures refused to die. "Brothers and sisters," I once heard a Negro preacher exhort, "let us make up our faces before the world, and our names shall sound throughout the land with honor! For we ourselves are our *true* names, not their epithets! So let us, I say, Make Up Our Faces and Our Minds!"

Perhaps my preacher had read T. S. Eliot, although I doubt it. And in actuality, it was unnecessary that he do so, for a concern with names and naming was very much a part of that special area of American culture from which I come, and it is precisely for this reason that this example should come to mind in a discussion of my own experience as a writer.

Undoubtedly, writers begin their *conditioning* as manipulators of words long before they become aware of literature—certain Freudians would say at the breast. Perhaps. But if so, that is far too early to be of use at this moment. Of this, though, I am certain: that despite the misconceptions of those educators who trace the reading difficulties experienced by large numbers of Negro children in Northern schools to their Southern background, these children are, in *their* familiar South, facile manipulators of words. I know, too, that the Negro community is deadly in its ability to create nicknames and to spot all that is ludicrous in an unlikely name or that which is incongruous in conduct. Names are not qualities; nor are words, in this particular sense, actions. To assume that they are could cost one his life many times a day. Language skills depend to a large extent upon a knowledge of the details, the manners, the objects, the folkways, the psychological patterns, of a given environment. Humor and wit depend upon much the same awareness, and so does the suggestive power of names.

"A small brown bowlegged Negro with the name 'Franklin D. Roosevelt Jones' might sound like a clown to someone who looks at him from the outside," said my friend Albert Murray, "but on the other hand he just might turn out to be a hell of a fireside operator. He might just lie back in all of that comic juxtaposition of names and manipulate you deaf, dumb and blind—and you not even suspecting it, because you're thrown out of stance by his name! There you are, so dazzled by the F.D.R. image—which you *know* you can't see—and so delighted with your own superior position that you don't realize that its *Jones* who must be confronted."

Well, as you must suspect, all of his speculation on the matter of names has a purpose, and now, because it is tied up so ironically with my own experience as a writer, I must turn to my own name.

For in the dim beginnings, before I ever thought consciously of writing, there was my own name, and there was, doubtless, a certain magic in it. From the start I was uncomfortable with it, and in my earliest years it caused me much puzzlement. Neither could I understand what a poet was, nor why, exactly, my father had chosen to name me after one. Perhaps I could have understood it perfectly well had he named me after his own father, but that name had been given to an older brother who died and thus was out of the question. But why hadn't he named me after a hero, such as Jack Johnson, or a soldier like Colonel Charles Young, or a great seaman like Admiral Dewey, or an educator like Booker T. Washington, or a great orator and abolitionist like Frederick Douglass? Or again, why hadn't he named me (as so many Negro parents had done) after President Teddy Roosevelt?

Instead, he named me after someone called Ralph Waldo Emerson, and then, when I was three, he died. It was too early for me to have understood his choice, although I'm sure he must have explained it many times, and it was also too soon for me to have made the connection between my name and my father's love for reading. Much later, after I began to write and work with words, I came to suspect that he was aware of the suggestive powers of names and of the magic involved in naming.

I recall an odd conversation with my mother during my early teens in which she mentioned their interest in, of all things, prenatal culture! But for a long time I actually knew only that my father read a lot, and that he admired this remote Mr. Emerson, who was something called a "poet and philosopher"—so much so that he named his second son after him.

I knew, also, that whatever his motives, the combination of names he'd given me caused me no end of trouble from the moment when I could talk well enough to respond to the ritualized question which grownups put to very young children. Emerson's name was quite familiar to Negroes in Oklahoma during those days when World War I was brewing, and adults, eager to show off their knowledge of literary figures, and obviously amused by the joke implicit in such a small brown nubbin of a boy carrying around such a heavy moniker, would invariably repeat my first two names and then to my great annoyance, they'd add "Emerson."

And I, in my confusion, would reply, "No, *no, I'm* not Emerson; he's the little boy who lives next door." Which only made them laugh all the louder. "Oh no," they'd say, "*you're* Ralph Waldo Emerson," while I had fantasies of blue murder.

For a while the presence next door of my little friend, Emerson, made it unnecessary for me to puzzle too often over this peculiar adult confusion. And since there were other Negro boys named Ralph in the city, I came to suspect that there was something about the combination of names which produced their laughter. Even today I know of only one other Ralph who had as much comedy made out of his name, a campus politician and deep-voiced orator whom I knew at Tuskegee, who was called in friendly ribbing, *Ralph Waldo Emerson Edgar Allan Poe*, spelled Powe. This must have been quite a trial for him, but I had been initiated much earlier.

During my early school years the name continued to puzzle me, for it constantly evoked in the faces of others some secret. It was as though I possessed some treasure or some defect, which was invisible to my own eyes and ears; something which I had but did not *possess*, like a piece of property in South Carolina, which was mine but which I could not have until some future time. I recall finding, about this time, while seeking adventure in back alleys—which possess for boys a superiority over playgrounds like that which kitchen utensils possess over toys designed for infants—a large photographic lens. I remember nothing of its optical qualities, of its speed or color correction, but it gleamed with crystal mystery and it was beautiful.

Mounted handsomely in a tube of shiny brass, it spoke to me of distant worlds of possibility. I played with it, looking through it with squinted eyes, holding it in shafts of sunlight, and tried to use it for a magic lantern. But most of this was as unrewarding as my attempts to make the music come from a phonograph record by holding the needle in my fingers.

I could burn holes through newspapers with it, or I could pretend that it was a telescope, the barrel of a cannon, or the third eye of a monster—*I* being the monster—but I could do nothing at all about its proper function of making images; nothing to make it yield its secret. But I could not discard it.

Older boys sought to get it away from me by offering knives or tops, agate marbles or whole zoos of grass snakes and horned toads in trade, but I held on to it. No one, not even the white boys I knew, had such a lens, and it was my own good luck to have found it. Thus I would hold on to it until such time as I could acquire the parts needed to make it function. Finally I put it aside and it remained buried in my box of treasures, dusty and dull, to be lost and forgotten as I grew older and became interested in music.

I had reached by now the grades where it was necessary to learn something about Mr. Emerson and what he had written, such as the "Concord Hymn" and the essay "Self-Reliance," and in following his advice, I reduced the "Waldo" to a simple and, I hoped, mysterious "W," and in my own reading I avoided his works like the plague. I could no more deal with my name—I shall never really master it—than I could find a creative use for my lens. Fortunately there were other problems to occupy my mind. Not that I forgot my fascination with names, but more about that later.

Negro Oklahoma City was starkly lacking in writers. In fact, there was only Roscoe Dungee, the editor of the local Negro newspaper and a very fine editorialist in that valuable tradition of personal journalism which is now rapidly disappearing; a writer who in his emphasis upon the possibilities for justice offered by the Constitution anticipated the anti-segregation struggle by decades. There were also a few reporters who drifted in and out, but these were about all. On the level of *conscious* culture the Negro community was biased in the direction of music.

These were the middle and late twenties, remember, and the state was still a new frontier state. The capital city was one of the great centers for southwestern jazz, along with Dallas and Kansas City. Orchestras which were to become famous within a few years were constantly coming and going. As were the blues singers—Ma Rainey and Ida Cox, and the old bands like that of King Oliver. But best of all, thanks to Mrs. Zelia N. Breaux, there was an active and enthusiastic school music program through which any child who had the interest and the talent could learn to play an instrument and take part in the band, the orchestra, the brass quartet. And there was a yearly operetta and a chorus and a glee club. Harmony was taught for four years and the music appreciation program was imperative. European folk dances were taught throughout the Negro school system, and we were also taught complicated patterns of military drill.

I tell you this to point out that although there were no incentives to write, there was ample opportunity to receive an artistic discipline. Indeed, once one picked up an instrument it was difficult to escape. If you chafed at the many rehearsals of the school band or orchestra and were drawn to the many small jazz groups, you were likely to discover that the jazzmen were apt to rehearse far more than the school band; it was only that they seemed to enjoy themselves better and to possess a freedom of imagination which we were denied at school. And one soon learned that the wild, transcendent moments which occurred at dances or "battles of music," moments in which memorable improvisations were ignited, depended upon a dedication to a discipline which was observed even when rehearsals had to take place in the crowded quarters of Halley Richardson's shoeshine parlor. It was not the place which counted, although a large hall with good acoustics was preferred, but what one did to perfect one's performance.

If this talk of musical discipline gives the impression that there were no forces working to nourish one who would one day blunder, after many a twist and turn, into writing, I am misleading you. And here I might give you a longish lecture on the Ironies and Uses of Segregation. When I was a small child there was no library for Negroes in our city; and not until a Negro minister invaded the main library did we get one. For it was discovered that there was no law, only custom, which held that we could not use these public facilities. The results were the quick renting of two large rooms in a Negro office building (the recent site of a pool hall), the hiring of a young Negro librarian, the installation of shelves and a hurried stocking of the walls with any and every book possible. It was, in those first days, something of a literary chaos.

But how fortunate for a boy who loved to read! I started with the fairy tales and quickly went through the junior fiction; then through the Westerns and the detective novels, and very soon I was reading the classics—only I didn't know it. There were also the Haldeman Julius Blue Books, which seem to have floated on the air down from Girard, Kansas; the syndicated columns of O. O. McIntyre, and the copies of *Vanity Fair* and the *Literary Digest* which my mother brought home from work—how could I ever join uncritically in the heavy-handed attacks on the so-called Big Media which have become so common today?

There were also the pulp magazines and, more important, that other library which I visited when I went to help my adopted grandfather, J. D. Randolph (my parents had been living in his rooming house when I was born), at his work as custodian of the law library of the Oklahoma State Capitol. Mr. Randolph had been one of the first teachers in what became Oklahoma City; and he'd also been one of the leaders of a group who walked from Gallatin, Tennessee, to the Oklahoma Territory. He was a tall man, as brown as smoked leather, who looked like the Indians with whom he'd herded horses in the early days.

And while his status was merely the custodian of the law library, I was to see the white legislators come down on many occasions to question him on points of law, and often I was to hear him answer without recourse to the uniform rows of books on the shelves. This was a thing to marvel at in itself, and the white lawmakers did so, but even more marvelous, ironic, intriguing, haunting—call it what you will—is the fact that the Negro who knew the answers was named after Jefferson Davis. What Tennessee lost, Oklahoma was to gain, and after gaining it (a gift of courage, intelligence, fortitude and grace), used it only in concealment and, one hopes, with embarrassment.

So, let us, I say, make up our faces and our minds!

Discussion Questions

1. Why was Ellison's name especially difficult for him to live with? In what way was his name part of a larger problem of self-definition? How was it tied up with his identity as a writer?

2. What was the significance of the large photographic lens that Ellison found as a young boy in South Carolina? How is the lens connected with the problem of his name?

3. Why does Ellison devote so much of his attention to the black community? What connection does he find between his role in the community and his identity? How do his views compare to those of James Baldwin?

4. What value does Ellison find in keeping one's given name, even if one is uncomfortable with it? Do you agree or disagree with him on this? Write a short essay in which you discuss the merits or the liabilities involved in changing one's name for religious, marital, or cultural-political reasons.

Nora Ephron

Nora Ephron was born in 1941 to parents who were both screenwriters. After graduating from Wellesley College, she worked as a reporter for the New York Post before becoming a freelance journalist and media critic. She continues to collect the best of her witty and wide-ranging essays in books such as Wallflower at the Orgy (1970) and Crazy Salad (1975). Her easy moving and confident style is achieved, she has said, by constant rewriting: "A piece that I turn in is probably in its twelfth draft." The following selection exemplifies a concern she has maintained throughout her career: the standards of her own profession.

The Boston Photographs

"I made all kinds of pictures because I thought it would be a good rescue shot over the ladder . . . never dreamed it would be anything else. . . . I kept having to move around because of the light set. The sky was bright and they were in deep shadow. I was making pictures with a motor drive and he, the fire fighter, was reaching up and, I don't know, everything started falling. I followed the girl down taking pictures . . . I made three or four frames. I realized what was going on and I completely turned around, because I didn't want to see her hit."

You probably saw the photographs. In most newspapers, there were three of them. The first showed some people on a fire escape—a fireman, a woman and a child. The fireman had a nice strong jaw and looked very brave. The woman was holding the child. Smoke was pouring from the building behind them. A rescue ladder was approaching, just a few feet away, and the fireman had one arm around the woman and one arm reaching out toward the ladder. The second picture showed the fire escape slipping off the building. The child had fallen on the escape and seemed about to slide off the edge. The woman was grasping desperately at the legs of the fireman, who had managed to grab the ladder. The third picture showed the woman and child in midair, falling to the ground. Their arms and legs were outstretched, horribly distended. A potted plant was falling too. The caption said that the woman, Diana Bryant, nineteen, died in the fall. The child landed on the woman's body and lived.

The pictures were taken by Stanley Forman, thirty, of the *Boston Herald American.* He used a motor-driven Nikon F set at 1/250, f5.6-S Because of the motor, the camera can click off three frames a second. More than four hundred newspapers in the United States alone carried the photographs: the tear sheets from

THE BOSTON PHOTOGRAPHS

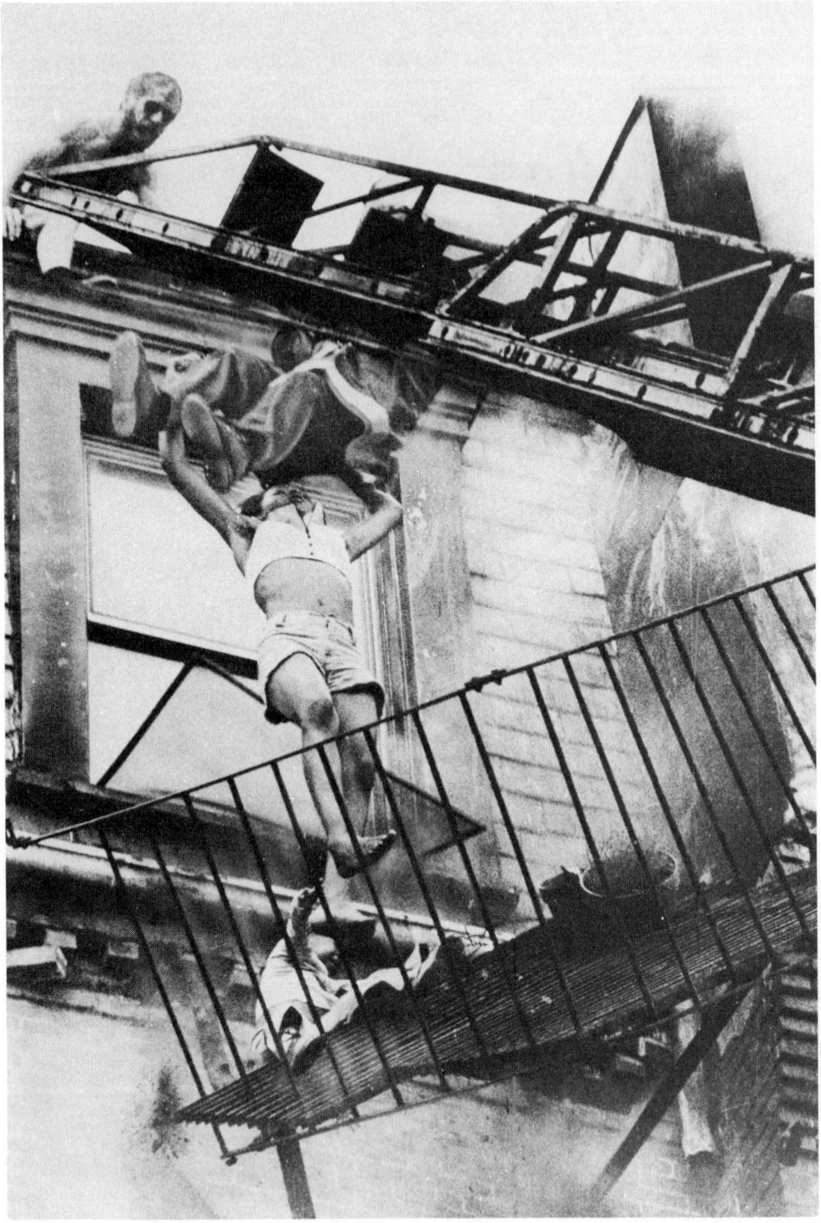

THE BOSTON PHOTOGRAPHS

overseas are still coming in. The *New York Times* ran them on the first page of its second section; a paper in south Georgia gave them nineteen columns; the *Chicago Tribune*, the *Washington Post* and the *Washington Star* filled almost half their front pages, the *Star* under a somewhat redundant headline that read: SENSATIONAL PHOTOS OF RESCUE ATTEMPT THAT FAILED.

The photographs are indeed sensational. They are pictures of death in action, of that split second when luck runs out, and it is impossible to look at them without feeling their extraordinary impact and remembering, in an almost subconscious way, the morbid fantasy of falling, falling off a building, falling to one's death. Beyond that, the pictures are classics, old-fashioned but perfect examples of photojournalism at its most spectacular. They're throwbacks, really, fire pictures, 1930s tabloid shots; at the same time they're technically superb and thoroughly modern—the sequence could not have been taken at all until the development of the motor-driven camera some sixteen years ago.

Most newspaper editors anticipate some reader reaction to photographs like Forman's; even so, the response around the country was enormous, and almost all of it was negative. I have read hundreds of the letters that were printed in letters-to-the-editor sections, and they repeat the same points. "Invading the privacy of death." "Cheap sensationalism." "I thought I was reading the *National Enquirer*." "Assigning the agony of a human being in terror of imminent death to the status of a side-show act." "A tawdry way to sell newspapers." The *Seattle Times* received sixty letters and calls; its managing editor even got a couple of them at home. A reader wrote the *Philadelphia Inquirer*: "*Jaws* and *Towering Inferno* are playing downtown; don't take business away from people who pay good money to advertise in your own paper." Another reader wrote the *Chicago Sun-Times*: "I shall try to hide my disappointment that Miss Bryant wasn't wearing a skirt when she fell to her death. You could have had some award-winning photographs of her underpants as her skirt billowed over her head, you voyeurs." Several newspaper editors wrote columns defending the pictures: Thomas Keevil of the *Costa Mesa* (California) *Daily Pilot* printed a ballot for readers to vote on whether they would have printed the pictures; Marshall L. Stone of Maine's *Bangor Daily News*, which refused to print the famous assassination picture of the Vietcong prisoner in Saigon, claimed that the Boston pictures showed the dangers of fire escapes and raised questions about slumlords. (The burning building was a five-story brick apartment house on Marlborough Street in the Back Bay section of Boston.)

For the last five years, the *Washington Post* has employed

various journalists as ombudsmen, whose job is to monitor the paper on behalf of the public. The *Post*'s current ombudsman is Charles Seib, former managing editor of the *Washington Star*; the day the Boston photographs appeared, the paper received over seventy calls in protest. As Seib later wrote in a column about the pictures, it was "the largest reaction to a published item that I have experienced in eight months as the *Post*'s ombudsman. . . .

"In the *Post*'s newsroom, on the other hand, I found no doubts, no second thoughts . . . the question was not whether they should be printed but how they should be displayed. When I talked to editors . . . they used words like 'interesting' and 'riveting' and 'gripping' to describe them. The pictures told of something about life in the ghetto, they said (although the neighborhood where the tragedy occurred is not a ghetto, I am told). They dramatized the need to check on the safety of fire escapes. They dramatically conveyed something that had happened, and that is the business we're in. They were news. . . .

"Was publication of that [third] picture a bow to the same taste for the morbidly sensational that makes gold mines of disaster movies? Most papers will not print the picture of a dead body except in the most unusual circumstances. Does the fact that the final picture was taken a millisecond before the young woman died make a difference? Most papers will not print a picture of a bare female breast. Is that a more inappropriate subject for display than the picture of a human being's last agonized instant of life?" Seib offered no answers to the questions he raised, but he went on to say that although as an editor he would probably have run the pictures, as a reader he was revolted by them.

In conclusion, Seib wrote: "Any editor who decided to print those pictures without giving at least a moment's thought to what purpose they served and what their effect was likely to be on the reader should ask another question: Have I become so preoccupied with manufacturing a product according to professional traditions and standards that I have forgotten about the consumer, the reader?"

It should be clear that the phone calls and letters and Seib's own reaction were occasioned by one factor alone: the death of the woman. Obviously, had she survived the fall, no one would have protested; the pictures would have had a completely different impact. Equally obviously, had the child died as well—or instead—Seib would undoubtedly have received ten times the phone calls he did. In each case, the pictures would have been exactly the same—only the captions, and thus the responses, would have been different.

But the questions Seib raises are worth discussing—though

not exactly for the reasons he mentions. For it may be that the real lesson of the Boston photographs is not the danger that editors will be forgetful of reader reaction, but that they will continue to censor pictures of death precisely because of that reaction. The protests Seib fielded were really a variation on an old theme—and we saw plenty of it during the Nixon-Agnew years—the "Why doesn't the press print the good news?" argument. In this case, of course, the objections were all dressed up and cleverly disguised as righteous indignation about the privacy of death. This is a form of puritanism that is often justifiable; just as often it is merely puritanical.

Seib takes it for granted that the widespread though fairly recent newspaper policy against printing pictures of dead bodies is a sound one; I don't know that it makes any sense at all. I recognize that printing pictures of corpses raises all sorts of problems about taste and titillation and sensationalism; the fact is, however, that people die. Death happens to be one of life's main events. And it is irresponsible—and more than that, inaccurate—for newspapers to fail to show it, or to show it only when an astonishing set of photos comes in over the Associated Press wire. Most papers covering fatal automobile accidents will print pictures of mangled cars. But the significance of fatal automobile accidents is not that a great deal of steel is twisted but that people die. Why not show it? That's what accidents are about. Throughout the Vietnam war, editors were reluctant to print atrocity pictures. Why *not* print them? That's what that war was about. Murder victims are almost never photographed; they are granted their privacy. But their relatives are relentlessly pictured on their way in and out of hospitals and morgues and funerals.

I'm not advocating that newspapers print these things in order to teach their readers a lesson. The *Post* editors justified their printing of the Boston pictures with several arguments in that direction; every one of them is irrelevant. The pictures don't show anything about slum life; the incident could have happened anywhere, and it did. It is extremely unlikely that anyone who saw them rushed out and had his fire escape strengthened. And the pictures were not news—at least they were not national news. It is not news in Washington, or New York, or Los Angeles that a woman was killed in a Boston fire. The only newsworthy thing about the pictures is that they were taken. They deserve to be printed because they are great pictures, breathtaking pictures of something that happened. That they disturb readers is exactly as it should be: that's why photojournalism is often more powerful than written journalism.

THE BOSTON PHOTOGRAPHS

Discussion Questions

1. How does Nora Ephron prepare her readers throughout her essay for one of her concluding statements: "They deserve to be printed because they are great pictures. . . ."?

2. List the technical terms from the vocabulary of photography that Nora Ephron quotes or uses at the beginning of the essay. How does her placement of these terms affect her tone in the essay? Do they, for example, make her seem unsympathetic to the victims? How does her having begun with these terms affect the reader's perception of the pictures?

3. What does Nora Ephron accomplish by beginning with the photographer's narration of the failed rescue rather than her own reactions to the photographs? What details does she add in her retelling of the incident? According to the author, why was public reaction so widespread and so negative? What seems to be her purpose in quoting so many of the responses? How do these public reactions differ from the responses of people in the newsroom?

4. Compare the author's explanation of why people have opposing views to that offered by Margaret Mead in "New Superstitions for Old."

5. Write an essay supporting or opposing Nora Ephron's thesis that the press rather than some other institution should be allowed to decide what is printed as news.

M. F. K. Fisher

"There is no disputing about tastes," advises an old Roman proverb. Yet, for the renowned American writer, M. F. K. Fisher, taste may be finally all that is worth arguing about. The author of many books on the fine art of eating, Fisher has throughout her career shown an inimitable taste for the fine art of writing prose as well.

Mary Frances Kennedy Fisher was born in 1908 in Albion, Michigan, and grew up in Whittier, California. Her first book, Serve It Forth *appeared in 1937 and was followed by such gastronomical studies as* Consider the Oyster *(1941),* How to Cook a Wolf *(1942),* The Gastronomical Me *(1943), and* An Alphabet for Gourmets *(1949). In 1949 she translated Jean Anthelme Brillat-Savarin's classic,* The Physiology of Taste. *Many of her early essays have been collected in* The Art of Eating: Five Gastronomical Works *(1976). But the joy of eating has not been her only subject. Besides novels and poetry, Fisher has written several autobiographical books, including* Among Friends *(1970),* A Considerable Town *(1978), and* As They Were *(1982), in which the following reminiscence appears.*

Young Hunger

It is very hard for people who have passed the age of, say, fifty to remember with any charity the hunger of their own puberty and adolescence when they are dealing with the young human animals who may be frolicking about them. Too often I have seen good people helpless with exasperation and real anger upon finding in the morning that cupboards and iceboxes have been stripped of their supplies by two or three youths—or even *one*—who apparently could have eaten four times their planned share at the dinner table the night before.

Such avidity is revolting, once past. But I can recall its intensity still; I am not yet too far from it to understand its ferocious demands when I see a fifteen-year-old boy wince and whiten at the prospect of waiting politely a few more hours for food, when his guts are howling for meat-bread-candy-fruit-cheese-milkmilkmilk—ANYTHING IN THE WORLD TO EAT.

I can still remember my almost insane desperation when I was about eighteen and was staying overnight with my comparatively aged godparents. I had come home alone from France in a bad continuous storm and was literally concave with solitude and hunger. The one night on the train seemed even rougher than those on board ship, and by the time I reached my godparents' home I was almost lightheaded.

I got there just in time for lunch. It is clear as ice in my mind: a little cup of very weak chicken broth, one salted cracker, one-half piece of thinly sliced toast, and then, ah then, a whole waffle, crisp and brown and with a piece of beautiful butter melting in its middle—which the maid deftly cut into four sections! One section she put on my godmother's plate. The next *two*, after a nod of approval from her mistress, she put on mine. My godfather ate the fourth.

There was a tiny pot of honey, and I dutifully put a dab of it on my piggish portion, and we all nibbled away and drank one cup apiece of tea with lemon. Both my godparents left part of their waffles.

It was simply that they were old and sedentary and quite out of habit of eating amply with younger people: a good thing for them, but pure hell for me. I did not have the sense to explain to them how starved I was—which I would not hesitate to do now. Instead I prowled around my bedroom while the house slumbered through its afternoon siesta wondering if I dared sneak to the strange kitchen for something, anything, to eat, and knowing I would rather die than meet the silent, stern maid or my nice gentle little hostess.

Later we walked slowly down to the village, and I was thinking sensuously of double malted ice-cream sodas at the corner drugstore, but there was no possibility of such heaven. When we got back to the quiet house, the maid brought my godfather a tall glass of exquisitely rich milk, with a handful of dried fruit on the saucer under it, because he had been ill; but as we sat and watched him unwillingly down it, his wife said softly that it was such a short time until dinner that she was sure I did not want to spoil my appetite, and I agreed with her because I was young and shy.

When I dressed, I noticed that the front of my pelvic basin jutted out like two bricks under my skirt: I looked like a scarecrow.

Dinner was very long, but all I can remember is that it had as *pièce de résistance*, half of the tiny chicken previously boiled for broth at luncheon, which my godmother carved carefully so that we should each have a bit of the breast and I, as guest, should have the leg, after a snippet had been sliced from it for her husband, who liked dark meat too.

There were hot biscuits, yes, the smallest I have ever seen, two apiece under a napkin on a silver dish. Because of them we had no dessert: it would be too rich, my godmother said.

We drank little cups of decaffeinized coffee on the screened porch in the hot Midwestern night, and when I went up to my room I saw that the maid had left a large glass of rich malted milk beside my poor godfather's bed.

My train would leave before five in the morning, and I slept little and unhappily, dreaming of the breakfast I would order on it. Of course when I finally saw it all before me, twinkling on the Pullman silver dishes, I could eat very little, from too much hunger and a sense of outrage.

I felt that my hosts had been indescribably rude to me, and selfish and conceited and stupid. Now I know that they were none of these things. They had simply forgotten about any but their own dwindling and cautious needs for nourishment. They had forgotten about being hungry, being young, being . . .

In an essay by Max Beerbohm about hosts and guests, the tyrants and the tyrannized, there is a story of what happened to him once when he was a schoolboy and someone sent him a hamper that held, not the usual collection of marmalade, sardines, and potted tongue, but twelve whole sausage-rolls.

"Of sausage-rolls I was particularly fond," he says. He could have dominated all his friends with them, of course, but "I carried the box up to my cubicle, and, having eaten two of the sausage-rolls, said nothing that day about the other ten, nor anything about them when, three days later, I had eaten them all—all, up there, alone."

What strange secret memories such a tale evokes! Is there a grown-up person anywhere who cannot remember some such shameful, almost insane act of greediness of his childhood? In recollection his scalp will prickle, and his palms will sweat, at the thought of the murderous risk he may have run from his outraged companions.

When I was about sixteen, and in boarding-school, we were allowed one bar of chocolate a day, which we were supposed to eat sometime between the sale of them at the little school bookstore at four-thirty and the seven o'clock dinner gong. I felt an almost unbearable hunger for them—not for one, but for three or four or five at a time, so that I should have *enough*, for once, in my yawning stomach.

I hid my own purchases for several days, no mean trick in a school where every drawer and cupboard was inspected, openly and snoopingly too, at least twice a week. I cannot remember now how I managed it, with such lack of privacy and my own almost insurmountable hunger every afternoon, but by Saturday I had probably ten chocolate bars—my own and a few I had bribed my friends who were trying to lose weight to buy for me.

I did not sign up for any of the usual weekend debauchery such as a walk to the village drugstore for a well-chaperoned double butterscotch and pecan sundae. Instead I lay languidly on my bed, trying to look as if I had a headache and pretending to read a very fancy book called, I think, *Martin Pippin in the Apple Orchard*, until the halls quieted.

Then I arranged all my own and my roommate's pillows in a

voluptuous pile, placed so that I could see whether a silent housemotherly foot stood outside the swaying monk's-cloth curtain that served as a door (to cut down our libidinous chitchat, the school board believed), and I put my hoard of Hersheys discreetly under a fold of the bedspread.

I unwrapped their rich brown covers and their tinfoil as silently as any prisoner chipping his way through a granite wall, and lay there breaking off the rather warm, rubbery, delicious pieces and feeling them melt down my gullet, and reading the lush symbolism of the book; and all the time I was hot and almost panting with the fear that people would suddenly walk in and see me there. And the strange thing is that nothing would have happened if they had!

It is true that I had more than my allotted share of candy, but that was not a crime. And my friends, full of their Saturday delights, would not have wanted ordinary chocolate. And anyway I had much more than I could eat, and was basically what Beerbohm calls, somewhat scornfully, "a host" and not "a guest": I loved to entertain people and dominate them with my generosity.

Then why was I breathless and nervous all during that solitary and not particularly enjoyable orgy? I suppose there is a Freudian explanation for it, or some other kind. Certainly the experience does not make me sound very attractive to myself. Even the certainty of being in good company is no real solace.

Discussion Questions

1. Do the details of M. F. K. Fisher's economic status given in the essay (for example, the maid, the boarding school) spoil or trivialize her point about hunger? How would added passages attesting to her awareness of real starvation in the world have affected her essay? Would raising such public issues in connection with her private experience have spoiled or trivialized her point about "young hunger"?

2. What is the effect of the author's use of ellipses marks (. . .) in the middle of her essay? Given the second part of that essay, would "selfish" or "greedy" or "neurotic" have adequately filled in the gap? Why or why not?

3. Write an essay about a frustration concerning food, a craving for food, or a food binge of your own.

4. Compare the evocations of a part of childhood to the essays by Guy Davenport, Lillian Hellman, and Vladimir Nabokov. What techniques involving details of the five senses does Fisher use in ways unique to her own style? What techniques of detail do the writers share?

E. M. Forster

Edward Morgan Forster (1879–1970) was born in London and educated at King's College, Cambridge, where, after an extended trip to Greece and Italy, he returned to receive his master's degree in 1910. He is the author of five novels, two of which, Howard's End (1910) and Passage to India (1924), rank among the major works of twentieth-century English fiction. Forster also wrote journalism, biography, literary criticism, and travel books. His short stories have been collected in two volumes, and, along with an influential critical study, Aspects of the Novel (1927), he has published several volumes of essays, including Abinger Harvest (1936) and Two Cheers for Democracy (1951), from which "Racial Exercise" is taken.

Racial Exercise

Let us do some easy exercises in Racial Purity.

And let me offer myself for dissection-purposes.

If I go the right way about it, I come of an old English family, but the right way is unfortunately a crooked one. It is far from easy going in the branches of my genealogical tree. I have to proceed via my father to his mother, thence to her mother, and thence to her father. If I follow this zigzag course I arrive in the satisfactory bosom of a family called Sykes, and have a clear run back through several centuries. The Sykes' go right away ever so far, right back to a certain Richard of Sykes Dyke who flourished somewhere about the year 1400. Whether inside their dyke, which lay in Cumberland, or outside it, which was Yorkshire, this family never did anything earth-shaking, still they did keep going in the documentary sense, they made money and married into it, they became mayors of Pontefract or Hull, they employed Miss Anna Seward as a governess, and, in the seventeenth century, one of them, a Quaker, was imprisoned on account of his opinions in York Castle, and died there. I come of an old English family, and am proud of it.

Unfortunately in other directions the prospect is less extensive. If I take a wrong turning and miss the Sykes', darkness descends on my origins almost at once. Mrs. James is a case in point, and a very mortifying one. Mrs. James was a widow who not so very long ago married one of my great-grandfathers. I am directly descended from her, know nothing whatever about her, and should like at all events to discover her maiden name. Vain quest. She disappears in the mists of antiquity, like Richard of Sykes Dyke, but much too soon. She might be anyone, she may not even have been Aryan. When her shadow crosses my mind, I do not feel to belong to an old family at all.

After that dissection, let us proceed to do our easy Racial Exercise.

It is this: Can you give the names of your eight great-grandparents?

The betting is eight to one that you cannot. The Royal Family could, some aristocrats could, and so could a few yeomen who have lived undisturbed in a quiet corner of England for a couple of hundred years. But most of the people I know (and probably most of the people who read these words) will fail. We can often get six or seven, seldom the whole eight. And the human mind is so dishonest and so snobby, that we instinctively reject the eighth as not mattering, and as playing no part in our biological make-up. As each of us looks back into his or her past, doors open upon darkness. Two doors at first—the father and the mother—through each of these two more, then the eight great-grandparents, the sixteen great-greats, then thirty-two ancestors... sixty-four... one hundred and twenty-eight... until the researcher reels. Even if the stocks producing us interbred, and so reduced the total of our progenitors by using some of them up on us twice, even if they practised the strict domestic economy of the Ptolemies, the total soon becomes enormous, and the Sykes' in it are nothing beside the Mrs. James'. On such a shady past as this—our common past—do we erect the ridiculous doctrine of Racial Purity.

In the future the situation will be slightly less ridiculous. Registers of marriage and birth will be kept more carefully, bastardy more cunningly detected, so that in a couple of hundred years millions of people will belong to Old Families. This should be a great comfort to them. It may also be a convenience, if governments continue to impose racial tests. Citizens will be in a position to point to an Aryan ancestry if their government is Aryan, to a Cretinist ancestry if it is Cretin, and so on, and if they cannot point in the direction required, they will be sterilised. This should be a great discomfort to them. Nor will the sterilisation help, for the mischief has already been done in our own day, the mess has been made, miscegenation has already taken place. Whether there ever was such an entity as a "pure race" is debatable, but there certainly is not one in Europe today—the internationalisms of the Roman Empire and of the Middle Ages have seen to that. Consequently there never can be a pure race in the future. Europe is mongrel forever, and so is America.

How extraordinary it is that governments which claim to be realistic should try to base themselves on anything so shadowy and romantic as race! A common language, a common religion, a common culture all belong to the present, evidence about them is available, they can be tested. But race belongs to the unknown and unknowable past. It depends upon who went to bed with whom in the year 1400, not to mention Mrs. James, and what historian will ever discover that? Community of race is an illusion. Yet belief in race is a growing psychological force, and we must reckon with it. People like to feel that they are all of a piece, and one of the ways of inducing that feeling is to tell them that they come of pure stock. That explains the ease with which the dictators are putting their pseudo-science across. No doubt they are not cynical about it, and take themselves in by what they say. But they have very cleverly hit on a weak spot in the human equipment—the desire to feel a hundred per cent, no matter what the percentage is in.

A German Professor was holding forth the other day on the subject of the origins of the German people. His attitude was that the purity of the Nordic stock is not yet proved and should not be spoken of as proved. But it should be spoken of as a fact, because it is one, and the proofs of its existence will be forthcoming as soon as scholars are sufficiently energetic and brave. He spoke of "courage" in research. According to his own lights, he was a disinterested researcher, for he refused to support what he knew to be true by arguments which he held to be false. The truth, being *a priori*, could afford to wait on its mountain top until the right path to it was found: the truth of Nordic purity which every German holds by instinct in his blood. In India I had friends who said they were descended from the Sun and looked down on those who merely came from the Moon, but they were not tense about it and seemed to forget about it between times, nor did they make it a basis for political violence and cruelty; it takes the west to do that.

Behind our problem of the eight great-grandparents stands the civilising figure of Mendel. I wish that Mendel's name was mentioned in current journalism as often as Freud's or Einstein's. He embodies a salutary principle, and even when we are superficial about him, he helps to impress it in our minds. He suggests that no stock is pure, and that it may at any moment throw up forms which are unexpected, and which it inherits from the past. His best-known experiments were with the seeds of the pea. It is impossible that human beings can be studied as precisely as peas—too many factors are involved. But they too keep throwing up recessive characteristics, and cause us to question the creed of racial purity. Mendel did not want to prove anything. He was not a "courageous" researcher, he was merely a researcher. Yet he has unwittingly put a valuable weapon into the hands of civilised people. We don't know what our ancestors were like or what our descendants will be like. We only know that we are all of us mongrels, dark haired and light haired, who must learn not to bite one another. Thanks to Mendel and to a few simple exercises we can see comparatively clearly into the problem of race, if we choose to look, and can do a little to combat the pompous and pernicious rubbish that is at present being prescribed in the high places of the earth.

Discussion Questions

1. What is the occasion for Forster's essay? What immediate situation is he responding to?

2. Why does Forster offer himself for "dissection-purposes" first? Why does he call it "dissection"? What is the effect on the reader of his starting with himself?

3. What does Forster mean when he says that Mendel was not a "'courageous' researcher, he was merely a researcher"? What is he criticizing in that distinction? How does the type of thinking that Forster objects to in this essay conform to J. B. Priestly's definition of block thinking?

4. You may want to try Forster's easy exercise. How far can you get?

SIGMUND FREUD

The founder of psychoanalysis, Sigmund Freud (1865–1939) was born in Moravia and spent most of his long life in Vienna. As a student he found it difficult to decide on a course of study: Biology, classics, history, philosophy, chemistry, and physiology all interested him and all would eventually play a part in his thinking. He finally settled on a career in medicine and began practice as a neurologist in 1886. His first book, which he coauthored with a prestigious Viennese physician, Josef Breuer, was a highly influential study of hysteria that led directly to Freud's theory of psychic repression and the psychoanalytic method of treatment.

Freud found in psychoanalysis a conceptual tool that helped him understand and explain an enormous range of individual and cultural phenomena, many of which are evidenced in the titles of his books: The Interpretation of Dreams *(1900),* The Psychopathology of Everyday Life *(1904),* Jokes and Their Relation to the Unconscious *(1905),* Leonardo da Vinci and a Memory of Childhood *(1910),* Civilization and Its Discontents *(1929), and* Moses and Monotheism *(1939).*

In 1936, Freud was elected to the Royal Society, and, after the Nazis took Austria in 1938, he moved to London, where he died a year later.

The Relation of the Poet to Day-Dreaming

We laymen have always wondered greatly—like the cardinal who put the question to Ariosto—how that strange being, the poet, comes by his material. What makes him able to carry us with him in such a way and to arouse emotions in us of which we thought ourselves perhaps not even capable? Our interest in the problem is only stimulated by the circumstance that if we ask poets themselves they give us no explanation of the matter, or at least no satisfactory explanation. The knowledge that not even the clearest insight into the factors conditioning the choice of imaginative material, or into the nature of the ability to fashion that material, will ever make writers of us does not in any way detract from our interest.

If we could only find some activity in ourselves, or in people like ourselves, which was in any way akin to the writing of imaginative works! If we could do so, then examination of it would give us a hope of obtaining some insight into the creative powers of imaginative writers. And indeed, there is some prospect of achieving this—writers themselves always try to lessen the distance between their kind and ordinary human beings; they so often assure us that every man is at heart a poet, and that the last poet will not die until the last human being does.

We ought surely to look in the child for the first traces of imaginative activity. The child's best loved and most absorbing occupation is play. Perhaps we may say that every child at play behaves like an imaginative writer, in that he creates a world of his own or, more truly, he rearranges the things of his world and orders it in a new way that pleases him better. It would be incorrect to think that he does not take this world seriously; on the contrary, he takes his play very seriously and expends a great deal of emotion on it. The opposite of play is not serious occupation but—reality. Notwithstanding the large affective cathexis of his play-world, the child distinguishes it perfectly from reality; only he likes to borrow the objects and circumstances that he imagines from the tangible and visible things of the real world. It is only this linking of it to reality that still distinguishes a child's 'play' from 'day-dreaming'.

Now the writer does the same as the child at play; he creates a world of phantasy which he takes very seriously; that is, he invests it with a great deal of affect, while separating it sharply from reality. Language has preserved this relationship between children's play and poetic creation. It designates certain kinds of imaginative creation, concerned with tangible objects and capable of representation, as 'plays'; the people who present them are called 'players'. The unreality of this poetical world of imagination, however, has very important consequences for literary technique; for many things which if they happened in real life could produce no pleasure can nevertheless give enjoyment in a play—many emotions which are essentially painful may become a source of enjoyment to the spectators and hearers of a poet's work.

There is another consideration relating to the contrast between reality and play on which we will dwell for a moment. Long after a child has grown up and stopped playing, after he has for decades attempted to grasp the realities of life with all seriousness, he may one day come to a state of mind in which the contrast between play and reality is again abrogated. The adult can remember with what intense seriousness he carried on his childish play; then by comparing his would-be serious occupations with his childhood's play, he manages to throw off the heavy burden of life and obtain the great pleasure of humour.

As they grow up, people cease to play, and appear to give up the pleasure they derived from play. But anyone who knows anything of the mental life of human beings is aware that hardly anything is more difficult to them than to give up a pleasure they have once tasted. Really we never can relinquish anything; we only exchange one thing for something else. When we appear to give something up, all we really do is to adopt a substitute. So when the human being grows up and ceases to play he only gives up the connection with real objects; instead of playing he then begins to create phantasy. He builds castles in the air and creates what are called day-dreams. I believe that the greater number of human beings create phantasies at times as long as they live. This is a fact which has been overlooked for a long time, and its importance has therefore not been properly appreciated.

The phantasies of human beings are less easy to observe than the play of children. Children do, it is true, play alone, or form with other children a closed world in their minds for the purposes of play; but a child does not conceal his play from adults, even though his playing is quite unconcerned with them. The adult, on the other hand, is ashamed of his daydreams and conceals them from other people; he cherishes them as his most intimate possessions and as a rule he would rather confess all his misdeeds than tell his day-dreams. For this reason he may believe that he is the only person who makes up such phantasies, without having any idea that everybody else tells themselves stories of the same kind. Day-dreaming is a continuation of play, nevertheless, and the motives which lie behind these two activities contain a very good reason for this different behaviour in the child at play and in the day-dreaming adult.

The play of children is determined by their wishes—really by the child's *one* wish, which is to be grown-up, the wish that helps to 'bring him up'. He always plays at being grown-up; in play he imitates what is known to him of the lives of adults. Now he has no reason to conceal this wish. With the adult it is otherwise; on the one hand, he knows that he is expected not to play any longer or to day-dream, but to be making his way in a real world. On the other hand, some of the wishes from which his phantasies spring are such as have to be entirely hidden; therefore he is ashamed of his phantasies as being childish and as something prohibited.

If they are concealed with so much secretiveness, you will ask, how do we know so much about the human propensity to create phantasies? Now there is a certain class of human beings upon whom not a god, indeed, but a stern goddess—Necessity—has laid the task of giving an account of what they suffer and what they enjoy. These people are the neurotics; among other things they have to confess their phantasies to the physician to whom they go in the hope of recovering through mental treatment. This is our best source of knowledge, and we have later found good reason to suppose that our patients tell us about themselves nothing that we could not also hear from healthy people.

Let us try to learn some of the characteristics of day-dreaming. We can begin by saying that happy people never make phantasies, only unsatisfied ones. Unsatisfied wishes are the driving power behind phantasies; every separate phantasy contains the fulfilment of a wish, and improves on unsatisfactory reality. The impelling wishes vary according to the sex, character and circumstances of the creator; they may be easily divided, however, into two principal groups. Either they are ambitious wishes, serving to exalt the person creating them, or they are erotic. In young women erotic wishes dominate the phantasies almost exclusively, for their ambition is generally comprised in their erotic longings; in young men egoistic and ambitious wishes assert themselves plainly enough alongside their erotic desires. But we will not lay stress on the distinction between these two trends; we prefer to emphasize the fact that they are often united. In many altar-pieces the portrait of the donor is to be found in one corner of the picture; and in the greater number of ambitious day-dreams, too, we can discover a woman in some corner, for whom the dreamer performs all his heroic deeds and at whose feet all his triumphs are to be laid. Here you see we have strong enough motives for concealment; a well-brought-up woman is, indeed, credited with only a minimum of erotic desire, while a young man has to learn to suppress the overweening self-regard he acquires in the indulgent atmosphere surrounding his childhood, so that he may find his proper place in a society that is full of other persons making similar claims.

We must not imagine that the various products of this impulse towards phantasy, castles in the air or day-dreams, are stereotyped or unchangeable. On the contrary, they fit themselves into the changing impressions of life, alter with the vicissitudes of life; every deep new impression gives them what might be called a 'date-stamp'. The relation of phantasies to time is altogether of great importance. One may say that a phantasy at one and the same moment hovers between three periods of time—the three periods of our ideation. The activity of phantasy in the mind is linked up with some current impression, occasioned by some event in the present, which had the power to rouse an intense desire. From there it wanders back to the memory of an early experience, generally belonging to infancy, in which this wish was fulfilled. Then it creates for itself a situation which is to emerge in the future, representing the fulfilment of the wish—this is the day-dream or phantasy, which now carries in it traces both of the occasion which engendered it and of some past memory. So past, present and future are threaded, as it were, on the string of the wish that runs through them all.

A very ordinary example may serve to make my statement clearer. Take the case of a poor orphan lad, to whom you have given the address of some employer where he may perhaps get work. On the way there he falls into a day-dream suitable to the situation from which it springs. The content of the phantasy will be somewhat as follows: He is taken on and pleases his new employer, makes himself indispensable in the business, is taken into the family of the employer, and marries the charming daughter of the house. Then he comes to conduct the business first as a partner, and then as successor to his father-in-law. In this way the dreamer regains what he had in his happy childhood, the protecting house, his loving parents and the first objects of his affection. You will see from such an example how the wish employs some event in the present to plan a future on the pattern of the past.

Much more could be said about phantasies, but I will only allude as briefly as possible to certain points. If phantasies become over-luxuriant and over-powerful, the necessary conditions for an outbreak of neurosis or psychosis are constituted; phantasies are also the first preliminary stage in the mind of the symptoms of illness of which our patients complain. A broad by-path here branches off into pathology.

I cannot pass over the relation of phantasies to dreams. Our nocturnal dreams are nothing but such phantasies, as we can make clear by interpreting them. Language, in its unrivalled wisdom, long ago decided the question of the essential nature of dreams by giving the name of 'day-dreams' to the airy creations of phantasy. If the meaning of our dreams usually remains obscure in spite of this clue, it is because of the circumstance that at night wishes of which we are ashamed also become active in us, wishes which we have to hide from ourselves, which were consequently repressed and pushed back into the unconscious. Such repressed wishes and their derivatives can therefore achieve expression only when almost completely disguised. When scientific work had succeeded in elucidating the distortion in dreams, it was no longer difficult to recognize that nocturnal dreams are fulfilments of desires in exactly the same way as day-dreams are—those phantasies with which we are all so familiar.

So much for day-dreaming; now for the poet! Shall we dare really to compare an imaginative writer with 'one who dreams in broad daylight', and his creations with day-dreams? Here, surely, a first distinction is forced upon us; we must distinguish between poets who, like the bygone creators of epics and tragedies, take over their material ready-made, and those who seem to create their material spontaneously. Let us keep to the latter, and let us also not choose for our comparison those writers who are most highly esteemed by critics. We will choose the less pretentious writers of romances, novels and stories, who are read all the same by the widest circles of men and women. There is one very marked characteristic in the productions of these writers which must strike us all: they all have a hero who is the centre of interest, for whom the author tries to win our sympathy by every possible means, and whom he places under the protection of a special providence. If at the end of one chapter the hero is left unconscious and bleeding from severe wounds, I am sure to find him at the beginning of the next being carefully tended and on the way to recovery; if the first volume ends in the hero being shipwrecked in a storm at sea, I am certain to hear at the beginning of the next of his hairbreadth escape—otherwise, indeed, the story could not continue. The feeling of security with which I follow the hero through his dangerous adventures is the same as that with which a real hero throws himself into the water to save a drowning man, or exposes himself to the fire of the enemy while storming a battery. It is this very feeling of being a hero which one of our best authors has well expressed in the famous phrase, '*Es kann dir nix g'schehen!*' It seems to me, however, that this significant mark of invulnerability very clearly betrays—His Majesty the Ego, the hero of all day-dreams and all novels.

The same relationship is hinted at in yet other characteristics of these egocentric stories. When all the women in a novel invariably fall in love with the hero, this can hardly be looked upon as a description of reality, but it is easily understood as an essential constituent of a day-dream. The same thing holds good when the other people in the story are sharply divided into good and bad, with complete disregard of the manifold variety in the traits of real human beings; the 'good' ones are those who help the ego in its character of hero, while the 'bad' are his enemies and rivals.

We do not in any way fail to recognize that many imaginative productions have travelled far from the original naïve day-dream, but I cannot suppress the surmise that even the most extreme variations could be brought into relationship with this model by an uninterrupted series of transitions. It has struck me in many so-called psychological novels, too, that only one person—once again the hero—is described from within; the author dwells in his soul and looks upon the other people from outside. The psychological novel in general probably owes its peculiarities to the tendency of modern writers to split up their ego by self-observation into many component-egos, and in this way to personify the conflicting trends in their own mental life in many heroes. There are certain novels, which might be called 'excentric,' that seem to stand in marked contradiction to the typical day-dream; in these the person introduced as the hero plays the least active part of anyone, and seems instead to let the actions and sufferings of other people pass him by like a spectator. Many of the later novels of Zola belong to this class. But I must say that the psychological analysis of people who are not writers, and who deviate in many things from the so-called norm, has shown us analogous variations in their daydreams in which the ego contents itself with the role of spectator.

If our comparison of the imaginative writer with the day-dreamer, and of poetic production with the day-dream, is to be of any value, it must show itself fruitful in some way or other. Let us try, for instance, to examine the works of writers in reference to the idea propounded above, the relation of the phantasy to the wish that runs through it and to the three periods of time; and with its help let us study the connection between the life of the writer and his productions. Hitherto it has not been known what preliminary ideas would constitute an approach to this problem; very often this relation has been regarded as much simpler than it is; but the insight gained from phantasies leads us to expect the following state of things. Some actual experience which made a strong impression on the writer had stirred up a memory of an earlier experience, generally belonging to childhood, which then arouses a wish that finds a fulfilment in the work in question, and in which elements of the recent event and the old memory should be discernible.

Do not be alarmed at the complexity of this formula; I myself expect that in reality it will prove itself to be too schematic, but that possibly it may contain a first means of approach to the true state of affairs. From some attempts I have made I think that this way of approaching works of the imagination might not be unfruitful. You will not forget that the stress laid on the writer's memories of his childhood, which perhaps seems so strange, is ultimately derived from the hypothesis that imaginative creation, like day-dreaming, is a continuation of and substitute for the play of childhood.

We will not neglect to refer also to that class of imaginative work which must be recognized not as spontaneous production, but as a re-fashioning of ready-made material. Here, too, the writer retains a certain amount of independence, which can express itself in the choice of material and in changes in the material chosen, which are often considerable. As far as it goes, this material is derived from the racial treasure-house of myths, legends and fairy-tales. The study of these creations of racial psychology is in no way complete, but it seems extremely probable that myths, for example, are distorted vestiges of the wish-phantasies of whole nations—the age-long dreams of young humanity.

You will say that, although writers came first in the title of this paper, I have told you far less about them than about phantasy. I am aware of that, and will try to excuse myself by pointing to the present state of our knowledge. I could only throw out suggestions and bring up interesting points which arise from the study of phantasies, and which pass beyond them to the problem of the choice of literary material. We have not touched on the other problem at all, *i.e.* what are the means which writers use to achieve those emotional reactions in us that are roused by their productions. But I would at least point out to you the path which leads from our discussion of day-dreams to the problems of the effect produced on us by imaginative works.

You will remember that we said the day-dreamer hid his phantasies carefully from other people because he had reason to be ashamed of them. I may now add that even if he were to communicate them to us, he would give us no pleasure by his disclosures. When we hear such phantasies they repel us, or at least leave us cold. But when a man of literary talent presents his plays, or relates what we take to be his personal day-dreams, we experience great pleasure arising probably from many sources. How the writer accomplishes this is his innermost secret; the essential *ars poetica* lies in the technique by which our feeling of repulsion is overcome, and this has certainly to do with those barriers erected between every individual being and all others. We can guess at two methods used in this technique. The writer softens the egotistical character of the day-dream by changes and disguises, and he bribes us by the offer of a purely formal, that is, aesthetic, pleasure in the presentation of his phantasies. The increment of pleasure which is offered us in order to release yet greater pleasure arising from deeper sources in the mind is called an 'incitement premium' or technically, 'fore-pleasure'. I am of opinion that all the aesthetic pleasure we gain from the works of imaginative writers is of the same type as this 'fore-pleasure,' and that the true enjoyment of literature proceeds from the release of tensions in our minds. Perhaps much that brings about this result consists in the writer's putting us into a position in which we can enjoy our own day-dreams without reproach or shame. Here we reach a path leading into novel, interesting and complicated researches, but we also, at least for the present, arrive at the end of the present discussion.

Discussion Questions

1. How does Freud extend the analogy between child's play and phantasy? List the characteristics they have in common. Can you think of any similarities Freud doesn't cover?

2. What important differences are there between child's play and phantasy? In what way are these differences important to Freud's argument?

3. What part do sex differences play in Freud's analysis? How are these differences borne out in his example of the "poor orphan lad"?

4. How does Freud's idea of a "poet" change as his essay proceeds? What sort of "poet" is Freud actually discussing?

5. What does Freud admit he falls short of explaining in this essay?

6. What Freud says about the relationship between phantasy and imaginative writing could also be said of the movies. Choose a new or old movie you have seen recently and in a brief essay discuss its phantasy elements. Try to select a film meant to be "realistic" so that your discussion of its "day-dream" elements has more point.

ERICH FROMM

Erich Fromm (1900–1980) was born in Frankfurt, Germany. He received his doctorate from Heidelberg in 1922 and then continued his education in psychoanalysis in Munich and Berlin. He left Germany during the Nazi rise to power and in 1934 moved to the United States, where he eventually became a citizen. He taught psychiatry and psychoanalysis at New York University, Columbia, Bennington, and the National University of Mexico. One of the most broadly popular psychoanalysts, Fromm specialized in the relationship between individuals and their culture and society. In his influential book, The Art of Loving (1956), Fromm maintained that "love is the only sane and satisfactory answer to the problem of human existence." Among his many books are Escape from Freedom (1941), The Sane Society (1955), Zen Buddhism and Psychoanalysis (1960), and The Well-Being of Man and Society: Essays on a Humanistic Psychology (1978).

The following selection originally appeared as a chapter in The Forgotten Language: An Introduction to the Understanding of Dreams, Fairy Tales, and Myths *(1951), a ground-breaking study of the interplay between individual fantasy and social control.*

The Nature of Symbolic Language

Let us assume you want to tell someone the difference between the taste of white wine and red wine. This may seem quite simple to you. *You* know the difference very well; why should it not be easy to explain it to someone else? Yet you find the greatest difficulty putting this taste difference into words. And probably you will end up by saying, "Now look here, I can't explain it to you. Just drink red wine and then white wine, and you will know what the difference is." You have no difficulty in finding words to explain the most complicated machine, and yet words seem to be futile to describe a simple taste experience.

Are we not confronted with the same difficulty when we try to explain a feeling experience? Let us take a mood in which you feel lost, deserted, where the world looks gray, a little frightening though not really dangerous. You want to describe this mood to a friend, but again you find yourself groping for words and eventually feel that nothing you have said is an adequate explanation of the many nuances of the mood. The following night you have a dream. You see yourself in the outskirts of a city just before dawn, the streets are empty except for a milk wagon, the houses look poor, the surroundings are unfamiliar, you have no means of accustomed transportation to places familiar to you and where you feel you belong. When you wake up and remember the dream, it occurs to you that the feeling you had in that dream was exactly the feeling of lostness and grayness you tried to describe to your friend the day before. It is just one picture, whose visualization took less than a second. And yet this picture is a more vivid and precise description than you could have given by talking *about* it at length. The picture you see in the dream is a *symbol* of something you felt.

What is a symbol? A symbol is often defined as "something

that stands for something else." This definition seems rather disappointing. It becomes more interesting, however, if we concern ourselves with those symbols which are sensory expressions of seeing, hearing, smelling, touching, standing for a "something else" which is an inner experience, a feeling or thought. A symbol of this kind is something outside ourselves; that which it symbolizes is something inside ourselves. Symbolic language is language in which we express inner experience as if it were a sensory experience, as if it were something we were doing or something that was done to us in the world of things. Symbolic language is language in which the world outside is a symbol of the world inside, a symbol for our souls and our minds.

If we define a symbol as "something which stands for something else," the crucial question is: *What is the specific connection between the symbol and that which it symbolizes?*

In answer to this question we can differentiate between three kinds of symbols: the *conventional,* the *accidental* and the *universal* symbol. As will become apparent presently, only the latter two kinds of symbols express inner experiences as if they were sensory experiences, and only they have the elements of symbolic language.

The *conventional* symbol is the best known of the three, since we employ it in everday language. If we see the word "table" or hear the sound "table," the letters T-A-B-L-E stand for something else. They stand for the thing table that we see, touch and use. What is the connection between the *word* "table" and the *thing* "table"? Is there any inherent relationship between them? Obviously not. The thing table has nothing to do with the sound table, and the only reason the word symbolizes the thing is the convention of calling this particular thing by a particular name. We learn this connection as children by the repeated experience of hearing the word in reference to the thing until a lasting association is formed so that we don't have to think to find the right word.

There are some words, however, where the association is not only conventional. When we say "phooey," for instance, we make with our lips a movement of dispelling the air quickly. It is an expression of disgust in which our mouths participate. By this quick expulsion of air we imitate and thus express our intention to expel something, to get it out of our system. In this case, as in some others, the symbol has an inherent connection with the feeling it symbolizes. But even if we assume that originally many or even all words had their origins in some such inherent connection between symbol and the symbolized, most words no longer have this meaning for us when we learn a language.

Words are not the only illustration for conventional symbols, although they are the most frequent and best-known ones. Pictures also can be conventional symbols. A flag, for instance, may stand for a specific country, and yet there is no connection between the specific colors and the country for which they stand. They have been accepted as denoting that particular country, and we translate the visual impression of the flag into the concept of that country, again on conventional grounds. Some pictorial symbols are not entirely conventional; for example, the cross. The cross can be merely a conventional symbol of the Christian church and in that respect no different from a flag. But the specific content of the cross referring to Jesus' death or, beyond that, to the interpenetration of the material and spiritual planes, puts the connection between the symbol and what it symbolizes beyond the level of mere conventional symbols.

The very opposite to the conventional symbol is the *accidental* symbol, although they have one thing in common: there is no intrinsic relationship between the symbol and that which it symbolizes. Let us assume that someone has had a saddening experience in a certain city; when he hears the name of that city, he will easily connect the name with a mood of sadness, just as he would connect it with a mood of joy had his experience been a happy one. Quite obviously there is nothing in the nature of the city that is either sad or joyful. It is the individual experience connected with the city that makes it a symbol of a mood.

The same reaction could occur in connection with a house, a street, a certain dress, certain scenery, or anything once connected with a specific mood. We might find ourselves dreaming that we are in a certain city. In fact, there may be no particular mood connected with it in the dream; all we see is a street or even simply the name of the city. We ask ourselves why we happened to think of that city in our sleep in a mood similar to the one symbolized by the city. The picture in the dream represents this mood, the city "stands for" the mood once experienced in it. Here the connection between the symbol and the experience symbolized is entirely accidental.

In contrast to the conventional symbol, the accidental symbol cannot be shared by anyone else except as we relate the events connected with the symbol. For this reason accidental symbols are rarely used in myths, fairy tales, or works of art written in symbolic language because they are not communicable unless the writer adds a lengthy comment to each symbol he uses. In dreams, however, accidental symbols are frequent, and later in this book I shall explain the method of understanding them.

The *universal* symbol is one in which there is an intrinsic relationship between the symbol and that which it represents. We have already given one example, that of the outskirts of the city. The sensory experience of a deserted, strange, poor environment has indeed a significant relationship to a mood of lostness and anxiety. True enough, if we have never been in the outskirts of a city we could not use that symbol, just as the word "table" would be meaningless had we never seen a table. This symbol is meaningful only to city dwellers and would be meaningless to people living in cultures that have no big cities. Many other universal symbols, however, are rooted in the experience of every human being. Take, for instance, the symbol of fire. We are fascinated by certain qualities of fire in a fireplace. First of all, by its aliveness. It changes continuously, it moves all the time, and yet there is constancy in it. It remains the same without being the same. It gives the impression of power, of energy, of grace and lightness. It is as if it were dancing and had an inexhaustible source of energy. When we use fire as a symbol, we describe the inner experience characterized by the same elements which we notice in the sensory experience of fire; the mood of energy, lightness, movement, grace, gaiety—sometimes one, sometimes another of these elements being predominant in the feeling.

Similar in some ways and different in others is the symbol of water—of the ocean or of the stream. Here, too, we find the blending of change and permanence, of constant movement and yet of permanence. We also feel the quality of aliveness, continuity and energy. But there is a difference; where fire is adventurous, quick, exciting, water is quiet, slow and steady. Fire has an element of surprise; water an element of predictability. Water symbolizes the mood of aliveness, too, but one which is "heavier," "slower," and more comforting than exciting.

That a phenomenon of the physical world can be the adequate expression of an inner experience, that the world of things can be a symbol of the world of the mind, is not surprising. We all know that our bodies express our minds. Blood rushes to our heads when we are furious, it rushes away from them when we are afraid; our hearts beat more quickly when we are angry, and the whole body has a different tonus if we are happy from the one it has when we are sad. We express our moods by our facial expressions and our attitudes and feelings by movements and gestures so precise that others recognize them more accurately from our gestures than from our words. Indeed, the body is a symbol—and not an allegory—of the mind. Deeply and genuinely felt emotion, and even any genuinely felt thought, is expressed in our whole organism. In the case of the universal symbol, we find the same connection between mental and physical experience. Certain physical phenomena suggest by their very nature certain emotional and mental experiences, and we express emotional experiences in the language of physical experiences, that is to say, symbolically.

The universal symbol is the only one in which the relationship between the symbol and that which is symbolized is not coincidental but intrinsic. It is rooted in the experience of the affinity between an emotion or thought, on the one hand, and a sensory experience, on the other. It can be called universal because it is shared by all men, in contrast not only to the accidental symbol, which is by its very nature entirely personal, but also to the conventional symbol, which is restricted to a group of people sharing the same convention. The universal symbol is rooted in the properties of our body, our senses, and our mind, which are common to all men and, therefore, not restricted to individuals or to specific groups. Indeed, the language of the universal symbol is the one common tongue developed by the human race, a language which it forgot before it succeeded in developing a universal conventional language.

There is no need to speak of a racial inheritance in order to explain the universal character of symbols. Every human being who shares the essential features of bodily and mental equipment with the rest of mankind is capable of speaking and understanding the symbolic language that is based upon these common properties. Just as we do not need to learn to cry when we are sad or to get red in the face when we are angry, and just as these reactions are not restricted to any particular race or group of people, symbolic language does not have to be learned and is not restricted to any segment of the human race. Evidence for this is to be found in the fact that symbolic language as it is employed in myths and dreams is found in all cultures in so-called primitive as well as such highly developed cultures as Egypt and Greece. Furthermore, the symbols used in these various cultures are strikingly similar since they all go back to the basic sensory as well as emotional experiences shared by men of all cultures. Added evidence is to be found in recent experiments in which people who had no knowledge of the theory of dream interpretation were able, under hypnosis, to interpret the symbolism of their dreams without any difficulty. After emerging from the hypnotic state and being asked to interpret the same dreams, they were puzzled and said, "Well, there is no meaning to them—it is just nonsense."

The foregoing statement needs qualification, however. Some symbols differ in meaning according to the difference in their realistic significance in various cultures. For instance, the function and consequently the meaning of the sun is different in northern countries and in tropical countries. In northern countries, where water is plentiful, all growth depends on sufficient sunshine. The sun is the warm, life-giving, protecting, loving power. In the Near East, where the heat of the sun is much more powerful, the sun is a dangerous and even threatening power from which man must protect himself, while water is felt to be the source of all life and the main condition for growth. We may speak of dialects of universal symbolic language, which are determined by those differences in natural conditions which cause certain symbols to have a different meaning in different regions of the earth.

Quite different from these "symbolic dialects" is the fact that many symbols have more than one meaning in accordance with different kinds of experiences which can be connected with one and the same natural phenomenon. Let us take up the symbol of fire again. If we watch fire in the fireplace, which is a source of pleasure and comfort, it is expressive of a mood of aliveness, warmth, and pleasure. But if we see a building or forest on fire, it conveys to us an experience of threat or terror, of the powerlessness of man against the elements of nature. Fire, then, can be the symbolic representation of inner aliveness and happiness as well as of fear, powerlessness, or of one's own destructive tendencies. The same holds true of the symbol water. Water can be a most destructive force when it is whipped up by a storm or when a swollen river floods its banks. Therefore, it can be the symbolic expression of horror and chaos as well as of comfort and peace.

Another illustration of the same principle is a symbol of a valley. The valley enclosed between mountains can arouse in us the feeling of security and comfort, of protection against all dangers from the outside. But the protecting mountains can also mean isolating walls which do not permit us to get out of the valley and thus the valley can become a symbol of imprisonment. The particular meaning of the symbol in any given place can only be determined from the whole context in which the symbol appears, and in terms of the predominant experiences of the person using the symbol. We shall return to this question in our discussion of dream symbolism.

A good illustration of the function of the universal symbol is a story, written in symbolic language, which is known to almost everyone in Western culture: the Book of Jonah. Jonah has heard God's voice telling him to go to Nineveh and preach to its inhabitants to give up their evil ways lest they be destroyed. Jonah cannot help hearing God's voice and that is why he is a prophet. But he is an unwilling prophet, who, though knowing what he should do, tries to run away from the command of God (or, as we may say, the voice of his conscience). He is a man who does not care for other human beings. He is a man with a strong sense of law and order, but without love.

How does the story express the inner processes in Jonah?

We are told that Jonah went down to Joppa and found a ship which should bring him to Tarshish. In mid-ocean a storm rises and, while everyone else is excited and afraid, Jonah goes into the ship's belly and falls into a deep sleep. The sailors, believing that God must have sent the storm because someone on the ship is to be punished, wake Jonah, who had told them he was trying to flee from God's command. He tells them to take him and cast him forth into the sea and that the sea would then become calm. The sailors (betraying a remarkable sense of humanity by first trying everything else before following his advice) eventually take Jonah and cast him into the sea, which immediately stops raging. Jonah is swallowed by a big fish and stays in the fish's belly three days and three nights. He prays to God to free him from this prison. God makes the fish vomit out Jonah unto the dry land and Jonah goes to Nineveh, fulfills God's command, and thus saves the inhabitants of the city.

The story is told as if these events had actually happened. However, it is written in symbolic language and all the realistic events described are symbols for the inner experiences of the hero. We find a sequence of symbols which follow one another: going into the ship, going into the ship's belly, falling asleep, being in the ocean, and being in the fish's belly. All these symbols stand for the same inner experience: for a condition of being protected and isolated, of safe withdrawal from communication with other human beings. They represent what could be represented in another symbol, the fetus in the mother's womb. Different as the ship's belly, deep sleep, the ocean, and a fish's belly are realistically, they are expressive of the same inner experience, of the blending between protection and isolation.

In the manifest story events happen in space and time: *first*, going into the ship's belly; *then*, falling asleep; *then*, being thrown into the ocean; *then*, being swallowed by the fish. One thing happens after the other and, although some events are obviously unrealistic, the story has its own logical consistency in terms of time and space. But if we understand that the writer did not intend to tell us the story of external events, but of the inner experience of a man torn between his conscience and his wish to escape from his inner voice, it becomes clear that his various actions following one after the other express the same mood in him; and that *sequence in time* is expressive of a *growing intensity* of the same feeling. In his attempt to escape from his obligation to his fellow men Jonah isolates himself more and more until, in the belly of the fish, the protective element has so given way to the imprisoning element that he can stand it no longer and is forced to pray to God to be released from where he had put himself. (This is a mechanism which we find so characteristic of neurosis. An attitude is assumed as a defense against a danger, but then it grows far beyond its original defense function and becomes a neurotic symptom from which the person tries to be relieved.) Thus Jonah's escape into protective isolation ends in the terror of being imprisoned, and he takes up his life at the point where he had tried to escape.

There is another difference between the logic of the manifest and of the latent story. In the manifest story the logical connection is one of causality of external events. Jonah wants to go overseas *because* he wants to flee from God, he falls asleep *because* he is tired, he is thrown overboard *because* he is supposed to be the reason for the storm, and he is swallowed by the fish *because* there are man-eating fish in the ocean. One event occurs because of a previous event. (The last part of the story is unrealistic but not illogical.) But in the latent story the logic is different. The various events are related to each other by their association with the same inner experience. What appears to be a causal sequence of external events stands for a connection of experiences linked with each other by their association in terms of inner events. This is as logical as the manifest story—but it is a logic of a different kind. If we turn now to an examination of the nature of the dream, the logic governing symbolic language will become more transparent.

Discussion Questions

1. In what way are "conventional" and "accidental" symbols similar? How do they differ? How does each differ from a "universal" symbol?

2. Reread Fromm's analysis of the story of Jonah. Is his interpretation a religious one? Why or why not? Why do you think Fromm focuses his analysis on the internal conflicts in Jonah rather than on the external events of the tale? Can you think of another way to interpret the story?

THE NATURE OF SYMBOLIC LANGUAGE

3. Compare Fromm's analysis of the Biblical story of Jonah to DuBois's analysis of Jacob and Esau. How would you describe the differences between these two Biblical interpretations?

4. What do universal symbols have in common? What can occasionally cause them to have different meanings? Do you think these different meanings weaken Fromm's case for their universality? Explain.

5. Advertising art often makes use of a symbolic language. Using Fromm's distinctions among various kinds of symbols, write an analysis of the symbolic language of an advertisement of your choice. It might also help to read Daniel J. Boorstin's "The Rhetoric of Democracy" as preparation for this assignment.

Robert Frost

Robert Frost (1874–1963) supported himself as a newspaper editor, school teacher, and farmer while writing the poetry that was not to find a commercial publisher in this country until after the success of A Boy's Will, *published in England in 1913. After he became better known, Frost continued to farm from time to time, but more consistently became a figure adorning colleges and universities—most especially Amherst and Michigan—where he worked first as an English teacher and later as a poet in residence. By the time of his death he had become the best loved and most widely known of American poets and was unofficial poet laureate to the nation. How closely education and poetry associated themselves for Frost may be learned from the following essay, which was first delivered as a talk before the Amherst College Alumni Council in 1930 and later appeared in* Selected Prose of Robert Frost *(1966).*

Education By Poetry

I am going to urge nothing in my talk. I am not an advocate. I am going to consider a matter, and commit a description. And I am going to describe other colleges than Amherst. Or, rather say all that is good can be taken as about Amherst; all that is bad will be about other colleges.

I know whole colleges where all American poetry is barred—whole colleges. I know whole colleges where all contemporary poetry is barred.

I once heard of a minister who turned his daughter—his poetry-writing daughter—out on the street to earn a living, because he said there should be no more books written; God wrote one book, and that was enough. (My friend George Russell "Æ" has read no literature, he protests, since just before Chaucer.)

That all seems sufficiently safe, and you can say one thing for it. It takes the onus off the poetry of having to be used to teach children anything. It comes pretty hard on poetry, I sometimes think—what it has to bear in the teaching process.

Then I know whole colleges where, though they let in older poetry, they manage to bar all that is poetical in it by treating it as something other than poetry. It is not so hard to do that. Their reason I have often hunted for. It may be that these people act from a kind of modesty. Who are professors that they should attempt to deal with a thing as high and as fine as poetry? Who are *they*? There is a certain manly modesty in that.

That is the best general way of settling the problem; treat all poetry as if it were something else than poetry, as if it were syntax, language, science. Then you can even come down into the American and into the contemporary without any special risk.

There is another reason they have, and that is that they are, first and foremost in life, markers. They have the marking problem to consider. Now, I stand here a teacher of many years' experience and I have never complained of having had to mark. I had rather mark anyone for anything—for his looks, carriage, his ideas, his correctness, his exactness, anything you please,—I would rather give him a mark in terms of letters, A, B, C, D, than have to use adjectives on him. We are all being marked by each other all the time, classified, ranked, put in our place, and I see no escape from that. I am no sentimentalist. You have got to mark, and you have got to mark, first of all, for accuracy, for correctness. But if I am going to give a mark, that is the least part of my marking. The hard part is the part beyond that, the part where the adventure begins.

One other way to rid the curriculum of the poetry nuisance has been considered. More merciful than the others it would neither abolish nor denature the poetry, but only turn it out to disport itself, with the plays and games—in no wise discredited, though given no credit for. Any one who liked to teach poetically could take his subject, whether English, Latin, Greek or French, out into the nowhere along with the poetry. One side of a sharp line would be left to the rigorous and righteous; the other side would be assigned to the flowery where they would know what could be expected of them. Grade marks where more easily given, of course, in the courses concentrating on correctness and exactness as the only forms of honesty recognized by plain people; a general indefinite mark of X in the courses that scatter brains over taste and opinion. On inquiry I have found no teacher willing to take position on either side of the line, either among the rigors or among the flowers. No one is willing to admit that his discipline is not partly in exactness. No one is willing to admit that his discipline is not partly in taste and enthusiasm.

How shall a man go through college without having been marked for taste and judgment? What will become of him? What will his end be? He will have to take continuation courses for college graduates. He will have to go to night schools. They are having night schools now, you know, for college graduates. Why? Because they have not been educated enough to find their way around in contemporary literature. They don't know what they may safely like in the libraries and galleries. They don't know how to judge an editorial when they see one. They don't know how to judge a political campaign. They don't know when they are being fooled by a metaphor, an analogy, a parable. And metaphor is, of course, what we are talking about. Education by poetry is education by metaphor.

Suppose we stop short of imagination, initiative, enthusiasm, inspiration and originality—dread words. Suppose we don't mark in such things at all. There are still two minimal things, that we have got to take care of, taste and judgment. Americans are supposed to have more judgment than taste, but taste is there to be dealt with. That is what poetry, the only art in the colleges of arts, is there for. I for my part would not be afraid to go in for enthusiasm. There is the enthusiasm like a blinding light, or the enthusiasm of the deafening shout, the crude enthusiasm that you get uneducated by poetry, outside of poetry. It is exemplified in what I might call "sunset raving." You look westward toward the sunset, or if you get up early enough, eastward toward the sunrise, and you rave. It is oh's and ah's with you and no more.

But the enthusiasm I mean is taken through the prism of the intellect and spread on the screen in a color, all the way from hyperbole at one end—or overstatement, at one end—to understatement at the other end. It is a long strip of dark lines and many colors. Such enthusiasm is one object of all teaching in poetry. I heard wonderful things said about Virgil yesterday, and many of them seemed to me crude enthusiasm, more like a deafening shout, many of them. But one speech had range, something of overstatement, something of statement, and something of understatement. It had all the colors of an enthusiasm passed through an idea.

I would be willing to throw away everything else but that: enthusiasm tamed by metaphor. Let me rest the case there. Enthusiasm tamed to metaphor, tamed to that much of it. I do not think anybody ever knows the discreet use of metaphor, his own and other people's, the discreet handling of metaphor, unless he has been properly educated in poetry.

Poetry begins in trivial metaphors, pretty metaphors, "grace" metaphors, and goes on to the profoundest thinking that we have. Poetry provides the one permissible way of saying one thing and meaning another. People say, "Why don't you say what you mean?" We never do that, do we, being all of us too much poets. We like to talk in parables and in hints and in indirections— whether from diffidence or some other instinct.

I have wanted in late years to go further and further in making metaphor the whole of thinking. I find some one now and then to agree with me that all thinking, except mathematical thinking, is metaphorical, or all thinking except scientific thinking. The mathematical might be difficult for me to bring in, but the scientific is easy enough.

Once on a time all the Greeks were busy telling each other what the All was—or was like unto. All was three elements, air, earth, and water (we once thought it was ninety elements; now we think it is only one). All was substance, said another. All was change, said a third. But best and most fruitful was Pythagoras' comparison of the universe with number. Number of what? Number of feet, pounds, and seconds was the answer, and we had science and all that has followed in science. The metaphor has held and held, breaking down only when it came to the spiritual and psychological or the out of the way places of the physical.

The other day we had a visitor here, a noted scientist, whose latest word to the world has been that the more accurately you know where a thing is, the less accurately you are able to state how fast it is moving. You can see why that would be so, without going back to Zeno's problem of the arrow's flight. In carrying numbers into the realm of space and at the same time into the realm of time you are mixing metaphors, that is all, and you are in trouble. They won't mix. The two don't go together.

Let's take two or three more of the metaphors now in use to live by. I have just spoken of one of the new ones, a charming mixed metaphor right in the realm of higher mathematics and higher physics: that the more accurately you state where a thing is, the less accurately you will be able to tell how fast it is moving. And, of course, everything is moving. Everything is an event now. Another metaphor. A thing, they say, is an event. Do you believe it is? Not quite. I believe it is almost an event. But I like the comparison of a thing with an event.

I notice another from the same quarter. "In the neighborhood of matter space is something like curved." Isn't that a good one! It seems to me that that is simply and utterly charming—to say that space is something like curved in the neighborhood of matter. "Something like."

Another amusing one is from—what is the book?—I can't say it now; but here is the metaphor. Its aim is to restore you to your ideas of free will. It wants to give you back your freedom of will. All right, here it is on a platter. You know that you can't tell by name what persons in a certain class will be dead ten years after graduation, but you can tell actuarially how many will be dead. Now, just so this scientist says of the particles of matter flying at a screen, striking a screen; you can't tell what individual particles will come, but you can say in general that a certain number will strike in a given time. It shows, you see, that the individual particle can come freely. I asked Bohr about that particularly, and he said, "Yes, it is so. It can come when it wills and as it wills; and the action of the individual particle is unpredictable. But it is not so of the action of the mass. There you can predict." He says, "That gives the individual atom its freedom, but the mass its necessity."

Another metaphor that has interested us in our time and has done all our thinking for us is the metaphor of evolution. Never mind going into the Latin word. The metaphor is simply the metaphor of the growing plant or of the growing thing. And somebody very brilliantly, quite a while ago, said that the whole universe, the whole of everything, was like unto a growing thing. That is all. I know the metaphor will break down at some point, but it has not failed everywhere. It is a very brilliant metaphor, I acknowledge, though I myself get too tired of the kind of essay that talks about the evolution of candy, we will say, or the evolution of elevators—the evolution of this, that, and the other. Everything is evolution. I emancipate myself by simply saying that I didn't get up the metaphor and so am not much interested in it.

What I am pointing out is that unless you are at home in the metaphor, unless you have had your proper poetical education in the metaphor, you are not safe anywhere. Because you are not at ease with figurative values: you don't know the metaphor in its strength and its weakness. You don't know how far you may expect to ride it and when it may break down with you. You are not safe in science; you are not safe in history. In history, for instance—to show that [it] is the same in history as elsewhere—I heard somebody say yesterday that Aeneas was to be likened unto (those words, "likened unto"!) George Washington. He was that type of national hero, the middle-class man, not thinking of being a hero at all, bent on building the future, bent on his children, his descendants. A good metaphor, as far as it goes, and you must know how far. And then he added that Odysseus should be likened unto Theodore Roosevelt. I don't think that is so good. Someone visiting Gibbon at the point of death, said he was the same Gibbon as of old, still at his parallels.

Take the way we have been led into our present position morally, the world over. It is by a sort of metaphorical gradient. There is a kind of thinking—to speak metaphorically—there is a kind of thinking you might say was endemic in the brothel. It is always there. And every now and then in some mysterious way it becomes epidemic in the world. And how does it do so? By using all the good words that virtue has invented to maintain virtue. It uses honesty, first,—frankness, sincerity—those words; picks them up, uses them. "In the name of honesty, let us see what we are." You know. And then it picks up the word joy. "Let us in the name of joy, which is the enemy of our ancestors, the Puritans . . . Let us in the name of joy, which is the enemy of the kill-joy Puritan . . ." You see. "Let us," and so on. And then, "In the name of health . . ." Health is another good word. And that is the metaphor Freudianism trades on, mental health. And the first thing we know, it has us all in up to the top knot. I suppose we may blame the artists a good deal, because they are great people to spread by metaphor. The stage too—the stage is always a good intermediary between the two worlds, the under and the upper—if I may say so without personal prejudice to the stage.

In all this I have only been saying that the devil can quote Scripture, which simply means that the good words you have lying around the devil can use for his purposes as well as anybody else. Never mind about my morality. I am not here to urge anything. I don't care whether the world is good or bad—not on any particular day.

Let me ask you to watch a metaphor breaking down here before you.

Somebody said to me a little while ago, "It is easy enough for me to think of the universe as a machine, as a mechanism."

I said, "You mean the universe is like a machine?"

He said, "No, I think it is one . . . Well, it is like . . ."

"I think you mean the universe is like a machine."

"All right. Let it go at that."

I asked him, "Did you ever see a machine without a pedal for the foot, or a lever for the hand, or a button for the finger?"

He said, "No—no."

I said, "All right. Is the universe like that?"

And he said, "No. I mean it is like a machine, only . . ."

". . . it is different from a machine," I said.

He wanted to go just that far with that metaphor and no further. And so do we all. All metaphor breaks down somewhere. That is the beauty of it. It is touch and go with the metaphor, and until you have lived with it long enough you don't know when it is going. You don't know how much you can get out of it and when it will cease to yield. It is a very living thing. It is as life itself.

I have heard this ever since I can remember, and ever since I have taught: the teacher must teach the pupil to think. I saw a teacher once going around in a great school and snapping pupils' heads with thumb and finger and saying, "Think." That was when thinking was becoming the fashion. The fashion hasn't yet quite gone out.

We still ask boys in college to think, as in the nineties, but we seldom tell them what thinking means; we seldom tell them it is just putting this and that together; it is just saying one thing in terms of another. To tell them is to set their feet on the first rung of a ladder the top of which sticks through the sky.

Greatest of all attempts to say one thing in terms of another is the philosophical attempt to say matter in terms of spirit, or spirit in terms of matter, to make the final unity. That is the greatest attempt that ever failed. We stop just short there. But it is the height of poetry, the height of all thinking, the height of all poetic thinking, that attempt to say matter in terms of spirit and spirit in terms of matter. It is wrong to call anybody a materialist simply because he tries to say spirit in terms of matter, as if that were a sin. Materialism is not the attempt to say all in terms of matter. The only materialist—be he poet, teacher, scientist, politician, or statesman—is the man who gets lost in his material without a gathering metaphor to throw it into shape and order. He is the lost soul.

We ask people to think, and we don't show them what thinking is. Somebody says we don't need to show them how to think; bye and bye they will think. We will give them the forms of sentences and, if they have any ideas, then they will know how to write them. But that is preposterous. All there is to writing is having ideas. To learn to write is to learn to have ideas.

The first little metaphor . . . Take some of the trivial ones. I would rather have trivial ones of my own to live by than the big ones of other people.

I remember a boy saying, "He is the kind of person that wounds with his shield." That may be a slender one, of course. It goes a good way in character description. It has poetic grace. "He is the kind that wounds with his shield."

The shield reminds me—just to linger a minute—the shield reminds me of the inverted shield spoken of in one of the books of the "Odyssey," the book that tells about the longest swim on record. I forget how long it lasted—several days, was it?—but at last as Odysseus came near the coast of Phaeacia, he saw it on the horizon "like an inverted shield."

There is a better metaphor in the same book. In the end Odysseus comes ashore and crawls up the beach to spend the night under a double olive tree, and it says, as in a lonely farmhouse where it is hard to get fire—I am not quoting exactly—where it is hard to start the fire again if it goes out, they cover the seeds of fire with ashes to preserve it for the night, so Odysseus covered himself with the leaves around him and went to sleep. There you have something that gives you character, something of Odysseus himself. "Seeds of fire." So Odysseus covered the seeds of fire in himself. You get the greatness of his nature.

But these are slighter metaphors than the ones we live by. They have their charm, their passing charm. They are as it were the first steps toward the great thoughts, grave thoughts, thoughts lasting to the end.

The metaphor whose manage we are best taught in poetry—that is all there is of thinking. It may not seem far for the mind to go but it is the mind's furthest. The richest accumulation of the ages is the noble metaphors we have rolled up.

I want to add one thing more that the experience of poetry is to anyone who comes close to poetry. There are two ways of coming close to poetry. One is by writing poetry. And some people think I want people to write poetry, but I don't; that is, I don't necessarily. I only want people to write poetry if they want to write poetry. I have never encouraged anybody to write poetry that did not want to write it, and I have not always encouraged those who did want to write it. That ought to be one's own funeral. It is a hard, hard life, as they say.

(I have just been to a city in the West, a city full of poets, a city they have made safe for poets. The whole city is so lovely that you do not have to write it up to make it poetry; it is ready-made for you. But, I don't know—the poetry written in that city might not seem like poetry if read outside of the city. It would be like the jokes made when you were drunk; you have to get drunk again to appreciate them.)

But as I say, there is another way to come close to poetry, fortunately, and that is in the reading of it, not as linguistics, not as history, not as anything but poetry. It is one of the hard things for a teacher to know how close a man has come in reading poetry. How do I know whether a man has come close to Keats in reading Keats? It is hard for me to know. I have lived with some boys a whole year over some of the poets and I have not felt sure whether they have come near what it was all about. One remark sometimes told me. One remark was their mark for the year; had to be—it was all I got that told me what I wanted to know. And that is enough, if it was the right remark, if it came close enough. I think a man might make twenty fool remarks if he made one good one some time in the year. His mark would depend on that good remark.

The closeness—everything depends on the closeness with which you come, and you ought to be marked for the closeness, for nothing else. And that will have to be estimated by chance remarks, not by question and answer. It is only by accident that you know some day how near a person has come.

The person who gets close enough to poetry, he is going to know more about the word *belief* than anybody else knows, even in religion nowadays. There are two or three places where we know belief outside of religion. One of them is at the age of fifteen to twenty, in our self-belief. A young man knows more about himself than he is able to prove to anyone. He has no knowledge that anybody else will accept as knowledge. In his foreknowledge he has something that is going to believe itself into fulfillment, into acceptance.

There is another belief like that, the belief in someone else, a relationship of two that is going to be believed into fulfillment. That is what we are talking about in our novels, the belief of love. And the disillusionment that the novels are full of is simply the disillusionment from disappointment in that belief. That belief can fail, of course.

Then there is a literary belief. Every time a poem is written, every time a short story is written, it is written not by cunning, but by belief. The beauty, the something, the little charm of the thing to be, is more felt than known. There is a common jest, one that always annoys me, on the writers, that they write the last end first, and then work up to it; that they lay a train toward one sentence that they think is pretty nice and have all fixed up to set like a trap to close with. No, it should not be that way at all. No one who has ever come close to the arts has failed to see the difference between things written that way, with cunning and device, and the kind that are believed into existence, that begin in something more felt than known. This you can realize quite as well—not quite as well, perhaps, but nearly as well—in reading as you can in writing. I would undertake to separate short stories on that principle; stories that have been believed into existence and stories that have been cunningly devised. And I could separate the poems still more easily.

Now I think—I happen to think—that those three beliefs that I speak of, the self-belief, the love-belief, and the art-belief, are all closely related to the God-belief, that the belief in God is a relationship you enter into with Him to bring about the future.

There is a national belief like that, too. One feels it. I have been where I came near getting up and walking out on the people who thought that they had to talk against nations, against nationalism, in order to curry favor with internationalism. Their metaphors are all mixed up. They think that because a Frenchman and an American and an Englishman can all sit down on the same platform and receive honors together, it must be that there is no such thing as nations. That kind of bad thinking springs from a source we all know. I should want to say to anyone like that: "Look! First I want to be a person. And I want you to be a person, and then we can be as interpersonal as you please. We can pull each other's noses—do all sorts of things. But, first of all, you have got to have the personality. First of all, you have got to have the nations and then they can be as international as they please with each other."

I should like to use another metaphor on them. I want my

palette, if I am a painter, I want my palette on my thumb or on my chair, all clean, pure, separate colors. Then I will do the mixing on the canvas. The canvas is where the work of art is, where we make the conquest. But we want the nations all separate, pure, distinct, things as separate as we can make them; and then in our thoughts, in our arts, and so on, we can do what we please about it.

But I go back. There are four beliefs that I know more about from having lived with poetry. One is the personal belief, which is a knowledge that you don't want to tell other people about because you cannot prove that you know. You are saying nothing about it till you see. The love belief, just the same, has that same shyness. It knows it cannot tell; only the outcome can tell. And the national belief we enter into socially with each other, all together, party of the first part, party of the second part, we enter into that to bring the future of the country. We cannot tell some people what it is we believe, partly, because they are too stupid to understand and partly because we are too proudly vague to explain. And anyway it has got to be fulfilled, and we are not talking until we know more, until we have something to show. And then the literary one in every work of art, not of cunning and craft, mind you, but of real art; that believing the thing into existence, saying as you go more than you even hoped you were going to be able to say, and coming with surprise to an end that you foreknew only with some sort of emotion. And then finally the relationship we enter into with God to believe the future in—to believe the hereafter in.

Discussion Questions

1. How does Frost connect the two themes of metaphor and belief? How does he prepare his reader for the connection?

2. What technique does Frost use in the following sentence and what meaning does it convey: "But if I am going to give a mark, that is the least part of my marking"?

3. Compare Frost's views of metaphor to those of the scientist Jacob Bronowski. Do the two see "likenesses" in the same way? Does Frost think of "explanations" in the same way?

4. Frost says that one can learn to "ride" a metaphor until it "breaks down." What is the basis of the metaphor he uses to express this thought? For example, does he compare the mental process to a merry-go-round? What kinds of things does he compare it to? How much confidence in a given metaphor does Frost's metaphor express?

5. Why is Frost dissatisfied with the metaphor of "evolution" when it is applied to things like "elevators"? Would Bronowski agree?

6. People often use the metaphor of "progress." One can progress in one's studies or in business negotiations, and one's civilization can be said to progress. What is the basis of this metaphor? To what does it compare the various experiences it describes? Where, if at all, do you find it "breaking down"?

7. "Problem" is another widely used metaphor ("he's giving me a problem," "the problem of starvation in Asia"). In a brief essay, try to explain the popularity of this metaphor. How does it arrange the vastly different experiences it describes so as to satisfy so many people?

Northrup Frye

One of the most widely known and frequently cited critics of the twentieth century, Northrup Frye was born in Canada in 1912. His contributions to the theory of literary criticism have been many and his contention that critical insight depends upon and is a function of an overall structure of literature or a "schematic" method, as he calls it, has intrigued, puzzled, and outraged readers since his first book, Fearful Symmetry: A Study of William Blake (1947). His latest book, The Great Code (1982) makes a vast and vastly learned inquiry into the literary structure of the Bible. In the following selection, originally presented in the form of a lecture, Frye outlines some of his principles concerning the fundamental differences between literary and real experiences and explores some of the implications of that distinction.

The Keys to Dreamland

I have been trying to explain literature by putting you in a primitive situation on an uninhabited island, where you could see the imagination working in the most direct and simple way. Now let's start with our own society, and see where literature belongs in that, if it does. Suppose you're walking down the street of a North American city. All around you is a highly artificial society, but you don't think of it as artificial: you're so accustomed to it that you think of it as natural. But suppose your imagination plays a little trick on you of a kind that it often does play, and you suddenly feel like a complete outsider, someone who's just blown in from Mars on a flying saucer. Instantly you see how conventionalized everything is: the clothes, the shop windows, the movement of the cars in traffic, the cropped hair and shaved faces of the men, the red lips and blue eyelids that women put on because they want to conventionalize their faces, or "look nice," as they say, which means the same thing. All this convention is pressing toward uniformity or likeness. To be outside the convention makes a person look queer, or, if he's driving a car, a menace to life and limb. The only exceptions are people who have decided to conform to different conventions, like nuns or beatniks. There's clearly a strong force making toward conformity in society, so strong that it seems to have something to do with the stability of society itself. In ordinary life even the most splendid things we can think of, like goodness and truth and beauty, all mean essentially what we're accustomed to. As I hinted just now in speaking of female make-up, most of our ideas of beauty are pure convention, and even truth has been defined as whatever doesn't disturb the pattern of what we already know.

When we move on to literature, we again find conventions, but this time we notice that they are conventions, because we're not so used to them. These conventions seem to have something to do with making literature as unlike life as possible. Chaucer represents people as making up stories in ten-syllable couplets. Shakespeare uses dramatic conventions, which means, for instance, that Iago has to smash Othello's marriage and dreams of future happiness and get him ready to murder his wife in a few minutes. Milton has two nudes in a garden haranguing each other in set speeches beginning with such lines as "Daughter of God and Man, immortal Eve"—Eve being Adam's daughter because she's just been extracted from his ribcase. Almost every story we read demands that we accept as fact something that we know to be nonsense: that good people always win, especially in love; that murders are complicated and ingenious puzzles to be solved by logic, and so on. It isn't only popular literature that demands this: more highbrow stories are apt to be more ironic, but irony has its conventions too. If we go further back into literature, we run into such conventions as the king's rash promise, the enraged cuckold, the cruel mistress of love poetry—never anything that we or any other time would recognize as the normal behavior of adult people, only the maddened ethics of fairyland.

Even the details of literature are equally perverse. Literature is a world where phoenixes and unicorns are quite as important as horses and dogs—and in literature some of the horses talk, like the ones in *Gulliver's Travels*. A random example is calling Shakespeare the "swan of Avon"—he was called that by Ben Jonson. The town of Stratford, Ontario, keeps swans in its river partly as a literary allusion. Poets of Shakespeare's day hated to admit that they were writing words on a page: they always insisted that they were producing music. In pastoral poetry they might be playing a flute (or more accurately an oboe), but every other kind of poetic effort was called song, with a harp, a lyre or a lute in the background, depending on how highbrow the song was. Singing suggests birds, and so for their typical songbird and emblem of themselves, the poets chose the swan, a bird that can't sing. Because it can't sing, they made up a legend that it sang once before death, when nobody was listening. But Shakespeare didn't burst into song before his death; he wrote two plays a year until he'd made enough money to retire, and spent the last five years of his life counting his take.

So however useful literature may be in improving one's imagination or vocabulary, it would be the wildest kind of pedantry to use it directly as a guide to life. Perhaps here we see one reason why the poet is not only very seldom a person one would turn to for insight into the state of the world, but often seems even more gullible and simple-minded than the rest of us. For the poet, the particular literary conventions he adopts are likely to become, for him, facts of life. If he finds that the kind of writing he's best at has a good deal to do with fairies, like Yeats, or a white goddess, like Graves, or a life-force, like Bernard Shaw, or episcopal sermons, like T. S. Elliot, or bullfights, like Hemingway, or exasperation at social hypocrisies, as with the so-called angry school, these things are apt to take on a reality for him that seems badly out of proportion to his contemporaries. His life may imitate literature in a way that may warp or even destroy his social personality, as Byron wore himself out at thirty-four with the strain of being Byronic. Life and literature, then are both conventionalized, and of the conventions of literature about all we can say is that they don't much resemble the conditions of life. It's when the two sets of conventions collide that we realize how different they are.

In fact, whenever literature gets too probable, too much like life, some self-defeating process, some mysterious law of diminishing returns, seems to set in. There's a vivid and expertly written novel by H. G. Wells called *Kipps,* about a lower-middle-class, inarticulate, very likeable Cockney, the kind of character we often find in Dickens. Kipps is carefully studied: he never says anything that a man like Kipps wouldn't say; he never sounds the "h" in home or head; nothing he does is out of line with what we expect such a person to be like. It's an admirable novel, well worth reading, and yet I have a nagging feeling that there's some inner secret in bringing him completely to life that Dickens would have and that Wells doesn't have. All right, then, what would Dickens have done? Well, one of the things that Dickens often does do is write *badly*. He might have given Kipps sentimental speeches and false heroics and all sorts of inappropriate verbiage to say; and some readers would have clucked and tut-tutted over these passages and explained to each other how bad Dickens's taste was and how uncertain his hold on character could be. Perhaps they'd be right too. But we'd have had Kipps a few times the way he'd look to himself or the way he'd sometimes wish he could be: that's part of his reality, and the effect would remain with us however much we disapproved of it. Whether I'm right about this book or not, and I'm not at all sure I am, I think my general principle is right. What we'd never see except in a book is often what we go to books to find. Whatever is completely lifelike in literature is a bit of a laboratory specimen there. To bring anything really to life in literature we can't be lifelike: we have to be literature-like.

The same thing is true even of the use of language. We're often taught that prose is the language of ordinary speech, which is usually true in literature. But in ordinary life prose is no more the language of ordinary speech than one's Sunday suit is a bathing suit. The people who actually speak prose are highly cultivated and articulate people, who've read a good many books, and even they can speak prose only to each other. If you read the beautiful sentences of Elizabeth Bennett's conversation in *Pride and Prejudice,* you can see how in that book they give a powerfully convincing impression of a sensible and intelligent girl. But any girl who talked as coherently as that on a street car would be stared at as though she had green hair. It isn't only the difference between 1813 and 1962 that's involved either, as you'll see if you compare her speech with her mother's. The poet Emily Dickinson complained that everybody said "What?" to her, until finally she practically gave up trying to talk altogether, and confined herself to writing notes.

All this is involved with the principle I've touched on before: the difference between literary and other kinds of writing. If we're writing to convey information, or for any practical reason, our writing is an act of will and intention: we mean what we say, and the words we use represent that meaning directly. It's different in literature, not because the poet doesn't mean what he says too, but because his real effort is one of putting words together. What's important is not what he may have meant to say, but what the words themselves say when they get fitted together. With a novelist it's rather the incidents in the story he tells that get fitted together—as D. H. Lawrence says, don't trust the novelist; trust his story. That's why so much of a writer's best writing is or seems to be involuntary. It's involuntary because the forms of literature itself are taking control of it, and these forms are what are embodied in the conventions of literature. Conventions, we see, have the same role in literature that they have in life: they impose certain patterns of order and stability on the writer. Only, if they're such different conventions, it seems clear that the order of words, or the structure of literature, is different from the social order.

The absence of any clear line of connection between literature and life comes out in the issues involved in censorship. Because of the large involuntary element in writing, works of literature can't be treated as embodiments of conscious will or intention, like people, and so no laws can be framed to control their behavior which assume a tendency to do this or an intention of doing that. Works of literature get into legal trouble because they offend some powerful religious or political interest, and this interest in its turn usually acquires or exploits the kind of social hysteria that's always revolving around sex. But it's impossible to give legal definitions of such terms as obscenity in relation to works of literature. What happens to the book depends mainly on the intelligence of the judge. If he's a sensible man we get a sensible decision; if he's an ass we get that sort of decision, but what we don't get is a legal decision, because the basis for one doesn't exist. The best we get is a precedent tending to discourage cranks and pressure groups from attacking serious books. If you read the casebook on the trial of *Lady Chatterley's Lover*, you may remember how bewildered the critics were when they were asked what the moral effect of the book would be. They weren't putting on an act: they didn't know. Novels can only be good or bad in their own categories. There's no such thing as a morally bad novel: its moral effect depends entirely on the moral quality of its reader, and nobody can predict what that will be. And if literature isn't morally bad it isn't morally good either. I suppose one reason why *Lady Chatterley's Lover* dramatized this question so vividly was that it's a rather preachy and self-conscious book: like the Sunday-school novels of my childhood, it bores me a little because it tries so hard to do me good.

So literature has no consistent connection with ordinary life, positive or negative. Here we touch on another important difference between structures of the imagination and structures of practical sense, which include the applied sciences. Imagination is certainly essential to science, applied or pure. Without a constructive power in the mind to make models of experience, get hunches and follow them out, play freely around with hypotheses, and so forth, no scientist could get anywhere. But all imaginative effort in practical fields has to meet the test of practicability, otherwise it's discarded. The imagination in literature has no such test to meet. You don't relate it directly to life or reality: you relate works of literature, as we've said earlier, to each other. Whatever value there is in studying literature, cultural or practical, comes from the total body of our reading, the castle of words we've built, and keep adding new wings to all the time.

So it's natural to swing to the opposite extreme and say that literature is really a refuge or escape from life, a self-contained world like the world of the dream, a world of play or make-believe to balance the world of work. Some literature is like that, and many people tell us that they only read to get away from reality for a bit. And I've suggested myself that the sense of escape, or at least detachment, does come into everybody's literary experience. But the real point of literature can hardly be that. Think of such writers as William Faulkner or François Mauriac, their great moral dignity, the intensity and compassion that they've studied the life around them with. Or think of James Joyce, spending seven years on one book and seventeen on another, and having them ridiculed or abused or banned by the customs when they did get published. Or of the poets Rilke and Valéry, waiting patiently for years in silence until what they had to say was ready to be said. There's a deadly seriousness in all this that even the most refined theories of fantasy or make-believe won't quite cover. Still, let's go along with the idea for a bit, because we're not getting on very fast with the relation of literature to life, or what we could call the horizontal perspective of literature. That seems to block us off on all sides.

The world of literature is a world where there is no reality except that of the human imagination. We see a great deal in it that reminds us vividly of the life we know. But in that very vividness there's something unreal. We can understand this more clearly with pictures, perhaps. There are trick-pictures—*trompe l'oeil*, the French call them—where the resemblance to life is very strong. An American painter of this school played a joke on his bitchy wife by painting one of her best napkins so expertly that she grabbed at the canvas trying to pull it off. But a painting as realistic as that isn't a reality but an illusion: it has the glittering unnatural clarity of a hallucination. The real realities, so to speak, are things that don't remind us directly of our own experience, but are such things as the wrath of Achilles or the jealousy of Othello, which are bigger and more intense experiences than anything we can reach—except in our imagination, which is what we're reaching with. Sometimes, as in the happy endings of comedies, or in the ideal world of romances, we seem to be looking at a pleasanter world than we ordinarily know. Sometimes, as in tragedy and satire, we seem to be looking at a world more devoted to suffering or absurdity than we ordinarily know. In literature we always seem to be looking either up or down. It's the vertical perspective that's important, not the horizontal one that looks out to life. Of course, in the greatest works of literature we get both the up and down views, often at the same time as different aspects of one event.

There are two halves to literary experience, then. Imagination gives us both a better and a worse world than the one we usually live with, and demands that we keep looking steadily at them both. I said in my first talk that the arts follow the path of the emotions, and of the tendency of the emotions to separate the world into a half that we like and a half that we don't like. Literature is not a world of dreams, but it would be if we had only one half without the other. If we had nothing but romances and comedies with happy endings, literature would express only a wish-fulfillment dream. Some people ask why poets want to write tragedies when the world's so full of them anyway, and suggest that enjoying such things has something morbid or gloating about it. It doesn't, but it might if there were nothing else in literature.

This point is worth spending another minute on. You recall that terrible scene in *King Lear* where Gloucester's eyes are put out on the stage. That's part of a play, and a play is supposed to be entertaining. Now in what sense can a scene like that be entertaining? The fact that it's not really happening is certainly important. It would be degrading to watch a real blinding scene, and far more so to get any pleasure out of watching it. Consequently, the entertainment doesn't consist in its reminding us of a real blinding scene. If it did, one of the great scenes of drama would turn into a piece of repulsive pornography. We couldn't stop anyone from reacting in this way, and it certainly wouldn't cure him, much less help the public, to start blaming or censoring Shakespeare for putting sadistic ideas in his head. But a reaction of that kind has nothing to do with drama. In a dramatic scene of cruelty and hatred we're seeing cruelty and hatred, which we know are permanently real things in human life, from the point of view of the imagination. What the imagination suggests is horror, not the paralyzing sickening horror of a real blinding scene, but an exuberant horror, full of the energy of repudiation. This is as powerful a rendering as we can ever get of life as we don't want it.

So we see that there are moral standards in literature after all, even though they have nothing to do with calling the police when we see a word in a book that's more familiar in sound than in print. One of the things Gloucester says in that scene is: "I am tied to the stake, and I must stand the course." In Shakespeare's day it was a favourite sport to tie a bear to a stake and set dogs on it until they killed it. The Puritans suppressed this sport, according to Macaulay, not because it gave pain to the bear but because it gave pleasure to the spectators. Macaulay may have intended his remark to be a sneer at the Puritans, but surely if the Puritans did feel this way they were one hundred per cent right. What other reason is there for abolishing public hangings? Whatever their motives, the Puritans and Shakespeare were operating in the same direction. Literature keeps presenting the most vicious things to us as entertainment, but what it appeals to is not any pleasure in these things, but the exhilaration of standing apart from them and being able to see them for what they are because they aren't really happening. The more exposed we are to this, the less likely we are to find an unthinking pleasure in cruel or evil things. As the eighteenth century said in a fine mouth-filling phrase, literature refines our sensibilities.

The top half of literature is the world expressed by such

words as sublime, inspiring, and the like, where what we feel is not detachment but absorption. This is the world of heroes and gods and titans and Rabelaisian giants, a world of powers and passions and moments of ecstasy far greater than anything we meet outside the imagination. Such forces would not only absorb but annihilate us if they entered ordinary life, but luckily the protecting wall of the imagination is here too. As the German poet Rilke says, we adore them because they disdain to destroy us. We seem to have got quite a long way from our emotions with their division of things into "I like this" and "I don't like this." Literature gives us an experience that stretches us vertically to the heights and depths of what the human mind can conceive, to what corresponds to the conceptions of heaven and hell in religion. In this perspective what I like or don't like disappears, because there's nothing left of me as a separate person: as a reader of literature I exist only as a representative of humanity as a whole. We'll see in the last talk how important this is.

No matter how much experience we may gather in life, we can never in life get the dimension of experience that the imagination gives us. Only the arts and sciences can do that, and of these, only literature gives us the whole sweep and range of human imagination as it sees itself. It seems to be very difficult for many people to understand the reality and intensity of literary experience. To give an example that you may think a bit irrelevant: why have so many people managed to convince themselves that Shakespeare did not write Shakespeare's plays, when there is not an atom of evidence that anybody else did? Apparently because they feel that poetry must be written out of personal experience, and that Shakespeare didn't have enough experience of the right kind. But Shakespeare's plays weren't produced by his experience: they were produced by his imagination, and the way to develop the imagination is to read a good book or two. As for us, we can't speak or think or comprehend even our own experience except within the limits of our own power over words, and those limits have been established for us by our great writers.

Literature, then, is not a dream-world: it's two dreams, a wish-fulfillment dream and an anxiety dream that are focused together, like a pair of glasses, and become a fully conscious vision. Art, according to Plato, is a dream for awakened minds, a work of imagination withdrawn from ordinary life, dominated by the same forces that dominate the dream, and yet giving us a perspective and dimension on reality that we don't get from any other approach to reality. So the poet and the dreamer are distinct, as Keats says. Ordinary life forms a community, and literature is among other things an art of communication, so it forms a community too. In ordinary life we fall into a private and separate subconscious every night, where we reshape the world according to a private and separate imagination. Underneath literature there's another kind of subconscious, which is social and not private, a need for forming a community around certain symbols, like the Queen and the flag, or around certain gods that represent order and stabililty, or becoming and change, or death and rebirth to a new life. This is the myth-making power of the human mind, which throws up and dissolves one civilization after another.

I've taken my title for this talk, "The Keys to Dreamland," from what is possibly the greatest single effort of the literary imagination in the twentieth century, Joyce's *Finnegans Wake*. In this book a man goes to sleep and falls, not into the Freudian separate or private subconscious, but into the deeper dream of man that creates and destroys his own societies. The entire book is written in the language of this dream. It's a subconscious language, mainly English, but connected by associations and puns with the eighteen or so other languages that Joyce knew. *Finnegans Wake* is not a book to read, but a book to decipher: as Joyce says, it's about a dreamer, but it's addressed to an ideal reader suffering from an ideal insomnia. The reader or critic, then, has a role complementing the poet's role. We need two powers in literature, a power to create and a power to understand.

In all our literary experience there are two kinds of response. There is the direct experience of the work itself, while we're reading a book or seeing a play, especially for the first time. This experience is uncritical, or rather pre-critical, so it's not infallible. If our experience is limited, we can be roused to enthusiasm or carried away by something that we can later see to have been second-rate or even phony. Then there is the conscious, critical response we make after we've finished reading or left the theatre, where we compare what we've experienced with other things of the same kind, and form a judgment of value and proportion on it. This critical response, with practice, gradually makes our pre-critical responses more sensitive and accurate, or improves our taste, as we say. But behind our responses to individual works, there's a bigger response to our literary experience as a whole, as a total possession.

The critic has always been called a judge of literature, which means, not that he's in a superior position to the poet, but that he ought to know something about literature, just as a judge's right to be on a bench depends on his knowledge of law. If he's up against something the size of Shakespeare, he's the one being judged. The critic's function is to interpret every work of literature in the light of all the literature he knows, to keep constantly struggling to understand what literature as a whole is about. Literature as a whole is not an aggregate of exhibits with red and blue ribbons attached to them, like a cat-show, but the range of articulate human imagination as it extends from the height of imaginative heaven to the depth of imaginative hell. Literature is a human apocalypse, man's revelation to man, and criticism is not a body of adjudications, but the awareness of that revelation, the last judgment of mankind.

Discussion Questions

1. What kind of readers does Frye seem to imagine his audience to be and what does he implicitly urge them to become?

2. By what various techniques does Frye urge his audience to see literary conventions as unlife-like? Are any of these techniques themselves conventions? How and why, for example, does Frye use the words "I," "you," and "we"? What different relations to his audience do these different terms create?

3. How does Frye differ from Robert Frost and from Sigmund Freud in his view of the uses of literature for life? In what ways are their views similar?

4. Write an essay comparing Frye's views of the ethics of censorship to those of Nora Ephron.

5. Frye says that "literature has no consistent connection with ordinary life, positive or negative." In what ways would Robert Frost disagree with this statement? In what ways would he agree?

6. Frye describes love poetry as based only on the "maddened ethics of fairyland." In a brief essay, describe these "ethics" (or those of the poetry in love songs) more fully. Compare them to those of real life.

PAUL FUSSELL

Paul Fussell was born in 1924 and served in the U.S. Army Infantry in World War II before completing his education at Pomona College and, later, Harvard. He went on to a teaching career in English at Connecticut College and Rutgers, but his army experience led to a continuing interest in military history while he pursued his studies in literary criticism and literary theory. Fussell has managed to produce outstanding essays and books in both areas, including Poetic Meter and Poetic Form *(1965) and* The Great War and Modern Memory *(1975). He has recently turned his attention to manners and morals, as the following title essay from his latest collection of essays shows.*

The Boy Scout Handbook

It's amazing how many interesting books humanistic criticism manages not to notice. Staring fixedly at its handful of teachable masterpieces, it seems content not to recognize that a vigorous literary-moral life constantly takes place just below (sometimes above) its vision. What a pity Lionel Trilling or Kenneth Burke never paused to examine the intersection of rhetoric and social motive among, say the Knights of Columbus or the Elks. That these are their fellow citizens is less important than that the desires and rituals of these groups are desires and rituals, and thus of permanent social and psychological consequence. The culture of the Boy Scouts deserves this sort of look-in, especially since the right sort of people don't know much about it.

The right sort consists, of course, of liberal intellectuals. They have often gazed uneasily at the Boy Scout movement. After all, a general, the scourge of the Boers, invented it; Kipling admired it; the Hitlerjugend (and the Soviet Pioneers) aped it. If its insistence that there is a God has not sufficed to alienate the enlightened, its khaki uniforms, lanyards, salutes, badges, and flag-worship have seemed to argue incipient militarism, if not outright fascism. The movement has often seemed its own worst enemy. Its appropriation of Norman Rockwell as its official Apelles has not endeared it to those of exquisite taste. Nor has its cause been promoted by events like the TV appearance a couple of years ago of the Chief Pardoner, Gerald Ford, rigged out in scout neckerchief, assuring us from the teleprompter that a Scout is Reverent. Then there are the leers and giggles triggered by the very word "scoutmaster," which in knowing circles is alone sufficient to promise comic pederastic narrative. "*All* scoutmasters are homosexuals," asserted George Orwell, who also insisted that "*All* tobacconists are Fascists."

But anyone who imagines that the scouting movement is either sinister or stupid or funny should spend a few hours with the latest edition of *The Official Boy Scout Handbook* (1979). Social, cultural, and literary historians could attend to it profitably as well, for after *The Red Cross First Aid Manual, The World Almanac,* and the Gideon Bible, it is probably the best-known book in this country. Since the first edition in 1910, twenty-nine million copies have been read in bed by flashlight. The first printing of this ninth edition is 600,000. We needn't take too seriously the ascription of authorship to William ("Green Bar Bill") Hillcourt, depicted on the title page as an elderly gentlemen bare-kneed in scout uniform and identified as Author, Naturalist, and World Scouter. He is clearly the Ann Page or Reddy Kilowatt of the movement, and although he's doubtless contributed to this handbook (by the same author is *Baden-Powell: The Two Lives of a Hero* [1965]), it bears all the marks of composition by committee, or "task force," as it's called here. But for all that, it's admirably written. And although a complex sentence is as rare as a reference to girls, the rhetoric of this new edition has made no compromise with what we are told is the new illiteracy of the young. The book assumes an audience prepared by a very good high-school education, undaunted by terms like *biosphere, ideology,* and *ecosystem.*

The pliability and adaptability of the scout movement explains its remarkable longevity, its capacity to flourish in a world dramatically different from its founder's. Like the Roman Catholic Church, the scout movement knows the difference between cosmetic and real change, and it happily embraces the one to avoid any truck with the other. Witness the new American flag patch, now worn at the top of the right sleeve. It betokens no access of jingoism or threat to a civilized internationalism. It simply conduces to dignity by imitating a similar affectation of police and fire departments in anarchic towns like New York City. The message of the flag patch is not "I am a fascist, straining to become old enough to purchase and wield guns." It is, rather, "I can be put to quasi-official use, and like a fireman or policeman I am trained in first aid and ready to help."

There are other innovations, none of them essential. The breeches of thirty years ago have yielded to trousers, although shorts are still in. The wide-brimmed army field hat of the First World War is a fixture still occasionally seen, but it is now augmented by headwear deriving from succeeding mass patriotic exercises: overseas caps and berets from World War II, and visor caps of the sort worn by General Westmoreland and sunbelt retirees. The scout handclasp has been changed, perhaps because it was discovered in the context of the new internationalism that the former one, in which the little finger was separated from the other three on the right hand, transmitted inappropriate suggestions in the Third World. The handclasp is now the normal civilian one, but given with the left hand. There's now much less emphasis on knots than formerly; as if to signal this change, the neckerchief is no longer religiously knotted at the tips. What used to be known as artificial respiration ("Out goes the bad air, in comes the good") has given way to "rescue breathing." The young are now being familiarized with the metric system. Some bright empiric has discovered that a paste made of meat tenderizer is the best remedy for painful insect stings. Constipation is not the bugbear it was a generation ago. And throughout there is a striking new lyricism. "Feel the wind blowing through your hair," the scout is adjured, just as he is exhorted to perceive that Being Prepared for life means learning "to live happy" and—equally important—"to die happy." There's more emphasis now on fun and less on duty; or rather, duty is validated because, properly viewed, it is a pleasure. (If that sounds like advice useful to grown-ups as well as to sprouts, you're beginning to get the point.)

There are only two possible causes of complaint. The term "free world" surfaces too often, although the phrase is mercifully uncapitalized. And the Deism is a bit insistent. The United States is defined as a country "whose people believe in a supreme being." The words "In God We Trust" on the coinage and currency are taken almost as a constitutional injunction. The camper is told to carry along the "Bible, Testament, or prayer book of your faith," even though, for light backpacking, he is advised to leave behind air mattress, knife and fork, and pancake turner. When the scout finds himself lost in the woods, he is to "stay put and have faith that someone will find you." In aid of this end, "Prayer will help." But the religiosity is so broad that it's harmless. The words "your church" are followed always by the phrase "or synagogue." The writers have done as well as they can considering that they're saddled with the immutable twelve points of Baden-Powell's Scout Law, stating unambiguously that "A Scout is Reverent" and "faithful to his religious duties." But if "You have the right to worship God in your own way," you must see to it that "others retain their right to worship God in their way." Likewise, if "you have the right to speak your mind without fear of prison or punishment," you must "ensure that right for others, even when you do not agree with them." If the book adheres to any politics, they can hardly be described as conservative; they are better described as slightly archaic liberal. It is broadly hinted that industrial corporations are prime threats to clean air and conservation. In every illustration depicting more than three boys, one is black. The section introducing the reader to some Great Americans pays respects not only to Franklin and Edison and John D. Rockefeller and Einstein; it also makes much of Walter Reuther and Samuel Gompers, as well as Harriet Tubman, Martin Luther King, and Whitney Young. There is a post-Watergate awareness that public officials must be watched closely. One's civic duties include the obligation to "keep up on what is going on around you" in order to "get involved" and "help change things that are not good."

Few books these days could be called compendia of good sense. This is one such, and its good sense is not merely about swimming safely and putting campfires "cold out." The good sense is psychological and ethical as well. Indeed, this handbook is among the very few remaining popular repositories of something like classical ethics, deriving from Aristotle and Cicero. Except for the handbook's adhesions to the motif of scenic beauty, it reads as if the Romantic movement had never taken place. The constant moral theme is the inestimable benefits of looking objectively outward and losing consciousness of self in the work to be done. To its young audience vulnerable to invitations to "trips" and trances and anxious self-absorption, the book calmly says: "Forget yourself." What a shame the psychobabblers of Marin County will never read it.

There is other invaluable advice, applicable to adults as well as to scouts. Some is practical, like "Never use flammable fluids to start a charcoal fire. They burn off fast, lighting only a little of the charcoal." Some is civic-moral: "Take a 2-hour walk where you live. Make a list of things that please you, another of things that should be improved." And then the kicker: "Set out to improve them." Some advice is even intellectual, and pleasantly uncompromising: "Reading trash all the time makes it impossible for anyone to be anything but a second-rate person." But the best advice is ethical: "Learn to think." "Gather knowledge." "Have initiative." "Respect the rights of others." Actually, there's hardly a better gauge for measuring the gross official misbehavior of the seventies than the ethics enshrined in this handbook. From its explicit ethics you can infer such propositions as "A scout does not tap his acquaintances' telephones," or "A scout does not bomb and invade a neutral country, and then lie about it," or "A scout does not prosecute war unless, as the Constitution provides, it has been declared by the Congress." Not to mention that because a scout is clean in thought, word, and deed, he does not, like Richard Nixon, designate his fellow citizens "shits" and then both record his filth and lie about the recordings ("A scout tells the truth").

Responding to Orwell's satiric analysis of "Boys' Weeklies"

forty years ago, the boys' author Frank Richards, stigmatized by Orwell as a manufacturer of excessively optimistic and falsely wholesome stories, observed that "The writer for young people should . . . endeavor to give his young readers a sense of stability and solid security, because it is good for them, and makes for happiness and peace of mind." Even if it is true, as Orwell objects, that the happiness of youth is a cruel delusion, then, says Richards, "Let youth be happy, or as happy as possible. Happiness is the best preparation for misery, if misery must come. At least the poor kid will have had something." In the current world of Making It and Getting Away with It, there are not many books devoted to associating happiness with virtue. The shelves of the CIA and the State Department must be bare of them. Horror swells around us like an oil spill," Terrence Des Pres said recently. "Not a day passes without more savagery and harm." He was commenting on Philip Hallie's *Lest Innocent Blood Be Shed,* an account of a whole French village's trustworthiness, loyalty, helpfulness, friendliness, courtesy, kindness, cheerfulness, and bravery in hiding scores of Jews during the Occupation. Des Pres concludes: *"Goodness. When was the last time anyone used that word in earnest, without irony, as anything more than a double cliché?" The Official Boy Scout Handbook,* for all its focus on Axmanship, Backpacking, Cooking, First Aid, Flowers, Hiking, Map and Compass, Semaphore, Trees, and Weather, is another book about goodness. No home, and certainly no government office, should be without a copy. The generously low price of $3.50 is enticing, and so is the place on the back cover where you're invited to inscribe your name.

Discussion Questions

1. Fussell says at the end of his essay that *The Boy Scout Handbook* "is another book about goodness." Suppose he had begun his essay with that point. How would the change make a change in the opening strategy? How would the change tend to make a different initial reaction for the reader of the piece? Would the change, for example, make the reader more or less willing to accept the writer's judgments? Explain.

2. Fussell writes that "since the first edition in 1910, twenty-nine million copies have been read in bed by flashlight." How is this mild joke about the book typical of his style? Find other jokes of the same sort. What attitudes do the jokes invite a reader to adopt toward the

author? Toward the book in question? What attitudes might Fussell think the reader is in danger of adopting, were it not for the jokes? How do these jokes differ from those made about people who do not believe in what the author sees as the principles embodied in the book?

3. Look up the words "breeches" and "trousers." Find some other examples in the essay of the writer's precise use of words often used loosely. Given the author's concern for his own language, what attitudes has he the right to adopt toward the language of the book? Would you react in the same way, for example, to his use of the word "goodness," were he less concerned with words elsewhere?

4. *The Boy Scout Handbook* contains the advice, "Reading all trash all the time makes it impossible for anyone to be anything but a second-rate person." Fussell characterizes this advice as "pleasantly uncompromising." Rewrite the advice in a style you think Fussell would consider "compromising." What aspects of Fussell's own style might be characterized as "pleasantly uncompromising"? Pick a sentence of his and rewrite it as above in order to discover some of the particular strengths of his style.

5. Fussell writes that "a vigorous literary-moral life constantly takes place just below (sometimes above)" the vision of "humanistic criticism." Make a list of books that seem to you to fit these categories. For what books would Fussell's essay serve as a model for a "review"? For what books would his strategies and techniques be inappropriate? Why?

MARTIN GARDNER

Born in Tulsa, Oklahoma, in 1914, Martin Gardner was educated at The University of Chicago, where he received a B.A. in 1936. He worked as a newspaper reporter and as a member of the editorial staff of a children's magazine before joining Scientific American *in 1957. From that time until his recent retirement, Gardner headed the highly popular Mathematical Games Department.*

In addition to his magazine work, his wide-ranging interests have led to a variety of books. Like one of his subjects, Lewis Carroll, Gardner combines a professional interest in mathematics with a fondness for science, philosophy, and literature as well. A brief, and by no means complete, list of his books shows his versatility: In the Name of Science *(1952),* Mathematics, Magic, and Mystery *(1956),* The Wizard of Oz and Who He Was *(1957),* The Annotated Alice *(1960),* Relativity for the Million *(1962),* The Annotated Ancient Mariner *(1965), and* The Annotated Casey at The Bat *(1967).*

In the following selection, Gardner brings his fondness for problem solving to the question of what kind of man could have written a poem so popular and so nearly anonymous.

The Harvard Man Who Put the Ease in Casey's Manner

A sly way to start an argument in a saloon is to quote "Casey at the Bat." It is so well known that hardly anyone knows it—but almost everyone, especially in saloons along toward closing time, is convinced he does. Not the whole thing, maybe, but certainly enough to lay down the law about it. If you really know the poem, and have paced your drinks wisely, you can win any number of bets. What was the score, for instance, when Casey came to bat? ("The score stood four to two with but one inning more to play.") What players were on base and how did they get there? (Look it up, why don't you?) Who—and this is the one to rock the boilermaker literati back on their barstools—who wrote "Casey at the Bat?"

The name may be on the tip of everyone's tongue but it's nice to be the one to blurt it out. The author of "Casey" was Ernest Lawrence Thayer, son of Edward Davis Thayer, a wealthy New England textile manufacturer. Ernest was born in Lawrence, Mass. on August 14, 1863. By the time he entered Harvard the family had moved to Worcester, where the elder Thayer ran one of his several woolen mills. At Harvard young Thayer made a brilliant record as a major in philosophy. The great William James was his teacher and friend. Thayer belonged to the Hasty Pudding Club. He was a member of the exclusive Fly Club and Delta Kappa Epsilon fraternity. He edited the college's humor magazine, the Harvard *Lampoon*. His best friend, Samuel E. Winslow (later a Congressman from Massachusetts), was captain of the senior baseball team. During his last year at Harvard, Thayer never missed a ball game.

Another friend of Thayer's college years was the business manager of the *Lampoon*, William Randolph Hearst. In 1885, when Thayer was graduated *magna cum laude*—he was Phi Beta Kappa and the Ivy orator of his class—Hearst was unceremoniously booted out of Harvard Yard. (He had a habit of playing practical jokes that no one in the faculty thought funny; for example, sending chamber pots to professors, their names inscribed thereon.) Hearst's father had recently bought the ailing *San Francisco Examiner*. Now that young Will was in want of something to occupy his time, the elder Hearst turned the paper over to him.

Thayer, in the meantime, after wandering around Europe with no particular goal, had settled in Paris to brush up on his French. Would he consider, Hearst cabled him, returning to the U.S. to write a humor column for the *Examiner's* Sunday supplement? To the great annoyance of his father, who expected him to take over American Woolen Mills someday, Thayer agreed.

Thayer's Sunday column, under the by-line of "Phin" (at Harvard his friends had called him Phinney), began in 1886. Every other Sunday he tossed into the column a comic ballad that he dashed off in a few hours. These ballads started in the fall of 1887 and continued for several months. Then ill health forced Thayer to return to Worcester. For a while he continued sending ballads to the *Examiner*. The last of them was "Casey." It ran on June 3, 1888, page 4, column 4, sandwiched between editorials on the left and a weekly column by Ambrose Bierce on the right.

No one paid much attention to the poem. Baseball fans in San Francisco chuckled over it and a few eastern papers reprinted it, but it probably would have been quickly forgotten had it not been for a sequence of improbable events. In New York City, a young comedian and bass singer, DeWolf Hopper, was appearing in a comic opera at Wallack's theater. One evening (the exact date is a matter of controversy; it was probably late in 1888 or sometime in 1889) the New York Giants and the Chicago White Stockings were invited to the show as guests of the management. What could he do on stage, Hopper asked himself, for the special benefit of these men? I have just the thing, said Archibald Clavering Gunter, a novelist and friend. He took from his pocket a ragged newspaper clipping that he had cut from the *Examiner* on a recent trip to San Francisco. It was "Casey."

This poem, insisted Gunter, is great. Why not memorize it and deliver it on stage? Hopper recited it in the middle of the second act, with the Giants in boxes on one side of the theater, the White Stockings in boxes on the other.

Hopper made the recitation a permanent part of his repertoire. It became his most famous bit. Wherever he went, whatever the show in which he was appearing, there were always curtain shouts for "Casey." By his own count, he recited it more than 10,000 times, experimenting with hundreds of slight variations in emphasis and gesture to keep his mind from wandering. It took him exactly five minutes and forty seconds to deliver the poem.

All over the U.S. newspapers and magazines began to reprint it. No one knew who Phin was. Editors either dropped the name altogether or substituted their own or a fictitious one. Stanzas were lost. Lines got botched by printers or rewritten by editors who fancied themselves able to improve the original. Scarcely two printings of the poem were the same. In one early reprinting (by *The Sporting Times*, July 29, 1888) Mudville was changed to Boston and Casey's name to Kelly in honor of Mike (King) Kelly, a famous Boston star, about whom the popular song "Slide, Kelly, Slide" had been written.

From time to time various Caseys who played baseball in the late 1800's claimed to have been the inspiration for the ballad, but Thayer emphatically denied that he had had any ballplayer in mind for any of the men mentioned in his ballad. When the *Syracuse Post-Standard* wrote to ask him about this, he replied with a letter that is reprinted in full in Lee Allen's entertaining book on baseball, *The Hot Stove League* (1955):

> The verses owe their existence to my enthusiasm for college baseball, not as a player, but as a fan [Thayer wrote]. The poem has no basis in fact. The only Casey actually involved, I am sure about him, was not a ballplayer. He was a big, dour Irish lad of my high school days. While in high school, I composed and printed myself a very tiny sheet, less than two inches by three. In one issue, I ventured to gag, as we say, this Casey boy. He didn't like it and he told me so, and, as he discoursed, his big, clenched, red hands were white at the knuckles. This Casey's name never again appeared in the *Monohippic Gazette*. But I suspect the incident, many years after, suggested the title for the poem. It was a taunt thrown to the winds. God grant he never catches me.

By 1900 almost everyone in America knew the poem but hardly anyone knew who wrote it. Hopper himself did not discover the author's identity until about five years after he began reciting it. One evening, having delivered the poem in a Worcester theater, he received a note inviting him to a local club to meet "Casey's" author. "Over the details of wassail that followed," Hopper wrote later, "I will draw a veil of charity." He did disclose, however, that the club members had persuaded Thayer himself to stand up and recite "Casey." It was, Hopper declared, the worst delivery of the poem he had ever heard. "In a sweet dulcet whisper he [Thayer] implored Casey to murder the umpire, and gave this cry of animal rage all the emphasis of a caterpillar."

Thayer remained in Worcester for many years, doing his best to please his father by managing one of the family mills. He kept quietly to himself, studying philosophy in his spare hours and reading classical literature, a gracious, charming, modest man, soft-spoken, slight of build, a bit hard of hearing and with only the lowest opinion of his own verse. He dashed off a few more comic ballads in 1896, for Hearst's *New York Journal*, but he never considered them worth collecting in a book.

> During my brief acquaintance with the *Examiner*, [Thayer once wrote] I put out large quantities of nonsense, both prose and verse, sounding the whole newspaper gamut from advertisements to editorials. In general quality "Casey" (at least to my judgment) is neither better nor worse than much of the other stuff. Its persistent vogue is simply unaccountable, and it would be hard to say, all things considered, if it has given me more pleasure than annoyance. The constant wrangling about authorship, from which I have tried to keep aloof, has certainly filled me with disgust.

Throughout his life, he refused to discuss payments for reprintings of "Casey." "All I ask is never to be reminded of it again," he told one publisher. "Make it anything you wish."

Never happy in the family mills, Thayer finally quit working for them altogether. After a few years of travel abroad he retired in 1912 to Santa Barbara, Calif. The following year—he was then fifty—he married Mrs. Rosalind Buel Hammett, a widow from St. Louis. They had no children.

Thayer remained in Santa Barbara until his death in 1940.

"Casey" has had many imitations, sequels and parodies. Two silent motion pictures were based on Thayer's poem. The first, in 1916, starred Hopper himself as the mighty Casey. Thayer is said to have refused to appear in a short introductory scene. A second *Casey at the Bat* was released in 1927, with Wallace Beery in the leading role. (I can still recall Beery, bat in one hand and beer mug in the other, whacking the ball so hard that an outfielder has to mount a horse to retrieve it.) More recently, an animated short by Walt Disney featured the voice of Jerry Colonna reciting the ballad.

Several flimsy paperback editions of the poem, with illustrations, came out around the turn of the century. A. C. McClurg published a more substantial edition in 1912 with pictures by Dan Sayre Groesbeck. In 1964 Prentice-Hall brought out a hard-cover "Casey," profusely illustrated by Paul Frame; that same year Franklin Watts issued another, with art by Leonard Everett Fisher and a short introduction by Casey Stengel. The poem has also been illustrated innumerable times for newspaper and magazine appearances. The variant readings—including revisions by Thayer himself—might well make a thesis for a graduate student desperate for a subject.

How can one explain "Casey's" undying popularity? It is not

great poetry. It was written carelessly. Parts of it are certainly doggerel. Yet it is almost impossible to read it several times without memorizing whole chunks, and there are lines so perfectly expressed, given the poem's intent, that one cannot imagine a word changed for the better. The late T. S. Eliot admired the ballad so much that he even wrote a parody about a cat, "Growl-tiger's Last Stand," in which many of Thayer's lines are echoed.

The poem's secret can be found, of all places, in the autobiography of George Santayana, another famous Harvard philosopher. Santayana was one of Thayer's associate editors on the *Lampoon*. "The man who gave the tone to the *Lampoon* at that time," Santayana writes, "was Ernest Thayer. . . . He seemed a man apart, his wit was not so much jocular as Mercutio-like, curious and whimsical, as if he saw the broken edges of things that appear whole. There was some obscurity in his play with words, and a feeling (which I shared) that the absurd side of things is pathetic. Probably nothing in his later performance may bear out what I have just said of him, because American life was then becoming unfavorable to idiosyncrasies of any sort, and the current smoothed and rounded out all the odd pebbles."

But Santayana was wrong. One thing *did* bear this out, and that was "Casey." It is precisely the blend of absurd and tragic that lies at the heart of Thayer's poem. Casey is the giant of baseball who, at his moment of greatest possible triumph, strikes out. A pathetic figure, yet comic because of the supreme arrogance and confidence with which he approached the plate: "There was ease in Casey's manner." It is the shock of contrast between the enormous buildup and the final fizzle that produces the poem's explosion point. The story of Casey has become an American myth because Casey is the incomparable symbol of the great and glorious poop-out.

One might argue that Thayer, with his extraordinary beginning at Harvard, his friendship with James and Santayana, his lifelong immersion in philosophy and the great books, was himself something of a Casey. In later years his friends were constantly urging him to write, but he would always shake his head and reply, "I have nothing to say." Not until just before his death, at the age of seventy-seven, did he make an attempt to put some serious thoughts on paper. By then it was too late. "*Now* I have something to say," he said, "and I am too weak to say it."

But posterity's judgments are hard to anticipate. Thayer's writing career was no strikeout. He swatted one magnificent, eternal home run—"Casey"—and as long as baseball is played on this old earth, on Mudville, the air will be shattered over and over again by the force of Casey's blow.

CASEY AT THE BAT

It looked extremely rocky for the Mudville nine that day;
The score stood two to four, with but one inning left to play.
So, when Cooney died at second, and Burrows did the same,
A pallor wreathed the features of the patrons of the game.

A straggling few got up to go, leaving there the rest,
With that hope which springs eternal within the human breast.
For they thought: "If only Casey could get a whack at that,"
They'd put even money now, with Casey at the bat.

But Flynn preceded Casey, and likewise so did Blake,
And the former was a pudd'n, and the latter was a fake.
So on that stricken multitude a deathlike silence sat;
For there seemed but little chance of Casey's getting to the bat.

But Flynn let drive a "single," to the wonderment of all.
And the much-despisèd Blakey "tore the cover off the ball."
And when the dust had lifted, and they saw what had occurred,
There was Blakey safe at second, and Flynn a-huggin' third.

Then from the gladdened multitude went up a joyous yell—
It rumbled in the mountaintops, it rattled in the dell;
It struck upon the hillside and rebounded on the flat;
For Casey, mighty Casey, was advancing to the bat.

There was ease in Casey's manner as he stepped into his place,
There was pride in Casey's bearing and a smile on Casey's face;
And when responding to the cheers he lightly doffed his hat,
No stranger in the crowd could doubt 'twas Casey at the bat.

Ten thousand eyes were on him as he rubbed his hands with dirt.
Five thousand tongues applauded when he wiped them on his shirt;
Then when the writhing pitcher ground the ball into his hip,
Defiance glanced in Casey's eye, a sneer curled Casey's lip.

And now the leather-covered sphere came hurtling through the air,
And Casey stood a-watching it in haughty grandeur there.
Close by the sturdy batsman the ball unheeded sped;
"That ain't my style," said Casey. "Strike one," the umpire said.

From the benches, black with people, there went up a muffled roar,
Like the beating of the storm waves on the stern and distant shore.
"Kill him! kill the umpire!" shouted someone on the stand;
And it's likely they'd have killed him had not Casey raised his hand.

With a smile of Christian charity great Casey's visage shone;
He stilled the rising tumult, he made the game go on;
He signaled to the pitcher, and once more the spheroid flew;
But Casey still ignored it, and the umpire said, "Strike two."

"Fraud!" cried the maddened thousands, and the echo answered "Fraud!"
But one scornful look from Casey and the audience was awed;
They saw his face grow stern and cold, they saw his muscles strain,
And they knew that Casey wouldn't let the ball go by again.

The sneer is gone from Casey's lips, his teeth are clenched in hate,
He pounds with cruel vengeance his bat upon the plate;
And now the pitcher holds the ball, and now he lets it go,
And now the air is shattered by the force of Casey's blow.

Oh, somewhere in this favored land the sun is shining bright,
The band is playing somewhere, and somewhere hearts are light;
And somewhere men are laughing, and somewhere children shout,
But there is no joy in Mudville—Mighty Casey has struck out!

—ERNEST LAWRENCE THAYER

Discussion Questions

1. How does Gardner's introductory paragraph set the tone of the essay as a whole? Suppose he had begun his essay with the second sentence of the second paragraph. What would be lost without the introduction? Is the theme of trivia contests taken up elsewhere? Does the casual opening qualify the high praise Gardner gives Thayer at the end of the essay?

2. Gardner says that while some lines of the poem are "certainly doggerel," there are others "so perfectly expressed, given the poem's intent, that one cannot imagine a word changed for the better." Pick some lines that seem to you to fit each category and write an essay in which you explain and justify your distinctions.

3. Gardner does not directly report the success or failure of Hopper's first recitation of the poem. Would it have made a better essay to have been more specific and emotional here? Does the omission do anything positive for the essay?

4. Gardner selects details from several aspects of Thayer's life apparently unrelated to his composition of the poem. Are they in fact related? How and in what ways? Are other details left out that you wish had been supplied?

5. Gardner tries to explain the popularity of the poem. Do you think he succeeds? Are there any aspects that he leaves out? Are there other ways of accounting for the poem's having lasted? Can you think of other popular poems or jingles that have lasted in the same way?

6. In an essay compare Gardner's brief biography to that by Basil Liddell Hart on General Sherman. Each writer associates his subject with only a few leading facts and events. How do these two biographers differ in their approaches?

WILLIAM GOLDING

William Golding was born in Cornwall, England, in 1911 and educated at Oxford University. During World War II he served in the Royal Navy, participating in the D-Day operations and rising to the rank of lieutenant in command of a rocket-launching ship. He has traveled widely and taught at many American universities. He is perhaps best known for his internationally bestselling novel, Lord of the Flies *(1954)*, which graphically illustrates, in its tale of English schoolboys stranded on an island, the human inclination to violence and savagery. Among his other novels are Pincer Martin *(1956)*, The Inheritors *(1962)*, Darkness Visible *(1979)*, and Rites of Passage *(1980)*. His essays have appeared in numerous periodicals and have been collected in The Hot Gates and Other Occasional Pieces *(1958)* and A Moving Target *(1982)*.

Thinking as a Hobby

While I was still a boy, I came to the conclusion that there were three grades of thinking; and since I was later to claim thinking as my hobby, I came to an even stranger conclusion—namely, that I myself could not think at all.

I must have been an unsatisfactory child for grownups to deal with. I remember how incomprehensible they appeared to me at first, but not, of course, how I appeared to them. It was the headmaster of my grammar school who first brought the subject of thinking before me—though neither in the way, nor with the result he intended. He had some statuettes in his study. They stood on a high cupboard behind his desk. One was a lady wearing nothing but a bath towel. She seemed frozen in an eternal panic lest the bath towel slip down any farther; and since she had no arms, she was in an unfortunate position to pull the towel up again. Next to her, crouched the statuette of a leopard, ready to spring down at the top drawer of a filing cabinet labeled A-AH. My innocence interpreted this as the victim's last, despairing cry. Beyond the leopard was a naked, muscular gentleman, who sat, looking down, with his chin on his fist and his elbow on his knee. He seemed utterly miserable.

Some time later, I learned about these statuettes. The headmaster had placed them where they would face delinquent children because they symbolized to him the whole of life. The naked lady was the Venus of Milo. She was Love. She was not worried about the towel. She was just busy being beautiful. The leopard was Nature, and he was being natural. The naked, muscular gentleman was not miserable. He was Rodin's Thinker, an image of pure thought. It is easy to buy small plaster models of what you think life is like.

I had better explain that I was a frequent visitor to the headmaster's study, because of the latest thing I had done or left undone. As we now say, I was not integrated. I was, if anything, disintegrated; and I was puzzled. Grownups never made sense. Whenever I found myself in a penal position before the headmaster's desk, with the statuettes glimmering whitely above him, I would sink my head, clasp my hands behind my back and writhe one shoe over the other.

The headmaster would look opaquely at me through flashing spectacles.

"What are we going to do with you?"

Well, what *were* they going to do with me? I would writhe my shoe some more and stare down at the worn rug.

"Look up, boy! Can't you look up?"

Then I would look up at the cupboard, where the naked lady was frozen in her panic and the muscular gentleman comtemplated the hindquarters of the leopard in endless gloom. I had nothing to say to the headmaster. His spectacles caught the light so that you could see nothing human behind them. There was no possibility of communication.

"Don't you ever think at all?"

No, I didn't think, wasn't thinking, couldn't think—I was simply waiting in anguish for the interview to stop.

"Then you'd better learn—hadn't you?"

On one occasion the headmaster leaped to his feet, reached up and plonked Rodin's masterpiece on the desk before me.

"That's what a man looks like when he's really thinking."

I surveyed the gentleman without interest or comprehension.

"Go back to your class."

Clearly there was something missing in me. Nature had endowed the rest of the human race with a sixth sense and left me out. This must be so, I mused, on my way back to the class, since whether I had broken a window, or failed to remember Boyle's Law, or been late for school, my teachers produced me one, adult answer: "Why can't you think?"

As I saw the case, I had broken the window because I had tried to hit Jack Arney with a cricket ball and missed him; I could not remember Boyle's Law because I had never bothered to learn it; and I was late for school because I preferred looking over the bridge into the river. In fact, I was wicked. Were my teachers, perhaps, so good that they could not understand the depths of my depravity? Were they clear, untormented people who could direct their every action by this mysterious business of thinking? The whole thing was incomprehensible. In my earlier years, I found even the statuette of the Thinker confusing. I did not believe any of my teachers were naked, ever. Like someone born deaf, but bitterly determined to find out about sound, I watched my teachers to find out about thought.

There was Mr. Houghton. He was always telling me to think. With a modest satisfaction, he would tell me that he had thought a bit himself. Then why did he spend so much time drinking? Or was there more sense in drinking than there appeared to be? But if not, and if drinking were in fact ruinous to health—and Mr. Houghton was ruined, there was no doubt about that—why was he always talking about the clean life and the virtues of fresh air? He would spread his arms wide with the action of a man who habitually spent his time striding along mountain ridges.

"Open air does me good, boys—I know it!"

Sometimes, exalted by his own oratory, he would leap from his desk and hustle us outside into a hideous wind.

"Now, boys! Deep breaths! Feel it right down inside you—huge draughts of God's good air!"

He would stand before us, rejoicing in his perfect health, an open-air man. He would put his hands on his waist and take a tremendous breath. You could hear the wind, trapped in the cavern of his chest and struggling with all the unnatural impediments. His body would reel with shock and his ruined face go white at the unaccustomed visitation. He would stagger back to his desk and collapse there, useless for the rest of the morning.

Mr. Houghton was given to high-minded monologues about the good life, sexless and full of duty. Yet in the middle of one of these monologues, if a girl passed the window, tapping along on her neat little feet, he would interrupt his discourse, his neck would turn of itself and he would watch her out of sight. In this instance, he seemed to me ruled not by thought but by an invisible and irresistible spring in his nape.

His neck was an object of great interest to me. Normally it bulged a bit over his collar. But Mr. Houghton had fought in the First World War alongside both Americans and French, and had come—by who knows what illogic?—to a settled detestation of both countries. If either country happened to be prominent in current affairs, no argument could make Mr. Houghton think well of it. He would bang the desk, his neck would bulge still further and go red. "You can say what you like," he would cry, "but I've thought about this—and I know what I think!"

Mr. Houghton thought with his neck.

There was Miss Parsons. She assured us that her dearest wish was our welfare, but I knew even then, with the mysterious clairvoyance of childhood, that what she wanted most was the husband she never got. There was Mr. Hands—and so on.

I have dealt at length with my teachers because this was my introduction to the nature of what is commonly called thought. Through them I discovered that thought is often full of unconscious prejudice, ignorance and hypocrisy. It will lecture on disinterested purity while its neck is being remorselessly twisted toward a skirt. Technically, it is about as proficient as most businessmen's golf, as honest as most politicians' intentions, or—to come near my own preoccupation—as coherent as most books that get written. It is what I came to call grade-three thinking, though more properly, it is feeling, rather than thought.

True, often there is a kind of innocence in prejudices, but in those days I viewed grade-three thinking with an intolerant contempt and an incautious mockery. I was delighted to confront a pious lady who hated the Germans with the proposition that we should love our enemies. She taught me a great truth in dealing with grade-three thinkers; because of her, I no longer dismiss lightly a mental process which for nine-tenths of the population is the nearest they will get to thought. They have immense solidarity. We had better respect them, for we are outnumbered and surrounded. A crowd of grade-three thinkers, all shouting the same thing, all warming their hands at the fire of their own prejudices, will not thank you for pointing out the contradictions in their beliefs. Man is a gregarious animal, and enjoys agreement as cows will graze all the same way on the side of a hill.

Grade-two thinking is the detection of contradictions. I reached grade two when I trapped the poor, pious lady. Grade-two thinkers do not stampede easily, though often they fall into the other fault and lap behind. Grade-two thinking is a withdrawal, with eyes and ears open. It became my hobby and brought satisfaction and loneliness in either hand. For grade-two thinking destroys without having the power to create. It set me watching the crowds cheering His Majesty and King and asking myself what all the fuss was about, without giving me anything positive to put in the place of that heady patriotism. But there were compensations. To hear people justify their habit of hunting foxes and tearing them to pieces by claiming that the foxes like it. To hear our Prime Minister talk about the great benefit we conferred on India by jailing people like Pandit Nehru and Gandhi. To hear American politicians talk about peace in one sentence and refuse to join the League of Nations in the next. Yes, there were moments of delight.

But I was growing toward adolescence and had to admit that Mr. Houghton was not the only one with an irresistible spring in his neck. I, too, felt the compulsive hand of nature and began to find that pointing out contradiction could be costly as well as fun.

There was Ruth, for example, a serious and attractive girl. I was an atheist at the time. Grade-two thinking is a menace to religion and knocks down sects like skittles. I put myself in a position to be converted by her with an hypocrisy worthy of grade three. She was a Methodist—or at least, her parents were, and Ruth had to follow suit. But, alas, instead of relying on the Holy Spirit to convert me, Ruth was foolish enough to open her pretty mouth in argument. She claimed that the Bible (King James Version) was literally inspired. I countered by saying that the Catholics believed in the literal inspiration of Saint Jerome's *Vulgate*, and the two books were different. Argument flagged.

At last she remarked that there were an awful lot of Methodists, and they couldn't be wrong, could they—not all those millions? That was too easy, said I restively (for the nearer you were to Ruth, the nicer she was to be near to) since there were more Roman Catholics than Methodists anyway; and they couldn't be wrong, could they—not all those hundreds of millions? An awful flicker of doubt appeared in her eyes. I slid my arm around her waist and murmured breathlessly that if we were counting heads, the Buddhists were the boys for my money. But Ruth had *really* wanted to do me good, because I was so nice. She fled. The combination of my arm and those countless Buddhists was too much for her.

That night her father visited my father and left, red-cheeked and indignant. I was given the third degree to find out what had happened. It was lucky we were both of us only fourteen. I lost Ruth and gained an undeserved reputation as a potential libertine.

So grade-two thinking could be dangerous. It was in this knowledge, at the age of fifteen, that I remember making a comment from the heights of grade two, on the limitations of grade three. One evening I found myself alone in the school hall, preparing it for a party. The door of the headmaster's study was open. I went in. The headmaster had ceased to thump Rodin's Thinker down on the desk as an example to the young. Perhaps he had not found any more candidates, but the statuettes were still there, glimmering and gathering dust on top of the cupboard. I stood on a chair and rearranged them. I stood Venus in her bath towel on the filing cabinet, so that now the top drawer caught its breath in a gasp of sexy excitement. "A-ah!" The portentous Thinker I placed on the edge of the cupboard so that he looked down at the bath towel and waited for it to slip.

Grade-two thinking, though it filled life with fun and excitment, did not make for content. To find out the deficiencies of our elders bolsters the young ego but does not make for personal security. I found that grade two was not only the power to point out contradictions. It took the swimmer some distance from the shore and left him there, out of his depth. I decided that Pontius Pilate was a typical grade-two thinker. "What is truth?" he said, a very common grade-two thought, but one that is used always as the end of an argument instead of the beginning. There is still a higher grade of thought which says, "What is truth?" and sets out to find it.

But these grade-one thinkers were few and far between. They did not visit my grammar school in the flesh though they were there in books. I aspired to them, partly because I was ambitious and partly because I now saw my hobby as an unsatisfactory thing if it went no further. If you set out to climb a mountain, however high you climb, you have failed if you cannot reach the top.

I *did* meet an undeniably grade-one thinker in my first year at Oxford. I was looking over a small bridge in Magdalen Deer Park, and a tiny mustached and hatted figure came and stood by my side. He was a German who had just fled from the Nazis to Oxford as a temporary refuge. His name was Einstein.

But Professor Einstein knew no English at that time and I knew only two words of German. I beamed at him, trying wordlessly to convey by my bearing all the affection and respect that the English felt for him. It is possible—and I have to make the admission—that I felt here were two grade-one thinkers standing side by side; yet I doubt if my face conveyed more than a formless awe. I would have given my Greek and Latin and French and a good slice of my English for enough German to communicate. But we were divided; he was as inscrutable as my headmaster. For perhaps five minutes we stood together on the bridge, undeniable grade-one thinker and breathless aspirant. With true greatness, Professor Einstein realized that my contact was better than none. He pointed to a trout wavering in midstream.

He spoke: "*Fisch.*"

My brain reeled. Here I was, mingling with the great, and yet helpless as the veriest grade-three thinker. Desperately I sought for some sign by which I might convey that I, too, revered pure reason. I nodded vehemently. In a brilliant flash I used up half of my German vocabulary.

"*Fisch. Ja Ja.*"

For perhaps another five minutes we stood side by side. Then Professor Einstein, his whole figure still conveying good will and amiability, drifted away out of sight.

I, too, would be a grade-one thinker. I was irreverent at the best of times. Political and religious systems, social customs, loyalties and traditions, they all came tumbling down like so many rotten apples off a tree. This was a fine hobby and a sensible substitute for cricket, since you could play it all the year round. I came up in the end with what must always remain the justification for grade-one thinking, its sign, seal and charter. I devised a coherent system for living. It was a moral system, which was wholly logical. Of course, as I readily admitted, conversion of the world to my way of thinking might be difficult, since my system did away with a number of trifles, such as big business, centralized government, armies, marriage. . . .

It was Ruth all over again. I had some very good friends who stood by me, and still do. But my acquaintances vanished, taking the girls with them. Young women seemed oddly contented with the world as it was. They valued the meaningless ceremony with a ring. Young men, while willing to concede the chaining sordidness of marriage, were hesitant about abandoning the organizations which they hoped would give them a career. A young man on the first rung of the Royal Navy, while perfectly agreeable to doing away with big business and marriage, got as rednecked as Mr. Houghton when I proposed a world without any battleships in it.

Had the game gone too far? Was it a game any longer? In those prewar days, I stood to lose a great deal, for the sake of a hobby.

Now you are expecting me to describe how I saw the folly of my ways and came back to the warm nest, where prejudices are so often called loyalties, where pointless actions are hallowed into custom by repetition, where we are content to say we think when all we do is feel.

But you would be wrong. I dropped my hobby and turned professional.

If I were to go back to the headmaster's study and find the dusty statuettes still there, I would arrange them differently. I would dust Venus and put her aside, for I have come to love her and know her for the fair thing she is. But I would put the Thinker, sunk in his desperate thought, where there were shadows before him—and at his back, I would put the leopard, crouched and ready to spring.

Discussion Questions

1. How do the three statuettes help Golding organize his essay? Using Erich Fromm's distinctions, can you tell whether the statuettes are conventional, accidental, or universal symbols? How do the statuettes connect with Golding's three types of thinking?

2. Look up "hobby" in a good dictionary and think about the word. Why does Golding call thinking a hobby? What does hobby convey? What does he imply is the opposite of a hobby? When is thinking not a hobby?

3. Compare Golding's essay on thinking with J. B. Priestly's essay on "Block Thinking." In your opinion, which writer views the act of thinking in a more positive way?

4. Reread the section of the essay in which Einstein appears. What is Golding's purpose in describing this encounter? How does Einstein represent "grade-one" thinking in this encounter? What do you think Golding means by "Grade-one thinking"? Why doesn't he describe grade-one thinking as explicitly as he does grades two and three? Try to describe grade-three thinking in an essay of your own.

STEPHEN JAY GOULD

Born in New York in 1941, Stephen Jay Gould was educated as a biologist at Antioch College and Columbia. He has combined his career as a teacher of biology and a research biologist at Harvard (he has written over a hundred scientific papers) with a number of popular books on aspects of science and a monthly column in the magazine Natural History. *His latest book is on the measurement and mismeasurement of "intelligence," and his recent collection of essays,* The Panda's Thumb (1980), *contains the following selection. In it, Gould gives a brief course in adaptive evolution and shows how and why Mickey Mouse has apparently grown younger as he has grown older in his first fifty years.*

A Biographical Homage to Mickey Mouse

Age often turns fire to placidity. Lytton Strachey, in his incisive portrait of Florence Nightingale, writes of her declining years:

> Destiny, having waited very patiently, played a queer trick on Miss Nightingale. The benevolence and public spirit of that long life had only been equalled by its acerbity. Her virtue had dwelt in hardness.... And now the sarcastic years brought the proud woman her punishment. She was not to die as she had lived. The sting was to be taken out of her; she was to be made soft; she was to be reduced to compliance and complacency.

I was therefore not surprised—although the analogy may strike some people as sacrilegious—to discover that the creature who gave his name as a synonym for insipidity had a gutsier youth. Mickey Mouse turned a respectable fifty last year. To mark the occasion, many theaters replayed his debut performance in *Steamboat Willie* (1928). The original Mickey was a rambunctious, even slightly sadistic fellow. In a remarkable sequence, exploiting the exciting new development of sound, Mickey and Minnie pummel, squeeze, and twist the animals on board to produce a rousing chorus of "Turkey in the Straw." They honk a duck with a tight embrace, crank a goat's tail, tweak a pig's nipples, bang a cow's teeth as a stand-in xylophone, and play bagpipe on her udder.

Christopher Finch, in his semiofficial pictorial history of Disney's work, comments: "The Mickey Mouse who hit the movie houses in the late twenties was not quite the well-behaved character most of us are familiar with today. He was mischievous, to say the least, and even displayed a streak of cruelty." But Mickey soon cleaned up his act, leaving to gossip and speculation only his unresolved relationship with Minnie and the status of Morty and Ferdie. Finch continues: "Mickey . . . had become virtually a national symbol, and as such he was expected to behave properly at all times. If he occasionally stepped out of line, any number of letters would arrive at the Studio from citizens and organizations who felt that the nation's moral well-being was in their hands. . . . Eventually he would be pressured into the role of straight man."

As Mickey's personality softened, his appearance changed. Many Disney fans are aware of this transformation through time, but few (I suspect) have recognized the coordinating theme behind all the alterations—in fact, I am not sure that the Disney artists themselves explicitly realized what they were doing, since the changes appeared in such a halting and piecemeal fashion. In short, the blander and inoffensive Mickey became progressively more juvenile in appearance. (Since Mickey's chronological age never altered—like most cartoon characters he stands impervious to the ravages of time—this change in appearance at a constant age is a true evolutionary transformation. Progressive juvenilization as an evolutionary phenomenon is called neoteny. More on this later.)

The characteristic changes of form during human growth have inspired a substantial biological literature. Since the head-end of an embryo differentiates first and grows more rapidly in utero than the foot-end (an antero-posterior gradient, in technical language), a newborn child possesses a relatively large head attached to a medium-sized body with diminutive legs and feet. This gradient is reversed through growth as legs and feet overtake the front end. Heads continue to grow but so much more slowly than the rest of the body that relative head size decreases.

In addition, a suite of changes pervades the head itself dur-

Mickey's evolution during 50 years (left to right). As Mickey became increasingly well behaved over the years, his appearance became more youthful. Measurements of three stages in his development revealed a

ing human growth. The brain grows very slowly after age three, and the bulbous cranium of a young child gives way to the more slanted, lower-browed configuration of adulthood. The eyes scarcely grow at all and relative eye size declines precipitously. But the jaw gets bigger and bigger. Children, compared with adults, have larger heads and eyes, smaller jaws, a more prominent, bulging cranium, and smaller, pudgier legs and feet. Adult heads are altogether more apish, I'm sorry to say.

Mickey, however, has traveled this ontogenetic pathway in reverse during his fifty years among us. He has assumed an ever more childlike appearance as the ratty character of *Steamboat Willie* became the cute and inoffensive host to a magic kingdom. By 1940, the former tweaker of pig's nipples gets a kick in the ass for insubordination (as the *Sorcerer's Apprentice* in *Fantasia*). By 1953, his last cartoon, he has gone fishing and cannot even subdue a squirting clam.

The Disney artists transformed Mickey in clever silence, often using suggestive devices that mimic nature's own changes by different routes. To give him the shorter and pudgier legs of youth, they lowered his pants line and covered his spindly legs with a baggy outfit. (His arms and legs also thickened substantially—and acquired joints for a floppier appearance.) His head grew relatively larger and its features more youthful. The length of Mickey's snout has not altered, but decreasing protrusion is more subtly suggested by a pronounced thickening. Mickey's eye has grown in two modes: first, by a major, discontinuous evolutionary shift as the entire eye of ancestral Mickey became the pupil of his descendants, and second, by gradual increase thereafter.

larger relative head size, larger eyes, and an enlarged cranium–all traits of juvenility. © Walt Disney Productions

Mickey's improvement in cranial bulging followed an interesting path since his evolution has always been constrained by the unaltered convention of representing his head as a circle with appended ears and an oblong snout. The circle's form could not be altered to provide a bulging cranium directly. Instead, Mickey's ears moved back, increasing the distance between nose and ears, and giving him a rounded, rather than a sloping, forehead.

To give these observations the cachet of quantitative science, I applied my best pair of dial calipers to three stages of the official phylogeny—the thin-nosed, ears-forward figure of the early 1930s (stage 1), the latter-day Jack of Mickey and the Beanstalk (1947, stage 2), and the modern mouse (stage 3). I measured three signs of Mickey's creeping juvenility: increasing eye size (maximum height) as a percentage of head length (base of the nose to top of rear ear); increasing head length as a percentage of body length; and increasing cranial vault size measured by rearward displacement of the front ear (base of the nose to top of front ear as a percentage of base of the nose to top of rear ear).

All three percentages increased steadily—eye size from 27 to 42 percent of head length; head length from 42.7 to 48.1 percent of body length; and nose to front ear from 71.7 to a whopping 95.6 percent of nose to rear ear. For comparison, I measured Mickey's young "nephew" Morty Mouse. In each case, Mickey has clearly been evolving toward youthful stages of his stock, although he still has a way to go for head length.

You may, indeed, now ask what an at least marginally respectable scientist has been doing with a mouse like that. In part, fiddling around and having fun, of course. (I still prefer *Pinocchio* to *Citizen Kane*.) But I do have a serious point—two, in fact—to make. We must first ask why Disney chose to change his most famous character so gradually and persistently in the same direction? National symbols are not altered capriciously and market researchers (for the doll industry in particular) have spent a good deal of time and practical effort learning what features appeal to people as cute and friendly. Biologists also have spent a great deal of time studying a similar subject in a wide range of animals.

In one of his most famous articles, Konrad Lorenz argues that humans use the characteristic differences in form between babies and adults as important behavioral cues. He believes that features of juvenility trigger "innate releasing mechanisms" for affection and nurturing in adult humans. When we see a living creature with babyish features, we feel an automatic surge of disarmimg tenderness. The adaptive value of this response can scarcely be questioned, for we must nurture our babies. Lorenz, by the way,

HOMAGE TO MICKEY MOUSE

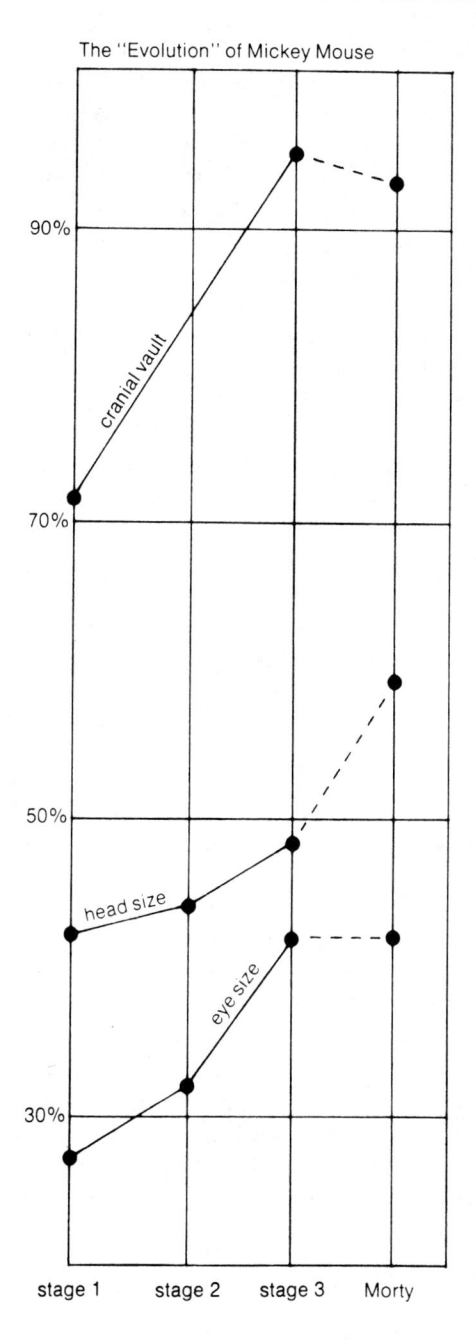

The "Evolution" of Mickey Mouse

At an early stage in his evolution, Mickey had a smaller head, cranial vault, and eyes. He evolved toward the characteristics of his young nephew Morty (connected to Mickey by a dotted line.)

lists among his releasers the very features of babyhood that Disney affixed progressively to Mickey: "a relatively large head, predominance of the brain capsule, large and low-lying eyes, bulging cheek region, short and thick extremities, a springy elastic consistency, and clumsy movements." (I propose to leave aside for this article the contentious issue of whether or not our affectionate response to babyish features is truly innate and inherited directly from ancestral primates—as Lorenz argues—or whether it is simply learned from our immediate experience with babies and grafted upon an evolutionary predisposition for attaching ties of affection to certain learned signals. My argument works equally well in either case for I only claim that babyish features tend to elicit strong feelings of affection in adult humans, whether the biological basis be direct programming or the capacity to learn and fix upon signals. I also treat as collateral to my point the major thesis of Lorenz's article—that we respond not to the totality or *Gestalt*, but to a set of specific features acting as releasers. This argument is important to Lorenz because he wants to argue for revolutionary identity in modes of behavior between other vertebrates and humans, and we know that many birds, for example, often respond to abstract features rather than *Gestalten*. Lorenz' article published in 1950, bears the title *Ganzheit und Teil in der tierischen und menschlichen Gemeinschaft*—"Entirety and part in animal and human society." Disney's piecemeal change of Mickey's appearance does make sense in this context—he operated in sequential fashion upon Lorenz's primary releasers.)

Lorenz emphasizes the power that juvenile features hold over us, and the abstract quality of their influence, by pointing out that we judge other animals by the same criteria—although the judgment may be utterly inappropriate in an evolutionary context. We are, in short, fooled by an evolved response to our own babies, and we transfer our reaction to the same set of features in other animals.

Many animals, for reasons having nothing to do with the inspiration of affection in humans, possess some features also shared by human babies but not by human adults—large eyes and a bulging forehead with retreating chin, in particular. We are drawn to them, we cultivate them as pets, we stop and admire them in the wild—while we reject their small-eyed, long-snouted relatives who might make more affectionate companions or objects of admiration. Lorenz points out that the German names of many animals with features mimicking human babies end in the diminutive suffix *chen*, even though the animals are often larger than close relatives without such features—*Rotkehlchen* (robin), *Eichhornchen* (squirrel), and *Kaninchen* (rabbit), for example.

In a fascinating section, Lorenz then enlarges upon our capacity for biologically inappropriate response to other animals, or even to inanimate objects that mimic human features. "The most amazing objects can acquire remarkable, highly specific emotional values by 'experiential attachment' of human properties.... Steeply rising, somewhat overhanging cliff faces or dark stormclouds piling up have the same, immediate display value as a human being who is standing at full height and leaning slightly forwards"—that is, threatening.

We cannot help regarding a camel as aloof and unfriendly because it mimics, quite unwittingly and for other reasons, the "gesture of haughty rejection" common to so many human cultures. In this gesture, we raise our heads, placing our nose above our eyes. We then half-close our eyes and blow out through our nose—the "harumph" of the stereotyped upperclass Englishman or his well-trained servant. "All this," Lorenz argues quite cogently, "symbolizes resistance against all sensory modalities emanating from the disdained counterpart." But the poor camel cannot help carrying its nose above its elongate eyes, with mouth

Humans feel affection for animals with juvenile features: large eyes, bulging craniums, retreating chins (left column). Small-eyed, long-snouted animals (right column) do not elicit the same response. From Studies in Animal and Human Behavior, *Vol. II, by Konrad Lorenz, 1971. Methuen & Co. Ltd.*

drawn down. As Lorenz reminds us, if you wish to know whether a camel will eat out of your hand or spit, look at its ears, not the rest of its face.

In his important book *Expression of the Emotions in Man and Animals*, published in 1872, Charles Darwin traced the evolutionary basis of many common gestures to originally adaptive actions in animals later internalized as symbols in humans. Thus, he argued for evolutionary continuity of emotion, not only of form. We snarl and raise our upper lip in fierce anger—to expose our nonexistent fighting canine tooth. Our gesture of disgust repeats the facial actions associated with the highly adaptive act of vomiting in necessary circumstances. Darwin concluded, much to the distress of many Victorian contemporaries: "With mankind some expressions, such as the bristling of the hair under the influence of extreme terror, or the uncovering of the teeth under that of furious rage, can hardly be understood, except on the belief that man once existed in a much lower and animal-like condition."

In any case, the abstract features of human childhood elicit powerful emotional responses in us, even when they occur in other animals. I submit that Mickey Mouse's evolutionary road down the course of his own growth in reverse reflects the unconscious discovery of this biological principle by Disney and his artists. In fact, the emotional status of most Disney characters rests on the same set of distinctions. To this extent, the magic kingdom trades on a biological illusion—our ability to abstract and our propensity to transfer inappropriately to other animals the fitting responses we make to changing form in the growth of our own bodies.

Donald Duck also adopts more juvenile features through time. His elongated beak recedes and his eyes enlarge; he converges on Huey, Louie, and Dewey as surely as Mickey approaches Morty. But Donald, having inherited the mantle of Mickey's original misbehavior, remains more adult in form with his projecting beak and more sloping forehead.

Mouse villains or sharpies, contrasted with Mickey, are always more adult in appearance, although they often share Mickey's chronological age. In 1936, for example, Disney made a short entitled *Mickey's Rival*. Mortimer, a dandy in a yellow sports car, intrudes upon Mickey and Minnie's quiet country picnic. The thoroughly disreputable Mortimer has a head only 29 percent of body length, to Mickey's 45, and a snout 80 percent of head length, compared with Mickey's 49. (Nonetheless, and was it ever different, Minnie transfers her affection until an obliging bull from a neighboring field dispatches Mickey's rival.) Consider also the exaggerated adult features of other Disney characters—the swaggering bully Peg-leg Pete or the simple if lovable, dolt Goofy.

As a second, serious biological comment on Mickey's odyssey in form, I note that his path to eternal youth repeats, in epitome, our own evolutionary story. For humans are neotenic. We have evolved by retaining to adulthood the originally juvenile features of our ancestors. Our australopithecine forebears, like Mickey in *Steamboat Willie*, had projecting jaws and low vaulted craniums.

Dandified, disreputable Mortimer (here stealing Minnie's affections) has strikingly more adult features than Mickey. His head is smaller in proportion to body length; his nose is a full 80 percent of head length. © Walt Disney Productions

Our embryonic skulls scarcely differ from those of chimpanzees. And we follow the same path of changing form through growth: relative decrease of the cranial vault since brains grow so much more slowly than bodies after birth, and continuous relative increase of the jaw. But while chimps accentuate these changes, producing an adult strikingly different in form from a baby, we proceed much more slowly down the same path and never get nearly so far. Thus, as adults, we retain juvenile features. To be sure, we change enough to produce a notable difference between baby and adult, but our alteration is far smaller than that experienced by chimps and other primates.

A marked slowdown of development rates has triggered our neoteny. Primates are slow developers among mammals, but we have accentuated the trend to a degree matched by no other mammal. We have very long periods of gestation, markedly extended childhoods, and the longest life span of any mammal. The morphological features of eternal youth have served us well. Our enlarged brain is, at least in part, a result of extending rapid prenatal growth rates to later ages. (In all mammals, the brain grows rapidly in utero but often very little after birth. We have extended this fetal phase into postnatal life.)

But the changes in timing themselves have been just as important. We are preeminently learning animals, and our extended childhood permits the transference of culture by education. Many animals display flexibility and play in childhood but follow rigidly programmed patterns as adults. Lorenz writes, in the same article cited above: "The characteristic which is so vital for the human peculiarity of the true man—that of always remaining in a state of development—is quite certainly a gift which we owe to the neotenous nature of mankind."

In short, we, like Mickey, never grow up although we, alas, do grow old. Best wishes to you, Mickey, for your next half-century. May we stay as young as you, but grow a bit wiser.

Discussion Questions

1. How does Gould make plain his affection for both his subjects, that is, evolution and Mickey Mouse?

2. What literary techniques does Gould use to make less imposing the empirical techniques and vocabulary of his profession?

3. Compare Gould's efforts to make evolution understandable with those of René Dubos.

4. Using some of Gould's techniques, apply a scientific analysis to another aspect of popular culture, for example, a statistical study of the frequency of "highways" in country and western songs.

5. Gould says, "We are, in short, fooled by an evolved response to our own babies, and we transfer our reaction to the same set of features in other animals." What evidence does he bring to support his claim? What would he say of someone who kept a snake (or a camel) as a pet?

6. Does Gould's analysis apply to cartoon figures other than those associated with Walt Disney? The Roadrunner, for example?

Cartoon villians are not the only Disney characters with exaggerated adult features. Goofy, like Mortimer, has a small head relative to body length and a prominent snout. © Walt Disney Productions

GRAHAM GREENE

Graham Greene, the author of over thirty novels and several collections of short stories and essays, was born in England in 1904. After graduating from Oxford, he supported his fiction-writing habit by working as a journalist and editor and eventually became director of a British publishing house. In 1926, he converted to Catholicism, a decision that affected nearly all his later writing.

Greene claims that as a writer he had "a vague ambition to create something legendary out of a contemporary thriller" and his novels frequently combine the ingredients of popular espionage fiction with serious religious themes. Not surprisingly, thirteen of his novels and two of his short stories have been made into films. Among his most famous works are Brighton Rock (1938), The Power and the Glory (1940), The Heart of the Matter (1948), The Quiet American (1955), The Honorary Consul (1973), and The Human Factor (1978). "The Revolver in the Corner Cupboard" first appeared in The Lost Childhood and Other Essays (1951) and was later included as an episode in Greene's autobiography. A Sort of Life (1971).

The Revolver in the Corner Cupboard

I can remember very clearly the afternoon I found the revolver in the brown deal corner cupboard in the bedroom which I shared with my elder brother. It was the early autumn of 1922. I was seventeen and terribly bored and in love with my sister's governess—one of those miserable, hopeless, romantic loves of adolescence that set in many minds the idea that love and despair are inextricable and that successful love hardly deserves the name. At that age one may fall irrevocably in love with failure, and success of any kind loses half its savour before it is experienced. Such a love is surrendered once and for all to the singer at the pavement's edge, the bankrupt, the old school friend who wants to touch you for a dollar. Perhaps in many so conditioned it is the love for God that mainly survives, because in his eyes they can imagine themselves remaining always drab, seedy, unsuccessful, and therefore worthy of notice.

The revolver was a small genteel object with six chambers like a tiny egg stand, and there was a cardboard box of bullets. It has only recently occurred to me that they may have been blanks; I always assumed them to be live ammunition, and I never mentioned the discovery to my brother because I had realized the moment I saw the revolver the use I intended to make of it. (I don't to this day know why he possessed it; certainly he had no licence, and he was only three years older than myself. A large family is as departmental as a Ministry.)

My brother was away—probably climbing in the Lake District—and until he returned the revolver was to all intents mine. I knew what to do with it because I had been reading a book (the name Ossendowski comes to mind as the possible author) describing how the White Russian officers, condemned to inaction in South Russia at the tail-end of the counter-revolutionary war, used to invent hazards with which to escape boredom. One man would slip a charge into a revolver and turn the chambers at random, and his companion would put the revolver to his head and pull the trigger. The chance, of course, was six to one in favour of life.

How easily one forgets emotions. If I were dealing now with an imaginary character, I would feel it necessary for verisimilitude to make him hesitate, put the revolver back into the cupboard, return to it again after an interval, reluctantly and fearfully, when the burden of boredom became too great. But in fact I think there was no hesitation at all, for the next I can remember is crossing Berkhamsted Common, gashed here and there between the gorse bushes with the stray trenches of the first Great War, towards the Ashridge beeches. Perhaps before I had made the discovery, boredom had already reached an intolerable depth.

I think the boredom was far deeper than the love. It had always been a feature of childhood: it would set in on the second day of the school holidays. The first day was all happiness, and, after the horrible confinement and publicity of school, seemed to consist of light, space and silence. But a prison conditions its inhabitants. I never wanted to return to it (and finally expressed my rebellion by the simple act of running away), but yet I was so conditioned that freedom bored me unutterably.

The psycho-analysis that followed my act of rebellion had fixed the boredom as hypo fixes the image on the negative. I emerged from those delightful months in London spent at my analyst's house—perhaps the happiest months of my life—correctly orientated, able to take a proper extrovert interest in my fellows (the jargon rises to the lips), but wrung dry. For years, it seemed to me, I could take no aesthetic interest in any visual thing at all: staring at a sight that others assured me was beautiful, I would feel nothing. I was fixed in my boredom. (Writing this I come on a remark of Rilke: "Psycho-analysis is too fundamental a help for me, it helps you once and for all, it clears you up, and to find myself finally cleared up one day might be even more helpless than this chaos.")

Now with the revolver in my pocket I was beginning to emerge. I had stumbled on the perfect cure. I was going to escape in one way or another, and because escape was inseparably connected with the Common in my mind, it was there that I went.

The wilderness of gorse, old trenches, abandoned butts was the unchanging backcloth of most of the adventures of childhood. It was to the Common I had decamped for my act of rebellion some years before, with the intention, expressed in a letter left after breakfast on the heavy black sideboard, that there I would stay, day and night, until either I had starved or my parents had given in; when I pictured war it was always in terms of this Common, and myself leading a guerilla campaign in the ragged waste, for no one, I was persuaded, knew its paths so intimately (how humiliating that in my own domestic campaign I was ambushed by my elder sister after a few hours).

Beyond the Common lay a wide grass ride known for some reason as Cold Harbour to which I would occasionally with some fear take a horse, and beyond this again stretched Ashridge Park, the smooth olive skin of beech trees and the thick last year's quagmire of leaves, dark like old pennies. Deliberately I chose my ground, I believe without any real fear—perhaps because I was uncertain myself whether I was play-acting; perhaps because so many acts which my elders would have regarded as neurotic, but which I still consider to have been under the circumstances highly reasonable, lay in the background of this more dangerous venture.

There had been, for example, perhaps five or six years before, the disappointing morning in the dark room by the linen cupboard on the eve of term when I had patiently drunk a quantity of hypo under the impression that it was poisonous: on another occasion the blue glass bottle of hay fever lotion which as it contained a small quantity of cocaine had probably been good for my mood: the bunch of deadly nightshade that I had eaten with only a slight narcotic effect: the twenty aspirins I had taken before swimming in the empty out-of-term school baths (I can still remember the curious sensation of swimming through wool): these acts may have removed all sense of strangeness as I slipped a bullet into a chamber and, holding the revolver behind my back, spun the chambers round.

Had I romantic thoughts about the governess? Undoubtedly I must have had, but I think that at the most they simply eased the medicine down. Boredom, aridity, those were the main emotions. Unhappy love has, I suppose, sometimes driven boys to suicide, but this was not suicide, whatever a coroner's jury might have said of it: it was a gamble with six chances to one against an inquest. The romantic flavour—the autumn scene, the small heavy compact shape lying in the fingers—that perhaps was a tribute to adolescent love, but the discovery that it was possible to enjoy again the visible world by risking its total loss was one I was bound to make sooner or later.

I put the muzzle of the revolver in my right ear and pulled the trigger. There was a minute click, and looking down at the chamber I could see that the charge had moved into place. I was out by one. I remember an extraordinary sense of jubilation. It was as if a light had been turned on. My heart was knocking in its cage, and I felt that life contained an infinite number of possibilities. It was like a young man's first successful experience of sex—as if in that Ashridge glade one had passed a test of manhood. I went home and put the revolver back in the corner cupboard.

The odd thing about this experience was that it was repeated several times. At fairly long intervals I found myself craving for the drug. I took the revolver with me when I went up to Oxford and I would walk out from Headington towards Elsfield down what is now a wide arterial road, smooth and shiny like the walls of a public lavatory. Then it was a sodden unfrequented country lane. The revolver would be whipped behind my back, the chambers twisted, the muzzle quickly and surreptitiously inserted beneath the black and ugly winter tree, the trigger pulled.

Slowly the effect of the drug wore off—I lost the sense of jubilation, I began to gain from the experience only the crude kick of excitement. It was like the difference between love and lust. And as the quality of the experience deteriorated so my sense of responsibility grew and worried me. I wrote a very bad piece of free verse (free because it was easier in that way to express my meaning without literary equivocation) describing how, in order to give a fictitious sense of danger, I would 'press the trigger of a revolver I already know to be empty.' This piece of verse I would leave permanently on my desk, so that if I lost my gamble, there would be incontrovertible evidence of an accident, and my parents, I thought, would be less troubled than by an apparent suicide—or than by the rather bizarre truth.

But it was back at Berkhamsted that I paid a permanent farewell to the drug. As I took my fifth dose it occurred to me that I wasn't even excited: I was beginning to pull the trigger about as casually as I might take an aspirin tablet. I decided to give the revolver—which was six-chambered—a sixth and last chance. Twirling the chambers round, I put the muzzle to my ear for the last time and heard the familiar empty click as the chambers revolved. I was through with the drug, and walking back over the Common, down the new road by the ruined castle, past the private entrance to the gritty old railway station—reserved for the use of Lord Brownlow—my mind was already busy on other plans. One campaign was over, but the war against boredom had got to go on.

I put the revolver back in the corner cupboard, and going downstairs I lied gently and convincingly to my parents that a friend had invited me to join him in Paris.

REVOLVER IN THE CORNER CUPBOARD

Discussion Questions

1. What is Greene's reason for wanting to play Russian roulette? How certain is he about his reason? How is his sense of that reason complicated by his playacting? Go through the essay and locate examples of Greene's sensitivity to acting and fiction.

2. In the opening sentence, why does Greene say "the" revolver? Suppose he had written "a" revolver. What difference does the definite article make?

3. Compare the techniques Graham Greene uses to describe an intense experience of youth to those employed by Richard Wright in "Innocence."

4. How does the language of drug-taking enter into Greene's suicidal experiences? How does the metaphor help him explain his behavior? Does the "drug" cure Greene's boredom? Is that why he stops? In the final paragraph, why does he emphasize the fact that he lied to his parents? Are there other instances of lying in the essay? Explain whether or not you think the character's emotions are different at the beginning and end of the essay.

S. I. HAYAKAWA

Born in Vancouver, Canada, in 1906, S. I. Hayakawa taught English in several American Universities and became a leader in and popularizer of the new study of semantics. His fame in this field led him to be appointed as acting President of San Francisco State University in 1968; colorful and unyielding actions as a president led to wider fame and the United States Senate in 1976.

In all his many books Hayakawa has tried to bring to the general reading public the insights into controversy and social conflict that the formal study of language can provide. In the selection that follows, from Language in Thought and Action (1938), he discusses the origin of the authority over words that most people grant to dictionaries.

How Dictionaries Are Made

It is widely believed that every word has a correct meaning, that we learn these meanings principally from teachers and grammarians (except that most of the time we don't bother to, so that we ordinarily speak "sloppy English"), and that dictionaries and grammars are the supreme authority in matters of meaning and usage. Few people ask by what authority the writers of dictionaries and grammars say what they say. I once got into a dispute with an Englishwoman over the pronunciation of a word and offered to look it up in the dictionary. The Englishwoman said firmly "What for? I am English. I was born and brought up in England. The way I speak *is* English." Such self-assurance about one's own language is not uncommon among the English. In the United States, however, anyone who is willing to quarrel with the dictionary is regarded as either eccentric or mad.

  Let us see how dictionaries are made and how the editors arrive at definitions. What follows applies, incidentally, only to those dictionary offices where first-hand, original research goes on—not those in which editors simply copy existing dictionaries. The task of writing a dictionary begins with the reading of vast amounts of the literature of the period or subject that the dictionary is to cover. As the editors read, they copy on cards every interesting or rare word, every unusual or peculiar occurrence of a common word, a large number of common words in their ordinary uses, and also the sentences in which each of these words appears, thus:

> pail
>
> The dairy *pails* bring home increase of milk
>
> Keats, Endymion
>
> 1, 44-45

That is to say, the context of each word is collected, along with the word itself. For a really big job of dictionary writing, such as the *Oxford English Dictionary* (usually bound in about twenty-five volumes), millions of such cards are collected, and the task of editing occupies decades. As the cards are collected, they are alphabetized and sorted. When the sorting is completed, there will be for each word anywhere from two to three to several hundred illustrative quotations, each on its card.

To define a word, then, the dictionary editor places before him the stack of cards illustrating that word; each of the cards represents an actual use of the word by a writer of some literary or historical importance. He reads the cards carefully, discards some, rereads the rest, and divides up the stack according to what he thinks are the several senses of the word. Finally, he writes his definitions, following the hard-and-fast rule that each definition *must* be based on what the quotations in front of him reveal about the meaning of the word. The editor cannot be influenced by what *he* thinks a given word *ought* to mean. He must work according to the cards or not at all.

The writing of a dictionary, therefore, is not a task of setting up authoritative statements about the "true meanings" of words, but a task of *recording,* to the best of one's ability, what various words *have meant* to authors in the distant or immediate past. *The writer of a dictionary is a historian, not a lawgiver.* If, for example, we had been writing a dictionary in 1890, or even as late as 1919, we could have said that the word "broadcast" means "to scatter" (seed, for example), but we could not have decreed that from 1921 on, the most common meaning of the word should become "to disseminate audible messages, etc., by radio transmission." To regard the dictionary as an "authority," therefore, is to credit the dictionary writer with gifts of prophecy which neither he nor anyone else possesses. In choosing our words when we speak or write, we can be *guided* by the historical record afforded us by the dictionary, but we cannot be *bound* by it, because new situations, new experiences, new inventions, new feelings, are always compelling us to give new uses to old words. Looking under a "hood," we should ordinarily have found, five hundred years ago, a monk; today, we find a motorcar engine.

Discussion Questions

1. To what new authority does Hayakawa's argument shift the question of a dictionary's authority concerning words?
2. What is the effect for Hayakawa's argument of his constant repetition of the word, "card"?
3. Compare Hayakawa's views of the nature of language to those of Robert Frost and Edmund Wilson.
4. Pick a word or group of words that seem to you to be changing in meaning at the present time. Using the Oxford English Dictionary, write a brief history of your choice and an explanation of its current condition.

Lillian Hellman

Born in New Orleans in 1906, Lillian Hellman became the country's leading female playwright before she was forty; a rank she has maintained ever since while expanding her activities as an author. For many years she has also worked as a screenwriter, adapting her own material and that of others. In addition, she has worked as a director of plays and has contributed lyrics to Leonard Bernstein's Theater Songs *(1965). The first volume of her autobiography,* An Unfinished Woman, *in which the selection that follows appears, won the National Book Award in Arts and Letters for 1969, and her second volume,* Pentimento *(1973), was nominated for that prize.*

The Fig Tree

There was a heavy fig tree on the lawn where the house turned the corner into the side street, and to the front and sides of the fig tree were three live oaks that hid the fig tree from my aunts' boardinghouse. I suppose I was eight or nine before I discovered the pleasures of the fig tree, and although I have lived in many houses since then, including a few I made for myself, I still think of it as my first and most beloved home.

    I learned early, in our strange life of living half in New York and half in New Orleans, that I made my New Orleans teachers uncomfortable because I was too far ahead of my schoolmates, and my New York teachers irritable because I was too far behind. But in New Orleans, I found a solution: I skipped school at least once a week and often twice, knowing that nobody cared or would report my absence. On those days I would set out for school done up in polished strapped shoes and a prim hat against what was known as "the climate," carrying my books and a little basket filled with delicious stuff my Aunt Jenny and Carrie, the cook, had made for my school lunch. I would round the corner of the side street, move on toward St. Charles Avenue, and sit on a bench as if I were waiting for a streetcar until the boarders and the neighbors had gone to work or settled down for the post-breakfast rest that all Southern ladies thought necessary. Then I would run back to the fig tree, dodging in and out of bushes to make sure the house had no dangers for me. The fig tree was heavy, solid, comfortable, and I had, through time, convinced myself that it wanted me, missed me when I was absent, and approved all the rigging I had done for the happy days I spent in its arms: I had made a sling to hold the school books, a pulley rope for my lunch basket, a hole for the bottle of afternoon cream-soda pop, a fishing pole and a smelly little bag of elderly bait, a pillow embroidered with a picture of

Henry Clay on a horse that I had stolen from Mrs. Stillman, one of my aunts' boarders, and a proper nail to hold my dress and shoes to keep them neat for the return to the house.

It was in that tree that I learned to read, filled with the passions that can only come to the bookish, grasping, very young, bewildered by almost all of what I read, sweating in the attempt to understand a world of adults I fled from in real life but desperately wanted to join in books. (I did not connect the grown men and women in literature with the grown men and women I saw around me. They were, to me, another species.)

It was in the fig tree that I learned that anything alive in water was of enormous excitement to me. True, the water was gutter water and the fishing could hardly be called that: sometimes the things that swam in New Orleans gutters were not pretty, but I didn't know what was pretty and I liked them all. After lunch—the men boarders returned for a large lunch and a siesta—the street would be safe again, with only the noise from Carrie and her helpers in the kitchen, and they could be counted on never to move past the back porch, or the chicken coop. Then I would come down from my tree to sit on the side street gutter with my pole and bait. Often I would catch a crab that had wandered in from the Gulf, more often I would catch my favorite, the crayfish, and sometimes I would, in that safe hour, have at least six of them for my basket. Then about 2:30, when house and street would stir again, I would go back to my tree for another few hours of reading or dozing or having what I called the ill hour. It is too long ago for me to know why I thought the hour "ill," but certainly I did not mean sick. I think I meant an intimation of sadness, a first recognition that there was so much to understand that one might never find one's way and the first signs, perhaps, that for a nature like mine, the way would not be easy. I cannot be sure that I felt all that then, although I can be sure that it was in the fig tree, a few years later, that I was first puzzled by the conflict which would haunt me, harm me, and benefit me the rest of my life: simply, the stubborn, relentless, driving desire to be alone as it came into conflict with the desire not to be alone when I wanted not to be. I already guessed that other people wouldn't allow that, although, as an only child, I pretended for the rest of my life that they would and must allow it to me.

Discussion Questions

1. Lillian Hellman admits that she has forgotten what she had named as the "ill hour." How does she relate what she is sure she remembers to what she is less sure of? What makes the admitted vagueness seem natural and probable?
2. What would the essay gain or lose from a more highly detailed physical description of the fig tree?
3. Compare Lillian Hellman's memories of early reading to those of Eudora Welty.
4. Describe a place or time in your own past of comparable importance to you.

ERNEST HEMINGWAY

The Nobel Prize-winning American writer, Ernest Hemingway (1899–1961), was born in Illinois. After a stint as a reporter for the Kansas City Star, *volunteered for Red Cross ambulance service in France and Italy during World War I. In 1921, he settled in Paris, a member of the expatriate group of American writers and artists who gravitated around Gertrude Stein and thought of themselves as a "lost generation." His first major collection of fiction,* In Our Time *(1925), established him as a leading practitioner of the short story and created a new "voice" for fiction, one that we can hear in the following descriptive essay, "The Clark's Fork Valley, Wyoming."*

Hemingway's best known novels are The Sun Also Rises *(1926),* A Farewell to Arms *(1929),* For Whom the Bell Tolls *(1940), and* The Old Man and the Sea *(1952). Besides his numerous pieces of journalism, Hemingway's nonfiction includes* Death in the Afternoon *(1932), an account of bullfighting,* Green Hills of Africa *(1935), an account of big-game hunting, and his posthumously published memoirs of Paris,* A Moveable Feast *(1964).*

The Clark's Fork Valley, Wyoming

At the end of summer, the big trout would be out in the centre of the stream; they were leaving the pools along the upper part of the river and dropping down to spend the winter in the deep water of the canyon. It was wonderful fly-fishing then in the first weeks of September. The native trout were sleek, shining, and heavy, and nearly all of them leaped when they took the fly. If you fished two flies, you would often have two big trout on and the need to handle them very delicately in that heavy current.

The nights were cold, and, if you woke in the night, you would hear the coyotes. But you did not want to get out on the stream too early in the day because the nights were so cold they chilled the water, and the sun had to be on the river until almost noon before the trout would start to feed.

You could ride in the morning, or sit in front of the cabin, lazy in the sun, and look across the valley where the hay was cut so the meadows were cropped brown and smooth to the line of quaking aspens along the river, now turning yellow in the fall. And on the hills rising beyond, the sage was silvery grey.

Up the river were the two peaks of Pilot and Index, where we would hunt mountain-sheep later in the month, and you sat in the sun and marvelled at the formal, clean-lined shape mountains can have at a distance, so that you remember them in the shapes they show from far away, and not as the broken rockslides you crossed, the jagged edges you pulled up by, and the narrow shelves you sweated along, afraid to look down, to round that peak that looked so smooth and geometrical. You climbed around it to come out on a clear space to look down to where an old ram and three young rams were feeding in the juniper bushes in a high, grassy pocket cupped against the broken rock of the peak.

The old ram was purple-grey, his rump was white, and when

he raised his head you saw the great heavy curl of his horns. It was the white of his rump that had betrayed him to you in the green of the junipers when you had lain in the lee of a rock, out of the wind, three miles away, looking carefully at every yard of the high country through a pair of good Zeiss glasses.

Now as you sat in front of the cabin, you remembered that down-hill shot and the young rams standing, their heads turned, staring at him, waiting for him to get up. They could not see you on that high ledge, nor wind you, and the shot made no more impression on them than a boulder falling.

You remembered the year we had built a cabin at the head of Timber Creek, and the big grizzly that tore it open every time we were away. The snow came late that year, and this bear would not hibernate, but spent his autumn tearing open cabins and ruining a trap-line. But he was so smart you never saw him in the day. Then you remembered coming on the three grizzlies in the high country at the head of Crandall Creek. You heard a crash of timber and thought it was a cow elk bolting, and then there they were, in the broken shadow, running with an easy, lurching smoothness, the afternoon sun making their coats a soft, bristling silver.

You remembered elk bugling in the fall, the bull so close you could see his chest muscles swell as he lifted his head, and still not see his head in the thick timber; but hear that deep, high mounting whistle and the answer from across another valley. You thought of all the heads you had turned down and refused to shoot, and you were pleased about every one of them.

You remembered the children learning to ride; how they did with different horses; and how they loved the country. You remembered how this country had looked when you first came into it, and the year you had to stay four months after you had brought the first car ever to come in for the swamp roads to freeze solid enough to get the car out. You could remember all the hunting and all the fishing and the riding in the summer sun and the dust of the pack-train, the silent riding in the hills in the sharp cold of fall going up after the cattle on the high range, finding them wild as deer and as quiet, only bawling noisily when they were all herded together being forced along down into the lower country.

Then there was the winter; the trees bare now, the snow blowing so you could not see, the saddle wet, then frozen as you came down-hill, breaking a trail through the snow, trying to keep your legs moving, and the sharp, warming taste of whiskey when you hit the ranch and changed your clothes in front of the big open fireplace. It's a good country.

THE CLARK'S FORK VALLEY, WYOMING

Discussion Questions

1. What is the effect of writing in the second person ("you")? Why doesn't Hemingway say "I"? Does Hemingway mean "you" the reader or someone else? Explain exactly who is meant by "you."

2. Examine Hemingway's vocabulary. What kind of words does he prefer? What kind of words does he seem reluctant to use?

3. What details about the country does Hemingway most cherish? What do these details have in common? What image of the natural world is conveyed in this essay? What does his sense of the natural world have in common with Edward Hoagland's?

4. How does Hemingway succeed in conveying senses of both a particular and a general time? Using his essay as a model, write a brief description of a spot on earth that you love. Avoid explicit evaluation and let your details express your affection and enthusiasm. Work into your essay memories that are both particular and general.

EDWARD HOAGLAND

The novelist, essayist, and travel writer Edward Hoagland was born in New York City in 1932 and graduated from Harvard University. In 1954, he received the Houghton-Mifflin Literary Fellowship Award for Cat Man, *the first of a series of literary honors that include an American Academy of Arts and Letters Travelling Fellowship, a Guggenheim Fellowship, an O. Henry Award, and a New York State Council on the Arts Award. Hoagland has taught at Rutgers, Sarah Lawrence, the University of Iowa, and Columbia, and his writing has appeared in such magazines as* Harper's, Commentary, The New Yorker, Esquire, *and the* New American Review. *Many of his highly personal essays deal with people and animals on the edge of survival. Some have been collected in the* Edward Hoagland Reader *(1979). Among his many critically acclaimed books are* The Courage of Turtles *(1971),* Walking the Dead Diamond River *(1973),* Red Wolves and Black Bears *(1976),* African Calliope: A Journey to the Sudan *(1979), and* The Tugman's Passage *(1982).*

The Courage of Turtles

Turtles are a kind of bird with the governor turned low. With the same attitude of removal, they cock a glance at what is going on, as if they need only to fly away. Until recently they were also a case of virtue rewarded, at least in the town where I grew up, because, being humble creatures, there were plenty of them. Even when we still had a few bobcats in the woods the local snapping turtles, growing up to forty pounds, were the largest carnivores. You would see them through the amber water, as big as greeny wash basins at the bottom of the pond, until they faded into the inscrutable mud as if they hadn't existed at all.

When I was ten I went to Dr. Green's Pond, a two-acre pond across the road. When I was twelve I walked a mile or so to Taggart's Pond, which was lusher, had big water snakes and a waterfall; and shortly after that I was bicycling way up to the adventuresome vastness of Mud Pond, a lake-sized body of water in the reservoir system of a Connecticut city, possessed of cat-backed little islands and empty shacks and a forest of pines and hardwoods along the shore. Otters, foxes and mink left their prints on the bank; there were pike and perch. As I got older, the estates and forgotten back lots in town were parceled out and sold for nice prices, yet, though the woods had shrunk, it seemed that fewer people walked in the woods. The new residents didn't know how to find them. Eventually, exploring, they did find them, and it required some ingenuity and doubling around on my part to go for eight miles without meeting someone. I was grown by now, I lived in New York, and that's what I wanted on the occasional weekends when I came out.

Since Mud Pond contained drinking water I had felt confident nothing untoward would happen there. For a long while the developers stayed away, until the drought of the mid-1960s. This event, squeezing the edges in, convinced the local water company that the pond really wasn't a necessity as a catch basin, however; so they bulldozed a hole in the earthen dam, bulldozed the banks to fill in the bottom, and landscaped the flow of water that remained to wind like an English brook and provide a domestic view for the houses which were planned. Most of the painted turtles of Mud Pond, who had been inaccessible as they sunned on their rocks wound up in boxes in boy's closets within a matter of days. Their footsteps in the dry leaves gave them away as they wandered forlornly. The snappers and the little musk turtles, neither of whom leave the water except once a year to lay their eggs, dug into the drying mud for another siege of hot weather, which they were accustomed to doing whenever the pond got low. But this time it was low for good; the mud baked over them and slowly entombed them. As for the ducks, I couldn't stroll in the woods and not feel guilty, because they were crouched beside every stagnant pothole, or were slinking between the bushes with their heads tucked into their shoulders so that I wouldn't see them. If they decided I had, they beat their way through the screen of trees, striking their wings dangerously, and wheeled about with that headlong, magnificent velocity to locate another poor puddle.

I used to catch possums and black snakes as well as turtles, and I kept dogs and goats. Some summers I worked in a menagerie with the big personalities of the animal kingdom, like elephants and rhinoceroses. I was twenty before these enthusiasms began to wane, and it was then that I picked turtles as the particular animal I wanted to keep in touch with. I was allergic to fur, for one thing, and turtles need minimal care and not much in the way of quarters. They're personable beasts. They see the same colors we do and they seem to see just as well, as one discovers in trying to sneak up on them. In the laboratory they unravel the twists of a maze with the hot-blooded rapidity of a mammal. Though they can't run as fast as a rat, they improve on their errors just as quickly, pausing at each crossroads to look left and right. And they rock rhythmically in place, as we often do, although they are hatched from eggs, not the womb. (A common explanation psychologists give for our pleasure in rocking quietly is that it recapitulates our mother's heartbeat *in utero*.)

Snakes, by contrast, are dryly silent and priapic. They are smooth movers, legalistic, unblinking, and they afford the humor which the humorless do. But they make challenging captives; sometimes they don't eat for months on a point of order—if the light isn't right, for instance. Alligators are sticklers too. They're like war-horses, or German shepherds, and with their bar-shaped, vertical pupils adding emphasis, they have the *idée fixe* of eating, eating, even when they choose to refuse all food and stubbornly die. They delight in tossing a salamander up towards the sky and grabbing him in their long mouths as he comes down. They're so eager that they get the jitters, and they're too much of a proposition for a casual aquarium like mine. Frogs are depressingly defenseless: that moist, extensive back, with the bones almost sticking through. Hold a frog and you're holding its skeleton. Frogs' tasty legs are the staff of life to many animals—herons, raccoons, ribbon snakes—though they themselves are hard to feed. It's not an enviable role to be the staff of life, and after frogs you descend down the evolutionary ladder a big step to fish.

Turtles cough, burp, whistle, grunt and hiss, and produce social judgments. They put their heads together amicably enough, but then one drives the other back with the suddenness of two dogs who have been conversing in tones too low for an onlooker to hear. They pee in fear when they're first caught, but exercise both pluck and optimism in trying to escape, walking for hundreds of yards within the confines of their pen, carrying the weight of that cumbersome box on legs which are cruelly positioned for walking. They don't feel that the contest is unfair; they keep plugging, rolling like sailorly souls—a bobbing, infirm gait, a brave, sea-legged momentum—stopping occasionally to study the lay of the land. For me, anyway, they manage to contain the rest of the animal world. They can stretch out their necks like a giraffe, or loom underwater like an apocryphal hippo. They browse on lettuce thrown on the water like a cow moose which is partly submerged. They have a penguin's alertness, combined with a build like a Brontosaurus when they rise up on tiptoe. Then they hunch and ponderously lunge like a grizzly going forward.

Baby turtles in a turtle bowl are a puzzle in geometrics. They're as decorative as pansy petals, but they are also self-directed building blocks, propping themselves on one another in different arrangements, before upending the tower. The timid individuals turn fearless, or vice versa. If one gets a bit arrogant he will push the others off the rock and afterwards climb down into the water and cling to the back of one of those he has bullied, tickling him with his hind feet until he bucks like a bronco. On the other hand, when this same milder-mannered fellow isn't exerting himself, he will stare right into the face of the sun for hours. What could be more lionlike? And he's at home in or out of the water and does lots of metaphysical tilting. He sinks and rises, with an infinity of levels to choose from; or, elongating himself, he climbs out on the land again to perambulate, sits boxed in his box, and finally slides back in the water, submerging into dreams.

I have five of these babies in a kidney-shaped bowl. The hatchling, who is a painted turtle, is not as large as the top joint of my thumb. He eats chicken gladly. Other foods he will attempt to eat but not with sufficient perseverance to succeed because he's so little. The yellow-bellied terrapin is probably a yearling, and he eats salad voraciously, but no meat, fish or fowl. The Cumberland terrapin won't touch salad or chicken but eats fish and all of the meats except bacon. The little snapper, with a black crenelated shell, feasts on any kind of meat, but rejects greens and fish. The fifth of the turtles is African. I acquired him only recently and don't know him well. A mottled brown, he unnerves the green turtles, dragging their food off to his lairs. He doesn't seem to want to be green—he bites the algae off his shell, hanging meanwhile at daring, steep, head-first angles.

The snapper was a Ferdinand until I provided him with deeper water. Now he snaps at my pencil with his downturned and fearsome mouth, his swollen face like a napalm victim's. The Cumberland has an elliptical red mark on the side of his green-and-yellow head. He is benign by nature and ought to be as elegant as his scientific name (*Pseudemys scripta elegans*), except he has contracted a disease of the air bladder which has permanently inflated it; he floats high in the water at an undignified slant and can't go under. There may have been internal bleeding, too, because his carapace is stained along its ridge. Unfortunately, like flowers, baby turtles often die. Their mouths fill up with a white fungus and their lungs with pneumonia. Their organs clog up from the rust in the water, or diet troubles, and, like a dying man's, their eyes and heads become too prominent. Toward the end, the edge of the shell becomes flabby as felt and folds around them like a shroud.

While they live they're like puppies. Although they're vivacious, they would be a bore to be with all the time, so I also have an adult wood turtle about six inches long. Her shell is the equal of any seashell for sculpturing, even a Cellini shell; it's like an old, dusty, richly engraved medallion dug out of a hillside. Her legs are salmon-orange bordered with black and protected by canted, heroic scales. Her plastron—the bottom shell—is splotched like a margay cat's coat, with black ocelli on a yellow background. It is convex to make room for the female organs inside, whereas a male's would be concave to help him fit tightly on top of her. Altogether, she exhibits every camouflage color on her limbs and shells. She has a turtleneck, a tail like an elephant's, wise old pachydermous hind legs and the face of a turkey—except that when I carry her she gazes at the passing ground with a hawk's eyes and mouth. Her feet fit to the fingers of my hand, one to each one, and she rides looking down. She can walk on the floor in perfect silence, but usually she lets her shell knock portentously, like a footstep, so that she resembles some grand, concise, slow-moving id. But if an earthworm is presented, she jerks swiftly ahead, poises above it and strikes like a mongoose, consuming it with wild vigor. Yet she will climb on my lap to eat bread or boiled eggs.

If put into a creek, she swims like a cutter, nosing forward to intercept a strange turtle and smell him. She drifts with the current to go downstream, maneuvering behind a rock when she wants to take stock, or sinking to the nether levels, while bubbles float up. Getting out, choosing her path, she will proceed a distance and dig into a pile of humus, thrusting herself to the coolest layer at the bottom. The hole closes over her until it's as small as a mouse's hole. She's not as aquatic as a musk turtle, not quite as terrestrial as the box turtles in the same woods, but because of her versatility she's marvelous, she's everywhere. And though she breathes the way we breathe, with scarcely perceptible movements of her chest, sometimes instead she pumps her throat ruminatively, like a pipe smoker sucking and puffing. She waits and blinks, pumping her throat, turning her head, then sets off like a loping tiger in slow motion, hurdling the jungly lumber, the pea vine and twigs. She estimates angles so well that when she rides over the rocks, sliding down a drop-off with her rugged front legs extended, she has the grace of a rodeo mare.

But she's well off to be with me rather than at Mud Pond. The other turtles have fled—those that aren't baked into the bottom. Creeping up the brooks to sad, constricted marshes, burdened as they are with that box on their backs, they're walking into a setup where all their enemies move thirty times faster than they. It's like the nightmare most of us have whimpered through, where we are weighted down disastrously while trying to flee; fleeing our home ground, we try to run.

I've seen turtles in still worse straits. On Broadway, in New York, there is a penny arcade which used to sell baby terrapins that were scrawled with bon mots in enamel paint, such as KISS ME BABY. The manager turned out to be a wholesaler as well, and once I asked him whether he had any larger turtles to sell. He took me upstairs to a loft room devoted to the turtle business. There were desks for the paper work and a series of racks that held shallow tin bins atop one another, each with several hundred babies crawling around in it. He was a smudgy-complexioned, serious fellow and he did have a few adult terrapins, but I was going to school and wasn't planning to buy; I'd only wanted to see them. They were aquatic turtles, but here they went without water, presumably for weeks, lurching about in those dry bins like handicapped citizens, living on gumption. An easel where the artist worked stood in the middle of the floor. She had a palette and a clip attachment for fastening the babies in place. She wore a smock and a beret, and was homely, short and eccentric-looking, with funny black hair, like some of the ladies who show their paintings in Washington Square in May. She had a cold, she was smoking, and her hand wasn't very steady, although she worked quickly enough. The smile that she produced for me would have looked giddy if she had been happier, or drunk. Of course the turtles' doom was sealed when she painted them, because their bodies inside would continue to grow but their shells would not. Gradually, invisibly, they would be crushed. Around us their bellies—two thousand belly shells—rubbed on the bins with a mournful, momentous hiss.

Somehow there were so many of them I didn't rescue one. Years later, however, I was walking on First Avenue when I noticed a basket of living turtles in front of a fish store. They were as dry as a heap of old bones in the sun; nevertheless, they were creeping over one another gimpily, doing their best to escape. I looked and was touched to discover that they appeared to be wood turtles, my favorites, so I bought one. In my apartment I looked closer and realized that in fact this was a diamond-back terrapin, which was bad news. Diamondbacks are tidewater turtles from brackish estuaries, and I had no sea water to keep him in. He spent his days thumping interminably against the baseboards, pushing for an opening through the wall. He drank thirstily but but would not eat and had none of the hearty, accepting qualities of wood turtles. He was morose, paler in color, sleeker and more Oriental in the carved ridges and rings that formed his shell. Though I felt sorry for him, finally I found his unrelenting presence exasperating. I carried him, struggling in a paper bag, across town to the Morton Street Pier on the Hudson. It was August but gray and windy. He was very surprised when I tossed him in; for the first time in our association, I think, he was afraid. He looked afraid as he bobbed about on top of the water, looking up at me from ten feet below. Though we were both accustomed to his resistance and rigidity, seeing him still pitiful, I recognized that I must have done the wrong thing. At least the river was salty, but it was also bottomless; the waves were too rough for him, and the tide was coming in, bumping him against the pilings underneath the pier. Too late, I realized that he wouldn't be able to swim to a peaceful inlet in New Jersey, even if he could figure out which way to swim. But since, short of diving in after him, there was nothing I could do, I walked away.

Discussion Questions

1. Why does Hoagland begin his essay by describing a variety of animals? How are these animals related to his main subject—turtles?
2. Hoagland says that for him turtles "manage to contain the rest of the animal world." How is this so and how is that observation demonstrated in the highly metaphorical language with which Hoagland describes the look and behavior of turtles?
3. Compare Hoagland's attitude toward animals to D. H. Lawrence's and E. B. White's. Which writer do you think has the greatest tendency to humanize animals? (In what sense, for example, can turtles be said to possess courage?) How does each writer try to avoid the pitfall—common when writing about animals—of sentimentality? Which writer do you think is least sentimental about animals? Which most?
4. How does the conclusion of Hoagland's essay affect you? Do you think that for someone who seems to know and care so much about turtles his disposal of the diamondback is callous? Or do you think it is realistic, even humane? Why or why not?

LANGSTON HUGHES

A prominent figure of the Harlem Renaissance of the 1920's, (James) Langston Hughes (1902–1967) wanted most of all to "explain the Negro condition in America." And he did so throughout a lifetime of enormous literary productivity; he published over sixty books of fiction, drama, poetry, journalism, essays, translations, and songs.

Hughes was born in Joplin, Missouri, and studied at Columbia University. He worked on freighters, in restaurants and in hotels to support himself while he pursued his one passion—writing. He frequently wrote for black newspapers, such as the Baltimore Afro-American *and the* Chicago Defender, *where his still-popular "Simple" tales originally appeared throughout the 1940's and 1950's. Among his most important books are* The Weary Blues *(1936), a collection of poetry that imaginatively integrates folk and jazz rhythms,* The Ways of White Folks *(1940),* Selected Poems *(1959), and* Fight For Freedom *(1962), a study of the NAACP. "Salvation" is reprinted from Hughes's autobiography,* The Big Sea *(1940).*

Salvation

I was saved from sin when I was going on thirteen. But not really saved. It happened like this. There was a big revival at my Auntie Reed's church. Every night for weeks there had been much preaching, singing, praying, and shouting, and some very hardened sinners had been brought to Christ, and the membership of the church had grown by leaps and bounds. Then just before the revival ended, they held a special meeting for children, "to bring the young lambs to the fold." My aunt spoke of it for days ahead. That night I was escorted to the front row and placed on the mourners' bench with all the other young sinners, who had not yet been brought to Jesus.

My aunt told me that when you were saved you saw a light, and something happened to you inside! And Jesus came into your life! And God was with you from then on! She said you could see and hear and feel Jesus in your soul. I believed her. I had heard a great many old people say the same thing and it seemed to me they ought to know. So I sat there calmly in the hot, crowded church, waiting for Jesus to come to me.

The preacher preached a wonderful rhythmical sermon, all moans and shouts and lonely cries and dire pictures of hell, and then he sang a song about the ninety and nine safe in the fold, but one little lamb was left out in the cold. Then he said: "Won't you come? Won't you come to Jesus? Young lambs, won't you come?" And he held out his arms to all us young sinners there on the mourners' bench. And the little girls cried. And some of them jumped up and went to Jesus right away. But most of us just sat there.

A great many old people came and knelt around us and prayed, old women with jet-black faces and braided hair, old men with work-gnarled hands. And the church sang a song about the lower lights are burning, some poor sinners to be saved. And the whole building rocked with prayer and song.

Still I kept waiting to *see* Jesus.

Finally all the young people had gone to the altar and were saved, but one boy and me. He was a rounder's son named Westley. Westley and I were surrounded by sisters and deacons praying. It was very hot in the church, and getting late now. Finally Westley said to me in a whisper: "God damn! I'm tired o' sitting here. Let's get up and be saved." So he got up and was saved.

Then I was left all alone on the mourner's bench. My aunt came and knelt at my knees and cried, while prayers and song swirled all around me in the little church. The whole congregation prayed for me alone, in a mighty wail of moans and voices. And I kept waiting serenely for Jesus, waiting, waiting—but he didn't come. I wanted to see him, but nothing happened to me. Nothing! I wanted something to happen to me, but nothing happened.

I heard the songs and the minister saying: "Why don't you come? My dear child, why don't you come to Jesus? Jesus is waiting for you. He wants you. Why don't you come? Sister Reed, what is this child's name?"

"Langston," my aunt sobbed.

"Langston, why don't you come? Why don't you come and be saved? Oh, Lamb of God! Why don't you come?"

Now it was really getting late. I began to be ashamed of myself, holding everything up so long. I began to wonder what God thought about Westley, who certainly hadn't seen Jesus either, but who was now sitting proudly on the platform, swinging his knickerbockered legs and grinning down at me, surrounded by deacons and old women on their knees praying. God had not struck Westley dead for taking his name in vain or for lying in the temple. So I decided that maybe to save further trouble, I'd better lie, too, and say that Jesus had come, and get up and be saved.

So I got up.

Suddenly the whole room broke into a sea of shouting, as they saw me rise. Waves of rejoicing swept the place. Women leaped in the air. My aunt threw her arms around me. The minister took me by the hand and led me to the platform.

When things quieted down, in a hushed silence, punctuated by a few ecstatic "Amens," all the new young lambs were blessed in the name of God. Then joyous singing filled the room.

That night, for the last time in my life but one—for I was a big boy twelve years old—I cried. I cried, in bed alone, and couldn't stop. I buried my head under the quilts, but my aunt heard me. She woke up and told my uncle I was crying because the Holy Ghost had come into my life, and because I had seen Jesus. But I was really crying because I couldn't bear to tell her that I had lied, that I had deceived everybody in the church, that I hadn't seen Jesus, and that now I didn't believe there was a Jesus any more, since he didn't come to help me.

Discussion Questions

1. Through which verbal devices does Hughes attempt to render the rhythmical spirit of the revival meeting? Point out a few examples of Hughes's style that show him imitating the language of the meeting.
2. Point out some of the ways in which Hughes holds himself apart from the revival meeting. How do you know from his writing style alone, for instance, that he is not completely identified with the rest of the people at the meeting?
3. What effect does the description of Westley have on Hughes's narrative? Why is Westley's introduction an effective narrative strategy?
4. Compare Hughes's narrative of a childhood episode to Richard Wright's. Both writers deal with lies. Which writer appears to take lying more seriously? Why? Is there anything in each writer's literary style that would suggest why this is so?
5. Using Hughes's narrative technique, describe an episode in your own life that brought into conflict your private and public selves.

Aldous Huxley

Aldous Huxley (1894–1963) was born in England into a famous intellectual family. His early training was scientific, but at the age of sixteen a disease of the eyes left him temporarily blind and frustrated his medical ambitions. His training came to serve him well, however, in his social satire and science fiction. Perhaps his most famous book in this mode is Brave New World (1932). Huxley wrote voluminously and in a wide variety of genres: besides novels, he wrote plays, screenplays, books of travel, and poetry along with polemical essays on artistic and literary criticism, manners and morals. His constant goal was the discovery of new capacities for the human mind, and this search led him into the exploration of many exotic mystical systems as well as into early experimentation with hallucinogenic drugs, for which he first coined the term, "psychedelic."

Selected Snobberies

All men are snobs about something. One is almost tempted to add: There is nothing about which men cannot feel snobbish. But this would doubtless be an exaggeration. There are certain disfiguring and mortal diseases about which there has probably never been any snobbery. I cannot imagine, for example, that there are any leprosy-snobs. More picturesque diseases, even when they are dangerous, and less dangerous diseases, particularly when they are the diseases of the rich, can be and very frequently are a source of snobbish self-importance. I have met several adolescent consumption-snobs, who thought that it would be romantic to fade away in the flower of youth, like Keats or Marie Bashkirtseff. Alas, the final stages of the consumptive fading are generally a good deal less romantic than these ingenuous young tubercle-snobs seem to imagine. To any one who has actually witnessed these final stages, the complacent poeticizings of these adolescents must seem as exasperating as they are profoundly pathetic. In the case of those commoner disease-snobs, whose claim to distinction is that they suffer from one of the maladies of the rich, exasperation is not tempered by very much sympathy. People who possess sufficient leisure, sufficient wealth, not to mention sufficient health, to go travelling from spa to spa, from doctor to fashionable doctor, in search of cures from problematical diseases (which, in so far as they exist at all, probably have their source in overeating) cannot expect us to be very lavish in our solicitude and pity.

    Disease-snobbery is only one out of a great multitude of snobberies, of which now some, now others, take pride of place in general esteem. For snobberies ebb and flow; their empire rises, declines, and falls in the most approved historical manner. What were good snobberies a hundred years ago are now out of fashion. Thus, the snobbery of family is everywhere on the decline. The snobbery of culture, still strong, has now to wrestle with an organized and active low-browism, with a snobbery of ignorance and stupidity unique, so far as I know in the whole of history. Hardly less characteristic of our age is that repulsive booze-snobbery, born of American Prohibition. The malefic influences of this snobbery are rapidly spreading all over the world. Even in France, where the existence of so many varities of delicious wine has hitherto imposed a judicious connoisseurship and has led to the branding of mere drinking as a brutish solecism, even in France the American booze-snobbery, with its odious accompaniments—a taste for hard drinks in general and for cocktails in particular—is making headway among the rich. Booze-snobbery has now made it socially permissible, and in some circles even rather creditable, for well-brought-up men and (this is the novelty) well-brought-up women of all ages, from fifteen to seventy, to be seen drunk, if not in public, at least in the very much tempered privacy of a party.

Modernity-snobbery, though not exclusive to our age, has come to assume an unprecedented importance. The reasons for this are simple and of a strictly economic character. Thanks to modern machinery, production is outrunning consumption. Organized waste among consumers is the first condition of our industrial prosperity. The sooner a consumer throws away the object he has bought and buys another, the better for the producer. At the same time, of course, the producer must do his bit by producing nothing but the most perishable articles. "The man who builds a skyscraper to last for more than forty years is a traitor to the building trade." The words are those of a great American contractor. Substitute motor car, boot, suit of clothes, etc., for skyscraper, and one year, three months, six months, and so on for forty years, and you have the gospel of any leader of any modern industry. The modernity-snob, it is obvious, is this industrialist's best friend. For modernity-snobs naturally tend to throw away their old possessions and buy new ones at a greater rate than those who are not modernity-snobs. Therefore it is in the producer's interest to encourage modernity-snobbery. Which in fact he does do—on an enormous scale and to the tune of millions and millions a year—by means of advertising. The newspapers do their best to help those who help them; and to the flood of advertisement is added a flood of less directly paid-for propaganda in favour of modernity-snobbery. The public is taught that up-to-dateness is one of the first duties of man. Docile, it accepts the reiterated suggestion. We are all modernity-snobs now.

Most of us are also art-snobs. There are two varieties of art-snobbery—the platonic and the unplatonic. Platonic art-snobs merely "take an interest" in art. Unplatonic art-snobs go further and actually buy art. Platonic art-snobbery is a hybrid or mule; for it is simultaneously a sub-species of culture-snobbery and of possession-snobbery. A collection of works of art is a collection of culture-symbols, and culture-symbols still carry social prestige. It is also a collection of wealth-symbols. For an art collection can represent money more effectively than a whole fleet of motor cars.

The value of art-snobbery to living artists is considerable. True, most art-snobs collect only the works of the dead; for an Old Master is both a safer investment and a holier culture-symbol than a living master. But some art-snobs are also modernity-snobs. There are enough of them, with the few eccentrics who like works of art for their own sake, to provide living artists with the means of subsistence.

The value of snobbery in general, its humanistic "point," consists in its power to stimulate activity. A society with plenty of snobberies is like a dog with plenty of fleas: it is not likely to become comatose. Every snobbery demands of its devotees unceasing efforts, a succession of sacrifices. The society-snob must be perpetually lion-hunting; the modernity-snob can never rest from trying to be up to date. Swiss doctors and the Best that has been thought or said must be the daily and nightly preoccupation of all the snobs respectively of disease and culture.

If we regard activity as being in itself a good, then we must count all snobberies as good; for all provoke activity. If, with the Buddhists, we regard all activity in this world of illusion as bad, then we shall condemn all snobberies out of hand. Most of us, I suppose, take up our position somewhere between the two extremes. We regard some activities as good, others as indifferent or downright bad. Our approval will be given only to such snobberies as excite what we regard as the better activities; the most professional intellectuals will approve of culture-snobbery (even while intensely disliking most individual culture-snobs), because it compels the Philistines to pay at least some slight tribute to the things of the mind and so helps to make the world less dangerously unsafe for ideas than it otherwise might have been. A manufacturer of motor cars, on the other hand, will rank the snobbery of possessions above culture-snobbery; he will do his best to persuade people that those who have fewer possessions, particularly possessions on four wheels, are inferior to those who have more possessions. And so on. Each hierarchy culminates in its own particular Pope.

Discussion Questions

1. Describe and explain as fully as you can Huxley's reasons for the view expressed in the sentence: "Every snobbery demands of its devotees unceasing efforts, a succession of sacrifices." What specific evidence does he bring to support this view? In what ways does the view seem a paradox? Does Huxley seem to expect his reader to see it as a paradox? Why or why not?

2. How does Huxley organize the succession of examples he chooses? What would be the effects of a different organization?

3. How does Huxley's analysis use techniques similar to those of Randall Jarrell? How, for example, does each writer employ lists? Whose sentences are commonly longer? Does there seem to be a different tone of voice created by differing habits of sentence length?

4. Write an essay explaining the values and assumptions underlying the following statements or ones like them: "I've never been any good with (mechanical things; mathematics; words)." What hidden snobberies are at work in statements like these?

5. Huxley says in his last sentence: "Each hierarchy culminates in its own Pope." Pick a contemporary hierarchy of snobbery and name its "Pope."

ADA LOUISE HUXTABLE

The distinguished historian and critic of architecture, Ada Louise Huxtable was born in New York City in 1921 and educated at Hunter College and New York University. The recipient of numerous honorary degrees, she has also been awarded Fulbright and Guggenheim Fellowships, the first Pulitzer Prize for distinguished criticism, and the American Association of University Women "Woman of the Year" Award in 1974. She recently received the prestigious McArthur Foundation award. In 1963–73 she was the architecture critic for the New York Times. Her most important books are Pier Luigi Nervi (1960), Classic New York (1964), and Kicked a Building Lately? (1976), from which the following essay on Houston is reprinted.

Houston

This is a car's-eye view of Houston—but is there any other? It is a short report on a fast trip to the city that has supplanted Los Angeles in current intellectual mythology as the city of the future. You'd better believe. Houston is the place that scholars flock to for the purpose of seeing what modern civilization has wrought. Correctly perceived and publicized as freeway city, mobile city, space city, strip city, and speculator city, it is being dissected by architects and urban historians as a case study in new forms and functions. It even requires a new definition of urbanity. Houston is *the* city of the second half of the twentieth century.

But what strikes the visitor accustomed to cities shaped by rivers, mountains, and distinguishing topography, by local identity and historical and cultural conditioning, is that this is instant city, and it is nowhere city.

Houston is totally without the normal rationales of geography and evolutionary social growth that have traditionally created urban centers and culture. From the time that the Allen brothers came here from New York in 1836 and bought the featureless land at the junction of two bayous (they could not get the site they really wanted), this city has been an act of real estate, rather than an act of God or man. Houston has been willed on the flat, uniform prairie not by some planned ideal, but by the expediency of land investment economics, first, and later by oil and petrochemical prosperity.

This is not meant to be an unfavorable judgment. It is simply an effort to convey the extraordinary character of this city—to suggest its unique importance, interest, and impact. Its affluence and eccentricities have been popularly celebrated. It is known to be devoutly conservative, passionately devoted to free enterprise and non-governmental interference. It is famous, or notorious, for the fact that, alone among the country's major cities, it has no zoning—no regulations on what anyone builds, anywhere—and the debate rages over whether this makes it better or worse than other cities. (It's a draw, with pluses and minuses that have a lot to do with special local conditions.)

Now the fifth largest city in the country, Houston has had its most phenomenal expansion since the Second World War. At last count, it covered over 500 square miles and had a population of 1.4 million, with a half million more in surrounding Harris County. A thousand new people move in every week. This record-setting growth has leap-frogged over open country without natural boundaries, without land use restrictions, moving on before anything is finished, for the kind of development as open-ended as the prairie. It has jumped across smaller, fully incorporated cities within the vast city limits. The municipality can legally annex 10 percent of its urban area in outlying land or communities every year, and the land grab has been continuous and relentless.

Houston is a study in paradoxes. There are pines and palm trees, skyscrapers and sprawl; Tudor townhouses stop abruptly as cows and prairie take over. It deals in incredible extremes of wealth and culture. In spite of its size, one can find no real center, no focus. "Downtown" boasts a concentration of suave towers, but they are already challenged by other, newer commercial centers of increasing magnitude that form equally important nodes on the freeway network that ties everything together. Nor are these new office and shopping complexes located to serve existing communities in the conventional sense. They are created in a vacuum, and people come by automobile, driving right into their parking garages. They rise from expressway ribbons and seas of cars.

Houston is all process and no plan. Gertrude Stein said of Oakland that there was no there, there. One might say of Houston that one never gets there. It feels as if one is always on the way, always arriving, always looking for the place where everything comes together. And yet as a city, a twentieth-century city, it works remarkably well. If one excepts horrendous morning and evening traffic jams as all of Houston moves to and from home and work, it is a lesson in how a mobile society functions, the values it endorses, and what kind of world it makes.

Houston is different from the time one rises in the morning to have the dark suddenly dispelled by a crimson aureole on a horizon that seems to stretch full circle, and a sun that appears to rise below eye level. (New Yorkers are accustomed to seeing only fractured bits and pieces of sky.) From a hotel of sophisticated excellence that might be Claridge's-on-the-prairie, furnished with an owner-oilman's private collection of redundant boiserie and Sevres, one drives past fountains of detergent blue.

Due north on Main Street is "downtown," a roughly 20-block cluster of commercial towers begun in the 1920s and thirties and doubled in size and numbers in the 1960s and seventies, sleek symbols of prosperity and power. They are paradigms of the corporate style. The names they bear are Tenneco, Shell Plaza, Pennzoil Place, Humble, and Houston Natural Gas, and their architects have national reputations.

In another paradox, in this country of open spaces, the towers are increasingly connected by tunnels underground. Houston's environment is strikingly "internalized" because of the area's extremes of heat and humidity. It is the indoors one seeks for large parts of the year, and that fact has profoundly affected how the city builds and lives.

The enclosed shopping center is Houston's equivalent of the traditional town plaza—a clear trend across the country. The Post Oak Galleria, a $20-million product of Houston developer Gerald Hines and architects Hellmuth, Obata and Kassabaum, with Neuhaus and Taylor, is characteristically large and opulent. A 420,000-square-foot, 600-foot long, three-level, covered shopping mall, it is part of a 33-acre commercial, office, and hotel complex off the West Loop Freeway, at the city's western edge.

The Galleria is the place to see and be seen: it is meeting place, promenade, and social center. It also offers restaurants, baubles from Tiffany and Nieman-Marcus, a galaxy of specialty shops equivalent to Madison Avenue, and an ice-skating rink comparable to Rockefeller Center's, all under a chandelier-hung glass roof. One can look up from the ice-skating to see joggers circling the oblong glass dome. The Galleria is now slated for an expansion larger than the original.

These enterprises do not require outdoor settings; they are magnets that can be placed anywhere. In fact, one seeks orientation by the freeways and their man-made landmarks (Southwest Freeway and Sharpstown, West Loop and Post Oak Tower) rather than by reference to organic patterns of growth. Climate, endless open topography, speculator economics and spectator consumerism, and, of course, the car have determined Houston's free-wheeling, vacuum-packed life and environment.

For spectator sports, one goes to the Astrodome to the southwest which has created its own environment—the Astrodomain [sic] of assiduously cultivated amusements and motels. Popular and commercial culture are well served in Houston. There is also high, or middle, culture, for which the "brutalist" forms of the Alley Theater by New York architect Ulrich Franzen, and the neutral packaging of Jones Hall for the performing arts, by the Houston firm of Caudill, Rowlett, Scott, have been created. They stand in the shadow of the downtown oil industry giants that have provided their funding.

Farther south on Main are the Fine Arts Museum, with its handsome extension by Mies van der Rohe, and the Contemporary Arts Association building, a sharp-edged, metal trapezoid by Gunnar Birkets. They cling together among odd vacant lots in a state of decaying or becoming, next to a psychoanalytic center.

Because the city has no zoning, these surreal juxtapositions prevail. A hamburger stand closes the formal vista of Philip Johnson's delicate, Miesian arcade at St. Thomas University. Transitional areas, such as Westheimer, not only mirror the city's untrammeled development in ten-year sections, but are freely altered as old houses are turned into new shops and restaurants, unhampered by zoning taboos. (Conventionally zoned cities simply rezone their deteriorating older residential neighborhoods to save their tax base and facilitate the same economic destiny. The process just takes a little longer.)

Houston's web of freeways is the consummate example of the twentieth-century phenomenon known as the commercial strip. The route of passage attracts sales, services, and schlock in continuous road-oriented structures—gas stations, drive-ins, and displays meant to catch the eye and fancy at 60 miles an hour. There are fixed and mobile signs, and signs larger than buildings ("buildingboards," according to students of the Pop environment). Style, extracted as symbols, becomes a kind of sign in itself, evoking images from Rapunzel to Monticello. There are miles of fluttering metallic pennants (used cars), a giant lobster with six shooters, cowboy hat, and scarf (seafood), a turning, life-size plaster bull (American International Charolais Association), and a revolving neon piano. The strip is full of intuitive wit, invention, and crass, but also real creativity—a breathtaking affront to normal sensibility that is never a bore.

Directly behind the freeways, one short turn takes the driver from the strip into pine and live oak-alleyed streets of comfortable and elegant residential communities (including the elite and affluent River Oaks). They have maintained their environmental purity by deed restrictions passed on from one generation of buyers to another.

Beyond these enclaves, anything goes. Residential development is a spin-the-wheel happening that hops, skips, and jumps outward, each project seemingly dropped from the sky—but always on the freeway. The southwest section, which was prairie before the 1950s, is now the American Dream incarnate. There is a continuing rivalry of you-name-it styles that favor French and Anglo-Saxon labels and details. If you live in Westminster, authentic-looking London street signs on high iron fences frame views of the flat Texas plains. You know you're home when you get to La Cour du Roi or Robin Hood Dell.

Because Houston is an urban invention, this kind of highly salable make-believe supplies instant history and architecture; it is an anchor to time and place where neither is defined. All of those values that accrue throughout centuries of civilization—identity, intimacy, scale, complexity, style—are simply created out of whole cloth, or whole prairie, with unabashed commercial eclecticism. How else to establish a sense of place or community, to indicate differences where none exist?

Houston is a continuous series of such cultural shocks. Its private patronage, on which the city depends for its public actions, has a cosmic range. There is the superb, *echt*-Houston eccentricity of Judge Roy Hofheinz's personal quarters in the Astrodome, done in a kind of Astrobaroque of throne chairs, gold phones, and temple dogs, with a pick-a-religion, fake stone chapel (good for bullfighters or politicians who want to meditate), shooting gallery, and presidential suite, tucked into the periphery of the stadium, complete with views of the Astros and Oilers. At the other end of the esthetic scale there is the Rothko Chapel, where the blood-dark paintings of the artist's pre-suicide days have been brought together by Dominique de Menil—a place of overwhelming, icy death. One welcomes the Texas sunshine.

Houston is not totally without planned features. It has large and handsome parks and the landscaped corridor of the Buffalo Bayou that are the result of philanthropic forethought. There are universities and a vast medical center.

But no one seems to feel the need for the public vision that older cities have of a hierarchy of places and buildings, an organized concept of function and form. Houston has a downtown singularly without amenities. The fact that money and population are flowing there from the rest of the country is considered cause for celebration, not for concern with the city's quality. This city bets on a different and brutal kind of distinction—of power, motion, and sheer energy. Its values are material fulfillment, mobility, and mass entertainment. Its returns are measured on its commercial investments. These contemporary ideals have little to do with the deeper or subtler aspects of the mind or spirit, or even with the more complex, human pleasure potential of a hedonistic culture.

When we build a new city, such as Houston, it is quite natural that we build in this image, using all of our hardware to serve its uses and desires. We create new values and new dimensions in time and space. The expanded, mobile city deals in distance and discontinuity; it "explodes" community. It substitutes fantasy for history. Houston is devoted to moon shots, not moon-viewing. The result is a significant, instructive, and disquieting city form.

What Houston possesses to an exceptional degree is an extraordinary, unlimited vitality. One wishes that it had a larger conceptual reach, that social and cultural and human patterns were as well understood as dollar dynamism. But this kind of vitality is the distinguishing mark of a great city in any age. And Houston today is the American present and future. It is an exciting and disturbing place.

Discussion Questions

1. Why is Houston considered the latest in modern civilization?
2. Huxtable claims that "Houston is a study in paradoxes." How does this rhetorical term help her organize her essay? How does it lead to patterns of description and criticism? Go through the essay, underlining Huxtable's paradoxical expressions.
3. Compare Huxtable's description of Houston with John McPhee's description of Atlantic City. How does each writer's approach differ? Where does Huxtable seem to be looking at Houston from? Where does McPhee seem to be observing from? How does each writer's perspective affect your view of each city?
4. How does Huxtable's experience as an architectural critic make itself felt in the essay? How does it inform her selection of detail? How does her knowledge of architecture help determine her sense of Houston's significance as a city? Do you think Huxtable would like to live in Houston? Why or why not? Write an essay that supports your views, using evidence from her account.

WILLIAM JAMES

One of the outstanding figures of American intellectual history, William James (1842–1910) was born in New York City and studied medicine at Harvard. In 1872 he became an instructor of physiology at Harvard and taught there until his retirement in 1907. James was the leading proponent of pragmatism and empirical philosophy, which stood for the hard-nosed values of practicality, particularity, and experiential data in philosophical thinking. "The whole function of philosophy," James declared, "ought to be to find out what definite difference it will make to you and me, at definite instants of our life, if this world-formula or that world-formula be the true one."

James's first major work, The Principles of Psychology *(1890–1894) included a chapter entitled "The Stream of Thought," which had a profound influence on the development of twentieth-century technique. His other principal works are* The Will to Believe *(1897),* The Varieties of Religious Experience *(1902),* Pragmatism *(1907), and* A Pluralistic Universe *(1909). The essay "Habit" appeared in 1915 as a separate work; it had originally been part of a chapter in* The Principles of Psychology.

Habit

"Habit a second nature! Habit is ten times nature," the Duke of Wellington is said to have exclaimed; and the degree to which this is true no one can probably appreciate as well as one who is a veteran soldier himself. The daily drill and the years of discipline end by fashioning a man completely over again, as to most of the possibilities of his conduct.

> There is a story, which is credible enough, though it may not be true, of a practical joker, who, seeing a discharged veteran carrying home his dinner, suddenly called out, "Attention!" whereupon the man instantly brought his hands down, and lost his mutton and potatoes in the gutter. The drill had been thorough, and its effects had become embodied in the man's nervous structure.[1]

Riderless cavalry-horses, at many a battle, have been seen to come together and go through their customary evolutions at the sound of the bugle-call. Most trained domestic animals, dogs and oxen, and omnibus- and car-horses, seem to be machines almost pure and simple, undoubtingly, unhesitatingly doing from minute to minute the duties they have been taught, and giving no sign that the possibility of an alternative ever suggests itself to their mind. Men grown old in prison have asked to be readmitted after being once set free. In a railroad accident to a travelling menagerie in the United States some time in 1884, a tiger, whose cage had broken open, is said to have emerged, but presently crept back again, as if too much bewildered by his new responsibilities, so that he was without difficulty secured.

Habit is thus the enormous fly-wheel of society, its most precious conservative agent. It alone is what keeps us all within the bounds of ordinance, and saves the children of fortune from

[1] Huxley, "Elementary Lessons in Physiology"

the envious uprisings of the poor. It alone prevents the hardest and most repulsive walks of life from being deserted by those brought up to tread therein. It keeps the fisherman and the deck-hand at sea through the winter, it holds the miner in his darkness, and nails the countryman to his log-cabin and his lonely farm through all the months of snow; it protects us from invasion by the natives of the desert and the frozen zone. It dooms us all to fight out the battle of life upon the lines of our nurture or our early choice, and to make the best of a pursuit that disagrees, because there is no other for which we are fitted, and it is too late to begin again. It keeps different social strata from mixing. Already at the age of twenty-five you see the professional mannerism settling down on the young commercial traveller, on the young doctor, on the young minister, on the young counsellor-at-law. You see the little lines of cleavage running through the character, the tricks of thought, the prejudices, the ways of the "shop," in a word, from which the man can by-and-by no more escape than his coat-sleeve can suddenly fall into a new set of folds. On the whole, it is best he should not escape. It is well for the world that in most of us, by the age of thirty, the character has set like plaster, and will never soften again.

If the period between twenty and thirty is the critical one in the formation of intellectual and professional habits, the period below twenty is more important still for the fixing of *personal* habits, properly so called, such as vocalization and pronunciation, gesture, motion, and address. Hardly ever is a language learned after twenty spoken without a foreign accent; hardly ever can a youth transferred to the society of his betters unlearn the nasality and other vices of speech bred in him by the associations of his growing years. Hardly ever, indeed, no matter how much money there be in his pocket, can he even learn to *dress* like a gentleman-born. The merchants offer their wares as eagerly to him as to the veriest "swell," but he simply *cannot* buy the right things. An invisible law, as strong as gravitation, keeps him within his orbit, arrayed this year as he was the last; and how his better-bred acquaintances contrive to get the things they wear will be for him a mystery till his dying day.

The great thing, then, in all education, is to *make our nervous system our ally instead of our enemy.* It is to fund and capitalize our acquisitions, and live at ease upon the interest of the fund. *For this we must make automatic and habitual, as early as possible, as many useful actions as we can,* and guard against the growing into ways that are likely to be disadvantageous to us, as we should guard against the plague. The more of the details of our daily life we can hand over to the effortless custody of automatism, the more our higher powers of mind will be set free for their own proper work. There is no more miserable human being than one in whom nothing is habitual but indecision, and for whom the lighting of every cigar, the drinking of every cup, the time of rising and going to bed every day, and the beginning of every bit of work, are subjects of express volitional deliberation. Full half the time of such a man goes to the deciding, or regretting, of matters which ought to be so ingrained in him as practically not to exist for his consciousness at all. If there be such daily duties not yet ingrained in any one of my readers, let him begin this very hour to set the matter right.

In Professor Bain's chapter on "The Moral Habits" there are some admirable practical remarks laid down. Two great maxims emerge from his treatment. The first is that in the acquisition of a new habit, or the leaving off of an old one, we must take care to *launch ourselves with as strong and decided an initiative as possible.* Accumulate all the possible circumstances which shall re-enforce the right motives; put yourself assiduously in conditions that encourage the new way; make engagements incompatible with the old; take a public pledge, if the case allows; in short, envelop your resolution with every aid you know. This will give your new beginning such a momentum that the temptation to break down will not occur as soon as it otherwise might; and every day during which a breakdown is postponed adds to the chances of its not occurring at all.

The second maxim is: *Never suffer an exception to occur till the new habit is securely rooted in your life.* Each lapse is like the letting fall of a ball of string which one is carefully winding up; a single slip undoes more than a great many turns will wind again. *Continuity* of training is the great means of making the nervous system act infallibly right. As Professor Bain says:

> The peculiarity of the moral habits, contradistinguishing them from the intellectual acquisitions, is the presence of two hostile powers, one to be gradually raised into the ascendant over the other. It is necessary, above all things, in such a situation, never to lose a battle. Every gain on the wrong side undoes the effect of many conquests on the right. The essential precaution, therefore, is so to regulate the two opposing powers that the one may have a series of uninterrupted successes, until repetition has fortified it to such a degree as to enable it to cope with the opposition, under any circumstances. This is the theoretically best career of mental progress.

The need of securing success at the *outset* is imperative. Failure at first is apt to dampen the energy of all future attempts, whereas past experience of success nerves one to future vigor.

Goethe says to a man who consulted him about an enterprise but mistrusted his own powers: "Ach! you need only blow on your hands!" And the remark illustrates the effect on Goethe's spirits of his own habitually successful career. Prof. Baumann, from whom I borrow the anecdote, says that the collapse of barbarian nations when Europeans come among them is due to their despair of ever succeeding as the new-comers do in the larger tasks of life. Old ways are broken and new ones not formed.

The question of "tapering-off," in abandoning such habits as drink and opium-indulgence, comes in here, and is a question about which experts differ within certain limits, and in regard to what may be best for an individual case. In the main, however, all expert opinion would agree that abrupt acquisition of the new habit is the best way, *if there be a real possibility of carrying it out.* We must be careful not to give the will so stiff a task as to insure its defeat at the very outset; but, *provided one can stand it,* a sharp period of suffering, and then a free time, is the best thing to aim at, whether in giving up a habit like that of opium, or in simply changing one's hours of rising or of work. It is surprising how soon a desire will die of inanition if it be *never* fed.

> One must learn, unmoved, looking neither to the right nor left, to walk firmly on the straight and narrow path, before one can begin "to make one's self over again." He who every day makes a fresh resolve is like one who, arriving at the edge of the ditch he is to leap, forever stops and returns for a fresh run. Without *unbroken* advance there is no such thing as *accumulation* of the ethical forces possible, and to make this possible, and to exercise us and habituate us in it, is the sovereign blessing of regular *work.*

A third maxim may be added to the preceding pair: *Seize the very first possible opportunity to act on every resolution you make, and on every emotional prompting you may experience in the direction of the habits you aspire to gain.* It is not in the moment of their forming, but in the moment of their producing *motor effects,* that resolves and aspirations communicate the new "set" to the brain. As the author last quoted remarks:

> The actual presence of the practical opportunity alone furnishes the fulcrum upon which the lever can rest, by means of which the moral will may multiply its strength, and raise itself aloft. He who has no solid ground to press against will never get beyond the stage of empty gesture-making.

No matter how full a reservoir of *maxims* one may possess, and no matter how good one's *sentiments* may be, if one have not taken advantage of every concrete opportunity to *act,* one's character may remain entirely unaffected for the better. With mere good intentions, hell is proverbially paved. And this is an obvious consequence of the principles we have laid down. A "character," as J. S. Mill says, "is a completely fashioned will"; and a will, in the sense in which he means it, is an aggregate of tendencies to act in a firm and prompt and definite way upon all the principal emergencies of life. A tendency to act only becomes effectively ingrained in us in proportion to the uninterrupted frequency with which the actions actually occur, and the brain "grows" to their use. Every time a resolve or a fine glow of feeling evaporates without bearing practical fruit is worse than a chance lost; it works so as positively to hinder future resolutions and emotions from taking the normal path of discharge. There is no more contemptible type of human character than that of the nerveless sentimentalist and dreamer, who spends his life in a weltering sea of sensibility and emotion, but who never does a manly concrete deed. Rousseau, inflaming all the mothers of France, by his eloquence, to follow Nature and nurse their babies themselves, while he sends his own children to the foundling hospital, is the classical example of what I mean. But every one of us in his measure, whenever, after glowing for an abstractly formulated Good, he practically ignores some actual case, among the squalid "other particulars" of which that same Good lurks disguised, treads straight on Rousseau's path. All Goods are disguised by the vulgarity of their concomitants, in this work-a-day world; but woe to him who can only recognize them when he thinks them in their pure and abstract form! The habit of excessive novel-reading and theatre-going will produce true monsters in this line. The weeping of a Russian lady over the fictitious personages in the play, while her coachman is freezing to death on his seat outside, is the sort of thing that everywhere happens on a less glaring scale. Even the habit of excessive indulgence in music, for those who are neither performers themselves nor musically gifted enough to take it in a purely intellectual way, has probably a relaxing effect upon the character. One becomes filled with emotions which habitually pass without prompting to any deed, and so the inertly sentimental condition is kept up. The remedy would be, never to suffer one's self to have an emotion at a concert, without expressing it afterward in *some* active way. Let the expression be the least thing in the world—speaking genially to one's aunt, or giving up one's seat in a horse-car, if nothing more heroic offers—but let it not fail to take place.

These latter cases make us aware that it is not simply *particular lines* of discharge, but also *general forms* of discharge, that seem to be grooved out by habit in the brain. Just as, if we let our emotions evaporate, they get into a way of evaporating; so there is reason to suppose that if we often flinch from making an effort, before we know it the effort-making capacity will be gone; and that, if we suffer the wandering of our attention, presently it will wander all the time. Attention and effort are, as we shall see later, but two names for the same psychic fact. To what brain-processes they correspond we do not know. The strongest reason for believing that they do depend on brain-processes at all, and are not pure acts of the spirit, is just this fact, that they seem in some degree subject to the law of habit, which is a material law. As a final practical maxim, relative to these habits of the will, we may, then, offer something like this: *Keep the faculty of effort alive in you by a little gratuitous exercise every day.* That is, be systematically ascetic or heroic in little unnecessary points, do every day or two something for no other reason than that you would rather not do it, so that when the hour of dire need draws nigh, it may find you not unnerved and untrained to stand the test. Asceticism of this sort is like the insurance which a man pays on his house and goods. The tax does him no good at the time, and possibly may never bring him a return. But if the fire *does* come, his having paid it will be his salvation from ruin. So with the man who has daily inured himself to habits of concentrated attention, energetic volition, and self-denial in unnecessary things. He will stand like a tower when everything rocks around him, and when his softer fellow-mortals are winnowed like chaff in the blast.

The physiological study of mental conditions is thus the most powerful ally of hortatory ethics. The hell to be endured hereafter, of which theology tells, is no worse than the hell we make for ourselves in this world by habitually fashioning our characters in the wrong way. Could the young but realize how soon they will become mere walking bundles of habits, they would give more heed to their conduct while in the plastic state. We are spinning our own fates, good or evil, and never to be undone. Every smallest stroke of virtue or of vice leaves its never so little scar. The drunken Rip Van Winkle, in Jefferson's play, excuses himself for every fresh dereliction by saying, "I won't count this time!" Well! he may not count it, and a kind Heaven may not count it; but it is being counted none the less. Down among his nerve-cells and fibres the molecules are counting it, registering and storing it up to be used against him when the next temptation comes. Nothing we ever do is, in strict scientific literalness, wiped out. Of course, this has its good side as well as its bad one. As we become permanent drunkards by so many separate drinks, so we become saints in the moral, and authorities and experts in the practical and scientific spheres, by so many separate acts and hours of work. Let no youth have any anxiety about the upshot of his education, whatever the line of it may be. If he keep faithfully busy each hour of the working-day, he may safely leave the final result to itself. He can with perfect certainty count on waking up some fine morning, to find himself one of the competent ones of his generation, in whatever pursuit he may have singled out. Silently, between all the details of his business, the *power of judging* in all that class of matter will have built itself up within him as a possession that will never pass away. Young people should know this truth in advance. The ignorance of it has probably engendered more discouragement and faint-heartedness in youths embarking on arduous careers than all other causes put together.

Discussion Questions

1. What does the Duke of Wellington's comment mean? Why does James begin with it?

2. James starts his essay with a military reference. Go through the selection and find other allusions that equate life with struggle and battle. What ethical view of life is behind James's respect for the physiological power of habit?

3. Most people today would argue with James when he says that it is best we should not escape our intellectual and professional habits. But why does he say this? In what sense is James's use of the word "habit" a positive one? How do we often use the term negatively?

4. Why doesn't James take into account other pressures on the individual—economic, social, political, and so forth? Do you find his reliance on the individual old fashioned? How might he respond to people who see themselves as "victims" of society or culture?

5. J. B. Priestly also talks about habits. Compare his essay to James's. Which writer do you think makes a more convincing case for the importance of habit in daily life?

6. Do you find James's final paragraph convincing, even scary? If so, explain what makes it effective. If not, on what grounds do you feel his exhortation can be dismissed?

Elizabeth Janeway

Born in Brooklyn, New York, in 1913, Elizabeth Janeway graduated from Barnard College, where she is currently a trustee and Distinguished Alumna. Since 1955, she has sponsored the Elizabeth Janeway Prize for Prose Writing, an award for Barnard College students. She has served as a judge for both the National Book Award and the Pulitzer Prize and has recently contributed to the Harvard Guide to Contemporary American Writing. *The author of six novels and four children's books, she has also published short stories and critical essays in a wide variety of newspapers and periodicals. She has written three important books on the women's movement:* Man's World, Woman's Place *(1971),* Between Myth and Morning: Women Awakening *(1974), and* Powers of the Weak *(1980). "Water" was her contribution to a commissioned collection of essays on basic things.*

Water

Water is a universal symbol. Tamed and trickling out of the tap, softened and fluoridated, warmed in the boiler by fires burning million-year-old oil, it is still not quite a commodity. Even for city dwellers some dim memory stirs from time to time of those ancient eons when water or the lack of it ruled everything—the sites of habitation, the paths through the wilderness, the limits of hunting grounds, famine and abundance, life and death. It can still shatter human hopes and plans. Thirty years ago, the top soil in the plains states rose into the sky and blew away. Men had ploughed grazing land, counting on rain to bind the soil where the tough grass roots had been cut, and the rain did not come. A migration as great as that of the Mongols poured out of the Dust Bowl toward California. Steinbeck, in *The Grapes of Wrath*, recorded what happened to one bit of flotsam on one stream of this Diaspora. Today, I read in the papers, the Russians are ploughing the virgin Siberian lands as, in the last century, we ploughed the Dakotas. But the stubborn old gods of rivers and rains have not yet submitted to Marxist-Leninist discipline. Disappointing harvests are reported.

Water. "It has caused more wars in the Middle East," writes Freya Stark in one of her brilliant travel books, "than even religion." In the Middle East, that is quite a feat. But there are historians who trace the breakdown of the ancient civilizations along the Tigris, the Euphrates and the Indus to wars and raiding parties which breached dams and ruined irrigation and drainage systems. Whether the cities fell first and the aqueducts and irrigation ditches silted up through neglect, or whether they were deliberately destroyed to strangle the cities, they have never been rebuilt. Let us imagine, in our smug pride of modernity, that engineers have yet become more powerful than statesmen, for even today, there is desert where once there was fertile land. Civilization takes water for granted, but that is civilization's mistake.

It's not a mistake, though, that will ever be made by those who live past the limits of "city water." Amidst all the denouncing of suburbia, let us give it credit for this: suburban dwellers must face some of the old facts of life, of living and of weather. In the country, water comes out of a well—save for that blessed, lucky trickle which flows to a favored few from a gravity-fed spring (and that is a trickle which, in August, may dwindle disastrously). Civilization, of course, has changed the Old Oaken Bucket into an electric motor pumping so many gallons a minute to a cistern from an artesian well, but it has not changed the nature of the emotions that go with procuring this water, only bunched them together into patches of intensity with stretches of complacence in between. But when the power goes out in a storm, so does the water supply.

Where we used to live, seventy miles from New York, the power had a habit of failing before the telephone lines went. Why this should be, I don't know. But the prudence of the telephone company in locating its poles and stringing its wires allowed messages to get through from neighbor to neighbor before the telephone lines went down and silence followed darkness. Thus, a spreading rash of calls would ripple out from the center of casualty: "We've lost our power. If you still have yours, fill the bathtubs quick." Then the householder (or his wife, if he was a commuter who spent his days in an ivory tower in the city) would go into action and fill tubs and buckets and pots and pans against the drought to come. After one ice storm, the water famine lasted for a week in some parts of the township, and luckier folk invited their neighbors in for baths.

From time to time, as families grew in size or new houses went up with their demanding machines for washing clothes and dishes, new wells had to be dug. Then the drillers would come with their rig and thump away at the ancient granite beneath our green countryside, and the owners would groan and shake a little, too, at the dollars that each hour of thumping represented. There was water, the drillers would report encouragingly, but not yet quite enough, three gallons a minute, five gallons a minute— would they never find the level that would deliver the necessary eight gallons a minute? On and on they went, like persevering, unsuccessful disciples of Moses, smiting the rock. Once a friend of ours, in despair after weeks of fruitless pounding, called in a water dowser. Our friend is the founder of one of the oldest and most respected public opinion polls. It seemed quaintly appropriate to think of an old man with a hazel twig in his hands questioning every foot of the poll taker's land on its water content. At last he said, "Dig here," and they dug, and found water. Of course, it was simply luck—whatever that means.

Water. It is a universal symbol, I wrote, but a symbol of what? Of birth and beginnings, as the scientists, the first chapter of Genesis and Dr. Freud all tell us? Life began in the sea, say the biochemists, when lightning discharges awoke, in the thin soup of almost life, some monstrous protein molecules which married each other: this is our most modern mythology. An older story tells us that the Spirit of God moved on the face of the waters even before His command created Light: which might, after all, be simply a more majestic way of describing the same event. As for Freud, when he had rummaged through enough people's heads and stitched thousands of fragments of dreams together, he came to the cautious conclusion that "to dream of being in water or passing through a stream often symbolized the act of birth." Which is a nice, pedantic, and quite useless conclusion, for it leaves us with another set of waters unexplained. What shall we make of "the bitter, salt, estranging sea," or the rivers of Styx and of Lethe, which are the rivers of death?

We must think again. Water can symbolize birth, as it can symbolize death, but essentially its meaning is greater and simpler, and includes both. At the deepest level, water stands as the symbol of Change. Indeed, when St. John, in the Revelations, wished to describe the eternal landscape that would follow upon the Day of Judgment, he said, "There was no more sea." Changeless eternity could go no further.

Water is the present tense. It flows. It will not take a shape of its own, but will fill indifferently any jug or pitcher or cup, and then flow out and on, indifferent still, forgetful and uninfluenced. Its strength is the strength of movement. Even "still waters" must "run deep." If they do not, we distrust them and have made a pejorative word for such unnatural behavior—"stagnant," or standing. In New Mexico, the Indians believe that water can die. Mary Austin records the legend:

> *At midnight drink no water*
> *For I have heard said*
> *That on the stroke of midnight*
> *All water goes dead.*

Water is always now. It demands the present participle for its description—gushing, flowing, pouring, sprinkling. As every gardener knows, last week's soaking and next week's rain might as well not exist, unless we manage to string them together by constructing tanks and cisterns and reservoirs. Thirst is immediate. Water cannot be an event, it must be a presence. To make it so must be a primary concern of any stable society, great or small.

Modern man is astonishingly modest about his achievements. I am not at all sure that this is a healthy state of mind. Might we not be more confident of our ability to deal with our future problems if we took a bit more pride in our successful solutions to problems of the past? Modesty is all very well for individuals, but civic pride can give a community a sense of wholeness and of its obligations to its citizens. We have somehow lost the knack of celebrating deeds of greatness today, and are apt to go off to the beach on the Fourth of July, each family by itself, instead of taking a little time to remember our heroes and refresh our pride.

I would like to see more holidays, and as one of them I would like to propose a Festival of the Waters. It might well be held on St. Swithin's Day. I imagine pilgrimages to the Tennessee Valley, to Grand Coulee and to Boulder Dam. I think of holiday tours along the St. Lawrence Seaway, with river steamers full of bands and picnickers toasting all that good sense, engineering training and peace between nations have wrought there. The irrigated valleys of California could show off their wealth.

Above all, each city should offer thanks to its sanitary engineers, who might appear with an accompanying guard of master plumbers—for even the grimmest nature may sweeten a little once it feels itself appreciated. The Mayor might read out the proud statistics citing the number of years since typhoid or cholera claimed a victim within his purlieus; and if the statistics should by any chance not be so proud, how quick the Mayor and the Department of Sanitation would be to improve them! And each year the ceremony would be crowned by the dedication of some new Wonder of Water: a handsome public pool, or a fountain with a bit of green about it, shining and leaping in the center of the city where passers-by could refresh their eyes. Or a boat basin. Or a new wing on the aquarium. Or—

But you see what I mean. Water is a universal symbol because it is a universal need. As we live now, it is beyond the power of the individual, in the vast majority of cases, to satisfy this need on his own. Only men working together can build reservoirs and aqueducts and dams and hydroelectric stations and sewage conversion plants and, soon no doubt, great structures to desalt the sea and make the desert blossom like the corn tassel and the alfalfa.

Our Festival of Waters, then, would be a holiday to celebrate the things that men working together can achieve. What could be more appropriate? For as we all know, the just and the unjust both get wet when it rains and thirsty when it does not. Too often, in the past, the just and the unjust have preferred to disagree and to create deserts rather than settle down and share out their water rights. But now our engineering knowledge is growing with the world's population, and with its need for water. Might not, for once, new skills combine with new needs? Might not the just and the unjust decide to work together, literally for dear life? And might not these projects to control the fluid strength and the eternal changeability of water teach us something about controlling the fluid strength and eternal changeability of human nature?

Discussion Questions

1. Why, according to Elizabeth Janeway, do suburbanites and country people take water less for granted than do city dwellers? Do you agree with this?

2. Do you think Janeway's proposal for a Festival of Waters is a good idea? What exactly does she want the Festival to celebrate? How does Janeway associate water and human nature?

3. How does Elizabeth Janeway make us see water as a precious commodity? In fact, why does she say that water "is still not quite a commodity"?

4. How does Elizabeth Janeway's use of "universal symbol" compare to Erich Fromm's use of the term?

5. One of Elizabeth Janeway's accomplishments in this brief essay is to make us aware of how extraordinary such an ordinary thing as water actually is. Using her essay as a model, choose another "ordinary" thing and, paying attention to its rich symbolic value, show your readers its "extraordinary" dimensions.

RANDALL JARRELL

Randall Jarrell (1914–1965) served in the Army Air Corps in World War II, from which he emerged to become America's most successful "war poet." He quickly expanded beyond that category and maintained an insistent and energetic voice in American poetry and poetic criticism until his death. Years of working as a teacher as well as a creator of poetry and an apparently limitless mastery of the literary past gave Jarrell an authority and an audience. But for reasons the following selection helps to make clear, Jarrell felt that the American public "has an unusual relationship to the poet: it doesn't even know that he is there." Still, the essay was originally published in the popular, "family" magazine, The Saturday Evening Post, *which makes clear that, in Jarrell's case at least, no one could help but know that he was there.*

The Taste of the Age

We all remember that Queen Victoria, when she died in 1901, had never got to see a helicopter, a television set, penicillin, an electric refrigerator; yet she *had* seen railroads, electric lights, textile machinery, the telegraph—she came about midway in the industrial and technological revolution that has transformed our world. But there are a good many other things, of a rather different sort, that Queen Victoria never got to see, because she came at the very beginning of another sort of half-technological, half-cultural revolution. Let me give some examples.

If the young Queen Victoria had said to the Duke of Wellington: "Sir, the Bureau of Public Relations of Our army is in a deplorable state," he would have answered: "What is a Bureau of Public Relations, ma'am?" When he and his generals wanted to tell lies, they had to tell them themselves; there was no organized institution set up to do it for them. But of course Queen Victoria couldn't have made any such remark, since she too had never heard of public relations. She had never seen, or heard about, or dreamed of an advertising agency; she had never seen—unless you count Barnum—a press agent; she had never seen a photograph of a sex slaying in a tabloid—had never seen a tabloid. People gossiped about her, but not in gossip columns; she had never heard a commentator, a soap opera, a quiz program. Queen Victoria—think of it!—had never heard a singing commercial, never seen an advertisement beginning: *Science says* . . . and if she *had* seen one she would only have retorted: "And what, pray, does the Archbishop of Canterbury say? What does dear good Albert say?"

When some comedian or wit—Sydney Smith, for example—told Queen Victoria jokes, they weren't supplied him by six well-paid gag writers, but just occurred to him. When Disraeli and

Gladstone made speeches for her government, the speeches weren't written for them by ghost writers; when Disraeli and Gladstone sent her lovingly or respectfully inscribed copies of their new books, they had written the books themselves. There they were, with the resources of an empire at their command, and they wrote the books themselves! And Queen Victoria had to read the books herself: nobody was willing—or able—to digest them for her in *Reader's Digest*, or to make movies of them, or to make radio or television programs of them, so that she could experience them painlessly and effortlessly. In those days people chewed their own food or went hungry; we have changed all that.

Queen Victoria never went to the movies and had an epic costing eight million dollars injected into her veins—she never went to the movies. She never read a drugstore book by Mickey Spillane; even if she had had a moral breakdown and had read a Bad Book, it would just have been *Under Two Flags* or something by Marie Corelli. She had never been interviewed by, or read the findings of, a Gallup Poll. She never read the report of a commission of sociologists subsidized by the Ford Foundation; she never Adjusted herself to her Group, or Shared the Experience of her Generation, or breathed a little deeper to feel herself a part of the Century of the Common Man—she *was* a part of it for almost two years, but she didn't know that that was what it was.

And all the other people in the world were just like Queen Victoria.

Isn't it plain that it is all *these* lacks that make Queen Victoria so old-fashioned, so finally and awfully different from us, rather than the fact that she never flew in an airplane, or took insulin, or had a hydrogen bomb dropped on her? Queen Victoria in a DC-7 would be Queen Victoria still—I can hear her saying to the stewardess: "We do not wish Dramamine"; but a Queen Victoria who listened every day to *John's Other Wife, Portia Faces Life*, and *Just Plain Bill*—that wouldn't be Queen Victoria at all!

There has been not one revolution, an industrial and technological revolution, there have been two; and this second, cultural revolution might be called the Revolution of the Word. People have learned to process words too—words, and the thoughts and attitudes they embody: we manufacture entertainment and consolation as efficiently as we manufacture anything else. One sees in stores ordinary old-fashioned oatmeal or cocoa; and, side by side with it, another kind called Instant Cocoa, Instant Oats. Most of our literature—I use the word in its broadest sense—is Instant Literature: the words are short, easy, instantly recognizable words, the thoughts are easy, familiar, instantly recognizable thoughts, the attitudes are familiar, already-agreed-upon, instantly acceptable attitudes. And if all this is true, can these productions be either truth or—in the narrower and higher sense—literature? The truth, as everybody knows, is sometimes complicated or hard to understand; is sometimes almost unrecognizably different from what we expected it to be; is sometimes difficult or, even, impossible to accept. But literature is necessarily mixed up with truth, isn't it?—our truth, truth as we know it; one can almost define literature as the union of a wish and a truth, or as a wish modified by a truth. But this Instant Literature is a wish reinforced by a cliché, a wish proved by a lie: Instant Literature—whether it is a soap opera, a Broadway play, or a historical, sexual best-seller—tells us always that life is not only what we wish it, but also what we think it. When people are treating him as a lunatic who has to be humored, Hamlet cries: "They fool me to the top of my bent"; and the makers of Instant Literature treat us exactly as advertisers treat the readers of advertisements—humor us, flatter our prejudices, pull our strings, show us that they know us for what they take us to be: impressionable, emotional, ignorant, somewhat weak-minded Common Men. They fool us to the top of our bent—and if we aren't fooled, they dismiss us as *a statistically negligible minority.*

An advertisement is a wish modified, if at all, by the Pure Food and Drug Act. Take a loaf of ordinary white bread that you buy at the grocery. As you eat it you know that you are eating it, and not the blotter, because the blotter isn't so bland; yet in the world of advertisements little boys ask their mother not to put any jam on their bread, it tastes so good without. This world of the advertisements is a literary world, of a kind: it is the world of Instant Literature. Think of some of the speeches we hear in political campaigns—aren't they too part of the world of Instant Literature? And the first story you read in *The Saturday Evening Post,* the first movie you go to at your neighborhood theater, the first dramatic program you hear on the radio, see on television—are these more like *Grimm's Tales* and *Alice in Wonderland* and *The Three Sisters* and *Oedipus Rex* and Shakespeare and the Bible, or are they more like political speeches and advertisements?

The greatest American industry—why has no one ever said so?—is the industry of using words. We pay tens of millions of people to spend their lives lying to us, or telling us the truth, or supplying us with a nourishing medicinal compound of the two. All of us are living in the middle of a dark wood—a bright Technicolored forest—of words, words, words. It is a forest in which the wind is never still: there isn't a tree in the forest that is not, for every moment of its life and our lives, persuading or ordering or seducing or overawing us into buying this, believing that, voting for the other.

And yet, the more words there are, the simpler the words get. The professional users of words process their product as if it were baby food and we babies: all we have to do is open our mouths and swallow. Most of our mental and moral food is quick-frozen, pre-digested, spoon-fed. E. M. Forster has said: "The only thing we learn from spoon-feeding is the shape of the spoon." Not only is this true—pretty soon, if anything doesn't have the shape of that spoon we won't swallow it, we can't swallow it. Our century has produced some great and much good literature, but the habitual readers of Instant Literature cannot read it, nor can they read the great and good literature of the past.

If Queen Victoria had got to read the *Reader's Digest*—awful thought!—she would have loved it; and it would have changed her. Everything in the world, in the *Reader's Digest*—I am using it as a convenient symbol for all that is like it—is a palatable, timely, ultimately reassuring anecdote, immediately comprehensible to everybody over, and to many under, the age of eight. Queen Victoria would notice that Albert kept quoting, from Shakespeare—that the Archbishop of Canterbury kept quoting, from the Bible—things that were very different from anything in the *Reader's Digest*. Sometimes these sentences were not reassuring but disquieting, sometimes they had big words or hard thoughts in them, sometimes the interest in them wasn't human, but literary or divine. After a while Queen Victoria would want Shakespeare and the Bible—would want Albert, even—digested for her beforehand by the *Reader's Digest*. And a little further on in the process of digestion, she would look from the *Reader's Digest* to some magazine the size of your palm, called *Quick* or *Pic* or *Click* or *The Week in TV*, and a strange half-sexual yearning would move like musk through her veins, and she would—

But I cannot, I will not say it. You and I know how she and Albert will end: sitting before the television set, staring into it, silent; and inside the set, there are Victoria and Albert, staring into the television camera, silent, and the master of ceremonies is saying to them: "No, I think you will find that *Bismarck* is the capital of North Dakota!"

But for so long as she still reads, Queen Victoria will be able to get the Bible and Shakespeare—though not, alas! Albert—in some specially prepared form. Fulton Oursler or Fulton J. Sheen or a thousand others are always rewriting the Bible; there are many comic-book versions of Shakespeare; and only the other day

I read an account of an interesting project of rewriting Shakespeare "for students":

> *Philadephia, Pa, Feb. 1.* (AP) Two high school teachers have published a simplified version of Shakespeare's "Julius Caesar" and plan to do the same for "Macbeth." Their goal is to make the plays more understandable to youth.
> The teachers, Jack A. Waypen and Leroy S. Layton, say if the Bible can be revised and modernized why not Shakespeare? They made 1,122 changes in "Julius Caesar" from single words to entire passages. They modernized obsolete words and expressions and substituted "you" for "thee" and "thou."
> Shakespeare had Brutus say in Act III, Scene I:
>
> *Fates, wee will know your pleasures;*
> *That we shall die, we know; 'tis but the time*
> *And drawing days out, that men stand upon.*
>
> In the Waypen-Layton version, Brutus says:
>
> *We will soon know what Fate decrees for us.*
> *That we shall die, we know. It's putting off*
> *The time of death that's of concern to men.*

Not being Shakespeare, I can't find a comment worthy of this, this project. I am tempted to say in an Elizabethan voice: "Ah, wayward Waypen, lascivious Layton, lay down thine errant pen!" And yet if I said this to them they would only reply earnestly, uncomprehendingly, sorrowfully: "Can't you give us some *con*structive criticism, not *de*structive? Why don't you say *your* errant pen, not *thine?* And *lascivious!* Mr. Jarrell, if you *have* to talk about that type subject, don't say *lascivious* Layton, say *sexy* Layton!"

Even Little Red Ridinghood is getting too hard for children, I read. The headline of the story is "CHILD'S BOOKS BEING MADE MORE SIMPLE;" the story comes from New York, is distributed by the International News Service, and is written by Miss Olga Curtis. Miss Curtis has interviewed Julius Kushner, the head of a firm that has been publishing children's books longer than anyone else in the country. He tells Miss Curtis:

"Non-essential details have disappeared from the 1953 Little Red Ridinghood story. Modern children enjoy their stories better stripped down to basic plot—for instance, Little Red Ridinghood meets wolf, Little Red Ridinghood escapes wolf. [I have a comment: the name Little Red Ridinghood seems to me both long and non-essential—why not call the child Red, and strip the story down to Red meets wolf, Red escapes wolf? At this rate, one could tell a child all of Grimm's tales between dinner and bedtime.]

"'We have to keep up with the mood of each generation,' Kushner explained. 'Today's children like stories condensed to essentials, and with visual and tactile appeal as well as interesting content.'

"'Modernizing old favorites,' Kushner said, 'is fundamentally a matter of simplifying.' Kushner added that today's children's books are intended to be activity games as well as reading matter. He mentioned books that make noises when pressed, and books with pop-up three-dimensional illustrations as examples of publishers' efforts to make each book a teaching aid as well as a story."

As one reads one sees before one, as if in a vision, the children's book of the future: a book that, pressed, says: *I'm your friend;* teaches the child that Crime Does Not Pay; does not exceed thirty words; can be used as a heating pad if the electric blanket breaks down; and has three-dimensional illustrations dyed with harmless vegetable coloring matter and flavored with pure vanilla. I can hear the children of the future crying: "Mother, read us another vanilla book!"

But by this time you must be thinking, as I am, of one of the more frightening things about our age: that much of the body of common knowledge that educated people (and many uneducated people) once had, has disappeared or is rapidly disappearing. Fairy tales, myths, proverbs, history—the Bible and Shakespeare and Dickens, the *Odyssey* and *Gulliver's Travels*—these and all the things like them are surprisingly often things that most of an audience won't understand an allusion to, a joke about. These things were the ground on which the people of the past came together. Much of the wit or charm or elevation of any writing or conversation with an atmosphere depends upon this presupposed, easily and affectionately remembered body of common knowledge; because of it we understand things, feel about things, as human beings and not as human animals.

Who teaches us all this? Our families, our friends, our schools, society in general. Most of all, we hope, our schools. When I say *schools* I mean grammar schools and high schools and colleges—but the first two are more important. Most people still don't go to college, and those who do don't get there until they are seventeen or eighteen. "Give us a child until he is seven and he is ours," a Jesuit is supposed to have said; the grammar schools and high schools of the United States have a child for ten years longer, and then he is—whose? Shakespeare's? Leroy S. Layton's? The

Reader's Digest's? When students at last leave high school or go on to college, what are they like?

Discussion Questions

1. Whom does Jarrell implicitly see as his audience? Do college students seem to be included? What efforts, if any, does he make to avoid sounding "preachy" to his audience?
2. In what various ways does Jarrell use Queen Victoria as a symbol?
3. How do Jarrell's views of literature and its functions compare with those of Robert Frost and Northrup Frye?
4. Find an example of what Jarrell calls "Instant Literature" and explain how far Jarrell's definition applies and what, if anything, it leaves unaccounted for.
5. Jarrell hopes that "Little Red Ridinghood" won't be "rewritten" as the Bible and Shakespeare have been. Would he, however, have approved of Russell Baker's version? Why or why not?
6. Jarrell does not say explicitly what he disapproves of in the "rewritten" passage from Shakespeare. Write an essay explaining what it is about the language of the new version Jarrell would have disliked.

SIR JAMES JEANS

The English mathematician, physicist, and astronomer Sir James Jeans (1877–1946) wrote his first book (on clocks) at the age of nine. In 1906, at the very early age of twenty-eight, he was elected a Fellow of the Royal Society, in spite of his career having been interrupted for two years by a severe illness. After teaching at Cambridge, his alma mater, *at Princeton, and then again at Cambridge, he retired in 1912 to devote himself to writing and research in several areas including the structure of stars. After 1929 he largely turned to the creation of popular essays and books on science, such as* The Stars in Their Courses, *from which the following essay is taken.*

Why the Sky Looks Blue

Imagine that we stand on any ordinary seaside pier, and watch the waves rolling in and striking against the iron columns of the pier. Large waves pay very little attention to the columns—they divide right and left and re-unite after passing each column, much as a regiment of soldiers would if a tree stood in their road; it is almost as though the columns had not been there. But the short waves and ripples find the columns of the pier a much more formidable obstacle. When the short waves impinge on the columns, they are reflected back and spread as new ripples in all direction. To use the technical term, they are "scattered." The obstacle provided by the iron columns hardly affects the long waves at all, but scatters the short ripples.

We have been watching a sort of working model of the way in which sunlight struggles through the earth's atmosphere. Between us on earth and outer space the atmosphere interposes innumerable obstacles in the form of molecules of air, tiny droplets of water, and small particles of dust. These are represented by the columns of the pier.

The waves of the sea represent the sunlight. We know that sunlight is a blend of lights of many colours—as we can prove for ourselves by passing it through a prism, or even through a jug of water, or as Nature demonstrates to us when she passes it through the raindrops of a summer shower and produces a rainbow. We also know that light consists of waves, and that the different colours of light are produced by waves of different lengths, red light by long waves and blue light by short waves. The mixture of waves which constitutes sunlight has to struggle through the obstacles it meets in the atmosphere, just as the mixture of waves at the seaside has to struggle past the columns of the pier. And these obstacles treat the light-waves much as the columns of the pier treat the sea-waves. The long waves which constitute red light are hardly affected, but the short waves which constitute blue light are scattered in all directions.

Thus, the different constituents of sunlight are treated in different ways as they struggle through the earth's atmosphere. A wave of blue light may be scattered by a dust particle, and turned out of its course. After a time a second dust particle again turns it out of its course, and so on, until finally it enters our eyes by a path as zigzag as that of a flash of lightning. Consequently the blue waves of the sunlight enter our eyes from all directions. And that is why the sky looks blue.

Discussion Questions

1. What level of scientific education does Jeans generally imagine his audience to have? Does he ever deviate from this general assumption? Through what techniques does he maintain his explanation at a particular level? For example, he is careful to give common alternative examples for the effects of a prism. Do his sentences vary in complexity?

2. In what different ways does Jeans build up the parts of his analysis and their relation to the whole of it? For example, how does each paragraph contribute to the whole? How does each successive example contribute?

3. Compare Jeans's analysis to that of Bronowski on "likenesses." What does each writer assume about scientific "explanation"? Do they entirely agree?

4. Use the technique of analogy to explain another natural phenomenon or technical device to a similar audience. You might, for example, explain how we hear sounds or how a computer works.

C. G. JUNG

The world-renowned Swiss psychologist and psychiatrist Carl Gustav Jung (1875–1961) was born in Basel, where he studied medicine at the University, before continuing studies in psychology in Paris. He met Sigmund Freud in 1907, but the close relationship that soon developed fell apart in 1912, when Jung proposed a rival theory of sexuality and the unconscious. In short, Jung's method of "analytical psychology" placed more emphasis than did Freud's upon immediate human conflicts and less upon the significance of childhood sexuality.

    Jung, after his quarrel with Freud, founded a new influential school of psychiatry at Zurich. Among his major works are The Theory of Psychoanalysis (1912), Psychology of the Unconscious (1916), Psychological Types (1923), Modern Man in Search of a Soul (1933), and Integration of the Personality (1939). English translations of his works have been collected in a nineteen-volume set published by the Bollingen Series of Princeton University Press. "A Vision of Life After Death" is excerpted from an episode in Jung's autobiography, Memories, Dreams, Reflections (1961).

A Vision of Life After Death

At the beginning of 1944 I broke my foot, and this misadventure was followed by a heart attack. In a state of unconsciousness I experienced deliriums and visions which must have begun when I hung on the edge of death and was being given oxygen and camphor injections. The images were so tremendous that I myself concluded that I was close to death. My nurse afterward told me, "It was as if you were surrounded by a bright glow." That was a phenomenon she had sometimes observed in the dying, she added. I had reached the outermost limit, and do not know whether I was in a dream or an ecstasy. At any rate, extremely strange things began to happen to me.

It seemed to me that I was high up in space. Far below I saw the globe of the earth, bathed in a gloriously blue light. I saw the deep blue sea and the continents. Far below my feet lay Ceylon, and in the distance ahead of me the subcontinent of India. My field of vision did not include the whole earth, but its global shape was plainly distinguishable and its outlines shone with a silvery gleam through that wonderful blue light. In many places the globe seemed colored, or spotted dark green like oxydized silver. Far away to the left lay a broad expanse—the reddish-yellow desert of Arabia; it was as though the silver of the earth had there assumed a reddish-gold hue. Then came the Red Sea, and far, far back—as if in the upper left of a map—I could just make out a bit of the Mediterranean. My gaze was directed chiefly toward that. Everything else appeared indistinct. I could also see the snow-covered Himalayas, but in that direction it was foggy or cloudy. I did not look to the right at all. I knew that I was on the point of departing from the earth.

Later I discovered how high in space one would have to be to have so extensive a view—approximately a thousand miles! The

A VISION OF LIFE AFTER DEATH

sight of the earth from this height was the most glorious thing I had ever seen.

After contemplating it for a while, I turned around. I had been standing with my back to the Indian Ocean, as it were, and my face to the north. Then it seemed to me that I made a turn to the south. Something new entered my field of vision. A short distance away I saw in space a tremendous dark block of stone, like a meteorite. It was about the size of my house, or even bigger. It was floating in space, and I myself was floating in space.

I had seen similar stones on the coast of the Gulf of Bengal. They were blocks of tawny granite, and some of them had been hollowed out into temples. My stone was one such gigantic dark block. An entrance led into a small antechamber. To the right of the entrance, a black Hindu sat silently in lotus posture upon a stone bench. He wore a white gown, and I knew that he expected me. Two steps led up to this antechamber, and inside, on the left, was the gate to the temple. Innumerable tiny niches, each with a saucer-like concavity filled with coconut oil and small burning wicks, surrounded the door with a wreath of bright flames. I had once actually seen this when I visited the Temple of the Holy Tooth at Kandy in Ceylon; the gate had been framed by several rows of burning oil lamps of this sort.

As I approached the steps leading up to the entrance into the rock, a strange thing happened: I had the feeling that everything was being sloughed away; everything I aimed at or wished for or thought, the whole phantasmagoria of earthly existence, fell away or was stripped from me—an extremely painful process. Nevertheless something remained; it was as if I now carried along with me everything I had ever experienced or done, everything that had happened around me. I might also say: it was with me, and I was it. I consisted of all that, so to speak. I consisted of my own history, and I felt with great certainty: this is what I am. "I am this bundle of what has been, and what has been accomplished."

This experience gave me a feeling of extreme poverty, but at the same time of great fullness. There was no longer anything I wanted or desired. I existed in an objective form; I was what I had been and lived. At first the sense of annihilation predominated, of having been stripped or pillaged; but suddenly that became of no consequence. Everything seemed to be past; what remained was a *fait accompli*, without any reference back to what had been. There was no longer any regret that something had dropped away or been taken away. On the contrary: I had everything that I was, and that was everything.

Something else engaged my attention: as I approached the

temple I had the certainty that I was about to enter an illuminated room and would meet there all those people to whom I belong in reality. There I would at last understand—this too was a certainty—what historical nexus I or my life fitted into. I would know what had been done before me, why I had come into being, and where my life was flowing. My life as I lived it had often seemed to me like a story that has no beginning and no end. I had the feeling that I was a historical fragment, an excerpt for which the preceding and succeeding text was missing. My life seemed to have been snipped out of a long chain of events, and many questions had remained unanswered. Why had it taken this course? Why had I brought these particular assumptions with me? What had I made of them? What will follow? I felt sure that I would receive an answer to all these questions as soon as I entered the rock temple. There I would learn why everything had been thus and not otherwise. There I would meet the people who knew the answer to my question about what had been before and what would come after.

While I was thinking over these matters, something happened that caught my attention. From below, from the direction of Europe, an image floated up. It was my doctor, Dr. H.—or, rather, his likeness—framed by a golden chain or a golden laurel wreath. I knew at once: "Aha, this is my doctor, of course, the one who has been treating me. But now he is coming in his primal form, as a *basileus* of Kos.[1] In life he was an avatar of this *basileus*, the temporal embodiment of the primal form, which has existed from the beginning. Now he is appearing in that primal form."

Presumably I too was in my primal form, though this was something I did not observe but simply took for granted. As he stood before me, a mute exchange of thought took place between us. Dr. H. had been delegated by the earth to deliver a message to me, to tell me that there was a protest against my going away. I had no right to leave the earth and must return. The moment I heard that, the vision ceased.

---

[1]*Basileus*: King; Kos: The birthplace of Hippocrates.

Discussion Questions

1. In the opening paragraph Jung says that he "experienced deliriums and visions." Note that he doesn't use the word "delirium" later to describe what happened to him. Why not? What distinction can you make between the two words, and why is the distinction important to make in this case?

2. How do you think Jung reacted to this experience afterwards? How skeptical does he appear to be in the passage? Suppose you said to him: "Very interesting, but it was only a dream brought on by the medication." How might he answer you?

3. Compare the notion of a life after death with that of Evelyn Waugh's in "Half in Love with Easeful Death." Which writer is more mystical? Which writer seems more religious to you?

4. Nearly everyone has had some sort of strange, uncanny experience. In a short personal essay, write about such an experience. Pay attention in your writing to how much your experience conforms to certain expectations: for example, do you think it's true that people who think they are suddenly about to die see their entire lives flash before them?

PAULINE KAEL

One of the most respected movie reviewers of our time, Pauline Kael began her prestigious career with The New Yorker *magazine in 1968. A prolific writer who admits she often discovers her thoughts in the process of writing, she successfully combines in her reviews an instinctive delight in movies (a term she prefers to "film") with a keen sense of artistic fakery and cant. Her reviews frequently branch out into larger aesthetic issues, inviting the reader to consider the entire movie business and its vital connections with American popular culture. She regards her many collections of reviews as a "record of the interaction of movies and our national life. . . ."*

Born in Sonoma County, California, in 1919, she attended the University of California, Berkeley, where she majored in philosophy. Before moving to New York City, she did movie reviews on radio and for several small journals. Her first book, I Lost It at the Movies *(1965) established her as a major critic and led to staff positions with* Life, McCall's, *and* The New Republic. *Since then she has written* Kiss Kiss Bang Bang *(1968),* Going Steady *(1970),* The Citizen Kane Book *(1971),* Reeling *(1976),* When the Lights Go Down *(1980), and* 5001 Nights at the Movies *(1982). Her collection of reviews,* Deeper into Movies, *won the National Book Award for 1974. In the following essay she looks at movies through another, somewhat alien, medium—television.*

Movies on Television

A few years ago, a jet on which I was returning to California after a trip to New York was instructed to delay landing for a half hour. The plane circled above the San Francisco area, and spread out under me were the farm where I was born, the little town where my grandparents were buried, the city where I had gone to school, the cemetery where my parents were, the homes of my brothers and sisters, Berkeley, where I had gone to college, and the house where at that moment, while I hovered high above, my little daughter and my dogs were awaiting my return. It was as though my whole life were suspended in time—as though no matter where you'd gone, what you'd done, the past were all still there, present, if you just got up high enough to attain the proper perspective.

Sometimes I get a comparable sensation when I turn from the news program or the discussion shows on television to the old movies. So much of what formed our tastes and shaped our experiences, and so much of the garbage of our youth that we never thought we'd see again—preserved and exposed to eyes and minds that might well want not to believe that this was an important part of our past. Now these movies are there for new generations, to whom they cannot possibly have the same impact or meaning, because they are all jumbled together, out of historical sequence. Even what may deserve an honorable position in movie history is somehow dishonored by being so available, so meaninglessly present. Everything is in hopeless disorder, and that is the way new generations experience our movie past. In the other arts, something like natural selection takes place: only the best or the most significant or influential or successful works compete for our attention. Moreover, those from the past are likely to be touched up to accord with the taste of the present. In popular music, old tunes are newly orchestrated. A small repertory of plays is continually reinterpreted for contemporary meanings—the great ones for new relevance, the not so great rewritten, tackily "brought up to date," or deliberately treated as period pieces. By contrast, movies, through the accidents of commerce, are sold in blocks or packages to television, the worst with the mediocre and the best, the successes with the failures, the forgotten with the half forgotten, the ones so dreary you don't know whether you ever saw them or just others like them with some so famous you can't be sure whether you actually saw them or only imagined what they were like. A lot of this stuff never really made it with any audience; it played in small towns or it was used to soak up the time just the way TV in bars does.

There are so many things that we, having lived through them, or passed over them, never want to think about again. But in movies nothing is cleaned away, sorted out, purposefully discarded. (The destruction of negatives in studio fires or deliberately, to save space, was as indiscriminate as the preservation and resale.) There's a kind of hopelessness about it: what does not deserve to last lasts, and so it all begins to seem one big pile of junk, and some people say, "Movies never really were any good—except maybe the Bogarts." If the same thing had happened in literature or music or painting—if we were constantly surrounded by the piled-up inventory of the past—it's conceivable that modern man's notions of culture and civilization would be very different. Movies, most of them produced as fodder to satisfy the appetite for pleasure and relaxation, turned out to have magical properties—indeed to *be* magical properties. This fodder can be fed to people over and over again. Yet, not altogether strangely, as the years wear on it doesn't please their palates, though many will go on swallowing it, just because nothing tastier is easily accessible. Watching old movies is like spending an evening with those people next door. They bore us, and we wouldn't go out of our way to see them; we drop in on them because they're so close. If it took some effort to see old movies, we might try to find out which were the good ones, and if people saw only the good ones maybe they would still respect old movies. As it is, people sit and watch movies that audiences walked out on thirty years ago. Like Lot's wife, we are tempted to take another look, attracted not by evil but by something that seems much more shameful—our own innocence. We don't try to reread the girls' and boys' "series" books of our adolescence—the very look of them is dismaying. The textbooks we studied in grammar school are probably more "dated" than the movies we saw then, but we never look at the old schoolbooks, whereas we keep seeing on TV the movies that represent the same stage in our lives and played much the same part in them—as things we learned from and, in spite of, went beyond.

Not all old movies look bad now, of course; the good ones are still good—surprisingly good, often, if you consider how much of the detail is lost on television. Not only the size but the shape of the image is changed, and, indeed, almost all the specifically visual elements are so distorted as to be all but completely destroyed. On television, a cattle drive or a cavalry charge or a chase—the climax of so many a big movie—loses the dimensions of space and distance that made it exciting, that sometimes made it great. And since the structural elements—the rhythm, the buildup, the suspense—are also partly destroyed by deletions and commercial breaks and the interruptions incidental to home viewing, it's amazing that the bare bones of performance, dialogue, story, good directing, and (especially important for close-range viewing) good editing can still make an old movie more entertaining than almost anything new on television. (That's why old movies are taking over television—or, more accurately, vice versa.) The verbal slapstick of the newspaper-life comedies—*Blessed Event, Roxie Hart, His Girl Friday*—may no longer be fresh (partly because it has been so widely imitated), but it's still funny. Movies with good, fast, energetic talk seem better than ever on television—still not great but, on television, better than what *is* great. (And as we listen to the tabloid journalists insulting the corrupt politicians, we respond once again to the happy effrontery of that period when the targets of popular satire were still small enough for us to laugh at without choking.) The wit of dialogue comedies like Preston Sturges's *Unfaithfully Yours* isn't much diminished, nor does a tight melodrama like *Double Indemnity* lose a great deal. Movies like Joseph L. Mankiewicz's *A Letter to Three Wives* and *All About Eve* look practically the same on television as in theatres, because they have almost no visual dimensions to lose. In them the camera serves primarily to show us the person who is going to speak the next presumably bright line—a scheme that on television, as in theatres, is acceptable only when the line *is* bright. Horror and fantasy films like Karl Freund's *The Mummy* or Robert Florey's *The Murders in the Rue Morgue*—even with the loss, through miniaturization, of imaginative special effects—are surprisingly effective, perhaps because they are so primitive in their appeal that the qualities of the imagery matter less than the basic suggestions. Fear counts for more than finesse, and viewing horror films is far more frightening at home than in the shared comfort of an audience that breaks the tension with derision.

Other kinds of movies lose much of what made them worth looking at—the films of von Sternberg, for example, designed in light and shadow, or the subtleties of Max Ophuls, or the lyricism of Satyajit Ray. In the box the work of these men is not as lively or as satisfying as the plain good movies of lesser directors. Reduced to the dead grays of a cheap television print, Orson Welles's *The Magnificent Ambersons*—an uneven work that is nevertheless a triumphant conquest of the movie medium—is as lifelessly dull as a newspaper Wirephoto of a great painting. But when people say of a "big" movie like *High Noon* that it has dated or that it doesn't hold up, what they are really saying is that their judgment was faulty or has changed. They may have overresponded to its publicity and reputation or to its attempt to deal with a social problem or an idea, and may have ignored the banalities surrounding that attempt; now that the idea doesn't seem so daring, they notice the rest. Perhaps it was a traditional drama that was new to them and that they thought was new to the world; everyone's "golden age of movies" is the period of his first moviegoing and just before—what he just missed or wasn't allowed to see. (The Bogart films came out just before today's college kids started going.)

Sometimes we suspect, and sometimes rightly, that our memory has improved a picture—that imaginatively we made it what we knew it could have been or should have been—and, fearing this, we may prefer memory to new contact. We'll remember it better if we don't see it again—we'll remember what it meant to us. The nostalgia we may have poured over a performer or over our recollections of a movie has a way of congealing when we try to renew the contact. But sometimes the experience of reseeing is wonderful—a confirmation of the general feeling that was all that remained with us from childhood. And we enjoy the fresh proof of the rightness of our responses that reseeing the film gives us. We re-experience what we once felt, and memories flood back. Then movies seem magical—all those *madeleines* waiting to be dipped in tea. What looks bad in old movies is the culture of which they were part and which they expressed—a tone of American life that we have forgotten. When we see First World War posters, we are far enough away from their patriotic primitivism to be amused at the emotions and sentiments to which they appealed. We can feel charmed but superior. It's not so easy to cut ourselves off from old movies and the old selves who responded to them, because they're not an isolated part of the past held up for derision and amusement and wonder. Although they belong to the same world as stories in *Liberty*, old radio shows, old phonograph records, an America still divided between hayseeds and city slickers, and although they may seem archaic, their pastness isn't so very past. It includes the last decade, last year, yesterday.

Though in advertising movies for TV the recentness is the lure, for many of us what constitutes the attraction is the datedness, and the earlier movies are more compelling than the ones of the fifties or the early sixties. Also, of course, the movies of the thirties and forties look better technically, because, ironically, the competition with television that made movies of the fifties and sixties enlarge their scope and their subject matter has resulted in their looking like a mess in the box—the sides of the image lopped off, the crowds and vistas a boring blur, the color altered, the epic themes incongruous and absurd on the little home screen. In a movie like *The Robe*, the large-scale production values that were depended on to attract TV viewers away from their sets become a negative factor. But even if the quality of the image were improved, these movies are too much like the ones we can see in theatres to be interesting at home. At home, we like to look at those stiff, carefully groomed actors of the thirties, with their clipped, Anglophile stage speech and their regular, clean-cut features—walking profiles, like the figures on Etruscan vases and almost as remote. And there is the faithless wife—how will she decide between her lover and her husband, when they seem as alike as two wax grooms on a wedding cake? For us, all three are doomed not by sin and disgrace but by history. Audiences of the period may have enjoyed these movies for their action, their story, their thrills, their wit, and all this high living. But through our window on the past we see the actors acting our other dramas as well. The Middle European immigrants had children who didn't speak the king's English and, after the Second World War, didn't even respect it so much. A flick of the dial and we are in the fifties amid the slouchers, with their thick lips, shapeless noses, and shaggy haircuts, waiting to say their lines until they think them out, then mumbling something that is barely speech. How long, O Warren Beatty, must we wait before we turn back to beautiful stick figures like Phillips Holmes?

We can take a shortcut through the hell of many lives, turning the dial from the social protest of the thirties to the films of the same writers and directors in the fifties—full of justifications for blabbing, which they shifted onto characters in oddly unrelated situations. We can see in the films of the forties the displaced artists of Europe—the anti-Nazi exiles like Conrad Veidt, the refugees like Peter Lorre, Fritz Kortner, and Alexander Granach. And what are they playing? Nazis, of course, because they have accents, and so for Americans—for the whole world—they become images of Nazi brutes. Or we can look at the patriotic sentiments of the Second World War years and those actresses, in their orgies or ersatz nobility, giving their lives—or, at the very least, their bodies—to save their country. It was sickening at the time; it's perversely amusing now—part of the spectacle of our common culture.

Probably in a few years some kid watching *The Sandpiper* on television will say what I recently heard a kid say about *Mrs. Miniver*: "And to think they really believed it in those days." Of course, we didn't. We didn't accept nearly as much in old movies as we may now fear we did. Many of us went to see big-name pictures just as we went to *The Night of the Iguana*, without believing a minute of it. The James Bond pictures are not to be "believed," but they tell us a lot about the conventions that audiences now accept, just as the confessional films of the thirties dealing with sin and illegitimacy and motherhood tell us about the sickly-sentimental tone of American entertainment in the midst of the Depression. Movies indicate what the producers thought people would pay to see—which was not always the same as what they *would* pay to see. Even what they enjoyed seeing does not tell us directly what they believed but only indirectly hints at the tone and style of a culture. There is no reason to assume that people twenty or thirty years ago were stupider than they are now. (Consider how *we* may be judged by people twenty years from now looking at today's movies.) Though it may not seem obvious to us now, part of the original appeal of old movies—which we certainly understood and responded to as children—was that, despite their sentimental tone, they helped to form the liberalized modern consciousness. This trash—and most of it was, and is, trash—probably taught us more about the world, and even about values, than our "education" did. Movies broke down barriers of all kinds, opened up the world, helped to make us aware. And they were almost always on the side of the mistreated, the socially despised. Almost all drama is. And, because movies were a mass medium, they had to be on the side of the poor.

Nor does it necessarily go without saying that the glimpses of something really good even in mediocre movies—the quickening of excitement at a great performance, the discovery of beauty in a gesture or a phrase or an image—made us understand the meaning of art as our teachers in appreciation courses never could. And—what is more difficult for those who are not movie lovers to grasp—even after this sense of the greater and the higher is developed, we still do not want to live only on the heights. We still want that pleasure of discovering things for ourselves; we need the sustenance of the ordinary, the commonplace, the almost-good as part of the anticipatory atmosphere. And though it all helps us to respond to the moments of greatness, it is not only for this that we want it. The educated person who became interested in cinema as an art form through Bergman or Fellini or Resnais is an alien to me (and my mind goes blank with hostility and indifference when he begins to talk). There isn't much for the art-cinema person on television; to look at a great movie, or even a poor movie carefully designed in terms of textures and contrasts, on television is, in general, maddening, because those movies lose too much. (Educational television, though, persists in this misguided effort to bring the television viewer movie classics.) There are few such movies anyway. But there are all the not-great movies, which we probably wouldn't bother going to see in museums or in theatre revivals—they're just not that important. Seeing them on television is a different kind of experience, with different values—partly because the movie past hasn't been filtered to conform to anyone's convenient favorite notions of film art. We make our own, admittedly small, discoveries or rediscoveries. There's Dan Dailey doing his advertising-wise number in *It's Always Fair Weather*, or Gene Kelly and Fred Astaire singing and dancing "The Babbitt and the Bromide" in *Ziegfeld Follies*. And it's like putting on a record of Ray Charles singing "Georgia on My Mind" or Frank Sinatra singing "Bim Bam Baby" or Elisabeth Schwarzkopf singing operetta, and feeling again the elation we felt the first time. Why should we deny these pleasures because there are other, more complex kinds of pleasure possible? It's true that these pleasures don't deepen, and they don't change *us*, but maybe that is part of what makes them seem our own—we realize that we have some emotions and responses that *don't* change as we get older.

People who see a movie for the first time on television don't remember it the same way that people do who saw it in a theatre. Even without the specific visual loss that results from the transfer to another medium, it's doubtful whether a movie could have as intense an impact as it had in its own time. Probably by definition, works that are not truly great cannot be as compelling out of their time. Sinclair Lewis's and Hemingway's novels were becoming archaic while their authors lived. Can *On the Waterfront* have the impact now that it had in 1954? Not quite. And revivals in movie theatres don't have the same kind of charge, either. There's something a little stale in the air, there's a different kind of audience. At a revival, we must allow for the period, or care because of the period. Television viewers seeing old movies for the first time can have very little sense of how and why new stars moved us when they appeared, of the excitement of new themes, of what these movies meant to us. They don't even know which were important in their time, which were "hits."

But they can discover *something* in old movies, and there are few discoveries to be made on dramatic shows produced for television. In comedies, the nervous tic of canned laughter neutralizes everything; the laughter is as false for the funny as for the unfunny and prevents us from responding to either. In general, performances in old movies don't suffer horribly on television except from cuts, and what kindles something like the early flash fire is the power of personality that comes through in those roles that made a star. Today's high school and college students seeing *East of Eden* and *Rebel Without a Cause* for the first time are almost as caught up in James Dean as the first generation of adolescent viewers was, experiencing that tender, romantic, marvelously masochistic identification with the boy who does everything wrong because he cares so much. And because Dean died young and hard, he is not just another actor who outlived his myth and became ordinary in stale roles—he is the symbol of misunderstood youth. He is inside the skin of moviegoing and television-watching youth—even educated youth—in a way that Keats and Shelley or John Cornford and Julian Bell are not. Youth can respond—though not so strongly—to many of our old heroes and heroines: to Gary Cooper, say, as the elegant, lean, amusingly silent romantic loner of his early Western and aviation films. (And they can more easily ignore the actor who sacrificed that character for blubbering righteous bathos.) Bogart found his myth late, and Dean fulfilled the romantic myth of self-destructiveness, so they look good on television. More often, television, by showing us actors before and after their key starring roles, is a myth-killer. But it keeps acting ability alive.

There is a kind of young television watcher seeing old movies for the first time who is surprisingly sensitive to their values and responds almost with the intensity of a moviegoer. But he's different from the moviegoer. For one thing, he's housebound, inactive, solitary. Unlike a moviegoer, he seems to have no need to discuss what he sees. The kind of television watcher I mean (and the ones I've met are all boys) seems to have extreme empathy with the material in the box (new TV shows as well as old movies, though rarely news), but he may not know how to enter into a conversation, or even how to come into a room or go out of it. He fell in love with his baby-sitter, so he remains a baby. He's unusually polite and intelligent, but in a mechanical way— just going through the motions, without interest. He gives the impression that he wants to withdraw from this human interference and get back to real life—the box. He is like a prisoner who has everything he wants in prison and is content to stay there. Yet, oddly, he and his fellows seem to be tuned in to each other; just as it sometimes seems that even a teen-ager locked in a closet would pick up the new dance steps at the same moment as other teen-agers, these televison watchers react to the same things at the same time. If they can find more intensity in this box than in their own living, then this box can provide *constantly* what we got at the movies only a few times a week. Why should they move away from it, or talk, or go out of the house, when they will only experience that as a loss? Of course, we can see why they should, and their inability to make connections outside is frighteningly suggestive of ways in which we, too, are cut off. It's a matter of degree. If we stay up half the night to watch old movies and can't face the day, it's partly, at least, because of the fascination of our own movie past; *they* live in a past they never had, like people who become obsessed by places they have only imaginative connections with—Brazil, Venezuela, Arabia Deserta. Either way, there is always something a little shameful about living in the past; we feel guilty, stupid—as if the pleasure we get needed some justification that we can't provide.

For some moviegoers, movies probably contribute to that self-defeating romanticizing of expectations which makes life a series of disappointments. They watch the same movies over and over on television, as if they were constantly returning to the scene of the crime—the life they were so busy dreaming about that they never lived it. They are paralyzed by longing, while those less romantic can leap the hurdle. I heard a story the other day about a man who ever since his school days had been worshipfully "in love with" a famous movie star, talking about her, fantasizing about her, following her career, with its ups and downs and its stormy romances and marriages to producers and agents and wealthy sportsmen and rich businessmen. Though he became successful himself, it never occurred to him that he could enter her terrain—she was so glamorously above him. Last week, he got a letter from an old classmate, to whom, years before, he had confided his adoration of the star; the classmate—an unattractive guy who had never done anything with his life and had a crummy job in a crummy business—had just married her.

Movies are a combination of art and mass medium, but television is so single in its purpose—selling—that it operates without that painful, poignant mixture of aspiration and effort and compromise. We almost never think of calling a television show "beautiful," or even of complaining about the absence of beauty, because we take it for granted that television operates without beauty. When we see on television photographic records of the past, like the pictures of Scott's Antarctic expedition or those series on the First World War, they seem almost too strong for the box, too pure for it. The past has a terror and a fascination and a beauty beyond almost anything else. We are looking at the dead, and they move and grin and wave at us; it's an almost unbearable experience. When our wonder and our grief are interrupted or followed by a commercial, we want to destroy the ugly box. Old movies don't tear us apart like that. They do something else, which we can take more of and take more easily: they give us a sense of the passage of life. Here is Elizabeth Taylor as a plump matron and here, an hour later, as an exquisite child. That charmingly petulant little gigolo with the skinny face and the mustache that seems the most substantial part of him—can he have developed into the great Laurence Olivier? Here is Orson Welles, as a young man, playing a handsome old man, and here is Orson Welles as he has really aged. Here are Bette Davis and Charles Boyer traversing the course of their lives from ingenue and juvenile, through major roles, into character parts—back and forth, endlessly, embodying the good and bad characters of many styles, many periods. We see the old character actors put out to pasture in television serials, playing gossipy neighbors or grumpy grandpas, and then we see them in their youth or middle age, in the roles that made them famous—and it's startling to find how good they were, how vital, after we've encountered them caricaturing themselves, feeding off their old roles. They have almost nothing left of that young actor we responded to—and still find ourselves responding to—except the distinctive voice and a few crotchets. There are those of us who, when we watch old movies, sit there murmuring the names as the actors appear (Florence Bates, Henry Daniell, Ernest Thesiger, Constance Collier, Edna May Oliver, Douglas Fowley), or we recognize them but can't remember their names, yet know how well we once knew them, experiencing the failure of memory as a loss of our own past until we can supply it (Maude Eburne or Porter Hall)—with great relief. After a few seconds, I can always remember them, though I cannot remember the names of my childhood companions or of the prizefighter I once dated, or even of the boy who took me to the senior prom. We are eager to hear again that line we know is coming. We hate to miss anything. Our memories are jarred by cuts. We want to see the movie to the end.

The graveyard of *Our Town* affords such a tiny perspective compared to this. Old movies on television are a gigantic, panoramic novel that we can tune in to and out of. People watch avidly for a few weeks or months or years and then give up; others tune in when they're away from home in lonely hotel rooms, or regularly, at home, a few nights a week or every night. The rest of the family may ignore the passing show, may often interrupt, because individual lines of dialogue or details of plot hardly seem to matter as they did originally. A movie on television is no longer just a drama in itself: it is part of a huge ongoing parade. To a new generation, what does it matter if a few gestures and a nuance are lost, when they know they can't watch the parade on all the channels at all hours anyway? It's like traffic on the street. The television generation knows there is no end; it all just goes on. When television watchers are surveyed and asked what kind of programming they want or how they feel television can be improved, some of them not only have no answers but can't understand the questions. What they get on their sets is television—that's it.

Discussion Questions

1. What distinction does Pauline Kael draw between movies and television? How does that distinction in part derive from her personal experiences? Would you make a similar distinction? Explain.

2. How would you describe her tone of voice? How does her choice of words affect her tone? Do you notice any words that seem out of place in a serious essay?

3. Why does Pauline Kael enjoy the dated movies of the 1930's and 1940's on television more than she does the recent films? What does she get out of old movies?

4. How do old movies contribute to a sense of the past? Are there any dangers in these versions of history? Explain.

5. She says that, though most of the old movies were "trash," they "probably taught us more about the world, and even about values, than our 'education' did." Do you agree? What sort of values would watching "trash" give us? How would Marshall McLuhan respond to her claim?

6. Though ages change, nostalgia remains constant. Choose a cultural phenomenon that has changed during the course of your lifetime—popular music that has moved from radio to television (MTV) or pinball machines to video games—and write an essay describing not only the effects this change had upon you but upon your sense of a new generation.

Rudyard Kipling

Born in India, to which he returned after an unhappy English education, Rudyard Kipling (1865–1936) began his career as a journalist in Lahore. He soon began to write the stories and poems that would make him the premier author and poet of the British overseas empire. Returning to England in 1899, he resolved to conquer the literary world and soon did so. In 1907 he received one of the first Nobel Prizes for Literature and many other honors followed. Kipling remained a dedicated traveler whether on a journalistic assignment (he covered the Boer War) or on his own. The books of essays that came out of his travels show him as a careful observer constantly trying to generalize from any experience. The following essay comes from his Brazilian Sketches (1927) and provides models for several techniques of description.

A Snake Farm

There is, at the far end of one of the never-ending suburbs of São Paulo, a snake farm where serums are prepared and dispensed against the bites of venomous serpents, which abound in these parts. Like most of the things that matter, it was one man's notion and work. Unluckily, the man himself was up or down coast at the time of our visit. But we found the "farm" sitting alone amid beautiful grounds in a faultless stretch of drive—a big, white, shuttered, remote pile in dead heat among the crashing (colours hit here) green of its cut lawns and the raw bosses and clumps of flowers.

One lawn, enclosed by a low wall, was dotted with two-foot-high white domed Kaffir kraals, each pierced by a tiny arch. A moat, a couple of feet wide, ran between the lawn and the bounding wall which overhung, a trifle, as it rose from the water. Nothing else showed, or moved or sounded, in all that heat and space and colour and overwhelming light, till a door in the face of the building opened, and one passed thankfully into cool stillness. A girl in white linen stole down a corridor that gave a glimpse of a hall full of bottles on shelves, and a faint smell of varnish, hard woods, and chemicals. Then a block of solid silence, while portraits of eminent men looked down from the pale walls. A far-off echoing step—and a young man came in, clad like an umpire, with shortish linen trousers, enticingly low shoes, and white socks, and beckoned us to the open, quivering air. His weapon was a stick with a piece of wire bent to right angles at one end of it. He led down to the walled enclosure, entered it across the moat, and stood among the tiny kraals as though making up his mind. Had he by any chance forgotten his leggings? Not in the least, I was told, but leggings were unnecessary as well as warm. And, talking of leggings, a snake cannot as a rule strike higher than a man's knee.

So, on many farms and factories, leggings are issued to the workmen in the fields. Do they wear them? Not unless they are chased into them. For one thing it is a new notion; and for another it bothers their free legs.

Now a decent, forest-bred snake hates glare as much as an elephant does. Hence the baby kraals, with their small single apertures. The young man felt inside one of these with his stick, and slung out a snake, which he named, balanced on the wire. The body dropped raspingly on the dry crab-grass at the edge of the moat and recovered itself like coiled lightning, its head already set, and cocked in watch upon the man. He half kicked towards it with his shoed foot. It half struck back, showed its death-coloured mouth, and sunk back into its coils, cursing a little. Perhaps it knew the routine, or was dizzy with the glare.

The young man passed from kraal to kraal, drawing out, always balanced on the wire, snake after snake, which he named, and pitched beside the first; and as each snake came to rest, its head was watching him as though it had been on that duty since The Expulsion. The recover after the throw-down is quicker than eye can follow, for if a snake be not right side up he is the most helpless of things; but the orientation of the head is quicker than the recover.

Then, as the dishevelled and indignant tangle of them grew, one was lifted out of its dark, who dropped from the wire clumsily, almost in a straight line, and lay belly-up, drawing painful breath through the length of him; being solely concerned with the business of dying, to which he was left. A little lithe thing, rather like a *karait,* raced over him into the moat, where it flashed anxiously up and down along the concrete, seeking escape. But the Architect of its Universe had foreseen that there should be no purchase in still water, and it crawled back, over the thoughtfully roughened lip, on to the prison side. A companion, making the best of the upheaval, floated along the moat effortless in a luxurious knot, but all the while his head was turned towards the man.

Some of the others in the heap kept slipping away to the nearest kraal just as worms slip into grass when the bait-can upsets.

There were rattlers among them—big and bad-tempered—who raised their heads and warned. The "rattle" is more like the "sizzle" of dry seeds in a bean, just enough to hint that there is death in the pot; and, curiously, it impresses any one who has once heard it as much behind secure walls as it does in the open. We had a companion who knew and seemed to love the snakes of his native land. He and the young man talked together about them (most of their names seemed to begin with *ja*) and to illustrate a point, one flat head was pinned down by the wire stick, caught behind the thin neck, and, with a "scraunch" like shelling prawns, the jaws were forced open to start the fangs. But they carried no venom at the moment, and the thing was thrown into the discard, as though it were a journal that had been read or a politician that had served his turn.

"Yes. All the snakes in this enclosure are venomous—some more than others—but all quite enough. They are collected. They last a year or eighteen months. They are not fed because the hungrier they are the more poisonous they grow." (This gift also the Serpent bequeathed to the Sons of Adam.) "Besides our regular collectors, the farmers send us snakes. For each snake, malignant or harmless, the Institute returns them a dose of serum; and also perforated boxes for sending us more snakes. Of course, the best serum is made from the same breed of snake as bit you. But people are often not accurate when they are bitten, so a 'general' serum is sent to the farmers. It cures—it cures surely—but it takes longer and it hurts a little more than the specialised serum. There is no danger in handling snakes if you know how, and if anything happens the injections are just around the corner. Are snakes man-hunters? Only one sort of snake really likes chasing men. The others all want to get away—the harmless snakes first, and then the poison ones. You see, a poisonous snake is never afraid. He does not hurry. Oh, yes! There is a tale of a snake that is attracted by the smell of wood- or tobacco-smoke, and will follow it up till it casts itself into the fire. True? Who knows? Snakes are all curious. Would you care to look at our harmless ones? They are put in another place, a little way off."

We moved along the wall of that death-compound, past an enclosure where the grass had not been cut for some time, and half hid the little kraals. Why? "Oh, that is where they breed. We leave them alone." It must have been imagination—for there was no breath of wind—that made one fancy a tussock of herbage parted and bowed as we looked, but, at any rate, one was glad to think that the A'tosis are left in peace sometimes, and have not to bare their teeth to strangers.

The harmless snakes lived in an enclosure with a vine-covered pergola, and an evergreen tree in the centre. The stems wove easily back and forth as they crowned the trellis; and in exact and perfect camouflage of curve and colour (when the eye had seized the trick) lay half-a-dozen or more long thin serpents waiting hopefully for birds that never lighted. The evergreen tree, also, was filled with snakes, said the young man, but the local birds knew too much. These particular snakes came of a breed that always hunted in this fashion. So they climbed hungrily and copied the vines and the mottling and disking of the sunlit leaves, and the shape of the twigs; and not till we had worked up to the unwinking eyes at the ends could we guess that they were anything else. The short grass beneath the wall was full of snakes, at first invisible, and then—till one saw nothing else—two and three overlapping, deep down among the blades. But, nakedly on the top, no more to be concealed than an orange, was a brilliant yellow-red snake with a rat tail, and when she struck at the young man's foot it was with a curious stiff, weaving, frantic motion like a choking dog. To make more fear, she spread out the ribs behind her neck, and somehow suggested a cobra. "She can bite a little—not much," said the young man and offered her a fold of linen trouser. She closed and bit, but at once dropped from it dry-mouthed, and hurried away with that stiff, beseeching, uplifted neck as though she were trying to escape from herself, or seeking a deliverer. (And why on earth she should have suggested Lady Macbeth in the sleep-walking scene is another mystery.) Meantime, our companion had identified a small graceful little creature as of a kind he had once brought down from the North, and sent up here. "I don't know whether she could *do* anything, but she didn't all the way from Pará to here; so she must have been all right." He was fondling her. She made no protest, but twined herself as prettily as Lilith round his arm.

Last of all was a small boa, who comes of a breed less forsaken than the rest, because boas have a rounded, almost man-jowl and little piggy noses. He was changing his skin—and was therefore half blind, as well as blackish and frayed along his outline. "He can bite, too, if he wants to; but up North where they keep them for pets against the rats, they *never* bite the people of their own house." We left him sullen and dazed, waiting for the change which will turn him green, purple, and gold again, and the young man gave our companion the snake that had taken his fancy—in a perforated paper box.

Then we went off to one of the distant museums where the Tarantulas are; and the life-size wax models of what happens to your limbs after you are bitten. Here again all was silence and heat, with one small girl student in white linen, and a blaze of flowers outside the pale hall. The models make one heave with disgust, but there were two, differentiating the mixed scratch of a harmless serpent's teeth from the sufficient double puncture of venomous fangs, that brought back, atop of the nausea, the memory of a night when a half-fainting man's leg was examined by match-light for certain signs, and he broke into helpless tears of relief on being told that he would live.

The Tarantulas are manifestly the creation of the Personal Devil. They are not larger than the clenched fist, and are nourished by putting in with each one a thin snake about a foot long who stays alive till the end of the fortnight next ensuing. Then the Tarantula kills and eats it at great leisure. One looks into beautiful gauze-roofed, glass-sided worlds, each with a red earth floor and a little tin of damped wool to maintain humidity for the tenant and its ration. In one cage, a lady had hatched out a multitude of babes about the size of halfpennies, and had added to her works by casting, it seemed, all her skin. A person is officially allowed twenty-four hours after having been bitten by such a lady; but he will not be able to attend to his own affairs in that time.

Then we returned to the outside blaze, on our way back, and passed another silent range of white buildings, where are the horses and such, through whose systems the poisons are attenuated and controlled, so that folk may live longer who would otherwise have died horribly.

Roughly speaking, the process begins with an infinitely small injection of poison into a carefully kept horse. He reacts, but lives (for the dose is well known now), and the injection is gradually increased till he can resist, proportionately, as much of the venom as opium-eaters can of laudanum. Then he is tapped for some pints of his blood, and of its serum, duly attenuated and sterilised, the anti-venom is made. When it is administered to a man in need, the two powers war together on the physical side, as one may see the powers of the spirit tearing the soul of a sinner "under conviction" before he finds salvation. Every muscle and nerve and blood corpuscle may be involved, as well as other powers that we know not of; but normally, after the throes and disintegrations, the body recovers and—since it is a sister of the soul—throws off and puts behind it in a very little while all that nightmare of experiences in restored health. But, they say, the process is not a pleasant one to watch; and men are thinking and working all their lives to make it less vehement.

Yet, after all, the only care for venomous bites is the foot of man making hard paths from hut to hut, field to field, and shrine to shrine, through the length and breadth of a land.

The A'tosis hate the look and texture of trodden ground, the smell of the cattle who come after, the hoes and axes that eat into the edges of their nesting-places, and the heavy wheels that make earthquakes beneath their sensitive bellies.

Discussion Questions

1. To how many senses does the description in Kipling's first paragraph appeal? Which senses besides vision does he emphasize most throughout the essay?

2. From what different areas of experience does Kipling draw his analogies? Which does he emphasize most and with what effect?

3. Compare Kipling's techniques of description to those of Joan Didion and Rachel Carson. To what comparative extent does Kipling make his own personality a part of his subject? How would you characterize that personality? Is he overbearing, insensitive? What words would you use in place of these?

4. Kipling often asks rhetorical questions in the essay and addresses a "you." What qualities does he seem to take for granted in the audience he writes for? Write a brief character sketch of that audience. About what is it curious? About what is it not? Where does Kipling's imagination of his audience most influence what he says?

D. H. LAWRENCE

The son of a coal miner, D. H. Lawrence (1885–1930) was born in Eastwood, Nottinghamshire, and studied to be an elementary school teacher at University College, Nottingham. He taught school until 1912, when he met Frieda Weekly, the German wife of his former foreign language professor. They left together for Germany and thus Lawrence embarked on a tumultuous marriage, a nomadic life, and a literary career. After World War I, Lawrence lived for a time in Italy, then traveled to Germany, Austria, Ceylon, and Australia. In 1922, he accepted an invitation to live in Taos, New Mexico and from there traveled to Mexico, where he became engrossed in ancient Aztec civilization. He then went back to London, back to Taos, back to Italy. His health, never strong, worsened while he worked in Florence on Lady Chatterley's Lover *(1928). After nearly two more restless years, Lawrence died of tuberculosis in a sanatorium on the French Riviera.*

Besides his many novels, Lawrence within a short lifetime managed to write short stories, poetry, drama, criticism, translations, psychological studies, and travel books. A British edition of his works runs to sixty volumes. Among his most important books are Sons and Lovers *(1913),* The Rainbow *(1915),* Women in Love *(1920),* Studies in Classic American Literature *(1923), and* St. Mawr *(1925). The autobiographical essay "Rex" first appeared in 1921 and is reprinted from* Phoenix: The Posthumous Papers of D. H. Lawrence *(1936).*

Rex

Since every family has its black sheep, it almost follows that every man must have a sooty uncle. Lucky if he hasn't two. However, it is only with my mother's brother that we are concerned. She had loved him dearly when he was a little blond boy. When he grew up black, she was always vowing she would never speak to him again. Yet when he put in an appearance, after years of absence, she invariably received him in a festive mood, and was even flirty with him.

He rolled up one day in a dog-cart, when I was a small boy. He was large and bullet-headed and blustering, and this time, sporty. Sometimes he was rather literary, sometimes coloured with business. But this time he was in checks, and was sporty. We viewed him from a distance.

The upshot was, would we rear a pup for him. Now my mother detested animals about the house. She could not bear the mix-up of human with animal life. Yet she consented to bring up the pup.

My uncle had taken a large, vulgar public-house in a large and vulgar town. It came to pass that I must fetch the pup. Strange for me, a member of the Band of Hope, to enter the big, noisy, smelly plate-glass and mahogany public-house. It was called The Good Omen. Strange to have my uncle towering over me in the passage, shouting "Hello, Johnny, what d'yer want?" He didn't know me. Strange to think he was my mother's brother, and that he had his bouts when he read Browning aloud with emotion and éclat.

I was given tea in a narrow, uncomfortable sort of living-room, half kitchen. Curious that such a palatial pub should show such miserable private accommodations, but so it was. There was I, unhappy, and glad to escape with the soft fat pup. It was winter-time, and I wore a big-flapped black overcoat, half cloak. Under the cloak-sleeves I hid the puppy, who trembled. It was Saturday, and the train was crowded, and he whimpered under my coat. I sat in mortal fear of being hauled out for travelling without a dog-ticket. However, we arrived, and my torments were for nothing.

The others were wildly excited over the puppy. He was small and fat and white, with a brown-and-black head: a fox terrier. My father said he had a lemon head—some such mysterious technical phraseology. It wasn't lemon at all, but coloured like a field bee. And he had a black spot at the root of his spine.

It was Saturday night—bath-night. He crawled on the hearth-rug like a fat white teacup, and licked the bare toes that had just been bathed.

"He ought to be called Spot," said one. But that was too ordinary. It was a great question, what to call him.

"Call him Rex—the King," said my mother, looking down on the fat, animated little teacup, who was chewing my sister's little toe and making her squeal with joy and tickles. We took the name in all seriousness.

"Rex—the King!" We thought it was just right. Not for years did I realize that it was a sarcasm on my mother's part. She must have wasted some twenty years or more of irony on our incurable naiveté.

It wasn't a successful name, really. Because my father and all the people in the street failed completely to pronounce the monosyllable Rex. They all said Rax. And it always distressed me. It always suggested to me seaweed, and rack-and-ruin. Poor Rex!

We loved him dearly. The first night we woke to hear him weeping and whinnying in loneliness at the foot of the stairs. When it could be borne no more, I slipped down for him, and he slept under the sheets.

"I won't have that little beast in the beds. Beds are not for dogs," declared my mother callously.

"He's as good as we are!" we cried, injured.

"Whether he is or not, he's not going in the beds."

I think now, my mother scorned us for our lack of pride. We were a little *infra dig.*, we children.

The second night, however, Rex wept the same and in the same way was comforted. The third night we heard our father plod downstairs, heard several slaps administered to the yelling dismayed puppy, and heard the amiable, but to us heartless voice saying "Shut it then! Shut thy noise, 'st hear? Stop in thy basket, stop there!"

"It's a shame!" we shouted, in muffled rebellion, from the sheets.

"I'll give you shame, if you don't hold your noise and go to sleep," called our mother from her room. Whereupon we shed angry tears and went to sleep. But there was a tension.

"Such a houseful of idiots would make me detest the little beast, even if he was better than he is," said my mother.

But as a matter of fact, she did not detest Rexie at all. She only had to pretend to do so, to balance our adoration. And in truth, she did not care for close contact with animals. She was too fastidious. My father, however, would take on a real dog's voice, talking to the puppy: a funny, high, sing-song falsetto which he seemed to produce at the top of his head. "'S a pretty little dog! 's a pretty little doggy!—ay!—yes!—he is, yes!—Wag thy strunt, then! Wag thy strunt, Rexie!—Ha-ha! Nay, tha munna—" This last as the puppy, wild with excitement at the strange falsetto voice, licked my father's nostrils and bit my father's nose with his sharp little teeth.

"'E makes blood come," said my father.

"Serves you right for being so silly with him," said my mother. It was odd to see her as she watched the man, my father, crouching and talking to the little dog and laughing strangely when the little creature bit his nose and toused his beard. What does a woman think of her husband at such a moment?

My mother amused herself over the names we called him.

"He's an angel—he's a little butterfly—Rexie, my sweet!"

"Sweet! A dirty little object!" interpolated my mother. She and he had a feud from the first. Of course he chewed boots and worried our stockings and swallowed our garters. The moment we took off our stockings he would dart away with one, we after him. Then as he hung, growling, vociferously, at one end of the stocking, we at the other, we would cry:

"Look at him, mother! He'll make holes in it again." Whereupon my mother darted at him and spanked him sharply.

"Let go, sir, you destructive little fiend."

But he didn't let go. He began to growl with real rage, and hung on viciously. Mite as he was, he defied her with a manly fury. He did not hate her, nor she him. But they had one long battle with one another.

"I'll teach you, my Jockey! Do you think I'm going to spend my life darning after your destructive little teeth! I'll show you if I will!"

But Rexie only growled more viciously. They both became really angry, whilst we children expostulated earnestly with both. He would not let her take the stocking from him.

"You should tell him properly, mother. He won't be driven," we said.

"I'll drive him further than he bargains for. I'll drive him out of my sight for ever, that I will," declared my mother, truly angry. He would put her into a real temper, with his tiny, growling defiance.

"He's sweet! A Rexie, a little Rexie!"

"A filthy little nuisance! Don't think I'll put up with him."

And to tell the truth, he was dirty at first. How could he be otherwise, so young! But my mother hated him for it. And perhaps this was the real start of their hostility. For he lived in the house with us. He would wrinkle his nose and show his tiny dagger-teeth in fury when he was thwarted, and his growls of real battle-rage against my mother rejoiced us as much as they angered her. But at last she caught him *in flagrante*. She pounced on him, rubbed his nose in the mess, and flung him out into the yard. He yelped with shame and disgust and indignation. I shall never forget the sight of him as he rolled over, then tried to turn his head away from the disgust of his own muzzle, shaking his little snout with a sort of horror, and trying to sneeze it off. My sister gave a yell of despair, and dashed out with a rag and a pan of water, weeping wildly. She sat in the middle of the yard with the befouled puppy, and shedding bitter tears she wiped him and washed him clean. Loudly she reproached my mother. "Look how much bigger you are than he is. It's a shame, it's a shame!"

"You ridiculous little lunatic, you've undone all the good it would do him, with your soft ways. Why is my life made a curse with animals! Haven't I enough as it is—"

There was a subdued tension afterwards. Rex was a little white chasm between us and our parent.

He became clean. But then another tragedy loomed. He must be docked. His floating puppy-tail must be docked short. This time my father was the enemy. My mother agreed with us that it was an unnecessary cruelty. But my father was adamant. "The dog'll look a fool all his life, if he's not docked." And there was no getting away from it. To add to the horror, poor Rex's tail must be *bitten* off. Why bitten? we asked aghast. We were assured that biting was the only way. A man would take the little tail and just nip it through with his teeth, at a certain joint. My father lifted his lips and bared his incisors, to suit the description. We shuddered. But we were in the hands of fate.

Rex was carried away, and a man called Rowbotham bit off the superfluity of his tail in the Nag's Head, for a quart of best and bitter. We lamented our poor diminished puppy, but agreed to find him more manly and *comme il faut*. We should always have been ashamed of his little whip of a tail, if it had not been shortened. My father said it had made a man of him.

Perhaps it had. For now his true nature came out. And his true nature, like so much else, was dual. First he was a fierce, canine little beast, a beast of rapine and blood. He longed to hunt, savagely. He lusted to set his teeth in his prey. It was no joke with him. The old canine Adam stood first in him, the dog with fangs and glaring eyes. He flew at us when we annoyed him. He flew at all intruders, particularly the postman. He was almost a peril to the neighbourhood. But not quite. Because close second in his nature stood that fatal need to love, the *besoin d'aimer* which at last makes an end of liberty. He had a terrible, terrible necessity to love, and this trammelled the native, savage hunting beast which he was. He was torn between two great impulses: the native impulse to hunt and kill, and the strange, secondary, supervening impulse to love and obey. If he had been left to my father and mother, he would have run wild and got himself shot. As it was, he loved us children with a fierce, joyous love. And we loved him.

When we came home from school we would see him standing at the end of the entry, cocking his head wistfully at the open country in front of him, and meditating whether to be off or not: a white, inquiring little figure, with green savage freedom in front of him. A cry from a far distance from one of us, and like a bullet he hurled himself down the road, in a mad game. Seeing him coming, my sister invariably turned and fled, shrieking with delighted terror. And he would leap straight up her back, and bite her and tear her clothes. But it was only an ecstasy of savage love, and she knew it. She didn't care if he tore her pinafores. But my mother did.

My mother was maddened by him. He was a little demon. At the least provocation, he flew. You had only to sweep the floor, and he bristled and sprang at the broom. Nor would he let go. With his scruff erect and his nostrils snorting rage, he would turn up the whites of his eyes at my mother, as she wrestled at the other end of the broom. "Leave go, sir, leave go!" She wrestled and stamped her foot, and he answered with horrid growls. In the end it was she who had to let go. Then she flew at him, and he flew at her. All the time we had him, he was within a hair's-breadth of savagely biting her. And she knew it. Yet he always kept sufficient self-control.

We children loved his temper. We would drag the bones from his mouth, and put him into such paroxysms of rage that he would twist his head right over and lay it on the ground upside-down, because he didn't know what to do with himself, the savage was so strong in him and he must fly at us. "He'll fly at your throat one of these days," said my father. Neither he nor my mother dared have touched Rex's bone. It was enough to see him bristle and roll the whites of his eyes when they came near. How near he must have been to driving his teeth right into us, cannot be told. He was a horrid sight snarling and crouching at us. But we only laughed and rebuked him. And he would whimper in the sheer torment of his need to attack us.

He never did hurt us. He never hurt anybody, though the neighbourhood was terrified of him. But he took to hunting. To my mother's disgust, he would bring large dead bleeding rats and lay them on the hearth-rug, and she had to take them up on a shovel. For he would not remove them. Occasionally he brought a mangled rabbit, and sometimes, alas, fragmentary poultry. We were in terror of prosecution. Once he came home bloody and feathery and rather sheepish-looking. We cleaned him and questioned him and abused him. Next day we heard of six dead ducks. Thank heaven no one had seen him.

But he was disobedient. If he saw a hen he was off, and calling would not bring him back. He was worst of all with my father, who would take him walks on Sunday morning. My mother would not walk a yard with him. Once, walking with my father, he rushed off at some sheep in a field. My father yelled in vain. The dog was at the sheep, and meant business. My father crawled through the hedge, and was upon him in time. And now the man was in a paroxysm of rage. He dragged the little beast into the road and thrashed him with a walking stick.

"Do you know you're thrashing that dog unmercifully?" said a passerby.

"Ay, an' mean to," shouted my father.

The curious thing was that Rex did not respect my father any the more, for the beatings he had from him. He took much more heed of us children, always.

But he let us down also. One fatal Saturday he disappeared. We hunted and called, but no Rex. We were bathed, and it was bedtime, but we would not go to bed. Instead we sat in a row in our nightdresses on the sofa, and wept without stopping. This drove our mother mad.

"Am I going to put up with it? Am I? And all for that hateful little beast of a dog! He shall go! If he's not gone now, he shall go."

Our father came in late, looking rather queer, with his hat over his eye. But in his staccato tippled fashion he tried to be consoling.

"Never mind, my duckie, I s'll look for him in the morning."

Sunday came—oh, such a Sunday. We cried, and didn't eat. We scoured the land, and for the first time realized how empty and wide the earth is, when you're looking for something. My father walked for many miles—all in vain. Sunday dinner, with rhubarb pudding, I remember, and an atmosphere of abject misery that was unbearable.

"Never," said my mother, "never shall an animal set foot in this house again, while I live. I knew what it would be! I knew."

The day wore on, and it was the black gloom of bed-time, when we heard a scratch and an impudent little whine at the door. In trotted Rex, mud-black, disreputable, and impudent. His air of offhand "How d'ye do!" was indescribable. He trotted around with *suffisance*, wagging his tail as if to say, "Yes, I've come back. But I didn't need to. I can carry on remarkably well by myself." Then he walked to his water, and drank noisily and ostentatiously. It was a slap in the eye for us.

He disappeared once or twice in this fashion. We never knew where he went. And we began to feel that his heart was not so golden as we had imagined it.

But one fatal day reappeared my uncle and the dog-cart. He whistled to Rex, and Rex trotted up. But when he wanted to examine the lusty, sturdy dog, Rex became suddenly still, then sprang free. Quite jauntily he trotted round—but out of reach of my uncle. He leaped up, licking our faces, and trying to make us play.

"Why, what ha' you done wi' the dog—you've made a fool of him. He's softer than grease. You've ruined him. You've made a damned fool of him," shouted my uncle.

Rex was captured and hauled off to the dog-cart and tied to the seat. He was in a frenzy. He yelped and shrieked and struggled, and was hit on the head, hard, with the butt-end of my uncle's whip, which only made him struggle more frantically. So we saw him driven away, our beloved Rex, frantically, madly fighting to get to us from the high dog-cart, and being knocked down, whilst we stood in the street in mute despair.

After which, black tears, and a little wound which is still alive in our hearts.

I saw Rex once again, when I had to call just once at The Good Omen. He must have heard my voice, for he was upon me in the passage before I knew where I was. And in the instant I knew how he loved us. He really loved us. And in the same instant there was my uncle with a whip, beating and kicking him back, and Rex cowering, bristling, snarling.

My uncle swore many oaths, how we had ruined the dog for ever, made him vicious, spoiled him for showing purposes, and been altogether a pack of mard-soft fools not fit to be trusted with any dog but a gutter-mongrel.

Poor Rex! We heard his temper was incurably vicious, and he had to be shot.

And it was our fault. We had loved him too much, and he had loved us too much. We never had another pet.

It is a strange thing, love. Nothing but love has made the dog lose his wild freedom, to become the servant of man. And this very servility or completeness of love makes him a term of deepest contempt—"You dog!"

We should not have loved Rex so much, and he should not have loved us. There should have been a measure. We tended, all of us, to overstep the limits of our own natures. He should have stayed outside human limits, we should have stayed outside canine limits. Nothing is more fatal than the disaster of too much love. My uncle was right, we had ruined the dog.

My uncle was a fool, for all that.

Discussion Questions

1. What is the mother's attitude toward dogs? Why doesn't she want the dog? Describe the tone she takes toward Rex. Does she simply hate the dog? What makes her tone complicated? How is her tone expressed in the name she gives the dog? Describe the tone she takes toward her children. In what ways is it similar to the tone she takes toward Rex?

2. Lawrence says that Rex's "true nature, like so much else, was dual." Describe Rex's dual nature. What else can that duality refer to? To what extent does the duality pervade the entire essay? Is it resolved at the end?

3. How does the uncle think the dog should be trained? Does Lawrence agree with him? Explain the meaning of the last two sentences of the essay. Compare Lawrence's conclusion to Edward Hoagland's in "The Courage of Turtles."

4. "Poor Rex! We heard his temper was incurably vicious, and he had to be shot." Write an essay that discusses the role of "temper" in this piece. How is "temper" expressed by the various characters? How does the uncle's temper differ from the mother's, the father's? What is it about Rex's temper that the children find so amusing?

HELEN LAWRENSON

Helen Lawrenson, who in the grand old manner consistently refused to release the year of her birth for the public record, was born sometime in the first few years of this century and died in 1982. She was educated at Vassar, and, after working as a reporter in her native upstate New York, she was employed by the Condé Nast magazine organization, eventually rising to become editor of Vanity Fair *in the 1930's. At the end of that decade, she left magazine editing to become a writer, and she subsequently appeared in forty-five national publications, with over seventy articles for* Esquire *magazine alone. Her first article there, "Latins Make Lousy Lovers," was one of the most famous magazine essays of the century. Her autobiographical books describing a highly varied and colorful life are* Stranger at the Party *(1975) and* Whistling Girl *(1978).*

The Bulls of Pamplona vs. the Ivy League

In former years, American university students have at times distinguished themselves by such newsworthy antics as the swallowing of live goldfish, pantie raids on the dormitories of girl undergraduates, and the pelting of police. Now there has emerged a new, more daring, and much more expensive manifestation of youthful exhilaration. The ultimate seal of sophistication today, the really smashingly cool thing to do, is to go to Spain to run with the bulls in Pamplona. Ernest Hemingway has a lot to answer for, come Judgment Day.

Although the annual rite in which young men prove their valor by running through the streets, pursued by fighting bulls, dates back to the seventeenth century—first record of it was in 1686—it was taurophile Hemingway who put it on the map for Americans, when in *The Sun Also Rises* he transported Jake and Lady Brett and their pals to Pamplona for a glamorously lost week of drunkenness, fornication, bulls, incessant song, and dancing in the streets. Three years ago, Darryl Zanuck made a movie of the book, with a glittering Pleiades headed by Ava Gardner and Tyrone Power. The result was a resurgence of interest in the original novel, plus some smart publicity by travel agencies—and the stampede was on. Princeton, Harvard, Yale, *et al* sprang to the challenge, and those students fortunate enough to wangle a European junket as a June graduation present made a beeline for Pamplona, snorting with eagerness to prove their coming-of-age, their initiation into manhood via the ritual of ordeal by bull, a sort of chic new *bar mitzvah* of the Ivy League age group. It was just as well that their indulgent parents were not present to view their frazzled, exuberant offspring cavorting sassily through the ancient Spanish streets in one wild, week-long, stupendous, and quite idiotic romp.

Last summer's fiesta hit an all-time high for foreign participation. If at times it seemed as if Americans predominated, it was probably because they were the noisiest, the scruffiest, and the only ones with beards, but there were a lot of French, a surprising number of Australians, some English, Italians and Germans, and a smattering of Japanese, Portuguese and Egyptians. Curt Jergens was the only recognizable delegate from the movie world, although there was a rumor that Brigitte Bardot was there. She wasn't, but her influence was pleasurably apparent in dozens of delectably curvy nymphs, pouting sexily, their tangled blonde hair worn in B.B.'s famous hair-do.

Ava Gardner didn't come this time, but no matter: all the Bennington and Sarah Lawrence girls felt just like her. They had seen the movie; they knew what to do. (One of the commonest phrases heard around the town was, "But in the movie, they did it *this* way!") Nor did Hemingway show, although most people thought he did. A stocky, stalwart, grizzly-bearded ringer impressively strolled the streets, bowing to admirers, and held court in cafés, signing autographs. Bulls were dedicated to him at the fights, and matadors outdid themselves trying to please him. It turned out he was from Indiana and had spent years in South America doing publicity for an oil company. The last two years he had lived in Spain, where he had become a bullfight *aficionado*. It must be admitted that he signed his own name to autographs—Kenneth H. Vanderford—but everyone thought he was Hemingway, just the same.

The San Fermin Festival properly begins on July 7th, but the crowds descend on Pamplona days in advance, by train, by car, or, most typically, zooming into town on motor scooters, two to a scooter, with helmets, sunglasses, knapsacks, and an almost visible nimbus of rather depressing zest. By the evening of July 6th, the Plaza del Castillo, the main square, is jammed with several thousand shouting, singing, dancing young men and girls, all gassed to the ears. There are times when it looks like a riotous combination of an American Legion Convention in Chicago and the Winter Carnival at Dartmouth. Impromptu bands snake-dance around, banging drums, tooting toy trumpets, blowing whistles, and singing songs which range from Spanish folk songs to Yale's good old *Whiffenpoof*. Men carry little plastic cameras with which they squirt water at the girls, and they also wear funny hats, from the outlandishly big Mexican-type straw hats, to the Basque beret. The traditional costume is white slacks, white shirt, and a red silk kerchief knotted around the neck, but the Americans stuck mostly to blue jeans, soiled sweat shirts, the red kerchiefs, and their beards. As soon as they hit town, they all bought *botas*, the Spanish leather flasks, or wine skins, out of which you drink by holding the *bota* at arm's length and letting a stream of red wine shoot into your open mouth. For beginners, it is pretty easy to miss, and most of them did. Wine stains were *de rigueur*, crimson badges of merit permanently displayed, since laundry and personal hygiene facilities are practically nonexistent during fiesta week. Every available room in the few hotels is booked weeks, months, often a year, in advance. The hundreds without reservations sleep in their cars or on the streets—when they sleep at all—almost nobody bathes or shaves or changes a shirt, and toward the end of the week the whole town begins to get a little gamey.

The running of the bulls, called the *encierro*, is at seven every morning. When the bulls arrive from the breeding ranches by train or bus, they are loaded in their cages onto trucks and driven to a corral on the outskirts of town. The night before each fight, they are taken to a smaller corral in the upper part of the city rampart, where they pass the night. The next morning, the police clear the streets through which the bulls will run, and see that all doors are closed. The young men who are going to run are assembled at a specified distance from the corral. On the dot of seven, a bell tolls—the bell called El Gallico (The Little Cock)—the police unlatch the corral door, a rocket is fired, and the six bulls, frightened by the explosion and goaded from behind by men with sharp sticks, rush headlong into the street and start running. The men start running too. It is my theory that the bulls are just as scared as the men, if not more so. Confused by the raucous tumult of shouts, screams, fireworks, bells, and the sound of a hundred or more very drunk young men pounding along the street beside and in front of them, the bulls' one communal thought seems to be get the hell away somewhere to a nice quiet corral.

The second rocket explosion means that all the bulls and their guardian oxen are in the street. They run from the corral through the town and into the bullfight ring, a distance of 825 meters. The normal time for this perilous sprint is two minutes; when it takes more, it means that accidents have occurred. There are always a lot of bumps, bruises, sprains and cuts, although most of them are the normal result of a large crowd racing pell mell down a narrow street, falling over each other in a euphoria blended of red wine, excitement, and the delicious consciousness of their own bravado. The worst injuries last summer were to two Americans, one of whom was hurt in an eye and the other had a hand smashed, but whether their wounds were the result of being trampled by their comrades or by the bulls is a question which must remain forever moot. One young Englishman, it is true, was gored five times by a bull on the last day of the festival, but he wasn't even running in the *encierro*. He was standing by the barrier in the bull ring, waiting to photograph the bulls as they entered the ring, after the run through town.

When all six bulls and the oxen have gone into the ring, another rocket announces that people can again go about the streets. Once in the ring, the oxen shepherd the bulls to the Plaza corral; and a group of young wild cows, the *vaquillas*, are let into the ring to harry the youths—and vice versa. The cows wear rubber balls tied over their horns, but they can do a lot of damage if they step on you, which is hard for them to avoid doing, as the young men chase them madly, shouting and pulling their tails.

If you want to watch the *encierro*, you have to get up at five-thirty or six in the morning, and this is what almost all the town does, every morning for a week. If you want to run in it, the thing to do is to stay up all night, drinking from *botas* and singing. There is everywhere great emphasis on the *encierro* as an intensely male ceremony; and descriptions of it refer to "this masculine and emotional act," "this male rite in which bravery, drama and horror paralyze the hearts of all onlookers," and so forth.

Many of the runners, especially the Americans, are not unaware of these thrilling tributes; and the chance to see themselves as casually heroic Hemingway heroes is a heady bait. Then, too, there looms large the delightful prospect of being able to tell about it in the future. Even if one should get hurt, the scars forever after can be explained with splendid nonchalance: "Oh, that! I got it running with the bulls in Pamplona." This is infinitely superior to falling off a bike, or possibly having nothing to flaunt but your chicken-pox scars.

The whole ritual, apart from the immediately irresistible quality always inherent in danger, probably provides a certain answer to the gnawing need to feel masculine, so increasingly prevalent and so seldom satisfied. A century ago, Thoreau was appalled by the thought that we had become what he called "a race of tit-men." (The phrase did not, of course, have the modern connotation. He referred to tit-mice, those birds incapable of soaring flight.) Today, there are even fewer examples of noble daring in thought or deed, even fewer opportunities to test that private, elemental faculty of courage which elevates the individual ego. Despite the temptation to regard it merely as a waste of adrenalin, perhaps Pamplona is today's inadequate and momentary chivalric gesture for youth. However, a modern Englishman, Harold Nicolson, has written somewhere, "Physical courage, I have been told, is among the noblest of man's virtues; but it is a dangerous quality when unaccompanied by intelligence."

Exhilarated by the *encierro,* the survivors skedaddle out of the ring and back through town again, dancing frantically, shouting and singing in a medley of languages, their grubby faces bleary-eyed with fatigue, like tired children at a party who don't know enough to go home and take their naps. They keep this up until many of them drop in the street and sleep where they fall, their *botas* cuddled in their arms. The tougher Spaniards reel through the streets, leaping at passing girls like greyhounds after a bone. Their sense of humor could never be described as squeamish: some of them hang dead fish and chicken legs on their belts and one, whom I shall never forget, had caught a small bird and forced its leg, breaking it, through the cloth visor of his cap. The bird dangled there, fluttering and peeping until, after several hours, it finally died.

The bullfights are held daily at 5:30, and Spain's best matadors perform with bulls from the ranches of such social bigwigs as the Viscount of Garcia-Grande, the Marquis of Villamarta, the brandy-rich Pedro Domecq family, and the famous Miura bull breeders from Sevilla. As many as ten different amateur orchestras play, often different tunes simultaneously, before the fights begin and the official band takes over. A near-by church belfry, a vantage point overlooking the ring, is crowded with priests, looking from a distance like white-faced bats, all peering down throughout the fights. Many priests are also present among the paying customers, arousing some curiosity among the Anglo-Saxons, who tend to regard bullfights as a spectacularly unecclesiastical diversion. Someone has said of bullfights that from every point of view they are indefensible, but fascinating. Certainly they are so integrated with Spanish culture that to any Spaniard a civilization without them is practically inconceivable. My host in Pamplona politely inquired if our New York bull ring was much larger and, on being told that we didn't have one, he kept muttering, "No bull ring! *Que raro!*"

For Americans, however, the fights are obviously an acquired taste, but they have become so stylish of late that any cultural status-seeker ignorant of the *Death in the Afternoon* tautology is put down as pretty small beer indeed. The youthful *aficionados* in Pamplona bandy glib references to *verónicas, quites* and *faenas,* appraising the different matadors with that hubristic air of finality which is so often the mark of the sciolist. I have found that bullfight fans are just about as boring in their conversational clichés and mystic attitudes as those people who are always talking about their sessions with their analysts.

However, the pretty girls, who are perversely attracted by heroic bloodshed, listen with an attention as rapt as it is stimulating, and try to nod knowingly at the right intervals. Pamplona during fiesta is one of the world's greatest pick-up centers. Crowds of men come unattached, on the theory that taking your own girl to Pamplona is like taking your own beer to Munich. I doubt if I've ever seen so many pretty girls in one place, all of them looking well-bred and chic and expensively reared. The plainest among them were girls who would have been outstanding in any other group: it was only that they were eclipsed at Pamplona by the number of really sensational beauties there: creamy-skinned Spaniards with aquamarine eyes; ravishing Roman girls with pale, full lips, violet eye shadow, and an unmatched Italianate elegance of dress; English girls with chablis-colored hair in high, wrapped beehives; dozens of vivid Americans, alluringly tawny, with lovely legs; and sultry French teen-age sorceresses, *Nouvelle Vague* style. There was one paralyzing Belgian beauty whose long, straight hair was the color of the under side of a mushroom, and on it she wore a witch's peaked hat of black straw, from under which peered her amazing face, pale and cool and delicate, with enormous navy blue eyes. She moved about like a young queen bee, always in the center of a swarm of buzzing males.

Everyone quite naturally talks to everyone else, of any age, and the atmosphere is prevailingly informal, from the beginning, without any of that hesitant nosing-around there is on shipboard or at other gala gatherings. Pamplona doesn't build up to a climax. It starts there. The first night I was there, two talkative Australians sat down beside me at the café table and promptly threw up. Far from dampening their spirits, this only seemed to increase the general hilarity, especially when we were joined by a flock of U.S. Army Air Force colonels and majors, in town from Madrid and Paris for the fiesta, who insisted on singing *Waltzing Matilda* over and over again as an international *beau geste*. The air was rife with back-slapping as the college boys discovered long-lost fraternity brothers—"What fraternity are you? A Phi Delt?! *Man*, what d'ya know about *that*?!"—and found out who had gone to Choate, and if not, where? . . . A Princeton man announced that he was going on to Greece, where he had been promised a date with Princess Sophia; and a newly hatched Harvard graduate, who had left his parents at the Hotel Bristol in Paris, kept everyone in stitches with his attempts at Spanish. . . . All the waiters were drunk, too, beaming foolishly at a Kentuckian who kept standing and reciting long passages from Byron and Shelley.... "Never, never eat polar-bear liver," said a young man with the hiccoughs. "It's absolutely loaded with vitamin D and too much can kill you." ... "Oh, I won't! I promise I won't," said the girl everyone called Zelda because she looked like an F. Scott Fitzgerald dream girl. She wore her hair in sort of a Twenties bob, and she had on a smart green and purple sheath, with ropes of green and purple beads around her neck; and she smiled all the time, a radiant, spontaneous smile of pure joy that lit up her whole face. She looked prettiest when she was very drunk, with her face and eyes and teeth all shining; and all the men were in love with her, in a nice way, even the Yale man who didn't take up with any of the pretty girls because he said he was trying to be loyal to his girl back home. "I'm pinned," he kept explaining.

This sort of thing went on, in a haze of red wine and Fundador, all day and all night for a solid week. The carnivals in New Orleans and Habana and Rio are not in the same league. Even in Spain, a land of fiestas, this one is the biggest blast of all. You lose your sense of time and identity. Bill Manville, a columnist on leave from the Greenwich Village *Voice*, explained it best when he said, "I arrived at eight o'clock last night and I feel as if I'd been here since I was eight years old." It was all too much. You felt as if you were living in a giant cliché—a giant Hemingway cliché—in which all the people became caricatures of themselves: the Princeton boys became more Princetonian, the Spaniards acted more Spanish, the brave bull runners got braver and more male, the lovely girls seemed lovelier with more abandon, the drunks became drunker.

The trouble was that it never stopped. It was in *Jurgen*, I think, that James Branch Cabell remarked that orgies are always more fun to read about than they are in real life. The *olla podrida* of sensations which is the Pamplona fiesta can really only be endured by the youthful, and even *they* are rather hard put to it toward the end to maintain the illusion of perpetual enjoyment. Making the Pamplona fiesta may be *the* thing to do, but I bet a lot of them are glad when it's over and they are relieved of the onus of proving their virility in public by acting like extras in an existentialist movie. The bulls aren't the only ones who are dead by the end of the week.

Discussion Questions

1. In what ways does Helen Lawrenson combine objective description with personal attitudes? Describe those attitudes as fully as you can, taking into account her own presence at what she describes.

2. Find a representative sentence or two of Helen Lawrenson's style at its most lively and describe the various techniques that work to create that liveliness.

3. Compare Helen Lawrenson's treatment of her topic with the essays of Aldous Huxley on snobs, G. K. Chesterton on sightseeing, and Graham Greene on the attraction of danger.

4. Pick a similarly popular novel or movie and describe the ways in which popular and fashionable behavior has been influenced by it.

5. Pick a contemporary college custom—a happy hour, a charity fund-raiser—and name some of the characteristics of behavior brought about by the event. In an essay, describe the affair as if you were a visitor from another country writing for an audience back home.

C. S. LEWIS

The educator and scholar, Clive Staples Lewis (1898–1963) was born in Belfast, Northern Ireland, and was a Fellow of Magdalen College, Oxford. From 1954 to 1963 he was professor of Medieval and Renaissance English at Cambridge University. A prolific writer, Lewis became internationally known for his essays and books on Christianity, especially The Screwtape Letters *(1942)*, The Abolition of Man *(1943)*, Miracles *(1947), and* Mere Christianity *(1952)*. The Allegory of Love *(1936) is a classic study of medieval literature. Lewis's best-selling children's novels have been collected in a seven-volume set entitled* The Chronicles of Narnia *(1965). Among his most popular books is the science-fiction trilogy,* Out of the Silent Planet *(1938)*, Perelandra *(1943), and* That Hideous Strength *(1945).*

"The Trouble with 'X'. . ." is reprinted from Undeceptions, Essays on Theology and Ethics *(1971), a collection of Lewis's religious writings edited by Walter Hooper.*

The Trouble with "X" . . .

I suppose I may assume that seven out of ten of those who read these lines are in some kind of difficulty about some other human being. Either at work or at home, either the people who employ you or those whom you employ, either those who share your house or those whose house you share, either your in-laws or parents or children, your wife or your husband, are making life harder for you than it need be even in these days. It is to be hoped that we do not often mention these difficulties (especially the domestic ones) to outsiders. But sometimes we do. An outside friend asks us why we are looking so glum; and the truth comes out.

On such occasions the outside friend usually says, "But why don't you tell them? Why don't you go to your wife (or husband, or father, or daughter, or boss, or landlady, or lodger) and have it all out? People are usually reasonable. All you've got to do is to make them see things in the right light. Explain it to them in a reasonable, quiet, friendly way." And we, whatever we say outwardly, think sadly to ourselves, "He doesn't know 'X.'" We do. We know how utterly hopeless it is to make "X" see reason. Either we've tried it over and over again—tried it till we are sick of trying it—or else we've never tried it because we saw from the beginning how useless it would be. We know that if we attempt to "have it all out with 'X'" there will either be a "scene," or else "X" will stare at us in blank amazement and say "I don't know what on earth you're talking about"; or else (which is perhaps worst of all) "X" will quite agree with us and promise to turn over a new leaf and put everything on a new footing—and then, twenty-four hours later, will be exactly the same as "X" has always been.

You know, in fact, that any attempt to talk things over with "X" will shipwreck on the old, fatal flaw in "X's" character. And you see, looking back, how all the plans you have ever made always have shipwrecked on that fatal flaw—on "X's" incurable jealousy, or laziness, or touchiness, or muddle-headedness, or bossiness, or ill temper, or changeableness. Up to a certain age you have perhaps had the illusion that some external stroke of good fortune—an improvement in health, a rise of salary, the end of the war—would solve your difficulty. But you know better now. The war is over, and you realize that even if the other things happened, "X" would still be "X," and you would still be up against the same old problem. Even if you became a millionaire, your husband would still be a bully, or your wife would still nag or your son would still drink, or you'd still have to have your mother-in-law to live with you.

It is a great step forward to realize that this is so; to face the fact that even if all external things went right, real happiness would still depend on the character of the people you have to live with—and that you can't alter their characters. And now comes the point. When you have seen this you have, for the first time, had a glimpse of what it must be like for God. For, of course, this is (in one way) just what God Himself is up against. He has provided a rich, beautiful world for people to live in. He has given them intelligence to show them how it can be used, and conscience to show them how it ought to be used. He has contrived that the things they need for their biological life (food, drink, rest, sleep, exercise) should be positively delightful to them. And, having done all this, He then sees all His plans spoiled—just as our little plans are spoiled—by the crookedness of the people themselves. All the things He has given them to be happy with they turn into occasions for quarrelling and jealousy, and excess and hoarding, and tomfoolery.

You may say it is very different for God because He could, if He pleased, alter people's characters, and we can't. But this difference doesn't go quite as deep as we may at first think. God has made it a rule for Himself that He won't alter people's character by force. He can and will alter them—but only if the people will let Him. In that way He has really and truly limited His power. Sometimes we wonder why He has done so, or even wish that He hadn't. But apparently He thinks it worth doing. He would rather have a world of free beings, with all its risks, than a world of people who did right like machines because they couldn't do anything else. The more we succeed in imagining what a world of perfect automatic beings would be like, the more, I think, we shall see His wisdom.

I said that when we see how all our plans shipwreck on the characters of the people we have to deal with, we are "in *one* way" seeing what it must be like for God. But only in one way. There are two respects in which God's view must be very different from ours. In the first place, He sees (like you) how all the people in your home or your job are in various degrees awkward or difficult; but when He looks into that home or factory or office He sees one more person of the same kind—the one you never do see. I mean, of course, yourself. That is the next great step in wisdom—to realize that you also are just that sort of person. You also have a fatal flaw in your character. All the hopes and plans of others have again and again shipwrecked on your character just as your hopes and plans have shipwrecked on theirs.

It is no good passing this over with some vague, general admission such as "Of course, I know I have my faults." It is important to realize that there is some really fatal flaw in you: something which gives the others just that same feeling of *despair* which their flaws give you. And it is almost certainly something you don't know about—like what the advertisements call "halitosis," which everyone notices except the person who has it. But why, you ask, don't the others tell me? Believe me, they have tried to tell you over and over again, and you just couldn't "take it." Perhaps a good deal of what you call their "nagging" or "bad temper" or "queerness" are just their attempts to make you see the truth. And even the faults you do know you don't know fully. You say, "I admit I lost my temper last night"; but the others know that you're always doing it, that you are a bad-tempered person. You say, "I admit I drank too much last Saturday"; but everyone else knows that you are a habitual drunkard.

That is one way in which God's view must differ from mine. He sees all the characters: I see all except my own. But the second difference is this. He loves the people in spite of their faults. He goes on loving. He does not let go. Don't say, "It's all very well for Him; He hasn't got to live with them." He has. He is inside them as well as outside them. He is *with* them far more intimately and closely and incessantly than we can ever be. Every vile thought within their minds (and ours), every moment of spite, envy, arrogance, greed and self-conceit comes right up against His patient and longing love, and grieves His spirit more than it grieves ours.

The more we can imitate God in both these respects, the more progress we shall make. We must love "X" more; and we must learn to see ourselves as a person of exactly the same kind. Some people say it is morbid to be always thinking of one's faults. That would be all very well if most of us could stop thinking of our own without soon beginning to think about those of other people. For unfortunately we *enjoy* thinking about other people's faults:

and in the proper sense of the word "morbid," that is the most morbid pleasure in the world.

We don't like rationing which is imposed upon us, but I suggest one form of rationing which we ought to impose on ourselves. Abstain from all thinking about other people's faults, unless your duties as a teacher or parent make it necessary to think about them. Whenever the thoughts come unnecessarily into one's mind, why not simply shove them away? And think of one's own faults instead? For there, with God's help, one *can* do something. Of all the awkward people in your house or job there is only one whom you can improve very much. That is the practical end at which to begin. And really, we'd better. The job has to be tackled some day: and every day we put it off will make it harder to begin.

What, after all, is the alternative? You see clearly enough that nothing, not even God with all His power, can make "X" really happy as long as "X" remains envious, self-centered, and spiteful. Be sure there is something inside you which, unless it is altered, will put it out of God's power to prevent your being eternally miserable. While that something remains there can be no Heaven for you, just as there can be no sweet smells for a man with a cold in the nose, and no music for a man who is deaf. It's not a question of God "sending" us to Hell. In each of us there is something growing up which will of itself *be Hell* unless it is nipped in the bud. The matter is serious: let us put ourselves in His hands at once—this very day, this hour.

Discussion Questions

1. What does Lewis assume about reticence and privacy in the opening paragraph? Do you think these values have changed since Lewis wrote the essay in 1948? If so, what might have caused those changes.

2. Look carefully at Lewis's strategy in his essay. What is the effect of starting out with the difficulties we may have with others and then turning the essay around to deal with the complaints others may have with us? Why didn't he begin by telling us to take a close look at ourselves?

3. What assumption does Lewis make about human character? Compare his essay to William James's on "Habit." How are their assumptions similar? In what way is much of their language similar? Where do they differ?

4. In a sense, the human problems Lewis is dealing with in this essay are not very different from the kinds of problems we see in the newspaper advice columns everyday. Yet, religious belief aside, how does Lewis's solution to problems differ from those usually rendered in the advice columns? Find a complaint in one of the popular columns that falls into the type of difficulty Lewis is talking about (it won't be hard to find one) and compare the columnist's response to Lewis's response. Look carefully at the style and vocabulary of each writer; how do these differ for the two writers?

WYNDHAM LEWIS

The British author and painter Wyndham Lewis (1882–1957) was born in a yacht off the Canadian coast. After studying in England and France, he settled in London and began to create the literary and artistic movement called Vorticism. He promoted his ideas in his review, Blast, to which Ezra Pound and T. S. Eliot both contributed. The magazine attempted to stimulate a creative renaissance by internationalizing the art of England, but did not survive World War I. Lewis wrote enormously and on a wide range of subjects, but the chief book for which he is remembered is Time and Western Man (1927), a revolutionary work from which the following essay is taken. After publishing some fiction in the 1930's, Lewis returned chiefly to work on his painting until his blindness a few years before his death.

In "The Secret of the Success of Charlie Chaplin," Lewis tries to explore what many people dismiss as "matters of taste or opinion." Lewis finds these matters far from resistant to analysis.

The Secret of the Success of Charlie Chaplin

The childish, puny stature of Chaplin—enabling him always to be the little David to the Goliath of some man chosen for his statuesque proportions—served him well. He was always the *little-fellow-put-upon*—the naïf, child-like individual, bullied by the massive brutes by whom he was surrounded, yet whom he invariably vanquished. The fact that the giants were always vanquished, that, like the heroes of Ossian, they rode forth to battle (against the Chaplins of this world), but that, like those distant celtic heroes, *they always fell*, never, of course, struck the Public as pathetic, too. For the pathos of the Public is of a sentimental and also a naïvely selfish order. It is *its own* pathos and triumphs that it wishes to hear about. It seldom rises to an understanding of other forms of pathos than that of the kind represented by Chaplin, and the indirect reference to "greatness" in a more general sense, conveyed by mere physical size, repels it.

In this pathos of *the small*—so magnificently exploited by Charlie Chaplin—the ordinary "revolutionary" motif for crowd-consumption is not far to seek. The Keystone giants by whom, in his early films, he was always confronted, who *oppressed, misunderstood* and *hunted* him, but whom he invariably overcame, were the symbols of authority and power. Chaplin is a great revolutionary propagandist. On the political side, the pity he awakens, and his peculiar appeal to the public, is that reserved for *the small man.*

But no one can have seen a Chaplin film without being conscious also of something else, quite different from mere smallness. There was something much more positive than scale alone, or absence of scale, being put across, you would feel. First, of course, was the feeling that you were in the presence of an unbounded optimism (for one so small, poor and lonely). The combination of

THE SUCCESS OF CHARLIE CHAPLIN

light-heartedness and a sort of scurrilous cunning, that his irresponsible epileptic shuffle gives, is overpowering. It is Pippa that is passing. God is in His Heaven; all's well with the world (of Chaplins at all events). And, secondly, you would experience the utmost confidence in your little hero's winning all his battles. The happy-ending (for the militant child-man) was foreshadowed in the awkward and stupid, lurching bulk of the Keystone giants; in the flea-like adroitness of their terrible little antagonist. It was the little skiff of Drake against the Armada over again. In brief, your hero was not only small, but very capable and very confident. Throughout he bore a charmed life.

To the *smallness,* and to the *charmed life,* you now have to add the child-factor. Chaplin, the greatest screen artist, is *a child-man,* rather than merely *a small man.* That was his charm and the nature of his aesthetic appeal, as it were. His little doll-like face, his stuck-on toy moustache, his tiny wrists, his small body, are those of a child as much as is the "four-foot-something" body of Miss Loos. And without the public being conscious of it, no doubt, it was as a child that he went to its heart, which, as far as the popular audience is concerned, is maternal.

As to the sex-side of this psychology, it would be unscientific, if you like, to forget that the feminist revolution has been in progress all around the creative activities of this great clown, throughout his career. In Chaplin the simple woman would see clearly a symbol of her little Tommy—or little Charlie—giving that great, big, arrogant, troublesome bully, Dad (even if her particular "man" was not a good specimen of the ruling-sex), a wallop. For the head of a crowd is like a pudding *en surprise.* Everything is put into it; it reacts to the spectacles that are presented to it partly under the direction of those spectacles, but mainly according to the directing synthesis of all that has fallen or been stuffed into it, coming from all that is going on around it.

That, I think, is the way in which Chaplin endeared himself to the great public of the mass-democracy. But he is certainly mistaken in supposing that that was also the secret of Napoleon's success.

Perhaps in the success of Charlie Chaplin we have the heart of the secret of the child-fashion. It is at least strange how many people answer to the Chaplin-Loos (wide-eyed, naïf) standard. Even in physical stature it is strange how many have sprung up—or have *not* sprung up. And very many more lend their best energies to approximating as far as possible to this popular child-type.

*I think it is an age to be small in, said an intelligent flea,
But I shall see!*

And on the other hand, the rôle of the giant, or a rôle involving any greatness, is deservedly unpopular. Men fly from suggestions of greatness as though such things were tainted, as indeed they are proscribed. In their own bosoms they carefully stamp out all tell-tale traces of a suspect ambition.

I do not wish to be personal, but the subject is such a very significant one that that objection must be overridden. Picasso, then, is very small as well; with, however, a slightly napoleonic austerity lacking in Chaplin; though he has the same bright, darting, knowing eyes, the same appearance of microscopic competence. He is built on strictly infantile lines. I could name many more less-known people who answer to this description. Nature is certainly busy somewhere, and has been busy for a long time, turning these *eternal sucklings* out in the flesh, and not only in the spirit. What is Nature about? Why is she specializing in this manner? That is a question for the professional physiologist and psychologist. Those are, however, the facts; which any one, with a few hours to spare, can observe for themselves. At that, for the present, I will leave the problem of the infant-cult.

Discussion Questions

1. In what ways and from what points of view does Wyndham Lewis analyze the concept of "smallness" and its antithesis "greatness"? Does he see the appeal of "smallness" in the same way as Stephen Jay Gould?

2. What areas of discourse does Lewis draw on for his analogies? For example, he uses comparisons from the Bible and from medicine ("epileptic shuffle"). Where else might he have gone for metaphoric language?

3. Compare Randall Jarrell's views on "instant literature" to Lewis's treatment of a similar theme in this essay. Who seems more objective about the popularity of "popular" entertainment?

4. Pick a contemporary figure popular for reasons different from those Lewis gives and try to analyze the reasons for his or her success.

5. Do you see any evidence today for what Lewis calls the "problem of the infant-cult"? Would, for example, Woody Allen make an example? Pretend that he would and write an essay using Lewis's analysis but giving evidence from your knowledge of Allen.

Basil Liddell Hart

The English military historian and theorist Basil Liddell Hart (1895–1970) was born in London and educated at Cambridge. His studies were interrupted by World War I, in which he served as a captain of infantry and was severely wounded. He remained in the army until 1927, writing some manuals of instruction that attracted early attention to him as a revolutionary thinker. His studies of the Mongol invasions and of the campaigns of Sherman led him to the views of mobile warfare that were unfortunately to have more influence on German than on English military planning for World War II.

In reading the following essay, it should be kept in mind that Liddell Hart's emphasis on Sherman's "relentlessness" pertains only to the destruction of war resources and property. The march of over 60,000 men through over 2,000 miles of enemy countryside produced almost no proven crimes of violence upon the civilian population.

William Tecumseh Sherman: The First Modern General

"The legitimate object of war is a more perfect peace"—this sentence inscribed on the statue of General Sherman at Washington is a paraphrase of the words he used at St. Louis on July 20th, 1865, and the key to his thought and conduct before, during, and after the war. Because of his restless manner, the occasional extravagance of his language, and the ceaseless stream of ideas which he poured out, superficial observers often regarded him as an erratic genius, brilliant but unstable. A close study and analysis of his letters—and no man has stripped his soul more nakedly or more often—yields a different impression. His consistency is seen to be almost unparalleled among the great figures of history, and for the reason that none was more governed by reason or less influenced by instinct. His one strong instinct was the instinct for government, for order, and it guided him—through observation, historical study, and reflection—to a profound distrust of the influence of instinct in "self-government" and to an equally profound conviction that logical reasoning was the only sure guide. Reason had lifted man above the animal, which instinct would never have done, and to it was due not only the national but the moral progress of mankind. Reason was the light of humanity, instinct but the discarded skin of reason in an earlier stage of growth. Hence Sherman had a logical faith in progress, which was the firmer because he realized that the progress of the human mind is infinitely gradual, that it must be measured by aeons, not by generations; and that it follows, if so gradually as to be almost imperceptible, in the wake of physical progress. No man of action has more completely attained the point of view of the scientific historian, who observes the movements of mankind with the same detachment as a bacteriologist observes bacilli under a microscope and yet with a sympathy that springs from his own common manhood. In Sherman's attainment of that philosophic pinnacle, soaring above the clouds of ignorance and passion, lies the explanation of much that seems perplexing and contradictory in his character—the dispassionateness of an impulsive man, the restfulness of a restless man, the patience of an impatient man, the sympathy of a relentless man.

It was logical, and due to reasoning that was purely logical, that he should first oppose war; then, conduct it with iron severity; and, finally, seize the first real opportunity to make a peace of complete absolution. He cared little that his name should be execrated by the people of the South if he could only cure them of a taste for war. And to cure them he deliberately aimed at the non-combatant foundation of the hostile war spirit instead of at its combatant roof. He cared as little that this aim might violate a conventional code of war, for so long as war was regarded as a chivalrous pastime, and its baseness obscured by a punctilious code, so long would it be invested with a halo of romance. Such a code and such a halo had helped the duel to survive long after less polite forms of murder had grown offensive to civilized taste and gone out of fashion. In Sherman's view law and war were two opposed states, and war began when law broke down. In other words, war was primarily an anarchical state of mind and only secondarily a matter of physical blows. Here we see the deeper meaning underlying Sherman's phrase "war is only justifiable among civilized nations to produce peace." In logic and in fact, peoples make war, armies merely end it. The corollary of this deduction was expressed in Sherman's declaration, "Therefore, I had to go through Georgia and let them see what war meant."

Law might not be perfect but at least it was the most practical form of expressing right yet devised by the human reason. War, in contrast, was an assertion by a human group that right was merely a question of superior or inferior might. To contradict this assertion Sherman had reluctantly lent himself to the war—not against the South but *"against anarchy"*—his ceaseless refrain. Vigorously rejecting that specious salve of conscience—"my country right or wrong," he would just as readily have lent himself to a war against the North if his reason had told him that there lay the cause of anarchy.

His logic may seem extreme, his implied verdict against the South may seem an inequitable assessment of the responsibility for the war, but the peace and prosperity which have since reigned in the United States, are its practical justification. And if the abolition of anarchy on a national scale has not been completed on the smaller social scale, it is because of the subsequent imperfection of law, because those who have made and multiplied the laws have fallen so far below Sherman's standard of foresight and wisdom. He was too imbued with realism to believe that the legislative and political system of the United States could be reformed from within, and justified his own abstention from the attempt by saying, "It is too much like the case of a girl who marries a drunken lover in the hopes to reform him. It never has succeeded and never will." But he had a boundless faith in the healing and recreative power of time plus prosperity. His creed was summed up in the concluding words of his post-war St. Louis speech, wherein he had pointed out that the reconstruction and economic improvement of the South meant the benefit of the whole—"Therefore, my friends, now that the war is over, let us all go to work and do what seems honest and just to restore our country to its former prosperity—*to its physical prosperity.* As to its political prosperity, I know nothing of it, and care far less about it."

His hatred of anarchy was not inspired by an abstract motive but by the essentially practical one that only in a state of order are prosperity and progress possible. Order was merely the means to the end—progress. For Sherman's consistency was not a static conservatism but a progress through order to a better order. An advance from a secure base to gain a base for a fresh advance. It may truly be said that he based his life on the principles which governed his generalship, and proved that they were universally applicable.

Moreover, both the generalship and the principles were evolutionary. At the beginning of the war Sherman's military thought ran on the same lines as that of the normal studious soldier. Although his civil experience had widened his intellectual range he had not yet appreciated how profoundly this experience affected the military sphere. Bred on Jomini's teachings, he had a great respect for orthodox doctrine, with its emphasis on the geometrical rather than on the psychological, on bodies rather than on wills, on numerical superiority rather than on surprise. Thus, like the other "educated" soldiers of the day, he was at first handicapped in comparison with a Grant, or a Forrest, who for want of such education applied pure common sense in solving the problems of war. But the Vicksburg campaign, Sherman's "first gleam of daylight," was also his light of revelation, and the road to Vicksburg his road to Damascus. The campaign revealed to him, more clearly than any previous experience, that strategy is not merely the forerunner but the master of tactics, that the purpose of strategy is to minimize fighting and that it fulfills this purpose by playing on the mind of the opponent—so as first to disturb and then to upset his balance of mind. The campaign revealed to him also that in war unexpectedness and mobility are the master-keys of generalship—opening many doors which no physical weight can force—and it demonstrated, in particular, the incalculable value of a deceptive direction and of cutting loose from communications.

Because of his intellectual superiority, the experience made a deeper impression on him than on the simple soldier from whose instinctive practice he had acquired it. It became the foundation of a new conception of strategy which took form in his mind and henceforth he applied it with progressive consistency, developing it more boldly with each successive proof of its efficacy. For his military character as well as his thought underwent evolution. His own past experience had combined with his outlook on the war to give him a natural bias towards the security of caution, and only gradually did this yield to a growing perception that in calculated audacity and unexpectedness lay an even better guarantee of security. Hence, we see his moves becoming progressively bolder during and after the Atlanta campaign—while, on examination, they seem progressively safer. In acquiring boldness, he had learnt to measure both his own capacity and the margin of safety perhaps more acutely than any other great commander. And the reason was that his boldness was itself the product of a closely reasoned theory of war which had evolved from reflection and was supported on unrivalled knowledge of the conditions of topography, transportation, and supply. This was the real security for his progress, the logical base for his logistical moves. More perhaps than any other commander he *knew* what he was aiming at and his capacity to attain it.

He had come to realize also that in war all conditions are more calculable, all obstacles more surmountable, than those of human resistance. And having begun the war with an orthodox belief in the sovereign efficacy of battle as a "cure-all" he had learnt that the theoretical ideal of the destruction of the enemy's armed forces on the battlefield is rarely borne out in practice and that to pursue it singlemindedly is to chase a will-o'-the-wisp. Because of his original orthodoxy it is all the more significant that he reached the conclusion that the way to decide wars and win battles was "more by the movement of troops than by fighting." This was his ultimate theory, constantly expressed. And of its practice he could say, as truly as Napoleon in Austria—"I have destroyed the enemy merely by marches."

To attain such a result he radically recast the customary code of organization and maintenance, and for his superior "manœuverability" he was dependent on the elasticity of his instrument as well as on the elasticity of his thought, his aim being to convert his army—"into a mobile machine willing and able to start at a minute's notice, and to subsist on the scantiest of food." He was able to demand from his men such sacrifice of comfort because he demanded so comparatively little sacrifice of life. His men had a supreme faith in his ability and will to spare them loss and the consequence was that when he called on them to fight they had both a willingness and a confidence in success that made them irresistible. The ardour of the charge which carried Fort McAlister was in "striking" contrast with the assaults made in other armies during the last lap of the war.

Sherman's greater distinction in history, however, is that he not only forged new master-keys of generalship to open military locks but fitted them to a new type of lock. Even above his greatness as a strategist is his greatness as a grand strategist. He perceived that the resisting power of a modern democracy depends more on the strength of the popular will than on the strength of its armies, and that this will in turn depends largely upon economic and social security. To interrupt the ordinary life of the people and quench hope of its resumption is more effective than any military result short of the complete destruction of the armies. The last is an ideal rarely attained in the past, and increasingly difficult since the appearance of nations in arms.

As the greater size of armies and the lengthening range of weapons have made it more difficult to defeat a hostile army decisively, so the growth of the press has tended to reduce the effects of any defeat. For, from patriotism or censorship, they disguise the reality of defeat and keep the people under a pleasant opiate. Hence, as Sherman appreciated, rude personal contact with the hostile forces is necessary to awaken the enemy people from these drugged dreams of unreality and to shock them into surrender.

In contrast, however, to the increased difficulty and reduced effect of victory in battle, interference with the enemy people has become both easier and more effective as civilization has become more complex and the distribution of comfort more general. These new conditions of war were first manifest in the American Civil War, although still immature because of the loose agrarian nature of the Southern Confederacy. It is thus the more notable that these conditions should have been appreciated and turned to decisive advantage. As that war was the first modern war, so was Sherman the first modern general. And hitherto the only one. For although the same conditions, now more highly developed and obvious, governed and ultimately decided the World War, no grand strategist exploited and directed them consciously towards the collapse of the hostile will. That war did not produce a second Sherman. Nor did the Armistice.

Indeed, it is only after the dust of that conflict has settled that we can fully appreciate Sherman's outlook on war and peace. And without that war no complete understanding of Sherman would have been possible. For he was not a typical man of his age, but the prototype of the most modern age, of that age upon whose threshold we now seem to be standing. Far better than his own contemporaries we can understand his combination of restless energy with an ironical, almost fatalistic, perception of the limited results of human effort; his insistence on reasoning from facts and distrust of all received opinions; his passionate sincerity and fondness for psychological analysis; his balanced pride in his own constructive achievements—never in his instinctive attributes or nominal dignities—and awareness of his own defects; his democratic simplicity of manner and sardonic distrust of democracy as a political panacea; his loyalty to a cause, not to an emblem—a loyalty all the greater because it sprang from appreciation of its practical necessity and not from blind worship of authority; his lack of any definite religious beliefs, but increased belief in righteousness of life; his contempt for all creeds, as strait-jackets of the reason, yet respect and admiring support for any one who, like Howard, carried his religion into the practice of daily life, even in war.

But to understand Sherman it is also essential to realize the effect of the war upon his character. Momentarily it hardened him, ultimately it mellowed him. Logic had become more toned by generosity, sincerity by tolerance, purpose by sympathy. The trend of his own interests had carried him from the mountain top to the market place; the evolution of his character, from the Old Testament to the New.

Discussion Questions

1. How does Liddell Hart connect the qualities of "the modern man" to those of "the modern general"?

2. How does the author convey the sense of greatness in his subject? Make some comparisons between the key terms he uses as themes (for example, "reason," "progress," and so forth) and those employed by Borges in his study of pseudo-greatness.

3. How does the author use paradox to organize his essay?

4. Pick a historical figure you admire, one about whom you know some basic facts, including any famous utterances. Ask yourself your general reasons for admiring the figure. Now, pick one fact that seems to serve as a key to understanding the figure's greatness or an aspect of that greatness. Using Liddell Hart's essay as a model, write a brief essay that links all your facts to your "key" fact with a view to explaining the main reasons for your admiration.

WALTER LIPPMANN

The prominent newspaper columnist and social philosopher Walter Lippmann (1889–1974) was born in New York City. After graduating from Harvard University, he spent many years on the staff of The New Republic. *In 1921, he moved to the New York* World, *and in 1931 began writing a widely respected column, "Today and Tomorrow," for the* Herald Tribune. *The column ran until the 1960's, and Lippmann received Pulitzer Prizes in 1957 and 1962.*

Lippmann's social philosophy was one of realistic liberalism; he opposed any form of collectivism and believed in a minimum of governmental interference in the economy. Among his most important books are Liberty and the News *(1920),* Public Opinion *(1922),* The Phantom Public *(1925),* The Good Society *(1937),* The Cold War *(1947), and* The Public Philosophy *(1955). The following essay has been reprinted from the August 1939* Atlantic Monthly.

The Indispensable Opposition

Were they pressed hard enough, most men would probably confess that political freedom—that is to say, the right to speak freely and to act in opposition—is a noble ideal rather than a practical necessity. As the case for freedom is generally put to-day, the argument lends itself to this feeling. It is made to appear that, whereas each man claims his freedom as a matter of right, the freedom he accords to other men is a matter of toleration. Thus, the defense of freedom of opinion tends to rest not on its substantial, beneficial, and indispensable consequences, but on a somewhat eccentric, a rather vaguely benevolent, attachment to an abstraction.

It is all very well to say with Voltaire, "I wholly disapprove of what you say, but will defend to the death your right to say it," but as a matter of fact most men will not defend to the death the rights of other men: if they disapprove sufficiently what other men say, they will somehow suppress those men if they can.

So, if this is the best that can be said for liberty of opinion, that a man must tolerate his opponents because everyone has a "right" to say what he pleases, then we shall find that liberty of opinion is a luxury, safe only in pleasant times when men can be tolerant because they are not deeply and vitally concerned.

Yet actually, as a matter of historic fact, there is a much stronger foundation for the great constitutional right of freedom of speech, and as a matter of practical human experience there is a much more compelling reason for cultivating the habits of free men. We take, it seems to me, a naïvely self-righteous view when we argue as if the right of our opponents to speak were something that we protect because we are magnanimous, noble, and unselfish. The compelling reason why, if liberty of opinion did not exist, we should have to invent it, why it will eventually have to be restored in all civilized countries where it is now suppressed, is that we must protect the right of our opponents to speak because we must hear what they have to say.

We miss the whole point when we imagine that we tolerate the freedom of our political opponents as we tolerate a howling baby next door, as we put up with the blasts from our neighbor's radio because we are too peaceable to heave a brick through the window. If this were all there is to freedom of opinion, that we are too good-natured or too timid to do anything about our opponents and our critics except to let them talk, it would be difficult to say whether we are tolerant because we are magnanimous or because we are lazy, because we have strong principles or because we lack serious convictions, whether we have the hospitality of an inquiring mind or the indifference of an empty mind. And so, if we truly wish to understand why freedom is necessary in a civilized society, we must begin by realizing that, because freedom of discussion improves our own opinions, the liberties of other men are our own vital necessity.

We are much closer to the essence of the matter, not when we quote Voltaire, but when we go to the doctor and pay him to ask us the most embarrassing questions and to prescribe the most disagreeable diet. When we pay the doctor to exercise complete freedom of speech about the cause and cure of our stomachache, we do not look upon ourselves as tolerant and magnanimous, and worthy to be admired by ourselves. We have enough common sense to know that if we threaten to put the doctor in jail because we do not like the diagnosis and the prescription it will be unpleasant for the doctor, to be sure, but equally unpleasant for our own stomachache. That is why even the most ferocious dictator would rather be treated by a doctor who was free to think and speak the truth than by his own Minister of Propaganda. For there is a point, the point at which things really matter, where the freedom of others is no longer a question of their right but of our own need.

The point at which we recognize this need is much higher in some men than in others. The totalitarian rulers think they do not need the freedom of an opposition: they exile, imprison, or shoot their opponents. We have concluded on the basis of practical experience, which goes back to Magna Carta and beyond, that we need the opposition. We pay the opposition salaries out of the public treasury.

In so far as the usual apology for freedom of speech ignores this experience, it becomes abstract and eccentric rather than concrete and human. The emphasis is generally put on the right to speak, as if all that mattered were that the doctor should be free to go out into the park and explain to the vacant air why I have a stomachache. Surely that is a miserable caricature of the great civic right which men have bled and died for. What really matters is that the doctor should tell *me* what ails me, that I should listen to him; that if I do not like what he says I should be free to call in another doctor; and that then the first doctor should have to listen to the second doctor; and that out of all the speaking and listening, the give-and-take of opinions, the truth should be arrived at.

This is the creative principle of freedom of speech, not that it is a system for the tolerating of error, but that it is a system for finding the truth. It may not produce the truth, or the whole truth all the time, or often, or in some cases ever. But if the truth can be found, there is no other system which will normally and habitually find so much truth. Until we have thoroughly understood this principle, we shall not know why we must value our liberty, or how we can protect and develop it.

Let us apply this principle to the system of public speech in a totalitarian state. We may, without any serious falsification, picture a condition of affairs in which the mass of the people are being addressed through one broadcasting system by one man and his chosen subordinates. The orators speak. The audience listens but cannot and dare not speak back. It is a system of one-way communication; the opinions of the rulers are broadcast outwardly to the mass of the people. But nothing comes back to the rulers from the people except the cheers; nothing returns in the way of knowledge of forgotten facts, hidden feelings, neglected truths, and practical suggestions.

But even a dictator cannot govern by his own one-way inspiration alone. In practice, therefore, the totalitarian rulers get back the reports of the secret police and of their party henchmen down among the crowd. If these reports are competent, the rulers may manage to remain in touch with public sentiment. Yet that is not enough to know what the audience feels. The rulers have also to make great decisions that have enormous consequences, and here their system provides virtually no help from the give-and-take of opinion in the nation. So they must either rely on their intuition, which cannot be permanently and continually inspired, or, if they are intelligent despots, encourage their trusted advisers and their technicians to speak and debate freely in their presence.

On the walls of the houses of Italian peasants one may see inscribed in large letters the legend, "Mussolini is always right." But if that legend is taken seriously by Italian ambassadors, by the Italian General Staff, and by the Ministry of Finance, then all one can say is heaven help Mussolini, heaven help Italy, and the new Emperor of Ethiopia.

For at some point, even in a totalitarian state, it is indispensable that there should exist the freedom of opinion which causes opposing opinions to be debated. As time goes on, that is less and less easy under a despotism; critical discussion disappears as the internal opposition is liquidated in favor of men who think and feel alike. That is why the early successes of despots, of Napoleon I and of Napoleon III, have usually been followed by an irreparable mistake. For in listening only to his yes men—the others being in exile or in concentration camps, or terrified—the despot shuts himself off from the truth that no man can dispense with.

We know all this well enough when we contemplate the dictatorships. But when we try to picture our own system, by way of contrast, what picture do we have in our minds? It is, is it not, that anyone may stand up on his own soapbox and say anything he pleases, like the individuals in Kipling's poem who sit each in his separate star and draw the Thing as they see it for the God of Things as they are. Kipling, perhaps, could do this, since he was a poet. But the ordinary mortal isolated on his separate star will have an hallucination, and a citizenry declaiming from separate soapboxes will poison the air with hot and nonsensical confusion.

If the democratic alternative to the totalitarian one-way broadcasts is a row of separate soap boxes, then I submit that the alternative is unworkable, is unreasonable, and is humanly unattractive. It is above all a false alternative. It is not true that liberty has developed among civilized men when anyone is free to set up a soapbox, is free to hire a hall where he may expound his opinions to those who are willing to listen. On the contrary, freedom of speech is established to achieve its essential purpose only when different opinions are expounded in the same hall to the same audience.

For, while the right to talk may be the beginning of freedom, the necessity of listening is what makes the right important. Even in Russia and Germany a man may still stand in an open field and speak his mind. What matters is not the utterance of opinions. What matters is the confrontation of opinions in debate. No man can care profoundly that every fool should say what he likes. Nothing has been accomplished if the wisest man proclaims his wisdom in the middle of the Sahara Desert. This is the shadow. We have the substance of liberty when the fool is compelled to listen to the wise man and learn; when the wise man is compelled to take account of the fool, and to instruct him; when the wise man can increase his wisdom by hearing the judgment of his peers.

That is why civilized men must cherish liberty—as a means of promoting the discovery of truth. So we must not fix our whole attention on the right of anyone to hire his own hall, to rent his own broadcasting station, to distribute his own pamphlets. These rights are incidental; and though they must be preserved, they can be preserved only by regarding them as incidental, as auxiliary to the substance of liberty that must be cherished and cultivated.

Freedom of speech is best conceived, therefore, by having in mind the picture of a place like the American Congress, an assembly where opposing views are represented, where ideas are not merely uttered but debated, or the British Parliament, where men who are free to speak are also compelled to answer. We may picture the true condition of freedom as existing in a place like a court of law, where witnesses testify and are cross-examined, where the lawyer argues against the opposing lawyer before the same judge and in the presence of one jury. We may picture freedom as existing in a forum where the speaker must respond to questions; in a gathering of scientists where the data, the hypothesis, and the conclusion are submitted to men competent to judge them; in a reputable newspaper which not only will publish the opinions of those who disagree but will reëxamine its own opinion in the light of what they say.

Thus the essence of freedom of opinion is not in mere toleration as such, but in the debate which toleration provides: it is not in the venting of opinion, but in the confrontation of opinion. That this is the practical substance can readily be understood when we remember how differently we feel and act about the censorship and regulation of opinion purveyed by different media of communication. We find then that, in so far as the medium makes difficult the confrontation of opinion in debate, we are driven towards censorship and regulation.

There is, for example, the whispering campaign, the circulation of anonymous rumors by men who cannot be compelled to prove what they say. They put the utmost strain on our tolerance, and there are few who do not rejoice when the anonymous slanderer is caught, exposed and punished. At a higher level there is the moving picture, a most powerful medium for conveying ideas, but a medium which does not permit debate. A moving picture cannot be answered effectively by another moving picture; in all free countries there is some censorship of the movies, and there would be more if the producers did not recognize their limitations by avoiding political controversy. There is then the radio. Here debate is difficult: it is not easy to make sure that the speaker is being answered in the presence of the same audience. Inevitably, there is some regulation of the radio.

When we reach the newspaper press, the opportunity for debate is so considerable that discontent cannot grow to the point where under normal conditions there is any disposition to regulate the press. But when newspapers abuse their power by injuring people who have no means of replying, a disposition to regulate the press appears. When we arrive at Congress we find that, because the membership of the House is so large, full debate is impracticable. So there are restrictive rules. On the other hand, in the Senate, where the conditions of full debate exist, there is almost absolute freedom of speech.

This shows us that the preservation and development of freedom of opinion are not only a matter of adhering to abstract legal rights, but also, and very urgently, a matter of organizing and arranging sufficient debate. Once we have a firm hold on the central principle, there are many practical conclusions to be drawn. We then realize that the defense of freedom of opinion consists primarily in perfecting the opportunity for an adequate give-and-take of opinion; it consists also in regulating the freedom of those revolutionists who cannot or will not permit or maintain debate when it does not suit their purposes.

We must insist that free oratory is only the beginning of free speech; it is not the end, but a means to an end. The end is to find the truth. The practical justification of civil liberty is not that self-expression is one of the rights of man. It is that the examination of opinion is one of the necessities of man. For experience tells us that it is only when freedom of opinion becomes the compulsion to debate that the seed which our fathers planted has produced its fruit. When that is understood, freedom will be cherished not because it is a vent for our opinions but because it is the surest method of correcting them.

The unexamined life, said Socrates, is unfit to be lived by man. This is the virtue of liberty, and the ground on which we may best justify our belief in it, that it tolerates error in order to serve the truth. When men are brought face to face with their opponents, forced to listen and learn and mend their ideas, they cease to be children and savages and begin to live like civilized men. Then only is freedom a reality, when men may voice their opinions because they must examine their opinions.

The only reason for dwelling on all this is that if we are to preserve democracy we must understand its principles. And the principle which distinguishes it from all other forms of government is that in a democracy the opposition not only is tolerated as constitutional but must be maintained because it is in fact indispensable.

The democratic system cannot be operated without effective

opposition. For, in making the great experiment of governing people by consent rather than by coercion, it is not sufficient that the party in power should have a majority. It is just as necessary that the party in power should never outrage the minority. That means that it must listen to the minority and be moved by the criticisms of the minority. That means that its measures must take account of the minority's objections, and that in administering measures it must remember that the minority may become the majority.

The opposition is indispensable. A good statesman, like any other sensible human being, always learns more from his opponents than from his fervent supporters. For his supporters will push him where the dangers are. So if he is wise he will often pray to be delivered from his friends, because they will ruin him. But, though it hurts, he ought also to pray never to be left without opponents; for they keep him on the path of reason and good sense.

The national unity of a free people depends upon a sufficiently even balance of political power to make it impracticable for the administration to be arbitrary and for the opposition to be revolutionary and irreconcilable. Where that balance no longer exists, democracy perishes. For unless all the citizens of a state are forced by circumstances to compromise, unless they feel that they can affect policy but that no one can wholly dominate it, unless by habit and necessity they have to give and take, freedom cannot be maintained.

Discussion Questions

1. What does Lippman find wrong with Voltaire's famous statement on freedom of speech?

2. Why doesn't Lippman care much about the rights of people to have opinions? What does he believe is more significant if freedom of speech is to be preserved in a society?

3. Why does Lippman argue that opposition is not only to be tolerated, but that it is *indispensable*? How do his views compare with those of Nora Ephron?

4. You have often heard it said, or perhaps you often say it yourself, that "everyone has the right to his or her own opinion." End of discussion, no? But if this right to an opinion is so obvious, then why are people so frequently criticized and punished in this society for exercising that right? Does, for example, a secretary of state have the right to make—even off the record—pro-Communist comments?

Does a secretary of agriculture have the right to make a racist joke? When public officials say such things they are usually severely criticized by the press—the great believer in the right of free opinion—and they often lose their jobs. Do officials give up their right to hold opinions when they take office, or are they allowed to have personal opinions but not allowed to express them? This is only one aspect of the problem of rights to opinions. Surely you can think of others. Make a list of the problems that arise because of "everyone's right to an opinion." Then choose one problem to focus on, and write an essay in which you present your opinion on the right to have opinions.

JACK LONDON

The American novelist, reporter, and social critic, Jack London (1876–1916) was born in poverty in San Francisco, California. He quit school at the age of fourteen and supported himself for a time as an oyster pirate on the Oakland waterfront. In 1894, after a semester at the University of California at Berkeley, he spent the winter prospecting for gold in the Klondike; instead of gold he found experiences and material that he would mine for a lifetime as a writer. His first collection of stories appeared in 1900 and was followed by a best-seller, The Call of the Wild *(1903).*

Nearly all of London's writing derives from first-hand experiences: The People of the Abyss *(1903), from which the following selection is reprinted, is based on his life in the London slums;* The Road *(1907), comes out of his days as a railroad tramp;* The Cruise of the Snark *(1911) recounts his sailing expedition to the South Pacific. London was not only one of the highest-paid and best-known writers of his day, he was among the most prolific—fifty books in seventeen years. Some of his other major works are* The Sea Wolf *(1904),* White Fang *(1906),* The Iron Heel *(1907), and* Martin Eden *(1909).*

The Carter and the Carpenter

The Carter,[1] with his clean-cut face, chin beard, and shaved upper lip, I should have taken in the United States for anything from a master workman to a well-to-do farmer. The Carpenter—well, I should have taken him for a carpenter. He looked it, lean and wiry, with shrewd, observant eyes, and hands that had grown twisted to the handles of tools through forty-seven years' work at the trade. The chief difficulty with these men was that they were old, and that their children, instead of growing up to take care of them, had died. Their years had told on them, and they had been forced out of the whirl of industry by the younger and stronger competitors who had taken their places.

These two men, turned away from the casual ward of the Whitechapel Workhouse, were bound with me for Poplar Workhouse. Not much of a show, they thought, but to chance it was all that remained to us. It was Poplar, or the streets and night. Both men were anxious for a bed, for they were "about gone," as they phrased it. The Carter, fifty-eight years of age, had spent the last three nights without shelter or sleep, while the Carpenter, sixty-five years of age, had been out five nights.

But, O dear, soft people, full of meat and blood, with white beds and airy rooms waiting for you each night, how can I make you know what it is to suffer as you would suffer if you spent a weary night on London's streets? Believe me, you would think a thousand centuries had come and gone before the east paled into dawn; you would shiver till you were ready to cry aloud with the pain of each aching muscle; and you would marvel that you could endure so much and live. Should you rest upon a bench, and your tired eyes close, depend upon it the policeman would rouse you

[1] A teamster; one who hauls freight in a wagon

and gruffly order you to "move on." You may rest upon the bench, and benches are few and far between; but if rest means sleep, on you must go, dragging your tired body through the endless streets. Should you, in desperate slyness, seek some forlorn alley or dark passageway and lie down, the omnipresent policeman will rout you out just the same. It is his business to rout you out. It is a law of the powers that be that you shall be routed out.

But when the dawn came, the nightmare over, you would hie you home to refresh yourself, and until you died you would tell the story of your adventure to groups of admiring friends. It would grow into a mighty story. Your little eight-hour night would become an Odyssey and you a Homer.

Not so with these homeless ones who walked to Poplar Workhouse with me. And there are thirty-five thousand of them, men and women, in London Town this night. Please don't remember it as you go to bed; if you are as soft as you ought to be you may not rest so well as usual. But for old men of sixty, seventy, and eighty, ill-fed, with neither meat nor blood, to greet the dawn unrefreshed, and to stagger through the day in mad search for crusts, with relentless night rushing down upon them again, and to do this five nights and days—O dear, soft people, full of meat and blood, how can you ever understand?

I walked up Mile End Road between the Carter and the Carpenter. Mile End Road is a wide thoroughfare, cutting the heart of East London, and there were tens of thousands of people abroad on it. I tell you this so that you may fully appreciate what I shall describe in the next paragraph. As I say, we walked along, and when they grew bitter and cursed the land, I cursed with them, cursed as an American waif would curse, stranded in a strange and terrible land. And, as I tried to lead them to believe, and succeeded in making them believe, they took me for a "seafaring man," who had spent his money in riotous living, lost his clothes (no unusual occurrence with seafaring men ashore), and was temporarily broke while looking for a ship. This accounted for my ignorance of English ways in general and casual wards in particular, and my curiosity concerning the same.

The Carter was hard put to keep the pace at which we walked (he told me that he had eaten nothing that day), but the Carpenter, lean and hungry, his gray and ragged overcoat flapping mournfully in the breeze, swung on in a long and tireless stride which reminded me strongly of the plains coyote. Both kept their eyes upon the pavement as they walked and talked, and every now and then one or the other would stoop and pick something up, never missing the stride the while. I thought it was cigar and cigarette stumps they were collecting, and for some time took no notice. Then I did notice.

From the slimy, spittle-drenched side-walk, they were picking up bits of orange peel, apple skin, and grape stems, and they were eating them. The pits of green gage plums they cracked between their teeth for the kernels inside. They picked up stray crumbs of bread the size of peas, apple cores so black and dirty one would not take them to be apple cores, and these things these two men took into their mouths, and chewed them, and swallowed them; and this, between six and seven o'clock in the evening of August 20, year of our Lord 1902, in the heart of the greatest, wealthiest, and most powerful empire the world has ever seen.

These two men talked. They were not fools. They were merely old. And, quite naturally, a-reek with pavement offal, they talked of bloody revolution. They talked as anarchists, fanatics, and madmen would talk. And who shall blame them? In spite of my three good meals that day, and the snug bed I could occupy if I wished, and my social philosophy, and my evolutionary belief in the slow development and metamorphosis of things—in spite of all this, I say, I felt impelled to talk rot with them or hold my tongue. Poor fools! Not of their sort are revolutions bred. And when they are dead and dust, which will be shortly, other fools will talk bloody revolution as they gather offal from the spittle-drenched side-walk along Mile End Road to Poplar Workhouse.

Being a foreigner, and a young man, the Carter and the Carpenter explained things to me and advised me. Their advice, by the way, was brief and to the point; it was to get out of the country. "As fast as God'll let me," I assured them; "I'll hit only the high places, till you won't be able to see my trail for smoke." They felt the force of my figures rather than understood them, and they nodded their heads approvingly.

"Actually make a man a criminal against 'is will," said the Carpenter. "'Ere I am, old, younger men takin' my place, my clothes gettin' shabbier an' shabbier, an' makin' it 'arder every day to get a job. I go to the casual ward for a bed. Must be there by two or three in the afternoon or I won't get in. You saw what happened today. What chance does that give me to look for work? S'pose I do get into the casual ward? Keep me in all day tomorrow, let me out mornin' o' next day. What then? The law sez I can't get in another casual ward that night less'n ten miles distant. Have to hurry an' walk to be there in time that day. What chance does that give me to look for a job? S'pose I don't walk. S'pose I look for a job? In no time there's night come, an' no bed. No sleep all night, nothin' to eat, what shape am I in the mornin' to look for work? Got to make up my sleep in the park somehow" (the vision of Christ's Church, Spitalfield, was strong on me) "an' get something to eat. An' there I am! Old, down, an' no chance to get up."

"Used to be a toll-gate 'ere," said the Carter, "Many's the time I've paid my toll 'ere in my cartin' days."

"I've 'ad three 'a'penny rolls in two days," the Carpenter announced, after a long pause in the conversation.

"Two of them I ate yesterday, an' the third to-day," he concluded, after another long pause.

"I ain't 'ad anything today," said the Carter. "An' I'm fagged out. My legs is hurtin' me somethin' fearful."

"The roll you get in the 'spike' is that 'ard you can't eat it nicely with less than a pint of water," said the Carpenter, for my benefit. And, on asking him what the "spike" was, he answered, "The casual ward. It's a cant word, you know."

But what surprised me was that he should have the word "cant" in his vocabulary that I found was no mean one before we parted.

I asked him what I may expect in the way of treatment, if we succeeded in getting into the Poplar Workhouse, and between them I was supplied with much information. Having taken a cold bath on entering, I would be given for supper six ounces of bread and "three parts of skilly." "Three parts" means three-quarters of a pint, and "skilly" is a fluid concoction of three quarts of oatmeal stirred into three buckets and a half of hot water.

"Milk and sugar, I suppose, and a silver spoon?" I queried.

"No fear. Salt's what you'll get, an' I've seen some places where you'd not get any spoon. 'Old 'er up an' let 'er run down, that's 'ow they do it."

"You do get good skilly at 'Ackney," said the Carter.

"Oh, wonderful skilly, that," praised the Carpenter, and each looked eloquently at the other.

"Flour an' water at St. George's in the East," said the Carter.

The Carpenter nodded. He has tried them all.

"Then what?" I demanded.

And I was informed that I was sent directly to bed. "Call you at half after five in the mornin', an' you get up an' take a 'sluice'—if there's any soap. Then breakfast, same as supper, three parts o' skilly an' a six-ounce loaf."

"'Tisn't always six ounces," corrected the Carter.

"'Tisn't, no; an' often that sour you can 'ardly eat it. When first I started I couldn't eat the skilly nor the bread, but now I can eat my own an' another man's portion."

"I could eat three other men's portions," said the Carter. "I 'aven't 'ad a bit this blessed day."

"Then what?"

"Then you've got to do your task, pick four pounds of oakum, or clean an' scrub, or break ten to eleven hundredweight o' stones. I don't 'ave to break stones; I'm past sixty, you see. They'll make you do it, though. You're young an' strong."

"What I don't like," grumbled the Carter, "is to be locked up in a cell to pick oakum. It's too much like prison."

"But suppose after you've had your night's sleep, you refuse to pick oakum, or break stones, or do any work at all?" I asked.

"No fear you'll refuse the second time; they'll run you in," answered the Carpenter. "Wouldn't advise you to try it on, my lad."

"Then comes dinner," he went on. "Eight ounces of bread, one and a 'arf ounces of cheese, an' cold water. Then you finish your task and 'ave supper, same as before, three parts o' skilly an' six ounces of bread. Then to bed, six o'clock, an' next mornin' you're turned loose, provided you've finished your task."

We had long since left Mile End Road, and after traversing a gloomy maze of narrow, winding streets, we came to Poplar Workhouse. On a low stone wall we spread our handkerchiefs, and each in his handkerchief put all his worldly possessions with the exception of the "bit o' baccy" down his sock. And then, as the last light was fading from the drab-colored sky, the wind blowing cheerless and cold, we stood, with our pitiful little bundles in our hands, a forlorn group at the workhouse door.

Three working girls came along, and one looked pityingly at me; as she passed I followed her with my eyes, and she still looked pityingly back at me. The old men she did not notice, Dear Christ, she pitied me, young and vigorous and strong, but she had no pity for the two old men who stood by my side! She was a young woman, and I was a young man, and what vague sex promptings impelled her to pity me put her sentiment on the lowest plane. Pity for old men is an altruistic feeling, and besides, the workhouse door is the accustomed place for old men. So she showed no pity for them, only for me, who deserved it least or not at all. Not in honor do gray hairs go down to the grave in London Town.

On one side the door was a bell handle, on the other side a press button.

"Ring the bell," said the Carter to me.

And just as I ordinarily would at anybody's door, I pulled out the handle and rang a peal.

"Oh! Oh!" they cried in one terrified voice. "Not so 'ard!"

I let go, and they looked reproachfully at me, as though I had imperilled their chance for a bed and three parts of skilly. Nobody came. Luckily, it was the wrong bell, and I felt better.

"Press the button," I said to the Carpenter.

"No, no, wait a bit," the Carter hurriedly interposed.

From all of which I drew the conclusion that a poorhouse porter, who commonly draws a yearly salary of from thirty to forty dollars, is a very finicky and important personage, and cannot be treated too fastidiously by—paupers.

So we waited, ten times a decent interval, when the Carter stealthily advanced a timid forefinger to the button, and gave it the faintest possible push. I have looked at waiting men where life and death was the issue; but anxious suspense showed less plainly on their faces than it showed on the faces of these two men as they waited for the coming of the porter.

He came. He barely looked at us. "Full up," he said, and shut the door.

"Another night of it," groaned the Carpenter. In the dim light the Carter looked wan and gray.

Indiscriminate charity is vicious, say the professional philanthropists. Well, I resolved to be vicious.

"Come on; get your knife out and come here," I said to the Carter, drawing him into a dark alley.

He glared at me in a frightened manner, and tried to draw back. Possibly he took me for a latter-day Jack-the-Ripper, with a penchant for elderly male paupers. Or he may have thought I was inveigling him into the commission of some desperate crime. Anyway, he was frightened.

It will be remembered, at the outset, that I sewed a pound inside my stoker's singlet under the arm-pit. This was my emergency fund, and I was now called upon to use it for the first time.

Not until I had gone through the acts of a contortionist, and shown the round coin sewed in, did I succeed in getting the Carter's help. Even then his hand was trembling so that I was afraid he would cut me instead of the stitches, and I was forced to take the knife away and do it myself. Out rolled the gold piece, a fortune in their hungry eyes; and away we stampeded for the nearest coffee-house.

Of course, I had to explain to them that I was merely an investigator, a social student, seeking to find out how the other half lived. And at once they shut up like clams. I was not of their kind; my speech had changed, the tones of my voice were different, in short, I was a superior, and they were superbly class conscious.

"What will you have?" I asked, as the waiter came for the order.

"Two slices an' a cup of tea," meekly said the Carter.

"Two slices an' a cup of tea," meekly said the Carpenter.

Stop a moment, and consider the situation. Here were two men, invited by me into the coffee-house. They had seen my gold piece, and they could understand that I was no pauper. One had eaten a ha'penny roll that day, the other had eaten nothing. And they called for "two slices an' a cup of tea!" Each man had given a tu'penny order. "Two slices," by the way, means two slices of bread and butter.

That was the same degraded humility that had characterized their attitude toward the poorhouse porter. But I wouldn't have it. Step by step I increased their orders—eggs, rashers of bacon, more eggs, more bacon, more tea, more slices, and so forth—they denying wistfully all the while that they cared for anything more, and devouring it ravenously as fast as it arrived.

"First cup o' tea I've 'ad in a fortnight," said the Carter.

"Wonderful tea, that," said the Carpenter.

They each drank two pints of it, and I assure you that it was slops. It resembled tea less than lager beer resembles champagne. Nay, it was "water-bewitched," and did not resemble tea at all.

It was curious, after the first shock, to notice the effect the food had on them. At first they were melancholy, and talked of the divers times they had contemplated suicide. The Carter, not a week before, had stood on the bridge and looked at the water, and pondered the question. Water, the Carpenter insisted with heat, was a bad route. He, for one, he knew, would struggle. A bullet was "'andier," but how under the sun was he to get hold of a revolver? That was the rub.

They grew more cheerful as the hot "tea" soaked in, and talked more about themselves. The Carter had buried his wife and children, with the exception of one son, who grew to manhood and helped him in his little business. Then the thing happened. The son, a man of thirty-one, died of the smallpox. No sooner was this over than the father came down with fever and went to the hospital for three months. Then he was done for. He came out weak, debilitated, no strong young son to stand by him, his little business gone glimmering, and not a farthing. The thing had happened, and the game was up. No chance for an old man to start again. Friends all poor and unable to help. He tried for work when they were putting up stands for the first coronation parade. "An' I got fair sick of the answer: 'No! no! no!' It rang in my ears at night when I tried to sleep, always the same, 'No! no! no!'" Only the past week he had answered an advertisement in Hackney, and on giving his age was told, "Oh, too old, too old by far."

The Carpenter had been born in the army, where his father

had served twenty-two years. Likewise, his two brothers had gone into the army; one, troop sergeant-major of the Seventh Hussars, dying in India after the Mutiny; the other, after nine years under Roberts in the East, had been lost in Egypt. The Carpenter had not gone into the army, so here he was, still on the planet.

"But 'ere, give me your 'and," he said, ripping open his ragged shirt. "I'm fit for the anatomist, that's all. I'm wastin' away, sir, actually wastin' away for want of food. Feel my ribs an' you'll see."

I put my hand under his shirt and felt. The skin was stretched like parchment over the bones, and the sensation produced was for all the world like running one's hand over a washboard.

"Seven years o' bliss I 'ad," he said. "A good missus and three bonnie lassies. But they all died. Scarlet fever took the girls inside a fortnight."

"After this, sir," said the Carter, indicating the spread, and desiring to turn the conversation into more cheerful channels; "after this, I wouldn't be able to eat a workhouse breakfast in the morning."

"Nor I," agreed the Carpenter, and they fell to discussing stomach delights and the fine dishes their respective wives had cooked in the old days.

"I've gone three days and never broke my fast," said the Carter.

"And I, five," his companion added, turning gloomy with the memory of it. "Five days once, with nothing on my stomach but a bit of orange peel, an' outraged nature wouldn't stand it, sir, an' I near died. Sometimes, walkin' the streets at night, I've been that desperate I've made up my mind to win the horse or lose the saddle. You know what I mean sir—to commit some big robbery. But when mornin' come, there was I, too weak from 'unger an' cold to 'arm a mouse."

As their poor vitals warmed to the food, they began to expand and wax boastful, and to talk politics. I can only say that they talked politics as well as the average middle-class man, and a great deal better than some of the middle-class men I have heard. What surprised me was the hold they had on the world, its geography and peoples, and on recent and contemporaneous history. As I say, they were not fools, these two men. They were merely old, and their children had undutifully failed to grow up and give them a place by the fire.

One last incident, as I bade them good-by on the corner, happy with a couple of shillings in their pockets and the certain prospect of a bed for the night. Lighting a cigarette, I was about to throw away the burning match when the Carter reached for it. I proffered him the box, but he said, "Never mind, won't waste it, sir." And while he lighted the cigarette I had given him, the Carpenter hurried with the filling of his pipe in order to have a go at the same match.

"It's wrong to waste," said he.

"Yes," I said, but I was thinking of the washboard ribs over which I had run my hand.

Discussion Questions

1. Who do you think are meant by the "dear, soft people" London addresses directly in this selection? Would you include yourself in that audience?

2. Why does London refer to the two homeless men by their occupations alone? What is the effect of his doing that?

3. Why does London call the carter and the carpenter's revolutionary politics "rot"? Does he approve of the existing social order? What is it about their political conversation that he dislikes?

4. Compare London's techniques of describing people different from himself to those of Gay Talese in "Punks and Pushers." Which writer tends to identify himself more closely with the men he is writing about? How does each of their approaches differ from George Orwell's in "Shooting an Elephant"?

5. Why does London wait so long to be charitable? Why does he call charity "vicious"? He says that his act of charity changed the attitude of the two men toward him, but did it affect his attitude toward them?

6. We occasionally find ourselves in the company of people less fortunate than ourselves. Think of an episode in your life when this has happened and write about the event from the perspective of having read London's account of such a confrontation. Direct your essay toward a consideration of what charity means to you.

NORMAN MAILER

Born in New Jersey in 1923, Norman Mailer grew up in Brooklyn and graduated from Harvard with a degree in engineering. He served with the infantry in the Phillipines during World War II and afterwards drew on the experience for his first novel, The Naked and the Dead *(1948). After two more novels,* Barbary Shore *(1951) and* The Deer Park *(1955), Mailer began a newspaper column with* The Village Voice *in 1956 and since then, with the exception of the novels* An American Dream *(1965),* Why Are We in Vietnam? *(1967), and* Ancient Evening *(1983), has concentrated on essays and literary journalism. He has recorded his views on nearly every social, cultural, and political change in America since the mid-1950's in such books and collections as* The White Negro *(1958),* Advertisements for Myself *(1959),* The Armies of the Night *(1968),* Miami and the Siege of Chicago *(1968),* Of a Fire on the Moon *(1970),* Existential Errands *(1972), and* The Prisoner of Sex *(1972).*

The following selection is the opening passage of Marilyn *(1973), Mailer's long biographical essay on the movie star Marilyn Monroe.*

Marilyn Monroe

So we think of Marilyn who was every man's love affair with America, Marilyn Monroe who was blonde and beautiful and had a sweet little rinky-dink of a voice and all the cleanliness of all the clean American backyards. She was our angel, the sweet angel of sex, and the sugar of sex came up from her like a resonance of sound in the clearest grain of a violin. Across five continents the men who knew the most about love would covet her, and the classical pimples of the adolescent working his first gas pump would also pump for her, since Marilyn was deliverance, a very Stradivarius of sex, so gorgeous, forgiving, humorous, compliant and tender that even the most mediocre musician would relax his lack of art in the dissolving magic of her violin. "Divine love always has met and always will meet every human need," was the sentiment she offered from the works of Mary Baker Eddy as "my prayer for you always" (to the man who may have been her first illicit lover), and if we change *love* to *sex*, we have the subtext in the promise. "Marilyn Monroe's sex," said the smile of the young star, "will meet every human need." She gave the feeling that if you made love to her, why then how could you not move more easily into sweets and the purchase of the full promise of future sweets, move into tender heavens where your flesh would be restored. She would ask no price. She was not the dark contract of those passionate brunette depths that speak of blood, vows taken for life, and the furies of vengeance if you are untrue to the depth of passion, no, Marilyn suggested sex might be difficult and dangerous with others, but ice cream with her. If your taste combined with her taste, how nice, how sweet would be that tender dream of flesh there to share.

In her early career, in the time of *Asphalt Jungle* when the sexual immanence of her face came up on the screen like a sweet peach bursting before one's eyes, she looked then like a new love ready and waiting between the sheets in the unexpected clean breath of a rare sexy morning, looked like she'd stepped fully clothed out of a chocolate box for Valentine's Day, so desirable as to fulfill each of the letters in that favorite word of the publicity flack, *curvaceous,* so curvaceous and yet without menace as to turn one's fingertips into ten happy prowlers. Sex was, yes, ice cream to her. "Take me," said her smile. "I'm easy. I'm happy. I'm an angel of sex, you bet."

What a jolt to the dream life of the nation that the angel died of an overdose. Whether calculated suicide by barbiturates or accidental suicide by losing count of how many barbiturates she had already taken, or an end even more sinister, no one was able to say. Her death was covered over with ambiguity even as Hemingway's was exploded into horror, and as the deaths and spiritual disasters of the decade of the Sixties came one by one to American Kings and Queens, as Jack Kennedy was killed, and Bobby, and Martin Luther King, as Jackie Kennedy married Aristotle Onassis and Teddy Kennedy went off the bridge at Chappaquiddick, so the decade that began with Hemingway as the monarch of American arts ended with Andy Warhol as its regent, and the ghost of Marilyn's death gave a lavender edge to that dramatic American design of the Sixties which seemed in retrospect to have done nothing so much as to bring Richard Nixon to the threshold of imperial power. "Romance is a nonsense bet," said the jolt in the electric shock, and so began that long decade of the Sixties which ended with televison living like an inchworm on the aesthetic gut of the drug-deadened American belly.

In what a light does that leave the last angel of the cinema! She was never for TV. She preferred a theatre and those hundreds of bodies in the dark, those wandering lights on the screen when the luminous life of her face grew ten feet tall. It was possible she knew better than anyone that she was the last of the myths to thrive in the long evening of the American dream—she had been born, after all, in the year Valentino died, and his footprints in the forecourt at Grauman's Chinese Theatre were the only ones that fit her feet. She was one of the last of cinema's aristocrats and may not have wanted to be examined, then *ingested,* in the neighborly reductive dimensions of America's living room. No, she belonged to the occult church of the film, and the last covens of Hollywood. She might be as modest in her voice and as soft in her flesh as the girl next door, but she was nonetheless larger than life up on the screen. Even down in the Eisenhower shank of the early Fifties she was already promising that a time was coming when sex would be easy and sweet, democratic provender for all. Her stomach, untrammeled by girdles or sheaths, popped forward in a full woman's belly, inelegant as hell, an avowal of a womb fairly salivating in seed—that belly which was never to have a child—and her breasts popped buds and burgeons of flesh over many a questing sweating moviegoer's face. She was a cornucopia. She excited dreams of honey for the horn.

Yet she was more. She was a presence. She was ambiguous. She was the angel of sex, and the angel was in her detachment. For she was separated from what she offered. "None but Marilyn Monroe," wrote Diana Trilling,

> could suggest such a purity of sexual delight. The boldness with which she could parade herself and yet never be gross, her sexual flamboyance and bravado which yet breathed an air of mystery and even reticence, her voice which carried such ripe overtones of erotic excitement and yet was the voice of a shy child—these complications were integral to her gift. And they described a young woman trapped in some never-never land of unawareness.

Or is it that behind the gift is the tender wistful hint of another mood? For she also seems to say, "When an absurd presence is perfect, some little god must have made it." At its best, the echo of her small and perfect creation reached to the horizon of our mind. We hear her speak in that tiny tinkly voice so much like a little dinner bell, and it tolled when she was dead across all that decade of the Sixties she had helped to create, across its promise, its excitement, its ghosts and its center of tragedy.

Since she was also a movie star of the most stubborn secretiveness and flamboyant candor, most conflicting arrogance and on-rushing inferiority; great populist of philosophers—she loved the working man—and most tyrannical of mates, a queen of a castrator who was ready to weep for a dying minnow; a lover of books who did not read, and a proud, inviolate artist who could haunch over to publicity when the heat was upon her faster than a whore could lust over a hot buck; a female spurt of wit and sensitive energy who could hang like a sloth for days in a muddy-mooded coma; a child-girl, yet an actress to loose a riot by dropping her glove at a premiere; a fountain of charm and a dreary bore; an ambulating cyclone of beauty when dressed to show, a dank hunched-up drab at her worst—with a bad smell!—a giant and an emotional pygmy; a lover of life and a cowardly hyena of death who drenched herself in chemical stupors; a sexual oven whose fire may rarely have been lit—she would go to bed with her brassiere on—she was certainly more and less than the silver witch of us all. In her ambition, so Faustian, and in her ignorance of culture's dimensions, in her liberation and her tyrannical desires, her noble democratic longings intimately contradicted by the widening pool of her narcissism (where every friend and slave must bathe), we can see the magnified mirror of ourselves, our exaggerated and now all but defeated generation, yes, she ran a reconnaissance through the Fifties, and left a message for us in her death, "Baby go boom." Now she is the ghost of the Sixties....

Discussion Questions

1. Mailer calls Marilyn Monroe a "sweet angel of sex." What conflicting elements do you find in this description? How do those conflicting elements help shape the course of his essay?

2. Mailer claims that Marilyn resisted television and wished to be "larger than life" upon the movie screen. In what ways does Mailer make her larger than life in his writing? Point to some of Mailer's terms and images that have an enlarging effect. "Angel," for example, is only one of several religious references in the essay; find others.

3. Read Wyndham Lewis's essay on the success of another classic movie star, Charlie Chaplin. How does each writer establish his subject's popular appeal? Does Lewis also try to make his subject "larger than life"? Which writer seems more objective? More logical? Which gives you a clearer sense of the reasons behind his subject's enormous popularity?

4. How does Mailer's account of Marilyn's death conform to his description of her personality? Write an essay that analyzes Mailer's techniques of biography.

WILLIAM MANCHESTER

The historian, biographer, and author of the highly controversial book on John F. Kennedy, The Death of a President, *William Manchester was born in Attleboro, Massachusetts, in 1922. His studies at the University of Massachusetts were interrupted by World War II, and he enlisted in the United States Marines, serving throughout the Pacific campaign and alone surviving among the men in his unit. He has described the war in the Pacific historically in his biography of Douglas MacArthur,* American Caesar, *and personally in his autobiography,* Goodbye, Darkness, *in which the following selection appears.*

How I Slew My First Man

Our Boeing 747 has been fleeing westward from darkened California, racing across the Pacific toward the sun, the incandescent eye of God, but slowly, three hours later than West Coast time, twilight gathers outside, veil upon lilac veil. This is what the French call *l'heure bleue*. Aquamarine becomes turquoise; turquoise, lavender; lavender, violet; violet, magenta; magenta, mulberry. Seen through my cocktail glass, the light fades as it deepens; it becomes opalescent, crepuscular. In the last waning moments of the day I can still feel the failing sunlight on my cheek, taste it in my martini. The plane rises before a spindrift; the darkening sky, broken by clouds like combers, boils and foams overhead. Then the whole weight of evening falls upon me. Old memories, phantoms repressed for more than a third of a century, begin to stir. I can almost hear the rhythm of surf on distant snow-white beaches. I have another drink, and then I learn, for the hundredth time, that you can't drown your troubles, not the real ones, because if they are real they can swim. One of my worst recollections, one I had buried in my deepest memory bank long ago, comes back with a clarity so blinding that I surge forward against the seat belt, appalled by it, filled with remorse and shame.

I am remembering the first man I slew.

There was this little hut on Motobu, perched atop a low rise overlooking the East China Sea. It was a fisherman's shack, so ordinary that scarcely anyone had noticed it. I did. I noticed it because I happened to glance in that direction at a crucial moment. The hut lay between us and B Company of the First Battalion. Word had been passed that that company had been taking sniper losses. They thought the sharpshooters were in spider holes, Jap foxholes, but as I was looking that way, I saw two B Company guys drop, and from the angle of their fall I knew the firing had to come from a window on the other side of that hut. At the same time, I saw that the shack had windows on *our* side, which meant that once the rifleman had B Company pinned down, he could turn toward us. I was dug in with Barney Cobb. We had excellent defilade ahead and the Twenty-second Marines on our right flank, but we had no protection from the hut, and our hole wasn't deep enough to let us sweat it out. Every time I glanced at that shack I was looking into the empty eye socket of death.

The situation was as clear as the deduction from a euclidean theorem, but my psychological state was extremely complicated. S. L. A. Marshall once observed that the typical fighting man is often at a disadvantage because he "comes from a civilization in which aggression, connected with the taking of life, is prohibited and unacceptable." This was especially true of me, whose horror of violence had been so deep-seated that I had been unable to trade punches with other boys. But since then life had become cheaper to me. "Two thousand pounds of education drops to a ten rupee," wrote Kipling of the fighting on India's North-West Frontier. My plight was not unlike that described by the famous sign in the Paris zoo: "Warning: This animal is vicious; when attacked, it defends itself." I was responding to a basic biological principle first set down by the German zoologist Heini Hediger in his *Skizzen zu einer Tierpsychologie um und im Zirkus*. Hediger noted that beyond a certain distance, which varies from one species to another, an animal will retreat, while within it, it will attack. He called these "flight distance" and "critical distance." Obviously I was within critical distance of the hut. It was time to bar the bridge, stick a finger in the dike—to do *something*. I could be quick or I could be dead.

My choices were limited. Moving inland was inconvenient; the enemy was there, too. I was on the extreme left of our perimeter, and somehow I couldn't quite see myself turning my back on the shack and fleeing through the rest of the battalion screaming, like Chicken Little, "A Jap's after me! A Jap's after me!" Of course, I could order one of my people to take out the sniper; but I played the role of the NCO in Kipling's poem who always looks after the black sheep, and if I ducked this one, they would never let me forget it. Also, I couldn't be certain that the order would be obeyed. I was a gangling, long-boned youth, wholly lacking in what the Marine Corps called "command presence"—charisma—and I led nineteen highly insubordinate men. I couldn't even be sure that Barney would budge. It is war, not politics, that makes strange bedfellows. The fact that I outranked Barney was in itself odd. He was a great blond buffalo of a youth, with stubby hair, a scraggly mustache, and a powerful build. Before the war he had swum breaststroke for Brown, and had left me far behind in two intercollegiate meets. I valued his respect for me, which cowardice would have wiped out. So I asked him if he had any grenades. He didn't; nobody in the section did. The grenade shortage was chronic. That sterile exchange bought a little time, but every moment lengthened my odds against the Nip sharpshooter. Finally, sweating with the greatest fear I had known till then, I took a deep breath, told Barney, "Cover me," and took off for the hut at Mach 2 speed in little bounds, zigzagging and dropping every dozen steps, remembering to roll as I dropped. I was nearly there, arrowing in, when I realized that I wasn't wearing my steel helmet. The only cover on my head was my cloth Raider cap. That was a violation of orders. I was out of uniform. I remember hoping, idiotically, that nobody would report me.

Utterly terrified, I jolted to a stop on the threshold of the shack. I could feel a twitching in my jaw, coming and going like a winky light signaling some disorder. Various valves were opening and closing in my stomach. My mouth was dry, my legs quaking, and my eyes out of focus. Then my vision cleared. I unlocked the safety of my Colt, kicked the door with my right foot, and leapt inside. My horror returned. I was in an empty room. There was another door opposite the one I had unhinged, which meant another room, which meant the sniper was in there—and had been warned by the crash of the outer door. But I had committed myself. Flight was impossible now. So I smashed into the other room and saw him as a blur to my right. I wheeled that way, crouched, gripped the pistol butt in both hands, and fired.

Not only was he the first Japanese soldier I had ever shot at; he was the only one I had seen at close quarters. He was a robin-fat, moon-faced, roly-poly little man with his thick, stubby, trunklike legs sheathed in faded khaki puttees and the rest of him squeezed into a uniform that was much too tight. Unlike me, he was wearing a tin hat, dressed to kill. But I was quite safe from him. His Arisaka rifle was strapped on in a sniper's harness, and though he had heard me, and was trying to turn toward me, the harness sling had him trapped. He couldn't disentangle himself from it. His eyes were rolling in panic. Realizing that he couldn't extricate his arms and defend himself, he was backing toward a corner with a curious, crablike motion.

My first shot had missed him, embedding itself in the straw wall, but the second caught him dead-on in the femoral artery. His left thigh blossomed, swiftly turning to mush. A wave of blood gushed from the wound; then another boiled out, sheeting across his legs, pooling on the earthen floor. Mutely he looked down at it. He dipped a hand in it and listlessly smeared his cheek red. His shoulders gave a little spasmodic jerk, as though someone had whacked him on the back; then he emitted a tremendous, raspy fart, slumped down, and died. I kept firing, wasting government property.

Already I thought I detected the dark brown effluvium of the freshly slain, a sour, pervasive emanation which is different from anything else you have known. Yet seeing death at that range, like smelling it, requires no previous experience. You instantly recognize the spastic convulsion and the rattle, which in his case was not loud, but deprecating and conciliatory, like the manners of civilian Japanese. He continued to sink until he reached the earthen floor. His eyes glazed over. Almost immediately a fly landed on his left eyeball. It was joined by another. I don't know how long I stood there staring. I knew from previous combat what lay ahead for the corpse. It would swell, then bloat, bursting out of the uniform. Then the face would turn from yellow to red, to purple, to green, to black. My father's account of the Argonne had omitted certain vital facts. A feeling of disgust and self-hatred clotted darkly in my throat, gagging me.

Jerking my head to shake off the stupor, I slipped a new, fully loaded magazine into the butt of my .45. Then I began to tremble, and next to shake, all over. I sobbed, in a voice still grainy with fear: "I'm sorry." Then I threw up all over myself. I recognized the half-digested C-ration beans dribbling down my front, smelled the vomit above the cordite. At the same time I noticed another odor; I had urinated in my skivvies. I pondered fleetingly why our excretions become so loathsome the instant they leave the body. Then Barney burst in on me, his carbine at the ready, his face gray, as though he, not I, had just become a partner in the firm of death. He ran over to the Nip's body, grabbed its stacking swivel—its neck—and let go, satisfied that it was a cadaver. I marveled at his courage; I couldn't have taken a step toward that corner. He approached me and then backed away, in revulsion, from my foul stench. He said: "Slim, you stink." I said nothing. I knew I had become a thing of tears and twitchings and dirtied pants. I remember wondering dumbly: *Is this what they mean by "conspicuous gallantry"?*

Discussion Questions

1. What is it about the atmosphere of the sunset that Manchester implies may have helped to evoke his memory? What would have been gained or lost by making the implication more explicit?

2. Manchester uses the ends of sentences and paragraphs in curious ways to modify his objective descriptions. What are the directions and effects of those modifications?

3. Compare the ways in which audiences are invited to respond to the idea of "territoriality" in Manchester's essay to those in that by René Dubos.

4. Describe a memory of a situation (for example, an accident or near accident) that involved a serious displacement of your ordinary self.

MARY MCCARTHY

Mary McCarthy was born in 1912 and orphaned at the age of six. After a convent education, she went to Vassar, where she studied English literature and helped to found a literary magazine. She began to work after graduation as a professional book and play reviewer in New York. She soon came to be known as a devastating and witty opponent of what she did not like. Her second husband, Edmund Wilson, the literary critic, encouraged her to write novels, among which her most famous was to be The Group (1963). She recently completed editing the posthumous papers of her close friend, the philosopher Hannah Arendt. The selection that follows is taken from her autobiography, Memoirs of a Catholic Girlhood (1957).

Catholic Education

If you are born and brought up a Catholic, you have absorbed a good deal of world history and the history of ideas before you are twelve, and it is like learning a language early; the effect is indelible. Nobody else in America, no other group, is in this fortunate position. Granted that Catholic history is biased, it is not dry or dead; its virtue for the student, indeed, is that it has been made to come alive by the violent partisanship which inflames it. This partisanship, moreover, acts as a magnet to attract stray pieces of information not ordinarily taught in American schools. While children in public schools were studying American history, we in the convent in the eighth grade were studying English history down to the time of Lord Palmerston; the reason for this was, of course, that English history, up to Henry VIII, was Catholic history, and, after that, with one or two interludes, it became anti-Catholic history. Naturally, we were taught to sympathize with Bloody Mary (never called that in the convent), Mary Queen of Scots, Philip of Spain, the martyr Jesuits, Charles I (married to a Catholic princess), James II (married first to a Protestant and then to Mary of Modena), the Old Pretender, Bonnie Prince Charlie; interest petered out with Peel and Catholic Emancipation. To me, it does not matter that this history was one-sided (this can always be remedied later); the important thing is to have learned the battles and the sovereigns, their consorts, mistresses, and prime ministers, to know the past of a foreign country in such detail that it becomes one's own. Had I stayed in the convent, we would have gone on to French history, and today I would know the list of French kings and their wives and ministers, because French history, up to the Revolution, was Catholic history, and Charlemagne, Joan of Arc, and Napoleon were all prominent Catholics.

Nor is it only a matter of knowing more, at an earlier age, so that it becomes a part of oneself; it is also a matter of feeling. To care for the quarrels of the past, to identify oneself passionately with a cause that became, politically speaking, a losing cause with the birth of the modern world, is to experience a kind of straining against reality, a rebellious nonconformity that, again, is rare in America, where children are instructed in the virtues of the system they live under, as though history had achieved a happy ending in American civics.

So much for the practical side. But it might be pointed out that to an American educator, my Catholic training would appear to have no utility whatever. What is the good, he would say, of hearing the drone of a dead language every day or of knowing that Saint Ursula, a Breton princess, was martyred at Cologne, together with ten thousand virgins? I have shown that such things proved to have a certain usefulness in later life—a usefulness that was not, however, intended at the time, for we did not study the lives of the saints in order to look at Italian painting or recite our catechism in order to read John Donne. Such an idea would be atrocious blasphemy. We learned those things for the glory of God, and the rest, so to speak, was added to us. Nor would it have made us study any harder if we had been assured that what we were learning was going to come in handy in later life, any more than children study arithmetic harder if they are promised it will help them later on in business. Nothing is more boring to a child than the principle of utility. The final usefulness of my Catholic training was to teach me, together with much that proved to be practical, a conception of something prior to and beyond utility ("Consider the lilies of the field; they toil not, neither do they spin"), an idea of sheer wastefulness that is always shocking to non-Catholics, who cannot bear, for example, the contrast between the rich churches and the poor people of southern Europe. Those churches, agreed, are a folly; so is the life of a dirty anchorite or of a cloistered, non-teaching nun—unprofitable for society and bad for the person concerned. But I prefer to think of them that way than to imagine them as an investment, shares bought in future salvation. I never really liked the doctrine of Indulgences—the notion that you could say five Hail Marys and knock off a year in Purgatory. This seemed to me to belong to my grandmother McCarthy's kind of Catholicism. What I liked in the Church, and what I recall with gratitude, was the sense of mystery and wonder, ashes put on one's forehead on Ash Wednesday, the blessing of the throat with candles on St. Blaise's Day, the purple palls put on the statues after Passion Sunday, which meant they were hiding their faces in mourning because Christ was going to be crucified, the ringing of the bell at the Sanctus, the burst of lilies at Easter—all this ritual, seeming slightly strange and having no purpose (except the throat-blessing), beyond commemoration of a Person Who had died a long time ago. In these exalted moments of altruism the soul was fired with reverence.

Discussion Questions

1. How would differing lists of examples from political and church history have differently affected the points that Mary McCarthy uses her lists to support?
2. Where and how does Mary McCarthy make her transitions and what effects for her argument do her transitions create?
3. Compare the values and assumptions about education expressed by Mary McCarthy to those of Jacques Barzun and Randall Jarrell.
4. Make an assessment of comparable length of your own education and what it may have taught you "prior to and beyond utility."

Marshall McLuhan

Herbert Marshall McLuhan (1911–1980) was educated at the University of Manitoba and received his doctorate from Cambridge in 1942. He taught at Fordham University and was Director of the Centre for Culture and Technology at the University of Toronto. In his book The Mechanical Bride *(1951), McLuhan undertook one of the earliest cultural analyses of how advertising works.* Understanding Media: The Extensions of Man *(1964), a wide-ranging study of the cultural effects of technology on our conventional notions of language, remains a milestone of twentieth-century thought.*

Besides literary essays and criticism, McLuhan also wrote The Gutenberg Galaxy: The Making of Typographic Man *(1967),* Culture Is Our Business *(1970),* The Medium Is the Massage: An Inventory of Effects *(1972), and* From Cliché to Archetype *(1972). "Classrooms Without Walls" (an allusion to Malraux's "Museum Without Walls") first appeared in a collection of essays edited by McLuhan,* Explorations in Communication *(1960).*

Classroom Without Walls

It's natural today to speak of "audio-visual aids" to teaching, for we still think of the book as norm, of other media as incidental. We also think of the new media (press, radio, TV) as *mass media* and think of the book as an individualistic form—individualistic because it isolated the reader in silence and helped create the Western "I." Yet it was the first product of mass production.

With it everybody could have the same books. It was impossible in medieval times for different students, different institutions, to have copies of the same book. Manuscripts, commentaries, were dictated. Students memorized. Instruction was almost entirely oral, done in groups. Solitary study was reserved for the advanced scholar. The first printed books were "visual aids" to oral instruction.

Before the printing press, the young learned by listening, watching, doing. So, until recently, our own rural children learned the language and skills of their elders. Learning took place outside the classroom. Only those aiming at professional careers went to school at all. Today in our cities, most learning occurs outside the classroom. The sheer quantity of information conveyed by press-magazines-film-TV-radio far exceeds the quantity of information conveyed by school instruction and texts. This challenge has destroyed the monopoly of the book as a teaching aid and cracked the very walls of the classroom so suddenly that we're confused, baffled.

In this violently upsetting social situation, many teachers naturally view the offerings of the new media as entertainment, rather than education. But this carries no conviction to the student. Find a classic that wasn't first regarded as light entertainment. Nearly all vernacular works were so regarded until the 19th century.

Many movies are obviously handled with a degree of insight and maturity at least equal to the level permitted in today's textbooks. Olivier's *Henry V* and *Richard III* assemble a wealth of scholarly and artistic skill, which reveals Shakespeare at a very high level, yet in a way easy for the young to enjoy.

The movie is to dramatic representation what the book was to the manuscript. It makes available to many and at many times and places what otherwise would be restricted to a few at few times and places. The movie, like the book, is a ditto device. TV shows to 50,000,000 simultaneously. Some feel that the value of experiencing a book is diminished by being extended to many minds. This notion is always implicit in the phrases "mass media," "mass entertainment"—useless phrases obscuring the fact that English itself is a mass medium.

Today we're beginning to realize that the new media aren't just mechanical gimmicks for creating worlds of illusion, but new languages with new and unique powers of expression. Historically, the resources of English have been shaped and expressed in constantly new and changing ways. The printing press changed not only the quantity of writing but also the character of language and the relations between author and public. Radio, film, TV pushed written English toward the spontaneous shifts and freedom of the spoken idiom. They aided us in the recovery of intense awareness of facial language and bodily gesture. If these "mass media" should serve only to weaken or corrupt previously achieved levels of verbal and pictorial culture, it won't be because there's anything inherently wrong with them. It will be because we've failed to master them as new languages in time to assimilate them to our total cultural heritage.

These new developments, under quiet analytic survey, point to a basic strategy of culture for the classroom. When the printed book first appeared, it threatened the oral procedures of teaching and created the classroom as we now know it. Instead of making his own text, his own grammar, the student started out with these tools. He could study not one but several languages. Today these new media threaten, instead of merely reinforce, the procedures of this traditional classroom. It's customary to answer this threat with denunciations of the unfortunate character and effect of movies and TV, just as the comic book was feared and scorned and rejected from the classroom. Its good and bad features in form and content, when carefully set beside other kinds of art and narrative, could have become a major asset to the teacher.

Where student interest is already focused is the natural point at which to be in the elucidation of other problems and interests.

The educational task is not only to provide basic tools of perception but also to develop judgment and discrimination with ordinary social experience.

Few students ever acquire skill in analysis of newspapers. Fewer have any ability to discuss a movie intelligently. To be articulate and discriminating about ordinary affairs and information is the mark of an educated man. It's misleading to suppose there's any basic difference between education and entertainment. This distinction merely relieves people of the responsibility of looking into the matter. It's like setting up a distinction between didactic and lyric poetry on the ground that one teaches, the other pleases. However, it's always been true that whatever pleases teaches more effectively.

Discussion Questions

1. Why does McLuhan distrust the phrases "mass media" and "mass entertainment"?

2. How do you think books helped "create the Western 'I'?" What is the Western "I"? Does McLuhan seem to favor it? How does he use the first person singular?

3. What kinds of educational material would McLuhan like to see included in a curriculum? Do you think his system of education would be an improvement? Why or why not? How does his system of education compare to Jacques Barzun's and Edmund Wilson's?

4. McLuhan claims that "to be articulate and discriminating about ordinary affairs and information is the mark of an educated man," but he stops short of informing us how one learns to be articulate and discriminating. Does one acquire the "ability to discuss a movie intelligently" by simply watching plenty of movies? What else is required in education besides educational material? How does one "develop judgment and discrimination"? Write an essay in which you discuss the marks of an educated person.

JOHN MCPHEE

John McPhee was born in Princeton, New Jersey, in 1931 and educated at Deerfield Academy, Princeton University, and Cambridge University. A staff writer for The New Yorker *magazine, McPhee also teaches a writing course—"The Literature of Fact"—at Princeton. His many books include* A Sense of Where You Are *(1965),* The Headmaster *(1966),* The Pine Barrens *(1968),* A Roomful of Hovings *(1969),* Oranges *(1967),* Levels of the Game *(1970),* The Crofter and the Laird *(1969),* The Deltoid Pumpkin Seed *(1973),* The Survival of the Bark Canoe *(1975), and* Coming into the Country *(1977).*

Two of his books were nominated for National Book Awards in the category of Science: Encounters with the Archdruid *(1972) and* The Curve of Binding Energy *(1974). In 1977, McPhee received an award from the American Academy and Institute of Arts and Letters. Recently, McPhee has written two books on geology:* Basin and Range *(1981) and* In Suspect Terrain *(1982).*

The following 1972 essay depicting the pre-gambling environment of Atlantic City is reprinted from McPhee's collection, Pieces of the Frame *(1975).*

The Search for Marvin Gardens

Go. I roll the dice—a six and a two. Through the air I move my token, the flatiron, to Vermont Avenue, where dog packs range.

•

The dogs are moving (some are limping) through ruins, rubble, fire damage, open garbage. Doorways are gone. Lath is visible in the crumbling walls of the buildings. The street sparkles with shattered glass. I have never seen, anywhere, so many broken windows. A sign—"Slow, Children at Play"—has been bent backward by an automobile. At the lighthouse, the dogs turn up Pacific and disappear. George Meade, Army engineer, built the lighthouse—brick upon brick, six hundred thousand bricks, to reach up high enough to throw a beam twenty miles over the sea. Meade, seven years later, saved the Union at Gettysburg.

•

I buy Vermont Avenue for $100. My opponent is a tall, shadowy figure, across from me, but I know him well, and I know his game like a favorite tune. If he can, he will always go for the quick kill. And when it is foolish to go for the quick kill he will be foolish. On the whole, though, he is a master assessor of percentages. It is a mistake to underestimate him. His eleven carries his top hat to St. Charles Place, which he buys for $140.

•

The sidewalks of St. Charles Place have been cracked to shards by through-growing weeds. There are no buildings. Mansions, hotels once stood here. A few street lamps now drop cones of light on broken glass and vacant space behind a chain-link fence that some great machine has in places bent to the ground.

Five plane trees—in full summer leaf, flecking the light—are all that live on St. Charles Place.

•

Block upon block gradually, we are cancelling each other out—in the blues, the lavenders, the oranges, the greens. My opponent follows a plan of his own devising. I use the Hornblower & Weeks opening and the Zuricher defense. The first game draws tight, will soon finish. In 1971, a group of people in Racine, Wisconsin, played for seven hundred and sixty-eight hours. A game begun a month later in Danville, California, lasted eight hundred and twenty hours. These are official records, and they stun us. We have been playing for eight minutes. It amazes us that Monopoly is thought of as a long game. It is possible to play to a complete, absolute, and final conclusion in less than fifteen minutes, all within the rules as written. My opponent and I have done so thousands of times. No wonder we are sitting across from each other now in this best-of-seven series for the international singles championship of the world.

•

On Illinois Avenue, three men lean out from second-story windows. A girl is coming down the street. She wears dungarees and a bright-red shirt, has ample breasts and a Hadendoan Afro, a black halo, two feet in diameter. Ice rattles in the glasses in the hands of the men.

"Hey, sister!"

"Come on up!"

She looks up, looks from one to another to the other, looks them flat in the eye.

"What for?" she says, and she walks on.

•

I buy Illinois for $240. It solidifies my chances, for I already own Kentucky and Indiana. My opponent pales. If he had landed first on Illinois, the game would have been over then and there, for he has houses built on Boardwalk and Park Place, we share the railroads equally, and we have cancelled each other everywhere else. We never trade.

•

In 1852, R. B. Osborne, an immigrant Englishman, civil engineer, surveyed the route of a railroad line that would run from Camden to Absecon Island, in New Jersey, traversing the state from the Delaware River to the barrier beaches of the sea. He then sketched in the plan of a "bathing village" that would surround the eastern terminus of the line. His pen flew glibly, framing and naming spacious avenues parallel to the shore—Mediterranean, Baltic, Oriental, Ventnor—and narrower transsecting avenues: North Carolina, Pennsylvania, Vermont, Connecticut, States, Virginia, Tennessee, New York, Kentucky, Indiana, Illinois. The place as a whole had no name, so when he had completed the plan Osborne wrote in large letters over the ocean, "Atlantic City." No one ever challenged the name, or the names of Osborne's streets. Monopoly was invented in the early nineteen-thirties by Charles B. Darrow, but Darrow was only transliterating what Osborne had created. The railroads, crucial to any player, were the making of Atlantic City. After the rails were down, houses and hotels burgeoned from Mediterranean and Baltic to New York and Kentucky. Properties—building lots—sold for as little as six dollars apiece and as much as a thousand dollars. The original investors in the railroads and the real estate called themselves the Camden & Atlantic Land Company. Reverently, I repeat their names: Dwight Bell, William Coffin, John DaCosta, Daniel Deal, William Fleming, Andrew Hay, Joseph Proter, Jonathan Pitney, Samuel Richards—founders, fathers, forerunners, archetypical masters of the quick kill.

•

My opponent and I are now in a deep situation of classical Monopoly. The torsion is almost perfect—Boardwalk and Park Place versus the brilliant reds. His cash position is weak, though, and if I escape him now he may fade. I land on Luxury Tax, contiguous to but in sanctuary from his power. I have four houses on Indiana. He lands there. He concedes.

•

Indiana Avenue was the address of the Brighton Hotel, gone now. The Brighton was exclusive—a word that no longer has retail value in the city. If you arrived by automobile and tried to register at the Brighton, you were sent away. Brighton-class people came in private railroad cars. Brighton-class people had other private railroad cars for their horses—dawn rides on the firm sand at water's edge, skirts flying. Colonel Anthony J. Drexel Biddle—the sort of name that would constrict throats in Philadelphia—lived, much of the year, in the Brighton.

•

Colonel Sanders' fried chicken is on Kentucky Avenue. So is Clifton's Club Harlem, with the Sepia Revue and the Sepia Follies, featuring the Honey Bees, the Fashions, and the Lords.

•

My opponent and I, many years ago, played 2,428 games of Monopoly in a single season. He was then a recent graduate of the Harvard Law School, and he was working for a downtown firm, looking up law. Two people we knew—one from Chase Manhattan, the other from Morgan, Stanley—tried to get into the game, but after a few rounds we found that they were not in the conversation and we sent them home. Monopoly should always be *mano a mano* anyway. My opponent won 1,199 games, and so did I. Thirty were ties. He was called into the Army, and we stopped just there. Now, in Game 2 of the series, I go immediately to jail, and again to jail while my opponent seines property. He is dumbfoundingly lucky. He wins in twelve minutes.

•

Visiting hours are daily, eleven to two; Sunday, eleven to one: evenings, six to nine. "NO MINORS, NO FOOD, Immediate Family Only Allowed in Jail." All this above a blue steel door in a blue cement wall in the windowless interior of the basement of the city hall. The desk sergeant sits opposite the door in the jail. In a cigar box in front of him are pills in every color, a banquet of fruit salad an inch and a half deep—leapers, co-pilots, footballs, truck drivers, peanuts, blue angels, yellow jackets, redbirds, rainbows. Near the desk are two soldiers, waiting to go through the blue door. They are about eighteen years old. One of them is trying hard to light a cigarette. His wrists are in steel cuffs. A military policeman waits, too. He is a year or so older than the soldiers, taller, studious in appearance, gentle, fat. On a bench against a wall sits a good-looking girl in slacks. The blue door rattles, swings heavily open. A turnkey stands in the doorway. "Don't you guys kill yourselves back there now," says the sergeant to the soldiers.

"One kid, he overdosed himself about ten and a half hours ago," says the M.P.

The M.P., the soldiers, the turnkey, and the girl on the bench are white. The sergeant is black. "If you take off the handcuffs, take off the belts," says the sergeant to the M.P. "I don't want them hanging themselves back there." The door shuts and its tumblers move. When it opens again, five minutes later, a young white man in sandals and dungarees and a blue polo shirt emerges. His hair is in a ponytail. He has no beard. He grins at the good-looking girl. She rises, joins him. The sergeant hands him a manila envelope. From it he removes his belt and a small notebook. He is out of jail, free. What did he do? He offended Atlantic City in some way. He spent a night in the jail. In the nineteen-thirties, men visiting Atlantic City went to jail, directly to jail, did not pass Go, for appearing in topless bathing suits on the beach. A city statute requiring all men to wear full-length bathing suits was not seriously challenged until 1937, and the first year in which a man could legally go bare-chested on the beach was 1940.

•

Game 3. After seventeen minutes, I am ready to begin construction on overpriced and sluggish Pacific, North Carolina, and Pennsylvania. Nothing else being open, opponent concedes.

•

The physical profile of streets perpendicular to the shore is something like a playground slide. It begins in the high skyline of Boardwalk hotels, plummets into warrens of "side-avenue" motels, crosses Pacific, slopes through church missions, convalescent homes, burlesque houses, rooming houses, and liquor stores, crosses Atlantic, and runs level through the bombed-out ghetto as far—Baltic, Mediterranean—as the eye can see. North Carolina Avenue, for example, is flanked at its beach end by the Chalfonte and the Haddon Hall (908 rooms, air-conditioned), where, according to one biographer, John Philip Sousa (1854—1932) first played when he was twenty-two, insisting, even then, that everyone call him by his entire name. Behind these big hotels, motels—Barbizon, Catalina—crouch. Between Pacific and Atlantic is an occasional house from 1910—wooden porch, wooden mullions, old yellow paint—and two churches, a package store, a strip show, a dealer in fruits and vegetables. Then, beyond Atlantic Avenue, North Carolina moves on into the vast ghetto, the bulk of the city, and it looks like Metz in 1919, Cologne in 1944. Nothing has actually exploded. It is not bomb damage. It is deep and complex decay. Roofs are off. Bricks are scattered in the street. People sit on porches, six deep, at nine on a Monday morning. When they go off to wait in unemployment lines, they wait sometimes two hours. Between Mediterranean and Baltic runs a chain-link fence, enclosing rubble. A patrol car sits idling by the curb. In the back seat is a German shepherd. A sign on the fence says, "Beware of Bad Dogs."

Mediterranean and Baltic are the principal avenues of the ghetto. Dogs are everywhere. A pack of seven passes me. Block after block, there are three-story brick row houses. Whole segments of them are abandoned, a thousand broken windows. Some parts are intact, occupied. A mattress lies in the street, soaking in a pool of water. Wet stuffing is coming out of the mattress. A postman is having a rye and a beer in the Plantation Bar at nine-fifteen in the morning. I ask him idly if he knows where Marvin Gardens is. He does not. "HOOKED AND NEED HELP? CONTACT N.A.R.C.O." "REVIVAL NOW GOING ON, CONDUCTED BY REVEREND H. HENDERSON OF TEXAS." These are signboards on Mediterranean and Baltic. The second one is upside down and leans against a boarded-up window of the Faith Temple Church of God in Christ. There is an old peeling poster on a warehouse wall showing a figure in an electric chair. "The Black Panther Manifesto" is the title of the poster, and its message is, or was, that "the fascists have already decided in advance to murder Chairman Bobby Seale in the electric chair." I pass an old woman who carries a bucket. She wears blue sneakers, worn through. Her feet spill out. She wears red socks, rolled at the knees. A white handkerchief, spread over her head, is knotted at the corners. Does she know where Marvin Gardens is? "I sure don't know," she says, setting down the bucket. "I sure don't know. I've heard of it somewhere, but I just can't say where." I walk on, through a block of shattered glass. The glass crunches underfoot like coarse sand. I remember when I first came here—a long train ride from Trenton, long ago, games of poker in the train—to play basketball against Atlantic City. We were half black, they were all black. We scored forty points, they scored eighty, or something like it. What I remember most is that they had glass backboards—glittering, pendent, expensive glass backboards, a rarity then in high schools, even in colleges, the only ones we played on all year.

    I turn on Pennsylvania, and start back toward the sea. The windows of the Hotel Astoria, on Pennsylvania near Baltic, are boarded up. A sheet of unpainted plywood is the door, and in it is a triangular peephole that now frames an eye. The plywood door opens. A man answers my question. Rooms there are six, seven, and ten dollars a week. I thank him for the information and move on, emerging from the ghetto at the Catholic Daughters of America Women's Guest House, between Atlantic and Pacific. Between Pacific and the Boardwalk are the blinking vacancy signs of the Aristocrat and Colton Manor motels. Pennsylvania terminates at the Sheraton-Seaside—thirty-two dollars a day, ocean corner. I take a walk on the Boardwalk and into the Holiday Inn (twenty-three stories). A guest is registering. "You reserved for Wednesday, and this is Monday," the clerk tells him. "But that's all right. We have *plenty* of rooms." The clerk is very young, female, and has soft brown hair that hangs below her waist. Her superior kicks her.

He is a middle-aged man with red spiderwebs in his face. He is jacketed and tied. He takes her aside. "Don't say 'plenty,'" he says. "Say 'You are fortunate, sir. We have rooms available.'"

The face of the young woman turns sour. "We have all the rooms you need," she says to the customer, and, to her superior, "How's that?"

•

Game 4. My opponent's luck has become abrasive. He has Boardwalk and Park Place, and has sealed the board.

•

Darrow was a plumber. He was, specifically, a radiator repairman who lived in Germantown, Pennsylvania. His first Monopoly board was a sheet of linoleum. On it he placed houses and hotels that he had carved from blocks of wood. The game he thus invented was brilliantly conceived, for it was an uncannily exact reflection of the business milieu at large. In its depth, range, and subtlety, in its luck-skill ratio, in its sense of infrastructure and socio-economic parameters, in its philosophical characteristics, it reached to the profundity of the financial community. It was as scientific as the stock market. It suggested the manner and means through which an underdeveloped world had been developed. It was chess at Wall Street level. "Advance token to the nearest Railroad and pay owner twice the rental to which he is otherwise entitled. If Railroad is unowned, you may buy it from the Bank. Get out of Jail, free. Advance token to nearest Utility. If unowned, you may buy it from the Bank. If owned, throw dice and pay owner a total ten times the amount thrown. You are assessed for street repairs: $40 per house, $115 per hotel. Pay poor tax of $15. Go to Jail. Go directly to Jail. Do not pass Go. Do not collect $200."

•

The turnkey opens the blue door. The turnkey is known to the inmates as Sidney K. Above his desk are ten closed-circuit TV screens—assorted viewpoints of the jail. There are three cellblocks—men, women, juvenile boys. Six days is the average stay. Showers twice a week. The steel doors and the equipment that operates them were made in San Antonio. The prisoners sleep on bunks of butcher block. There are no mattresses. There are three prisoners to a cell. In winter, it is cold in here. Prisoners burn newspapers to keep warm. Cell corners are black with smudge. The jail is three years old. The men's block echoes with chatter. The man in the cell nearest Sidney K. is pacing. His shirt is covered with broad stains of blood. The block for juvenile boys is, by contrast, utterly silent—empty corridor, empty cells. There is only one prisoner. He is small and black and appears to be thirteen. He says he is sixteen and that he has been alone in here for three days.

"Why are you here? What did you do?"

"I hit a jitney driver."

●

The series stands at three all. We have split the fifth and sixth games. We are scrambling for property. Around the board we fairly fly. We move so fast because we do our own banking and search our own deeds. My opponent grows tense.

●

Ventnor Avenue, a street of delicatessens and doctors' offices, is leafy with plane trees and hydrangeas, the city flower. Water Works is on the mainland. The water comes over in submarine pipes. Electric Company gets power from across the state, on the Delaware River, in Deepwater. States Avenue, now a wasteland like St. Charles, once had gardens running down the middle of the street, a horse-drawn trolley, private homes. States Avenue was as exclusive as the Brighton. Only an apartment house, a small motel, and the All Wars Memorial Building—monadnocks spaced widely apart—stand along States Avenue now. Pawnshops, convalescent homes, and the Paradise Soul Saving Station are on Virginia Avenue. The soul-saving station is pink, orange, and yellow. In the windows flanking the door of the Virginia Money Loan Office are Nikons, Polaroids, Yashicas, Sony TVs, Underwood typewriters, Singer sewing machines, and pictures of Christ. On the far side of town, beside a single track and locked up most of the time, is the new railroad station, a small hut made of glazed firebrick, all that is left of the lines that built the city. An authentic phrenologist works on New York Avenue close to Frank's Extra Dry Bar and a church where the sermon today is "Death in the Pot." The church is of pink brick, has blue and amber windows and two red doors. St. James Place, narrow and twisting, is lined with boarding houses that have wooden porches on each of three stories, suggesting a New Orleans made of salt-bleached pine. In a vacant lot on Tennessee is a white Ford station wagon stripped to the chassis. The windows are smashed. A plastic Clorox bottle sits on the driver's seat. The wind has pressed newspaper against the chain-link fence around the lot. Atlantic Avenue, the city's principal thoroughfare, could be seventeen American Main Streets placed end to end—discount vitamins and Vienna Corset shops, movie theatres, shoe stores, and funeral homes. The Boardwalk is made of yellow pine and Douglas fir, soaked in pentachlorophenol. Downbeach, it reaches far beyond the city. Signs everywhere—on windows, lampposts, trash baskets—proclaim "Bienvenue Canadiens!" The salt air is full of Canadian French. In the Claridge Hotel, on Park Place, I ask a clerk if she knows where Marvin Gardens is. She says, "Is it a floral shop?" I ask a cabdriver, parked outside. He says, "Never heard of it." Park Place is one block long, Pacific to Boardwalk. On the roof of the Claridge is the Solarium, the highest point in town—panoramic view of the ocean, the bay, the salt-water ghetto. I look down at the rooftops of the side-avenue motels and into swimming pools. There are hundreds of people around the rooftop pools, sunbathing, reading—many more people than are on the beach. Walls, windows, and a block of sky are all that is visible from these pools—no sand, no sea. The pools are craters, and with the people around them they are countersunk into the motels.

•

The seventh, and final, game is ten minutes old and I have hotels on Oriental, Vermont, and Connecticut. I have Tennessee and St. James. I have North Carolina and Pacific. I have Boardwalk, Atlantic, Ventnor, Illinois, Indiana. My fingers are forming a "V." I have mortgaged most of these properties in order to pay for others, and I have mortgaged the others to pay for the hotels. I have seven dollars. I will pay off the mortgages and build my reserves with income from the three hotels. My cash position may be low, but I feel like a rocket in an underground silo. Meanwhile, if I could go to jail for a time I could pause there, wait there, until my opponent, in his inescapable rounds, pays the rates of my hotels. Jail, at times, is the strategic place to be. I roll boxcars from the Reading and move the flatiron to Community Chest. "Go to Jail. Go directly to Jail."

•

The prisoners, of course, have no pens and no pencils. They take paper napkins, roll them tight as crayons, char the ends with matches, and write on the walls. The things they write are not entirely idiomatic; for example, "In God We Trust." All is in carbon. Time is required in the writing. "Only humanity could know of such pain." "God So Loved the World." "There is no greater pain than life itself." In the women's block now there are six blacks, giggling, and a white asleep in red shoes. She is drunk. The others are pushers, prostitutes, an auto-thief, a burglar caught with pistol in purse. A sixteen-year-old accused of murder was in here last week. These words are written on the wall of a now empty cell: "Laying here I see two bunks about six inches thick, not counting the one I'm laying on, which is hard as brick. No cushion for my back. No pillow for my head. Just a couple scratchy blankets which is best to use it's said. I wake up in the morning so shivery and cold, waiting and waiting till I am told the food is coming. It's on its way. It's not worth waiting for, but I eat it anyway. I know one thing when they set me free I'm gonna be good if it kills me."

•

How many years must a game be played to produce an Anthony J. Drexel Biddle and chestnut geldings on the beach? About half a century was the original answer, from the first railroad to Biddle at his peak. Biddle, at his peak, hit an Atlantic City streetcar conductor with his fist, laid him out with one punch. This increased Biddle's legend. He did not go to jail. While John Philip Sousa led his band along the Boardwalk playing "The Stars and Stripes Forever" and Jack Dempsey ran up and down in training for his fight with Gene Tunney, the city crossed the high curve of its parabola. Al Capone held conventions here—upstairs with his sleeves rolled, apportioning among his lieutenant governors the states of the Eastern seaboard. The natural history of an American resort proceeds from Indians to French Canadians via Biddles and Capones. French Canadians, whatever they may be at home, are Visigoths here. Bienvenue Visigoths!

•

My opponent plods along incredibly well. He has got his fourth railroad, and patiently, unbelievably, he has picked up my potential winners until he has blocked me everywhere but Marvin Gardens. He has avoided, in the fifty-dollar zoning, my increasingly petty hotels. His cash flow swells. His railroads are costing me two hundred dollars a minute. He is building hotels on States, Virginia, and St. Charles. He has temporarily reversed the current. With the yellow monopolies and my blue monopolies, I could probably defeat his lavenders and his railroads. I have Atlantic and Ventnor. I need Marvin Gardens. My only hope is Marvin Gardens.

•

There is a plaque at Boardwalk and Park Place, and on it in relief is the leonine profile of a man who looks like an officer in a metropolitan bank—"Charles B. Darrow, 1889—1967, inventor of the game of Monopoly." "Darrow," I address him, aloud. "Where is Marvin Gardens?" There is, of course, no answer. Bronze, impassive, Darrow looks south down the Boardwalk. "Mr. Darrow, please, where is Marvin Gardens?" Nothing. Not a sign. He just looks south down the Boardwalk.

•

My opponent accepts the trophy with his natural ease, and I make, from notes, remarks that are even less graceful than his.

•

Marvin Gardens is the one color-block Monopoly property that is not in Atlantic City. It is a suburb within a suburb secluded. It is a planned compound of seventy-two handsome houses set on curvilinear private streets under yews and cedars, poplars and willows. The compound was built around 1920, in Margate, New Jersey, and consists of solid buildings of stucco, brick, and wood, with slate roofs, tile roofs, multi-mullioned porches, Giraldic towers, and Spanish grilles. Marvin Gardens, the ultimate outwash of Monopoly, is a citadel and sanctuary of the middle class. "We're heavily patrolled by police here. We don't take no chances. Me? I'm living here nine years. I paid seventeen thousand dollars and I've been offered thirty. Number one, I don't want to move. Number two, I don't need the money. I have four bedrooms, two and a half baths, front den, back den. No basement. The Atlantic is down there. Six feet down and you float. A lot of people have a hard time finding this place. People that lived in Atlantic City all their life don't know how to find it. They don't know where the hell they're going. They just know it's south, down the Boardwalk."

Discussion Questions

1. The popular game of Monopoly, as you have just learned, is based on the street plan of Atlantic City, New Jersey. Why didn't McPhee begin his essay by telling his reader just that? What does he gain by starting as he does?

2. What contrasts does McPhee make between Atlantic City as it appears in a game and Atlantic City as it appears in real life? How do these contrasts deepen as the essay proceeds?

3. How does McPhee build narrative into his simultaneous descriptions? What two stories emerge and how are they connected and contrasted? How does his method of description differ from Ada Louise Huxtable's in "Houston" and V. S. Naipaul's in "The New Tehran"?

4. In this essay McPhee shows us how a popular game can reflect the larger dimensions of a society. Choose a popular game that you find or once found engaging (for example, PacMan, poker, or Parcheesi) and write an essay in which you show how the game mirrors some of the broader characteristics of society.

MARGARET MEAD

One of the most widely read anthropologists, Margaret Mead (1901–1978) was raised in Philadelphia. She graduated from Barnard College and received her doctorate from Columbia University in 1925. In that year she traveled to the South Pacific to study adolescent behavior; out of her field work she wrote Coming of Age in Somoa *(1928), a controversial classic of cultural anthropology. This was followed by* Growing Up in New Guinea *(1930), and* Sex and Temperament in Three Primitive Societies *(1935). For many years she served as curator of ethnology at the American Museum of Natural History.*

In the 1940's Mead turned her attention to contemporary culture and society. In one of her most famous books, Male and Female: A Study of the Sexes in a Changing World *(1949) she brought an anthropological perspective to western sexual behavior. Among her other many books are* Continuities in Cultural Evolution *(1964),* Culture and Commitment *(1970), and a personal account of her early days in field work,* Blackberry Winter *(1972). The following essay is reprinted from* A Way of Seeing *(1970), a book she coauthored with Rhoda Mentraux, a French anthropologist.*

New Superstitions for Old

Once in a while there is a day when everything seems to run smoothly and even the riskiest venture comes out exactly right. You exclaim, "This is my lucky day!" Then as an afterthought you say, "Knock on wood!" Of course, you do not really believe that knocking on wood will ward off danger. Still, boasting about your own good luck gives you a slightly uneasy feeling—and you carry out the little protective ritual. If someone challenged you at that moment, you would probably say, "Oh, that's nothing. Just an old superstition."

But when you come to think about it, what is a superstition?

In the contemporary world most people treat old folk beliefs as superstitions—the belief, for instance, that there are lucky and unlucky days or numbers, that future events can be read from omens, that there are protective charms or that what happens can be influenced by casting spells. We have excluded magic from our current world view, for we know that natural events have natural causes.

In a religious context, where truths cannot be demonstrated, we accept them as a matter of faith. Superstitions, however, belong to the category of beliefs, practices and ways of thinking that have been discarded because they are inconsistent with scientific knowledge. It is easy to say that other people are superstitious because they believe what we regard to be untrue. "Superstition" used in that sense is a derogatory term for the beliefs of other people that we do not share. But there is more to it than that. For superstitions lead a kind of half life in a twilight world where, sometimes, we partly suspend our disbelief and act as if magic worked.

Actually, almost every day, even in the most sophisticated home, something is likely to happen that evokes the memory of some old folk belief. The salt spills. A knife falls to the floor. Your nose tickles. Then perhaps, with a slightly embarrassed smile, the person who spilled the salt tosses a pinch over his left shoulder. Or someone recites the old rhyme, "Knife falls, gentleman calls." Or as you rub your nose you think, That means a letter. I wonder who's writing? No one takes these small responses very seriously or gives them more than a passing thought. Sometimes people will preface one of these ritual acts—walking around instead of under a ladder or hastily closing an umbrella that has been opened inside a house—with such a remark as "I remember my great-aunt used to . . ." or "Germans used to say you ought not . . ." And then, having placed the belief at some distance away in time or space, they carry out the ritual.

Everyone also remembers a few of the observances of childhood—wishing on the first star; looking at the new moon over the right shoulder; avoiding the cracks in the sidewalk on the way to school while chanting, "Step on a crack, break your mother's back"; wishing on white horses, on loads of hay, on covered bridges, on red cars; saying quickly, "Bread-and-butter" when a post or a tree separated you from the friend you were walking with. The adult may not actually recite the formula "Star light, star bright . . ." and may not quite turn to look at the new moon, but his mood is tempered by a little of the old thrill that came when the observance was still freighted with magic.

Superstition can also be used with another meaning. When I discuss the religious beliefs of other peoples, especially primitive peoples, I am often asked, "Do they really have a religion, or is it all just superstition?" The point of contrast here is not between a scientific and a magical view of the world but between the clear, theologically defensible religious beliefs of members of civilized societies and what we regard as the false and childish views of the heathen who "bow down to wood and stone." Within the civilized religions, however, where membership includes believers who are educated and urbane and others who are ignorant and simple, one always finds traditions and practices that the more sophisticated will dismiss offhand as "just superstition" but that guide the steps of those who live by older ways. Mostly these are very ancient beliefs, some handed on from one religion to another and carried from country to country around the world.

Very commonly, people associate superstition with the past, with very old ways of thinking that have been supplanted by modern knowledge. But new superstitions are continually coming into being and flourishing in our society. Listening to mothers in the park in the 1930's, one heard them say, "Now, don't you run out into the sun, or Polio will get you." In the 1940's elderly people explained to one another in tones of resignation, "It was the Virus that got him down." And every year the cosmetics industry offers us new magic—cures for baldness, lotions that will give every woman radiant skin, hair coloring that will restore to the middle-aged the charm and romance of youth—results that are promised if we will just follow the simple directions. Families and individuals also have their cherished, private superstitions. You must leave by the back door when you are going on a journey, or you must wear a green dress when you are taking an examination. It is a kind of joke, of course, but it makes you feel safe.

These old half-beliefs and new half-beliefs reflect the keenness of our wish to have something come true or to prevent something bad from happening. We do not always recognize new superstitions for what they are, and we will follow the old ones because someone's faith long ago matches our contemporary hopes and fears. In the past people "knew" that a black cat crossing one's path was a bad omen, and they turned back home. Today we are fearful of taking a journey and would give anything to turn back—and then we notice a black cat running across the road in front of us.

Child psychologists recognize the value of the toy a child holds in his hand at bedtime. It is different from his thumb, with which he can close himself in from the rest of the world, and it is different from the real world, to which he is learning to relate himself. Psychologists call these toys—these furry animals and old, cozy baby blankets—"transitional objects"; that is, objects that help the child move back and forth between the exactions of everyday life and the world of wish and dream.

Superstitions have some of the qualities of these transitional objects. They help people pass between the areas of life where what happens has to be accepted without proof and the areas where sequences of events are explicable in terms of cause and effect, based on knowledge. Bacteria and viruses that cause sickness have been identified; the cause of symptoms can be diagnosed and a rational course of treatment prescribed. Magical charms no longer are needed to treat the sick; modern medicine has brought the whole sequence of events into the secular world. But people often act as if this change had not taken place. Laymen still treat germs as if they were invisible, malign spirits, and physicians sometimes prescribe antibiotics as if they were magic substances.

Over time, more and more of life has become subject to the controls of knowledge. However, this is never a one-way process.

Scientific investigation is continually increasing our knowledge. But if we are to make good use of this knowledge, we must not only rid our minds of old, superseded beliefs and fragments of magical practice, but also recognize new superstitions for what they are. Both are generated by our wishes, our fears and our feeling of helplessness in difficult situations.

Civilized peoples are not alone in having grasped the idea of superstitions—beliefs and practices that are superseded but that still may evoke compliance. The idea is one that is familiar to every people, however primitive, that I have ever known. Every society has a core of transcendent beliefs—beliefs about the nature of the universe, the world and man—that no one doubts or questions. Every society also has a fund of knowledge related to practical life—about the succession of day and night and of the seasons; about correct ways of planting seeds so that they will germinate and grow; about the processes involved in making dyes or the steps necessary to remove the deadly poison from manioc roots so they become edible. Island peoples know how the winds shift and they know the star toward which they must point the prow of the canoe exactly so that as the sun rises they will see the first fringing palms on the shore toward which they are sailing.

This knowledge, based on repeated observations of reliable sequences, leads to ideas and hypotheses of the kind that underlie scientific thinking. And gradually as scientific knowledge, once developed without conscious plan, has become a great self-corrective system and the foundation for rational planning and action, old magical beliefs and observances have had to be discarded.

But it takes time for new ways of thinking to take hold, and often the transition is only partial. Older, more direct beliefs live on in the hearts and minds of elderly people. And they are learned by children who, generation after generation, start out life as hopefully and fearfully as their forebears did. Taking their first steps away from home, children use the old rituals and invent new ones to protect themselves against the strangeness of the world into which they are venturing.

So whatever has been rejected as no longer true, as limited, provincial and idolatrous, still leads a half life. People may say, "It's just a superstition," but they continue to invoke the ritual's protection or potency. In this transitional, twilight state such beliefs come to resemble dreaming. In the dream world a thing can be either good or bad; a cause can be an effect and an effect can be a cause. Do warts come from touching toads, or does touching a toad cure the wart? Is sneezing a good omen or a bad omen? You can have it either way—or both ways at once. In the same sense, the half-acceptance and half-denial accorded superstitions give us the best of both worlds.

Superstitions are sometimes smiled at and sometimes frowned upon as observances characteristic of the old-fashioned, the unenlightened, children, peasants, servants, immigrants, foreigners or backwoods people. Nevertheless, they give all of us ways of moving back and forth among the different worlds in which we live—the sacred, the secular and the scientific. They allow us to keep a private world also, where, smiling a little, we can banish danger with a gesture and summon luck with a rhyme, make the sun shine in spite of storm clouds, force the stranger to do our bidding, keep an enemy at bay and straighten the paths of those we love.

Discussion Questions

1. How do the new superstitions differ from the old? What do they have in common with the old?

2. What attitude does Mead have toward superstitions? Does she use the term in a derogatory way? How is her attitude reflected in her style? How, in her opinion, do superstitions originate?

3. Why doesn't scientific knowledge necessarily drive out superstitions? How can scientific knowledge lead to superstitions? Compare her attitude towards superstition to J. H. Plumb's attitude in "The Stars in Their Day."

4. As Mead points out, nearly all of us possess some sort of superstition. Think about some of the things you do to ensure good luck or avoid bad luck. After thinking carefully about the role of this superstition in your life, write a short essay describing the superstition, examining its origins, and discussing the sense of security it gives you. How do Mead's ideas about superstition relate to your own experiences?

H. L. MENCKEN

H. L. Mencken (1880–1956) lived almost his entire life in Baltimore and wrote for almost forty years in the Baltimore Sun. In addition, he edited for years The American Mercury and The Smart Set, both influential literary magazines in the early part of the century. A wide-ranging literary, cultural, and social critic, Mencken gave the enlivening sense of being against almost everything. But though he constantly attacked "professors," he also wrote the immensely scholarly The American Language (1919). Though he railed against ideologues and the "booboisie" who made up the electorate, he constantly expressed his faith in the country that he saw as "bulletproof." His style, in the words of Louis Kronenberger, "hid a conservative's taste under a firebrands's vocabulary."

In the following selection, we see Mencken at his paradoxical best: on the side of what he calls the "average man" and inveighing very intellectually against "intellectuals."

Criminology

The more I read the hand-books of the new criminology, the more I am convinced that it stands on a level with dogmatic theology, chiropractic and the New Thought—in brief, that it is mainly buncombe. That it has materially civilized punishment I do not, of course, deny; what I question is its doctrine as to the primary causes of crime. The average man, as everyone knows, puts those causes in the domain of free will. The criminal, in his view, is simply a scoundrel who has deliberately chosen to break the law and injure his fellow-men. *Ergo,* he deserves to be punished swiftly and mercilessly. The new criminologists, in swinging away from that naive view, have obviously gone too far in the other direction. They find themselves, in the end, embracing a determinism that is as childlike as the free will of the man in the street. Crime, as they depict it, becomes a sort of disease, either inherited or acquired by contagion, and as devoid of moral content or significance as smallpox. The criminal is no longer a black-hearted villain, to be put down by force, but a poor brother who has succumbed to the laws of Mendel and the swinish stupidity of society. The aim of punishment is not to make him sweat, but to dissuade and rehabilitate him. In every pickpocket there is a potential Good Man. All this, gradually gaining credit, has greatly ameliorated punishments. They have not only lost their old barbaric quality; they have also diminished quantitatively. Men do not sit in prison as long as they used to; the parole boards turn them out almost as fast as the cops shove them in. The result is a public discontent that must be manifest. Whenever a criminal of any eminence comes to trial there are loud bellows against any show of mercy to him, and demands that he be punished to the limit. One never hears complaints any more that the courts are too savage; one hears only complaints that they are too soft and sentimental.

I am a congenital disbeliever in laws, and have only the most formal respect for the juridic process and its learned protagonists; nevertheless, it seems to me that there is a certain reasonableness in this unhappiness. For what it indicates, basically, is simply the inability of the average man to grasp the determinism of the new criminologists. He cannot imagine an apparently voluntary act that is determined, or even materially conditioned, from without. He can think of crime only in terms of free will, and so thinking of it, he believes that it ought to be punished in the ancient Christian manner, i. e., according to the damage flowing out of it, and not according to the temptations behind it. Certainly this is not an illogical ground to take. In all the other relations of life the average man sees free will accepted as axiomatic: he could not imagine a world in which it was denied. His religion is based squarely upon it: he knows, by the oath of his pastor, that his free acts can lift him to Heaven or cast him down to Hell. He works as a matter of free will, and is punished inevitably if he lags. His marriage, as he sees it, was a free will compact, and though he has some secret doubt, perhaps, that its issue came that way, he nevertheless orders his relations with his children on the same basis, and assumes it in judging them. In other words, he lives in a world in which free will is apparently omnipotent, and in which it is presumed even when there is no direct evidence for it. All his daily concerns are free will concerns. Well, what the criminologists ask him to do is to separate one special concern from the rest, and hand it over to determinism. They damn legislators for passing harsh laws, and judges and jailers for executing them—free will. They denounce society for "coercing" morons into crime—free will again. And then they argue that the criminals are no more than helpless victims of circumstance, like motes dancing along a sunbeam—determinism in its purest and sweetest form.

No wonder the plain man baulks! Suppose an analogous suspension of the usual rules were attempted in some other field. Suppose it were argued seriously that free will had nothing to do with, say, the execution of contracts. Suppose an employer who failed to pay his workmen on Saturday were excused on the ground that he was the helpless victim of an evil heredity or of the stupidity of society, and thus not to be blamed for dissipating his money on Ford parts, women, foreign missions, or drink? Suppose the workman who had got out a mechanic's lien against him and sought to levy on his assets were denounced as a cruel and medieval fellow, and at odds with human progress? Certainly there would be a horrible hullabaloo, and equally certainly it would be justified. For whatever the theoretical arguments for determinism—and I am prepared to go even further in granting them than the criminologists go—it must be plain that the everyday affairs of the world are ordered on an assumption of free will, and that it is impossible, practically speaking, to get rid of it. Society itself, indeed, is grounded upon that assumption. Imagining it as determined is possible only to professional philosophers, whose other imaginings are surely not such as to give any authority to this one. The plain man simply gives up the effort as hopeless—and perhaps as also a bit anarchistic and un-Christian. So he is sniffish when the new criminologists begin to prattle their facile determinism, and when he observes it getting credit from the regular agents of the law he lets a loud whoop of protest. I do not believe he is naturally cruel and vindictive; on the contrary, he is very apt to be maudlingly sentimental. But sentiment is one thing, and what seems to him to be a palpably false philosophy is quite another. He no more favors letting criminals go on the ground that they can't help themselves than he favors giving money to foreign missions, or the Red Cross, or the Y.M.C.A on the ground that it is his inescapable duty. In all of these cases he is willing to be persuaded, but in none of them is he willing to be dragooned.

Thus I fear that the criminologists of the new school only pile up trouble for themselves, and indirectly their pets, when they attempt to revise so radically the immemorial human view of crime. If they kept quiet in the department of responsibility, they would be heard with far more attention and respect in the department of punishment, where they really have something apposite and useful to say. Their influence here, in fact, is already immense, and it works much good. Our prisons are no longer quite as sordid and demoralizing as they used to be. They are still bad enough, in all conscience, but they are not as bad as they were. Here there is room for yet more improvement, and it cries aloud to be made. The men to work out its details are the criminologists. They have studied the effects of the prevailing punishments, and know where those punishments succeed or fail. They are happily devoid of that proud ignorance which is one of the boasts of the average judge, and they lack the unpleasant zeal of district attorneys, jail wardens and other such professional blood-letters. They need only offer the proofs that this or that punishment is ineffective to see it abandoned for something better, or, at all events, less obviously bad. But when they begin to talk of criminals in terms of pathology, even of social pathology, they speak a language that the plain man cannot understand and doesn't want to hear. He believes that crime, in the overwhelming majority of cases, is a voluntary matter, and that it ought to pay its own way and bury its own dead. He is not bothered about curing criminals, or otherwise redeeming them. He is intent only upon punishing them, and the more swiftly and certainly that business is achieved the better he is satisfied. Every time it is delayed by theorizing about the criminal's heredity and environment, and the duty that society owes to him, the plain man breaks into indignation. Only too often that indignation has been wreaked upon criminology and the criminologists. More American States, of late, have gone back to capital punishment than have abandoned it. What set the tide to running that way was surely not mere blood-lust. It was simply a natural reaction against the doctrine that murder is mainly an accidental and unfortunate matter, and devoid of moral content, like slipping on an icy sidewalk or becoming the father of twins.

Discussion Questions

1. Mencken explains moral issues (like "guilt") by seeing them as secondary to more general philosophical issues (like "free will"). What does this force a would-be opponent to do?

2. Compare Mencken's ideas about the modern "plain man" to those of Randall Jarrell. What similarities and differences appear? What worries each writer most?

3. How does Mencken's use of hypothetical examples support his case? Would appreciably more or fewer of them work in the same way?

4. Many other issues may be seen in terms of fate as "illness" or in terms of free will as "vice." Pick another social problem (for example, drunkenness or compulsive gambling) and apply Mencken's mode of analysis to it. In an essay, argue for or against the "average man's" point of view.

5. In conceding a useful contribution of criminology, Mencken says "They need only offer the proofs that this or that punishment is ineffective to see it abandoned for something better, or in all events less obviously bad." Do you share this view? Write an essay supporting or opposing its truth.

Jessica Mitford

Jessica Mitford was born in England in 1917, one of the six daughters of the second Baron of Redesdale. Like all her sisters, she was educated at home and like her sister Nancy became a writer only later in her life. However, with the publication in 1963 of The American Way of Death *she came to be known as "The Queen of the Muckrakers" and went on to cover (or uncover) such topics as "fat farms," television executives, and snobbish, overpriced restaurants. Her* Poisonpensmanship: The Gentle Art of Muckraking *(1979) collects many of her most famous essays, all of which display a style that expresses both zest for the hunt and contempt for the prey.*

On Embalming

Embalming is indeed a most extraordinary procedure, and one must wonder at the docility of Americans who each year pay hundreds of millions of dollars for its perpetuation, blissfully ignorant of what it is all about, what is done, how it is done. Not one in ten thousand has any idea of what actually takes place. Books on the subject are extremely hard to come by. They are not to be found in most libraries or bookshops.

In an era when huge television audiences watch surgical operations in the comfort of their living rooms, when, thanks to the animated cartoon, the geography of the digestive system has become familiar territory even to the nursery school set, in a land where the satisfaction of curiosity about almost all matters is a national pastime, the secrecy surrounding embalming can, surely, hardly be attributed to the inherent gruesomeness of the subject. Custom in this regard has within this century suffered a complete reversal. In the early days of American embalming, when it was performed in the home of the deceased, it was almost mandatory for some relative to stay by the embalmer's side and witness the procedure. Today, family members who might wish to be in attendance would certainly be dissuaded by the funeral director. All others, except apprentices, are excluded by law from the preparation room.

A close look at what does actually take place may explain in large measure the undertaker's intractable reticence concerning a procedure that has become his major *raison d'être*. Is it possible he fears that public information about embalming might lead patrons to wonder if they really want this service? If the funeral men are loath to discuss the subject outside the trade, the reader may, understandably, be equally loath to go on reading at this point. For those who have the stomach for it, let us part the formaldehyde curtain. . . .

The body is first laid out in the undertaker's morgue—or rather, Mr. Jones is reposing in the preparation room—to be readied to bid the world farewell.

The preparation room in any of the better funeral establishments has the tiled and sterile look of a surgery, and indeed the embalmer-restorative artist who does his chores there is beginning to adopt the term "dermasurgeon" (appropriately corrupted by some mortician-writers as "demisurgeon") to describe his calling. His equipment, consisting of scalpels, scissors, augers, forceps, clamps, needles, pumps, tubes, bowls and basins, is crudely imitative of the surgeon's, as is his technique, acquired in a nine- or twelve-month post-high-school course in an embalming school. He is supplied by an advanced chemical industry with a bewildering array of fluids, sprays, pastes, oils, powders, creams, to fix or soften tissue, shrink or distend it as needed, dry it here, restore the moisture there. There are cosmetics, waxes and paints to fill and cover features, even plaster of Paris to replace entire limbs. There are ingenious aids to prop and stabilize the cadaver: a Vari-Pose Head Rest, the Edwards Arm and Hand Positioner, the Repose Block (to support the shoulders during the embalming), and the Throop Foot Positioner, which resembles an old-fashioned stocks.

Mr. John H. Eckels, president of the Eckels College of Mortuary Science, thus describes the first part of the embalming procedure: "In the hands of a skilled practitioner, this work may be done in a comparatively short time and without mutilating the body other than by slight incision—so slight that it scarcely would cause serious inconvenience if made upon a living person. It is necessary to remove the blood, and doing this not only helps in the disinfecting, but removes the principal cause of disfigurements due to discoloration."

Another textbook discusses the all-important time element: "The earlier this is done, the better, for every hour that elapses between death and embalming will add to the problems and complications encountered. . . ." Just how soon should one get going on the embalming? The author tells us, "On the basis of such scanty information made available to this profession through its rudimentary and haphazard system of technical research, we must conclude that the best results are to be obtained if the subject is embalmed before his life is completely extinct—that is, before cellular death has occurred. In the average case, this would mean within an hour after somatic death." For those who feel that there is something a little rudimentary, not to say haphazard, about this advice, a comforting thought is offered by another writer. Speaking of fears entertained in early days of premature burial, he points out, "One of the effects of embalming by chemical injection, however, has been to dispel fears of live burial." How true; once the blood is removed, chances of live burial are indeed remote.

To return to Mr. Jones, the blood is drained out through the veins and replaced by embalming fluid pumped in through the arteries. As noted in *The Principles and Practices of Embalming*, "every operator has a favorite injection and drainage point—a fact which becomes a handicap only if he fails or refuses to forsake his favorites when conditions demand it." Typical favorites are the carotid artery, femoral artery, jugular vein, subclavian vein. There are various choices of embalming fluid. If Flextone is used, it will produce a "mild, flexible rigidity. The skin retains a velvety softness, the tissues are rubbery and pliable. Ideal for women and children." It may be blended with B. and G. Products Company's Lyf-Lyk tint, which is guaranteed to reproduce "nature's own skin texture . . . the velvety appearance of living tissue." Suntone comes in three separate tints: Suntan; Special Cosmetic Tint, a pink shade "especially indicated for young female subjects"; and Regular Cosmetic Tint, moderately pink.

About three to six gallons of a dyed and perfumed solution of formaldehyde, glycerin, borax, phenol, alcohol and water is soon circulating through Mr. Jones, whose mouth has been sewn together with a "needle directed upward between the upper lip and gum and brought out through the left nostril," with the corners raised slightly "for a more pleasant expression." If he should be bucktoothed, his teeth are cleaned with Bon Ami and coated with colorless nail polish. His eyes, meanwhile, are closed with flesh-tinted eye caps and eye cement.

The next step is to have at Mr. Jones with a thing called a trocar. This is a long, hollow needle attached to a tube. It is jabbed into the abdomen, poked around the entrails and chest cavity, the contents of which are pumped out and replaced with "cavity fluid." This done, and the hole in the abdomen sewn up, Mr. Jones's face is heavily creamed (to protect the skin from burns which may be caused by leakage of the chemicals), and he is covered with a sheet and left unmolested for a while. But not for long—there is more, much more, in store for him. He has been embalmed, but not yet restored, and the best time to start the restorative work is eight to ten hours after embalming, when the tissues have become firm and dry.

The object of all this attention to the corpse, it must be remembered, is to make it presentable for viewing in an attitude of healthy repose. "Our customs require the presentation of our dead in the semblance of normality . . . unmarred by the ravages of illness, disease or mutilation," says Mr. J. Sheridan Mayer in his *Restorative Art.* This is rather a large order since few people die in the full bloom of health, unravaged by illness and unmarked by some disfigurement. The funeral industry is equal to the challenge: "In some cases the gruesome appearance of a mutilated or disease-ridden subject may be quite discouraging. The task of restoration may seem impossible and shake the confidence of the embalmer. This is the time for intestinal fortitude and determination. Once the formative work is begun and affected tissues are cleaned or removed, all doubts of success vanish. It is surprising and gratifying to discover the results which may be obtained."

The embalmer, having allowed an appropriate interval to elapse, returns to the attack, but now he brings into play the skill and equipment of sculptor and cosmetician. Is a hand missing? Casting one in plaster of Paris is a simple matter. "For replacement purposes, only a cast of the back of the hand is necessary; this is within the ability of the average operator and is quite adequate." If a lip or two, a nose or an ear should be missing, the embalmer has at hand a variety of restorative waxes with which to model replacements. Pores and skin texture are simulated by stippling with a little brush, and over this cosmetics are laid on. Head off? Decapitation cases are rather routinely handled. Ragged edges are trimmed, and head joined to torso with a series of splints, wires and sutures. It is a good idea to have a little something at the neck—a scarf or high collar—when time for viewing comes. Swollen mouth? Cut out tissue as needed from inside the lips. If too much is removed, the surface contour can easily be restored by padding with cotton. Swollen necks and cheeks are reduced by removing tissue through vertical incisions made down each side of the neck. "When the deceased is casketed, the pillow will hide the sutured incision . . . as an extra precaution against leakage, the suture may be painted with liquid sealer."

The opposite condition is more likely to present itself—that of emaciation. His hypodermic syringe now loaded with massage cream, the embalmer seeks out and fills the hollowed and sunken areas by injection. In this procedure the backs of the hands and fingers and the under-chin area should not be neglected.

Positioning the lips is a problem that recurrently challenges the ingenuity of the embalmer. Closed too tightly, they tend to give a stern, even disapproving expression. Ideally, embalmers feel, the lips should give the impression of being ever so slightly parted, the upper lip protruding slightly for a more youthful appearance. This takes some engineering, however, as the lips tend to drift apart. Lip drift can sometimes be remedied by pushing one or two straight pins through the inner margin of the lower lip and then inserting them between the two front upper teeth. If Mr. Jones happens to have no teeth, the pins can just as easily be anchored in his Armstrong Face Former and Denture Replacer. Another method to maintain lip closure is to dislocate the lower jaw, which is then held in its new position by a wire run through holes which have been drilled through the upper and lower jaws at the midline. As the French are fond of saying, *il faut souffrir pour être belle.*[1]

If Mr. Jones has died of jaundice, the embalming fluid will very likely turn him green. Does this deter the embalmer? Not if he has intestinal fortitude. Masking pastes and cosmetics are heavily laid on, burial garments and casket interiors are color-correlated with particular care, and Jones is displayed beneath rose-colored lights. Friends will say, "How *well* he looks." Death by carbon monoxide, on the other hand, can be rather a good thing from the embalmer's viewpoint: "One advantage is the fact that this type of discoloration is an exaggerated form of a natural pink coloration." This is nice because the healthy glow is already present and needs but little attention.

The patching and filling completed, Mr. Jones is now shaved, washed, and dressed. Cream-based cosmetic, available in pink, flesh, suntan, brunette and blond, is applied to his hands and face, his hair shampooed and combed (and, in the case of Mrs. Jones, set), his hands manicured. For the horny-handed son of toil special care must be taken; cream should be applied to remove ingrained grime, and the nails cleaned. "If he were not in the habit of having them manicured in life, trimming and shaping is advised for better appearance—never questioned by kin."

Jones is now ready for casketing (this is the present participle of the verb "to casket"). In this operation his right shoulder should be depressed slightly "to turn the body a bit to the right and soften the appearance of lying flat on the back." Positioning the hands is a matter of importance, and special rubber positioning blocks may be used. The hands should be cupped slightly for a more lifelike, relaxed appearance. Proper placement of the body requires a delicate sense of balance. It should lie as high as possible in the casket, yet not so high that the lid, when lowered, will hit the nose. On the other hand, we are cautioned, placing the body too low "creates the impression that the body is in a box."

[1] One must suffer to be beautiful.

Jones is next wheeled into the appointed slumber room where a few last touches may be added—his favorite pipe placed in his hand or, if he was a great reader, a book propped into position. (In the case of little Master Jones a Teddy bear may be clutched.) Here he will hold open house for a few days, visiting hours 10 A.M. to 9 P.M.

Discussion Questions

1. The name for the occupation of which embalming is a part has changed within the twentieth century from "undertaker" to "mortician" to "funeral director." What values and assumptions about death and the handling of death underlie each of these terms?

2. How does the alternation between "Mr. Jones" and "the corpse" affect Jessica Mitford's point?

3. Compare the treatment of funeral rites here to the treatment given by Evelyn Waugh.

4. Pick another aspect of life that is taboo in a way similar to the handling of corpses (for example, sewage disposal). What aspects of Jessica Mitford's satiric techniques could be used on your topic and which would need modification?

Ashley Montague

One of the best known anthropologists in the world, Ashley Montague was born in England in 1905 and in 1927 came to the United States where he completed his studies at Columbia. He has claimed his main interest as "the relation of cultural factors to the physical and behavioral evolution of man." In the service of this interest, Montague has attacked many myths, most especially what he calls the "most dangerous" myth, that which involves the concept of "race" as an absolute term and which holds a simple-minded view of evolution. His first work against this myth was published in the early 1940's when ideas of "racial superiority and inferiority" were being tragically enacted in Nazi Germany and Soviet Russia. In Germany, Jews were considered an "inferior race" and thereby a danger of polluting through intermarriage the superior race's "scientific" evolution toward even greater superiority. In Russia former capitalists were thought somehow to have transmitted their tendencies to their children who were therefore also a danger to the state and who were therefore also eliminated.

Social Change and Human Change

An embarrassment of clichés would, perhaps, be the fairest description of what most people conceive to be the nature of human nature. Such stereotypes as "You can't change human nature," "It is only human nature," and that we shall always have with us wars, juvenile delinquents, murderers, politicians, poverty, and pornography, because it is in the nature of the beast, are only too banally familiar.

All these disorders, and many others, are taken to be expressions of human nature. But they are not. They are expressions of a learned, an acquired nature. And, indeed, it were better not to speak of nature in this connection in order to avoid any possible confusion between genuinely natural phenomena and artifactual learned or acquired behavior.

The only thing natural for man as a behaving human being is to be unnatural. It is because of his ability to be unnatural that man has been able to make the natural do his bidding, to put a noose around the natural and draw it to himself. Man is human because he has transcended the natural in himself and in his environment; because he has made himself and he has made the human environment, and in large part remade the natural environment. Man is human because he has moved into a wholly new zone of adaptation, the dimension of the man-made part of the environment, the extrasomatic environment of communication through symboling, that is to say, *culture*.

Beyond all other creatures man is the creature who adapts to his environment entirely through learned, that is cultural, responses. The "entirely" here does not, of course, refer to such complex responses as respiration, food and liquid intake and the other basic responses without the satisfaction of which the organism could not survive. But even these basic needs are in many fundamental ways affected both in their expression and satisfaction by cultural pressures.

Whatever a human being comes to know and do as a human being he must learn from other human beings. Man is, as a result of his peculiar and unique mode of evolution, the most plastic, the most malleable, and the most educable of all creatures. If one were to settle upon the one trait which beyond all others distinguishes man from everything else in the world, it is man's educability.

Having been abandoned by the trees, man's forest-dwelling ancestors were forced to adapt themselves to a life on the savannas, the open plains. This entailed the transition from a herbivorous to an omnivorous diet and to hunting instead of merely food-gathering. Hunting puts a high positive selection pressure upon problem-solving abilities and a negative selection pressure upon unthinking automatic reactions. Success in the hunt is impeded by instinct and advanced by quick thinking, by intelligence, that is, by the ability to make the appropriate response to the particular challenge of the environment.

In response to such challenges man's genetic system gradually changed in a feedback relation to the cultural demands. The cultural challenges, having produced changes by selection in the genetic constitution (the genotype), were in turn challenged by the carriers of the new gene combinations, so that as cultural advances were made in this way there was a continuing selective pressure exerted upon the genotype, resulting in further genetic change.

It is only in recent years that this feedback relation between culture and genotype has come to be recognized. What this means is that man's social behavior has played a fundamental, *the* fundamental, role in the evolution of man as a human being and as a physical organism. That is to say, even man's peculiar physical traits have been significantly influenced in their evolution to their present form by cultural factors.

What, in brief, the selective pressures that have been operative in the evolution of man have produced is a creature who can learn to live in any environment in which it is possible to live. There is only one creature on this earth that can do that, and that is man. This extraordinary creature, unique in the history of our world, prospers best in environments in which he is challenged to acquire, to learn his *responses,* rather than to react to those challenges with fixed and inappropriate *reactions.* What a world of meaning lies in those statements for all who have anything to do with the education, the making, of human beings! A matter to which we shall return.

In all animals genes determine potentialities and the limits of their possible development. The realization and ultimate expression of those potentialities are to a large extent determined by the environment. In no animal is that anywhere nearly as true as it is in man. Thus heredity is the result of the interaction between the genetically determined potentialities and the environmental stimulations which those genic potentialities undergo. Genic potentialities for being human are not enough to make a behaving human being; for *that* the behaving human environment, actively provided by other human beings, is necessary.

Hence, no matter what the normal limits of the genically determined potentialities may be, given those potentialities for being human, the most important and indispensably necessary condition for the development of human behavior is the socializing human enviroment provided by human socializers. Without one or more such socializers there can be no social human beings. As Aristotle remarked more than 2,000 years ago, "The nature of a man is not what he is born as, but what he is born for." And what man is born for is the realization of his potentialities in adaptation to whatever environments in which he finds himself. And with a genetic constitution that enables him to adapt himself to every possible environment, he is abundantly able to do that—*provided he is adequately taught.*

As an instinctless creature man comes into the world naked and with a cry, and just as his body is clothed or not according to the customs prevailing in the culture in which he is born, so his potentialities are tailored into the required behaviors according to the patterns of culture prevailing in his particular segment of society. Man is custom-made. The product of the cultural patterning or organization of his raw potentialities constitutes human nature, and that human nature will vary according to the cultures in which it has been conditioned.

That being so, and since cultural or social change occurs in all societies, changes in human societies will be reflected by changes in human nature. The record of man's history abundantly testifies to that fact. Indeed, changes in human nature must always depend upon social changes. Human change *is* social change. These quite elementary, simple, and verifiable statements are fundamental. They at once provide us with the surgent hope and the constructive foundations for a creative approach to the making of human beings.

I have said that man is the creature who prospers best when he is challenged to acquire, to learn and develop his responses rather than to react with stereotyped and inappropriate behaviors. And what a challenge those words should constitute to every educator! Intelligence, the ability to make the most appropriate response to any particular challenge, the supreme problem-solving ability, has been a vitally important factor in the evolution of man. It is an ability as vitally important today as it ever was—if anything, even more important. And it is as vitally necessary for the healthy functioning of the organism today—indeed, even more vital than it ever was. And yet our so-called educational systems specialize in training students in an incapacity to think, in the absorption of large quantities of facts learned, for the most part uncritically, and regurgitated upon certain ceremonial occasions known as examinations. Such individuals go through life regurgitating stereotypes under the impression that they are engaged in thinking. We pride ourselves on the fact that we can make machines that think like human beings and overlook the fact that we have long been making millions of human beings who think like machines.

Lack of skill in thinking can be lethal. A stereotype regurgitator has become a servo-mechanism, a starting device for initiating automatic reactions. Such starting devices are now proliferating at a disastrously accelerating rate and threaten the continuing quality of humanity as never before. Through thinking soundly man changes for the better. By thinking unsoundly or not at all man changes for the worse. And it must always be remembered that by virtue of his educability man is capable of learning not only more sound things but also more unsound things than any other creature, and that the result of this is not intelligence but confusion. So that social change may be sound so that human change shall be sound, the primary requirement is teaching the young how to think critically, originally, imaginatively, and daringly.

In the nuclear scientific age we need to teach children to understand why it is that nuclear science is far too important to leave to the nuclear scientists; and why, indeed, all science is too important to leave to scientists; that science is not enough; that science must be controlled by humanity, just as humanity must, in a feedback relation, be in continuous reciprocal interaction with science, for the mutual enrichment of both and of mankind.

The best guarantee of advancing social change is the ability to think; and by the ability to think I mean the ability to think soundly. The future, no less, of the world depends upon our ability to teach the young how to think soundly from their earliest beginnings.

Indispensably necessary as the ability to think is, it is not sufficient; for man is not alone a thinking creature, he is also a feeling creature. And just as he has to be taught to think, so, too, he has to be taught how to feel. The potentialities are there, but they require education; and by education I mean *educare*, to nourish and to cause to grow, those potentialities for being able to relate oneself warmly, lovingly, and creatively toward others. This group of potentialities, the capacity to love, is developed in precisely the same way as are one's other social capacities, by learning. And one learns to love in only one way: by being loved.

The growth and development of the ability to love has played a major role in the evolution of the human species. With the loss of instincts and the increasing dependency upon others for learning how to be human to which this loss led, deepening of involvement—as a capacity and an ability—in the welfare of the dependent child became a trait of correspondingly increasing survival value.

I have repeatedly urged that in view of the evolutionary facts and what we have learned of the nature of human development our educational institutions, to be worthy of the name, must become institutes for the training in the science and art of human relations. That all else must be regarded as secondary to this, and that the three R's must come to be regarded as secondary skills in the service of the primary of all skills, the art of creative interaction with others. Toward this end I conceive the educator's function to be that of one who joins learning to loving-kindness in himself and in his pupils. There is nothing in the innate nature of man which constitutes in any sense a barrier toward the achievement of this end. On the other hand, innate nature has an orientation and a directiveness which seeks realization in just that way. And nature is so malleable, so plastic, so educable a thing, that it can be adjusted to any kind of social change considered desirable.

Discussion Questions

1. How, if at all, does Montague reconcile his insistence on the "unnatural" nature of man, the "artifactual learned or acquired behavior" with his opposition to the "absorption of large quantities of facts"?

2. How do Montague's puns and paradoxes (for example, man is "custom-made") work to exemplify what he means by "critical thinking"?

3. Compare Montague's views of education to those of Robert Frost and Jacques Barzun.

4. Write a curriculum or a part of a curriculum that would seem to be in keeping with Montague's educational views. For example, compose an appropriate final examination in your own major field or list the courses that should be taught in the ideal college to every student.

5. How would Ashley Montague respond to the assertion of Lewis Mumford's first paragraph that sports become spectacles when a population has become "drilled, regimented, and depressed"?

Samuel Eliot Morison

The distinguished historian Samuel Eliot Morison (1887–1976) was born and died in Boston where he lived and worked for most of his life. Educated at Harvard, he went on to study in France and England before returning to Harvard to serve as professor and professor emeritus from 1925 until the year of his death. Of his many books, his Pulitzer Prize-winning biography of Columbus, Admiral of the Ocean Sea *(1942) and his fifteen-volume* History of United States Naval Operations in World War II *(1947–60) mark only some high points in over sixty years of prolific historical writing. His pleas for historical writing that is readable by the general public are being echoed by many historians today. The essay appeared in his collection,* By Land and by Sea *(1953).*

History as a Literary Art

Exploring American history has been a very absorbing and exciting business now for three quarters of a century. Thousands of graduate students have produced thousands of monographs on every aspect of the history of the Americas. But the American reading public for the most part is blissfully ignorant of this vast output. When John Citizen feels the urge to read history, he goes to the novels of Kenneth Roberts or Margaret Mitchell, not to the histories of Professor this or Doctor that. Why?

Because American historians, in their eagerness to present facts and their laudable anxiety to tell the truth, have neglected the literary aspects of their craft. They have forgotten that there is an art of writing history.

Even the earliest colonial historians like William Bradford and Robert Beverley knew that; they put conscious art into their narratives. And the historians of our classical period, Prescott and Motley, Irving and Bancroft, Parkman and Fiske, were great literary craftsmen. Their many-volumed works sold in sufficient quantities to give them handsome returns; even today they are widely read. But the first generation of seminar-trained historians, educated in Germany or by teachers trained there, imagined that history would tell itself, provided one were honest, thorough, and painstaking. Some of them went so far as to regard history as pure science and to assert that writers thereof had no more business trying to be "literary" than did writers of statistical reports or performers of scientific experiments. Professors warned their pupils (quite unnecessarily) against "fine writing," and endeavored to protect their innocence from the seductive charm of Washington Irving or the masculine glamour of Macaulay. And in this flight of history from literature the public was left behind. American history became a bore to the reader and a drug on the market; even historians with something to say and the talent for saying it (Henry Adams, for instance) could not sell their books. The most popular American histories of the period 1890—1905 were those of John Fiske, a philosopher who had no historical training, but wrote with life and movement.

Theodore Roosevelt in his presidential address before the American Historical Association in 1912 made a ringing plea to the young historian to do better:

> He must ever remember that while the worst offense of which he can be guilty is to write vividly and inaccurately, yet that unless he writes vividly he cannot write truthfully; for no amount of dull, painstaking detail will sum up the whole truth unless the genius is there to paint the truth.

And although American historians cannot hope as Theodore Roosevelt did to "watch the nearing chariots of the champions," or look forward to the day when "for us the war-horns of King Olaf shall wail across the flood, and the harps sound high at festivals in forgotten halls," we may indeed "show how the land which the pioneers won slowly and with incredible hardship was filled in two generations by the overflow from the countries of western and central Europe." We may describe the race, class, and religious conflicts that immigration has engendered, and trace the rise of the labor movement with a literary art that compels people to read about it. You do not need chariots and horsemen, harps and war-horns to make history interesting.

Theodore Roosevelt's trumpet call fell largely on deaf ears, at least in the academic historical profession. A whole generation has passed without producing any really great works on American history. Plenty of good books, valuable books, and new interpretations and explorations of the past; but none with fire in the eye, none to make a young man want to fight for his country in war or live to make it a better country in peace. There has been a sort of chain reaction of dullness. Professors who have risen to positions of eminence by writing dull, solid, valuable monographs that nobody reads outside the profession, teach graduate students to write dull, solid, valuable monographs like theirs; the road to academic security is that of writing dull, solid, valuable monographs. And so the young men who have a gift for good writing either leave the historical field for something more exciting, or write more dull, solid, valuable monographs. The few professional historians who have had a popular following or appeal during the last thirty years are either men like Allan Nevins who were trained in some juicier profession like journalism, or men and women like the Beards who had the sense to break loose young from academic trammels.

In the meantime, the American public has become so sated by dull history textbooks in school and college that it won't read history unless disguised as something else under a title such as "The Flowering of Florida," "The Epic of the East," or "The Growth of the American Republic." Or, more often, they get what history they want from historical novels.

Now I submit, this is a very bad situation. The tremendous plowing up of the past by well-trained scholars is all to the good, so far as it goes. Scholars know more about America's past than ever; they are opening new furrows and finding new artifacts, from aboriginal arrowheads to early twentieth-century corset stays. But they are heaping up the pay dirt for others. Journalists, novelists, and free-lance writers are the ones that extract the gold; and they deserve every ounce they get because they are the ones who know how to write histories that people care to read. What I want to see is a few more Ph.D.'s in history winning book-of-the-month adoptions and reaping the harvest of dividends. They can do it, too, if they will only use the same industry at presenting history as they do in compiling it.

Mind you, I intend no disparagement of historians who choose to devote their entire energies to teaching. Great teachers do far more good to the cause of history than mediocre writers. Such men, for instance, as the late H. Morse Stephens, who stopped writing (which he never liked) as soon as he obtained a chair in this country, and the late Edwin F. Gay, who never began writing, inspired thousands of young men and initiated scores of valuable books. Thank God for these gifted teachers, I say; universities should seek out, encourage, and promote them far more than they do. My remarks are addressed to young people who have the urge to write history, and wish to write it effectively.

There are no special rules for writing history; any good manual of rhetoric or teacher of composition will supply the rules for writing English. But what terrible stuff passes for English in Ph.D. dissertations, monographs, and articles in historical reviews! Long, involved sentences that one has to read two or three times in order to grasp their meaning; poverty in vocabulary, ineptness of expression, weakness in paragraph structure, frequent misuse of words, and, of late, the introduction of pseudo-scientific and psychological jargon. There is no fundamental cure for this except better teaching of English in our schools and colleges, and by every teacher, whatever his other subject may be. If historical writing is infinitely better in France than in America, and far better in the British Isles and Canada than in the United States, it is because every French and British teacher of history drills his pupils in their mother tongue, requiring a constant stream of essays and reports, and criticizing written work not only as history but as literature. The American university teacher who gives honor grades to students who have not yet learned to write English, for industrious compilations of facts or feats of memory, is wanting in professional pride or competency.

Of course, what we should all like to attain in writing history is style. "The sense of style," says Whitehead in his *Aims of Education*, "is an aesthetic sense, based on admiration for the direct attainment of a foreseen end, simply and without waste. Style in art, style in literature, style in science, style in logic, style in practical execution, have fundamentally the same aesthetic qualities, namely attainment and restraint. Style, in its finest sense, is the last acquirement of the educated mind; it is also the most useful. It pervades the whole being. . . . Style is the ultimate morality of mind."

Unfortunately, there is no royal road to style. It cannot be attained by mere industry; it can never be achieved through imitation, although it may be promoted by example. Reading the greatest literary artists among historians will help; but do not forget that what was acceptable style in 1850 might seem turgid today. We can still read Macaulay with admiration and pleasure, we can still learn paragraph structure and other things from Macaulay, but anyone who tried to imitate Macaulay today would be a pompous ass.

Just as Voltaire's ideal curé advises his flock not to worry about going to heaven, but to do right and probably by God's grace they will get there; so the young writer of history had better concentrate on day-by-day improvement in craftmanship. Then perhaps he may find some day that his prose appeals to a large popular audience; that, in other words, he has achieved style through simple, honest, straightforward writing.

A few hints as to the craft may be useful to budding historians. First and foremost, *get writing!* Young scholars generally wish to secure the last fact before writing anything, like General McClellan refusing to advance (as people said) until the last mule was shod. It is a terrible strain, isn't it, to sit down at a desk with your notes all neatly docketed, and begin to write? You pretend to your wife that you mustn't be interrupted; but, actually, you welcome a ring of the telephone, a knock at the door, or a bellow from the baby as an excuse to break off. Finally, after smoking sundry cigarettes and pacing about the house two or three times, you commit a lame paragraph or two to paper. By the time you get to the third, one bit of information you want is lacking. What a relief! Now you must go back to the library or the archives to do some more digging. That's where you are happy! And what you turn up there leads to more questions and prolongs the delicious process of research. Half the pleas I have heard from graduate students for more time or another grant-in-aid are mere excuses to postpone the painful drudgery of writing.

There is the "indispensablest beauty in knowing how to get done," said Carlyle. In every research there comes a point, which you should recognize like a call of conscience, when you must get down to writing. And when you once are writing, go on writing as long as you can; there will be plenty of time later to shove in the footnotes or return to the library for extra information. Above all, *start* writing. Nothing is more pathetic than the "gonna" historian, who from graduate school on is always "gonna" write a magnum opus but never completes his research on the subject, and dies without anything to show for a lifetime's work.

Dictation is usually fatal to good historical writing. Write out your first draft in longhand or, if you compose easily on the typewriter, type it out yourself, revise with pencil or pen, and have it retyped clean. Don't stop to consult your notes for every clause or sentence; it is better to get what you have to say clearly in your mind and dash it off; then, after you have it down, return to your notes and compose your next few pages or paragraphs. After a little experience you may well find that you think best with your fingers on the typewriter keys or your fountain pen poised over the paper. For me, the mere writing of a few words seems to point up vague thoughts and make jumbled facts array themselves in neat order. Whichever method you choose, composing before you write or as you write, do not return to your raw material or verify facts and quotations or insert footnotes until you have written a substantial amount, an amount that will increase with practice. It is significant that two of our greatest American historians, Prescott and Parkman, were nearly blind during a good part of their active careers. They had to have the sources read to them and turn the matter over and over in their minds before they could give anything out; and when they gave, *they gave!*

Now, the purpose of this quick, warm synthesis between research, thinking, and writing is to attain the three prime qualities of historical composition—clarity, vigor, and objectivity. You must think about your facts, analyze your material, and decide exactly what you mean before you can write it so that the average reader will understand. Do not fall into the fallacy of supposing that "facts speak for themselves." Most of the facts that you excavate, like other relics of past human activity, are dumb things; it is for you to make them speak by proper selection, arrangement, and emphasis. Dump your entire collection of facts on paper, and the result will be unreadable if not incomprehensible.

So, too, with vigor. If your whole paragraph or chapter is but a hypothesis, say so at the beginning, but do not bore and confuse the reader with numerous "buts," "excepts," "perhapses," "howevers," and "possiblys." Use direct rather than indirect statements, the active rather than the passive voice, and make every sentence and paragraph an organic whole. Above all, if you are writing historical narrative, make it move. Do not take time out in the middle of a political or military campaign to introduce special developments or literary trends, as McMaster did to the confusion of his readers. Place those admittedly important matters in a chapter or chapters by themselves so that your reader's attention will not be lost by constant interruption.

That brings us to the third essential quality—objectivity. Keep the reader constantly in mind. You are not writing history for yourself or for the professors who are supposed to know more about it than you do. Assume that you are writing for intelligent people who know nothing about your particular subject but whom you wish to interest and attract. I once asked the late Senator Beveridge why his *Life of John Marshall*, despite its great length and scholarly apparatus, was so popular. He replied: "The trouble with you professors of history is that you write for each other. I write for people almost completely ignorant of American history, as I was when I began my research."

A few more details. Even if the work you are writing does not call for footnotes, keep them in your copy until the last draft, for they will enable you to check up on your facts, statements, and quotations. And since accuracy is the prime virtue of the historian, this checking must be done, either by the author or by someone else. You will be surprised by the mistakes that creep in between a first rough draft and a final typed copy. And the better you write, the more your critics will enjoy finding misquotations and inaccuracies.

The matter of handling quotations seems to be a difficult one for young historians. There is nothing that adds so much to the charm and effectiveness of a history as good quotations from the sources, especially if the period be somewhat remote. But there is nothing so disgusting to the reader as long, tedious, broken quotations in small print, especially those in which, to make sense, the author has to interpolate words in brackets. Young writers are prone to use quotations in places where their own words would be better, and to incorporate in the text source excerpts that belong in footnotes or appendices. Avoid ending chapters with quotations, and never close your book with one.

Above all, do not be afraid to revise and rewrite. Reading aloud is a good test—historians' wives have to stand a lot of that! A candid friend who is not a historian and so represents the audience you are trying to reach, is perhaps the best "dog" to try it on. Even if he has little critical sense, it is encouraging to have him stay awake. My good friend Lucien Price years ago listened with a pained expression to a bit of my early work. "Now, just what do you mean by that?" he asked after a long, involved, pedantic, and quote-larded paragraph. I told him in words of one syllable, or perhaps two. "Fine!" said he, "I understand that. Now write down what you said; throw the other away!"

Undoubtedly the writer of history can enrich his mind and broaden his literary experience as well as better his craftsmanship by his choice of leisure reading. If he is so fortunate as to have had a classical education, no time will be better spent in making him an effective historian than in reading Latin and Greek authors. Both these ancient languages are such superb instruments of thought that a knowledge of them cures slipshod English and helps one to attain a clear, muscular style. All our greatest historical stylists—notably Prescott, Parkman, Fiske, and Frederick J. Turner—had a classical education and read the ancient historians in the original before they approached American history.

If you have little Latin and less Greek and feel unable to spare the time and effort to add them to your stock of tools, read the ancient classics in the best literary translations, such as North's Plutarch, Rawlinson's Herodotus, John J. Chapman's Æschylus, Gilbert Murray's Euripides, and, above all, Jowett's or Livingstone's Thucydides. Through them you will gain the content and spirit of the ancient classics, which will break down your provincialism, refresh your spirit, and give you a better philosphical insight into the ways of mankind than most of such works as the new science of psychology has brought forth. Moreover, you will be acquiring the same background as many of the great Americans of the past generations, thus aiding your understanding of them.

The reading of English classics will tend in the same diretion, and will also be a painless and unconscious means of improving your literary style. Almost every English or American writer of distinction is indebted to Shakespeare and the English Bible. The Authorized Version is not only the great source book of spiritual experience of English-speaking peoples; it is a treasury of plain, pungent words and muscular phrases, beautiful in themselves and with long associations, which we are apt to replace by smooth words lacking in punch, or by hackneyed or involved phrases. Here are a few examples chosen in five minutes from my desk Bible: I Samuel i, 28: "I have lent him to the Lord." What an apt phrase for anyone bringing up their son for the Church! Why say "loaned" instead of "lent"? Isaiah xxii, 5: "For it is a day of trouble, and of treading down, and of perplexity." In brief, just what we are going through today. But most modern historians would not feel that they were giving the reader his money's worth unless they wrote: "It is an era of agitation, of a progressive decline in the standard of living, and of uncertainty as to the correct policy." Romans xi, 25: "Wise in your own conceits." This epigram has often been used, but a modern writer would be tempted to express the thought in some such cumbrous manner as "Expert within the limits of your own fallacious theories."

Of course much of the Biblical phraseology is obsolete, and there are other literary quarries for historians. You can find many appropriate words, phrases, similes, and epigrams in American authors such as Mark Twain, Emerson, and Thoreau. I have heard an English economist push home a point to a learned audience with a quotation from *Alice in Wonderland*; American historians might make more use of *Huckleberry Finn*.

The historian can learn much from the novelist. Most writers of fiction are superior to all but the best historians in characterization and description. If you have difficulty in making people and events seem real, see if you cannot learn the technique from American novelists such as Sherwood Anderson, Joseph Hergesheimer and Margaret Mitchell. For me, the greatest master of all is Henry James. He used a relatively simple and limited vocabulary; but what miracles he wrought with it! What precise and perfect use he makes of words to convey the essence of a human situation to the reader! If you are not yet acquainted with Henry James, try the selection of his shorter novels and stories edited by Clifton Fadiman, and then read some of the longer novels, like *Roderick Hudson* and *The American*. And, incidentally, you will learn more about the top layers of American and European society in the second half of the nineteenth century than you can ever glean from the works of social historians.

What is the place of imagination in history? An historian or biographer is under restrictions unknown to a novelist. He has no right to override facts by his own imagination. If he is writing on a remote or obscure subject about which few facts are available, his imagination may legitimately weave them into a pattern. But to be honest he must make clear what is fact and what is hypothesis. The quality of imagination, if properly restrained by the conditions of historical discipline, is of great assistance in enabling one to discover problems to be solved, to grasp the significance of facts, to form hypotheses, to discern causes in their first beginnings, and, above all, to relate the past creatively to the present. There are many opportunities in historical narrative for bold, imaginative expressions. "A complete statement in the imaginative form of an important truth arrests attention," wrote Emerson, "and is repeated and remembered." Imagination used in this way invests an otherwise pedestrian narrative with vivid and exciting qualities.

Finally, the historian should have frequent recourse to the book of life. The richer his personal experience, the wider his human contacts, the more likely he is to effect a living contact with his audience. In writing, similes drawn from the current experience of this mechanical age rather than those rifled from the literary baggage of past eras, are the ones that will go home to his reader. Service on a jury or a local committee may be a revelation as to the political thoughts and habits of mankind. A month's labor in a modern factory would help any young academician to clarify his ideas of labor and capital. A camping trip in the woods will tell him things about Western pioneering that he can never learn in books. The great historians, with few exceptions, are those who have not merely studied, but lived; and whose studies have ranged over a much wider field than the period or subject of which they write.

The veterans of World War II who, for the most part, have completed their studies in college or graduate school, should not regard the years of their war service as wasted. Rather should they realize that the war gave them a rich experience of life, which is the best equipment for a historian. They have "been around," they have seen mankind at his best and his worst, they have shared the joy and passion of a mighty effort and they can read man's doings in the past with far greater understanding than if they had spent these years in sheltered academic groves.

To these young men especially, and to all young men I say (as the poet Chapman said to the young Elizabethan): "Be free, all worthy spirits, and stretch yourselves!" Bring all your knowledge of life to bear on everything that you write. Never let yourself bog down in pedantry and detail. Bring History, the most humane and noble form of letters, back to the proud position she once held; knowing that your words, if they be read and remembered, will enter into the stream of life, and perhaps move men to thought and action centuries hence, as do those of Thucydides after more than two thousand years.

Discussion Questions

1. Find a representative paragraph or so and describe those virtues of style that Morison himself embodies. Do his stylistic strengths include those he argues for in historical writing?
2. Morison says that one can still learn paragraphing from Macaulay. What are the virtues of Morison's own paragraphing techniques?
3. To what extent does Morison's style meet the critical standards of George Orwell in "Politics and the English Language" and of Edmund Wilson?
4. Morison once called the general style of this essay "hortatory." Write an essay that compares Morison's hortatory manner with that of another essayist in this collection.

John Muir

Born in Scotland, Muir (1838–1914) emigrated with his family to the United States while only a child. His father, a typical pioneer, over and over again would clear the land and create a farm, only to sell it to buy an even larger tract of wilderness farther west. Muir became an explorer and naturalist and was one of the first advocates of forest preservation. He was influential in the establishment of several National Parks, and his writings strongly affected the conservation programs of both Grover Cleveland and Theodore Roosevelt. The following selection is from his Memoirs of My Boyhood and Youth *(1913).*

Digging a Well

We called our second farm Hickory Hill, from its many fine hickory trees and the long gentle slope leading up to it. Compared with Fountain Lake farm it lay high and dry. The land was better, but it had no living water, no spring or stream or meadow or lake. A well ninety feet deep had to be dug, all except the first ten feet or so in fine-grained sandstone. When the sandstone was struck, my father, on the advice of a man who had worked in mines, tried to blast the rock; but from lack of skill the blasting went on very slowly, and father decided to have me do all the work with mason's chisels, a long, hard job, with a good deal of danger in it. I had to sit cramped in a space about three feet in diameter, and wearily chip, chip, with heavy hammer and chisels from early morning until dark, day after day, for weeks and months. In the morning, father and David lowered me in a wooden bucket by a windlass, hauled up what chips were left from the night before, then went away to the farm work and left me until noon, when they hoisted me out for dinner. After dinner I was promptly lowered again, the forenoon's accumulation of chips hoisted out of the way, and I was left until night.

One morning, after the dreary bore was about eighty feet deep, my life was all but lost in deadly choke-damp,—carbonic acid gas that had settled at the bottom during the night. Instead of clearing away the chips as usual when I was lowered to the bottom, I swayed back and forth and began to sink under the poison. Father, alarmed that I did not make any noise, shouted, "What's keeping you so still?" to which he got no reply. Just as I was settling down against the side of the wall, I happened to catch a glimpse of a branch of a bur-oak tree which leaned out over the mouth of the shaft. This suddenly awakened me, and to father's excited shouting I feebly murmured, "Take me out." But when he began to hoist he found I was not in the bucket and in wild alarm shouted, "Get in! Get in the bucket and hold on! Hold on!" Somehow I managed to get into the bucket, and that is all I remembered until I was dragged out, violently gasping for breath.

One of our near neighbors, a stone mason and miner by the name of William Duncan, came to see me, and after hearing the particulars of the accident he solemnly said: "Weel, Johnnie, it's God's mercy that you're alive. Many a companion of mine have I seen dead with choke-damp, but none that I ever saw or heard of was so near to death in it as you were and escaped without help." Mr. Duncan taught father to throw water down the shaft to absorb the gas, and also to drop a bundle of brush or hay attached to a light rope, dropping it again and again to carry down pure air and stir up the poison. When, after a day or two, I had recovered from the shock, father lowered me again to my work, after taking the precaution to test the air with a candle and stir it up well with a brush-and-hay bundle. The weary hammer-and-chisel-chipping went on as before, only more slowly, until ninety feet down, when at last I struck a fine, hearty gush of water. Constant dropping wears away stone. So does constant chipping, while at the same time wearing away the chipper. Father never spent an hour in that well. He trusted me to sink it straight and plumb, and I did, and built a fine covered top over it, and swung two iron-bound buckets in it from which we all drank for many a day.

Discussion Questions

1. William Manchester and Graham Greene also describe what it is like to pass through danger. What methods do those writers share with Muir? How does Muir differ in his manner from each of the other writers?

2. Where does Muir's general manner seem to change? Does it in fact change? If you think it does, tell from what to what. If you think it does not, show how it more particularly defines itself.

3. How does Muir convey the difficulty of his work? How, especially, does he create a sense of the passage of time? How does he convey both his attitude toward his father at the time of the event and his attitude at the time of describing the event? How is his task with regard to his father like that of Ralph Ellison? In what similar and in what different ways does each writer meet his task?

4. Rewrite the last two sentences in such a way as to give an entirely new sense of what the event meant to Muir. How do your sentences differ from his? What about his last two sentences is most representative of his general style? Find some names to describe that style.

LEWIS MUMFORD

Seven of Lewis Mumford's books are on architecture and city planning, but the subjects of his writing include history, religion, sociology, and the fine arts. His work in any one field almost always draws on the strengths of his interests in others. Born in New York in 1895, Mumford had an early passion for electricity. He wrote his first publications in this area and served as a naval radio operator in World War I. He studied at City College, Columbia, and The New School for Social Research before beginning his own investigations into the nature of modern life, one of whose aspects he analyzes in the following essay.

Sport and the "Bitch-Goddess"

The romantic movements were important as a corrective to the machine because they called attention to essential elements in life that were left out of the mechanical world-picture: they themselves prepared some of the materials for a richer synthesis. But there is within modern civilization a whole series of compensatory functions that, so far from making better integration possible, only serve to stabilize the existing state—and finally they themselves become part of the very regimentation they exist to combat. The chief of these institutions is perhaps mass-sports. One may define these sports as those forms of organized play in which the spectator is more important than the player, and in which a good part of the meaning is lost when the game is played for itself. Mass-sport is primarily a spectacle.

Unlike play, mass-sport usually requires an element of mortal chance or hazard as one of its main ingredients: but instead of the chance's occurring spontaneously, as in mountain climbing, it must be increased when the spectacle begins to bore the spectators. Play in one form or another is found in every human society and among a great many animal species: but sport in the sense of a mass-spectacle, with death to add to the underlying excitement, comes into existence when a population has been drilled and regimented and depressed to such an extent that it needs at least a vicarious participation in difficult feats of strength or skill or heroism in order to sustain its waning life-sense. The demand for circuses, and when the milder spectacles are still insufficiently life-arousing, the demand for sadistic exploits and finally for blood is characteristic of civilizations that are losing their grip: Rome under the Caesars, Mexico at the time of Montezuma, Germany under the Nazis. These forms of surrogate manliness and bravado are the surest signs of a collective impotence and a pervasive death wish. The dangerous symptoms of that ultimate decay one finds everywhere today in machine civilization under the guise of mass-sport.

The invention of new forms of sport and the conversion of play into sport were two of the distinctive marks of the last century: baseball is an example of the first, and the transformation of tennis and golf into tournament spectacles, within our day, is an example of the second. Unlike play, sport has an existence in our mechanical civilization even in its most abstract possible manifestation: the crowd that does not witness the ball game will huddle around the scoreboard in the metropolis to watch the change of counters. If it does not see the aviator finish a record flight around the world, it will listen over the radio to the report of his landing and hear the frantic shouts of the mob on the field: should the hero attempt to avoid a public reception and parade, he would be regarded as cheating. At times, as in horse-racing, the elements may be reduced to names and betting odds: participation need go no further than the newspaper and the betting booth, provided that the element of chance be there. Since the principal aim of our mechanical routine in industry is to reduce the domain of chance, it is in the glorification of chance and the unexpected, which sport provides, that the element extruded by the machine returns, with an accumulated emotional charge, to life in general. In the latest forms of mass-sport, like air races and motor races, the thrill of the spectacle is intensified by the promise of immediate death or fatal injury. The cry of horror that escapes from the crowd when the motor car overturns or the airplane crashes is not one of surprise but of fulfilled expectation: is it not fundamentally for the sake of exciting just such bloodlust that the competition itself is held and widely attended? By means of the talking picture that spectacle and that thrill are repeated in a thousand theatres throughout the world as a mere incident in the presentation of the weeks' news: so that a steady habituation to blood-letting and exhibitionistic murder and suicide accompanies the spread of the machine and, becoming stale by repetition in its milder forms, encourages the demand for more massive and desperate exhibitions of brutality.

Sport presents three main elements: the spectacle, the competition, and the personalities of the gladiators. The spectacle itself introduces the esthetic element, so often lacking in the paleotechnic industrial environment itself. The race is run or the game is played within a frame of spectators, tightly massed: the movements of this mass, their cries, their songs, their cheers, are a constant accompaniment of the spectacle: they play, in effect, the part of the Greek chorus in the new machine-drama, announcing what is about to occur and underlining the events of the contest. Through his place in the chorus, the spectator finds his special release: usually cut off from close physical associations by his impersonal routine, he is now at one with a primitive undifferentiated group. His muscles contract or relax with the progress of the game, his breath comes quick or slow, his shouts heighten the excitement of the moment and increase his internal sense of the drama: in moments of frenzy he pounds his neighbor's back or embraces him. The spectator feels himself contributing by his presence to the victory of his side, and sometimes, more by hostility to the enemy than encouragement to the friend, he does perhaps exercise a visible effect on the contest. It is a relief from the passive role of taking orders and automatically filling them, of conforming by means of a reduced "I" to a magnified "It," for in the sports arena the spectator has the illusion of being completely mobilized and utilized. Moreover, the spectacle itself is one of the richest satisfactions for the esthetic sense that the machine civilization offers to those that have no key to any other form of culture: the spectator knows the style of his favorite contestants in the way that the painter knows the characteristic line or palette of his master, and he reacts to the bowler, the pitcher, the punter, the server, the air ace, with a view, not only to his success in scoring, but to the esthetic spectacle itself. This point has been stressed in bullfighting; but of course it applies to every form of sport. There remains, nevertheless, a conflict between the desire for a skilled exhibition and the desire for a brutal outcome: the maceration or death of one or more of the contestants.

Now in the competition two elements are in conflict: chance and record-making. Chance is the sauce that stimulates the excitement of the spectator and increases his zest for gambling: whippet-racing and horse-racing are as effective in this relation as games where a greater degree of human skill is involved. But the habits of the mechanical régime are as difficult to combat in sport as in the realm of sexual behavior: hence one of the most significant elements in modern sport is the fact that an abstract interest in record-making has become one of its main preoccupations. To cut the fifth of a second off the time of running a race, to swim the English channel twenty-minutes faster than another swimmer, to stay up in the air an hour longer than one's rival did—these interests come into the competition and turn it from a purely human contest to one in which the real opponent is the previous record: time takes the place of a visible rival. Sometimes, as in dance marathons or flag-pole squattings, the record goes to feats of inane endurance: the blankest and dreariest of sub-human spectacles.

With the increase in professionalized skill that accompanies this change, the element of chance is further reduced: the sport, which was originally a drama, becomes an exhibition. As soon as specialism reaches this point, the whole performance is arranged as far as possible for the end of making possible the victory of the popular favorite: the other contestants are, so to say, thrown to the lions. Instead of "Fair Play" the rule now becomes "Success at Any Price."

Finally, in addition to the spectacle and the competition, there comes onto the stage, further to differentiate sport from play, the new type of popular hero, the professional player or sportsman. He is as specialized for the vocation as a soldier or an opera singer: he represents virility, courage, gameness, those talents in exercising and commanding the body which have so small a part in the new mechanical regimen itself: if the hero is a girl, her qualities must be Amazonian in character. The sports hero represents the masculine virtues, the Mars complex, as the popular motion picture actress or the bathing beauty contestant represents Venus. He exhibits that complete skill to which the amateur vainly aspires. Instead of being looked upon as a servile and ignoble being, because of the very perfection of his physical efforts, as the Athenians in Socrates' time looked upon the professional athletes and dancers, this new hero represents the summit of the amateur's effort, not at pleasure but at efficiency. The hero is handsomely paid for his efforts, as well as being rewarded by praise and publicity, and he thus further restores to sport its connection with the very commercialized existence from which it is supposed to provide relief—restores it and thereby sanctifies it. The few heroes who resist this vulgarization—notably Lindbergh—fall into popular or at least into journalistic disfavor, for they are only playing the less important part of the game. The really successful sports hero, to satisfy the mass-demand, must be midway between a pander and a prostitute.

Sport, then, in this mechanized society, is no longer a mere game empty of any reward other than the playing: it is a profitable business: millions are invested in arenas, equipment, and players, and the maintenance of sport becomes as important as the maintenance of any other form of profit-making mechanism. And the technique of mass sport infects other activities: scientific expeditions and geographic explorations are conducted in the manner of a speed stunt or a prizefight—*and for the same reason.* Business or recreation or mass spectacle, sport is always a means: even when it is reduced to athletic and military exercises held with great pomp within the sports arenas, the aim is to gather a record-breaking crowd of performers and spectators, and thus testify to the success or importance of the movement that is represented. Thus sport, which began originally, perhaps, as a spontaneous reaction against the machine, has become one of the mass-duties of the machine age. It is a part of that universal regimentation of life—for the sake of private profits or nationalistic exploit—from which its excitement provides a temporary and only a superficial release. Sport has turned out, in short, to be one of the least effective reactions against the machine. There is only one other reaction less effective in its final result: the most ambitious as well as the most disastrous. I mean war.

Discussion Questions

1. Within his essay, Mumford never defines explicitly what he means by the "Bitch-goddess." What definition does his essay as a whole imply for that term, which, as his quotation marks show, is not of his own making?

2. In what ways does Mumford organize his argument? How would the effectiveness of his argument have been changed by different methods of organization? Suppose he had begun with the points he makes at the end, for example. How would that change have dictated other changes in his argument?

3. How does Mumford's view on the public exposure of death compare to that of Nora Ephron? Where would he stand, on the evidence of this essay, on the issue of censorship?

4. Pick a form of recreation as yet outside Mumford's notion of mass sport (for example, Frisbee contests). Explain why the sport does not fit Mumford's definition and speculate on two different possibilities for its future.

5. Drawing examples from your own experience and observations, write an essay in which you defend or attack Mumford's assertion that "the thrill of the spectacle is intensified by the promise of immediate death or fatal injury."

Vladimir Nabokov

Vladimir Nabokov (1899–1977) described his life concisely as that of "an American writer born in Russia and educated in England, where I studied French Literature before spending fifteen years in Germany." Born into the Russian nobility, Nabokov escaped to England in 1919 at the end of the civil war that followed the Russian Revolution. By the time he escaped from the Nazis just before the final collapse of France in May of 1940, Nabokov had achieved a full career as a Russian novelist and poet among the large community of his fellow exiles in Western Europe. Coming to the United States, he began a new career as a writer in English, a language that, like French, he had known since childhood. After he had taught for many years at Wellesley and Cornell, the success of his most famous book, Lolita, in 1958 allowed him for the first time to devote all his efforts to writing. Today nearly forty of his books are still in print. The following essay makes up a part of his autobiography, Speak, Memory (1966).

Colored Hearing

As far back as I remember myself (with interest, with amusement, seldom with admiration or disgust), I have been subject to mild hallucinations. Some are aural, others are optical, and by none have I profited much. The fatidic accents that restrained Socrates or egged on Joaneta Darc have degenerated with me to the level of something one happens to hear between lifting and clapping down the receiver of a busy party-line telephone. Just before falling asleep, I often become aware of a kind of one-sided conversation going on in an adjacent section of my mind, quite independently from the actual trend of my thoughts. It is a neutral, detached, anonymous voice, which I catch saying words of no importance to me whatever—an English or a Russian sentence, not even addressed to me, and so trivial that I hardly dare give samples, lest the flatness I wish to convey be marred by a molehill of sense. This silly phenomenon seems to be the auditory counterpart of certain praedormitary visions, which I also know well. What I mean is not the bright mental image (as, for instance, the face of a beloved parent long dead) conjured up by a wing-stroke of the will; *that* is one of the bravest movements a human spirit can make. Nor am I alluding to the so-called *muscae volitantes*—shadows cast upon the retinal rods by motes in the vitreous humor, which are seen as transparent threads drifting across the visual field. Perhaps nearer to the hypnagogic mirages I am thinking of is the colored spot, the stab of an afterimage, with which the lamp one has just turned off wounds the palpebral night. However, a shock of this sort is not really a necessary starting point for the slow, steady development of the visions that pass before my closed eyes. They come and go, without the drowsy observer's participation, but are essentially different from dream pictures for he is still master of his senses. They are often grotesque. I am pestered by roguish profiles, by some coarse-featured and florid dwarf with a swelling nostril or ear. At times, however, my photisms take on a rather soothing *flou* quality, and then I see—projected, as it were, upon the inside of the eyelid—gray figures walking between beehives, or small black parrots gradually vanishing among mountain snows, or a mauve remoteness melting beyond moving masts.

On top of all this I present a fine case of colored hearing. Perhaps "hearing" is not quite accurate, since the color sensation seems to be produced by the very act of my orally forming a given letter while I imagine its outline. The long *a* of the English alphabet (and it is this alphabet I have in mind farther on unless otherwise stated) has for me the tint of weathered wood, but a French *a* evokes polished ebony. This black group also includes hard *g* (vulcanized rubber) and *r* (a sooty rag being ripped). Oatmeal *n*, noodle-limp *l*, and the ivory-backed hand mirror of *o* take care of the whites. I am puzzled by my French *on* which I see as the brimming tension-surface of alcohol in a small glass. Passing on to the blue group, there is steely *x*, thundercloud *z*, and huckleberry *k*. Since a subtle interaction exists between sound and shape, I see *q* as browner than *k*, while *s* is not the light blue of *c*, but a curious mixture of azure and mother-of-pearl. Adjacent tints do not merge, and diphthongs do not have special colors of their own, unless represented by a single character in some other language (thus the fluffy-gray, three-stemmed Russian letter that stands for *sh*, a letter as old as the rushes of the Nile, influences its English representation).

I hasten to complete my list before I am interrupted. In the green group, there are alder-leaf *f*, the unripe apple of *p*, and pistachio *t*. Dull green, combined somehow with violet, is the best I can do for *w*. The yellows comprise various *e*'s and *i*'s, creamy *d*, bright-golden *y*, and *u*, whose alphabetical value I can express only by "brassy with an olive sheen." In the brown group, there are the rich rubbery tone of soft *g*, paler *j*, and the drab shoelace of *h*. Finally, among the reds, *b* has the tone called burnt sienna by painters, *m* is a fold of pink flannel, and today I have at last perfectly matched *v* with "Rose Quartz" in Maerz and Paul's *Dictionary of Color*. The word for rainbow, a primary, but decidedly muddy, rainbow, is in my private language the hardly pronounceable: *kzspygv*. The first author to discuss *audition colorée* was, as far as I know, an albino physician in 1812, in Erlangen.

The confessions of a synesthete must sound tedious and pretentious to those who are protected from such leakings and drafts by more solid walls than mine are. To my mother, though, this all seemed quite normal. The matter came up, one day in my seventh year, as I was using a heap of old alphabet blocks to build a tower. I casually remarked to her that their colors were all wrong. We discovered then that some of her letters had the same tint as mine and that, besides, she was optically affected by musical notes. These evoked no chromatisms in me whatsoever. Music, I regret to say, affects me merely as an arbitrary succession of more or less irritating sounds. Under certain emotional circumstances I can stand the spasms of a rich violin, but the concert piano and all wind instruments bore me in small doses and flay me in larger ones. Despite the number of operas I was exposed to every winter (I must have attended *Ruslan* and *Pikovaya Dama* at least a dozen times in the course of half as many years), my weak responsiveness to music was completely overrun by the visual torment of not being able to read over Pimen's shoulder or of trying in vain to imagine the hawkmoths in the dim bloom of Juliet's garden.

My mother did everything to encourage the general sensitiveness I had to visual stimulation. How many were the aquarelles she painted for me; what a revelation it was when she showed me the lilac tree that grows out of mixed blue and red! Sometimes, in our St. Petersburg house, from a secret compartment in the wall of her dressing room (and my birth room), she would produce a mass of jewelry for my bedtime amusement. I was very small then, and those flashing tiaras and chokers and rings seemed to me hardly inferior in mystery and enchantment to the illumination in the city during imperial fêtes, when, in the padded stillness of a frosty night, giant monograms, crowns, and other armorial designs, made of colored electric bulbs—sapphire, emerald, ruby—glowed with a kind of charmed constraint above snow-lined cornices on housefronts along residential streets.

Discussion Questions

1. In what ways, if any, does Nabokov attempt to avoid seeming self-centered in writing about himself? For example, how does his first paragraph define the relation of himself as an author to himself as a subject? Does he maintain this relation throughout the essay?

2. At times Nabokov uses highly specialized diction (for example, "fatidic," "hypnagogic," "palpebral"). What would have been gained for his essay or lost by using more common synonyms or circumlocutions?

3. Compare the sense of childhood that Nabokov creates to the evocations of Richard Wright and John Muir.

4. Write a description of an odd mental phenomenon of your own (for example, déjà vu—the feeling of having been through an experience before—or a slip of the tongue).

5. In his last paragraph, Nabokov implies a change in his values concerning the relative "mystery and enchantment" of jewels and colored electric light bulbs. Which did he value most as a child? Which does he value most now? How would you describe the tone of voice in which you "hear" the sentence in which he expresses the distinction? For example, does it sound "off-hand," "stuck up," "cynical"? What terms would you use in place of these? Why?

V. S. NAIPAUL

V. S. Naipaul was born in the Hindu community of Trinidad in 1932. At the age of eighteen he went to England to study and in 1954 settled in London, where he began his career as a writer and where he has lived ever since. He has written seventeen books and has received numerous literary prizes. His works of fiction include The Mystic Masseur (1957); Miguel Street (1959), a collection of stories based on his Trinidadian childhood; A House for Mr. Biswas (1961); In a Free State (1971), which won England's prestigious Booker Prize; and his most famous novel, A Bend in the River (1979).

Naipaul began traveling in 1960: The Middle Passage (1962) is an account of Caribbean colonial society; An Area of Darkness (1964) is a personal record of a year spent in India, the land of his grandparents, where he returned a decade later to write India: A Wounded Civilization (1977). The following description of revolutionary Tehran is reprinted from Naipaul's Islamic journey, Among the Believers (1981).

The New Tehran

We made a technical stop at Kuwait, to refuel; no one left the plane. It was dark, but dawn was not far off. The light began to come; the night vanished. And we saw that the airport—such a pattern of electric lights from above—had been built on sand. The air that came through the ventilators was warm. It was 40 degrees Centigrade outside, 104 Fahrenheit, and the true day had not begun.

Tehran was going to be cooler, the steward said. It was an hour's flight to the northeast: more desert, oblongs of pale vegetation here and there, and here and there gathers of rippled earth that sometimes rose to mountains.

After all that I had heard about the Shah's big ideas for his country, the airport building at Tehran was a disappointment. The arrival hall was like a big shed. Blank rectangular patches edged with reddish dust—ghost pictures in ghostly frames—showed where, no doubt, there had been photographs of the Shah and his family or his monuments. Revolutionary leaflets and caricatures were taped down on walls and pillars; and—also taped down: sticky paper and handwritten notices giving a curious informality to great events—there were colour photographs of the Ayatollah Khomeini, as hard-eyed and sensual and unreliable and roguish-looking as any enemy might have portrayed him.

The airport branch of the Melli Bank—rough tables, three clerks, a lot of paper, a littered floor—was like an Indian bazaar stall. A handwritten notice on the counter said: *Dear Guests. God is the Greatest. Welcome to the Islamic Republic of Iran.* Bits of sticky brown paper dotted the customs notice boards that advised passengers of their allowances. The brown paper did away with the liquor allowance; it was part of the Islamic welcome.

The luggage track, which should have been rolling out our

luggage, didn't move for a long time. And the Iranian passengers (the physician and his family among them), with their London shopping bags, seemed to become different people. At London airport they had been Iranians, people from the fairyland of oil and money, spenders; now, in the shabby arrival hall, patient in their own setting and among their own kind, they looked like country folk who had gone to town.

The customs man had a little black brush moustache. He asked, "Whisky?" His pronunciation of the word, and his smile, seemed to turn the query into a joke. When I said no he took my word and smilingly waved me out into the summer brightness, to face the post-revolutionary rapaciousness of the airport taxi men, who after six months were more than ever animated by memories of the old days, when the world's salesmen came to Tehran, there were never enough hotel rooms, and no driver pined for a fare.

The colours of the city were as dusty and pale as they had appeared from the air. Dust blew about the road, coated the trees, dimmed the colours of cars. Bricks and plaster were the colour of dust; unfinished buildings looked abandoned and crumbling; and walls, like abstracts of the time, were scribbled over in the Persian script and stencilled with portraits of Khomeini.

On the outskirts of the city, in what looked like waste ground, I saw a low khaki-coloured tent, a queue of men and veiled women, and some semi-uniformed men. I thought of refugees from the countryside, dole queues. But then—seeing another tent and another queue in front of an unfinished apartment block—I remembered it was the day of an election, the second test of the people's will since the revolution. The first had been a referendum; the people had voted then for an Islamic republic. This election was for an "Assembly of Experts," who would work out an Islamic constitution. Khomeini had advised that priests should be elected.

Experts were necessary, because an Islamic constitution couldn't simply be adopted. No such thing existed or had ever existed. An Islamic constitution was something that had to be put together; and it had to be something of which the Prophet would have approved. The trouble there was that the Prophet, creating his seventh-century Arabian state, guided always by divine revelation, had very much ruled as his own man. That was where the priests came in. They might not have ideas about a constitution—a constitution was, after all, a concept from outside the Muslim world; but, with their knowledge of the Koran and the doings of the Prophet, the priests would know what was un-Islamic.

My hotel was in central Tehran. It was one of the older hotels of the city. It was behind a high wall; it had a gateman's lodge, an asphalted circular drive, patches of lawn with shrubs and trees. It was in better order than I had imagined; there were even a few cars. But the building the driver took me to had a chain across the glass door. Someone shouted from the other side of the compound. The building we had gone to was closed. It was the older building of the hotel; during the boom they had built a new block, and now it was only that block that was open.

A number of young men—the hotel taxi drivers, to whom the cars outside belonged—were sitting idly together in one corner of the lobby, near the desk. Away from that corner the lobby was empty. In the middle of the floor there was a very large patterned carpet; the chairs arranged about it appeared to await a crowd. There were glass walls on two sides. On one side was the courtyard, with the dusty shrubs and pines and the parked hotel taxis; on the other side, going up to the hotel wall, was a small paved pool area, untenanted, glaring in the light, with metal chairs stacked up below an open shed.

The room to which I was taken up was of a good size, with sturdy wooden furniture, and with wood panelling three or four feet up the side walls. The glass wall at the end faced North Tehran; a glass door opened onto a balcony. But the air-conditioning duct was leaking through its exhaust grille, and the blue carpet tiling in the vestibule was sodden and stained.

The hotel man—it was hard, in the idleness of the hotel, to attach the professional status of "boy" to him, though he wore the uniform—smiled and pointed to the floor above and said, "Bathroom," as though explanation was all that was required. The man he sent up spoke about condensation; he made the drips seem normal, even necessary. And then—explanations abruptly abandoned—I was given another room.

It was furnished like the first and had the same view. On the television set here, though, there was a white card, folded down the middle and standing upright. It gave the week's programmes on the "international," English-language service of Iranian television. The service had long been suspended. The card was six months old. The revolution had come suddenly to this hotel.

It was Ramadan, the Muslim fasting month; it was Friday, the sabbath; and it was an election day. Tehran was unusually quiet, but I didn't know that; and when in the afternoon I went walking I felt I was in a city where a calamity had occurred. The shops in the main streets were closed and protected by steel gates. Signs on every floor shrieked the names of imported things—Seiko, Citizen, Rolex, Mary Quant of Chelsea, Aiwa—and on that closed afternoon they were like names from Tehran's past.

THE NEW TEHRAN

The pavements were broken. Many shop signs were broken or had lost some of their raised letters. Dust and grime were so general, and on illuminated signs looked so much like the effect of smoke, that buildings that had been burnt out in old fires did not immediately catch the eye. Building work seemed to have been suspended; rubble heaps and gravel heaps looked old, settled.

On the walls were posters of the revolution, and in the pavement kiosks there were magazines of the revolution. The cover of one had a composite photograph of the Shah as a bathing beauty: the head of the Shah attached to the body of a woman in a bikini—but the bikini had been brushed over with a broad stroke of black, not to offend modesty. In another caricature the Shah, jacketed, his tie slackened, sat on a lavatory seat with his trousers down, and with a Tommy gun in his hand. A suitcase beside him was labelled *To Israel* and *Bahama*; an open canvas bag showed a bottle of whisky and a copy of *Time* magazine.

Young men in tight, open-necked shirts dawdled on the broken pavements. They were handsome men of a clear racial type, small, broad-shouldered, narrow-waisted. They were working men of peasant antecedents, and there was some little air of vanity and danger about them that afternoon: they must have been keyed up by the communal Friday prayers. In their clothes, and especially their shirts, there was that touch of flashiness which—going by what I had seen in India—I associated with people who had just emerged from traditional ways and now possessed the idea that, in clothes as in other things, they could choose for themselves.

The afternoon cars and motorcycles went by, driven in the Iranian way. I saw two collisions. One shop had changed its name. It was now Our Fried Chicken, no longer the chicken of Kentucky, and the figure of the Southern colonel had been fudged into something quite meaningless (except to those who remembered the colonel). Revolutionary Guards, young men with guns, soon ceased to be surprising; they were part of the revolutionary sabbath scene. There were crowds outside the cinemas; and, Ramadan though it was, people were buying pistachio nuts and sweets from the *confiseries*—so called—that were open.

Far to the north, at the end of a long avenue of plane trees, an avenue laid out by the Shah's father, was the Royal Tehran Hilton. It was "royal" no longer. The word had been taken off the main roadside sign and hacked away from the entrance; but inside the hotel the word survived like a rooted weed, popping up fresh and clean on napkins, bills, menus, crockery.

The lounge was nearly empty; the silence there, among waiters and scattered patrons, was like the silence of embarrassment.

Iranian samovars were part of the décor. (There had been some foreign trade in these samovars as decorative ethnic objects; two years or so before, I had seen a number of them in the London stores, converted into lamp bases.) Alcohol could no longer be served; but for the smart (and non-Christian) who needed to sip a nonalcoholic drink in style, there was Orange Blossom or Virgin Mary or Swinger.

Chez Maurice was the Hilton's French restaurant. It was done up in an appropriate way, with brownish paper, a dark-coloured dado, and sconce lights. On the glass panels of one wall white letters, set in little arcs, said: *Vins et Liqueurs, Le Patron Mange Içi, Gratinée à Toute Heure.* In the large room, which might have seated a hundred, there was only a party of five, and they were as subdued as the people in the lounge. The soup I had, like the sturgeon which followed it, was heavy with a brown paste. But the waiters still undid napkins and moved and served with panache; it added to the embarrassment.

Every table was laid. Every table had a fresh rose, and pre-revolutionary give-aways; the coloured postcard (the restaurant had been founded four years before, in 1975); the little ten-page note pad that diners in places like this were thought to need: *Chez Maurice, Tehran's Most Distinctive Restaurant, Le Restaurant le Plus Sélect de Tehran.* Six months after the revolution these toys—pads, postcards—still existed; when they were used up there would be no more.

The pool at the side of the hotel was closed, for chemical cleaning, according to the notice. But the great concrete shell next door, the planned extension to the Royal Tehran Hilton, had been abandoned, with all the building materials on the site and the cranes. There were no "passengers" now, the waiter said; and the contractors had left the country. From the Hilton you could look across to the other hills of North Tehran and see other unfinished, hollow buildings that looked just as abandoned. The revolution had caught the "international" city of North Tehran in mid-creation.

And I thought, when I went back to my hotel, that there was an unintended symbolism in the revolutionary poster on the glass front door. The poster was printed on both sides. The side that faced the courtyard was straightforward, a guerrilla pin-up of Yassir Arafat of the Palestine Liberation Organization in dark glasses and checkered red headdress.

On the reverse was an allegorical painting of blood and revenge. In the foreground there was a flat landscape: a flat, featureless land bisected by a straight black road, marked down the middle by a broken white line. On this road a veiled woman, seen from the back, lay half collapsed, using her last strength to lift up her child as if to heaven. The woman had a bloodied back; there was blood on the black road. Out of that blood, higher up the road, giant red tulips had grown, breaking up the heavy crust of the black road with the white markings; and above the tulips, in the sky, was the face of Khomeini, the saviour, frowning.

Khomeini saved and avenged. But the tulips he had called up from the blood of martyrs had damaged the modern road (so carefully rendered by the artist) for good; that road in the wilderness now led nowhere.

Also, in this allegory of the revolution, personality had been allowed only to the avenger. The wounded woman, small in the foreground, with whose pain the upheaval began, was veiled and faceless; she was her pain alone. It was the allegorist's or caricaturist's licence; and it wouldn't have been remarkable if there hadn't been so many faceless people in the posters and drawings I had seen that day.

In one election poster a faceless crowd—the veiled women reduced to simple triangular outlines—held up photographs of candidates of a particular party. In a newspaper the face of Ali, the Shia hero, the cousin and son-in-law of the Prophet, was shown as a surrealist outline, transparent against a landscape. In one poster Khomeini himself had been faceless, his features (within the outline of turban, cheeks, and beard) replaced by a clenched fist.

Facelessness had begun to seem like an Islamic motif. And it was, indeed, the subject of protest in *Iran Week* (lettering like *Newsweek*), a postrevolutionary English-language paper I had bought in a kiosk. The paper was for the revolution, but it was protesting against what had begun to come with the revolution, all the Islamic bans on alcohol, Western television programmes, fashions, music, mixed bathing, women's sports, dancing. The cover illustration showed a twisted sitting-room where walls had been replaced by iron bars. The family posing for their picture in this room—father, mother, two children—were dressed in Western clothes; but where their faces should have been there were white blanks.

Individualism was to be surrendered to the saviour and avenger. But when the revolution was over, individualism—in the great city the Shah had built—was to be cherished again. That seemed to be the message of the *Iran Week* cover.

Discussion Questions

1. What sense of Tehran does Naipaul's detailed description convey? He never once in the essay renders a direct opinion, but how does his attitude emerge?

2. What is the allegorical meaning of the Khomeini poster Naipaul notices on the hotel door? How would his interpretation of the picture differ from an Islamic interpretation?

3. Compare Naipaul's techniques of observation in this essay to Simone de Beauvoir's, Ada Louise Huxtable's and John McPhee's. To which of these writers is Naipaul most similar? In what way? Which of these writers seems closest to the city he or she is observing? Which is most detached? How do the writers manage to create a sense of a society and culture from urban details alone?

4. Choose a city that you have visited and with Naipaul's descriptive techniques in mind, write a short essay in which you show your attitude toward the place through selection of details alone.

José Ortega y Gasset

The Spanish philosopher José Ortega y Gasset (1883–1955) was born in Madrid, received a Jesuit education, and took his doctorate at the University of Madrid, where he subsequently taught metaphysics. A humanist, Ortega believed that the immediate conditions of human life constituted the basic reality ("I am I, and my circumstance"), an intellectual position that can be seen in the following selection from one of his most important books, The Dehumanization of Art (1925; translated 1948).

Ortega left Spain at the outbreak of the Civil War in 1936 and lived for nearly ten years in France and Argentina before returning to Europe in 1943 to lecture in Lisbon. In 1948 he founded the Institute of Humanities in Madrid. The English translations of his major works include The Modern Theme (1931), The Revolt of the Masses (1932), and Towards a Philosophy of History (1941).

Emotional Reality

A great man is dying. His wife is by his bedside. A doctor takes the dying man's pulse. In the background two more persons are discovered: a reporter who is present for professional reasons, and a painter whom mere chance has brought here. Wife, doctor, reporter, and painter witness one and the same event. Nonetheless, this identical event—a man's death—impresses each of them in a different way. So different indeed that the several aspects have hardly anything in common. What this scene means to the wife who is all grief has so little to do with what it means to the painter who looks on impassively that it seems doubtful whether the two can be said to be present at the same event.

It thus becomes clear that one and the same reality may split up into many diverse realities when it is beheld from different points of view. And we cannot help asking ourselves: Which of all these realities must then be regarded as the real and authentic one? The answer, no matter how we decide, cannot but be arbitrary. Any preference can be founded on caprice only. All these realities are equivalent, each being authentic for its corresponding point of view. All we can do is to classify the points of view and to determine which among them seems, in a practical way, most normal or most spontaneous. Thus we arrive at a conception of reality that is by no means absolute, but at least practical and normative.

As for the points of view of the four persons present at the deathbed, the clearest means of distinguishing them is by measuring one of their dimensions, namely the emotional distance between each person and the event they all witness. For the wife of the dying man the distance shrinks to almost nothing. What is happening so tortures her soul and absorbs her mind that it becomes one with her person. Or to put it inversely, the wife is drawn into the scene, she is part of it. A thing can be seen, an event can be observed, only when we have separated it from ourselves and it has ceased to form a living part of our being. Thus the wife is not present at the scene, she is in it. She does not behold it, she "lives" it.

The doctor is several degrees removed. To him this is a professional case. He is not drawn into the event with the frantic and blinding anxiety of the poor woman. However it is his bounden duty as a doctor to take a serious interest, he carries responsibility, perhaps his professional honor is at stake. Hence he too, albeit in a less integral and less intimate way, takes part in the event. He is involved in it not with his heart but with the professional portion of his self. He too "lives" the scene although with an agitation originating not in the emotional center, but in the professional surface, of his existence.

When we now put ourselves in the place of the reporter we realize that we have travelled a long distance away from the tragic event. So far indeed that we have lost all emotional contact with it. The reporter, like the doctor, has been brought here for professional reasons and not out of a spontaneous human interest. But while the doctor's profession requires him to interfere, the reporter's requires him precisely to stay aloof; he has to confine himself to observing. To him the event is a mere scene, a pure spectacle on which he is expected to report in his newspaper column. He takes no feeling part in what is happening here, he is emotionally free, an outsider. He does not "live" the scene, he observes it. Yet he observes it with a view to telling his readers about it. He wants to interest them, to move them, and if possible to make them weep as though they each had been the dying man's best friend. From his schooldays he remembers Horace's recipe: *"Si vis me flere dolendum est primum ipsi tibi"*—if you want me to weep you must first grieve yourself.

Obedient to Horace the reporter is anxious to pretend emotion, hoping that it will benefit his literary performance. If he does not "live" the scene he at least pretends to "live" it.

The painter, in fine, completely unconcerned, does nothing but keep his eyes open. What is happening here is none of his business; he is, as it were, a hundred miles removed from it. His is a purely perceptive attitude; indeed, he fails to perceive the event in its entirety. The tragic inner meaning escapes his attention which is directed exclusively toward the visual part—color values, lights, and shadows. In the painter we find a maximum of distance and a minimum of feeling intervention.

The inevitable dullness of this analysis will, I hope, be excused if it now enables us to speak in a clear and precise way of a scale of emotional distances between ourselves and reality. In this scale, the degree of closeness is equivalent to the degree of feeling participation; the degree of remoteness, on the other hand, marks the degree to which we have freed ourselves from the real event, thus objectifying it and turning it into a theme of pure observation. At one end of the scale the world—persons, things, situations—is given to us in the aspect of "lived" reality; at the other end we see everything in the aspect of "observed" reality.

At this point we must make a remark that is essential in aesthetics and without which neither old art nor new art can be satisfactorily analyzed. Among the diverse aspects of reality we find one from which all the others derive and which they all presuppose: "lived" reality. If nobody had ever "lived" in pure and frantic abandonment a man's death, the doctor would not bother, the readers would not understand the reporter's pathos, and the canvas on which the painter limned a person on a bed surrounded by mourning figures would be meaningless. The same holds for any object, be it a person, a thing, or a situation. The primal aspect of an apple is that in which I see it when I am about to eat it. All its other possible forms—when it appears, for instance, in a Baroque ornament, or on a still life of Cézanne's, or in the eternal metaphor of a girl's apple cheeks—preserve more or less that original aspect. A painting or a poem without any vestiges of "lived" forms would be unintelligible, i.e., nothing—as a discourse is nothing whose every word is emptied of its customary meaning.

That is to say, in the scale of realities "lived" reality holds a peculiar primacy which compels us to regard it as "the" reality. Instead of "lived" reality we may say "human" reality. The painter who impassively witnesses the death scene appears "inhuman." In other words, the human point of view is that in which we "live" situations, persons, things. And, vice versa, realities—a woman, a countryside, an event—are human when they present the aspect in which they are usually "lived."

As an example, the importance of which will appear later, let us mention that among the realities which constitute the world are our ideas. We use our ideas in a "human" way when we employ them for thinking things. Thinking of Napoleon, for example, we are normally concerned with the great man of that name. A psychologist, on the other hand, adopts an unusual, "inhuman" attitude when he forgets about Napoleon and, prying into his own mind, tries to analyze his idea of Napoleon as such idea. His perspective is the opposite of that prevailing in spontaneous life. The idea, instead of functioning as the means to think an object with, is itself made the object and the aim of thinking.

Discussion Questions

1. Why do the wife, doctor, reporter, and painter perceive the dying man differently? What do their perceptions have in common? What about the dying man? Why aren't his perceptions accounted for in Ortega y Gasset's "reality scale"? Why aren't Ortega y Gasset's?

2. What does Ortega y Gasset mean by "lived reality"? Aren't all the participants in the scene alive? Explain the value he places on this term.

3. Is Ortega y Gasset simply saying that the different people perceive things differently, or is he driving at something else? How does his perceptual scale apply to George Orwell's points of view in "A Hanging"?

4. Try illustrating Ortega y Gasset's "reality scale" with some other phenomenon—a football game, a courtroom trial, a rock concert, and so forth. Rank participants according to their degree of emotional closeness to the scene. How does the "reality scale" help you understand the human dimensions of the event? What problems do you encounter in the ranking? Do you think your role as ranker becomes an issue?

GEORGE ORWELL

George Orwell was the pen name of Eric Arthur Blair (1903–1950), an Englishman born in Bengal. Blair won a scholarship to Eton and afterwards served with the Indian Imperial Police in Burma from 1922 to 1927. Outraged by the evils of British imperialism—though he never neglected to point out native evils as well—Blair quit the police and tramped about in a semi-disguised fashion through the working-class districts of London and Paris. Out of these experiences he wrote his first book, Down and Out in Paris and London (1933), which he published under the pseudonym of George Orwell.

Orwell's politics were complex. Though he often wrote from a leftist, anti-imperialist point of view, he was fiercely anti-communist and anti-Stalinist, positions he powerfully expressed in Homage to Catalonia (1938) and Animal Farm (1945). His most famous novel—one of the best-known works of fiction in this century —is Nineteen Eighty-Four (1949), a terrifying portrayal of modern totalitarian systems ("Big Brother Is Watching You"). The following three essays appeared in Shooting an Elephant and Other Essays (1950).

Shooting an Elephant

In Moulmein, in lower Burma, I was hated by large numbers of people—the only time in my life that I have been important enough for this to happen to me. I was sub-divisional police officer of the town, and in an aimless, petty kind of way anti-European feeling was very bitter. No one had the guts to raise a riot, but if a European woman went through the bazaars alone somebody would probably spit betel juice over her dress. As a police officer I was an obvious target and was baited whenever it seemed safe to do so. When a nimble Burman tripped me up on the football field and the referee (another Burman) looked the other way, the crowd yelled with hideous laughter. This happened more than once. In the end the sneering yellow faces of young men that met me everywhere, the insults hooted after me when I was at a safe distance, got badly on my nerves. The young Buddhist priests were the worst of all. There were several thousands of them in the town and none of them seemed to have anything to do except stand on street corners and jeer at Europeans.

All this was perplexing and upsetting. For at that time I had already made up my mind that imperialism was an evil thing and the sooner I chucked up my job and got out of it the better. Theoretically—and secretly, of course—I was all for the Burmese and all against their oppressors, the British. As for the job I was doing, I hated it more bitterly than I can perhaps make clear. In a job like that you see the dirty work of Empire at close quarters. The wretched prisoners huddling in the stinking cages of the lock-ups, the grey, cowed faces of the long-term convicts, the scarred buttocks of the men who had been flogged with bamboos—all these oppressed me with an intolerable sense of guilt. But I could get nothing into perspective. I was young and ill-educated and I had had to think out my problems in the utter silence that is imposed on every Englishman in the East. I did not even know that the British Empire is dying, still less did I know that it is a great deal better than the younger empires that are going to supplant it. All I knew was that I was stuck between my hatred of the empire I served and my rage against the evil-spirited little beasts who tried to make my job impossible. With one part of my mind I thought of the British Raj as an unbreakable tyranny, as something clamped down, in *saecula saeculorum,* upon the will of prostrate peoples; with another part I thought that the greatest joy in the world would be to drive a bayonet into a Buddhist priest's guts. Feelings like these are the normal by-products of imperialism; ask any Anglo-Indian official, if you can catch him off duty.

One day something happened which in a roundabout way was enlightening. It was a tiny incident in itself, but it gave me a better glimpse than I had had before of the real nature of imperialism—the real motive for which despotic governments act. Early one morning the sub-inspector at a police station the other end of the town rang me up on the 'phone and said that an elephant was ravaging the bazaar. Would I please come and do something about it? I did not know what I could do, but I wanted to see what was happening and I got on to a pony and started out. I took my rifle, an old .44 Winchester and much too small to kill an elephant, but I thought the noise might be useful *in terrorem.* Various Burmans stopped me on the way and told me about the elephant's doings. It was not, of course, a wild elephant, but a tame one which had gone "must." It had been chained up, as tame elephants always are when their attack of "must" is due, but on the previous night it had broken its chain and escaped. Its mahout, the only person who could manage it when it was in that state, had set out in pursuit, but had taken the wrong direction and was now twelve hours' journey away, and in the morning the elephant had suddenly reappeared in the town. The Burmese population had no weapons and were quite helpless against it. It had already destroyed somebody's bamboo hut, killed a cow and raided some fruit-stalls and devoured the stock; also it had met the municipal rubbish van and, when the driver jumped out and took to his heels, had turned the van over and inflicted violences upon it.

The Burmese sub-inspector and some Indian constables were waiting for me in the quarter where the elephant had been seen. It was a very poor quarter, a labyrinth of squalid bamboo huts, thatched with palm-leaf, winding all over a steep hillside. I remember that it was a cloudy, stuffy morning at the beginning of the rains. We began questioning the people as to where the elephant had gone and, as usual, failed to get any definite information. That is invariably the case in the East; a story always sounds clear enough at a distance, but the nearer you get to the scene of events the vaguer it becomes. Some of the people said that the elephant had gone in one direction, some said that he had gone in another, some professed not even to have heard of any elephant. I had almost made up my mind that the whole story was a pack of lies, when we heard yells a little distance away. There was a loud, scandalized cry of "Go away, child! Go away this instant!" and an old woman with a switch in her hand came round the corner of a hut, violently shooing away a crowd of naked children. Some more women followed, clicking their tongues and exclaiming; evidently there was something that the children ought not to have seen. I rounded the hut and saw a man's dead body sprawling in the mud. He was an Indian, a black Dravidian coolie, almost naked, and he could not have been dead many minutes. The people said that the elephant had come suddenly upon him round the corner of the hut, caught him with its trunk, put its foot on his back and ground him into the earth. This was the rainy season and the ground was soft, and his face had scored a trench a foot deep and a couple of yards long. He was lying on his belly with arms crucified and head sharply twisted to one side. His face was coated with mud, the eyes wide open, the teeth bared and grinning with an expression of unendurable agony. (Never tell me, by the way, that the dead look peaceful. Most of the corpses I have seen looked devilish.) The friction of the great beast's foot had stripped the skin from his back as neatly as one skins a rabbit. As soon as I saw the dead man I sent an orderly to a friend's house nearby to borrow an elephant rifle. I had already sent back the pony, not wanting it to go mad with fright and throw me if it smelt the elephant.

The orderly came back in a few minutes with a rifle and five cartridges, and meanwhile some Burmans had arrived and told us that the elephant was in the paddy fields below, only a few hundred yards away. As I started forward practically the whole population of the quarter flocked out of the houses and followed me. They had seen the rifle and were all shouting excitedly that I was going to shoot the elephant. They had not shown much interest in the elephant when he was merely ravaging their homes, but it was different now that he was going to be shot. It was a bit of fun to them, as it would be to an English crowd; besides they wanted the meat. It made me vaguely uneasy. I had no intention of shooting the elephant—I had merely sent for the rifle to defend myself if necessary—and it is always unnerving to have a crowd following you. I marched down the hill, looking and feeling a fool, with the rifle over my shoulder and an ever-growing army of people jostling at my heels. At the bottom, when you got away from the huts, there was a metalled road and beyond that a miry waste of paddy fields a thousand yards across, not yet ploughed but soggy from the first rains and dotted with coarse grass. The elephant was standing eight yards from the road, his left side towards us. He took not the slightest notice of the crowd's approach. He was tearing up branches of grass, beating them against his knees to clean them and stuffing them into his mouth.

I had halted on the road. As soon as I saw the elephant I knew with perfect certainty that I ought not to shoot him. It is a serious matter to shoot a working elephant—it is comparable to destroying a huge and costly piece of machinery—and obviously one ought not to do it if it can possibly be avoided. And at that distance, peacefully eating, the elephant looked no more dangerous than a cow. I thought then and I think now that his attack of "must" was already passing off; in which case he would merely wander harmlessly about until the mahout came back and caught him. Moreover, I did not in the least want to shoot him. I decided that I would watch him for a little while to make sure that he did not turn savage again, and then go home.

But at that moment I glanced round at the crowd that had followed me. It was an immense crowd, two thousand at the least and growing every minute. It blocked the road for a long distance on either side. I looked at the sea of yellow faces above the garish clothes—faces all happy and excited over this bit of fun, all certain that the elephant was going to be shot. They were watching me as they would watch a conjurer about to perform a trick. They did not like me, but with the magical rifle in my hands I was momentarily worth watching. And suddenly I realized that I should have to shoot the elephant after all. The people expected it of me and I had got to do it; I could feel their two thousand wills pressing me forward, irresistibly. And it was at this moment, as I stood there with the rifle in my hands, that I first grasped the hollowness, the futility of the white man's dominion in the East. Here was I, the white man with his gun, standing in front of the unarmed native crowd—seemingly the leading actor of the piece; but in reality I was only an absurd puppet pushed to and fro by the will of those yellow faces behind. I perceived in this moment that when the white man turns tyrant it is his own freedom that he destroys. He becomes a sort of hollow, posing dummy, the conventionalized figure of a sahib. For it is the condition of his rule that he shall spend his life in trying to impress the "natives," and so in every crisis he has got to do what the "natives" expect of him. He wears a mask, and his face grows to fit it. I had got to shoot the elephant. I had committed myself to doing it when I sent for the rifle. A sahib has got to act like a sahib; he has got to appear resolute, to know his own mind and do definite things. To come all that way, rifle in hand, with two thousand people marching at my heels, and then to trail feebly away, having done nothing—no, that was impossible. The crowd would laugh at me. And my whole life, every white man's life in the East, was one long struggle not to be laughed at.

But I did not want to shoot the elephant. I watched him beating his bunch of grass against his knees, with that preoccupied grandmotherly air that elephants have. It seemed to me that it would be murder to shoot him. At that age I was not squeamish about killing animals, but I had never shot an elephant and never wanted to. (Somehow it always seems worse to kill a *large* animal.) Besides, there was the beast's owner to be considered. Alive, the elephant was worth at least a hundred pounds; dead, he would only be worth the value of his tusks, five pounds, possibly. But I had got to act quickly. I turned to some experienced-looking Burmans who had been there when we arrived, and asked them how the elephant had been behaving. They all said the same thing: he took no notice of you if you left him alone, but he might charge if you went too close to him.

It was perfectly clear to me what I ought to do. I ought to walk up to within, say, twenty-five yards of the elephant and test his behavior. If he charged, I could shoot; if he took no notice of me, it would be safe to leave him until the mahout came back. But also I knew that I was going to do no such thing. I was a poor shot with a rifle and the ground was soft mud into which one would sink at every step. If the elephant charged and I missed him, I should have about as much chance as a toad under a steam-roller. But even then I was not thinking particularly of my own skin, only of the watchful yellow faces behind. For at that moment, with the crowd watching me, I was not afraid in the ordinary sense, as I would have been if I had been alone. A white man mustn't be frightened in front of "natives"; and so, in general, he isn't frightened. The sole thought in my mind was that if anything went wrong those two thousand Burmans would see me pursued, caught, trampled on and reduced to a grinning corpse like that Indian up the hill. And if that happened it was quite probable that some of them would laugh. That would never do. There was only one alternative. I shoved the cartridges into the magazine and lay down on the road to get a better aim.

The crowd grew very still, and a deep, low, happy sigh, as of people who see the theatre curtain go up at last, breathed from innumerable throats. They were going to have their bit of fun after all. The rifle was a beautiful German thing with cross-hair sights. I did not then know that in shooting an elephant one would shoot to cut an imaginary bar running from ear-hole to ear-hole. I ought, therefore, as the elephant was sideways on, to have aimed straight at his ear-hole; actually I aimed several inches in front of this, thinking the brain would be further forward.

When I pulled the trigger I did not hear the bang or feel the kick—one never does when a shot goes home—but I heard the devilish roar of glee that went up from the crowd. In that instant, in too short a time, one would have thought, even for the bullet to get there, a mysterious, terrible change had come over the elephant. He neither stirred nor fell, but every line of his body had altered. He looked suddenly stricken, shrunken, immensely old, as though the frightful impact of the bullet had paralysed him without knocking him down. At last, after what seemed a long time—it might have been five seconds, I dare say—he sagged flabbily to his knees. His mouth slobbered. An enormous senility seemed to have settled upon him. One could have imagined him thousands of years old. I fired again into the same spot. At the second shot he did not collapse but climbed with desperate slowness to his feet and stood weakly upright, with legs sagging and head drooping. I fired a third time. That was the shot that did for him. You could see the agony of it jolt his whole body and knock the last remnant of strength from his legs. But in falling he seemed for a moment to rise, for as his hind legs collapsed beneath him he seemed to tower upward like a huge rock toppling, his trunk reaching skywards like a tree. He trumpeted, for the first and only time. And then down he came, his belly towards me, with a crash that seemed to shake the ground even where I lay.

I got up. The Burmans were already racing past me across the mud. It was obvious that the elephant would never rise again, but he was not dead. He was breathing very rhythmically with long rattling gasps, his great mound of a side painfully rising and falling. His mouth was wide open—I could see far down into caverns of pale pink throat. I waited a long time for him to die, but his breathing did not weaken. Finally I fired my two remaining shots into the spot where I thought his heart must be. The thick blood welled out of him like red velvet, but still he did not die. His body did not even jerk when the shots hit him, the tortured breathing continued without a pause. He was dying, very slowly and in great agony, but in some world remote from me where not even a bullet could damage him further. I felt that I had got to put an end to that dreadful noise. It seemed dreadful to see the great beast lying there, powerless to move and yet powerless to die, and not even to be able to finish him. I sent back for my small rifle and poured shot after shot into his heart and down his throat. They seemed to make no impression. The tortured gasps continued as steadily as the ticking of a clock.

In the end I could not stand it any longer and went away. I heard later that it took him half an hour to die. Burmans were bringing dahs and baskets even before I left, and I was told they had stripped his body almost to the bones by the afternoon.

Afterwards, of course, there were endless discussions about the shooting of the elephant. The owner was furious, but he was only an Indian and could do nothing. Besides, legally I had done the right thing, for a mad elephant has to be killed, like a mad dog, if its owner fails to control it. Among the Europeans opinion was divided. The older men said I was right, the younger men said it was a damn shame to shoot an elephant for killing a coolie, because an elephant was worth more than any damn Coringhee coolie. And afterwards I was very glad that the coolie had been killed; it put me legally in the right and it gave me a sufficient pretext for shooting the elephant. I often wondered whether any of the others grasped that I had done it solely to avoid looking a fool.

Discussion Questions

1. Orwell says that secretly he was "all for the Burmese and all against their oppressors." Yet how are his emotions and behavior more complex than this political statement suggests?

2. How does the final paragraph affect you? Why does Orwell recount various opinions about the shooting? Why is he "very glad that the coolie had been killed"?

3. Does Orwell shoot the elephant *because* it killed a man? Explain his motive as accurately as you can. How does Orwell connect his motive to imperialist politics? How does his thinking in this essay conform to William Golding's discussion of the three grades of thought?

4. Orwell is noted for his ability to make social and political *-isms* vivid and dramatic. He says of shooting the elephant, for example, that "it was a tiny incident in itself, but it gave me a better glimpse than I had had before of the real nature of imperialism, the real motives for which despotic governments act." Using his essay as a model, write about a moment in your life when larger forces (social, political, hereditary, racial, and so forth) became crystallized in a single incident.

A Hanging

It was in Burma, a sodden morning of the rains. A sickly light, like yellow tinfoil, was slanting over the high walls into the jail yard. We were waiting outside the condemned cells, a row of sheds fronted with double bars, like small animal cages. Each cell measured about ten feet by ten and was quite bare within except for a plank bed and a pot for drinking water. In some of them brown, silent men were squatting at the inner bars, with their blankets draped round them. These were the condemned men, due to be hanged within the next week or two.

One prisoner had been brought out of his cell. He was a Hindu, a puny wisp of a man, with a shaven head and vague liquid eyes. He had a thick, sprouting moustache, absurdly too big for his body, rather like the moustache of a comic man on the films. Six tall Indian warders were guarding him and getting him ready for the gallows. Two of them stood by with rifles and fixed bayonets, while the others handcuffed him, passed a chain through his handcuffs and fixed it to their belts, and lashed his arms tight to his sides. They crowded very close about him, with their hands always on him in a careful, caressing grip, as though all the while feeling him to make sure he was there. It was like men handling a fish which is still alive and may jump back into the water. But he stood quite unresisting, yielding his arms limply to the ropes, as though he hardly noticed what was happening.

Eight o'clock struck and a bugle call, desolately thin in the wet air, floated from the distant barracks. The superintendent of the jail, who was standing apart from the rest of us, moodily prodding the gravel with his stick, raised his head at the sound. He was an army doctor, with a grey toothbrush moustache and a gruff voice. "For God's sake hurry up, Francis," he said irritably. "The man ought to have been dead by this time. Aren't you ready yet?"

Francis, the head jailer, a fat Dravidian in a white drill suit and gold spectacles, waved his black hand. "Yes sir, yes sir," he bubbled. "All iss satisfactorily prepared. The hangman iss waiting. We shall proceed."

"Well, quick march, then. The prisoners can't get their breakfast till this job's over."

We set out for the gallows. Two warders marched on either side of the prisoner, with their rifles at the slope; two others marched close against him, gripping him by arm and shoulder, as though at once pushing and supporting him. The rest of us, magistrates and the like, followed behind. Suddenly, when we had gone ten yards, the procession stopped short without any order or warning. A dreadful thing had happened—a dog, come goodness knows whence, had appeared in the yard. It came bounding among us with a loud volley of barks, and leapt round us wagging its whole body, wild with glee at finding so many human beings together. It was a large woolly dog, half Airedale, half pariah. For a moment it pranced round us, and then, before anyone could stop it, it had made a dash for the prisoner, and jumping up tried to lick his face. Everyone stood aghast, too taken aback even to grab at the dog.

"Who let that bloody brute in here?" said the superintendent angrily. "Catch it, someone!"

A warder detached from the escort, charged clumsily after the dog, but it danced and gambolled just out of his reach, taking everything as part of the game. A young Eurasian jailer picked up a handful of gravel and tried to stone the dog away, but it dodged the stones and came after us again. Its yaps echoed from the jail walls. The prisoner, in the grasp of the two warders, looked on incuriously, as though this was another formality of the hanging. It was several minutes before someone managed to catch the dog. Then we put my handkerchief through its collar and moved off once more, with the dog still straining and whimpering.

It was about forty yards to the gallows. I watched the bare brown back of the prisoner marching in front of me. He walked clumsily with his bound arms, but quite steadily, with that bobbing gait of the Indian who never straightens his knees. At each step his muscles slid neatly into place, the lock of hair on his scalp danced up and down, his feet printed themselves on the wet gravel. And once, in spite of the men who gripped him by each shoulder, he stepped slightly aside to avoid a puddle on the path.

It is curious, but till that moment I had never realized what it means to destroy a healthy, conscious man. When I saw the prisoner step aside to avoid the puddle I saw the mystery, the unspeakable wrongness, of cutting a life short when it is in full tide.

This man was not dying, he was alive just as we are alive. All the organs of his body were working—bowels digesting food, skin renewing itself, nails growing, tissues forming—all toiling away in solemn foolery. His nails would still be growing when he stood on the drop, when he was falling through the air with a tenth-of-a-second to live. His eyes saw the yellow gravel and the grey walls, and his brain still remembered, foresaw, reasoned—reasoned even about puddles. He and we were a party of men walking together, seeing, hearing, feeling, understanding the same world; and in two minutes, with a sudden snap, one of us would be gone—one mind less, one world less.

The gallows stood in a small yard, separate from the main grounds of the prison, and overgrown with tall prickly weeds. It was a brick erection like three sides of a shed, with planking on top, and above that two beams and a crossbar with the rope dangling. The hangman, a grey-haired convict in the white uniform of the prison, was waiting beside his machine. He greeted us with a servile crouch as we entered. At a word from Francis the two warders, gripping the prisoner more closely than ever, half led half pushed him to the gallows and helped him clumsily up the ladder. Then the hangman climbed up and fixed the rope round the prisoner's neck.

We stood waiting, five yards away. The warders had formed in a rough circle round the gallows. And then, when the noose was fixed, the prisoner began crying out to his god. It was a high, reiterated cry of "Ram! Ram! Ram! Ram!" not urgent and fearful like a prayer or cry for help, but steady, rhythmical, almost like the tolling of a bell. The dog answered the sound with a whine. The hangman, still standing on the gallows, produced a small cotton bag like a flour bag and drew it down over the prisoner's face. But the sound, muffled by the cloth, still persisted, over and over again: "Ram! Ram! Ram! Ram! Ram!"

The hangman climbed down and stood ready, holding the lever. Minutes seemed to pass. The steady, muffled crying from the prisoner went on and on, "Ram! Ram! Ram!" never faltering for an instant. The superintendent, his head on his chest, was slowly poking the ground with his stick; perhaps he was counting the cries, allowing the prisoner a fixed number—fifty, perhaps, or a hundred. Everyone had changed colour. The Indians had gone grey like bad coffee, and one or two of the bayonets were wavering. We looked at the lashed, hooded man on the drop, and listened to his cries—each cry another second of life; the same thought was in all our minds: oh, kill him quickly, get it over, stop that abominable noise!

Suddenly the superintendent made up his mind. Throwing up his head he made a swift motion with his stick. "Chalo!" he shouted almost fiercely.

There was a clanking noise, and then dead silence. The prisoner had vanished, and the rope was twisting on itself. I let go of the dog, and it galloped immediately to the back of the gallows; but when it got there it stopped short, barked, and then retreated into a corner of the yard, where it stood among the weeds, looking timorously out at us. We went round the gallows to inspect the prisoner's body. He was dangling with his toes pointed straight downwards, very slowly revolving, as dead as a stone.

The superintendent reached out with his stick and poked the bare brown body; it oscillated slightly. "*He's* all right," said the superintendent. He backed out from under the gallows, and blew out a deep breath. The moody look had gone out of his face quite suddenly. He glanced at his wrist-watch. "Eight minutes past eight. Well, that's all for this morning, thank God."

The warders unfixed bayonets and marched away. The dog, sobered and conscious of having misbehaved itself, slipped after them. We walked out of the gallows yard, past the condemned cells with their waiting prisoners, into the big central yard of the prison. The convicts, under the command of warders armed with lathis, were already receiving their breakfast. They squatted in long rows, each man holding a tin pannikin, while two warders with buckets marched round ladling out rice; it seemed quite a homely, jolly scene, after the hanging. An enormous relief had come upon us now that the job was done. One felt an impulse to sing, to break into a run, to snigger. All at once everyone began chattering gaily.

The Eurasian boy walking beside me nodded towards the way we had come, with a knowing smile: "Do you know, sir, our friend (he meant the dead man) when he heard his appeal had been dismissed, he pissed on the floor of the cell. From fright. Kindly take one of my cigarettes, sir. Do you not admire my new silver case, sir? From the boxwallah, two rupees eight annas. Classy European style."

Several people laughed—at what, nobody seemed certain.

Francis was walking by the superintendent, talking garrulously: "Well, sir, all has passed off with the utmost satisfactoriness. It was all finished—flick! like that. It iss not always so—oah, no! I have known cases where the doctor wass obliged to go beneath the gallows and pull the prissoner's legs to ensure decease. Most disagreeable!"

"Wriggling about, eh? That's bad," said the superintendent.

"Ach, sir, it iss worse when they become refractory! One man, I recall, clung to the bars of hiss cage when we went to take him out. You will scarcely credit, sir, that it took six warders to dislodge him, three pulling at each leg. We reasoned with him. 'My dear fellow,' we said, 'think of all the pain and trouble you are causing to us!' But no, he would not listen! Ach, he wass very troublesome!"

I found that I was laughing quite loudly. Everyone was laughing. Even the superintendent grinned in a tolerant way. "You'd better all come out and have a drink," he said quite genially. "I've got a bottle of whisky in the car. We could do with it."

We went through the big double gates of the prison into the road. "Pulling at his legs!" exclaimed a Burmese magistrate suddenly, and burst into a loud chuckling. We all began laughing again. At that moment Francis' anecdote seemed extraordinarily funny. We all had a drink together, native and European alike, quite amicably. The dead man was a hundred yards away.

Discussion Questions

1. Why doesn't Orwell tell us the reason for the execution? After the hanging, why do the men start joking and laughing? What is funny?

2. Why does Orwell introduce the dog into this narrative? Why isn't the dog irrelevant? Why does he call its intrusion "dreadful"?

3. Why is the fact that the prisoner steps aside to avoid a puddle so important to Orwell? What mysteries does it disclose? Find a similar use of detail in George Orwell's "Shooting an Elephant."

4. Using Orwell's essay as a model, write about an unpleasant incident you have witnessed (for example, an accident, a death, a crime, an act of violence) as part of a group of people. Describe the incident and let your choice of details establish both your response and that of the group.

Politics and the English Language

Most people who bother with the matter at all would admit that the English language is in a bad way, but it is generally assumed that we cannot by conscious action do anything about it. Our civilization is decadent and our language—so the argument runs—must inevitably share in the general collapse. It follows that any struggle against the abuse of language is a sentimental archaism, like preferring candles to electric light or hansom cabs to aeroplanes. Underneath this lies the half-conscious belief that language is a natural growth and not an instrument which we shape for our own purposes.

Now, it is clear that the decline of a language must ultimately have political and economic causes: it is not due simply to the bad influence of this or that individual writer. But an effect can become a cause, reinforcing the original cause and producing the same effect in an intensified form, and so on indefinitely. A man may take to drink because he feels himself to be a failure, and then fail all the more completely because he drinks. It is rather the same thing that is happening to the English language. It becomes ugly and inaccurate because our thoughts are foolish, but the slovenliness of our language makes it easier for us to have foolish thoughts. The point is that the process is reversible. Modern English, especially written English, is full of bad habits which spread by imitation and which can be avoided if one is willing to take the necessary trouble. If one gets rid of these habits one can think more clearly, and to think clearly is a necessary first step towards political regeneration: so that the fight against bad English is not frivolous and is not the exclusive concern of professional writers. I will come back to this presently, and I hope that by that time the meaning of what I have said here will have become clearer. Meanwhile, here are five specimens of the English language as it is now habitually written.

These five passages have not been picked out because they are especially bad—I could have quoted far worse if I had chosen—but because they illustrate various of the mental vices from which we now suffer. They are a little below the average, but are fairly representative samples. I number them so that I can refer back to them when necessary:

> (1) I am not, indeed, sure whether it is not true to say that the Milton who once seemed not unlike a seventeenth-century Shelley had not become, out of an experience ever more bitter in each year, more alien [sic] to the founder of that Jesuit sect which nothing could induce him to tolerate.
> Professor Harold Laski
> (Essay in *Freedom of Expression*).

> (2) Above all, we cannot play ducks and drakes with a native battery of idioms which prescribes such egregious collocations of vocables as the Basic *put up with* for *tolerate* or *put at a loss* for *bewilder*.
> Professor Lancelot Hogben
> (*Interglossa*).

> (3) On the one side we have the free personality: by definition it is not neurotic, for it has neither conflict nor dream. Its desires, such as they are, are transparent, for they are just what institutional approval keeps in the forefront of consciousness; another institutional pattern would alter their number and intensity; there is little in them that is natural, irreducible, or culturally dangerous. But *on the other side*, the social bond itself is nothing but the mutual reflection of these self-secure integrities. Recall the definition of love. Is not this the very picture of a small academic? Where is there a place in this hall of mirrors for either personality or fraternity?
> Essay on psychology in *Politics*
> (New York).

> (4) All the "best people" from the gentlemen's clubs, and all the frantic fascist captains, united in common hatred of Socialism and bestial horror of the rising tide of the mass revolutionary movement, have turned to acts of provocation, to foul incendiarism, to medieval legends of poisoned wells, to legalize their own destruction of proletarian organizations, and rouse the agitated petty-bourgeoisie to chauvinistic fervor on behalf of the fight against the revolutionary way out of the crisis.
> Communist pamphlet.

> (5) If a new spirit *is* to be infused into this old country, there is one thorny and contentious reform which must be tackled, and that is the humanization and galvanization of the B.B.C. Timidity here will bespeak canker and atrophy of the soul. The heart of Britain may be sound and of strong beat, for instance, but the British lion's roar at present is like that of Bottom in Shakespeare's *Midsummer Night's Dream*—as gentle as any sucking dove. A virile new Britain cannot continue indefinitely to be traduced in the eyes, or rather ears, of

the world by the effete languors of Langham Place, brazenly masquerading as "standard English." When the Voice of Britain is heard at nine o'clock, better far and infinitely less ludicrous to hear aitches honestly dropped than the present priggish, inflated, inhibited, school-ma'amish arch braying of blameless bashful mewing maidens!

Letter in *Tribune*

Each of these passages has faults of its own, but, quite apart from avoidable ugliness, two qualities are common to all of them. The first is staleness of imagery; the other is lack of precision. The writer either has a meaning and cannot express it, or he inadvertently says something else, or he is almost indifferent as to whether his words mean anything or not. This mixture of vagueness and sheer incompetence is the most marked characteristic of modern English prose, and especially of any kind of political writing. As soon as certain topics are raised, the concrete melts into the abstract and no one seems able to think of turns of speech that are not hackneyed: prose consists less and less of *words* chosen for the sake of their meaning, and more and more of *phrases* tacked together like the sections of a prefabricated hen-house. I list below, with notes and examples, various of the tricks by means of which the work of prose-construction is habitually dodged:

Dying Metaphors

A newly invented metaphor assists thought by evoking a visual image, while on the other hand a metaphor which is technically "dead" (e.g. *iron resolution*) has in effect reverted to being an ordinary word and can generally be used without loss of vividness. But in between these two classes there is a huge dump of worn-out metaphors which have lost all evocative power and are merely used because they save people the trouble of inventing phrases for themselves. Examples are: *Ring the changes on, take up the cudgels for, toe the line, ride roughshod over, stand shoulder to shoulder with, play into the hands of, no axe to grind, grist to the mill, fishing in troubled waters, on the order of the day, Achilles' heel, swan song, hotbed.* Many of these are used without knowledge of their meaning (what is a "rift," for instance?), and incompatible metaphors are frequently mixed, a sure sign that the writer is not interested in what he is saying. Some metaphors now current have been twisted out of their original meaning without those who use them even being aware of the fact. For example, *toe the line* is sometimes written *tow the line*. Another example is *the hammer and the anvil*, now always used with the implication that the anvil gets the worst of it. In real life it is always the anvil that breaks the hammer, never the other way about: a writer who stopped to think what he was saying would be aware of this, and would avoid perverting the original phrase.

Operators or Verbal False Limbs

These save the trouble of picking out appropriate verbs and nouns, and at the same time pad each sentence with extra syllables which give it an appearance of symmetry. Characteristic phrases are *render inoperative, militate against, make contact with, be subjected to, give rise to, give grounds for, have the effect of, play a leading part (role) in, make itself felt, take effect, exhibit a tendency to, serve the purpose of,* etc., etc. The keynote is the elimination of simple verbs. Instead of being a single word such as *break, stop, spoil, mend, kill,* a verb becomes a *phrase,* made up of a noun or adjective tacked on to some general-purpose verb such as *prove, serve, form, play, render.* In addition, the passive voice is wherever possible used in preference to the active, and noun constructions are used instead of gerunds (*by examination of* instead of *by examining*). The range of verbs is further cut down by means of the *-ize* and *de-* formations, and the banal statements are given an appearance of profundity by means of the *not un-* formation. Simple conjunctions and prepositions are replaced by such phrases as *with respect to, having regard to, the fact that, by dint of, in view of, in the interests of, on the hypothesis that;* and the ends of sentences are saved from anticlimax by such resounding commonplaces as *greatly to be desired, cannot be left out of account, a development to be expected in the near future, deserving of serious consideration, brought to a satisfactory conclusion,* and so on and so forth.

Pretentious Diction

Words like *phenomenon, element, individual* (as noun), *objective, categorical, effective, virtual, basic, primary, promote, constitute, exhibit, exploit, utilize, eliminate, liquidate* are used to dress up simple statements and give an air of scientific impartiality to biased judgments. Adjectives like *epoch-making, epic, historic, unforgettable, triumphant, age-old, inevitable, inexorable, veritable,* are used to dignify the sordid processes of international politics, while writing that aims at glorifying war usually takes on an archaic color, its characteristic words being: *realm, throne, chariot, mailed fist, trident, sword, shield, buckler, banner, jackboot, clarion.* Foreign words and expressions such as *cul de sac, ancien régime, deus ex machina, mutatis mutandis, status quo, gleichschaltung, Weltanschauung,* are used to give an air of culture and elegance. Except for the useful abbreviations *i.e., e.g.,* and *etc.,* there is no real need for any of the hundreds of foreign phrases now current in English. Bad writers, and especially scientific, political and sociological writers, are nearly always haunted by the notion that Latin or Greek words are grander than Saxon ones, and unnecessary words like *expedite, ameliorate, predict, extraneous, deracinated, clandestine, subaqueous* and hundreds of others constantly gain ground from their Anglo-Saxon opposite numbers.[1] The jargon peculiar to Marxist writing (*hyena, hangman, cannibal, petty bourgeois, these gentry, lacquey, flunkey, mad dog, White Guard,* etc.) consists largely of words and phrases translated from Russian, German or French; but the normal way of coining a new word is to use a Latin or Greek root with the appropriate affix and, where necessary, the *-ize* formation. It is often easier to make up words of this kind (*deregionalize, impermissible, extramarital, non-fragmentary* and so forth) than to think up the English words that will cover one's meaning. The result, in general, is an increase in slovenliness and vagueness.

Meaningless Words

In certain kinds of writing, particularly in art criticism and literary criticism, it is normal to come across long passages which are almost completely lacking in meaning.[2] Words like *romantic, plastic, values, human, dead, sentimental, natural, vitality,* as used in art criticism, are strictly meaningless, in the sense that they not only do not point to any discoverable object, but are hardly ever expected to do so by the reader. When one critic writes, "The outstanding feature of Mr. X's work is its living quality," while another writes, "The immediately striking thing about

---

[1] An interesting illustration of this is the way in which the English flower names which were in use till very recently are being ousted by Greek ones, *snapdragon* becoming *antirrhinum, forget-me-not* becoming *myosotis,* etc. It is hard to see any practical reason for this change of fashion; it is probably due to an instinctive turning-away from the more homely word and a vague feeling that the Greek word is scientific.

[2] Example: "Comfort's catholicity of perception and image, strangely Whitmanesque in range, almost the exact opposite in aesthetic compulsion, continues to evoke that trembling atmospheric accumulative hinting at a cruel, an inexorably serene timelessness.... Wrey Gardiner scores by aiming at simple bull's-eyes with precision. Only they are not so simple, and through this contented sadness runs more than the surface bitter-sweet of resignation." (*Poetry Quarterly*).

Mr. X's work is its peculiar deadness," the reader accepts this as a simple difference of opinion. If words like *black* and *white* were involved, instead of the jargon words *dead* and *living*, he would see at once that language was being used in an improper way. Many political words are similarly abused. The word *Fascism* has now no meaning except in so far as it signifies "something not desirable." The words *democracy, socialism, freedom, patriotic, realistic, justice,* have each of them several different meanings which cannot be reconciled with one another. In the case of a word like *democracy,* not only is there no agreed definition, but the attempt to make one is resisted from all sides. It is almost universally felt that when we call a country democratic we are praising it: consequently the defenders of every kind of régime claim that it is a democracy, and fear that they might have to stop using the word if it were tied down to any one meaning. Words of this kind are often used in a consciously dishonest way. That is, the person who uses them has his own private definition, but allows his hearer to think he means something quite different. Statements like *Marshal Pétain was a true patriot, The Soviet Press is the freest in the world, The Catholic Church is opposed to persecution,* are almost always made with intent to deceive. Other words used in variable meanings, in most cases more or less dishonestly, are: *class, totalitarian, science, progressive, reactionary, bourgeois, equality.*

Now that I have made this catalogue of swindles and perversions, let me give another example of the kind of writing that they lead to. This time it must of its nature be an imaginary one. I am going to translate a passage of good English into modern English of the worst sort. Here is a well-known verse from *Ecclesiastes*:

> I returned and saw under the sun, that the race is not to the swift, nor the battle to the strong, neither yet bread to the wise, nor yet riches to men of understanding, nor yet favour to men of skill; but time and chance happeneth to them all.

Here it is in modern English:

> Objective consideration of contemporary phenomena compels the conclusion that success or failure in competitive activities exhibits no tendency to be commensurate with innate capacity, but that a considerable element of the unpredictable must invariably be taken into account.

This is a parody, but not a very gross one. Exhibit (3), above, for instance, contains several patches of the same kind of English. It will be seen that I have not made a full translation. The beginning and ending of the sentence follow the original meaning fairly closely, but in the middle the concrete illustrations—race, battle, bread—dissolve into the vague phrase "success or failure in competitive activities." This had to be so, because no modern writer of the kind I am discussing—no one capable of using phrases like "objective consideration of contemporary phenomena"—would ever tabulate his thoughts in that precise and detailed way. The whole tendency of modern prose is away from concreteness. Now analyse these two sentences a little more closely. The first contains forty-nine words but only sixty syllables, and all its words are those of everyday life. The second contains thirty-eight words of ninety syllables: eighteen of its words are from Latin roots, and one from Greek. The first sentence contains six vivid images, and only one phrase ("time and chance") that could be called vague. The second contains not a single fresh, arresting phrase, and in spite of its ninety syllables it gives only a shortened version of the meaning contained in the first. Yet without a doubt it is the second kind of sentence that is gaining ground in modern English. I do not want to exaggerate. This kind of writing is not yet universal, and outcrops of simplicity will occur here and there in the worst-written page. Still, if you or I were told to write a few lines on the uncertainty of human fortunes, we should probably come much nearer to my imaginary sentence than to the one from *Ecclesiastes*.

As I have tried to show, modern writing at its worst does not consist in picking out words for the sake of their meaning and inventing images in order to make the meaning clearer. It consists in gumming together long strips of words which have already been set in order by someone else, and making the results presentable by sheer humbug. The attraction of this way of writing is that it is easy. It is easier—even quicker, once you have the habit—to say *In my opinion it is not an unjustifiable assumption that* than to say *I think*. If you use readymade phrases, you not only don't have to hunt about for words; you also don't have to bother with the rhythms of your sentences, since these phrases are generally so arranged as to be more or less euphonious. When you are composing in a hurry—when you are dictating to a stenographer, for instance, or making a public speech—it is natural to fall into a pretentious, Latinized style. Tags like *a consideration which we should do well to bear in mind* or *a conclusion to which all of us would readily assent* will save many a sentence from coming down with a bump. By using stale metaphors, similes and idioms, you save much mental effort, at the cost of leaving your meaning vague, not only for your reader but for yourself. This is the significance of mixed metaphors. The sole aim of a metaphor is to call up a visual image. When these images clash—as in *The Fas-*

cist octopus has sung its swan song, the jackboot is thrown into the melting pot—it can be taken as certain that the writer is not seeing a mental image of the objects he is naming; in other words he is not really thinking. Look again at the examples I gave at the beginning of this essay. Professor Laski (1) uses five negatives in fifty-three words. One of these is superfluous, making nonsense of the whole passage, and in addition there is the slip *alien* for *akin*, making further nonsense, and several avoidable pieces of clumsiness which increase the general vagueness. Professor Hogben (2) plays ducks and drakes with a battery which is able to write prescriptions, and, while disapproving of the everyday phrase *put up with*, is unwilling to look *egregious* up in the dictionary and see what it means; (3), if one takes an uncharitable attitude towards it, is simply meaningless: probably one could work out is intended meaning by reading the whole of the article in which it occurs. In (4), the writer knows more or less what he wants to say, but an accumulation of stale phrases chokes him like tea leaves blocking a sink. In (5), words and meaning have almost parted company. People who write in this manner usually have a general emotional meaning—they dislike one thing and want to express solidarity with another—but they are not interested in the detail of what they are saying. A scrupulous writer, in every sentence that he writes, will ask himself at least four questions, thus: What am I trying to say? What words will express it? What image or idiom will make it clearer? Is this image fresh enough to have an effect? And he will probably ask himself two more: Could I put it more shortly? Have I said anything that is avoidably ugly? But you are not obliged to go to all this trouble. You can shirk it by simply throwing your mind open and letting the ready-made phrases come crowding in. They will construct your sentences for you—even think your thoughts for you, to a certain extent—and at need they will perform the important service of partially concealing your meaning even from yourself. It is at this point that the special connection between politics and the debasement of language becomes clear.

In our time it is broadly true that political writing is bad writing. Where it is not true, it will generally be found that the writer is some kind of rebel, expressing his private opinions and not a "party line." Orthodoxy, of whatever color, seems to demand a lifeless, imitative style. The political dialects to be found in pamphlets, leading articles, manifestos, White Papers and the speeches of under-secretaries do, of course, vary from party to party, but they are all alike in that one almost never finds in them a fresh, vivid, home-made turn of speech. When one watches some tired hack on the platform mechanically repeating the familiar phrases—*bestial atrocities, iron heel, bloodstained tyranny, free peoples of the world, stand shoulder to shoulder*—one often has a curious feeling that one is not watching a live human being but some kind of dummy: a feeling which suddenly becomes stronger at moments when the light catches the speaker's spectacles and turns them into blank discs which seem to have no eyes behind them. And this is not altogether fanciful. A speaker who uses that kind of phraseology has gone some distance towards turning himself into a machine. The appropriate noises are coming out of his larynx, but his brain is not involved as it would be if he were choosing his words for himself. If the speech he is making is one that he is accustomed to make over and over again, he may be almost unconscious of what he is saying, as one is when one utters the responses in church. And this reduced state of consciousness, if not indispensable, is at any rate favorable to political conformity.

In our time, political speech and writing are largely the defence of the indefensible. Things like the continuance of British rule in India, the Russian purges and deportations, the dropping of the atom bombs on Japan, can indeed be defended, but only by arguments which are too brutal for most people to face, and which do not square with the professed aims of political parties. Thus political language has to consist largely of euphemism, question-begging and sheer cloudy vagueness. Defenseless villages are bombarded from the air, the inhabitants driven out into the countryside, the cattle machine-gunned, the huts set on fire with incendiary bullets: this is called *pacification*. Millions of peasants are robbed of their farms and sent trudging along the roads with no more than they can carry: this is called *transfer of population* or *rectification of frontiers*. People are imprisoned for years without trial, or shot in the back of the neck or sent to die of scurvy in Arctic lumber camps: this is called *elimination of unreliable elements*. Such phraseology is needed if one wants to name things without calling up mental pictures of them. Consider for instance some comfortable English professor defending Russian totalitarianism. He cannot say outright, "I believe in killing off your opponents when you can get good results by doing so." Probably, therefore, he will say something like this:

> While freely conceding that the Soviet régime exhibits certain features which the humanitarian may be inclined to deplore, we must, I think, agree that a certain curtailment of the right to political opposition is an unavoidable concomitant of transitional periods, and that the rigors which the Russian people have been called upon to undergo have been amply justified in the sphere of concrete achievement.

The inflated style is itself a kind of euphemism. A mass of Latin words falls upon the facts like soft snow, blurring the outlines and covering up all the details. The great enemy of clear language is insincerity. When there is a gap between one's real and one's declared aims, one turns as it were instinctively to long words and exhausted idioms, like cuttlefish squirting out ink. In our age there is no such thing as "keeping out of politics." All issues are political issues, and politics itself is a mass of lies, evasions, folly, hatred and schizophrenia. When the general atmosphere is bad, language must suffer. I should expect to find—this is a guess which I have not sufficient knowledge to verify—that the German, Russian and Italian languages have all deteriorated in the last ten or fifteen years, as a result of dictatorship.

But if thought corrupts language, language can also corrupt thought. A bad usage can spread by tradition and imitation, even among people who should and do know better. The debased language that I have been discussing is in some ways very convenient. Phrases like *a not unjustifiable assumption, leaves much to be desired, would serve no good purpose, a consideration which we should do well to bear in mind,* are a continuous temptation, a packet of aspirins always at one's elbow. Look back through this essay, and for certain you will find that I have again and again committed the very faults I am protesting against. By this morning's post I have received a pamphlet dealing with conditions in Germany. The author tells me that he "felt impelled" to write it. I open it at random, and here is almost the first sentence that I see: "[The Allies] have an opportunity not only of achieving a radical transformation of Germany's social and political structure in such a way as to avoid a nationalistic reaction in Germany itself, but at the same time of laying the foundations of a cooperative and unified Europe." You see, he "feels impelled" to write—feels, presumably, that he has something new to say—and yet his words, like cavalry horses answering the bugle, group themselves automatically into the familiar dreary pattern. This invasion of one's mind by ready-made phrases (*lay the foundations, achieve a radical transformation*) can only be prevented if one is constantly on guard against them, and every such phrase anaesthetizes a portion of one's brain.

I said earlier that the decadence of our language is probably curable. Those who deny this would argue, if they produced an argument at all, that language merely reflects existing social conditions, and that we cannot influence its development by any direct tinkering with words and constructions. So far as the general tone or spirit of a language goes, this may be true, but it is not true in detail. Silly words and expressions have often disappeared, not through any evolutionary process but owing to the conscious action of a minority. Two recent examples were *explore every avenue* and *leave no stone unturned,* which were killed by the jeers of a few journalists. There is a long list of flyblown metaphors which could similarly be got rid of if enough people would interest themselves in the job; and it should also be possible to laugh the *not un-* formation out of existence,[3] to reduce the amount of Latin and Greek in the average sentence, to drive out foreign phrases and strayed scientific words, and, in general, to make pretentiousness unfashionable. But all these are minor points. The defence of the English language implies more than this, and perhaps it is best to start by saying what it does *not* imply.

To begin with it has nothing to do with archaism, with the salvaging of obsolete words and turns of speech, or with the setting up of a "standard English" which must never be departed from. On the contrary, it is especially concerned with the scrapping of every word or idiom which has outworn its usefulness. It has nothing to do with correct grammar and syntax, which are of no importance so long as one makes one's meaning clear, or with the avoidance of Americanisms, or with having what is called a "good prose style." On the other hand it is not concerned with fake simplicity and the attempt to make written English colloquial. Nor does it even imply in every case preferring the Saxon word to the Latin one, though it does imply using the fewest and shortest words that will cover one's meaning. What is above all needed is to let the meaning choose the word, and not the other way about. In prose, the worst thing one can do with words is to surrender to them. When you think of a concrete object, you think wordlessly, and then, if you want to describe the thing you have been visualizing you probably hunt about till you find the exact words that seem to fit it. When you think of something abstract you are more inclined to use words from the start, and unless you make a conscious effort to prevent it, the existing dialect will come rushing in and do the job for you, at the expense of blurring or even changing your meaning. Probably it is better to put off using words as long as possible and get one's meaning as clear as one can through pictures or sensations. Afterwards one can choose— not simply *accept*—the phrases that will best cover the meaning, and then switch round and decide what impression one's words are likely to make on another person. This last effort of the mind

---

[3]One can cure oneself of the *not un-* formation by memorizing this sentence: A not unblack dog was chasing a not unsmall rabbit across a not ungreen field.

cuts out all stale or mixed images, all prefabricated phrases, needless repetitions, and humbug and vagueness generally. But one can often be in doubt about the effect of a word or a phrase, and one needs rules that one can rely on when instinct fails. I think the following rules will cover most cases:

(i) Never use a metaphor, simile or other figure of speech which you are used to seeing in print.
(ii) Never use a long word where a short one will do.
(iii) If it is possible to cut a word out, always cut it out.
(iv) Never use the passive where you can use the active.
(v) Never use a foreign phrase, a scientific word or a jargon word if you can think of an everyday English equivalent.
(vi) Break any of these rules sooner than say anything outright barbarous.

These rules sound elementary, and so they are, but they demand a deep change in attitude in anyone who has grown used to writing in the style now fashionable. One could keep all of them and still write bad English, but one could not write the kind of stuff that I quoted in those five specimens at the beginning of this article.

I have not here been considering the literary use of language, but merely language as an instrument for expressing and not for concealing or preventing thought. Stuart Chase and others have come near to claiming that all abstract words are meaningless, and have used this as a pretext for advocating a kind of political quietism. Since you don't know what Fascism is, how can you struggle against Fascism? One need not swallow such absurdities as this, but one ought to recognize that the present political chaos is connected with the decay of language, and that one can probably bring about some improvement by starting at the verbal end. If you simplify your English, you are freed from the worst follies of orthodoxy. You cannot speak any of the necessary dialects, and when you make a stupid remark its stupidity will be obvious, even to yourself. Political language—and with variations this is true of all political parties, from Conservatives to Anarchists—is designed to make lies sound truthful and murder respectable, and to give an appearance of solidity to pure wind. One cannot change this all in a moment, but one can at least change one's own habits, and from time to time one can even, if one jeers loudly enough, send some worn-out and useless phrase—some *jackboot, Achilles' heel, hotbed, melting pot, acid test, veritable inferno* or other lump of verbal refuse—into the dustbin where it belongs.

Discussion Questions

1. What connection does Orwell see between language and politics? What problems arise from this connection? What solution does he offer?

2. How do Orwell's standards of concreteness apply to his other essays? Read "Shooting an Elephant" and "A Hanging" and discuss whether Orwell practices what he preaches.

3. Compare Orwell's essay to Russell Baker's "Little Red Riding Hood Revisited." Are both writers concerned with the same problem?

4. Orwell makes it clear in this essay that a careful writer must be "constantly on guard against" ready-made phrases. Try this experiment in class. Write as quickly as you can (say in ten minutes) a one-page essay responding to the topic "Everyone has a right to his or her own opinion." Afterwards, break into small discussion groups and together make a list of the ready-made phrases and stale idioms that invaded the compositions. Underline these on your paper. Then take the paper home and rewrite the essay, this time guarding against the kind of soft-headed writing that Orwell despises.

DOROTHY PARKER

Dorothy Parker (1893–1967) grew up in Manhattan and was educated in private schools in New York and New Jersey. In 1916 she took an editorial job with Vogue magazine, which led a year later to a position as drama critic for one of the premier magazines of the day, Vanity Fair. On the Vanity Fair staff she met the writers and wits who formed the Algonquin Round Table and in no time she was an accepted member, wisecracking with the best of them. In 1925, she was one of several writers who helped launch The New Yorker, where she published poems, stories, and reviews until 1955. She covered the Spanish Civil War as a newspaper correspondent and afterwards went to Hollywood with her second husband to collaborate on screenplays.

Her clever, caustic, and quotable light verse appeared in Enough Rope (1926), Sunset Gun (1928), and Death and Taxes (1931), all of which were collected in Not So Deep a Well (1936). The stories and sketches of Laments for the Living (1930) and After Such Pleasures (1933) were collected in Here Lies (1939).

Mrs. Post Enlarges on Etiquette

Emily Post's *Etiquette* is out again, this time in a new and an enlarged edition, and so the question of what to do with my evenings has been all fixed up for me. There will be an empty chair at the deal table at Tony's, when the youngsters gather to discuss life, sex, literature, the drama, what is a gentleman, and whether or not to go on to Helen Morgan's Club when the place closes; for I shall be at home among my book. I am going in for a course of study at the knee of Mrs. Post. Maybe, some time in the misty future, I shall be Asked Out, and I shall be ready. You won't catch me being intentionally haughty to subordinates or refusing to be a pallbearer for any reason except serious ill health. I shall live down the old days, and with the help of Mrs. Post and God (always mention a lady's name first) there will come a time when you will be perfectly safe in inviting me to your house, which should never be called a residence except in printing or engraving.

It will not be a grueling study, for the sprightliness of Mrs. Post's style makes the textbook as fascinating as it is instructive. Her characters, introduced for the sake of example, are called by no such unimaginative titles as Mrs. A., or Miss Z., or Mr. X.; they are Mrs. Worldly, Mr. Bachelor, the Gildings, Mrs. Oldname, Mrs. Neighbor, Mrs. Stranger, Mrs. Kindhart, and Mr. and Mrs. Nono Better. This gives the work all the force and the application of a morality play.

It is true that occasionally the author's invention plucks at the coverlet, and she can do no better by her brain-children than to name them Mr. Jones and Mrs. Smith. But it must be said, in fairness, that the Joneses and the Smiths are the horrible examples, the confirmed pullers of social boners. They deserve no more. They go about saying "*Shake hands with Mr. Smith*" or "*I want to make you acquainted with Mrs. Smith*" or "*Will you permit me to recall myself to you?"* or *"Pardon* me!*"* or *"Permit me to assist you"* or even *"Pleased to meet you!"* One pictures them as small people, darting about the outskirts of parties, fetching plates of salad and glasses of punch, applauding a little too enthusiastically at the end of a song, laughing a little too long at the point of an anecdote. If you could allow yourself any sympathy for such white trash, you might find something pathetic in their eagerness to please, their desperate readiness to be friendly. But one must, after all, draw that line somewhere, and Mr. Jones, no matter how expensively he is dressed, always gives the effect of being in his shirt-sleeves, while Mrs. Smith is so unmistakably the daughter of a hundred Elks. Let them be dismissed by somebody's phrase (I wish to heaven it were mine)—"the sort of people who buy their silver."

These people in Mrs. Post's book live and breathe; as Heywood Broun once said of the characters in a play, "they have souls and elbows." Take Mrs. Worldly, for instance, Mrs. Post's heroine. The woman will live in American letters. I know of no character in the literature of the last quarter-century who is such a complete pain in the neck.

See her at that moment when a younger woman seeks to introduce herself. Says the young woman: "'Aren't you Mrs. Worldly?' Mrs. Worldly, with rather freezing politeness, says 'Yes,' and waits." And the young woman, who is evidently a glutton for punishment, neither lets her wait from then on nor replies, "Well, Mrs. Worldly, and how would you like a good sock in the nose, you old meat-axe?" Instead she flounders along with some cock-and-bull story about being a sister of Millicent Manners, at which Mrs. Worldly says, "I want very much to hear you sing some time," which marks her peak of enthusiasm throughout the entire book.

See Mrs. Worldly, too, in her intimate moments at home. "Mrs. Worldly seemingly pays no attention, but nothing escapes her. She can walk through a room without appearing to look either to the right or left, yet if the slightest detail is amiss, an ornament out of place, or there is one dull button on a footman's livery, her house telephone is rung at once!" Or watch her on that awful night when she attends the dinner where everything goes wrong. "In removing the plates, Delia, the assistant, takes them up by piling one on top of the other, clashing them together as she does so. You can feel Mrs. Worldly looking with almost hypnotized fascination—as her attention might be drawn to a street accident against her will."

There is also the practical-joker side to Mrs. W. Thus does Mrs. Post tell us about that: "For example, Mrs. Worldly writes:

"'Dear Mrs. Neighbor:

"'Will you and your husband dine with us very informally on Tuesday, the tenth, etc.'

"Whereupon, the Neighbors arrive, he in a dinner coat, she in her simplest evening dress, and find a dinner of fourteen people and every detail as formal as it is possible to make it.... In certain houses—such as the Worldlys' for instance—formality is inevitable, no matter how informal may be her 'will you dine informally' intention."

One of Mrs. Post's minor characters, a certain young Struthers, also stands sharply out of her pages. She has caught him perfectly in that scene which she entitles "Informal Visiting Often Arranged by Telephone" (and a darn good name for it, too). We find him at the moment when he is calling up Millicent Gilding, and saying, "'Are you going to be in this afternoon?' She says, 'Yes, but not until a quarter of six.' He says ,'Fine, I'll come then.' Or she says, 'I'm sorry, I'm playing bridge with Pauline—but I'll be in tomorrow!' He says, 'All right, I'll come tomorrow.'" Who, ah, who among us does not know a young Struthers?

As one delves deeper and deeper into *Etiquette*, disquieting thoughts come. That old Is-It-Worth-It Blues starts up again, softly, perhaps, but plainly. Those who have mastered etiquette, who are entirely, impeccably right, would seem to arrive at a point of exquisite dullness. The letters and the conversations of the correct, as quoted by Mrs. Post, seem scarcely worth the striving for. The rules for the finding of topics of conversation fall damply on the spirit. "You talk of something you have been doing or thinking about—planting a garden, planning a journey, contemplating a journey, or similar safe topics. Not at all a bad plan is to ask advice: "We want to motor through the South. Do you know about the roads?" Or, "I'm thinking of buying a radio. Which make do you think is best?"

I may dispute Mrs. Post. If she says that is the way you should talk, then, indubitably, that is the way you should talk. But though it be at the cost of that future social success I am counting on, there is no force great enough ever to make me say, "I'm thinking of buying a radio."

It is restful, always, in a book of many rules—and *Etiquette* has six hundred and eighty-four pages of things you must and mustn't do—to find something that can never touch you, some law that will never affect your ways....

And in *Etiquette*, too, I had the sweetly restful moment of chancing on a law which I need not bother to memorize, let come no matter what. It is in that section called "The Retort Courteous to One You Have Forgotten," although it took a deal of dragging to get it in under that head. "If," it runs, "after being introduced to you, Mr. Jones" (of course, it would be Mr. Jones that would do it) "calls you by a wrong name, you let it pass, at first, but if he persists you may say: "If you please, my name is Stimson.""

No, Mrs. Post; persistent though Mr. Smith be, I may not say, "If you please, my name is Stimson." The most a lady may do is give him the wrong telephone number.

Discussion Questions

1. How would you describe Dorothy Parker's tone of voice in the opening paragraph? How seriously does she seem to take the book she is reviewing?

2. Why does she focus so closely on Emily Post's characters? How does this affect the way she reviews *Etiquette*? What does she make *Etiquette* sound like?

3. What does Dorothy Parker object to about Emily Post's advice on "topics of conversation"?

4. Compare Dorothy Parker's review of Emily Post's *Etiquette* to Paul Fussell's review of another publishing institution, *The Boy Scout Handbook*. How might Parker have responded to Fussell's topic? What does she do that Fussell avoids?

5. What is the joke in the last paragraph? How does it summarize Parker's attitude toward the book?

6. Though advice books on proper behavior still sell, psychological self-help books are probably more typical of our time. Choose any contemporary self-help book (for example, one of Wayne Dyer's, Leo Buscaglia's, and so forth), and, using Parker's methods, write a review of it for your class.

S. J. Perelman

S. J. Perelman (1909–1979) was born in Brooklyn and educated at Brown. His career embraced such apparently disparate things as cartooning, reediting the 1897 Sears, Roebuck and Company Catalog, and writing the screenplays Monkey Business and Duck Soup for the Marx Brothers. He won an Oscar for the screenplay of Around the World in 80 Days. Perelman described himself as basically a feuilletonist, a writer of short pieces for popular magazines. Once called the funniest man alive, Perelman, in the baroque wordplay of his "sketches," has been seen by the critic Richard Poirier as having influenced the odd stylistic effects of such contemporary avant garde writers as Thomas Pynchon.

Dental or Mental, I Say It's Spinach

A few days ago, under the heading, MAN LEAPS OUT WINDOW AS DENTIST GETS FORCEPS, *The New York Times* reported the unusual case of a man who leaped out a window as the dentist got the forceps. Briefly, the circumstances were these. A citizen in Staten Island tottered into a dental parlor and, indicating an aching molar, moaned, "It's killing me. You've got to pull it out." The dentist grinned like a Cheshire cat—*The New York Times* nelected to say so, but a Cheshire cat who was present at the time grinned like a dentist—and reached for his instruments. "There was a leap and a crash," continues the account. "The astonished dentist saw his patient spring through the closed window and drop ten feet to the sidewalk, where he lay dazed." The casualty was subsequently treated at a nearby hospital for abrasion and shock by Drs. J. G. Abrazian and Walter Shock, and then, like a worm, crept back to the dentist, apologized and offered to pay for the damage. On one point, however, he remained curiously adamant. He still has his tooth.

As a party who recently spent a whole morning with his knees braced against a dentist's chest, whimpering "Don't—don't—I'll do anything, but don't drill!" I am probably the only man in America equipped to sympathize with a set of thirty-two flawless little pearls of assorted sizes, I never once relaxed my vigilant stewardship of same. From the age of six onward, I constantly polished the enamel with peanut brittle, massaged the incisors twice daily with lollipops, and chewed taffy and chocolate-covered caramels faithfully to exercise the gums. As for consulting a dentist regularly, my punctuality practically amounted to a fetish. Every twelve years I would drop whatever I was doing and allow wild Caucasian ponies to drag me to a reputable orthodonist. I guess you might say I was hipped on the subject of dental care.

When, therefore, I inadvertently stubbed a tooth on a submerged cherry in an old-fashioned last week and my toupee ricocheted off the ceiling, I felt both dismayed and betrayed. By eleven the next morning, I was seated in the antechamber of one Russell Pipgrass, D.D.S., limply holding a copy of the *National Geographic* upside down and pretending to be absorbed in Magyar folkways. Through the door communicating with the arena throbbed a thin, blood-curdling whine like a circular saw biting into a green plank. Suddenly an ear-splitting shriek rose above it, receding into a choked gurgle. I nonchalantly tapped out my cigarette in my eardrum and leaned over to the nurse, a Medusa type with serpents writhing out from under her prim white coif.

"Ah—er—pardon me," I observed, swallowing a bit of emery paper I had been chewing. "Did you hear anything just then?"

"Why, no," she replied, primly tucking back a snake under her cap. "What do you mean?"

"A—kind of a scratchy sound," I faltered.

"Oh, that," she sniffed carelessly. "Impacted wisdom tooth. We have to go in through the skull for those, you know." Murmuring some inconsequential excuse about lunching with a man in Sandusky, Ohio, I dropped to the floor and was creeping toward the corridor on all fours when Dr. Pipgrass emerged, rubbing his hands. "Well, here's an unexpected windfall!" he crackled, his eyes gleaming with cupidity. "Look out—slam the door on him!" Before I could dodge past, he pinioned me in a hammer lock and bore me, kicking and struggling, into his web. He was trying to wrestle me into the chair when the nurse raced in, brandishing a heavy glass ash tray.

"Here, hit him with this!" she panted.

"No, no, we mustn't bruise him," muttered Pipgrass. "Their relatives always ask a lot of silly questions." They finally made me comfy by strapping me into the chair with a half a dozen towels, tilted my feet up and pried open my teeth with a spoon. "Now then, where are his X-rays?" demanded the doctor.

"We haven't any," returned the nurse. "This is the first time he's been here."

"Well, bring me any X-rays," her employer barked. "What difference does it make? When you've seen one tooth, you've seen them all." He held up the X-rays against the light and examined them critically. "Well, friend, you're in a peck of trouble," he said at length. "You may as well know the worst. These are the teeth of an eighty-year-old man. You got here just in time." Plucking a horrendous nozzle from the rack, he shot compressed air down my gullet that sent me into a strangled paroxysm, and peered curiously at my inlays.

"Who put those in, a steamfitter?" he sneered. "You ought to be arrested for walking around with a job like that." He turned abruptly at the rustle of greenbacks and glared at his nurse. "See here, Miss Smedley, how many times have I told you not to count the patient's money in front of him? Take the wallet outside and go through it there." She nodded shamefacedly and slunk out. "That's the kind of thing that creates a bad impression on the layman," growled Dr. Pipgrass, poking at my tongue with a sharp stick. "Now what seems to be the trouble in there?"

"Ong ong ong," I wheezed.

"H'm'm'm, a cleft palate," he mused. "Just as I feared. And you've got between four and five thousand cavities. While we're at it, I think we'd better tear out those lowers with a jackhammer and put in some nice expensive crowns. Excuse me." He quickly dialed a telephone number. "Is that you, Irene?" he asked. "Russell. Listen, on that white mink coat we were talking about at breakfast—go right ahead, I've changed my mind. . . . No, I'll tell you later. He's filthy with it."

"Look Doctor," I said with a casual yawn. "It's nothing really—just a funny tickling sensation in that rear tooth. I'll be back Tuesday—a year from Tuesday."

"Yes, yes," he interrupted, patting me reassuringly. "Don't be afraid now; this won't hurt a bit." With a slow, cunning smile, he produced from behind his back a hypodermic of the type used on brewery horses and, distending my lip, plunged it into the gum. The tip of my nose instantly froze, and my tongue took on the proportions of a bolt of flannel. I tried to cry out, but my larynx was out to lunch. Seizing the opportunity, Pipgrass snatched up his drill, took a firm purchase on my hair and teed off. A mixture of sensation roughly comparable to being alternately stilettoed and inflated with a bicycle pump overcame me; two thin wisps of smoke curled upward slowly from my ears. Fortunately, I had been schooled from boyhood to withstand pain without flinching, and beyond an occasional scream that rattled the windows, I bore myself with the stoicism of a red man. Scarcely ninety minutes later, Dr. Pipgrass thrust aside the drill, wiped his streaming forehead and shook the mass of protoplasm before him.

"Well, we're in the home stretch," he announced brightly, extracting a rubber sheet from a drawer. "We'll put this dam on you and fill her in a jiffy. You don't get claustrophobia, do you?"

"Wh-what's that?" I squeaked.

"Fear of being buried alive," he explained smoothly. "Kind of a stifling feeling. Your heart starts racing and you think you're going crazy. Pure imagination, of course." He pinned the rubber sheet over my face, slipped it over the tooth and left me alone with my thoughts. In less time than it takes to relate, I was a graduate member, *summa cum laude*, of the Claustrophobia Club. My face had turned a stunning shade of green, my heart was going like Big Ben, and a set of castanets in my knees was playing the "Malagueña." Summoning my last reserves of strength, I cast off my bonds and catapulted through the anteroom to freedom. I bequeathed Pipgrass a fleece-lined overcoat worth sixty-eight dollars, and he's welcome to it; I'll string along nicely with this big wad of chewing gum over my tooth. On me it looks good.

Discussion Questions

1. What is the joke in Perelman's title and what does it do for his essay as a whole? What about the joke, if anything, has become dated? What, if anything, still seems funny today?

2. Make a complete list of Perelman's similes and describe any pattern or patterns you see in his choices of comparison.

3. Compare Perelman's techniques of humor to those of Michael Arlen and Lillian Ross. What, if anything, do the writers share?

4. Using some of Perelman's techniques, write an essay on any phobia or phobias you have suffered from. How, for example, would Perelman have exaggerated (and thereby lightened) the terrors and menaces of being trapped in a darkened elevator between floors late at night?

J. H. Plumb

The English historian J. H. Plumb was born in 1911 and until his retirement was professor of modern English history at Cambridge. In all his many books, essays, and reviews, his style embodies a balanced and unprejudiced mode of inquiry along with that sense of "history as a literary art" called for by S. E. Morison. Plumb's work has therefore proved popular both with professional historians and with the general public. The following essay on astrology comes from a collection titled In the Light of History (1972) and presents a model of techniques for writing on a specialized and complicated historical topic to a wide range of readers.

The Stars in Their Day

Are you Taurus or Gemini, Pisces or Capricorn? Does your eye furtively glance at the column headed "The Stars and You" and are you relieved when you read that you could have a "speculative benefit" or worried when you see "changeability in relationships may pose problems"? Or does a slightly sheepish, shame-faced smile flutter across your face as you turn hurriedly to another page in your newspaper?

I suspect it strikes few readers that the silly astrological columns are the sad end of an extraordinary human enterprise stretching back to the very dawn of history. The persistence of the belief that the movements of the stars are related to man's destiny goes back to the very earliest days of the neolithic revolution, if not beyond. And the fact that popular, non-elite newspapers in America, England, France, Germany, Italy, India, indeed in all non-communist countries, find it worthwhile to publish astrological columns day in day out, indicates the persistence of that belief. And as well as popular astrologers, high priests of the cult still exist, dedicated astrologers, masters of intricate calculations, who cast horoscopes and predict the fate of individuals with the conviction of a scientist, men and women who believe as intensely in the stars as the magicians of ancient China.

True, over the last three centuries the belief in the stars has steadily weakened and the market for horoscopes dwindled. With the coming of industrial society and the scientific revolution which has given us an accurate knowledge of the stars, astrology has become the plaything of the credulous and the ill-educated. But two hundred years ago its power in the West was still strong: both Cagliostro and Casanova cast horoscopes and interpreted the stars in order to bamboozle aristocrats, merchants and attractive women. A further hundred years back, however, the stars were still playing a vital part in human affairs, although historians rarely pay any attention to this aspect of seventeenth-century belief.

The Earl of Shaftesbury, the violent Whig who nearly toppled Charles II from his throne by exploiting the hysteria of the Popish Plot in 1678—1679, believed absolutely in astrology. John Locke, the rationalist philosopher, lived in his household, but made no impression it would seem on this aspect of Shaftesbury's beliefs. A Dutch doctor who dabbled in the occult had cast his horoscope and so, Shaftesbury thought, foretold all that would happen to him. Nor was Shaftesbury an isolated crank. The great German general, Wallenstein, who dominated the Thirty Years' War, took no action, military or political, without consulting the stars, and no one thought him either eccentric or pagan.

Astrology in these centuries lived quite comfortably with Christianity. Many kings kept astrologers at Court and consulted them regularly. Dr. John Dee, the great Elizabethan magician, who consulted the spirits in a polished obsidian mirror which he had somehow or other acquired from Aztec Mexico via Spain, also used the stars to predict the future. He created a sense of fear, but the great Elizabethans consulted him and he died comfortably enough in his bed and not at the stake. Magic he might practice, but even in that age, terrified as it was by the fear of witchcraft, he survived. The stars were beyond the Devil and his works. They belonged to the mechanism of the universe, a piece of God's handiwork: therefore good and open to interpretation. And, in this respect, Catholic and Protestant did not differ, and a belief in astrology covered all creeds and heresies: Protestant, Catholic, Jew and Moslem did not differ in this particular. And in this respect, at least, they were at one with the Hindus and Chinese, and with the remoter civilizations of the Middle East. The stars dominated the lives of Sumerians, Akkadians, Babylonians and Egyptians.

The greatest historian of classical China, Ssŭ-ma Chi'en, gloried in the title of the Grand Astrologer, possibly because the earliest archives to be kept systematically were those which dealt with astrological matters. Indeed the Chinese not only consulted the stars but devised the most elaborate instruments to determine their precise conjunction at a precise moment of time. One of the most elaborate and complex astronomic clocks of antiquity was built by the Chinese so that the position of the stars, even if the heavens were cloudy, would be known, should the empress conceive when the emperor paid a visit to her bed, for Heaven would naturally be disclosing its hand at such an auspicious moment, either to foretell happiness or doom.

Long before the Chinese had developed their elaborate system of star-gazing, the Assyrians and Egyptians had been studying the heavens just as intensely. Of all civilizations, perhaps, the Assyrian was the most addicted to astrology and no king of Babylon would act in minor, let alone major, matters without consulting them. A great reference library was built up in their palaces, so that prediction and result could be studied and referred to. By the time Babylon fell the Assyrian astrologers and divinators had reference material which dated back nearly a thousand years. The ancient Egyptians too studied the stars and believed in their benign or malevolent influence. Nor was belief in astrology derived from a single center for, without any contact with Europe, the Mayas in the Yucatán and Guatemala built huge observatories and watched the stars. From China to Peru throughout many millennia, men's lives were star-haunted and the heavens wrote in cryptic symbols the fate of nations and the destiny of men.

So those foolish columns in the newspapers have a long, long history; a history heaving with portent. The stars have terrified men, made them jubilant, provided dreams of ecstasy and fear and, above all, strengthened a sense of unalterable fate, not only in the heart of the peasant and craftsman, but also in emperors and kings, priests and soldiers. It is easy, of course, to see how relevant initially the position of the stars was to all communities which depended on the soil, for changes in the constellations indicated the coming of spring or winter or foretold that rains would come in Yucatán or the Nile flood in Egypt, events which, if delayed or inadequate, could mean famine. To the peasant the sky and the seasons were in mysterious harmony, yet capable of discord. The constellations might appear and yet the rains, in spite of sacrifice and religious observance, stay away; and then for years the juxtaposition could be close. The will of the gods and the stars were interconnected but not obvious: they needed to be studied with intense and minute care, and only then could they be used safely for prediction.

But humanity's need for the stars goes deeper than the need to discern the changing seasons or the coming of rain and water, deeper than the need to foretell the fate of kings, or the hopes and fears of men. There is a need in man to know and to rationalize his universe through magic and through very precise and detailed knowledge. He derives a sense of security from knowledge, whether it be the very precise and detailed knowledge of territory, of its trees and flowers and animals, such as the most primitive tribes of men acquire, or from the complexities of the modern science of physics or biology. His aim has always been both to control his environment and to banish anxiety. Man has always been, as it were, scientifically orientated even if his earlier and more primitive sciences did not work very well. Only gradually did he learn the precise way to investigate and control (perhaps one should rather say exploit) his environment, but he put the same intellectual effort, the same passion to observe and to accumulate knowledge into his earlier attempts.

Magicians, astrologers, were but mankind's first scientists. They were men of great intelligence and keen observation, no different in quality from Newton or Rutherford and, essentially, dedicated to the same task. Many of their facts were right and beautifully observed; their pursuits led them to invent instruments of great ingenuity. What was wrong were their premises. And in the vaporings of a Katrina one sees the pathetic end of a once majestic and comprehensive study of destiny: a science which for thousands of years interpreted men's hopes and fears and which seemed to give them a chance of evading disaster and controlling their fate.

Discussion Questions

1. In what ways does Plumb work to combine his praise of astrology with his acknowledgment of its limitations? What ends besides the "pathetic" end of the "science" does he invite his readers to imagine?

2. How do the first sentences in Plumb's paragraphs change in the course of his essay? What are the purposes and effects of the changes? How do the first sentences reflect the nature of the paragraphs they introduce?

3. Compare Plumb's views of the motives and methods of science with those of other writers on the topic like Jacob Bronowski, Annie Dillard, and Robert Frost.

4. Pick another area of human inquiry or activity that is now viewed as absurd or distasteful (for example, phrenology or bearbaiting) and try to account for both the former popularity and present decline.

KATHERINE ANNE PORTER

Katherine Anne Porter (1890–1980) was born in Texas. As a young woman, she worked for newspapers, played minor parts in early movies, and studied Mayan and Aztec art in Mexico. Though she had always wanted to write, it was not until she was thirty years old that she was able to publish her first short story, "Maria Concepción," which, by her own account, she rewrote "fifteen or sixteen times." She made her greatest success as a writer of short stories, though she did produce a novel, Ship of Fools (1962). Her Collected Stories won both the National Book Award and The Pulitzer Prize in 1966. Of her writing she has said, "My whole attempt has been to discover and understand human motives, human feelings, to make a distillation of what human relations and experiences my mind has been able to absorb."

In addition to her long career as a writer, Katherine Anne Porter lectured and taught literature at many universities and became the first female faculty member at Washington and Lee. She wrote much nonfiction including The Never-Ending Wrong (1977), a personal memory of the Sacco and Vanzetti trial. Her Collected Essays appeared in 1970. The following essay is taken from The Days Before (1952). It makes an early contribution to a question still much debated today.

The Future Is Now

Not so long ago I was reading in a magazine with an enormous circulation some instructions as to how to behave if and when we see that flash brighter than the sun which means that the atom bomb has arrived. I read of course with the intense interest of one who has everything to learn on this subject; but at the end, the advice dwindled to this: the only real safety seems to lie in simply being somewhere else at the time, the further away the better; the next best, failing access to deep shelters, bombproof cellars and all, is to get under a stout table—that is, just what you might do if someone were throwing bricks through your window and you were too nervous to throw them back.

The comic anticlimax to what I had been taking as a serious educational piece surprised me into real laughter, hearty and carefree. It is such a relief to be told the truth, or even just the facts; so pleasant not to be coddled with unreasonable hopes. That very evening I was drawn away from my work table to my fifth-story window by one of those shrill terror-screaming sirens which our excitement-loving city government used then to affect for so many occasions: A fire? Police chasing a gangster? Somebody being got to the hospital in a hurry? Some distinguished public guest being transferred from one point to another? Strange aircraft coming over, maybe? Under the lights of the corner crossing of the great avenue, a huge closed vehicle whizzed past, screaming. I never knew what it was, had not in fact expected to know; no one I could possibly ask would know. Now that we have bells clamoring away instead for such events, we all have one doubt less, if perhaps one expectancy more. The single siren's voice means to tell us only one thing.

But at that doubtful moment, framed in a lighted window level with mine in the apartment house across the street, I saw a young man in a white T-shirt and white shorts at work polishing a long, beautiful dark table top. It was obviously his own table in his own flat, and he was enjoying his occupation. He was bent over in perfect concentration, rubbing, sandpapering, running the flat of his palm over the surface, standing back now and then to get the sheen of light on the fine wood. I am sure he had not even raised his head at the noise of the siren, much less had he come to the window. I stood there admiring his workmanlike devotion to a good job worth doing, and there flashed through me one of those pure fallacies of feeling which suddenly overleap reason: surely all that effort and energy so irreproachably employed were not going to be wasted on a table that was to be used merely for crawling under at some unspecified date. Then why take all those pains to make it beautiful? Any sort of old board would do.

I was shocked at this treachery of the lurking Foul Fiend (despair *is* a foul fiend, and this was despair) I stood a moment longer, looking out and around, trying to collect my feelings, trying to think a little. Two windows away and a floor down in the house across the street, a young woman was lolling in a deep chair, reading and eating fruit from a little basket. On the sidewalk, a boy and a girl dressed alike in checkerboard cotton shirts and skin-tight blue denims, a costume which displayed acutely the structural differences of their shapes, strolled along with their arms around each other. I believe this custom of lovers walking enwreathed in public was imported by our soldiers of the First World War from France, from Paris indeed. "You didn't see that sort of thing here before," certain members of the older generation were heard to remark quite often, in a tone of voice. Well, one sees quite a lot of it now, and it is a very pretty, reassuring sight. Other citizens of all sizes and kinds and ages were crossing back and forth; lights flashed red and green, punctually. Motors zoomed by, and over the great city—but where am I going? I never read other peoples' descriptions of great cities, more particularly if it is a great city I know. It doesn't belong here anyway, except that I had again that quieting sense of the continuity of human experience on this earth, its perpetual aspirations, set-backs, failures and re-beginnings in eternal hope; and that, with some appreciable differences of dress, customs and means of conveyance, so people have lived and moved in the cities they have built for more millennia than we are yet able to account for, and will no doubt build and live for as many more.

Why did this console me? I cannot say; my mind is of the sort that can often be soothed with large generalities of that nature. The silence of the spaces between the stars does not affright me, as it did Pascal, because I am unable to imagine it except poetically; and my awe is not for the silence and space of the endless universe but for the inspired imagination of man, who can think and feel so, and turn a phrase like that to communicate it to us. Then too, I like the kind of honesty and directness of the young soldier who lately answered someone who asked him if he knew what he was fighting for. "I sure do," he said, "I am fighting to live." And as for the future, I was once reading the first writings of a young girl, an apprentice author, who was quite impatient to get on with the business and find her way into print. There is very little one can say of use in such matters, but I advised her against haste—she could so easily regret it. "Give yourself time," I said, "the future will take care of itself." This opinionated young person looked down her little nose at me and said, "The future is now." She may have heard the phrase somewhere and liked it, or she may just have naturally belonged to that school of metaphysics; I am sure she was too young to have investigated the thought deeply. But maybe she was right and the future does arrive every day and it is all we have, from one second to the next.

So I glanced again at the young man at work, a proper-looking candidate for the armed services, and realized the plain, homely fact: he was not preparing a possible shelter, something to cower under trembling; he was restoring a beautiful surface to put his books and papers on, to serve his plates from, to hold his cocktail tray and his lamp. He was full of the deep, right, instinctive, human belief that he and the table were going to be around together for a long time. Even if he is off to the army next week, it will be there when he gets back. At the very least, he is doing something he feels is worth doing now, and that is no small thing.

At once the difficulty, and the hope, of our special time in this world of Western Europe and America is that we have been brought up for many generations in the belief, however tacit, that all humanity was almost unanimously engaged in going forward, naturally to better things and to higher reaches. Since the eighteenth century at least when the Encyclopedists seized upon the Platonic theory that the highest pleasure of mankind was pursuit of the good, the true, and the beautiful, progress, in precisely the sense of perpetual, gradual amelioration of the hard human lot, has been taught popularly not just as theory of possibility but as an article of faith and the groundwork of a whole political doctrine. Mr. Toynbee has even simplified this view for us with picture diagrams of various sections of humanity, each in its own cycle rising to its own height, struggling beautifully on from craggy level to level, but always upward. Whole peoples are arrested at certain points, and perish there, but others go on. There is also the school of thought, Oriental and very ancient, which gives to life the spiral shape, and the spiral moves by nature upward. Even adherents of the circular or recurring-cycle school, also ancient and honorable, somehow do finally allow that the circle is a thread that spins itself out one layer above another, so that even though it is perpetually at every moment passing over a place it had been before, yet by its own width it will have risen just so much higher.

These are admirable attempts to get a little meaning and order into our view of our destiny, in that same spirit which moves the artist to labor with his little handful of chaos, bringing it to coherency within a frame; but on the visible evidence we must admit that in human nature the spirit of contradiction more than holds its own. Mankind has always built a little more than he has hitherto been able or willing to destroy; got more children than he has been able to kill; invented more laws and customs than he had any intention of observing; founded more religions than he was able to practice or even to believe in; made in general many more promises than he could keep; and has been known more than once to commit suicide through mere fear of death. Now in our time, in his pride to explore his universe to its unimaginable limits and to exceed his possible powers, he has at last produced an embarrassing series of engines too powerful for their containers and too tricky for their mechanicians; millions of labor-saving gadgets which can be rendered totally useless by the mere failure of the public power plants, and has reduced himself to such helplessness that a dozen or less of the enemy could disable a whole city by throwing a few switches. This paradoxical creature has committed all these extravagances and created all these dangers and sufferings in a quest—we are told—for peace and security.

How much of this are we to believe, when with the pride of Lucifer, the recklessness of Icarus, the boldness of Prometheus and the intellectual curiosity of Adam and Eve (yes, intellectual; the serpent promised them wisdom if . . .) man has obviously outreached himself, to the point where he cannot understand his own science or control his own inventions. Indeed he has become as the gods, who have over and over again suffered defeat and downfall at the hands of their creatures. Having devised the most exquisite and instantaneous means of communication to all corners of the earth, for years upon years friends were unable even to get a postcard message to each other across national frontiers. The newspapers assure us that from the kitchen tap there flows a chemical, cheap and available, to make a bomb more disturbing to the imagination even than the one we so appallingly have; yet no machine has been invented to purify that water so that it will not spoil even the best tea or coffee. Or at any rate, it is not in use. We are proud possessors of rocket bombs that go higher and farther and faster than any ever before, and there is some talk of a rocket ship shortly to take off for the moon. (My plan is to stow away.) We may indeed reach the moon some day, and I dare predict that will happen before we have devised a decent system of city garbage disposal.

This lunatic atom bomb has succeeded in rousing the people of all nations to the highest point of unanimous moral dudgeon; great numbers of persons are frightened who never really had much cause to be frightened before. This world has always been a desperately dangerous place to live for the greater part of the earth's inhabitants; it was, however reluctantly, endured as the natural state of affairs. Yet the invention of every new weapon of war has always been greeted with horror and righteous indignation, especially by those who failed to invent it, or who were threatened with it first . . . bows and arrows, stone cannon balls, gunpowder, flintlocks, pistols, the dumdum bullet, the Maxim silencer, the machine gun, poison gas, armored tanks, and on and on to the grand climax—if it should prove to be—of the experiment on Hiroshima. Nagasaki was bombed too, remember? Or were we already growing accustomed to the idea? And as for Hiroshima, surely it could not have been the notion of sudden death of others that shocked us? How could it be, when in two great wars within one generation we have become familiar with millions of shocking deaths, by sudden violence of most cruel devices, and by agonies prolonged for years in prisons and hospitals and concentration camps. We take with apparent calmness the news of the deaths of millions by flood, famine, plague—no, all the frontiers of danger are down now, no one is safe, no one, and that, alas, really means all of us. It is our own deaths we fear, and so let's out with it and give up our fine debauch of moralistic frenzy over Hiroshima. I fail entirely to see why it is more criminal to kill a few thousand persons in one instant than it is to kill the same number slowly over a given stretch of time. If I have a choice, I'd as lief be killed by an atom bomb as by a hand grenade or a flame thrower. If dropping the atom bomb is an immoral act, then the making of it was too; and writing of the formula was a crime, since those who wrote it must have known what such a contrivance was good for. So, morally speaking, the bomb is only a magnified hand grenade, and the crime, if crime it is, is still murder. It was never anything else. Our protocriminal then was the man who first struck fire from flint, for from that moment we have been coming steadily to this day and this weapon and this use of it. What would you have advised instead? That the human race should have gone on sitting in caves gnawing raw meat and beating each other over the head with the bones?

And yet it may be that what we have is a world not on the verge of flying apart, but an uncreated one—still in shapeless fragments waiting to be put together properly. I imagine that when we want something better, we may have it: at perhaps no greater price than we have already paid for the worse.

Discussion Questions

1. In her first paragraph, the author sees the idea of a table as a bomb shelter as a "comic anticlimax." In what other ways might she have viewed the suggestion? How, if at all, does she prepare her reader for the way she comes to view the suggestion? What words and phrases in the first paragraph seem at first reading or on rereading potentially comic?

2. How would you define the tone of voice suggested by the remark quoted in paragraph 4, "You didn't see that sort of thing here before?" Does the author ever employ a similar tone of voice? How would you define her usual tone in the essay?

3. How does the author's description of the origin of her title illuminate the particular sense in which she used the phrase "the future is now"?

4. "We may indeed reach the moon some day, and I dare predict that will happen before we have devised a decent system of city garbage disposal." The author's prediction about one aspect of her future came true. Does this make you tend to agree with her more general argument, or is the prediction separable?

5. Write an essay in which you support or refute Katherine Anne Porter's thesis, in her next-to-last paragraph, that the "fine debauch of moralistic frenzy over Hiroshima" is a direct result of fear of our own deaths.

J. B. PRIESTLY

J. B. Priestly, the author of nearly thirty novels and numerous plays, critical studies, and essays, was born in Yorkshire, England, in 1894. He began writing for newspapers at the age of sixteen, was educated at Cambridge, and served with the British infantry during World War I. A nationally known broadcaster and screenwriter, Priestly is married to the archeologist and writer Jacquetta Hawkes.

Among Priestly's many collections of essays are Papers from Lilliput (1922), Apes and Angels (1928), Delight (1949), Thoughts in the Wilderness (1957), in which the following essay originally appeared, and Essays of Five Decades (1968). Priestly has also written an autobiography, Instead of the Trees (1977).

Block Thinking

My children being too old for such things, my grandchildren still too young, I do not know if they still exist; but there used to be offered in the toyshops sheets of cardboard to which were fixed the miniature outfits of bus conductors, soldiers, cowboys, and so forth. A small boy presented with one of these outfits could at once transform himself, to his own deep satisfaction, into the fascinating figure of his daydreams. All you had to do was put on the hat, take the gun, the whistle, the badge: there you were, completely outfitted.

Now it seems to me that during the last twenty years there has been a great deal of this Complete Outfitting far away from toyshops, in the world of our beliefs and opinions. It might also be called Block Thinking. Neat sets of beliefs and opinions are fastened together; and you are expected to take the lot. Either live in one Block or go and find a room in the next Block. Stay in the street outside, and you will be sniped at from all the windows. A Completely Outfitted man, a good Block Thinker, would rather have a fellow from the other Block, properly Outfitted, than tolerate a ditherer without a Block and Outfit. Let him shuffle off to the wilderness where he belongs!

I remember the hours I spent in the Thirties arguing with people who thought they were much cleverer than I was. (I am not very clever, but a bit cleverer than I look, like many seemingly gormless West Riding men.) They would try to prove to me that I had no choice except between Fascism and Communism. Your money or your life? Black or Red? So they were joining the C.P.; and most of them since have written long articles and books—and not done badly out of them—explaining that when they were Communists they were not really Communists. It all seems sadly out of date now, of course, but the attitude of mind is still with us, the Blocks and Outfits still in fashion. Probably the same people, grown no wiser, have the same contempt for my lack of insight and decision now that they had then. What Block are you in? Where is your Outfit? Bah!

Let us say, for example, that you believe that when the men responsible for atom bombs and other horrors solemnly warn their audiences, composed of people who never asked for any of this, that they live in a perilous age, those audiences should throw their chairs at the platform, to show what they think of such impudence. Write something to this effect, perhaps omitting the chair-throwing but making your protest, and immediately messages arrive from the Pacifist Block, telling you that you only need more courage and consistency to be entitled to wear the Outfit. Yet you may be anything but a turner of cheeks. You may believe in the most murderous direct defence of your own homes and persons, with pistols and lead pipes for men, sharp knives for the girls, holding that if the other fellows do not want to be killed, they should not obey orders to leave their own homes and ruin other people's. You may believe, as I do, that if the citizens of Great Powers were more sharply militant, less like sheep, then States would soon be less like wolves.

Again, your attitude towards Science may be ambivalent, as mine is. You may be profoundly sceptical about scientific humanism and its air-conditioned cybernetics utopia round the corner. You may feel that pseudo-scientific thought about man and the universe, sinking into the popular mind, has done much to create a mood of despair, making men feel homeless exiles, caught in a blind machine. You may take a sour view of recent contributions of nuclear physics to human progress, and discover in its professors a certain irresponsibility. But if you say these things in print, there arrives a triumphant messenger from the Catholic Block, crying: "What did we tell you? Now admit, you are one of us." Whereas you may be not one of them at all, may feel entitled to be as sceptical abut the Pope and the priests as you are about the British Association. A man may think that scientists should make narrower claims and take longer-term views and yet not want to climb on to the Angst-wagon of Original Sin and Guilt and Sex-lit-with-Hellfire.

This brings a loud cheer from the Rationalist Block. But it does not follow that you can join it. The accommodation it offers may seem much too small. For though you may not believe, with the Block gang, that man reached his noblest height in the thirteenth century and that the Renaissance was a blot on our history, you may yet hold that men need some form of religion, and that it is our misfortune if we find ourselves without one, among a litter of symbols that have lost their magic. You may know, as I do, men and women who never enter a church to worship there, yet seem more deeply possessed by genuine religious feeling than most of the ecclesiastical propagandists, hell-fire novelists, cold and cautious advocates of a Christian Society without faith, hope, or charity.

It is true that if a writer does not belong to a Block, goes about without a Complete Outfit, he suffers from many disadvantages. He has to think for himself, and thus may appear slow-witted as well as vague and "woolly." (You are always "woolly" if you have no Outfit.) He has no access to a Block list of witty retorts and crushing counter-arguments. He may still be groping and fumbling about while his Outfitted opponent has whipped out the cowboy gun, the bus-conductor's bell, the policeman's whistle. A sound Block man has more respect for a fellow from the opposite Block than he has for woolly ditherers, and nine times out of ten would rather leave one Block for another than stay outside in the rain. Once they have worn a Complete Outfit, most men feel naked without one.

What is most important, however, is that a writer solidly established in a Block can count on its support. At a time when critical standards are uncertain, when independent judgment is fast disappearing, when the prizes are few and so increasingly valuable, this Block support is almost worth a gold mine. Thus, there are some aesthetic enterprises that are hardly likely to succeed without some assistance from the Inverts' Block—called by a sardonic friend of mine "the Girls' Friendly Society"—which enthusiastically gives its praise and patronage to whatever is decorative, "amusing," "good theatre," witty in the right way, and likely to make heterosexual relationships look ridiculous: all of which is probably the stiff price we are paying in London for our stupid laws against inversion.

Clearly nothing can be achieved in politics without a Block. Even those of us who mistrust Block thinking, Complete Outfits on cards, would have to form some sort of Block to assert our essential liberalism. (Though guerrillas have been known to succeed against regular armies.) Where I disagree with many of my correspondents is in believing that a man is not necessarily useless just because he remains outside the Blocks. Many of us feel that this is a time when it is better to be "woolly" than Completely Outfitted. For men are in despair. Most people who join the Blocks, accepting with relief some ready-made system, do it out of despair. That is why they are so often angry and intolerant, having arrived at their decision not by way of hope and love but through despair and terror. You can smell all this in the very air of our time: we seem to live among savage rats and screaming mice. We are in despair because we begin to feel that our problems are beyond our solution, our dilemmas intolerable. But the worst way out of this situation may be to hurry to the nearest Block and to man the guns there. This will settle nothing except perhaps the hash of Western Man.

We must think, and think in a fresh, creative fashion. One glimmering of a new idea, in our situation, is worth all the blaze and fury of the Block systems, with their propaganda and anathemas. For, as possible solutions, not as power systems, they are all out of date. The Outfit is Complete just because it is done with. Every Block known to me is old-fashioned, like all fortresses. Every man who joins one, proudly accepting its logic and consistency, has really stopped trying to shape the future. It is he, and not the vague woollies outside, who had given it up as a hopeless job. For example, what is the world's Number One Problem? Not one Block will give the right answer. Yet there it is glaring at us: "What can we do now that will prevent our great-grandchildren from eating one another?" But perhaps here I do some of the Block systems an injustice; for at least they are working hard to prevent our having any great-grandchildren.

Our remote ancestors, we are told, were not impressive creatures, they cut a poor figure among the great beasts of the forest; they had no huge claws and teeth, no scaly armour, no wings, no great turn of speed, not even the power of rapid reproduction: all the odds seemed heavily against them. But they had one miraculous trick—they could adapt themselves to make the best of changing conditions; they were flexible and experimental. And now that we have conquered—and nearly ruined—the earth, now when we ourselves change our conditions often at appalling speed and almost blindly, we are in sore need of all the adaptability our species can still discover in itself. We must think freshly, think fast, improvise, experiment, and be tolerant of one another's mistakes. Despair and hate are not going to help us. And neither, I fancy, is Block thinking.

Discussion Questions

1. What do children's play Outfits and Block Thinking have in common?
2. What is "woolly thinking"? Is J. B. Priestly using it as a derogatory term? What advantages do Block Thinkers have over woolly thinkers? What is the most characteristic feature of Block Thinking?
3. What does Priestly consider the most serious problem facing the world today? How will woolly thinking help? Compare his treatment of poor thinking to E. M. Forster's in "Racial Exercise."
4. Think of some contemporary form of Block Thinking and in a brief essay demonstrate how the Block is constructed from one or two basic principles, allegiances, or ideas.

LILLIAN ROSS

As a journalist with The New Yorker *magazine, Lillian Ross developed the craft of reporting into an art form and thus laid the groundwork for what critics now call the New Journalism. In her articles and essays the writer often seems to vanish, leaving the reader with the impression that detail and quotation alone can amply convey their overall significance without any authorial intrusion. This objective style of writing characterizes much of Lillian Ross's work, especially the short pieces, such as "The Vinyl Santa," that she crafted over the years for the "Talk of the Town" section of* The New Yorker *and that she collected in* Talk Stories *(1966) and* Talks *(1983).*

Lillian Ross was born in Syracuse, New York, in 1927 and since 1948 has regularly contributed fiction, biographical sketches, and reporting to The New Yorker. *In 1952, she published her first book,* Picture, *a reportorial account in the form of a novel dealing with the filming of Stephen Crane's classic,* The Red Badge of Courage. *Besides several volumes of short stories, she has also written* Portrait of Hemingway *(1961),* Reporting *(1964),* Adlai Stevenson *(1966),* Reporting Two *(1969), and* Moments with Chaplin *(1978).*

The Vinyl Santa

Our lighted fireproof plastic Christmas bells are strung all through the house, not a creature is stirring, and our mail-order catalogues—now piled high on the back porch—have been under surveillance since August, when they started coming in from Atlantic City, New Jersey; Oshkosh, Wisconsin; Evanston, Illinois; Chicago, Illinois; Falls Church, Virginia; Omaha, Nebraska; Vineland, New Jersey; Northport, New York; New York, New York; and elsewhere, including points across the seas. We did our shopping during Indian summer, without leaving our chair. Our house is full. Our task is completed. We are ready.

On our front door is a "Deck the Door Knob of red-and-green felt with touches of glittering gold that has three jingly bells to say 'Hi! and Merry Christmas!' to all comers." On our windows are "Press-On Window Scenes" of snowmen and reindeer, and the windows are further ornamented with "Giant, 29-inch Personal Balls Artistically Hand-Lettered with the Family Name." Mounted outside on the wall of the house are "The Three Wise Men in Full Color in a Procession of Heavy Weatherproof Methyl-methacrylate Plastic." Each Wise Man is three feet tall and illuminated. A "Life-Size Climbing Vinyl Santa" is on the rooftop, and on the front lawn we have "3-D Thirty-Inch High Full Color Carollers of Strong Vinylite Carolling 'Oh, Come All Ye Faithful!'" In place of our regular doorbell we have a "glowing, jingling Santa stamped with the family name with a cord that visitors pull that raises Santa's arms in welcome, jingling bright brass bells." The garage door is covered with a "Giant Door Greeter Five Feet High and Six Feet Wide, Reading 'Merry Christmas.'" Indoors, all our rooms have been sprayed either wih "Bayberry Mist, the forest-fresh scent-of-Christmas" or with the "pungent, spicy, exotic, sweet and rare frankincense-and-myrrh spray—gift of the Magi to the newborn Babe." Each light switch is covered with a "Switchplate-Santa made of white felt with red bell-bedecked cap—the switch comes through his open mouth, the sight of which will make you feel jolly." The towels on the bathroom racks are hand-printed with designs of sleighs and candy canes. The rug next to the tub has "Jolly Old Santa centered in deep, soft, plushy, white pile, and he's wreathed in smiles and in cherries, too, for 'round his head is a gay, cherry wreath." All the mirrors in the house are plastered with red, green, and white pleated tissue cutouts of angels with self-adhesive backs. In the dining room, "Full Size Santa Mugs of Bright Red-and-White Glazed Ceramic are 'Ready' for a 'Spot' of Holiday Cheer." In the living room, we have a "giant holiday chandelier of metallic foil discs reflecting a rainbow of colors," and "giant four-foot electric candles in festive red-and-white candy stripes are glowing cheerfully from their rock-steady base to their dripping wax 'flame.'" On the hall table stands our "Electric Musical Church, five inches high, with inspirational strains of 'Silent Night' pealing reverently from behind lighted colorfully stained windows."

The tree is trimmed, all the way from a "Perforated Golden Star Making the Sun Envious of Its Brilliance, as though the Blazing Star of Bethlehem Were Pausing in Its Orbit at Your Home," down to the "Christmas Tree Bib Covered with a Profusion of Christmas Designs and Colors" on the floor. Reflecting the light of the Perforated Golden Star, which is made of anodized aluminum with "Hundreds of Holes through which the Light Twinkles just like a Real Star," hang dozens of "Personalized Tree Balls with Names of the Family Nicely Applied in Shimmering, Non-Tarnishing Glitter." Bare spots on the tree are filled in with "Luminous Tree Icicles of Plastic," "Luminous, Plastic, Heavenly Angel Babes Who Have Left the Milky Way," "Handcarved Wooden Angels Holding Hymnals on Gilded Hanging Strings," "Frosty White Pine Cones Lit with Colored Bulbs," "Miniature Felt Money Bags Gayly Trimmed in Assorted Designs of Yuletide," and "Yummy-Yum-Yum Santa Sweetest Holiday Lollipops."

On Christmas morning, there will be plenty of laughs when everybody gets dressed. Dad will be wearing his "Personalized Holiday Ringing Bell Shorts of White Sanforized Cotton with Santa Claus Handpainted in All His Glory on One Side with a Tinkling Bell on the Tassel of His Cap and Dad's name embroidered in Contrasting Red on the Other." Big Sister will have on "Bright Red Holiday Stretch Socks of Bright Red Nylon Embossed with Contrasting White Holiday Motif." Little Sister and Mom will have on matching "Candy Striped Flannelette Housecoats." Brother will have on a "Clip-On Bow Tie of Red Felt in a Holly Pattern" and also "The Host with the Most Bright Red Felt Vest with Colorful Christmas Accent." Auntie will have on "Ringing Bell Panties Boasting a Ribbon Bedecked Candy Cane Handpainted in Brilliant Yuletide Colors with a Real Tinkling Bell for Extra Cheer." And Shep will have on his own "Personalized Dog Galoshes Embossed with Dog Claus on the Toes." Odds and ends under the tree will include a "Jingle Bell Apron that Plays a Merry Tune with Every Movement," "Donner and Blitzen Salt and Pepper Shakers," a set of "Holly Jewelry for the Holly-Days," a "Ten Commandments Bookmark of Ten Radiant Gold-Plated Squares that Look Like Ancient Scrolled Pages of the Old Testament with the Commandments Etched Upon Them," and "Hi-Fi Bible Stories on a Personalized Record." And our Christmas dinner will be prepared with the help of the "No Cooking Cookbook, with a Collection of Easy-To-Fix Recipes for Busy Mothers that Turns Canned and Frozen Foods into a Banquet of Gourmet Dishes."

Discussion Questions

1. Where, specifically, do the details of "The Vinyl Santa" come from? What do they all have in common?

2. No personal comments appear in this Christmas sketch, but how can you infer the writer's point of view?

3. What is the effect of the accumulation of detail? What verbal characteristics do the details share?

4. How does Lillian Ross's use of detail compare with Gwendolyn Brooks's on the same subject. Could you change the details of Ross's sketch to produce an entirely different point of view?

5. Good writers are almost scientifically alert to specimens of language within a culture. What sort of language is Ross responding to in this sketch? Using her objective method, select another such specimen of language—for example, the idiom of sports broadcasting or the clipped style of newspaper headlines. Write a brief essay in which you deal with a subject not quite appropriate to that language almost entirely in the conventions of that language. What attitude toward your subject emerges?

BERTRAND RUSSELL

The English philosopher Bertrand Russell (1872–1970) had first earned a reputation in mathematical logic before he branched out into other, less specialized fields. His Principles of Mathematics *appeared in 1903 and was followed by an enormously influential three-volume collaboration with Alfred North Whitehead,* Principia Mathematica *(1910–1913). In 1908, Russell was elected to the Royal Society, and in 1910 was appointed a lecturer at Cambridge, a position he lost as a result of the active anti-draft role he took during World War I. In 1918, he was sentenced to six months in prison for writing a pacifist article. In later years, Russell campaigned against the atomic bomb and was an outspoken opponent of the Vietnam war. In 1950, he received the Nobel Prize for Literature.*

Russell lectured widely throughout the United States in the 1930's, returning to England in 1944, where he continued his efforts at popular education by presenting British Broadcasting Corporation programs. His numerous books include The A. B. C. of Atoms *(1923),* The A. B. C. of Relativity *(1925),* Marriage and Morals *(1929),* The Conquest of Happiness *(1930),* An Inquiry into Meaning and Truth *(1940),* A History of Western Philosophy *(1945),* Unpopular Essays *(1950), and* Human Society in Ethics and Politics *(1954). Russell's* Autobiography *appeared in three volumes between 1967 and 1969. The following essay is reprinted from* In Praise of Idleness and Other Essays *(1935).*

Education and Discipline

Any serious educational theory must consist of two parts: a conception of the ends of life, and a science of psychological dynamics, i.e., of the laws of mental change. Two men who differ as to the ends of life cannot hope to agree about education. The educational machine, throughout Western civilization, is dominated by two ethical theories: that of Christianity, and that of nationalism. These two, when taken seriously, are incompatible, as is becoming evident in Germany. For my part, I hold that, where they differ, Christianity is preferable, but where they agree, both are mistaken. The conception which I should substitute as the purpose of education is civilization, a term which, as I meant it, has a definition which is partly individual, partly social. It consists, in the individual, of both intellectual and moral qualities: intellectually, a certain minimum of general knowledge, technical skill in one's own profession, and a habit of forming opinions on evidence; morally, of impartiality, kindliness, and a modicum of self-control. I should add a quality which is neither moral nor intellectual, but perhaps physiological: zest and joy of life. In communities, civilization demands respect for law, justice as between man and man, purposes not involving permanent injury to any section of the human race, and intelligent adaptation of means to ends.

If these are to be the purpose of education, it is a question for the science of psychology to consider what can be done towards realizing them, and, in particular, what degree of freedom is likely to prove most effective.

On the question of freedom in education there are at present three main schools of thought, deriving partly from differences as to ends and partly from differences in psychological theory. There are those who say that children should be completely free, however bad they may be; there are those who say they should be completely subject to authority, however good they may be; and there are those who say they should be free, but in spite of freedom they should be always good. This last party is larger than it has any logical right to be; children, like adults, will not all be virtuous if they are all free. The belief that liberty will insure moral perfection is a relic of Rousseauism, and would not survive a study of animals and babies. Those who hold this belief think that education should have no positive purpose, but should merely offer an environment suitable for spontaneous development. I cannot agree with this school, which seems too individualistic, and unduly indifferent to the importance of knowledge. We live in communities which require cooperation, and it would be utopian to expect all the necessary cooperation to result from spontaneous impulse. The existence of a large population on a limited area is only possible owing to science and technique; education must, therefore, hand on the necessary minimum of these. The educators who allow most freedom are men whose success depends upon a degree of benevolence, self-control, and trained intelligence which can hardly be generated where every impulse is left unchecked; their merits, therefore, are not likely to be perpetuated if their methods are undiluted. Education, viewed from a social standpoint, must be something more positive than a mere opportunity for growth. It must, of course, provide this, but it must also provide a mental and moral equipment which children cannot acquire entirely for themselves.

The arguments in favor of a great degree of freedom in education are derived not from man's natural goodness, but from the effects of authority, both on those who suffer it and on those who exercise it. Those who are subject to authority become either submissive or rebellious, and each attitude has its drawbacks.

The submissive lose initiative, both in thought and action; moreover, the anger generated by the feeling of being thwarted tends to find an outlet in bullying those who are weaker. That is why tyrannical institutions are self-perpetuating: what a man has suffered from his father he inflicts upon his son, and the humiliations which he remembers having endured at his public school he passes on to "natives" when he becomes an empire-builder. Thus an unduly authoritative education turns the pupils into timid tyrants, incapable of either claiming or tolerating originality in word or deed. The effect upon the educators is even worse: they tend to become sadistic disciplinarians, glad to inspire terror, and content to inspire nothing else. As these men represent knowledge, the pupils acquire a horror of knowledge, which, among the English upper class, is supposed to be part of human nature, but is really part of the well-grounded hatred of the authoritarian pedagogue.

Rebels, on the other hand, though they may be necessary, can hardly be just to what exists. Moreover, there are many ways of rebelling, and only a small minority of these are wise. Galileo was a rebel and was wise; believers in the flat-earth theory are equally rebels, but are foolish. There is a great danger in the tendency to suppose that opposition to authority is essentially meritorious and that unconventional opinions are bound to be correct: no useful purpose is served by smashing lamp-posts or maintaining Shakespeare to be no poet. Yet this excessive rebelliousness is often the effect that too much authority has on spirited pupils. And when rebels become educators, they sometimes encourage defiance in their pupils, for whom at the same time they are trying to produce a perfect environment, although these two aims are scarcely compatible.

What is wanted is neither submissiveness nor rebellion, but good nature, and general friendliness both to people and to new ideas. These qualities are due in part to physical causes, to which old-fashioned educators paid too little attention; but they are due still more to freedom from the feeling of baffled impotence which arises when vital impulses are thwarted. If the young are to grow into friendly adults, it is necessary, in most cases, that they should feel their environment friendly. This requires that there should be a certain sympathy with the child's important desires, and not merely an attempt to use him for some abstract end such as the glory of God or the greatness of one's country. And, in teaching, every attempt should be made to cause the pupil to feel that it is worth his while to know what is being taught—at least when this is true. When the pupil cooperates willingly, he learns twice as fast and with half the fatigue. All these are valid reasons for a very great degree of freedom.

It is easy, however, to carry the argument too far. It is not desirable that children, in avoiding the vices of the slave, should acquire those of the aristocrat. Consideration for others, not only in great matters, but also in little everyday things, is an essential element in civilization, without which social life would be intolerable. I am not thinking of mere forms of politeness, such as saying "please" and "thank you": formal manners are most fully developed among barbarians, and diminish with every advance in culture. I am thinking rather of willingness to take a fair share of necessary work, to be obliging in small ways that save trouble on the balance. It is not desirable to give a child a sense of omnipotence, or a belief that adults exist only to minister to the pleasures of the young. And those who disapprove of the existence of the idle rich are hardly consistent if they bring up their children without any sense that work is necessary, and without the habits that make continuous application possible.

There is another consideration to which some advocates of freedom attach too little importance. In a community of children which is left without adult interference there is a tyranny of the stronger, which is likely to be far more brutal than most adult tyranny. If two children of two or three years old are left to play together, they will, after a few fights, discover which is bound to be the victor, and the other will then become a slave. Where the number of children is larger, one or two acquire complete mastery, and the others have far less liberty than they would have if the adults interfered to protect the weaker and less pugnacious. Consideration for others does not, with most children, arise spontaneously, but has to be taught, and can hardly be taught except by the exercise of authority. This is perhaps the most important argument against the abdication of the adults.

I do not think that educators have yet solved the problem of combining the desirable forms of freedom with the necessary minimum of moral training. The right solution, it must be admitted, is often made impossible by parents before the child is brought to an enlightened school. Just as psychoanalysts, from their clinical experience, conclude that we are all mad, so the authorities in modern schools, from their contact with pupils whose parents have made them unmanageable, are disposed to conclude that all children are "difficult" and all parents utterly foolish. Children who have been driven wild by parental tyranny (which often takes the form of solicitous affection) may require a longer or shorter period of complete liberty before they can view any adult without suspicion. But children who have been sensibly handled at home can bear to be checked in minor ways, so long as they feel that they are being helped in the ways that they themselves regard as important. Adults who like children, and are not reduced to a condition of nervous exhaustion by their company, can achieve a great deal in the way of discipline without ceasing to be regarded with friendly feelings by their pupils.

I think modern educational theorists are inclined to attach too much importance to the negative virture of not interfering with children, and too little to the positive merit of enjoying their company. If you have the sort of liking for children that many people have for horses or dogs, they will be apt to respond to your suggestions, and to accept prohibitions, perhaps with some good-humored grumbling, but without resentment. It is no use to have the sort of liking that consists in regarding them as a field for valuable social endeavor, or—what amounts to the same thing—as an outlet for power-impulses. No child will be grateful for an interest in him that springs from the thought that he will have a vote to be secured for your party or a body to be sacrificed to king and country. The desirable sort of interest is that which consists in spontaneous pleasure in the presence of children, without any ulterior purpose. Teachers who have this quality will seldom need to interfere with children's freedom, but will be able to do so, when necessary, without causing psychological damage.

Unfortunately, it is utterly impossible for overworked teachers to preserve an instinctive liking for children; they are bound to come to feel towards them as the proverbial confectioner's apprentice does towards macaroons. I do not think that education ought to be any one's whole profession: it should be undertaken for at most two hours a day by people whose remaining hours are spent away from children. The society of the young is fatiguing, especially when strict discipline is avoided. Fatigue, in the end, produces irritation, which is likely to express itself somehow, whatever theories the harassed teacher may have taught himself or herself to believe. The necessary friendliness cannot be preserved by self-control alone. But where it exists, it should be unnecessary to have rules in advance as to how "naughty" children are to be treated, since impulse is likely to lead to the right decision, and almost any decision will be right if the child feels that you like him. No rules, however wise, are a subtitute for affection and tact.

Discussion Questions

1. Good sense is often an attempt to find a middle ground between two extremes. How is "good sense" expressed in this essay? What are the advantages of this procedure? What are its limitations?

2. How does Russell rely on classification to provide an outline for his essay? Break his essay down into its parts to see what its skeleton looks like.

3. Compare McLuhan's "Classroom Without Walls" to Russell's essay. How would Russell have responded to McLuhan's idea of what a classroom should be like? Would he have agreed with McLuhan's educational purpose? With his means to achieve it?

4. Why does Russell attach such importance to "general friendliness"? What educational value does this quality possess for him? Why do

you think so few educators today stress it? What term might today's educators use in place of "friendliness"?

5. Think about your own education. What aspects of freedom or discipline would have made it a better experience for you? Using Bertrand Russell's essay as a model, discuss in a short essay of your own the human qualities you think educational theories should be based on.

Logan Pearsall Smith

Logan Pearsall Smith (1865–1946) was born in New Jersey into a cultivated Quaker family. A first cousin, Miss M. Carey Thomas, was the President of Bryn Mawr; one of his sisters married the art critic, Bernhard Berenson; another sister was the first wife of Bertrand Russell. After some study at Haverford and Harvard, Smith worked in his father's business until he was persuaded to join his parents in England. He remained there for the rest of his long life, becoming an expert on English usage and collecting his dryly ironic and severely self-limited essays in books like his *Trivia* (1917). Before his death he had achieved a unique reputation as a writer and came to be seen as a holdover from an earlier age, as one of Henry James's American expatriates come to life.

Words from the Sea

Metaphorical idioms, and, indeed, many grammatical idioms also, come to us in great numbers from special occupations and popular forms of sport. Each form of human activity has its own vocabulary, its terms to describe its materials, its methods, its difficulties, and its aims; and from these vocabularies not only words, but idiomatic phrases often make their way into the standard language. Our speech is never adequate to express the inexhaustible richness of life, with all its relations and thoughts and feelings; the standard language is hampered, too, by many impediments in the always difficult process of word-formation, and is therefore ready to seize on any of the special terms which are already current, and to which it can give the wide significance it desires. Then, too, the idioms and happy phrases invented by people engaged in popular sports and occupations being terse, colloquial, vivid, and charged with eager life, are just the kind that are sought for and welcomed in animated speech. Sailors at sea, hunters with their dogs, labourers in the fields, cooks in their kitchens, needing in some crisis a vigorous phrase of command or warning or reprobation, have often hit on some expressive collocation of words, some vivid and homely metaphor from the objects before them; and these phrases and metaphors, striking the fancy of their companions, have been adopted into the vocabulary of their special sport or occupation. Soon a number of these phrases are found to be capable of a wider use; often for convenience, often with a touch of humour, they come to be applied to analogous situations; a sailor applies his sea-phrases to the situations in which he finds himself on land; the fisherman (as indeed we see in the Gospels) talks of life in terms of fishing; the housewife helps herself out with metaphors from her kitchen or her farmyard; the sportsman expresses himself in the idioms of his sport; and little by little the most vivid and most useful of these phrases make their way into the common vocabulary and come to be understood by all.

In any analysis of the sources of our English idioms those which come to us from the sea will be found to be especially numerous. The vigorous expressive speech of sailors is rich in technical idioms of its own, and many of these have passed, with metaphorical signification, into the speech of Englishmen on land. The sea origin of the following is sufficiently obvious:

To take the helm,
To take in a reef,
To set afloat,
To turn adrift,
To cut the painter,
To have, or take, in tow,
To put about,
To tide over,
To steer clear of,
To touch bottom,
To be in the same boat with,
To put in one's oar,
To rest on one's oars,
To sail near the wind,
To sail before the wind,
To sail in,
To take the wind out of some one's sails,
To hang in the wind,
To go with, or against, the stream,
To keep one's head above water,
To keep one's weather eye open,
To look out for squalls,
To weather, or ride out, the storm,
To pour oil on troubled waters,
To hoist or lower one's flag,
To nail one's flag to the mast.

All at sea,
Half seas over,
Three sheets in the wind,
On the top of the wave,
On one's beam ends,
On the rocks,
On the wrong tack,
At a low ebb,
In the wake of,
In low water,
In deep water,
In troubled waters,
In full sail,
Over head and ears,
Left stranded,
Between wind and water,
High-water mark,
Plain sailing,
Leeway to make up,
Breakers ahead,
The cut of one's jib,
Not a shot in the locker.
When one's ship comes home,
Shipshape and Bristol fashion,

And less obvious in their nautical origin the following:

To find one's bearings,
To bear a hand,
To bear down upon,
To give a wide berth to,
To keep aloof,
To fall foul of [collide],
To make way,
To give way,
To see how the land lies,
To box the compass,
To speak by the card [of the compass],
To break the ice,
To throw over [overboard],
To go by the board,
To run high,
To turn in,
To go ahead,
To sheer off,
To know the ropes,
To put about,
To cut and run,
To pipe the eye,
To come down with a run.
To forge ahead.

All hands,
All told,
Hard up (of the helm),
Hard lines,
Hard and fast,
High and dry,
Hand over hand,
Under way,
On the stocks,
The lay of the land,
The coast is clear.
At close quarters.

Discussion Questions

1. What kinds of idioms does Smith himself employ in his introductory remarks, and what effects do they create in his style?

2. What principles govern Smith's technique of listing and how do they contribute to the essay as a whole?

3. Compare Smith's approach to language to those of Robert Frost and S. I. Hayakawa.

4. Find another occupation (for example, agriculture or military life) that has been a source of common idioms and list as many as you can. How would you design a method to make a more systematic and exhaustive list?

SUSAN SONTAG

Susan Sontag was born in New York City in 1933. She graduated from the University of Chicago, and studied religion and philosophy at Harvard and at the Union Theological Seminary. She began writing essays for Partisan Review in the early 1960's, and since then has achieved a reputation as one of America's leading intellectuals. Her wide-ranging concerns can be seen in her three collections of essays, Against Interpretation (1966), Styles of Radical Will (1969), and Under the Sign of Saturn (1980), in which she writes about film, Marxism, theater, popular taste, pornography, revolutionary politics, fascism, and a large number of prominent European artists and thinkers. Indeed, there are few living writers who have done more to introduce contemporary European thought to American culture. She has written two other nonfiction books: the award-winning On Photography (1977) and Illness As Metaphor (1978).

The recipient of numerous awards and fellowships, Susan Sontag has written and directed three films. She is also the author of two novels, The Benefactor (1963) and Death Kit (1967), as well as a collection of short stories, I etcetera (1978). The following selection is the opening of an essay on science fiction films, "The Imagination of Disaster," which originally appeared in Commentary in 1965 and which, despite the date, is still an accurate account of an ever-popular genre.

Science Fiction Films: The Imagination of Disaster

The typical science fiction film has a form as predictable as a Western, and is made up of elements which, to a practiced eye, are as classic as the saloon brawl, the blonde schoolteacher from the East, and the gun duel on the deserted main street.

One model scenario proceeds through five phases.

(1) The arrival of the thing. (Emergence of the monsters, landing of the alien spaceship, etc.) This is usually witnessed or suspected by just one person, a young scientist on a field trip. Nobody, neither his neighbors nor his colleagues, will believe him for some time. The hero is not married, but has a sympathetic though also incredulous girl friend.

(2) Confirmation of the hero's report by a host of witnesses to a great act of destruction. (If the invaders are beings from another planet, a fruitless attempt to parley with them and get them to leave peacefully.) The local police are summoned to deal with the situation and massacred.

(3) In the capital of the country, conferences between scientists and the military take place, with the hero lecturing before a chart, map, or blackboard. A national emergency is declared. Reports of further destruction. Authorities from other countries arrive in black limousines. All international tensions are suspended in view of the planetary emergency. This stage often includes a rapid montage of news broadcasts in various languages, a meeting at the the UN, and more conferences between the military and the scientists. Plans are made for destroying the enemy.

(4) Further atrocities. At some point the hero's girl friend is in grave danger. Massive counter-attacks by international forces, with brilliant displays of rocketry, rays, and other advanced

weapons; are all unsuccessful. Enormous military casualties, usually by incineration. Cities are destroyed and/or evacuated. There is an obligatory scene here of panicked crowds stampeding along a highway or a big bridge, being waved on by numerous policemen who, if the film is Japanese, are immaculately white-gloved, preternaturally calm, and call out in dubbed English, "Keep moving. There is no need to be alarmed."

(5) More conferences, whose motif is: "They must be vulnerable to something." Throughout the hero has been working in his lab to this end. The final strategy, upon which all hopes depend, is drawn up; the ultimate weapon—often a superpowerful, as yet untested, nuclear device—is mounted. Countdown. Final repulse of the monster or invaders. Mutual congratulations, while the hero and girl friend embrace cheek to cheek and scan the skies sturdily. "But have we seen the last of them?"

The film I have just described should be in color and on a wide screen. Another typical scenario, which follows, is simpler and suited to black-and-white films with a lower budget. It has four phases.

(1) The hero (usually, but not always, a scientist) and his girl friend, or his wife and two children, are disporting themselves in some innocent ultra-normal middle-class surroundings—their house in a small town, or on vacation (camping, boating). Suddenly, someone starts behaving strangely; or some innocent form of vegetation becomes monstrously enlarged and ambulatory. If a character is pictured driving an automobile, something gruesome looms up in the middle of the road. If it is night, strange lights hurtle across the sky.

(2) After following the thing's tracks, or determining that It is radioactive, or poking around a huge crater—in short, conducting some sort of crude investigation—the hero tries to warn the local authorities, without effect; nobody believes anything is amiss. The hero knows better. If the thing is tangible, the house is elaborately barricaded. If the invading alien is an invisible parasite, a doctor or friend is called in, who is himself rather quickly killed or "taken possession of" by the thing.

(3) The advice of whoever further is consulted proves useless. Meanwhile, It continues to claim other victims in the town,

which remains implausibly isolated from the rest of the world. General helplessness.
(4) One of two possibilities. Either the hero prepares to do battle alone, accidentally discovers the thing's one vulnerable point, and destroys it. Or, he somehow manages to get out of town and succeeds in laying his case before competent authorities. They, along the lines of the first script but abridged, deploy a complex technology which (after initial setbacks) finally prevails against the invaders.

Another version of the second script opens with the scientist-hero in his laboratory, which is located in the basement or on the grounds of his tasteful, prosperous house. Through his experiments, he unwittingly causes a frightful metamorphosis in some class of plants or animals which turn carnivorous and go on a rampage. Or else, his experiments have caused him to be injured (sometimes irrevocably) or "invaded" himself. Perhaps he has been experimenting with radiation, or has built a machine to communicate with beings from other planets or transport him to other places or times.

Another version of the first script involves the discovery of some fundamental alteration in the conditions of existence of our planet, brought about by nuclear testing, which will lead to the extinction in a few months of all human life. For example: the temperature of the earth is becoming too high or too low to support life, or the earth is cracking in two, or it is gradually being blanketed by lethal fallout.

A third script, somewhat but not altogether different from the first two, concerns a journey through space—to the moon, or some other planet. What the space-voyagers discover commonly is that the alien terrain is in a state of dire emergency, itself threatened by extra-planetary invaders or nearing extinction through the practice of nuclear warfare. The terminal dramas of the first and second scripts are played out there, to which is added the problem of getting away from the doomed and/or hostile planet and back to Earth.

Discussion Questions

1. How does Susan Sontag convey the predictability of science fiction films? To what extent is her assessment of this predictability a

negative criticism of such films? To what extent is the predictability an essential ingredient of the films?

2. How are Sontag's two typical scenarios different? What do they have in common? How does the tone in which she narrates these scenarios indicate her feelings about them?

3. Why do you think westerns and science fiction films follow such prescribed forms? The derivative mentality of movie people? Other factors? Has it to do with their subject matter? The expectations of their audiences? How would you construct a movie scenario for the events detailed in Barbara Tuchman's "This Is the End of the World: The Black Death"?

4. Susan Sontag's essay was written in 1965. Do you think her versions of science fiction films are still applicable? Think of some of the classic science fiction films you have seen (or some of the most recent) and discuss how well they conform to Sontag's model scenarios.

GAY TALESE

Born in New Jersey in 1932, Gay Talese graduated from the University of Alabama and spent ten years as a staff writer for The New York Times, a position that afforded him the inside information for his best-selling history of the Times entitled The Kingdom and the Power (1969). In another best seller, Honor Thy Father (1971), Talese reported on the intimate life of a Mafia family. His writing style, a deliberate blend of factual detail and fictional technique, won him much acclaim, and he is credited—along with Tom Wolfe—as one of the founders of the New Journalism. As Talese put it, the New Journalism, "though often reading like fiction," is "as reliable as the most reliable reportage although it seeks a larger truth than is possible through the mere compilation of verifiable facts, the use of direct quotations, and adherence to the rigid organizational style of the older form." Talese's reputation survives, however, not because he practiced the New Journalism, but because within that mode he adhered to age-old standards of good writing.

Talese's articles have appeared in a variety of magazines, and his most recent book, Thy Neighbor's Wife (1980) is a comprehensively researched account of sex in America. The following account of the construction of the Verrazano Bridge is taken from "The Bridge," which appeared in his collection of essays, Fame and Obscurity (1970).

Punks and Pushers

Building a bridge is like combat; the language is of the barracks, and the men are organized along the lines of the noncommissioned officers' caste. At the very bottom, comparable to the Army recruit, are the apprentices—called "punks." They climb catwalks with buckets of bolts, learn through observation and turns on the tools, occasionally are sent down for coffee and water, seldom hear thanks. Within two or three years, most punks have become full-fledged bridgemen, qualified to heat, catch, or drive rivets; to raise, weld, or connect steel—but it is the last job, connecting the steel, that most captures their fancy. The steel connectors stand highest on the bridge, their sweat taking minutes to hit the ground, and when the derricks hoist up new steel, the connectors reach out and grab it with their hands, swing it into position, bang it with bolts and mallets, link it temporarily to the steel already in place, and leave the rest to the riveting gangs.

Connecting steel is the closest thing to aerial art, except the men must build a new sky stage for each show, and that is what makes it so dangerous—that and the fact that young connectors sometimes like to grandstand a bit, like to show the old men how it is done, and so they sometimes swing on the cables too much, or stand on unconnected steel, or run across narrow beams on windy days instead of straddling as they should—and sometimes they get so daring they die.

Once the steel is in place, riveting gangs move in to make it permanent. The fast, four-man riveting gangs are wondrous to watch. They toss rivets around as gracefully as infielders, driving in more than a thousand a day, each man knowing the others' moves, some having traveled together for years as a team. One man is called the "heater," and he sweats on the bridge all day over a kind of barbecue pit of flaming coal, cooking rivets until they are red—but not so red that they will buckle or blister. The heater must be a good cook, a chef, must think he is cooking sausages not rivets, because the other three men in the riveting gang are very particular people.

Once the rivet is red, but not too red, the heater tong-tosses it fifty, or sixty, or seventy feet, a perfect strike to the "catcher," who snares it out of the air with his metal mitt. Then the catcher relays the rivet to the third man, who stands nearby and is called the "bucker-up"—and who, with a long cylindrical tool named after the anatomical pride of a stud horse, bucks the rivet into the prescribed hole and holds it there while the fourth man, the riveter, moves in from the other side and begins to rattle his gun against the rivet's front end until the soft tip of the rivet has been flattened and made round and full against the hole. When the rivet cools, it is as permanent as the bridge itself.

Each gang—whether it be a riveting gang, connecting gang or raising gang—is under the direct supervision of a foreman called a "pusher." (One night in a Brooklyn bar, an Indian pusher named Mike Tarbell was arrested by two plainsclothesmen who had overheard his occupation, and Tarbell was to spend three days in court and lose $175 in wages before convincing the judge that he was not a pusher of dope, only of bridgemen.)

The pusher, like an Army corporal who is bucking for sergeant, drives his gang to be the best, the fastest, because he knows that along the bridge other pushers are doing the same thing. They all know that the company officials keep daily records of the productivity of each gang. The officials know which gang lifted the most steel, drove the most rivets, spun the most cable—and if the pusher is ambitious, wants to be promoted someday to a better job on the bridge, pushing is the only way.

But if he pushes too hard, resulting in accidents or death, then he is in trouble with the bridge company. While the bridge company encourages competition between gangs, because it wants to see the bridge finished fast, wants to see traffic jams up there and hear the clink of coins at toll gates, it does not want any accidents or deaths to upset the schedule or get into the newspapers or degrade the company's safety record with the insurance men. So the pusher is caught in the middle. If he is not lucky, if there is death in his gang, he may be blamed and be dropped back into the gang himself, and another workman will be promoted to pusher. But if he is lucky, and his gang works fast and well, then he someday might become an assistant superintendent on the bridge—a "walkin' boss."

The walkin' boss, of which there usually are four on a big

bridge where four hundred or five hundred men are employed, commands a section of the span. One walkin' boss may be in charge of the section between an anchorage and a tower, another from that tower to the center of the span, a third from the center of the span to the other tower, the fourth from that tower to the other anchorage—and all they do all day is walk up and down, up and down, strutting like gamecocks, a look of suspicion in their eyes as they glance sideways to see that the pushers are pushing, the punks are punking, and the young steel connectors are not behaving like acrobats on the cables.

The thing that concerns walkin' bosses most is that they impress *the* boss, who is the superintendent, and is comparable to a top sergeant. The superintendent is usually the toughest, loudest, foulest-mouthed, best bridgeman on the whole job, and he lets everybody know it. He usually spends most of his day at a headquarters shack built along the shore near the anchorage of the bridge, there to communicate with the engineers, designers, and other white-collar officers from the bridge company. The walkin' bosses up on the bridge represent him and keep him informed, but about two or three times a day the superintendent will leave his shack and visit the bridge, and when he struts across the span the whole thing seems to stiffen. The men are all heads down at work, the punks seem petrified.

The superintendent selected to supervise the construction of the span and the building of the cables for the Verrazano-Narrows Bridge was a six-foot, fifty-nine-year-old, hot-tempered man named John Murphy, who, behind his back, was known as "Hard Nose" or "Short Fuse."

He was a broad-shouldered and chesty man with a thin strong nose and jaw, with pale blue eyes and thinning white hair—but the most distinguishing thing about him was his red face, a face so red that if he ever blushed, which he rarely did, nobody would know it. The red hard face—the result of forty years' booming in the high wind and hot sun of a hundred bridges and skyscrapers around America—gave Murphy the appearance of always being boiling mad at something, which he usually was.

He had been born, like so many boomers, in a small town without horizons—in this case, Rexton, a hamlet of three hundred in New Brunswick, Canada. The flu epidemic that had swept through Rexton in the spring of 1919, when Murphy was sixteen years old killed his mother and father, an uncle and two cousins, and left him largely responsible for the support of his five younger brothers and sisters. So he went to work driving timber in Maine, and, when that got slow, he moved down to Pennsylvania and learned the bridge business, distinguishing himself as a steel connector because he was young and fearless. He was considered one of the best connectors on the George Washington Bridge, which he worked on in 1930 and 1931, and since then he had gone from one job to another, booming all the way up to Alaska to put a bridge across the Tanana River, and then back east again on other bridges and buildings.

In 1959 he was the superintendent in charge of putting up the Pan Am, the fifty-nine-story skyscraper in mid-Manhattan, and after that he was appointed to head the Verrazano job by the American Bridge Company, a division of United States Steel that had the contract to put up the bridge's span and steel cables.

When Hard Nose Murphy arrived at the bridge site in the early spring of 1962, the long, undramatic, sloppy, yet so vital part of bridge construction—the foundations—was finished, and the two 693-foot towers were rising.

The foundation construction for the two towers, done by J. Rich Steers, Inc., and the Frederick Snare Corporation, if not an aesthetic operation that would appeal to the adventurers in high steel, nevertheless was a most difficult and challenging task, because the two caissons sunk in the Narrows had been among the largest ever built. They were 229 feet long and 129 feet wide, and each had sixty-six circular dredging holes—each hole being seventeen feet in diameter—and, from a distance, the concrete caissons looked like gigantic chunks of Swiss cheese.

Building the caisson that would support the pedestal which would in turn bear the foundation for the Staten Island tower had required 47,000 cubic yards of concrete, and before it settled on firm sand 105 feet below the surface, 81,500 cubic yards of muck and sand had to be lifted up through the dredging holes by clamshell buckets suspended from cranes. The caisson for the Brooklyn tower had to be sunk to about 170 feet below sea level, had required 83,000 cubic yards of concrete, and 143,600 cubic yards of muck and sand had to be dredged up.

The foundations, the ones that anchor the bridge to Staten Island and Brooklyn, were concrete blocks the height of a ten-story building, each triangular-shaped, and holding, within their hollows, all the ends of the cable strands that stretch across the bridge. These two anchorages, built by the Arthur A. Johnson Corporation and Peter Kiewit Sons' Company, hold back the 240,000,000-pound pull of the bridge's four cables.

It had taken a little more than two years to complete the four foundations, and it had been a day-and-night grind, unappreciated by sidewalk superintendents and, in fact, protested by two hundred Staten Islanders on March 29, 1961; they claimed, in a petition presented to Richmond County District Attorney John M. Braisted, Jr., that the foundation construction between 6 P.M. and 6 A.M. was ruining the sleep of a thousand persons within a one-mile radius. In Brooklyn, the Bay Ridge neighborhood also was cluttered with cranes and earth-moving equipment as work on the approachway to the bridge continued, and the people still were hating Moses, and some had cried foul after he had awarded a $20,000,000 contract, without competitive bidding, to a construction company that employs his son-in-law. All concerned in the transaction immediately denied there was anything irregular about it.

But when Hard Nose Murphy arrived, things were getting better; the bridge was finally crawling up out of the water, and the people had something to *see*—some visible justification for all the noise at night—and in the afternoons some old Brooklyn men with nothing to do would line the shore watching the robin-red towers climb higher and higher.

The towers had been made in sections in steel plants and had been floated by barge to the bridge site. The Harris Structural Steel Company had made the Brooklyn tower, while Bethlehem made the Staten Island tower—both to O. H. Ammann's specifications. After the tower sections had arrived at the bridge site, they were lifted up by floating derricks anchored alongside the tower piers. After the first three tiers of each tower leg had been locked into place, soaring at this point to about 120 feet, the floating derricks were replaced by "creepers"—derricks, each with a lifting capacity of more than one hundred tons, that crept up the towers on tracks bolted to the sides of the tower legs. As the towers got higher, the creepers were raised until, finally, the towers had reached their pinnacle of 693 feet.

While the construction of towers possesses the element of danger, it is not really much different from building a tall building or an enormous lighthouse; after the third or fourth story is built, it is all the same the rest of the way up. The real art and drama in bridge building begins after the towers are up; then the men have to reach out from these towers and begin to stretch the cables and link the span over the sea.

This would be Murphy's problem, and as he sat in one of the Harris Company's boats on this morning in May, 1962, idly watching from the water as the Staten Island tower loomed up to its tenth tier, he was saying to one of the engineers in the boat, "You know, every time I see a bridge in this stage, I can't help but think of all the problems we got coming next—all the mistakes, all the cursing, all the goddamned sweat and the death we gotta go through to finish this thing. . . ."

The engineer nodded, and then they both watched quietly again as the derricks, swelling at the veins, continued to hoist large chunks of steel through the sky.

Discussion Questions

1. Gay Talese is a writer, not a construction worker; why was it important for him to know the vocabulary of bridge construction? How does that vocabulary affect your sense of his expertise? Of his presence in the essay?

2. Where does Talese change his description from the general to the particular? Why did he organize his essay in this fashion?

3. How does Talese create a sense of the glamour of bridge construction? Point to terms in the essay that you think contribute to the romance of the job. What does his technique have in common with Tom Wolfe's in "The Right Stuff"?

4. Nearly all occupations consist of specialized tasks within a hierarchical structure. In a short essay, using Talese's method of objective description, write about a job that you have had or now have. Make sure to work into your essay the vocabulary of the job and a description of the processes and people involved.

LEWIS THOMAS

A *physician, professor, and an award-winning essayist, Lewis Thomas was born in Flushing, New York, in 1913. He taught medicine at the University of Minnesota, served as dean at the Yale Medical School, and is currently director of the Memorial Sloan-Kettering Cancer Center. Although he has written several hundred scientific articles, Thomas did not start writing essays professionally until 1970, when he began contributing to the prestigious* New England Journal of Medicine. *His first collection of essays,* Lives of a Cell *(1974) won the National Book Award in Arts and Letters and immediately became a classic, one of the few contemporary books that compellingly bridges the languages of the sciences and of the humanities.*

The playful "Notes on Punctuation" was collected in Thomas's second book, Medusa and the Snail *(1979). His most recent book is* The Youngest Science: Notes of a Medicine Watcher *(1983).*

Notes on Punctuation

There are no precise rules about punctuation (Fowler lays out some general advice (as best he can under the complex circumstances of English prose (he points out, for example, that we possess only four stops (the comma, the semicolon, the colon and the period (the question mark and exclamation point are not, strictly speaking, stops; they are indicators of tone (oddly enough, the Greeks, employed the semicolon for their question mark (it produces a strange sensation to read a Greek sentence which is a straightforward question: Why weepest thou; (instead of Why weepest thou? (and, of course, there are parentheses (which are surely a kind of punctuation making this whole matter much more complicated by having to count up the left-handed parentheses in order to be sure of closing with the right number (but if the parentheses were left out, with nothing to work with but the stops, we would have considerably more flexibility in the deploying of layers of meaning than if we tried to separate all the clauses by physical barriers (and in the latter case, while we might have more precision and exactitude for our meaning, we would lose the essential flavor of language, which is its wonderful ambiguity)))))))))))).

The commas are the most useful and usable of all the stops. It is highly important to put them in place as you go along. If you try to come back after doing a paragraph and stick them in the various spots that tempt you you will discover that they tend to swarm like minnows into all sorts of crevices whose existence you hadn't realized and before you know it the whole long sentence becomes immobilized and lashed up squirming in commas. Better to use them sparingly, and with affection, precisely when the need for each one arises, nicely, by itself.

I have grown fond of semicolons in recent years. The semicolon tells you that there is still some question about the preceding full sentence; something needs to be added; it reminds you sometimes of the Greek usage. It is almost always a greater pleasure to come across a semicolon than a period. The period tells you that that is that; if you didn't get all the meaning you wanted or expected, anyway you got all the writer intended to parcel out and now you have to move along. But with a semicolon there you get a pleasant little feeling of expectancy; there is more to come; read on; it will get clearer.

Colons are a lot less attractive, for several reasons: firstly, they give you the feeling of being rather ordered around, or at least having your nose pointed in a direction you might not be inclined to take if left to yourself, and, secondly, you suspect you're in for one of those sentences that will be labeling the points to be made: firstly, secondly and so forth, with the implication that you haven't sense enough to keep track of a sequence of notions without having them numbered. Also, many writers use this system loosely and incompletely, starting out with number one and number two as though counting off on their fingers but then going on and on without the succession of labels you've been led to expect, leaving you floundering about searching for the ninethly or seventeenthly that ought to be there but isn't.

Exclamation points are the most irritating of all. Look! they say, look at what I just said! How amazing is my thought! It is like being forced to watch someone else's small child jumping up and down crazily in the center of the living room shouting to attract attention. If a sentence really has something of importance to say, something quite remarkable, it doesn't need a mark to point it out. And if it is really, after all, a banal sentence needing more zing, the exclamation point simply emphasizes its banality!

Quotation marks should be used honestly and sparingly, when there is a genuine quotation at hand, and it is necessary to be very rigorous about the words enclosed by the marks. If something is to be quoted, the *exact* words must be used. If part of it must be left out because of space limitations, it is good manners to insert three dots to indicate the omission, but it is unethetical to do this if it means connecting two thoughts which the original author did not intend to have tied together. Above all, quotation marks should not be used for ideas that you'd like to disown, things in the air so to speak. Nor should they be put in place around clichés; if you want to use a cliché you must take full responsibility for it yourself and not try to fob it off on anon., or on society. The most objectionable misuse of quotation marks, but one which illustrates the dangers of misuse in ordinary prose, is seen in advertising, especially in advertisements for small restaurants, for example "just around the corner," or "a good place to eat." No single, identifiable, citable person ever really said, for the record, "just around the corner," much less "a good place to eat," least likely of all for restaurants of the type that use this type of prose.

The dash is a handy device, informal and essentially playful, telling you that you're about to take off on a different tack but still in some way connected with the present course—only you have to remember that the dash is there, and either put a second dash at the end of the notion to let the reader know that he's back on course, or else end the sentence, as here, with a period.

The greatest danger in punctuation is for poetry. Here it is necessary to be as economical and parsimonious with commas and periods as with the words themselves, and any marks that seem to carry their own subtle meanings, like dashes and little rows of periods, even semicolons and question marks, should be left out altogether rather than inserted to clog up the thing with ambiguity. A single exclamation point in a poem, no matter what else the poem has to say, is enough to destroy the whole work.

The things I like best in T. S. Eliot's poetry, especially in the *Four Quartets*, are the semicolons. You cannot hear them, but they are there, laying out the connections between the images and the ideas. Sometimes you get a glimpse of a semicolon coming, a few lines farther on, and it is like climbing a steep path through woods and seeing a wooden bench just at a bend in the road ahead, a place where you can expect to sit for a moment, catching your breath.

Commas can't do this sort of thing; they can only tell you how the different parts of a complicated thought are to be fitted together, but you can't sit, not even take a breath, just because of a comma,

Discussion Questions

1. In what ways does Thomas use punctuation to make his points about punctuation? How does he call attention to the use of commas? What does he want us to do with commas?

2. These notes on punctuation do not sound like the kind of information you would receive from a grammar handbook—why not? Try revising Thomas's second paragraph by inserting commas where you think they ought to go. How does this affect the writing?

3. Compare Lewis Thomas's sense of the importance of stylistic conventions to that of John Updike in "Crush vs. Whip."

4. Thomas does not cover all of the types of writing conventions. Using his essay as a model, choose a convention that he doesn't write about (capitalization, the apostrophe, and so forth) and in one or two paragraphs demonstrate how you feel about that convention.

JAMES THURBER

The noted humorist James Thurber (1894–1961) was born in Columbus, Ohio. He graduated from Ohio State University and, after World War I, worked as a reporter for several newspapers. In 1927, he started writing humor and drawing cartoons for The New Yorker, *an occupation—and preoccupation—that would last his entire life. In his essays, sketches, short stories, fables, and parables, he ranged from a light-hearted satirical stance toward conventional American dreams to a heavier-hitting ironic attitude toward human illusion in general.*

Besides his children's fantasies and his plays, Thurber's many books include a satire on sex manuals, Is Sex Necessary? (1929), *which he wrote with* New Yorker *colleague E. B. White;* The Owl in the Attic and Other Perplexities *(1931);* The Last Flower *(1939);* Fables for Our Time and Famous Poems Illustrated *(1940);* My World—and Welcome to It *(1942);* Men, Women, and Dogs *(1943);* Thurber Country *(1953);* Alarms and Diversions *(1957). The following comic reminiscence is from one of Thurber's best-known books,* My Life and Hard Times *(1933).*

University Days

I passed all the other courses that I took at my University, but I could never pass botany. This was because all botany students had to spend several hours a week in a laboratory looking through a microscope at plant cells, and I could never see through a microscope. I never once saw a cell through a microscope. This used to enrage my instructor. He would wander around the laboratory pleased with the progress all the students were making in drawing the involved and, so I am told, interesting structure of flower cells, until he came to me. I would just be standing there. "I can't see anything," I would say. He would begin patiently enough, explaining how anybody can see through a microscope, but he would always end up in a fury, claiming that I could *too* see through a microscope but just pretended that I couldn't. "It takes away from the beauty of flowers anyway," I used to tell him. "We are not concerned with beauty in this course," he would say. "We are concerned solely with what I may call the *mechanics* of flars." "Well," I'd say, "I can't see anything." "Try it just once again," he'd say, and I would put my eye to the microscope and see nothing at all, except now and again a nebulous milky substance—a phenomenon of maladjustment. You were supposed to see a vivid, restless clockwork of sharply defined plant cells. "I see what looks like a lot of milk," I would tell him. This, he claimed, was the result of my not having adjusted the microscope properly, so he would readjust it for me, or rather, for himself. And I would look again and see milk.

I finally took a deferred pass, as they called it, and waited a year and tried again. (You had to pass one of the biological sciences or you couldn't graduate.) The professor had come back from vacation brown as a berry, bright-eyed, and eager to explain cell-structure again to his classes. "Well," he said to me, cheerily, when we met in the first laboratory hour of the semester, "we're going to see cells this time, aren't we?" "Yes, sir," I said. Students to right of me and to left of me and in front of me were seeing cells; what's more, they were quietly drawing pictures of them in their notebooks. Of course, I didn't see anything.

"We'll try it," the professor said to me, grimly, "with every adjustment of the microscope known to man. As God is my witness, I'll arrange this glass so that you see cells through it or I'll give up teaching. In twenty-two years of botany, I—" He cut off abruptly for he was beginning to quiver all over, like Lionel Barrymore, and he genuinely wished to hold onto his temper; his scenes with me had taken a great deal out of him.

So we tried it with every adjustment of the microscope known to man. With only one of them did I see anything but blackness or the familiar lacteal opacity, and that time I saw, to my pleasure and amazement, a variegated constellation of flecks, specks, and dots. These I hastily drew. The instructor, noting my activity, came back from an adjoining desk, a smile on his lips and his eyebrows high in hope. He looked at my cell drawing. "What's that?" he demanded, with a hint of a squeal in his voice. "That's what I saw," I said. "You didn't, you didn't, you *did*n't!" he screamed, losing control of his temper instantly, and he bent over and squinted into the microscope. His head snapped up. "That's your eye!" he shouted. "You've fixed the lens so that it reflects! You've drawn your eye!"

Another course that I didn't like, but somehow managed to pass, was economics. I went to that class straight from the botany class, which didn't help me any in understanding either subject. I used to get them mixed up. But not as mixed up as another student in my economics class who came there direct from a physics laboratory. He was a tackle on the football team, named Bolenciecwcz. At that time Ohio State University had one of the best football teams in the country, and Bolenciecwcz was one of its outstanding stars. In order to be eligible to play it was necessary for him to keep up in his studies, a very difficult matter, for while he was not dumber than an ox he was not any smarter. Most of his professors were lenient and helped him along. None gave him more hints, in answering questions, or asked him simpler ones than the economics professor, a thin, timid man named Bassum. One day when we were on the subject of transportation and distribution, it came Bolenciecwcz's turn to answer a question. "Name one means of transportation," the professor said to him. No light came into the big tackle's eyes. "Just any means of transportation," said the professor. Bolenciecwcz sat staring at him. "That is," pursued the pro-

He was beginning to quiver all over like Lionel Barrymore.

fessor, "any medium, agency, or method of going from one place to another." Bolenciecwcz had the look of a man who is being led into a trap. "You may choose among steam, horse-drawn, or electrically propelled vehicles," said the instructor. "I might suggest the one which we commonly take in making long journeys across land." There was a profound silence in which everybody stirred uneasily, including Bolenciecwcz and Mr. Bassum. Mr. Bassum abruptly broke this silence in an amazing manner. "Choo-choo-choo," he said, in a low voice, and turned instantly scarlet. He glanced appealingly around the room. All of us, of course, shared Mr. Bassum's desire that Bolenciecwcz should stay abreast of the class in economics, for the Illinois game, one of the hardest and most important of the season, was only a week off. "Toot, toot, too-toooooooot!" some student with a deep voice moaned, and we all looked encouragingly at Bolenciecwcz. Somebody else gave a fine imitation of a locomotive letting off steam. Mr. Bassum himself rounded off the little show. "Ding, dong, ding, dong," he said, hopefully. Bolenciecwcz was staring at the floor now, trying to think, his great brow furrowed, his huge hands rubbing together, his face red.

"How did you come to college this year, Mr. Bolenciecwcz?" asked the professor. "*Chuff*a chuffa, *chuff*a chuffa."

"M'father sent me," said the football player.

"What on?" asked Bassum.

"I git an 'lowance," said the tackle, in a low, husky voice, obviously embarrassed.

"No, no," said Bassum. "Name a means of transportation. What did you *ride* here on?"

"Train," said Bolenciecwcz.

"Quite right," said the professor. "Now, Mr. Nugent, will you tell us—"

If I went through anguish in botany and economics—for different reasons—gymnasium work was even worse. I don't even like to think about it. They wouldn't let you play games or join in the exercises with your glasses on and I couldn't see with mine off. I bumped into professors, horizontal bars, agricultural students, and swinging iron rings. Not being able to see, I could take it but I couldn't dish it out. Also, in order to pass gymnasium (and you had to pass it to graduate) you had to learn to swim if you didn't know how. I didn't like the swimming pool, I didn't like swimming, and I didn't like the swimming instructor, and after all these years I still don't. I never swam but I passed my gym work anyway, by having another student give my gymnasium number (978) and swim across the pool in my place. He was a quiet, amiable blonde youth, number 473, and he would have seen through a microscope for me if we could have got away with it, but we couldn't get away with it. Another thing I didn't like about gymnasium work was that they made you strip the day you registered.

Bolenciecwcz was trying to think.

It is impossible for me to be happy when I am stripped and being asked a lot of questions. Still, I did better than a lanky agricultural student who was cross-examined just before I was. They asked each student what college he was in—that is, whether Arts, Engineering, Commerce, or Agriculture. "What college are you in?" the instructor snapped at the youth in front of me. "Ohio State University," he said promptly.

It wasn't that agricultural student but it was another a whole lot like him who decided to take up journalism, possibly on the ground that when farming went to hell he could fall back on newspaper work. He didn't realize, of course, that that would be very much like falling back full-length on a kit of carpenter's tools. Haskins didn't seem cut out for journalism, being too embarrassed to talk to anybody and unable to use a typewriter, but the editor of the college paper assigned him to the cow barns, the sheep house, the horse pavilion, and the animal husbandry department generally. This was a genuinely big "beat," for it took up five times as much ground and got ten times as great a legislative appropriation as the College of Liberal Arts. The agricultural student knew animals, but nevertheless his stories were dull and colorlessly written. He took all afternoon on each of them, on account of having to hunt for each letter on the typewriter. Once in a while he had to ask somebody to help him hunt. "C" and "L," in particular, were hard letters for him to find. His editor finally got pretty much annoyed at the farmer-journalist because his pieces were so uninteresting. "See here, Haskins," he snapped at him one day, "Why is it we never have anything hot from you on the horse pavilion? Here we have two hundred head of horses on this campus—more than any other university in the Western Conference except Purdue—and yet you never get any real low down on them. Now shoot over to the horse barns and dig up something lively." Haskins shambled out and came back in about an hour; he said he had something. "Well, start it off snappily," said the editor. "Something people will read." Haskins set to work and in a couple of hours brought a sheet of typewritten paper to the desk; it was a two-hundred word story about some disease that had broken out among the horses. Its opening sentence was simple but arresting. It read: "Who has noticed the sores on the tops of the horses in the animal husbandry building?"

Ohio State was a land grant university and therefore two years of military drill was compulsory. We drilled with old Springfield rifles and studied the tactics of the Civil War even though the World War was going on at the time. At 11 o'clock each morning thousands of freshmen and sophomores used to deploy over the campus, moodily creeping up on the old chemistry building. It was good training for the kind of warfare that was waged at Shiloh but it had no connection with what was going on in Europe. Some people used to think there was German money behind it, but they didn't dare say so or they would have been thrown in jail as German spies. It was a period of muddy thought and marked, I believe, the decline of higher education in the Middle West.

As a soldier I was never any good at all. Most of the cadets were glumly indifferent soldiers, but I was no good at all. Once General Littlefield, who was commandant of the cadet corps, popped up in front of me during regimental drill and snapped. "You are the main trouble with this university!" I think he meant that my type was the main trouble with the university but he may have meant me individually. I was mediocre at drill, certainly—that is, until my senior year. By that time I had drilled longer than anybody else in the Western Conference, having failed at military at the end of each preceding year so that I had to do it all over again. I was the only senior still in uniform. The uniform which, when new, had made me look like an interurban railway conductor, now that it had become faded and too tight made me look like Bert Williams in his bellboy act. This had a definitely bad effect on my morale. Even so, I had become by sheer practise little short of wonderful at squad manoeuvres.

One day General Littlefield picked our company out of the whole regiment and tried to get it mixed up by putting it through one movement after another as fast as we could execute them: squads right, squads left, squads on right into line, squads right about, squads left front into line, etc. In about three minutes one hundred and nine men were marching in one direction and I was marching away from them at an angle of forty degrees, all alone. "Company, halt!" shouted General Littlefield. "That man is the only man who has it right!" I was made a corporal for my achievement.

The next day General Littlefield summoned me to his office. He was swatting flies when I went in. I was silent and he was silent too, for a long time. I don't think he remembered me or why he had sent for me, but he didn't want to admit it. He swatted some more flies, keeping his eyes on them narrowly before he let go with the swatter. "Button up your coat!" he snapped. Looking back on it now I can see that he meant me although he was looking at a fly, but I just stood there. Another fly came to rest on a paper in front of the general and began rubbing its hind legs together. The general lifted the swatter cautiously. I moved restlessly and the fly flew away. "You startled him!" barked General Littlefield, looking at me severely. I said I was sorry. "That won't help the situation!" snapped the General, with cold military logic. I didn't see what I could do except offer to chase some more flies toward his desk, but I didn't say anything. He stared out the window at the faraway figures of co-eds crossing the campus toward the library. Finally, he told me I could go. So I went. He either didn't know which cadet I was or else he forgot what he wanted to see me about. It may have been that he wished to apologize for having called me the main trouble with the university; or maybe he had decided to compliment me on my brilliant drilling of the day before and then at the last minute decided not to. I don't know. I don't think about it much any more.

Discussion Questions

1. How does Thurber turn his economics course into a single joke? How does he characterize himself in gym and military training? What image of himself does he convey? Why doesn't he mind conveying this image? In Thurber's world, what is important and what isn't?

2. How does Thurber compress his experience with botany into a single anecdote? What is funny about the experience? Do you think his failure to pass botany disturbed him?

3. What is wrong with Haskins's lead? Why does Thurber find it amusing? Compare Thurber's sense of literary style to John Updike's in "Crush Vs. Whip."

4. Thurber attended college during World War I, yet some of his experiences may seem familiar to you. Using his essay as a model, write a short autobiographical account of your university days. Try to encapsulate your experiences with courses or professors into single anecdotes.

Barbara Tuchman

The two-time Pulitzer Prize-winning historian Barbara Tuchman was born in New York City in 1912. After graduating from Radcliffe College in 1933, she worked as a researcher for the Institute of Pacific Relations and later as a staff writer and foreign correspondent for the Nation. *Between 1970 and 1973 she served as president of the Society of American Historians. In 1978 she received the American Academy of Arts and Sciences gold medal for history, and in 1979 became the first woman elected for the National Endowment for the Humanities' Jefferson Lectureship.*

As a nonacademic historian, Barbara Tuchman brings a strong literary approach to the writing of history—"I am a writer whose subject is history," she claims. Among her books are The Zimmermann Telegram *(1958),* The Guns of August *(1962),* The Proud Tower: A Portrait of the World Before the War, 1890—1914 *(1966),* Stilwell and the American Experience in China, 1911—1945 *(1972), and a collection of essays,* Practicing History *(1981). The following account of the Black Death is reprinted from* A Distant Mirror: The Calamitous Fourteenth Century *(1978).*

This is the End of the World: The Black Death

In October 1347, two months after the fall of Calais, Genoese trading ships put into the harbor of Messina in Sicily with dead and dying men at the oars. The ships had come from the Black Sea port of Caffa (now Feodosiȳa) in the Crimea, where the Genoese maintained a trading post. The diseased sailors showed strange black swellings about the size of an egg or an apple in the armpits and groin. The swellings oozed blood and pus and were followed by spreading boils and black blotches on the skin from internal bleeding. The sick suffered severe pain and died quickly within five days of the first symptoms. As the disease spread, other symptoms of continuous fever and spitting of blood appeared instead of the swellings or buboes. These victims coughed and sweated heavily and died even more quickly, within three days or less, sometimes in 24 hours. In both types everything that issued from the body—breath, sweat, blood from the buboes and lungs, bloody urine, and blood-blackened excrement—smelled foul. Depression and despair accompanied the physical symptoms, and before the end "death is seen seated on the face."

The disease was bubonic plague, present in two forms: one that infected the bloodstream, causing the buboes and internal bleeding, and was spread by contact; and a second, more virulent pneumonic type that infected the lungs and was spread by respiratory infection. The presence of both at once cause the high mortality and speed of contagion. So lethal was the disease that cases were known of persons going to bed well and dying before they woke, of doctors catching the illness at a bedside and dying before the patient. So rapidly did it spread from one to another that to a French physician, Simon de Covino, it seemed as if one sick person "could infect the whole world." The malignity of the pestilence appeared more terrible because its victims knew no prevention and no remedy.

THIS IS THE END OF THE WORLD

The physical suffering of the disease and its aspect of evil mystery were expressed in a strange Welsh lament which saw "death coming into our midst like black smoke, a plague which cuts off the young, a rootless phantom which has no mercy for fair countenance. Woe is me of the shilling in the armpit! It is seething, terrible . . . a head that gives pain and causes a loud cry . . . a painful angry knob . . . Great is its seething like a burning cinder . . . a grievous thing of ashy color." Its eruption is ugly like the "seeds of black peas, broken fragments of brittle sea-coal . . . the early ornaments of black death, cinders of the peelings of the cockle weed, a mixed multitude, a black plague like halfpence, like berries. . . ."

Rumors of a terrible plague supposedly arising in China and spreading through Tartary (Central Asia) to India and Persia, Mesopotamia, Syria, Egypt, and all of Asia Minor had reached Europe in 1346. They told of a death toll so devasting that all of India was said to be depopulated, whole territories covered by dead bodies, other areas with no one left alive. As added up by Pope Clement VI at Avignon, the total of reported dead reached 23,840,000. In the absence of a concept of contagion, no serious alarm was felt in Europe until the trading ships brought their black burden of pestilence into Messina while other infected ships from the Levant carried it to Genoa and Venice.

By January 1348 it penetrated France via Marseille, and North Africa via Tunis. Shipborne along coasts and navigable rivers, it spread westward from Marseille through the ports of Languedoc to Spain and northward up the Rhône to Avignon, where it arrived in March. It reached Narbonne, Montpellier, Carcassonne, and Toulouse between February and May, and at the same time in Italy spread to Rome and Florence and their hinterlands. Between June and August it reached Bordeaux, Lyon, and Paris, spread to Burgundy and Normandy, and crossed the Channel from Normandy into southern England. From Italy during the same summer it crossed the Alps into Switzerland and reached eastward to Hungary.

In a given area the plague accomplished its kill within four to six months and then faded, except in the larger cities, where, rooting into the close-quartered population, it abated during the winter, only to reappear in spring and rage for another six months.

In 1349 it resumed in Paris, spread to Picardy, Flanders, and the Low Countries, and from England to Scotland and Ireland as well as to Norway, where a ghost ship with a cargo of wool and a dead crew drifted offshore until it ran aground near Bergen. From there the plague passed into Sweden, Denmark, Prussia, Iceland, and as far as Greenland. Leaving a strange pocket of immunity in

Bohemia, and Russia unattacked until 1351, it had passed from most of Europe by mid-1350. Although the mortality rate was erratic, ranging from one fifth in some places to nine tenths or almost total elimination in others, the overall estimate of modern demographers has settled—for the area extending from India to Iceland—around the same figure expressed in Froissart's casual words: "a third of the world died." His estimate, the common one at the time, was not an inspired guess but a borrowing of St. John's figure for mortality from plague in Revelation, the favorite guide to human affairs of the Middle Ages.

A third of Europe would have meant about 20 million deaths. No one knows in truth how many died. Contemporary reports were an awed impression, not an accurate count. In crowded Avignon, it was said, 400 died daily; 7,000 houses emptied by death were shut up; a single graveyard received 11,000 corpses in six weeks; half the city's inhabitants reportedly died, including 9 cardinals or one third of the total, and 70 lesser prelates. Watching the endlessly passing death carts, chroniclers let normal exaggeration take wings and put the Avignon death toll at 62,000 and even at 120,000, although the city's total population was probably less than 50,000.

When graveyards filled up, bodies at Avignon were thrown into the Rhône until mass burial pits were dug for dumping the corpses. In London in such pits corpses piled up in layers until they overflowed. Everywhere reports speak of the sick dying too fast for the living to bury. Corpses were dragged out of homes and left in front of doorways. Morning light revealed new piles of bodies. In Florence the dead were gathered up by the Compagnia della Misericordia—founded in 1244 to care for the sick—whose members wore red robes and hoods masking the face except for the eyes. When their efforts failed, the dead lay putrid in the streets for days at a time. When no coffins were to be had, the bodies were laid on boards, two or three at once, to be carried to graveyards or common pits. Families dumped their own relatives into the pits, or buried them so hastily and thinly "that dogs dragged them forth and devoured their bodies."

Amid accumulating death and fear of contagion, people died without last rites and were buried without prayers, a prospect that terrified the last hours of the stricken. A bishop in England gave permission to laymen to make confession to each other as was done by the Apostles, "or if no man is present then even to a woman," and if no priest could be found to administer extreme unction, "then faith must suffice." Clement VI found it necessary to grant remissions of sin to all who died of the plague because so many were unattended by priests. "And no bells tolled," wrote a chronicler of Siena, "and nobody wept no matter what his loss because almost everyone expected death. . . . And people said and believed, 'This is the end of the world.'"

In Paris, where the plague lasted through 1349, the reported death rate was 800 a day, in Pisa 500, in Vienna 500 to 600. The total dead in Paris numbered 50,000 or half the population. Florence, weakened by the famine of 1347, lost three to four fifths of its citizens, Venice two thirds, Hamburg and Bremen, though smaller in size, about the same proportion. Cities, as centers of transportation, were more likely to be affected than villages, although once a village was infected, its death rate was equally high. At Givry, a prosperous village in Burgundy of 1,200 to 1,500 people, the parish register records 615 deaths in the space of fourteen weeks, compared to an average of thirty deaths a year in the previous decade. In three villages of Cambridgeshire, manorial records show a death rate of 47 percent, 57 percent, and in one case 70 percent. When the last survivors, too few to carry on, moved away, a deserted village sank back into the wilderness and disappeared from the map altogether, leaving only a grass-covered ghostly outline to show where mortals once had lived.

In enclosed places such as monasteries and prisons, the infection of one person usually meant that of all, as happened in the Franciscan convents of Carcassonne and Marseille, where every inmate without exception died. Of the 140 Dominicans at Montpellier only seven survived. Petrarch's brother Gherardo, member of a Carthusian monastery, buried the prior and 34 fellow monks one by one, sometimes three a day, until he was left alone with his dog and fled to look for a place that would take him in. Watching every comrade die, men in such places could not but wonder whether the strange peril that filled the air had not been sent to exterminate the human race. In Kilkenny, Ireland, Brother John Clyn of the Friars Minor, another monk left alone among dead men, kept a record of what had happened lest "things which should be remembered perish with time and vanish from the memory of those who come after us." Sensing "the whole world, as it were, placed within the grasp of the Evil One," and waiting for death to visit him too, he wrote, "I leave parchment to continue this work, if perchance any man survive and any of the race of Adam escape this pestilence and carry on the work which I have begun." Brother John, as noted by another hand, died of the pestilence, but he foiled oblivion.

The largest cities of Europe, with populations of about 100,000, were Paris and Florence, Venice and Genoa. At the next level, with more than 50,000, were Ghent and Bruges in Flanders, Milan, Bologna, Rome, Naples, and Palermo, and Cologne. London hovered below 50,000, the only city in England except York with more than 10,000. At the level of 20,000 to 50,000 were Bordeaux, Toulouse, Montpellier, Marseille, and Lyon in France, Barcelona, Seville, and Toledo in Spain, Siena, Pisa, and other secondary cities in Italy, and the Hanseatic trading cities of the Empire. The plague raged through them all, killing anywhere from one third to two thirds of their inhabitants. Italy, with a total population of 10 to 11 million, probably suffered the heaviest toll. Following the Florentine bankruptcies, the crop failures and workers' riots of 1346—47, the revolt of Cola di Rienzi that plunged Rome into anarchy, the plague came as the peak of successive calamities. As if the world were indeed in the grasp of the Evil One, its first appearance on the European mainland in January 1348 coincided with a fearsome earthquake that carved a path of wreckage from Naples up to Venice. Houses collapsed, church towers toppled, villages were crushed, and the destruction reached as far as Germany and Greece. Emotional response, dulled by horrors, underwent a kind of atrophy epitomized by the chronicler who wrote, "And in these days was burying without sorrow and wedding without friendschippe."

In Siena, where more than half the inhabitants died of the plague, work was abandoned on the great cathedral, planned to be the largest in the world, and never resumed, owing to loss of workers and master masons and "the melancholy and grief" of the survivors. The cathedral's truncated transept still stands in permanent witness to the sweep of death's scythe. Angolo di Tura, a chronicler of Siena, recorded the fear of contagion that froze every other instinct. "Father abandoned child, wife husband, one brother another," he wrote, "for this plague seemed to strike through the breath and sight. And so they died. And no one could be found to bury the dead for money or friendship. . . . And I, Angolo di Tura, called the Fat, buried my five children with my own hands, and so did many others likewise."

There were many to echo his account of inhumanity and few to balance it, for the plague was not the kind of calamity that inspired mutual help. Its loathsomeness and deadliness did not herd people together in mutual distress, but only prompted their desire to escape each other. "Magistrates and notaries refused to come and make the wills of the dying," reported a Franciscan friar of Piazza in Sicily; what was worse, "even the priests did not come to hear their confessions." A clerk of the Archbishop of Canterbury reported the same of English priests who "turned away from the care of their benefices from fear of death." Cases of parents deserting children and children their parents were reported across Europe from Scotland to Russia. The calamity chilled the hearts of men, wrote Boccaccio in his famous account of the plague in Florence that serves as introduction to the *Decameron*. "One man shunned another . . . kinsfolk held aloof, brother was forsaken by brother, oftentimes husband by wife; nay, what is more, and scarcely to be believed, fathers and mothers were found to abandon their own children to their fate, untended, unvisited as if they had been strangers." Exaggeration and literary pessimism were common in the 14th century, but the Pope's physician, Guy de Chauliac, was a sober, careful observer who reported the same phenomenon: "A father did not visit his son, nor the son his father. Charity was dead."

Yet not entirely. In Paris, according to the chronicler Jean de Venette, the nuns of the Hôtel Dieu or municipal hospital, "having no fear of death, tended the sick with all sweetness and humility." New nuns repeatedly took the places of those who died, until the majority "many times renewed by death now rest in peace with Christ as we may piously believe."

When the plague entered northern France in July 1348, it settled first in Normandy and, checked by winter, gave Picardy a deceptive interim until the next summer. Either in mourning or warning, black flags were flown from church towers of the worst-stricken villages of Normandy. "And in that time," wrote a monk of the abbey of Fourcarment, "the mortality was so great among the people of Normandy that those of Picardy mocked them." The same unneighborly reaction was reported of the Scots, separated by a winter's immunity from the English. Delighted to hear of the disease that was scourging the "southrons," they gathered forces for an invasion, "laughing at their enemies." Before they could move, the savage mortality fell upon them too, scattering some in death and the rest in panic to spread the infection as they fled.

In Picardy in the summer of 1349 the pestilence penetrated the castle of Coucy to kill Enguerrand's mother, Catherine, and her new husband. Whether her nine-year-old son escaped by chance or was perhaps living elsewhere with one of his guardians is unrecorded. In nearby Amiens, tannery workers, responding quickly to losses in the labor force, combined to bargain for higher wages. In another place villagers were seen dancing to drums and trumpets, and on being asked the reason, answered that, seeing their neighbors die day by day while their village remained immune, they believed they could keep the plague from entering "by the jollity that is in us. That is why we dance." Further north in Tournai on the border of Flanders, Gilles li Muisis, Abbot of St. Martin's, kept one of the epidemic's most vivid accounts. The passing bells rang all day and all night, he recorded, because sextons were anxious to obtain their fees while they could. Filled with the sound of mourning, the city became oppressed by fear, so that the authorities forbade the tolling of bells and the wearing of black and restricted funeral services to two mourners. The silencing of funeral bells and of criers' announcements of deaths was ordained by most cities. Siena imposed a fine on the wearing of mourning clothes by all except widows.

Flight was the chief recourse of those who could afford it or arrange it. The rich fled to their country places like Boccaccio's young patricians of Florence, who settled in a pastoral palace "removed on every side from the roads" with "wells of cool water and vaults of rare wines." The urban poor died in their burrows, "and only the stench of their bodies informed neighbors of their death." That the poor were more heavily afflicted than the rich was clearly remarked at the time, in the north as in the south. A Scottish chronicler, John of Fordun, stated flatly that the pest "attacked especially the meaner sort and common people—seldom the magnates." Simon de Covino of Montpellier made the same observation. He ascribed it to the misery and want and hard lives that made the poor more susceptible, which was half the truth. Close contact and lack of sanitation was the unrecognized other half. It was noticed too that the young died in greater proportion than the old; Simon de Covino compared the disappearance of youth to the withering of flowers in the fields.

In the countryside peasants dropped dead on the roads, in the fields, in their houses. Survivors in growing helplessness fell into apathy, leaving ripe wheat uncut and livestock untended. Oxen and asses, sheep and goats, pigs and chickens ran wild and they too, according to local reports, succumbed to the pest. English sheep, bearers of the precious wool, died throughout the country. The chronicler Henry Knighton, canon of Leicester Abbey, reported 5,000 dead in one field alone, "their bodies so corrupted by the plague that neither beast nor bird would touch them," and spreading an appalling stench. In the Austrian Alps wolves came down to prey upon sheep and then, "as if alarmed by some invisible warning, turned and fled back into the wilderness." In remote Dalmatia bolder wolves descended upon a plague-stricken city and attacked human survivors. For want of herdsmen, cattle strayed from place to place and died in hedgerows and ditches. Dogs and cats fell like the rest.

The dearth of labor held a fearful prospect because the 14th century lived close to the annual harvest both for food and for next year's seed. "So few servants and laborers were left," wrote Knighton, "that no one knew where to turn for help." The sense of a vanishing future created a kind of dementia of despair. A Bavarian chronicler of Neuberg on the Danube recorded that "Men and women . . . wandered around as if mad" and let their cattle stray "because no one had any inclination to concern themselves about the future." Fields went uncultivated, spring seed unsown. Second growth with nature's awful energy crept back over cleared land, dikes crumbled, salt water reinvaded and soured the lowlands. With so few hands remaining to restore the work of centuries, people felt, in Walsingham's words, that "the world could never again regain its former prosperity."

Though the death rate was higher among the anonymous poor, the known and the great died too. King Alfonso XI of Castile was the only reigning monarch killed by the pest, but his neighbor King Pedro of Aragon lost his wife, Queen Leonora, his daughter Marie, and a niece in the space of six months. John Cantacuzene, Emperor of Byzantium, lost his son. In France the lame Queen Jeanne and her daughter-in-law Bonne de Luxemburg, wife of the Dauphin, both died in 1349 in the same phase that took the life of Enguerrand's mother. Jeanne, Queen of Navarre, daughter of Louis X, was another victim. Edward III's second daughter, Joanna, who was on her way to marry Pedro, the heir of Castile, died in Bordeaux. Women appear to have been more vulnerable than men, perhaps because, being more housebound, they were more exposed to fleas. Boccaccio's mistress Fiammetta, illegitimate daughter of the King of Naples, died, as did Laura, the beloved—whether real or fictional—of Petrarch. Reaching out to us in the future, Petrarch cried, "Oh happy posterity who will not experience such abysmal woe and will look upon our testimony as a fable."

In Florence Giovanni Villani, the great historian of his time, died at 68 in the midst of an unfinished sentence: ". . . *e dure questo pistolenza fino a* . . . (in the midst of this pestilence there came to an end . . .)." Siena's master painters, the brothers Ambrogio and Pietro Lorenzetti, whose names never appear after 1348, presumably perished in the plague, as did Andrea Pisano, architect and sculptor of Florence. William of Ockham and the English mystic Richard Rolle of Hampole both disappear from mention after 1349. Francisco Datini, merchant of Prato, lost both his parents and two siblings. Curious sweeps of mortality afflicted certain bodies of merchants in London. All eight wardens of the Company of Cutters, all six wardens of the Hatters, and four wardens of the Goldsmiths died before July 1350. Sir John Pulteney, master draper and four times Mayor of London, was a victim, likewise Sir John Montgomery, Governor of Calais.

Among the clergy and doctors the mortality was naturally high because of the nature of their professions. Out of 24 physicians in Venice, 20 were said to have lost their lives in the plague, although, according to another account, some were believed to have fled or to have shut themselves up in their houses. At Montpellier, site of the leading medieval medical school, the physician Simon de Covino reported that, despite the great number of doctors, "hardly one of them escaped." In Avignon, Guy de Chauliac confessed that he performed his medical visits only because he dared not stay away for fear of infamy, but "I was in continual fear." He claimed to have contracted the disease but to have cured himself by his own treatment; if so, he was one of the few who recovered.

Clerical mortality varied with rank. Although the one-third toll of cardinals reflects the same proportion as the whole, this was probably due to their concentration in Avignon. In England, in strange and almost sinister procession, the Archbishop of Canterbury, John Stratford, died in August 1348, his appointed successor died in May 1349, and the next appointee three months later, all three within a year. Despite such weird vagaries, prelates in general managed to sustain a higher survival rate than the lesser clergy. Among bishops the deaths have been estimated at about one in twenty. The loss of priests, even if many avoided their fearful duty of attending the dying, was about the same as among the population as a whole.

Government officials, whose loss contributed to the general chaos, found, on the whole, no special shelter. In Siena four of the nine members of the governing oligarchy died, in France one third of the royal notaries, in Bristol 15 out of the 52 members of the Town Council or almost one third. Tax-collecting obviously suffered, with the result that Phillip VI was unable to collect more than a fraction of the subsidy granted him by the Estates in the winter of 1347—48.

Lawlessness and debauchery accompanied the plague as they had during the great plague of Athens of 430 B.C., when according to Thucydides, men grew bold in the indulgence of pleasure: "For seeing how the rich died in a moment and those who had nothing immediately inherited their property, they reflected that life and riches were alike transitory and they resolved to enjoy themselves while they could." Human behavior is timeless. When St. John had his vision of plague in Revelation, he knew from some experience or race memory that those who survived "repented not of the work of their hands. . . . Neither repented they of their murders, nor of their sorceries, nor of their fornication, nor of their thefts."

Discussion Questions

1. How does Tuchman convey a vivid sense of the catastrophic proportions of the Plague?
2. What didn't fourteenth century people know about the disease? Why did it seem to strike the poor more frequently than the rich?
3. Why does Tuchman say that "Human behavior is timeless"? What assumption about history is contained in such a statement? Does that assumption have any effect on the shape of her essay? How does her essay conform to Samuel Eliot Morison's standard of literary art?
4. The Black Death, though it decimated populations, may seem very remote to modern readers who think Legionnaire's Disease and Acquired Immune Deficiency Syndrome are dreadful menaces. Yet less than seventy years ago, the 1918 influenza, one of the most terrifying world-wide holocausts in history, took the lives of 20,000,000 people within a few months—548,000 died in the United States alone. Do some research on the 1918 influenza and, using Tuchman's methods as a guide, write an essay on the awesome force of the disease.

JOHN UPDIKE

Born in Reading, Pennsylvania, in 1932, the son of a high-school teacher, John Updike grew up in nearby Shillington, the setting of many of his stories. After his graduation from Harvard in 1954, he studied at Oxford and the Ruskin School of Drawing and Fine Art. For a few years he worked on the staff of The New Yorker, *where he still frequently contributes stories, reviews, and poems. One of the most prolific and versatile of contemporary writers, Updike has since 1958 published twelve novels, seven volumes of short stories, four books of poetry, three collections of essays, and a play.*

Among his best-known books are The Centaur *(1963),* Pigeon Feathers *(1963),* Couples *(1968),* Bech: A Book *(1970), and the series that so far makes up a trilogy,* Rabbit, Run *(1960),* Rabbit Redux *(1971), and the award-winning* Rabbit Is Rich *(1981). "Crush Vs. Whip" is reprinted from* Assorted Prose *(1965).*

Crush Vs. Whip

Apparently, the St. Louis Cardinals are much more friable than they used to be, for a paper in San Francisco recently ran the headline "GIANTS CRUSH CARDINALS, 3–1." Now, we don't want to suggest that our city's eldest franchise has got in with a group of orange squeezers who don't know real pulverization when they see it. There's been too much of such carping already. When a boy leaves home, a mother's duty is to hold her tongue, we always say. While voices around us cried that the West Coast was, variously, a vile limbo, an obscure religious sect, a figment of Walter O'Malley's fevered imagination, and a tar pit of busherism certain to fossilize whatever it enveloped, we kept mum. As a reward to ourself for restraint, therefore, we *will* offer some advice about the science or art of baseball-headline verbs. These we have seen evolve from a simple matter of "WIN" and "LOSE" into a structure of periphrasis as complex as heraldry in feudalism's decadence. New York City, now a quaint port known principally for her historical monuments, once boasted three—we swear it, *three*—baseball teams and a dozen daily newspapers. The lore accumulated here should be passed on to headline writers in all the fresh, brash towns likely to be visited as the major leagues, driven by a dark fatality, continue their migration toward Asia.

The correct verb, San Francisco, is "WHIP." Notice the vigor, force, and scorn obtained, quite without hyperbole. This table may prove helpful:

      3–1—WHIP
      3–2—SHADE
      2–1—EDGE
      1–0—(Pitcher's name) BLANKS[1]

[1] Below, in smaller type, you may have "Twirls 3-(4-, 5-) Hitter." Two-hitters are "spun." For a one-hitter, write "Robbed of No-hitter."

Turning back and working upward, we come to 4—2, known professionally as "the golden mean," or "absolute zero." The score is uniquely characterless. The bland terms "BEAT" and "DEFEAT" are called in from the bullpen (meaning an area in which pitchers not actually in the game may "warm up"). However, 4—1 gets the coveted verb "VANQUISH." Rule: Any three-run margin, *provided the winning total does not exceed ten*, may be described as a vanquishing. If, however, the margin is a mere two runs and the losing total is five or more, "OUTSLUG" is considered very tasty. You will notice, S.F., the trend called Mounting Polysyllabism, which culminates, at the altitude of double digits, in that trio of Latin-root rhymers, "ANNIHILATE," "OBLITERATE," and "HUMILIATE." E.g., "A's ANNIHILATE O's, 13—2."

Special cases:

1. If the home team is on the short end of the score, certain laws of mutation apply. "SHADE" becomes "SQUEAK BY." For "OUTSLUG," put "WIN OUT IN SLOPPY CONTEST." By a judicious exploitation of "BOW," the home team, while losing, can be given the active position in the sentence and an appearance of graciousness as well.

2. Many novice banner writers, elevated from the 2-col. obscurity of Class A ball to the black-cap. screamers of the big leagues, fumble the concept of "SWEEP." It *always* takes a plural object. Doubleheaders and series can be swept, but not regulation single games. (The minimal "WIN STREAK" is three games long; five makes a "SURGE.") A team that neither sweeps nor is swept splits. A headline familiar to New Englanders is "SOX SPLIT."

3. Which brings up the delicate matter of punning, or paronomasia. Each Baltimore journal is restricted by secret covenant to one "BIRDS SOAR" every two weeks. Milwaukee, with a stronger team, is permitted twelve instances of "braves scalp" before the All-Star game. "TIGERS CLAW" and "CUBS LICK" tend to take care of themselves. As for you, San Francisco, the lack of any synonyms for "giant" briefer than "behemoth" and "Brobdingnagian," together with the longstanding failure of New York's own writers to figure out exactly what giants *do* (intimidate? stomp?), rather lets you out of the fun. In view of this, and in view of the team's present surprising record, you may therefore write "GIANTS A-MAYS." But don't do it more than once a month: moderation in all things, S.F.

Discussion Questions

1. Who is Updike making fun of in this essay? For what reason?
2. What is *periphrasis*? How does it work in Updike's essay? Make up a few examples of your own. What is *paronomasia*? Make up a few examples of that rhetorical device: What, for example, might today's Milwaukee Brewers do to another team?
3. How would you characterize Updike's tone? Who is he addressing throughout most of the essay? What do you think Updike has learned from such other humorous writers in this collection as James Thurber and S. J. Perleman?
4. Part of Updike's fun in this essay is applying classical rhetorical terminology to such everyday language as sports headlines. Updike uses baseball. How do similar verbal distinctions apply to other sports: how might you headline a 52–6 football game or a 101–100 basketball final score?

EVELYN WAUGH

In his autobiography, A Little Learning, *Evelyn Waugh (1903–1966) claimed that he had tried desperately but unsuccessfully to resist entering the "family trade" of writing. His father, Arthur, was a well-known man of letters, a critic, an editor, and a publisher; his older brother, Alec, was a novelist; and two of Waugh's own children, Auberon and Harriet, became writers. Waugh himself gave in and became famous not only for his satiric novels (among them* Decline and Fall, Vile Bodies, *and* A Handful of Dust) *but for his many travel books and essays as well. One genre often fed the others. The essay that follows, for example, led to his novel,* The Loved One.

Half in Love with Easeful Death

In a thousand years or so, when the first archaeologists from beyond the date-line unload their boat on the sands of Southern California, they will find much the same scene as confronted the Franciscan Missionaries. A dry landscape will extend from the ocean to the mountains. Bel Air and Beverly Hills will lie naked save for scrub and cactus, all their flimsy multitude of architectural styles turned long ago to dust, while the horned toad and the turkey buzzard leave their faint imprint on the dunes that will drift on Sunset Boulevard.

For Los Angeles, when its brief history comes to an end, will fall swiftly and silently. Too far dispersed for effective bombardment, too unimportant strategically for the use of expensive atomic devices, it will be destroyed by drought. Its water comes 250 miles from the Colorado River. A handful of parachutists or partisans anywhere along that vital aqueduct can make the coastal strip uninhabitable. Bones will whiten along the Santa Fé trail as the great recession struggles Eastwards. Nature will re-assert herself and the seasons gently obliterate the vast, deserted suburb. Its history will pass from memory to legend until, centuries later, as we have supposed, the archaeologists prick their ears at the cryptic references in the texts of the twentieth century to a cult which once flourished on this forgotten strand; of the idol Oscar—sexless image of infertility—of the great Star Goddesses who were once noisily worshipped there in a Holy Wood.

Without the testimony of tombs the science of archaeology could barely exist, and it will be a commonplace among the scholars of 2947 that the great cultural decline of the twentieth century was first evident in the grave-yard. The wish to furnish the dead with magnificent habitations, to make an enduring record of their virtues and victories, to honour them and edify their descendants, raised all the great monuments of antiquity, the pyramids, the Taj Mahal, St. Peter's at Rome, and was the mainspring of all the visual arts. It died, mysteriously and suddenly, at the end of the nineteenth century. England, once very rich in sepulchral statuary, commemorated her fallen soldiers of the First World War by a simple inscription in the floor of an Abbey built nine centuries earlier to shelter the remains of a Saxon king. Rich patrons of art who in an earlier century would have spent the last decade of their lives in planning their own elaborate obsequies, deposed that their ashes should be broadcast from aeroplanes. The more practical Germans sent their corpses to the soap boiler. Only the primitive heathens of Russia observed a once-universal tradition in their shrine to Lenin.

All this will be a commonplace in the schools of 2947. The discoveries, therefore, of the Holy Wood Archaeological Expedition will be revolutionary, for when they have excavated and catalogued, and speculated hopelessly about the meaning of, a temple designed in the shape of a Derby hat and a concrete pavement covered with diverse monopedic prints, and have surveyed the featureless ruins of the great film studios, their steps will inevitably tend northward to what was once Glendale, and there they will encounter, on a gentle slope among embosoming hills, mellowed but still-rooted as the rocks, something to confound all the accepted generalizations, a necropolis of the age of the Pharaohs, created in the middle of the impious twentieth century, the vast structure of Forest Lawn Memorial Park.

We can touch hands across the millennium with these discoverers, for it is in the same mood of incredulous awe that the visitor of our own age must approach this stupendous property. Visitors, indeed, flock there—in twice the numbers that frequent the Metropolitan Museum in New York—and with good reaon, for there are many splendid collections of Art elsewhere but Forest Lawn is entirely unique. Behind the largest wrought-iron gates in the world lie 300 acres of park-land, judiciously planted with evergreen (for no plant which sheds its leaf has a place there). The lawns, watered and drained by 80 miles of pipe, do not at first betray their solemn purpose. Even the names given to their various sections—Eventide, Babyland, Graceland, Inspiration Slope, Slumberland, Sweet Memories, Vesperland, Dawn of Tomorrow—are none of them specifically suggestive of the grave-yard. The visitor is soothed by countless radios concealed about the vegetation, which ceaselessly discourse the 'Hindu' and other popular melodies, and the amplified twittering of caged birds. It is only when he leaves the 7 1/2 miles of paved roadway that he becomes aware of the thousands of little bronze plates which lie in the grass. Commenting on this peculiarity in the *Art Guide of Forest Lawn with Interpretations* Mr. Bruce Barton, author of *What can a man believe?* says: 'The cemeteries of the world cry out man's utter hopelessness in the face of death. Their symbols are pagan and pessimistic . . . Here sorrow sees no ghastly monuments, but only life and hope.' The Christian visitor might here remark that by far the commonest feature of other grave-yards is still the Cross, a symbol in which previous generations have found more Life and Hope than in the most elaborately watered evergreen shrub. This reproach will soon be removed in Forest Lawn's own grand way by a new acquisition, a prodigious canvas of the Crucifixion which took thirty years of the Polish painter, Jan Styka's life to complete; it will require a vast new building to house it. A miniature, 1/49th of the area of the original, now occupies one whole side of the largest hall in Forest Lawn and an explanatory speech has been recorded for the gramophone, identifying the hundreds of figures which in the original abound in life size. The canvas has had an unhappy history. Shipped to the U.S.A. in 1904 for the St. Louis Exhibition, it was impounded for excise dues and sold, without profit to the artist, to its importer, who was, however, unable to find a pavilion large enough to house it. Since then it has lain about in warehouses, a prey to 'silver fish,' and has been shown only once, in the Chicago Opera House, where it filled the entire stage and extended far into the auditorium. Soon it will form a suitable addition to the wonders of Forest Lawn.

These can be only briefly indicated in an essay of this length. There is the largest assembly of marble statuary in the United States, mostly secular in character, animals, children and even sculptured toys predominating; some of it erotic, and some of it enigmatically allegorical. There is also what is claimed to be the finest collection of stained glass in America, the glory of which is 'The Last Supper' in the Court of Honour; the original by Leonardo da Vinci has here, in the words of *Pictorial Forest Lawn*, been 'recreated in vibrant, glowing and indestructible colours.'

There are gardens and terraces, and a huge range of buildings, the most prominent of which is the rather Italian Mausoleum. There in marble fronted tiers lie the coffins, gallery after gallery of them, surrounded by statuary and stained glass. Each niche bears a bronze plaque with the inmate's name, sometimes in magnified counterfeit of his signature. Each has a pair of bronze vases which a modest investment can keep perpetually replenished with fresh flowers. Adjacent lies the Columbarium, where stand urns of ashes from the Crematory. There is the Tudor-style Administration Building, the Mortuary (Tudor exterior, Georgian interior) and the more functional Crematory. All are designed to defy the operations of time; they are in 'Class A steel and concrete,' proof against fire and earthquake. The Mausoleum alone, we are told, contains enough steel and concrete for a sixty storey office building, and its foundations penetrate thirty-three feet into solid rock.

The Memorial Court of Honour is the crowning achievement of this group. 'Beneath the rare marbles of its floor are crypts which money cannot purchase, reserved as gifts of honoured interment for Americans whose lives shall have been crowned with genius.' There have so far been two recipients of this gift, Gutzon Borglum, the first sculptor in history to employ dynamite instead of the chisel, and Mrs. Carrie Jacobs-Bond, author and composer of 'The End of a Perfect Day,' at whose funeral last year, which cost 25,000 dollars, Dr. Eaton, the Chairman of Forest Lawn, pronounced the solemn words: 'By the authority vested in me by the Council of Regents, I do herewith pronounce Carrie Jacobs-Bond an immortal of the Memorial Court of Honour.'

There is at the highest point a water-tower named 'The Tower of Legends,' where at the dawn of Easter Sunday a number of white doves are liberated in the presence of a huge concourse whose singing is broadcast 'from coast to coast.' Of this building 'a noted art authority' has remarked: 'It depicts, more truly than any structure I have ever seen, real American architecture. It deserves the attention of the world' (*Art Guide*). But this precious edifice, alas, is due for demolition and will soon give place to the non-sectarian, Bishopless 'Cathedral' which is to house Jan Styka's masterpiece and provide in its shade fresh galleries of urns and coffins.

There are already three non-sectarian churches, 'The Little Church of the Flowers,' 'The Wee Kirk o' the Heather' and 'The Church of the Recessional.' The first is, with modifications, a replica of Stoke Poges Church where Gray wrote his *Elegy*; the second a reconstruction of the ruins of a chapel at Glencairn, Dumfriesshire where Annie Laurie worshipped; the third, again with modifications, is a replica of the parish church of Rottingdean in Sussex where Rudyard Kipling is claimed by Dr. Eaton to have been inspired—by heaven knows what aberration of oratory from the pulpit so artlessly reproduced—to write *Kim*. The American visitor may well be surprised at the overwhelmingly British character of these places of worship in a State which has never enjoyed the blessings of British rule and is now inhabited by the most cosmopolitan people in the United States. The British visitor is surprised also at the modifications.

It is odd to find a church dedicated to Kipling, whose religion was highly idiosyncratic. The building is used not only for funerals but for weddings and christenings. Its courtyard is used for betrothals; there is a stone ring, named by Dr. Eaton the ring of Aldyth, through which the young lover is invited to clasp hands and swear fidelity to what Kipling described as 'a rag and a bone and hank of hair.' Round the courtyard are incised the texts of *Recessional, If,* and *When earth's last picture is painted.* The interior of St. Margaret's, Rottingdean, is not particularly remarkable among the many ancient parish churches of England, but the architects of Forest Lawn have used their ingenuity to enliven it. One aisle has been constructed of glass instead of stone, and filled with pot-plants and caged canaries; a chapel, hidden in what is no doubt thought to be devotional half-darkness, is illuminated by a spotlit painting of Bourgereau's entitled 'Song of the Angels'; in a kind of sacristy relics of the patron saint are exposed to veneration. They are not what ecclesiastics call 'major relics'; some photographs by the Topical Press, a rifle scoresheet signed by the poet, the photostatic copy of a letter to Sir Roderick Jones expressing Kipling's hope of attending a christening, a copy of Lady Jones's popular novel, *National Velvet,* an oleograph text from a nearby cottage; and so forth.

What will the archaeologists of 2947 make of all this and of the countless other rareties of the place? What webs of conjecture will be spun by the professors of Comparative Religion? We know with what confidence they define the intimate beliefs of remote ages. They flourished in the nineteenth century. Then G. K. Chesterton, in a masterly book, sadly neglected in Europe but honoured in the U.S.A.—*The Everlasting Man*—gently exposed their fatuity. But they will flourish again, for it is a brand of scholarship well suited to dreamy natures who are not troubled by the itch of precise thought. What will the professors of the future make of Forest Lawn? What do we make of it ourselves? Here is the thing, under our noses, a first class anthropological puzzle of our own period and neighbourhood. What does it mean?

First, of course, it is self-evidently a successful commercial undertaking. The works of sculpture enhance the value of the grave sites; the unification in a single business of all the allied crafts of undertaking is practical and, I believe, unique. But all this is the least interesting feature.

Secondly, the Park is a monument to local tradition. Europeans, whose traditions are measured in centuries, are wrong to suppose that American traditions, because they are a matter of decades, are the less powerful. They are a recent, swift and wiry growth. Southern California has developed a local character which is unique in the United States. The territory was won by military conquest less than a century ago. In the generations that followed the Spanish culture was obliterated, and survives today only in reconstructions. The main immigrations took place in living memory, and still continue. In 1930 it was calculated that of the million and a quarter inhabitants of Los Angeles half had arrived in the previous five years; only one tenth could claim longer than fifteen years' standing. In the last seventeen years the balance has changed still more in the newcomers' favour. Of this vast influx the rich came first. There was no pioneer period in which hungry young people won a living from the land. Elderly people from the East and Middle West brought their money with them to enjoy it in the sunshine, and they set up a tradition of leisure which is apparent today in the pathological sloth of the hotel servants and the aimless, genial coffee-house chatter which the Film executives call 'conferences.'

It is not the leisure of Palm Beach and Monte Carlo where busy men go for a holiday. It is the leisure of those whose work is done. Here on the ultimate, sunset-shore they warm their old bodies and believe themselves alive, opening their scaly eyes two or three times a day to browse on salads and fruits. They have long forgotten the lands that gave them birth and the arts and trades they once practised. Here you find, forgetful and forgotten, men and women you supposed to be long dead, editors of defunct newspapers, playwrights and artists who were once the glory of long-demolished theatres, and round them congregate the priests of countless preposterous cults to soothe them into the cocoon-state in which they will slough their old bodies. The ideal is to shade off, so finely that it becomes imperceptible, the moment of transition, and it is to this process that Forest Lawn is the most conspicuous monument.

Dr. Eaton has set up his Credo at the entrance. 'I believe in a happy Eternal Life,' he says. 'I believe those of us left behind should be glad in the certain belief that those gone before have entered into that happier Life.' This theme is repeated on Coleus Terrace: 'Be happy because they for whom you mourn are happy—far happier than ever before.' And again in Vesperland: '... Happy because Forest Lawn has eradicated the old customs of Death and depicts Life not Death.'

The implication of these texts is clear. Forest Lawn has consciously turned its back on the 'old customs of death,' the grim traditional alternatives of Heaven and Hell, and promises immediate eternal happiness for all its inmates. Similar claims are made for other holy places—the Ganges, Debra Lebanos in Abyssinia, and so on. Some of the simpler crusaders probably believed that they would go straight to Heaven if they died in the Holy Land. But there is a catch in most of these dispensations, a sincere repentance, sometimes an arduous pilgrimage, sometimes a monastic rule in the closing years. Dr. Eaton is the first man to offer eternal salvation at an inclusive charge as part of his undertaking service.

There is a vital theological point on which Dr. Eaton gives no *ex cathedra* definition. Does burial in Forest Lawn itself sanctify, or is sanctity the necessary qualification for admission? Discrimination is exercised. There is no room for the negro or the Chinaman, however devout; avowed atheists are welcome, but notorious ill-doers are not. Al Capone, for example, had he applied, would have been excluded, although he died fortified by the last rites of his Church. 'Fatty' Arbuckle was refused burial, because, although acquitted by three juries of the crime imputed to him by rumour, he had been found guilty, twenty years or so earlier, of giving a rowdy party. Suicides, on the other hand, who, in 'the old customs of death' would lie at a crossroads, impaled, come in considerable numbers and, often, particularly in cases of hanging, present peculiar problems to the embalmer.

Embalming is so widely practised in California that many believe it to be a legal obligation. At Forest Lawn the bodies lie in state, sometimes on sofas, sometimes in open coffins, in apartments furnished like those of a luxurious hotel, and named 'Slumber Rooms.' Here the bereaved see them for the last time, fresh from the final beauty parlour, looking rather smaller than in life and much more dandified. There is a hint of the bassinette about these coffins, with their linings of quilted and padded satin and their frilled silk pillows. There is more than a hint, indeed, throughout Forest Lawn that death is a form of infancy, a Wordsworthian return to innocence. 'I am the Spirit of Forest Lawn,' wrote K. C. Beaton, in less than Wordsworthian phrase: 'I speak in the language of the Duck Baby,[1] happy childhood at play.' We are very far here from the traditional conception of an adult soul naked at the judgment seat and a body turning to corruption. There is usually a marble skeleton lurking somewhere among the marble draperies and quartered escutcheons of the

---

[1] A bronze figure by Edith Barrett Parsons representing a laughing nude child with poultry. It inspired Leo Robinson's poem "After the lights went out".

tombs of the high renaissance; often you find, gruesomely portrayed, the corpse half decayed with marble worms writhing in the marble adipocere. These macabre achievements were done with a simple moral purpose—to remind a highly civilized people that beauty was skin deep and pomp was mortal. In those realistic times Hell waited for the wicked and a long purgation for all but the saints, but Heaven, if at last attained, was a place of perfect knowledge. In Forest Lawn, as the builder claims, these old values are reversed. The body does not decay; it lives on, more chic in death than ever before, in its indestructible class A steel and concrete shelf; the soul goes straight from the Slumber Room to Paradise, where it enjoys an endless infancy—one of a great Caucasian nursery-party where Knights of Pythias toddle on chubby unsteady legs beside a Borglum whose baby-fingers could never direct a pneumatic drill and a Carrie Jacobs-Bond whose artless ditties are for the Duck Baby alone.

That, I think, is the message. To those of us too old-fashioned to listen respectfully, there is the hope that we may find ourselves, one day beyond time, standing at the balustrade of Heaven among the unrecognizably grown-up denizens of Forest Lawn, and, leaning there beside them, amicably gaze down on Southern California, and share with them the huge joke of what the Professors of Anthropology will make of it all.

Discussion Questions

1. What, if anything, in Waugh's values and assumptions earlier in the essay makes it possible for him to imagine himself at the end "amicably" gazing down along with some of the people he has just satirized?

2. Waugh stops imagining an archeological expedition of the future just as he comes to the subject of Forest Lawn. In what ways has his beginning prepared you for the attitudes he takes toward the enterprise? How, for example, does his initial discussion of Hollywood as seen in the future make the same kinds of ironic criticisms?

3. Compare Waugh's description of the indignities of Forest Lawn to Jessica Mitford's description of embalming. Do the two authors build from similar or different values and assumptions about the real meaning of death? Give some examples to support your decision.

4. Pick something common in contemporary life (for example, a shopping mall) and try to describe it from the perspective of a distant future. Focus on details that reveal the values and assumptions of people who take such facility for granted as part of everyday life.

H. G. WELLS

Herbert George Wells (1866–1946), the English novelist and journalist, was born in Kent, the son of a lady's maid and a small shopkeeper who also played professional cricket. Wells had a spotty education but was an omnivorous reader and after failing to make a go at various apprenticeships, won at eighteen a scholarship that enabled him to graduate from London University in 1888. After teaching science for a few years, Wells turned to journalism, and in 1895 wrote his first novel, The Time Machine, *which was an immediate success and which was followed by a number of scientific romances, including* The Invisible Man *(1897),* The War of the Worlds *(1898), and* Tales of Space and Time *(1899).*

By 1900 Wells had begun to turn his attention to sociology; he wrote several successful novels dealing with the aspirations of the lower-middle class: Kipps *(1905),* Tono-Bungay *(1909), and* The History of Mr. Polly *(1910). He joined the socialist movement in 1903 and out of that commitment wrote many studies of society from a utopian perspective, a point of view that was shattered by World War I. After the War, he decided that only popular education could ensure human progress, so he wrote* The Outline of History *(1920),* The Science of Life *(1931), and* The Work, Wealth and Happiness of Mankind *(1932). Wells grew increasingly pessimistic during World War II and wrote several bleak depictions of mankind's prospects. The following selection, however, from* The Future in America *(1906) shows Wells writing in his earlier, more optimistic vein.*

Ellis Island

I visited Ellis Island yesterday. It chanced to be a good day for my purpose. For the first time in its history this filter of immigrant humanity has this week proved inadequate to the demand upon it. It was choked, and half a score of gravid liners were lying uncomfortably up the harbor, replete with twenty thousand or so of crude Americans from Ireland and Poland and Italy and Syria and Finland and Albania; men, women, children, dirt, and bags together.

Of immigration I shall have to write later; what concerns me now is chiefly the wholesale and multitudinous quality of that place and its work. I made my way with my introduction along white passages and through traps and a maze of metal lattices that did for a while succeed in catching and imprisoning me, to Commissioner Wachorn, in his quiet, green-toned office. There, for a time, I sat judicially and heard him deal methodically, swiftly, sympathetically, with case after case, a string of appeals against the sentences of deportation pronounced in the busy little courts below. First would come one dingy and strangely garbed group of wild-eyed aliens, and then another: Roumanian gypsies, South Italians, Ruthenians, Swedes, each under the intelligent guidance of a uniformed interpreter, and a case would be started, a report made to Washington, and they would drop out again, hopeful or sullen or fearful as the evidence might trend. . . .

Down-stairs we find the courts, and these seen, we traverse long refectories, long aisles of tables, and close-packed dormitories with banks of steel mattresses, tier above tier, and galleries and passages innumerable, perplexing intricacy that slowly grows systematic with the Commissioner's explanations.

Here is a huge, gray, untidy waiting-room, like a big railway-depot room, full of a sinister crowd of miserable people, loafing about or sitting dejectedly, whom America refuses, and here a second and a third such chamber each with its tragic and evil-looking crowd that hates us, and that even ventures to groan and hiss at us a little for our glimpse of its large dirty spectacle of hopeless failure, and here, squalid enough indeed, but still to some degree hopeful, are the appeal cases as yet undecided. In one place, at a bank of ranges, works an army of men cooks, in another spins the big machinery of the Ellis Island laundry, washing blankets, drying blankets, day in and day out, a big clean steamy space of hurry and rotation. Then, I recall a neat apartment lined to the ceiling with little drawers, a card-index of the names and nationalities and significant circumstances of upward of a million and a half of people who have gone on and who are yet liable to recall.

The central hall is the key of this impression. All day long, through an intricate series of metal pens, the long procession files, step by step, bearing bundles and trunks and boxes, past this examiner and that, past the quick, alert medical officers, the tallymen and the clerks. At every point immigrants are being picked out and set aside for further medical examination, for further questions, for the busy little courts; but the main procession satisfies conditions, passes on. It is a daily procession that, with a yard of space to each, would stretch over three miles, that any week in the year would more than equal in numbers that daily procession of the unemployed that is becoming a regular feature of the London winter, that in a year could put a cordon round London or New York of close-marching people, could populate a new Boston, that in a century—What in a century will it all amount to? . . .

On they go, from this pen to that, pen by pen, towards a desk at a little metal wicket—the gate of America. Through this metal wicket drips the immigration stream—all day long, every two or three seconds an immigrant, with a valise or a bundle, passes the little desk and goes on past the well-managed money-changing place, past the carefully organized separating ways that go to this railway or that, past the guiding, protecting officials—into a new world. The great majority are young men and young women, between seventeen and thirty, good, youthful, hopeful, peasant stock. They stand in a long string, waiting to go through that wicket, with bundles, with little tin boxes, with cheap portmanteaus, with odd packages, in pairs, in families, alone, women with children, men with strings of dependents, young couples. All day that string of human beads waits there, jerks forward, waits again; all day and every day, constantly replenished, constantly dropping the end beads through the wicket, till the units mount to hundreds and the hundreds to thousands. . . .

Yes, Ellis Island is quietly immense. It gives one a visible image of one aspect at least of this world-large process of filling and growing and synthesis, which is America.

"Look there!" said the Commissioner, taking me by the arm and pointing, and I saw a monster steamship far away, and already a big bulk looming up the Narrows. "It's the *Kaiser Wilhelm der Grosse*. She's got—I forget the exact figures, but let us say—eight hundred and fifty-three more for us. She'll have to keep them until Friday at the earliest. And there's more behind her, and more strung out all across the Atlantic."

In one record day this month 21,000 immigrants came into the port of New York alone; in one week over 50,000. This year the total will be 1,200,000 souls, pouring in, finding work at once, producing no fall in wages. They start digging and building and making. Just think of the dimensions of it!

Discussion Questions

1. What is Wells's attitude toward America in this passage? Do you find him critical of the Ellis Island procedure? How might a more recent description of Ellis Island read?

2. In the opening paragraph, why does Wells decribe Ellis Island as "this filter of immigrant humanity"? How does this image influence his eyewitness report?

3. What metaphors does Wells use to describe the vast crowd of immigrants? How do these metaphors affect your sense of the people? What is his attitude toward the immigrants? Does he make discriminations among them?

4. In this passage, Wells is pretty much a sightseer. How does his method of "sightseeing" compare to that recommended by G. K. Chesterton? What change in attitude would make Wells less a sightseer and more at one with the people and place he is observing?

5. Imagine yourself as one of the immigrants at Ellis Island at the time Wells is writing. Where might you be coming from? What might be your thoughts and worries at this moment? Refashioning Wells's details, write an essay about immigration as though you were actually experiencing it.

EUDORA WELTY

Eudora Welty was born in Jackson, Mississippi, in 1909, and she continues to make that community her home. She attended the Mississippi State College for Women, graduated from the University of Wisconsin, and studied at the Columbia University School of Business. During the Depression, she traveled through Mississippi for the Works Progress Administration, taking the photographs that she printed years later in One Time, One Place *(1971). In 1941, she published her first collection of stories,* A Curtain of Green and Other Stories, *which she followed the next year with her first novel,* The Robber Bridegroom. *Since then, she has produced several collections of short stories and four novels:* The Delta Wedding *(1946),* The Ponder Heart *(1954),* Losing Battles *(1970), and the Pulitzer Prize-winning novel* The Optimist's Daughter *(1972).*

Though she is known primarily as a writer of fiction, Eudora Welty has a fine reputation as an essayist and critic. Her articles and reviews have appeared in such journals as The Yale Review, The Southern Review, The Atlantic Monthly, Harper's Bazaar, The New Republic, The Hudson Review, Esquire, *and* The New York Times. *Her two studies,* Place in Fiction *(1958) and* Three Papers on Fiction *(1962) are frequently cited in criticism of the modern short story. The following autobiographical essay is reprinted from* The Eye of the Story: Selected Essays and Reviews *(1978).*

A Sweet Devouring

When I used to ask my mother which we were, rich or poor, she refused to tell me. I was then nine years old and of course what I was dying to hear was that we were poor. I was reading a book called *Five Little Peppers* and my heart was set on baking a cake for my mother in a stove with a hole in it. Some version of rich, crusty old Mr. King—up till that time not living on our street—was sure to come down the hill in his wheelchair and rescue me if anything went wrong. But before I could start a cake at all I had to find out if we were poor, and poor *enough*; and my mother wouldn't tell me, she said she was too busy. I couldn't wait too long; I had to go on reading and soon Polly Pepper got into more trouble, some that was a little harder on her and easier on me.

Trouble, the backbone of literature, was still to me the original property of the fairy tale, and as long as there was plenty of trouble for everybody and the rewards for it were falling in the right spots, reading was all smooth sailing. At that age a child reads with higher appetite and gratification, and with those two stars sailing closer together, than ever again in his growing up. The home shelves had been providing me all along with the usual books, and I read them with love—but snap, I finished them. I read everything just alike—snap. I even came to the *Tales from Maria Edgeworth* and went right ahead, without feeling the bump—then. It *was* noticeable that when her characters suffered she punished them for it, instead of rewarding them as a reader had rather been led to hope. In her stories, the children had to make their choice between being unhappy and good about it and being unhappy and bad about it, and then she helped them to choose wrong. In *The Purple Jar*, it will be remembered, there was the little girl being taken through the shops by her mother and her downfall coming when she chooses to buy something beautiful instead of something necessary. The purple jar, when the shop sends it out, proves to have been purple only so long as it was filled with purple water, and her mother knew it all the time. They don't deliver the water. That's only the cue for stones to start coming through the hole in the victim's worn-out shoe. She bravely agrees she must keep walking on stones until such time as she is offered another choice between the beautiful and the useful. Her father tells her as far as he is concerned she can stay in the house. If I had been at all easy to disappoint, that story would have disappointed me. Of course, I did feel, what is the good of walking on rocks if they are going to let the water out of the jar too? And it seemed to me that even the illustrator fell down on the characters in that book, not alone Maria Edgeworth, for when a rich, crusty old gentleman gave Simple Susan a guinea for some kind deed she'd done him, there was a picture of the transaction and where was the guinea? I couldn't make out a feather. But I liked *reading* the book all right—except that I finished it.

My mother took me to the Public Library and introduced me: "Let her have any book she wants, except *Elsie Dinsmore*." I looked for the book I couldn't have and it was a row. That was how I learned about the Series Books. The *Five Little Peppers* belonged, so did *The Wizard of Oz*, so did *The Little Colonel*, so did *The Green Fairy Book*. There were many of everything, generations of everybody, instead of one. I wasn't coming to the end of reading, after all—I was saved.

Our library in those days was a big rotunda lined with shelves. A copy of *V.V.'s Eyes* seemed to follow you wherever you went, even after you'd read it. I didn't know what I liked, I just knew what there was a lot of. After *Randy's Spring* there came *Randy's Summer*, *Randy's Fall* and *Randy's Winter*. True, I didn't care very much myself for her spring, but it didn't occur to me that I might not care for her summer, and then her summer didn't prejudice me against her fall, and I still had hopes as I moved on to her winter. I was disappointed in her whole year, as it turned out, but a thing like that didn't keep me from wanting to read every word of it. The pleasures of reading itself—who doesn't remember?—were like those of a Christmas cake, a sweet devouring. The "Randy Books" failed chiefly in being so soon over. Four seasons doesn't make a series.

All that summer I used to put on a second petticoat (our librarian wouldn't let you past the front door if she could see through you), ride my bicycle up the hill and "through the Capitol" (shortcut) to the library with my two read books in the basket (two was the limit you could take out at one time when you were a child and also as long as you lived), and tiptoe in ("Silence") and exchange them for two more in two minutes. Selection was no object. I coasted the two new books home, jumped out of my petticoat, read (I suppose I ate and bathed and answered questions put to me), then in all hope put my petticoat back on and rode those two books back to the library to get my next two.

The librarian was the lady in town who wanted to be it. She called me by my full name and said, "Does your mother know where you are? You know good and well the fixed rule of this library: *Nobody is going to come running back here with any book on the same day they took it out.* Get both those things out of here and don't come back till tomorrow. And I can practically see through you."

My great-aunt in Virginia, who understood better about needing more to read than you *could* read, sent me a book so big it had to be read on the floor—a bound volume of six or eight issues of *St. Nicholas* from a previous year. In the very first pages a serial began: *The Lucky Stone* by Abbie Farwell Brown. The illustrations were right down my alley: a heroine so poor she was ragged, a witch with an extremely pointed hat, a rich, crusty old gentleman in—better than a wheelchair—a runaway carriage; and I set to. I gobbled up installment after installment through the whole luxurious book, through the last one, and then came the words, turning me to *un*lucky stone: "To be concluded." The book had come to an end and *The Lucky Stone* wasn't finished! The witch had it! I couldn't believe this infidelity from my aunt. I still had my secret childhood feeling that if you hunted long enough in a book's pages, you could find what you were looking for, and long after I knew books better than that, I used to hunt again for the end of *The Lucky Stone*. It never occurred to me that the story had an existence anywhere else outside the pages of that single green-bound book. The last chapter was just something I would have to do without. Polly Pepper could do it. And then suddenly I tried something—I read it again, as much as I had of it. I was in love with books at least partly for what they looked like; I loved the printed page.

In my little circle books were almost never given for Christmas, they cost too much. But the year before, I'd been given a book and got a shock. It was from the same classmate who had told me there was no Santa Claus. She gave me a book, all right— *Poems by Another Little Girl*. It looked like a real book, was printed like a real book—but it was *by her*. Homemade poems? Illusion-dispelling was her favorite game. She was in such a hurry, she had such a pile to get rid of—her mother's electric runabout was stacked to the bud vases with copies—that she hadn't even time to say, "Merry Christmas!" With only the same raucous laugh with which she had told me, "Been filling my own stocking for years!" she shot me her book, received my Japanese pencil box with a moonlight scene on the lid and a sharpened pencil inside, jumped back into the car and was sped away by her mother. I stood right where they had left me, on the curb in my Little Nurse's uniform, and read that book, and I had no better way to prove when I got through than I had when I started that this was not a real book. But of course it wasn't. The printed page is not absolutely everything.

Then this Christmas was coming, and my grandfather in Ohio sent along in his box of presents an envelope with money in it for me to buy myself the book I wanted.

I went to Kress's. Not everybody knew Kress's sold books, but children just before Christmas know eveything Kress's ever sold or will sell. My father had showed us the mirror he was giving my mother to hang above her desk, and Kress's is where my brother and I went to reproduce that by buying a mirror together to give her ourselves, and where our little brother then made us take him and he bought her one his size for fifteen cents. Kress's had also its version of the Series Books, called, exactly like another series, "The Camp Fire Girls," beginning with *The Camp Fire Girls in the Woods*.

I believe they were ten cents each and I had a dollar. But they weren't all that easy to buy, because the series stuck, and to buy some of it was like breaking into a loaf of French bread. Then after you got home, each single book was as hard to open as a box stuck in its varnish, and when it gave way it popped like a firecracker. The covers once prized apart would never close; those books once open stayed open and lay on their backs helplessly fluttering their leaves like a turned-over June bug. They were as light as a matchbox. They were printed on yellowed paper with corners that crumbled, if you pinched on them too hard, like old graham crackers, and they smelled like attic trunks, caramelized glue, their own confinement with one another and, over all, the Kress's smell—bandannas, peanuts and sandalwood from the incense counter. Even without reading them I loved them. It was hard, that year, that Christmas is a day you can't read.

What could have happened to those books?—but I can tell you about the leading character. His name was Mr. Holmes. He was not a Camp Fire Girl: he wanted to catch one. Through every book of the series he gave chase. He pursued Bessie and Zara—those were the Camp Fire Girls—and kept scooping them up in his touring car, while they just as regularly got away from him. Once Bessie escaped from the second floor of a strange inn by climbing down a gutter pipe. Once she escaped by driving away from Mr. Holmes in his own automobile, which she had learned to drive by watching him. What Mr. Holmes wanted with them— either Bessie or Zara would do—didn't give me pause; I was too young to be a Camp Fire Girl; I was just keeping up. I wasn't alarmed by Mr. Holmes—when I cared for a chill, I knew to go to Dr. Fu Manchu, who had his own series in the library. I wasn't fascinated either. There was one thing I wanted from those books, and that was for me to have ten to read at one blow.

Who in the world wrote those books? I knew all the time they were the false "Camp Fire Girls" and the ones in the library were the authorized. But book reviewers sometimes say of a book that if anyone else had written it, it might not have been this good, and I found it out as a child—their warning is justified. This was a proven case, although a case of the true not being as good as the false. In the true series the characters were either totally different or missing (Mr. Holmes was missing), and there was too much time given to teamwork. The Kress's Campers, besides getting into a more reliable kind of trouble than the Carnegie Campers, had adventures that even they themselves weren't aware of: the pages were in wrong. There were transposed pages, repeated pages, and whole sections in upside down. There was no way of telling if there was anything missing. But if you knew your way in the woods at all, you could enjoy yourself tracking it down. I read the library "Camp Fire Girls," since that's what they were there for, but though they could be read by poorer light they were not as good.

And yet, in a way, the false Campers were no better either. I wonder whether I felt some flaw at the heart of things or whether I was just tired of not having any taste; but it seemed to me when I had finished that the last nine of those books weren't as good as the first one. And the same went for all Series Books. As long as they are keeping a series going, I was afraid, nothing can really happen. The whole thing is one grand prevention. For my greed, I might have unwittingly dealt with myself in the same way Maria Edgeworth dealt with the one who put her all into the purple jar—I had received word it was just colored water.

And then I went again to the home shelves and my lucky hand reached and found Mark Twain—twenty-four volumes, not a series, and good all the way through.

Discussion Questions

1. Does Welty find reading a sensuous or an intellectual pleasure? Why doesn't she enjoy Series Books?
2. What does a "sweet devouring" mean? Why does Welty use this metaphor? Why does she enjoy books with "plenty of trouble for everybody?"
3. Explain what Welty finds wrong with *Poems by Another Little Girl*. What doesn't she like about the other little girl? What does Welty want from books? Compare her attitude toward reading to Lillian Hellman's in "A Fig Tree."
4. People today who recall their childhoods are perhaps more likely to remember favorite TV shows than favorite books. Do you think anything is lost because of this? Write an essay comparing both childhood experiences—watching TV and reading children's books. Discuss the special pleasures of each. Which do you remember more vividly, with more pleasure?

PAUL WEST

Paul West was born in Derbyshire, England, in 1930. He was educated at the University of Birmingham, where he received his B.A.; at Oxford, where he did graduate work; and, after coming to the United States, at Columbia, where he received an M.A. He has made his career since as a professor of English at many universities while amassing an ever-growing number of essays and books of fiction, nonfiction, poetry, and criticism. His Words for a Deaf Daughter *(1969) received many citations as one of the best books of the year. He won the* Paris Review Aga Khan Prize for Fiction *in 1974.*

West's style has been described as one of "torrential fluency" and as "at once exhausting and curiously elating." The essay that follows on the Vehicle Assembly Building (or VAB) of the Kennedy Space Center first appeared in the literary-architectural magazine Sites *and shows West's attempts to bring language up to the pitch of his extraordinary feelings in the face of extraordinary architecture.*

The VAB Beside the Sea

In route to the Vehicle Assembly Building, which is Cape Canaveral's Cheops, we pause to inspect the steel trussed tower of a mobile service structure which, the driver says, is for sale. Even now, people are bidding for it. Like some dun red oil-rig trailing one black umbilical cable and two white ones, it looks forlorn, nerveless, dead, its winches dangling in the breeze that cannot stir them, like kidneys in an old-style butcher's window. It belongs beside a disused railroad or in a museum of constructivist art, and I can't connect it intimately with rockets or blockhouse consoles, which proves only that I am not a utility pipeline. There it stands or rears, part of nothing, awaiting the dismantler, with, on the second-up of its five platforms, something rusty and inert (a bit of iron crane or parapet) that looks just like a marooned corgi dog waiting to be taken down and home.

The dog's image remains even as we arrive at the toe of the fabled VAB, plunked there next to Banana Creek like some titanic cruciform bathroom-fitting overflown by vultures and equipped (as the driver says) with a gravity ventilation system that changes the air hourly lest fog or clouds form in the vast interior. In the fill beneath this building there are pieces of prehistoric mammoth bones (how fitting) and petrified wood 25,000 years old, resting on 4425 steel pipe pilings which, driven to bearing on the limestone rock, went through to a salty chemical solution beneath. The VAB just might have become the biggest wet cell battery in the world; electrolysis began, and cathodic protection had to be affixed to neutralize the current and prevent the foundation from corroding. The VAB might also, had it not been settled firm, have blown over (or even away) in high winds, like a Paul Bunyanesque kite; the wind-tunnel test model did.

So that a completely assembled rocket can be removed, the

VAB's narrowest two sides lift upward in seven stages: seven doors that ascend one behind the other until all seven pack into the black balustrade at the top of the tapered runway that extends from the roof to the top runner of bottom leaves that part and roll aside. Either wall has two sets of, all told, eight doors, so the VAB has four ways in and out, twenty-eight vertical and four horizontal doors. It retracts its doors as planes their wheels, as conjurers palm cards, an open sesame of sequence that converts itself into a squat Stonehenge with four tall black slots. As our driver says, in his diffidently jubilant way, some days you can see a complete rocket, mounted on a giant trestle and held rigid by a launch tower that has a hammerhead on top, being inched out for its debut, the whole assembly on the white platform of the dun-blue crawler-transporter.

I have seen pictures of such an event, and astounding as they are, as if a monolith that is troll and lighthouse in one were being spirited away by a strip-mining shovel out of which a bass groaning leaks. Ah, the macro-magic of four bulldozers in unison! The earth aches. The gulls go mad. The caterpillar engines churn. The loose Alabama Riverstone Crawlerway, about the width of the New Jersey Turnpike, creaks and spits while the rough green grass of the median goes unscathed. It's an event for Jonathan Swift's Brobdingnagians, a slowness you can hardly stand, an ingenious displacement of eighteen million pounds that seem so high, so precarious, the move evokes a Spanish religious procession in which this, the *pièce de résistance*, is the victim already nailed to the stake and being towed at a sadistic dawdle to where the fire will be. If a rocket-on-the-move is meant to summon up images, all of which pertain yet only in part, it succeeds; but of course it is meant to do nothing of the kind, any more than the lander is. I can't fend off, though, overtones from half the rites in history: Ku Klux Klan; totem poles from as far apart as British Columbia and New Guinea; skyscrapers and the Eiffel Tower; wizards in conical hats and condemned men lashed to stretchers borne upright to the execution wall; the Colossus of Rhodes; Jack and the beanstalk; druid, dust devil, and tornado. A plinthed obelisk creeps away at something like the speed of Beckett's Bom who, in *How It Is*, worms his way across the intergalactic wastes at a mere ten or fifteen yards an eon. Something Mayan eases a new Simon Stylites to the brink of the solar system. Who on earth could watch unmoved, with mind unplucked-at, with imagination calm and wise?

"Right through that door, folks," calls the driver, his face akin to that of "Ed" (acronym for electric dummy, the half-robot used in tests at the manned spacecraft center in Houston). Anemically impassive, he motions at a dark slot punched in the flank of the VAB ziggurat: a dwarf door, or so it seems, even at a distance of only twenty yards. But I stay put, catching a glimpse of orange-brown roof on the lowest block of the VAB. It's the color of Mediterranean walls, whereas the entire southern face, at least in today's harsh light, is black and white, the exact color-scheme of Tudor cottages. Then I notice something else about the VAB: the western pair of up-sliding doors faces only a parking lot (or what is being used as such) and a stretch of Banana Creek, whereas the other pair opens to the crawlerway. What the nearest fifty or sixty cars are parked upon doesn't look at all like the groomed mineral that leads to complex 39. Are the west doors, I wonder, a vertical false bottom? They conceal, as I discover on entering, an enormous Navy balloon, yellow and finless, roped like an animal in a clamming house.

On my right, shining fit to beat the band, are Apollo and Soyuz, perched on struts: mock-ups, of course, but arrestingly frozen on the point of clinch, Apollo sepia, Soyuz white with tan solar panels extended and a bright yellow stripe on its wasp waist. They hover in this vast granary like insects preparing to mate. You can see into the tunnel protruding from Apollo, and Soyuz's rear end has seven symmetrically arranged holes, like a certain kind of vase. Looking upward along the blatant taper of perspective, I stare into serried arc-lamps mounted on successive iron galleries reminiscent of jails. If you so situate yourself as to peer up through one of Soyuz's panels, you see only yourself reflected. Every echo clangs. Light strays in through high glass criss-crossed with girders whose pattern reappears on each gallery, much enlarged. End toward us, the big balloon has dark seams which furnish it with lines of latitude and a polar circle. Except for a triangular green patch over what otherwise might indeed be Greenland, or Ford Range, if you're geocentric, Ortygia or Thule I if you dote on Mars. A gymnasium for Atlas, this, with props to match, ponderable only in the presence of mild guards. I am glad to re-enter the fog outside, where I stroll fifty yards to look into the five nozzles of a discarded Saturn V at rest like a giant rolling pin, in each of which I could stand up, from each of which an F-1 engine vents 1.5 million pounds of thrust made by mixing kerosene with liquid oxygen. I hear the thunder in this tunnel assembled by Boeing in New Orleans: a shell echoing a sea on fire. Then I find I have no idea which bus of six or seven is mine, aboard which, as exhorted, I will keep on sitting in the same seat, once I've located it.

Reseated, I review the monstrous edifice I have just left,

whose bloat statistics—130 million cubic feet, 526 feet high, maximum wind-sway one foot—don't quite enact it. What's inside, from 141 lifting devices (as small as one-ton hoists, as big as the two 250-ton bridge cranes) to the two enormous bays, fills the mind more substantially, as do comparisons. Its cubic capacity is equal to that of the Pentagon plus the Merchandise Mart in Chicago. It is twenty-five feet shorter than the Washington Monument. It is twice as long as a football field. Of such mind-benders are TWA Comperes made. Yet for sheer metaphysical grasp, the cowboy star Roy Rodgers wins the palm: "You could sure store a lot of hay in there," or books, elephants, Ramadas.

It takes forty-five minutes to open one of the VAB's doors.

The sixteen high-speed elevators travel at a maximum speed of 700 feet per minute.

The working platforms, which encircle (or engirdle) the vehicle stages during preparation, are like a column of file drawers that retract against the walls when the rocket is removed.

A crane operator here, you're told, qualifies only by lowering an unthinkably heavy, water-ballasted weight onto a raw egg without cracking the shell.

I have a hunch that Dante would have been at home in the VAB.

The launch control center is connected to the VAB by a corridor six floors above ground, but the tour omits it, so I miss making corroborations I hardly need. "Not so much a building as an almost living brain," as architect Max Urbahn describes it, the LCC has huge louver-like windows in the east wall, through which the firing crews can watch the liftoff (whereas inside the old-style blockhouses they saw it only via periscope or closed-circuit TV). It looks like a brand-new bank or an ultra-white contemporary sideboard with concertina drawers.

On the way back, the driver says next to nothing, just points out the radar dishes that receive from space, and I have to make what I can of what the pale green NASA map labels: propellant servicing, haulover canal, Met. Lab., ordnance storage (not hard to guess), reclamation area, suspect car siding, and MIMS (I'm, still guessing), and UC 17, 54 wt7, FCA 2 (at which I don't even try). Ink-black clouds have gathered above the VAB, whereas over the sea the sky is total blue. Sprinting to the Vega as outsize raindrops begin to fall, I realize I haven't seen the piece of lunar rock on display inside, but I pass it up. I shall be back. Meanwhile I'm glad to be dry in the clammy vinyl interior of a car named after one of the stars that make up the summer triangle, so called, which makes the night sky less blank than the sight and sound of the VAB—that drab slab of a lab—itself.

Discussion Questions

1. West seems to assume that anyone would be moved by the sight of the VAB when he asks, "Who on earth could watch unmoved, with a mind unplucked-at, with imagination calm and wise?" Through what means does he express how moved he is? What kind of imagination does he substitute for one "calm and wise"? How does he show his mind as "plucked-at" by what he sees?

2. West praises "comparisons" at the expense of "statistics." From what various areas of discourse are his own comparisons drawn? For example, his first sentence compares the VAB to Cheops or the Great Pyramid of Egypt, another example of architecture. To what *besides* architecture does West compare the VAB?

3. How do the ways in which West creates a sense of place differ from those of Evelyn Waugh, Simone de Beauvoir, and Ada Louise Huxtable? In what ways does West resemble each of these authors?

4. Write a brief essay about an example of architecture that "plucks" at your mind.

EDITH WHARTON

Edith Wharton (1862–1937) was born into a socially prominent New York City family and received a private education that afforded her numerous trips abroad. She began writing in 1880 for the Atlantic Monthly *and in 1899 published her first collection of short stories,* The Greater Inclination. *After writing one of her most successful novels,* The House of Mirth *(1905), Wharton settled permanently in France, though she continued to write about American life in such novels as* Ethan Frome *(1911),* Summer *(1917), and the Pulitzer Prize-winning* The Age of Innocence *(1920). In 1930, she became the first woman to receive the prestigious gold medal of the National Institute of Arts and Letters.*

Wharton was not only a prolific writer of fiction, but she also produced a great deal of distinguished nonfiction: essays, criticism, autobiography, and travel books. Among her most important works of nonfiction are A Motor-Flight Through France *(1908),* In Morocco *(1920),* The Writing of Fiction *(1925), and* A Backward Glance *(1934), in which appeared the following amusing recollection of Henry James—a great writer here seen imprisoned by the power of his distinctive style.*

Henry James Asks Directions

Not infrequently, on my annual visit to Qu'acre, I "took off" from Lamb House, where I also went annually for a visit to Henry James. The motor run between Rye and Windsor being an easy one, I was often accompanied by Henry James, who generally arranged to have his visit to Qu'acre coincide with mine. James, who was a frequent companion on our English motor-trips, was firmly convinced that, because he lived in England, and our chauffeur (an American) did not, it was necessary that the latter should be guided by him through the intricacies of the English country-side. Signposts were rare in England in those days, and for many years afterward, and a truly British reserve seemed to make the local authorities reluctant to communicate with the invading stranger. Indeed, considerable difficulty existed as to the formulating of advice and instructions, and I remember in one village the agitated warning: "Motorists! Beware of the children!"—while in general there was a marked absence of indications as to the whereabouts of the next village.

It chanced, however, that Charles Cook, our faithful and skilful driver, was a born path-finder, while James's sense of direction was non-existent, or rather actively but always erroneously alert; and the consequences of his intervention were always bewildering, and sometimes extremely fatiguing. The first time that my husband and I went to Lamb House by motor (coming from France) James, who had travelled to Folkestone by train to meet us, insisted on seating himself next to Cook, on the plea that the roads across Romney marsh formed such a tangle that only an old inhabitant could guide us to Rye. The suggestion resulted in our turning around and around in our tracks till long after dark, though Rye, conspicuous on its conical hill, was just ahead of us, and Cook could easily have landed us there in time for tea.

Another year we had been motoring in the west country, and on the way back were to spend a night at Malvern. As we approached (at the close of a dark rainy afternoon) I saw James growing restless, and was not surprised to hear him say: "My dear, I once spent a summer at Malvern, and know it very well, and as it is rather difficult to find the way to the hotel, it might be well if Edward were to change places with me, and let me sit beside Cook." My husband of course acceded (although with doubt in his heart), and James having taken his place, we awaited the result. Malvern, if I am not mistaken, is encircled by a sort of upper boulevard, of the kind called in Italy a *strada di circonvallazione*, and for an hour we circled about above the outspread city, while James vainly tried to remember which particular street led down most directly to our hotel. At each corner (literally) he stopped the motor, and we heard a muttering, first confident and then anguished. "This—this, my dear Cook, yes . . . this certainly is the right corner. But no; stay! A moment longer, please—in this light it's so difficult . . . appearances are so misleading. . . It may be . . . yes! I think it *is* the next turn . . . 'a little farther lend thy guiding hand' . . . that is, drive on; but slowly, please, my dear Cook; *very* slowly!" And at the next corner the same agitated monologue would be repeated; till at length Cook, the mildest of men, interrupted gently: "I guess any turn'll get us down into the town, Mr. James, and after that I can ask—" and late, hungry and exhausted we arrived at length at our destination, James still convinced that the next turn would have been the right one, if only we had been more patient.

The most absurd of these episodes occurred on another rainy evening, when James and I chanced to arrive at Windsor long after dark. We must have been driven by a strange chauffeur—perhaps Cook was on a holiday; at any rate, having fallen into the lazy habit of trusting to him to know the way, I found myself at a loss to direct his substitute to the King's Road. While I was hesitating, and peering out into the darkness, James spied an ancient doddering man who had stopped in the rain to gaze at us. "Wait a moment, my dear—I'll ask him where we are"; and leaning out he signalled to the spectator.

"My good man, if you'll be good enough to come here, please; a little nearer—so," and as the old man came up: "My friend, to put it to you in two words, this lady and I have just arrived here from *Slough*; that is to say, to be more strictly accurate, we have recently *passed through* Slough on our way here, having actually motored to Windsor from Rye, which was our point of departure; and the darkness having overtaken us, we should be much obliged if you would tell us where we now are in relation, say, to the High Street, which, as you of course know, leads to the Castle, after leaving on the left hand the turn down to the railway station."

I was not surprised to have this extraordinary appeal met by silence, and a dazed expression on the old wrinkled face at the window; nor to have James go on: "In short" (his invariable prelude to a fresh series of explanatory ramifications), "in short", my good man, what I want to put to you in a word is this: supposing we have already (as I have reason to think we have) driven past the turn down to the railway station (which, in that case, by the way, would probably not have been on our left hand, but on our right), where are we now in relation to. . ."

"Oh, please," I interrupted, feeling myself utterly unable to sit through another parenthesis, "do ask him where the King's Road is."

"Ah—? The King's Road? Just so! Quite right! Can you, as a matter of fact, my good man, tell us where, in relation to our present position, the King's Road exactly *is*?"

"Ye're in it," said the aged face at the window.

Discussion Questions

1. What is the humor of this anecdote based on? The French poet Baudelaire said that laughter is based on feelings of superiority. Who is being superior to whom in this passage?

2. How does James's sense of direction match his verbal style? Point out a few of the similarities. Does he seem aware of these similarities?

3. Is Wharton's attitude toward James one of anger? Annoyance? Amusement? Explain. How is her style different from James's? Compare her evocation of character through dialogue with that of Michael Arlen.

4. Discuss the everyday activity of giving and asking for directions. What verbal skill is involved? How can people make the activity more complicated than it should be?

E. B. WHITE

The noted American essayist and humorist Elwyn Brooks White was born in Mt. Vernon, New York, in 1899 and graduated from Cornell in 1921. After working as a journalist for a few years, White joined the newly founded New Yorker *magazine and wrote the popular "Talk of the Town" column. From 1938 to 1943 he contributed essays to* Harper's *and in 1945 resumed his association with* The New Yorker, *this time as a free lance writer. In 1960, he received the National Institute of Arts and Letters gold medal. He is the author of two much loved children's books,* Stuart Little *(1945) and* Charlotte's Web *(1952).*

In 1929, White coauthored a humorous book with James Thurber, Is Sex Necessary? *His other books include* Alice Through Cellophane *(1933),* Every Day Is Saturday *(1934),* Quo Vadimus? or the Case for the Bicycle *(1939),* One Man's Meat *(1942),* The Second Tree from the Corner *(1954), and* The Points of My Compass *(1962). His revision of his former college writing teacher's book, William Strunk, Jr.'s* Elements of Style *(1959), remains one of the most widely recommended manuals of its kind. The following selection is reprinted from* Essays of E. B. White *(1977).*

Death of a Pig

I spent several days and nights in mid-September with an ailing pig and I feel driven to account for this stretch of time, more particularly since the pig died at last, and I lived, and things might easily have gone the other way round and none left to do the accounting. Even now, so close to the event, I cannot recall the hours sharply and am not ready to say whether death came on the third night or the fourth night. This uncertainty afflicts me with a sense of personal deterioration; if I were in decent health I would know how many nights I had sat up with a pig.

The scheme of buying a spring pig in blossomtime, feeding it through summer and fall, and butchering it when the solid cold weather arrives, is a familiar scheme to me and follows an antique pattern. It is a tragedy enacted on most farms with perfect fidelity to the original script. The murder, being premeditated, is in the first degree but is quick and skillful, and the smoked bacon and ham provide a ceremonial ending whose fitness is seldom questioned.

Once in a while something slips—one of the actors goes up in his lines and the whole performance stumbles and halts. My pig simply failed to show up for a meal. The alarm spread rapidly. The classic outline of the tragedy was lost. I found myself cast suddenly in the role of pig's friend and physician—a farcical character with an enema bag for a prop. I had a presentiment, the very first afternoon, that the play would never regain its balance and that my sympathies were now wholly with the pig. This was slapstick—the sort of dramatic treatment that instantly appealed to my old dachshund, Fred, who joined the vigil, held the bag, and, when all was over, presided at the interment. When we slid the body into the grave, we both were shaken to the core. The loss we felt was not the loss of ham but the loss of pig. He had evidently become precious to me, not that he represented a distant nourishment in a hungry time, but that he had suffered in a suffering world. But I'm running ahead of my story and shall have to go back.

My pigpen is at the bottom of an old orchard below the house. The pigs I have raised have lived in a faded building that once was an icehouse. There is a pleasant yard to move about in, shaded by an apple tree that overhangs the low rail fence. A pig couldn't ask for anything better—or none has, at any rate. The sawdust in the icehouse makes a comfortable bottom in which to root, and a warm bed. This sawdust, however, came under suspicion when the pig took sick. One of my neighbors said he thought the pig would have done better on new ground—the same principle that applies in planting potatoes. He said there might be something unhealthy about the sawdust, that he never thought well of sawdust.

It was about four o'clock in the afternoon when I first noticed that there was something wrong with the pig. He failed to appear at the trough for his supper, and when a pig (or a child) refuses supper a chill wave of fear runs through any household, or icehousehold. After examining my pig, who was stretched out in the sawdust inside the building, I went to the phone and cranked it four times. Mr. Dameron answered. "What's good for a sick pig?" I asked. (There is never any identification needed on a country phone; the person on the other end knows who is talking by the sound of the voice and by the character of the question.)

"I don't know, I never had a sick pig," said Mr Dameron, "but I can find out quick enough. You hang up and I'll call Henry."

Mr. Dameron was back on the line again in five minutes. "Henry says roll him over on his back and give him two ounces of castor oil or sweet oil, and if that doesn't do the trick give him an injection of soapy water. He says he's almost sure the pig's plugged up, and even if he's wrong, it can't do any harm."

I thanked Mr. Dameron. I didn't go right down to the pig, though. I sank into a chair and sat still for a few minutes to think about my troubles, and then I got up and went to the barn, catching up on some odds and ends that needed tending to. Unconsciously I held off, for an hour, the deed by which I would officially recognize the collapse of the performance of raising a pig; I wanted no interruption in the regularity of feeding, the steadiness of growth, the even succession of days. I wanted no interruption, wanted no oil, no deviation. I just wanted to keep on raising a pig, full meal after full meal, spring into summer into fall. I didn't even know whether there were two ounces of castor oil on the place.

Shortly after five o'clock I remembered that we had been invited out to dinner that night and realized that if I were to dose a pig there was no time to lose. The dinner date seemed a familiar conflict: I move in a desultory society and often a week or two will roll by without my going to anybody's house to dinner or anyone's coming to mine, but when an occasion does arise, and I am summoned, something usually turns up (an hour or two in advance) to make all human intercourse seem vastly inappropriate. I have come to believe that there is in hostesses a special power of divination, and that they deliberately arrange dinners to coincide with pig failure or some other sort of failure. At any rate, it was after five o'clock and I knew I could put off no longer the evil hour.

When my son and I arrived at the pigyard, armed with a small bottle of castor oil and a length of clothesline, the pig had emerged from his house and was standing in the middle of his yard, listlessly. He gave us a slim greeting. I could see that he felt uncomfortable and uncertain. I had brought the clothesline thinking I'd have to tie him (the pig weighed more than a hundred pounds) but we never used it. My son reached down, grabbed both front legs, upset him quickly, and when he opened his mouth to scream I turned the oil into his throat—a pink, corrugated area I had never seen before. I had just time to read the label while the neck of the bottle was in his mouth. It said Puretest. The screams, slightly muffled by oil, were pitched in the hysterically high range of pig-sound, as though torture were being carried out, but they didn't last long: it was all over rather suddenly, and, his legs released, the pig righted himself.

In the upset position the corners of his mouth had been turned down, giving him a frowning expression. Back on his feet again he regained the set smile that a pig wears even in sickness. He stood his ground, sucking slightly at the residue of oil; a few drops leaked out of his lips while his wicked eyes, shaded by their coy little lashes, turned on me in disgust and hatred. I scratched him gently with oily fingers and he remained quiet, as though trying to recall the satisfaction of being scratched when in health, and seeming to rehearse in his mind the indignity to which he had just been subjected. I noticed, as I stood there, four or five small dark spots on his back near the tail end, reddish brown in color, each about the size of a housefly. I could not make out what they were. They did not look troublesome but at the same time they did not look like mere surface bruises or chafe marks. Rather they seemed blemishes of internal origin. His stiff white bristles almost completely hid them and I had to part the bristles with my fingers to get a good look.

Several hours later, a few minutes before midnight, having dined well and at someone else's expense, I returned to the pighouse with a flashlight. The patient was asleep. Kneeling, I felt his ears (as you might put your hand on the forehead of a child) and they seemed cool, and then with the light made a careful examination of the yard and the house for sign that the oil had worked. I found none and went to bed.

We had been having an unseasonable spell of weather—hot, close days, with the fog shutting in every night, scaling for a few hours in midday, then creeping back again at dark, drifting in first over the trees on the point, then suddenly blowing across the fields, blotting out the world and taking possession of houses, men, and animals. Everyone kept hoping for a break, but the break failed to come. Next day was another hot one. I visited the pig before breakfast and tried to tempt him with a little milk in his trough. He just stared at it, while I made a sucking sound through my teeth to remind him of past pleasures of the feast. With very small, timid pigs, weanlings, this ruse is often quite successful and will encourage them to eat; but with a large, sick pig the ruse is senseless and the sound I made must have made him feel, if anything, more miserable. He not only did not crave food, he felt a positive revulsion to it. I found a place under the apple tree where he had vomited in the night.

At this point, although a depression had settled over me, I didn't suppose that I was going to lose my pig. From the lustiness of a healthy pig a man derives a feeling of personal lustiness; the stuff that goes into the trough and is received with such enthusiasm is an earnest of some later feast of his own, and when this suddenly comes to an end and the food lies stale and untouched, souring in the sun, the pig's imbalance becomes the man's, vicariously, and life seems insecure, displaced, transitory.

As my own spirits declined, along with the pig's, the spirits of my vile old dachshund rose. The frequency of our trips down the footpath through the orchard to the pigyard delighted him, although he suffers greatly from arthritis, moves with difficulty, and would be bedridden if he could find anyone willing to serve him meals on a tray.

He never missed a chance to visit the pig with me, and he made many professional calls on his own. You could see him down there at all hours, his white face parting the grass along the fence as he wobbled and stumbled about, his stethoscope dangling—a happy quack, writing his villainous prescriptions and grinning his corrosive grin. When the enema bag appeared, and the bucket of warm suds, his happiness was complete, and he managed to squeeze his enormous body between the two lowest rails of the yard and then assumed full charge of the irrigation. Once, when I lowered the bag to check the flow, he reached in and hurriedly drank a few mouthfuls of the suds to test their potency. I have noticed that Fred will feverishly consume any substance that is associated with trouble—the bitter flavor is to his liking. When the bag was above reach, he concentrated on the pig and was everywhere at once, a tower of strength and inconvenience. The pig, curiously enough, stood rather quietly through this colonic carnival, and the enema, though ineffective, was not as difficult as I had anticipated.

I discovered, though, that once having given a pig an enema there is no turning back, no chance of resuming one of life's more stereotyped roles. The pig's lot and mine were inextricably bound now, as though the rubber tube were the silver cord. From then until the time of his death I held the pig steadily in the bowl of my mind; the task of trying to deliver him from his misery became a strong obsession. His suffering soon became the embodiment of all earthly wretchedness. Along toward the end of the afternoon, defeated in physicking, I phoned the veterinary twenty miles away and placed the case formally in his hands. He was full of questions, and when I casually mentioned the dark spots on the pig's back, his voice changed its tone.

"I don't want to scare you," he said, "but when there are spots, erysipelas has to be considered."

Together we considered erysipelas, with frequent interruptions from the telephone operator, who wasn't sure the connection had been established.

"If a pig has erysipelas can he give it to a person?" I asked.

"Yes, he can," replied the vet.

"Have they answered?" asked the operator.

"Yes, they have," I said. Then I addressed the vet again. "You better come over here and examine this pig right away."

"I can't come myself," said the vet, "but McFarland can come this evening if that's all right. Mac knows more about pigs than I do anyway. You needn't worry too much about the spots. To indicate erysipelas they would have to be deep hemorrhagic infarcts."

"Deep hemorrhagic what?" I asked.

"Infarcts," said the vet.

"Have they answered?" asked the operator.

"Well," I said, "I don't know what you'd call these spots, except they're about the size of a housefly. If the pig has erysipelas I guess I have it, too, by this time, because we've been very close lately."

"McFarland will be over," said the vet.

I hung up. My throat felt dry and I went to the cupboard and got a bottle of whiskey. Deep hemorrhagic infarcts—the phrase began fastening its hooks in my head. I had assumed that there could be nothing much wrong with a pig during the months it was being groomed for murder; my confidence in the essential health and endurance of pigs had been strong and deep, particularly in the health of pigs that belonged to me and that were part of my proud scheme. The awakening had been violent and I minded it all the more because I knew that what could be true of my pig could be true also of the rest of my tidy world. I tried to put this distasteful idea from me, but it kept recurring. I took a short drink of the whiskey and then, although I wanted to go down to the yard and look for fresh signs, I was scared to. I was certain I had erysipelas.

It was long after dark and the supper dishes had been put away when a car drove in and McFarland got out. He had a girl with him. I could just make her out in the darkness—she seemed young and pretty. "This is Miss Owen," he said. "We've been having a picnic supper on the shore, that's why I'm late."

McFarland stood in the driveway and stripped off his jacket, then his shirt. His stocky arms and capable hands showed up in my flashlight's gleam as I helped him find his coverall and get zipped up. The rear seat of his car contained an astonishing amount of paraphernalia, which he soon overhauled, selecting a chain, a syringe, a bottle of oil, a rubber tube, and some other things I couldn't identify. Miss Owen said she'd go along with us and see the pig. I led the way down the warm slope of the orchard, my light picking out the path for them, and we all three climbed the fence, entered the pighouse, and squatted by the pig while McFarland took a rectal reading. My flashlight picked up the glitter of an engagement ring on the girl's hand.

"No elevation," said McFarland, twisting the thermometer in the light. "You needn't worry about erysipelas." He ran his hand slowly over the pig's stomach and at one point the pig cried out in pain.

"Poor piggledy-wiggledy!" said Miss Owen.

The treatment I had been giving the pig for two days was then repeated, somewhat more expertly, by the doctor, Miss Owen and I handing him things as he needed them—holding the chain that he had looped around the pig's upper jaw, holding the syringe, holding the bottle stopper, the end of the tube, all of us working in darkness and in comfort, working with the instinctive teamwork induced by emergency conditions, the pig unprotesting, the house shadowy, protecting, intimate. I went to bed tired but with a feeling of relief that I had turned over part of the responsibility of the case to a licensed doctor. I was beginning to think, that the pig was not going to live.

He died twenty-four hours later, or it might have been forty-eight—there is a blur in time here, and I may have lost or picked up a day in the telling and the pig one in the dying. At intervals during the last day I took cool fresh water down to him and at such times as he found the strength to get to his feet he would stand with head in the pail and snuffle his snout around. He drank a few sips but no more; yet it seemed to comfort him to dip his nose in water and bobble it about, sucking in and blowing out through his teeth. Much of the time, now, he lay indoors half buried in sawdust. Once, near the last, while I was attending him I saw him try to make a bed for himself but he lacked the strength, and when he set his snout into the dust he was unable to plow even the little furrow he needed to lie down in.

He came out of the house to die. When I went down, before going to bed, he lay stretched in the yard a few feet from the door. I knelt, saw that he was dead, and left him there: his face had a mild look, expressive neither of deep peace nor of deep suffering, although I think he had suffered a good deal. I went back up to the house and to bed, and cried internally—deep hemorrhagic intears. I didn't wake till nearly eight the next morning, and when I looked out the open window the grave was already being dug, down beyond the dump under a wild apple. I could hear the spade strike against the small rocks that blocked the way. Never send to know for whom the grave is dug, I said to myself, it's dug for thee. Fred, I well knew, was supervising the work of digging, so I ate breakfast slowly.

It was a Saturday morning. The thicket in which I found the gravediggers at work was dark and warm, the sky overcast. Here, among alders and young hackmatacks, at the foot of the apple tree, Lennie had dug a beautiful hole, five feet long, three feet wide, three feet deep. He was standing in it, removing the last spadefuls of earth while Fred patrolled the brink in simple but impressive circles, disturbing the loose earth of the mound so that it trickled back in. There had been no rain in weeks and the soil, even three feet down, was dry and powdery. As I stood and stared, an enormous earthworm which had been partially exposed by the spade at the bottom dug itself deeper and made a slow withdrawal, seeking even remoter moistures at even lonelier depths. And just as Lennie stepped out and rested his spade against the tree and lit a cigarette, a small green apple separated itself from a branch overhead and fell into the hole. Everything about this last scene seemed overwritten—the dismal sky, the shabby woods, the imminence of rain, the worm (legendary bedfellow of the dead), the apple (conventional garnish of a pig).

But even so, there was a directness and dispatch about animal burial, I thought, that made it a more decent affair than human burial: there was no stopover in the undertaker's foul parlor, no wreath nor spray; and when we hitched a line to the pig's hind legs and dragged him swiftly from his yard, throwing our weight into the harness and leaving a wake of crushed grass and smoothed rubble over the dump, ours was a businesslike procession, with Fred, the dishonorable pallbearer, staggering along in the rear, his perverse bereavement showing in every seam in his face; and the post-mortem performed handily and swiftly right at the edge of the grave, so that the inwards that had caused the pig's death preceded him into the ground and he lay at last resting squarely on the cause of his own undoing.

I threw in the first shovelful, and then we worked rapidly and without talk, until the job was complete. I picked up the rope, made it fast to Fred's collar (he is a notorious ghoul), and we all three filed back up the path to the house, Fred bringing up the rear and holding back every inch of the way, feigning unusual stiffness. I noticed that although he weighed far less than the pig, he was harder to drag, being possessed of the vital spark.

The news of the death of my pig traveled fast and far, and I received many expressions of sympathy from friends and neighbors, for no one took the event lightly and the premature expiration of a pig is, I soon discovered, a departure which the community marks solemnly on its calendar, a sorrow in which it feels fully involved. I have written this account in penitence and in grief, as a man who failed to raise his pig, and to explain my deviation from the classic course of so many raised pigs. The grave in the woods is unmarked, but Fred can direct the mourner to it unerringly and with immense good will, and I know he and I shall often revisit it, singly and together, in seasons of reflection and despair, on flagless memorial days of our own choosing.

Discussion Questions

1. Why doesn't White's pig have a name? Why does the dachshund? What does this fact tell us about White's relation to his pig?

2. How does White establish from the outset his feeling of identification with the pig? Find examples of this technique elsewhere in the essay.

3. Compare this essay to D. H. Lawrence's "Rex" and Edward Hoagland's "The Courage of Turtles." How does each writer establish his relation to animals? Which talks most to his animal? Which writer seems to have the closest attachment to his animal? Which writer seems most worried about being sentimental?

4. White maintains a humorous tone even when he is writing about something he finds depressing. Choose an unpleasant episode from your own life and write about it in such a way that it alone does not dominate your tone and mood.

The Essayist

The essayist is a self-liberated man, sustained by the childish belief that everything he thinks about, everything that happens to him, is of general interest. He is a fellow who thoroughly enjoys his work, just as people who take bird walks enjoy theirs. Each new excursion of the essayist, each new "attempt," differs from the last and takes him into new country. This delights him. Only a person who is congenitally self-centered has the effrontery and the stamina to write essays.

There are as many kinds of essays as there are human attitudes or poses, as many essay flavors as there are Howard Johnson ice creams. The essayist arises in the morning and, if he has work to do, selects his garb from an unusually extensive wardrobe: he can pull on any sort of shirt, be any sort of person, according to his mood or his subject matter—philosopher, scold, jester, raconteur, confidant, pundit, devil's advocate, enthusiast. I like the essay, have always liked it, and even as a child was at work, attempting to inflict my young thoughts and experiences on others by putting them on paper. I early broke into print in the pages of *St. Nicholas*. I tend still to fall back on the essay form (or lack of form) when an idea strikes me, but I am not fooled about the place of the essay in twentieth century American letters—it stands a short distance down the line. The essayist, unlike the novelist, the poet, and the playwright, must be content in his self-imposed role of second-class citizen. A writer who has his sights trained on the Nobel Prize or other earthly triumphs had best write a novel, a poem, or a play, and leave the essayist to ramble about, content with living a free life and enjoying the satisfactions of a somewhat undisciplined existence. (Dr. Johnson called the essay "an irregular, undigested piece"; this happy practitioner has no wish to quarrel with the good doctor's characterization.)

There is one thing the essayist cannot do, though—he cannot indulge himself in deceit or in concealment, for he will be found out in no time. Desmond MacCarthy, in his introductory remarks to the 1928 E. P. Dutton & Company edition of Montaigne, observes that Montaigne "had the gift of natural candour. . . ." It is the basic ingredient. And even the essayist's escape from discipline is only a partial escape: the essay, although a relaxed form, imposes its own disciplines, raises its own problems, and these disciplines and problems soon become apparent and (we all hope) act as a deterrent to anyone wielding a pen merely because he entertains random thoughts or is in a happy or wandering mood.

I think some people find the essay the last resort of the egoist, a much too self-conscious and self-serving form for their tastes; they feel that it is presumptuous of a writer to assume that his little excursions or his small observations will interest the reader. There is some justice in their complaint. I have always been aware that I am by nature self-absorbed and egoistical; to write of myself to the extent I have done indicates a too great attention to my own life, not enough to the lives of others. I have worn many shirts, and not all of them have been a good fit. But when I am discouraged or downcast I need only fling open the door of my closet, and there, hidden behind everything else, hangs the mantle of Michel de Montaigne, smelling slightly of camphor.

Discussion Questions

1. White includes himself in the hope that the "disciplines and problems" of the essay will "act as a deterrent to anyone wielding a pen merely because he entertains random thoughts or is in a happy or wandering mood." Yet in the beginning of the piece he claims for himself a sensibility very like what he hopes will be deterred. Is this really a contradiction? In what ways does White construct his essay to avoid the charges of "randomness" or "wandering?" Could, for example, the order of his paragraphs be changed without changing the essay for the worse?

2. White claims there is one thing the essayist cannot do. What qualities of White's writing would you point to as showing him without "deceit" and "concealment"?

3. White creates a partial list of roles the essayist may adopt: "philosopher, scold, jester, raconteur, confidant, pundit, devil's advocate, enthusiast." Which, if any, of these roles define the role White

adopts in this essay? Name a role not in the list which defines White as a writer here.

4. What other writer in the collection comes closest to White's manner as an essayist? Who seems most unlike White in the role he adopts as an essayist?

EDMUND WILSON

Edmund Wilson (1895–1972) was born in Red Bank, New Jersey, and graduated from Princeton University in 1916. He worked as a reporter, served in the Army Intelligence Corps during World War I, and in 1921 became managing editor of the prestigious magazine, Vanity Fair. Between 1926 and 1931, Wilson worked on the staff of the New Republic, and from 1944 to 1948 was a book reviewer for The New Yorker. In 1956, he received the National Institute of Arts and Letters Gold Medal for essays and criticism, and in 1966 was awarded the National Medal for Literature.

Although Wilson wrote poetry, plays, and fiction, he is best known for his social criticism and literary essays, which chronicled the state of American letters through five decades. Among his most important books are Axel's Castle: A Study in the Imaginative Literature of 1870—1930 (1931), the book which established his reputation; To the Finland Station (1940); The Wound and the Bow (1941); The Shores of Light (1952); The Scrolls from the Dead Sea (1955; 1969); and Patriotic Gore: Studies in the Literature of the American Civil War (1962). The following selection, dealing with one of Wilson's favorite subjects, is a complete essay from A Piece of My Mind: Reflections at Sixty (1956).

The Problem of English

And what about the teaching of English? What, exactly, does it mean to "teach English" in the United States?

Again I revert to my own experience. As a child, I imagined that a permanent antagonism existed between my father and me, that I was always, in tastes and opinions, on the opposite side from him. This was due, I can see, looking back, to a certain intellectual intolerance on my side as well as on his. But he was not an easy man to talk to: he almost eliminated give-and-take, for his conversation mostly consisted of either asking people questions in order to elicit information or telling them what to think. Our dinners at home, when we had no guests and there were only my parents and I, were likely to turn into lectures. My mother at her end of the table was—prematurely—so very deaf that she could not have any real interchange with my father at the other end, and my conversation with him usually took the form either of his asking my view of some question, then immediately squelching this view and setting me right on the subject, or of explaining at length, but with an expert lucidity, some basic point of law or government. So much did I take for granted our polarization that I was startled to realize one day that I was imitating my father's signature—my name was the same as his—which, like his writing in general, was completely illegible but quite beautiful in a graphic way, as if he had invented a calligraphy in order to conceal his meaning from everyone except himself. This handwriting had thus also its arrogance as well as its curious elegance and I found myself emulating these.

But it was not until after my father's death—in 1923—that I had a new revelation of the extent of my mimicry of him. In going through his speeches, briefs and other papers, I became for the first time aware how well he had expressed himself. His style had,

I saw, a purity quite exceptional in a public—or quasi-public—figure in New Jersey in the early nineteen hundreds, and his language was always distinguished by a silvery quality of clearness—I remember how he used to make fun of the pompous labored prose of Cleveland—which led me to understand his enthusiasm for the style of Stevenson, which I myself rather disliked. I realized now—and again with surprise—that I had been imitating this literary style as well as his penmanship. For my methods in writing had seemed to me personal: though I had imitated Shaw, Henry James and a number of other writers, I had consciously corrected these tendencies and was unconscious of my principal model. Since I had rarely heard my father in court or listened to his public speeches, I must have picked up his style mainly from his dinner-table lectures.

Some years after my father's death, I began making notes of his vocabulary and his characteristic phrases, and for the first time I took account of how old-fashioned his English was. He would say, for example, "It rains" or "It snows"—as the characters in Jane Austen do—instead of "It is raining," "It is snowing"; "It makes no matter" for "It doesn't matter." He would sometimes correct himself if he fell into the current usage of "*a* hotel" and make it "*an* hotel." He was the only living person I have ever known who used the exclamation "Zounds!" He was incapable of any other profanity, never even said "Good God!" or "Damn!" and his "Zounds" had a nuance of humor, but he did not regard it as a period piece. He was especially fond of such metaphors as "weltering around in a Dead Sea of mediocrity"—something I was warned not to do, when my school marks were not up to scratch—it was the worst fate with which he could threaten me. He was very much annoyed one day when, on our way home from one of his speeches, I undertook to inform him that the word he had wanted to use was *cataclysm*, not *cataclasm*. *Cataclasm* was then so archaic that I did not even know it existed and that it differed in meaning from *cataclysm*. I decided, in any case, at the moment of discovering in the writing of his papers the model for my literary style that this model was a valuable heritage, like the table pieces of silver of the Paul Revere silversmith period which had come to me from his side of the family.

Later on, at my prep school—Hill—I had been trained in traditional English by an extremely able English teacher—Dr. John A. Lester—who was himself an Englishman. He drilled us in sentence structure, grammar, the devices of "rhetoric" and prosody, as if we had been studying a foreign language; and we were made to take very seriously—as I have never, indeed, ceased to do—the great Trinity: Lucidity, Force and Ease. I have valued this training so much that I have always contended that English ought to be taught in this country by Englishmen. But this brings us to the crux of the problem: should Americans attempt to learn British English: and, if so, to what extent? There have been moments when I have seriously wondered whether my pieces of pre-revolutionary silver were adequate for modern use. I have sometimes become so bored with the language in which I wrote articles—the monotony of the vocabulary and the recurrence of routine formulas—that I would find it a great relief to get away from this kind of writing and give myself a freer hand in a play or a piece of fiction in which I could make people talk as contemporary Americans did. I also tried injecting some current slang into my purely critical writing, but I found that this was likely to jar and that I later had to take it out. With my own education based mainly on the literature and language of England, I sometimes envied H. L. Mencken, with his half-German education, which seemed to make it easier for him to play on "the American language." I was then and still am all in favor of the free development and the literary use of a semi-independent American language, but I cannot face without a shrinking the state of things predicted by Mencken, in which illiterate usage would eventually prevail in the United States—so that our grammar would be reduced to, for example, such conjugations—or non-conjugations—as *I was, he was; we was, you was, they was.* It is not so much, however, that our few surviving inflections are important as that the logic of syntax should not be lost. With all the considerable divergence between British and American idiom, the structure of the language is still the same—or ought to be the same, for otherwise we should have no structure: we should get nothing but woolly writing, incapable of expressing anything either elegantly or exactly.

I am aware of the special problems that exist in American public schools—that in localities where most of the pupils are the children of foreign parents, themselves illiterate in their native tongues, the instructor must sometimes be satisfied to teach them any English at all, that to exact from them a standard of correctitude becomes quite out of the question. I know that in some of our schools it is even as much as the teacher can do to avoid being murdered by his more aggressive students. But there ought to be institutions in which the abler kind of student can be taught to handle language competently. In my ideal university, I should have, as a general requirement, most rigorous courses in English, and I should have them all taught by Englishmen. Every student in every department would have to pass examinations in the accurate writing of English. Those specializing in scientific fields as well as the philosophers and historians would have their papers graded—except, of course, the kind that consist of equations—by the teachers in the English department as well as by their other professors, and, although it might be sometimes unfair to make it an invincible rule that no incompetent writer should ever be allowed to graduate, the gradings for precise expression should be given a good deal of importance.

The use of the English language as an instrument for analysis and exposition is one inheritance from England that we cannot afford to scrap. In the sciences, this logical and concrete style—as I have heard a Russian scientist say—possesses certain decided advantages over either German or French, which both, in their respective ways, so much tend to run to abstractions. In English it is easier to follow the argument, to see what the data are and to know what conclusions have been drawn from them in terms of a practical process. It is handier to describe a species, a country, a disease, a geological formation; to lay down the rules for a game, to give directions for navigation. In America, we have done a good deal to make a mess of this excellent medium. In my youthful days as an editor, I had once to prepare for publication a series of articles by the late John Dewey on a trip he had made to China. This ought really not to have involved him in obscurity, since he was merely telling what he had seen and the opinions to which it had led him; but when I came to edit the articles, I found that they both called for and resisted revision in a peculiarly exasperating way. It was not only a question here of clarifying the author's statements but of finding out what he meant; and when you did get the sense of his meaning, there was no way of straightening out the language: you would have had to try to give his meaning in a language of a different kind. But John Dewey, as I presently found out—though typical—was not by any means the worst American writer on education. Later on, the liberal weekly for which I worked ran a supplement on this subject, and the articles we received were incredible. How, I wondered, could a man set up as an authority on teaching the young when he was not himself sufficiently well-educated to have mastered the rudiments of writing. As for my experience with articles by experts in anthropology and sociology, it has led me to conclude that the requirement, in my ideal university, of having the papers in every department passed by a professor of English might result in revolutionizing these subjects—if indeed the second of them survived at all.

But even in the "Humanities" department there is a serious crisis in literacy. How can you write about a literary subject—

especially some great artisan of speech—when you yourself are hardly articulate, can scarcely express the most commonplace thoughts? At most, you can unearth a few unknown facts, point out some unsuspected sources. If you even, with no knowledge of the literary art, do not attempt anything more interesting than the dreary *"exposition des textes"* that has become a kind of standard academic product, you are likely to misread a language which you have never properly learned. Among the products of American teachers of such feeble qualifications, I have encountered some appalling cases. Some years ago—in 1939—I taught at the summer school of one of the biggest—and, I believe, one of the best—of the Western universities. A man who had been giving a course in contemporary English literature had gone abroad for the summer, and I was asked to grade the papers of his students, who had taken their examination after he left. Among the authors studied were Virginia Woolf, Yeats and Joyce—one of the greatest of English poets and two of the greatest masters of the harmonics of English prose; but the papers of the students dismayed me as a hideous revelation of the abysses of non-education that are possible in the United States. Hardly one of them could write and punctuate a respectable English sentence. One paper—like Molly Bloom's soliloquy—had been poured out with no punctuation except for an occasional full stop. In response to the question: "Explain the symbolism of Yeats's *The Winding Stair*," another of the examinees had written the following answer: "As Yeats goes up the winding stair he had a kind of a feeling like his old aristocratic past is coming back on him again." This was clearly not the fault of the teacher, a highly competent Britisher, well known as a writer on the subjects he was teaching. The failure had occurred further back. The truth was, of course, that such students should never have been allowed to take such a course at all. They ought to have been learning the use of the comma and the difference between conjunction and a preposition; they ought to have been standing at blackboards diagramming compound sentences. Another incredible example: a young man, the friend of a friend, once brought me for my criticism a manuscript of his poems. So many kinds of liberties are countenanced—in the way of off-rhymes and irregular rhythms—in the writing of modern poetry that I did not at first question these verses from the technical point of view, but I gradually became suspicious, and when I called the attention of the author to bad metric and impossible rhymes, I discovered not only that he knew nothing of metrics, had never been told that such a thing existed, but that he did not even understand rhyme, not having grasped the principle that it is the syllables with the accent that have to match, that you cannot rhyme *picture* with *pure*. Yet he had been graduated from an Eastern university which, if not very strong in the Humanities, is of excellent reputation and supposed to keep up a decent standard. He had specialized in American literature and had also had a course in Shakespeare, but it had never been explained to him at any point what kind of verse Shakespeare had written; he seemed, in fact, to have read it as prose. As for is own productions, he had simply seen modern poems in the current "avant-garde" magazines, and had tried to turn out something of the kind himself. (This experience has left with me terrible doubts about some of the stuff that is printed as verse in these literary magazines.) I ought to mention that this touching young man had also been going to classes intended for instruction in the writing of verse at the YMHA in New York, where his writings had been subjected to the scrutiny of a not-unknown poet. But, even after this, it remained for me to break it to him that poetry was an art with rules. It was not that he was stupid: on the contrary, I gave him an hour's instruction and found that he could soon identify the various metrical feet of which till that moment he had never heard. Still another student—from the largest university in the East—told me that he "wanted to write" and turned out to be equally ignorant of the medium that Shakespeare used. He was under the impression that blank verse was any verse that did not rhyme. He had taken one of those courses of miscellaneous classics in translation that are a feature of the modern curriculum, and had been through *The Divine Comedy* without being able to say whether it was written in prose or verse. He did not seem even to know whether the English translation was prose or verse. I was not able to tell him, because he did not know the name of the translator.

Discussion Questions

1. Why does Wilson begin this essay on education with an account of his father? What did he learn from his father about the English language?

2. Why does Wilson use the image of "table pieces of silver of the Paul Revere Silversmith period"? What does it suggest about his father? About Wilson's own relation to the English language?

3. What does Wilson mean by the "logic of syntax"? Why is it important? How is it a part of the problem of English?

4. Compare Wilson's essay to George Orwell's "Politics and the English Language." Does each writer worry about language for the same reasons? What does Orwell see as the "problem of English"? Then read Boorstin's "The Rhetoric of Democracy." Is he, too, worried about the English language?

5. With these three essays in mind, write a paper on "Advertising and the English language." Select an example of advertising language (a popular slogan, a sales pitch, a headline, and so forth) that you think distorts the English language in some way. Describe the verbal characteristics of the advertisement and explain why you think its misuse of English could have serious consequences.

Tom Wolfe

Tom Wolfe was born in 1931, grew up in Richmond, Virginia, and was educated at Washington and Lee University and Yale University, where he received a Ph.D. in American Studies. He worked as a reporter for the Springfield (Massachussetts) Union, the Washington Post, *and the* New York Herald Tribune. *A frequent contributor to many magazines, especially* Esquire *and* Harper's, *Wolfe has won two Washington Newspaper Guild Awards, and in 1980 received the Columbia Journalism Award for distinguished service to the field of journalism.*

Wolfe's first book, The Kandy-Kolored Tangerine-Flake Streamline Baby *appeared in 1965, and he has since then produced seven more books, a collection of his satirical drawings,* In Our Time *(1980), and an anthology,* The New Journalism *(1973). Among his best-known books are* The Electric Kool-Aid Acid Test *(1968),* Radical Chic & Mau-Mauing the Flak Catchers *(1970),* The Painted Word *(1975), and* From Bauhaus to Our House *(1981). Wolfe's genius for capturing a style or attitude with an enduring phrase ("radical chic," "the me-generation") was also apparent in* The Right Stuff *(1979), the book from which the following selection is drawn, and whose title remains one of the most popular expressions of our time.*

The Right Stuff

Anyone who travels very much on airlines in the United States soon gets to know the voice of *the airline pilot* . . . coming over the intercom . . . with a particular drawl, a particular folksiness, a particular down-home calmness that is so exaggerated it begins to parody itself (nevertheless!—it's reassuring) . . . the voice that tells you, as the airliner is caught in thunderheads and goes bolting up and down a thousand feet at a single gulp, to check your seat belts because "it might get a little choppy" . . . the voice that tells you (on a flight from Phoenix preparing for its final approach into Kennedy Airport, New York, just after dawn): "Now, folks, uh . . . this is the captain . . . ummmm . . . We've got a little ol' red light up here on the control panel that's tryin' to tell us that the *lan*din' gears're not . . . uh . . . *lock*in' into position when we lower 'em . . . Now . . . *I* don't believe that little ol' red light knows what its *talk*in' about—I believe it's that little ol' red *light* that iddn' workin' right" . . . faint chuckle, long pause, as if to say, *I'm not even sure all this is really worth going into–still, it may amuse you* . . . "But . . . I guess to play it by the rules, we oughta *hum*or that little ol' light . . . so we're gonna take her down to about, oh, two or three hundred feet over the runway at Kennedy, and the folks down there on the ground are gonna see if they caint give us a *vis*ual inspection of those ol' landin' gears"—with which he is obviously on intimate ol' buddy terms, as with every other working part of this mighty ship—"and if I'm right . . . they're gonna tell us everything is copa*cet*ic all the way aroun' an' we'll jes take her on in" . . . and, after a couple of low passes over the field, the voice returns: "Well, folks, those folks down there on the ground—it must be too early for 'em or somethin'—I 'spect they still got the *sleep*ers in their eyes . . . 'cause they say they caint tell if those ol' landin' gears are all the way down or not . . . But, you

702

know, up here in the cockpit we're convinced they're all the way down, so we're jes gonna take her on in . . . And oh" . . . (*I almost forgot*) . . . "while we take a little swing out over the ocean an' empty some of that surplus fuel we're not gonna be needin' anymore—that's what you might be seein' comin' out of the wings—our lovely little ladies . . . if they'll be so kind . . . they're gonna go up and down the aisles and show yu how we do what we call 'assumin' the position' " . . . another faint chuckle (*We do this often, and it's so much fun, we even have a funny little name for it*) . . . and the stewardesses, a bit grimmer, by the looks of them, than *that voice*, start telling the passengers to take their glasses off and take the ballpoint pens and other sharp objects out of their pockets, and they show them *the position*, with the head lowered . . . while down on the field at Kennedy the little yellow emergency trucks start roaring across the field—and even though in your pounding heart and your sweating palms and your broiling brainpan you *know* this is a critical moment in your life, you still can't quite bring yourself to b*elieve* it, because if it were . . . how could *the captain*, the man who knows the actual situation most intimately . . . how could he keep on drawlin' and chucklin' and driftin' and lollygaggin' in that particular voice of his—

Well!—who doesn't know that voice! And who can forget it!—even after he is proved right and the emergency is over.

That particular voice may sound vaguely Southern or Southwestern, but it is specifically Appalachian in origin. It originated in the mountains of West Virginia, in the coal country, in Lincoln County, so far up in the hollows that, as the saying went, "they had to pipe in daylight." In the late 1940's and early 1950's this up-hollow voice drifted down from on high, from over the high desert of California, down, down, down, from the upper reaches of the Brotherhood into all phases of American aviation. It was amazing. It was *Pygmalion* in reverse. Military pilots and then, soon, airline pilots, from Maine and Massachusetts and the Dakotas and Oregon and everywhere else began to talk in that poker-hollow West Virginia drawl, or as close to it as they could bend their native accents. It was the drawl of the most righteous of all the possessors of the right stuff: Chuck Yeager.

Yeager had started out as the equivalent, in the Second World War, of the legendary Frank Luke of the 27th Aero Squadron in the First. Which is to say, he was the boondocker, the boy from the back country, with only a high-school education, no credentials, no cachet or polish of any sort, who took off the feedstore overalls and put on a uniform and climbed into an airplane and lit up the skies over Europe.

Yeager grew up in Hamlin, West Virginia, a town on the Mud River not far from Nitro, Hurricane Whirlwind, Salt Rock, Mud, Sod, Crum, Leet, Dollie, Ruth, and Alum Creek. His father was a gas driller (drilling for natural gas in the coalfields), his older brother was a gas driller, and he would have been a gas driller had he not enlisted in the Army Air Force in 1941 at the age of eighteen. In 1943, at twenty he became a flight officer, i.e., a non-com who was allowed to fly, and went to England to fly fighter planes over France and Germany. Even in the tumult of the war Yeager was somewhat puzzling to a lot of other pilots. He was a short, wiry, but muscular little guy with dark curly hair and a tough-looking face that seemed (to strangers) to be saying: "You best not be lookin' me in the eye, you peckerwood, or I'll put four more holes in your nose." But that wasn't what was puzzling. What was puzzling was the way Yeager talked. He seemed to talk with some older forms of English elocution, syntax, and conjugation that had been preserved uphollow in the Appalachians. There were people up there who never said they disapproved of anything, they said: "I don't hold with it." In the present tense they were willing to *help* out, like anyone else; but in the past tense they only *holped*. "H'it weren't nothin' I hold with, but I holped him out with it, anyways."

In his first eight missions, at the age of twenty, Yeager shot down two German fighters. On his ninth he was shot down over German-occupied French territory, suffering flak wounds; he bailed out, was picked up by the French underground, which smuggled him across the Pyrenees into Spain disguised as a peasant. In Spain he was jailed briefly, then released, whereupon he made it back to England and returned to combat during the Allied invasion of France. On October 12, 1944, Yeager took on and shot down five German fighter planes in succession. On November 6, flying a propeller-driven P-51 Mustang, he shot down one of the new jet fighters the Germans had developed, the Messerschmitt-262, and damaged two more, and on November 20 he shot down four FW-190s. It was a true Frank Luke-style display of warrior fury and personal prowess. By the end of the war he had thirteen and a half kills. He was twenty-two years old.

In 1946 and 1947 Yeager was trained as a test pilot at Wright Field in Dayton. He amazed his instructors with his ability at stunt-team flying, not to mention the unofficial business of hassling. That plus his up-hollow drawl had everybody saying, "He's a natural-born stick 'n' rudder man." Nevertheless, there was something extraordinary about it when a man so young, with so little experience in flight test, was selected to go to Muroc Field in California for the X-1 project.

Muroc was up in the high elevations of the Mojave Desert. It looked like some fossil landscape that had long since been left behind by the rest of terrestrial evolution. It was full of huge dry lake beds, the biggest being Rogers Lake. Other than sagebrush the only vegetation was Joshua trees, twisted freaks of the plant world that looked like a cross between cactus and Japanese bonsai. They had a dark petrified green color and horribly crippled branches. At dusk the Joshua trees stood out in silhouette on the fossil wasteland like some arthritic nightmare. In the summer the temperature went up to 110 degrees as a matter of course, and the dry lake beds were covered in sand, and there would be windstorms and sandstorms right out of a Foreign Legion movie. At night it would drop to near freezing, and in December it would start raining, and the dry lakes would fill up with a few inches of water, and some sort of putrid prehistoric shrimps would work their way up from out of the ooze, and sea gulls would come flying in a hundred miles or more from the ocean, over the mountains, to gobble up these squirming little throwbacks. A person had to see it to believe it: flocks of sea gulls wheeling around in the air out in the middle of the high desert in the dead of winter and grazing on antediluvian crustaceans in the primordial ooze.

When the wind blew the few inches of water back and forth across the lake beds, they became absolutely smooth and level. And when the water evaporated in the spring, and the sun baked the ground hard, the lake beds became the greatest natural landing fields ever discovered, and also the biggest, with miles of room for error. That was highly desirable, given the nature of the enterprise at Muroc.

Besides the wind, sand, tumbleweed, and Joshua trees, there was nothing at Muroc except for two quonset-style hangars, side by side, a couple of gasoline pumps, a single concrete runway, a few tarpaper shacks, and some tents. The officers stayed in the shacks marked "barracks," and lesser souls stayed in the tents and froze all night and fried all day. Every road into the property had a guardhouse on it manned by soldiers. The enterprise the Army had undertaken in this godforsaken place was the development of supersonic jet and rocket planes.

At the end of the war the Army had discovered that the Germans not only had the world's first jet fighter but also a rocket plane that had gone 596 miles an hour in tests. Just after the war a British jet, the Gloster Meteor, jumped the official world speed record from 469 to 606 in a single day. The next great plateau would be Mach 1, the speed of sound, and the Army Air Force considered it crucial to achieve it first.

The speed of sound, Mach 1, was known (thanks to the work

of the physicist Ernst Mach) to vary at different altitudes, temperatures, and wind speeds. On a calm 60-degree day at sea level it was about 760 miles an hour, while at 40,000 feet, where the temperature would be at least sixty below, it was about 660 miles an hour. Evil and baffling things happened in the transonic zone, which began at about .7 Mach. Wind tunnels choked out at such velocities. Pilots who approachd the speed of sound in dives reported that the controls would lock or "freeze" or even alter their normal functions. Pilots had crashed and died because they couldn't budge the stick. Just last year Geoffrey de Havilland, son of the famous British aircraft designer and builder, had tried to take one of his father's DH 108s to Mach 1. The ship started buffeting and then disintegrated, and he was killed. This led engineers to speculate that the g-forces became infinite at Mach 1, causing the aircraft to implode. They started talking about "the sonic wall" and "the sound barrier."

So this was the task that a handful of pilots, engineers, and mechanics had at Muroc. The place was utterly primitive, nothing but bare bones, bleached tarpaulins, and corrugated tin rippling in the heat with caloric waves; and for an ambitious young pilot it was perfect. Muroc seemed like an outpost on the dome of the world, open only to a righteous few, closed off to the rest of humanity, including even the Army Air Force brass of command control, which was at Wright Field. The commanding officer at Muroc was only a colonel, and his superiors at Wright did not relish junkets to the Muroc rat shacks in the first place. But to pilots this prehistoric throwback of an airfield became . . . shrimp heaven! the rat-shack plains of Olympus!

Low Rent Septic Tank Perfection . . . yes; and not excluding those traditional essentials for the blissful hot young pilot: Flying & Drinking and Drinking & Driving.

Just beyond the base, to the southwest, there was a rickety wind-blown 1930's style establishment called Pancho's Fly Inn, owned, run, and bartended by a woman named Pancho Barnes. Pancho Barnes wore tight white sweaters and tight pants, after the mode of Barbara Stanwyck in *Double Indemnity*. She was only forty-one when Yeager arrived at Muroc, but her face was so weatherbeaten, had so many hard miles on it, that she looked older, especially to the young pilots at the base. She also shocked the pants off them with her vulcanized tongue. Everybody she didn't like was an old bastard or a sonofabitch. People she liked were old bastards and sonsabitches, too. "I tol' 'at ol' bastard to get 'is ass on over here and I'd g'im a drink." But Pancho Barnes was anything but Low Rent. She was the granddaughter of the man who designed the old Mount Lowe cable-car system, Thaddeus S. C. Lowe. Her maiden name was Florence Leontine Lowe. She was brought up in San Marino, which adjoined Pasadena and was one of Los Angeles' wealthiest suburbs, and her first husband—she was married four times—was the pastor of the Pasadena Episcopal Church, the Rev. C. Rankin Barnes. Mrs. Barnes seemed to have few of the conventional community interests of a Pasadena matron. In the late 1920's, by boat and plane, she ran guns for Mexican revolutionaries and picked up the nickname Pancho. In 1930 she broke Amelia Earhart's airspeed record for women. Then she barnstormed around the country as the featured performer of "Pancho Barnes's Mystery Circus of the Air." She always greeted her public in jodhpurs and riding boots, a flight jacket, a white scarf, and a white sweater that showed off her terrific Barbara Stanwyck chest. Pancho's desert Fly Inn had an airstrip, a swimming pool, a dude ranch corral, plenty of acreage for horseback riding, a big old guest house for the lodgers, and a connecting building that was the bar and restaurant. In the barroom the floors, the tables, the chairs, the walls, the beams, the bar were of the sort known as extremely weather-beaten, and the screen doors kept banging. Nobody putting together such a place for a movie about flying in the old days would ever dare make it as dilapidated and generally go-to-hell as it actually was. Behind the bar were many pictures of airplanes and pilots, lavishly autographed and inscribed, badly framed and crookedly hung. There was an old piano that had been dried out and cracked to the point of hopeless desiccation. On a good night a huddle of drunken aviators could be heard trying to bang, slosh, and navigate their way through old Cole Porter tunes. On average nights the tunes were not that good to start with. When the screen door banged and a man walked through the door into the saloon, every eye in the place checked him out. If he wasn't known as somebody who had something to do with flying at Muroc, he would be eyed like some lame goddamned mouseshit sheepherder from *Shane*.

The plane the Air Force wanted to break the sound barrier with was called the X-1. The Bell Aircraft Corporation had built it under an Army contract. The core of the ship was a rocket of the type first developed by a young Navy inventor, Robert Truax, during the war. The fuselage was shaped like a 50-caliber bullet—an object that was known to go supersonic smoothly. Military pilots seldom drew major test assignments; they went to highly paid civilians working for the aircraft corporations. The prime pilot for the X-1 was a man whom Bell regarded as the best of the breed. This man looked like a movie star. He looked like a pilot from out of *Hell's Angels*. And on top of everything else there was his name: Slick Goodlin.

The idea in testing the X-1 was to nurse it carefully into the transonic zone, up to seven-tenths, eight-tenths, nine-tenths the speed of sound (.7 Mach, .8 Mach, .9 Mach) before attempting the speed of sound itself, Mach 1, even though Bell and the Army already knew the X-1 had the rocket power to go to Mach 1 and beyond, if there *was* any *beyond*. The consensus of aviators and engineers, after Geoffrey de Havilland's death, was that the speed of sound was an absolute, like the firmness of the earth. The sound barrier was a farm you could buy in the sky. So Slick Goodlin began to probe the transonic zone in the X-1, going up to .8 Mach. Every time he came down he'd have a riveting tale to tell. The buffeting, it was so fierce—and the listeners, their imaginations aflame, could practically see poor Geoffrey de Havilland disintegrating in midair. And the goddammned aerodynamics—and the listeners got a picture of a man in ballroom pumps skidding across a sheet of ice, pursued by bears. A controversy arose over just how much bonus Slick Goodlin should receive for assaulting the dread Mach 1 itself. Bonuses for contract test pilots were not unusual; but the figure of $150,000 was now bruited about. The army balked, and Yeager got the job. He took it for $283 a month, or $3,396 a year; which is to say, his regular Army captain's pay.

The only trouble they had with Yeager was in holding him back. On his first powered flight in the X-1 he immediately executed an unauthorized zero-g roll with a full load of rocket fuel, then stood the ship on its tail and went up to .85 Mach in a vertical climb, also unauthorized. On subsequent flights, at speeds between .85 Mach and .9 Mach, Yeager ran into most known airfoil problems—loss of elevator, aileron, and rudder control, heavy trim pressures, Dutch rolls, pitching and buffeting, the lot—yet was convinced, after edging over .9 Mach, that this would all get better, not worse, as you reached Mach 1. The attempt to push beyond Mach 1—"breaking the sound barrier"—was set for October 14, 1947. Not being an engineer, Yeager didn't believe the "barrier" existed.

Discussion Questions

1. Why does Wolfe begin his essay with an account of the typical airline pilot's voice? How does it help describe Yeager? Why have pilots adopted this manner and tone of voice?
2. What is the purpose of introducing Pancho Barnes into Yeager's story? What does she add to the story? How is *her* voice characterized?
3. What is the "right stuff"? Why does Yeager have it? Does Pancho Barnes have it? Does Slick Goodlin? Explain why or why not.
4. Compare Wolfe's essay to Gay Talese's "Punks and Pushers." In what way does a sense of the "right stuff" function in Talese's piece? How does each writer translate the "right stuff" into a quality of voice?
5. Think of someone you know who has the "right stuff." In a short essay, describe that person's looks, style, voice, and achievement in a way that *shows* your reader—not just tells—what *you* think the "right stuff" is.

Virginia Woolf

The highly influential English novelist, essayist, and critic Virginia Woolf (1882–1941) was born in London, the daughter of a prominent scholar, Sir Leslie Stephen, who took charge of her education. In 1912, she married Leonard Woolf, a social critic, and together they started a printing press and became the center of a group of writers, intellectuals, and artists known as the Bloomsbury Group. Her first novels did not satisfy her desire for experimentation and originality, and it was not until Jacob's Room *(1922) that she was able to stress the interaction of time and consciousness within individual lives that became the distinctive theme of her four major novels,* Mrs. Dalloway *(1925),* To the Lighthouse *(1927),* Orlando *(1928), and* The Waves *(1931).*

A perceptive reader, Woolf wrote widely on books and writers; her critical and literary essays are collected in The Common Reader *(1925),* The Common Reader: Second Series *(1932), and* Granite and Rainbow *(1958). The following selection is the title piece of one of her best known essay collections,* The Death of the Moth *(1942).*

The Death of the Moth

    Moths that fly by day are not properly to be called moths; they do not excite that pleasant sense of dark autumn nights and ivy-blossom which the commonest yellow-underwing asleep in the shadow of the curtain never fails to rouse in us. They are hybrid creatures, neither gay like butterflies nor sombre like their own species. Nevertheless the present specimen, with his narrow hay-coloured wings, fringed wih a tassel of the same colour, seemed to be content with life. It was a pleasant morning, mid-September, mild, benignant, yet with a keener breath than that of the summer months. The plough was already scoring the field opposite the window, and where the share had been, the earth was pressed flat and gleamed with moisture. Such vigour came rolling in from the fields and then down beyond that it was difficult to keep the eyes strictly turned upon the book. The rooks too were keeping one of their annual festivities; soaring round the tree tops until it looked as if a vast net with thousands of black knots in it had been cast up into the air; which, after a few moments sank slowly down upon the trees until every twig seemed to have a knot at the end of it. Then, suddenly, the net would be thrown into the air again in a wider circle this time, with the utmost clamour and vociferation, as though to be thrown into the air and settle slowly down upon the tree tops were a tremendously exciting experience.
    The same energy which inspired the rooks, the ploughmen, the horses, and even, it seemed, the lean bare-backed downs, sent the moth fluttering from side to side of his square of the window pane. One could not help watching him. One was, indeed, conscious of a queer feeling of pity for him. The possibilities of pleasure seemed that morning so enormous and so various that to have only a moth's part in life, and a day moth's at that, appeared a hard

fate, and his zest in enjoying his meagre opportunities to the full, pathetic. He flew vigorously to one corner of his compartment, and, after waiting there a second, flew across to the other. What remained for him but to fly to a third corner and then to a fourth? That was all he could do, in spite of the size of the downs, the width of the sky, the far-off smoke of houses, and the romantic voice, now and then, of a steamer out at sea. What he could do he did. Watching him, it seemed as if a fibre, very thin but pure, of the enormous energy of the world had been thrust into his frail and diminutive body. As often as he crossed the pane, I could fancy that a thread of vital light became visible. He was little or nothing but life.

Yet, because he was so small, and so simple a form of the energy that was rolling in at the open window and driving its way through so many narrow and intricate corridors in my own brain and in those of other human beings, there was something marvelous as well as pathetic about him. It was as if someone had taken a tiny bead of pure life and decking it as lightly as possible with down and feathers, had set it dancing and zigzagging to show us the true nature of life. Thus displayed one could not get over the strangeness of it. One is apt to forget all about life, seeing it humped and bossed and garnished and cumbered so that it has to move with the greatest circumspection and dignity. Again, the thought of all that life might have been had he been born in any other shape caused one to view his simple activities with a kind of pity.

After a time, tired by his dancing apparently, he settled on the window ledge in the sun, and, the queer spectacle being at an end, I forgot about him. Then, looking up, my eye was caught by him. He was trying to resume his dancing, but seemed either so stiff or so awkward that he could only flutter to the bottom of the windowpane; and when he tried to fly across it he failed. Being intent on other matters I watched these futile attempts for a time without thinking, unconsciously waiting for him to resume his flight, as one waits for a machine, that has stopped momentarily, to start again without considering the reason of its failure. After perhaps a seventh attempt he slipped from the wooden ledge and fell, fluttering his wings, on to his back on the window sill. The helplessness of his attitude roused me. It flashed upon me that he was in difficulties; he could no longer raise himself; his legs struggled vainly. But, as I stretched out a pencil, meaning to help him to right himself, it came over me that the failure and awkwardness were the approach of death. I laid the pencil down again.

The legs agitated themselves once more. I looked as if for the enemy against which he struggled. I looked out of doors. What had happened there? Presumably it was midday, and work in the fields had stopped. Stillness and quiet had replaced the previous animation. The birds had taken themselves off to feed in the brooks. The horses stood still. Yet the power was there all the same, massed outside indifferent, impersonal, not attending to anything in particular. Somehow it was opposed to the little hay-coloured moth. It was useless to try to do anything. One could only watch the extraordinary efforts made by those tiny legs against an oncoming doom which could, had it chosen, have submerged an entire city, not merely a city, but masses of human beings; nothing, I knew, had any chance against death. Nevertheless after a pause of exhaustion the legs fluttered again. It was superb this last protest, and so frantic that he succeeded at last in righting himself. One's sympathies, of course, were all on the side of life. Also, when there was nobody to care or to know, this gigantic effort on the part of an insignificant little moth, against a power of such magnitude, to retain what no one else valued or desired to keep, moved one strangely. Again, somehow, one saw life, a pure bead. I lifted the pencil again, useless though I knew it to be. But even as I did so, the unmistakable tokens of death showed themselves. The body relaxed, and instantly grew stiff. The struggle was over. The insignificant little creature now knew death. As I looked at the dead moth, this minute wayside triumph of so great a force over so mean an antagonist filled me with wonder. Just as life had been strange a few minutes before, so death was now as strange. The moth having righted himself now lay most decently and uncomplainingly composed. O yes, he seemed to say, death is stronger than I am.

Discussion Questions

1. How does the description of the moth at the beginning of the essay differ from its description at the end? What is the significance of that difference?

2. What connections does Virginia Woolf make between what is happening to the moth and what is happening outside the window? Why are these connections important to her essay?

3. Compare this essay to E. B. White's "The Death of a Pig." Which writer has the greater tendency to internalize the experiences of a

dying creature? Which writer seems more emotionally affected? How does each writer try to avoid the pitfalls of sentimentality? Do you think they succeed at doing so?

4. What is meant by the sentence, "He was little or nothing but life"? Write an essay in which you describe how "life" is given concrete embodiment throughout the essay. Consider the connection Virginia Woolf establishes between life and the outside world. What is the author's connection with this world? Do you see any significance in the detail of the pencil?

RICHARD WRIGHT

Richard Wright (1909–1960) was born into an impoverished black sharecropper family near Natchez, Mississippi. He grew up in Memphis and after working at several menial jobs, left for Chicago, only to find more menial work. Though his sporadic formal education ended with the ninth grade, he managed to educate himself through a disciplined program of reading ("it had been only through books . . . that I had managed to keep myself alive"). After working with the Federal Writer's Project in Chicago, Wright moved to New York City, where he wrote for the Daily Worker *and prepared the government-sponsored* Guide to Harlem *(1937).*

Wright's first published book was a series of novellas, Uncle Tom's Children *(1938), which he followed with the novel that permanently established his reputation,* Native Son *(1940), and then with his internationally successful autobiography,* Black Boy *(1945), from which the following episode is reprinted. In the 1930's Wright had joined the Communist party, but by 1942 had abandoned it and by 1947, when he moved to France, had become a vehement anti-communist. His later works include several collections of political essays and travel books:* Black Power *(1954),* The Color Curtain *(1956), and* White Man, Listen! *(1957).*

Innocence

In Memphis we lived in a one-story brick tenement. The stone buildings and the concrete pavements looked bleak and hostile to me. The absence of green, growing things made the city seem dead. Living space for the four of us—my mother, my brother, my father, and me—was a kitchen and a bedroom. In the front and rear were paved areas in which my brother and I could play, but for days I was afraid to go into the strange city streets alone.

It was in this tenement that the personality of my father first came fully into the orbit of my concern. He worked as a night porter in a Beale Street drugstore and he became important and forbidding to me only when I learned that I could not make noise when he was asleep in the daytime. He was the lawgiver in our family and I never laughed in his presence. I used to lurk timidly in the kitchen doorway and watch his huge body sitting slumped at the table. I stared at him with awe as he gulped his beer from a tin bucket, as he ate long and heavily, sighed, belched, closed his eyes to nod on a stuffed belly. He was quite fat and his bloated stomach always lapped over his belt. He was always a stranger to me, always somehow alien and remote.

One morning my brother and I, while playing in the rear of our flat, found a stray kitten that set up a loud, persistent meowing. We fed it some scraps of food and gave it water, but it still meowed. My father, clad in his underwear, stumbled sleepily to the back door and demanded that we keep quiet. We told him that it was the kitten that was making the noise and he ordered us to drive it away. We tried to make the kitten leave, but it would not budge. My father took a hand.

"Scat!" he shouted.

The scrawny kitten lingered, brushing itself against our legs, and meowing plaintively.

"Kill that damn thing!" my father exploded. "Do anything, but get it away from here!"

He went inside, grumbling. I resented his shouting and it irked me that I could never make him feel my resentment. How could I hit back at him? Oh, yes . . . He had said to kill the kitten and I would kill it! I knew that he had not really meant for me to kill the kitten, but my deep hate of him urged me toward a literal acceptance of his word.

"He said for us to kill the kitten," I told my brother.

"He didn't mean it," my brother said.

"He did, and I'm going to kill 'im."

"Then he *will* howl," my brother said.

"He can't howl if he's dead," I said.

"He didn't really say kill 'im," my brother potested.

"He did!" I said. "And you heard him!"

My brother ran away in fright. I found a piece of rope, made a noose, slipped it about the kitten's neck, pulled it over a nail, then jerked the animal clear of the ground. It gasped, slobbered, spun, doubled, clawed the air frantically; finally its mouth gaped and its pink-white tongue shot out stiffly. I tied the rope to a nail and went to find my brother. He was crouching behind a corner of the building.

"I killed 'im," I whispered.

"You did bad," my brother said.

"Now Papa can sleep," I said, deeply satisfied.

"He didn't mean for you to kill 'im," my brother said.

"Then why did he *tell* me to do it?" I demanded.

My brother could not answer; he stared fearfully at the dangling kitten.

"That kitten's going to get you," he warned me.

"That kitten can't even breathe now," I said.

"I'm going to tell," my brother said, running into the house.

I waited, resolving to defend myself with my father's rash words, anticipating my enjoyment in repeating them to him even though I knew that he had spoken them in anger. My mother hurried toward me, drying her hands upon her apron. She stopped and paled when she saw the kitten suspended from the rope.

"What in God's name have you done?" she asked.

"The kitten was making noise and Papa said to kill it," I explained.

"You little fool!" she said. "Your father's going to beat you for this!"

"But he told me to kill it," I said.

"You shut your mouth!"

She grabbed my hand and dragged me to my father's bedside and told him what I had done.

"You know better than that!" my father stormed.

"You told me to kill 'im," I said.

"I told you to drive him away," he said.

"You told me to kill 'im," I countered positively.

"You get out of my eyes before I smack you down!" my father bellowed in disgust, then turned over in bed.

I had had my first triumph over my father. I had made him believe that I had taken his words literally. He could not punish me now without risking his authority. I was happy because I had at last found a way to throw my criticism of him into his face. I had made him feel that, if he whipped me for killing the kitten, I would never give serious weight to his words again. I had made him know that I felt he was cruel and I had done it without his punishing me.

But my mother, being more imaginative, retaliated with an assault upon my sensibilities that crushed me with the moral horror involved in taking a life. All that afternoon she directed toward me calculated words that spawned in my mind a horde of invisible demons bent upon exacting vengeance for what I had done. As evening drew near, anxiety filled me and I was afraid to go into an empty room alone.

"You owe a debt you can never pay," my mother said.

"I'm sorry," I mumbled.

"Being sorry can't make that kitten live again," she said.

Then, just before I was to go to bed, she uttered a paralyzing injunction: she ordered me to go out into the dark, dig a grave, and bury the kitten.

"No!" I screamed, feeling that if I went out of doors some evil spirit would whisk me away.

"Get out there and bury that poor kitten," she ordered.

"I'm scared!"

"And wasn't that kitten scared when you put that rope around its neck?" she asked.

"But it was only a kitten," I explained.

"But it was alive," she said. "Can you make it live again?"

"But Papa said to kill it," I said, trying to shift the moral blame upon my father.

My mother whacked me across my mouth with the flat palm of her hand.

"You stop that lying! You knew what he meant!"

"I didn't!" I bawled.

She shoved a tiny spade into my hands.

"Go out there and dig a hole and bury that kitten!"

I stumbled out into the black night, sobbing, my legs wobbly from fear. Though I knew that I had killed the kitten, my mother's words had made it live again in my mind. What would that kitten do to me when I touched it? Would it claw at my eyes? As I groped toward the dead kitten, my mother lingered behind me, unseen in the dark, her disembodied voice egging me on.

"Mama, come and stand by me," I begged.

"You didn't stand by that kitten, so why should I stand by you?" she asked tauntingly from the menacing darkness.

"I can't touch it," I whimpered, feeling that the kitten staring at me with reproachful eyes.

"Untie it!" she ordered.

Shuddering, I fumbled at the rope and the kitten dropped to the pavement with a thud that echoed in my mind for many days and nights. Then, obeying my mother's floating voice, I hunted for a spot of earth, dug a shallow hole, and buried the stiff kitten; as I handled its cold body my skin prickled. When I had completed the burial, I sighed and started back to the flat, but my mother caught hold of my hand and led me again to the kitten's grave.

"Shut your eyes and repeat after me," she said.

I closed my eyes tightly, my hand clinging to hers.

"Dear God, our Father, forgive me, for I knew not what I was doing . . ."

"Dear God, our Father, forgive me, for I knew not what I was doing," I repeated.

"And spare my poor life, even though I did not spare the life of the kitten . . ."

"And spare my poor life, even though I did not spare the life of the kitten," I repeated.

"And while I sleep tonight, do not snatch the breath of life from me . . ."

I opened my mouth but no words came. My mind was frozen with horror. I pictured myself gasping for breath and dying in my sleep. I broke away from my mother and ran into the night, crying, shaking with dread.

"No," I sobbed.

My mother called to me many times, but I would not go to her.

"Well, I suppose you've learned your lesson," she said at last.

Contrite, I went to bed, hoping that I would never see another kitten.

Discussion Questions

1. Why does Wright kill the kitten? How does he excuse his behavior? Do you find his argument convincing?

2. After he kills the kitten, how does Wright talk to his brother, father, and mother? How are these conversations similar? What effect does this repetition have on the reader?

3. How does Wright's mother react to the death of the kitten? Why doesn't she take seriously his argument that he was told to kill it? Why can't Wright get away with his excuse that he was simply doing what he was told? Who is correct, Wright or his mother? Explain.

4. Compare Wright's treatment of the theme of "lying" to Langston Hughes's in "Salvation" and Graham Greene's in "The Revolver in the Corner Cupboard."

5. How does this episode in Wright's life refer to a larger issue than a dead kitten? Using Wright's account as an example, relate an incident from your own past in which you tried to duck moral responsibility.

DISCIPLINES AND THEMES

I. HUMANITIES

Literature

Jorge Luis Borges	The Disinterested Killer Bill Harrigan	78
Ralph Ellison	Hidden Name and Complex Fate	188
Sigmund Freud	The Relation of the Poet to Day-Dreaming	218
Robert Frost	Education By Poetry	238
Northrup Frye	The Keys to Dreamland	250
Paul Fussell	The Boy Scout Handbook	261
Martin Gardner	The Harvard Man Who Put the Ease in Casey's Manner	268
Randall Jarrell	The Taste of the Age	354
Samuel Eliot Morison	History as a Literary Art	501
Eudora Welty	A Sweet Devouring	663
Edith Wharton	Henry James Asks Directions	676
E. B. White	The Essayist	690
Edmund Wilson	The Problem of English	693

Language

Russell Baker	Little Red Riding Hood Revisited	34
James Baldwin	If Black English Isn't a Language, Then Tell Me, What Is?	38
Daniel Boorstin	The Rhetoric of Democracy	66
Sigmund Freud	The Relation of the Poet to Day-Dreaming	218
Erich Fromm	The Nature of Symbolic Language	228
Robert Frost	Education By Poetry	238
Northrup Frye	The Keys to Dreamland	250
Paul Fussell	The Boy Scout Handbook	261
Martin Gardner	The Harvard Man Who Put the Ease in Casey's Manner	268
S. I. Hayakawa	How Dictionaries Are Made	304
George Orwell	Politics and the English Language	553

Lillian Ross	*The Vinyl Santa*	594
Logan Pearsall Smith	*Words from the Sea*	605
Lewis Thomas	*Notes on Punctuation*	623
John Updike	*Crush Vs. Whip*	646
Edmund Wilson	*The Problem of English*	693

Autobiography and Biography

James Agee	*Knoxville: Summer 1915*	1
Jorge Luis Borges	*The Disinterested Killer Bill Harrigan*	78
Gwendolyn Brooks	*Dreams of a Black Christmas*	87
Robert Coles	*Children of Affluence*	119
Guy Davenport	*Finding*	138
Joan Didion	*On Keeping a Notebook*	149
Ralph Ellison	*Hidden Name and Complex Fate*	188
M. F. K. Fisher	*Young Hunger*	208
Martin Gardner	*The Harvard Man Who Put the Ease in Casey's Manner*	268
Graham Greene	*The Revolver in the Corner Cupboard*	298
Lillian Hellman	*The Fig Tree*	308
Langston Hughes	*Salvation*	324
C. G. Jung	*A Vision of Life After Death*	365
D. H. Lawrence	*Rex*	389
Basil Liddell Hart	*William Tecumseh Sherman: The First Modern General*	417
Norman Mailer	*Marilyn Monroe*	444
William Manchester	*How I Slew My First Man*	449
Mary McCarthy	*Catholic Education*	455
John Muir	*Digging a Well*	512
Vladimir Nabokov	*Colored Hearing*	522
George Orwell	*Shooting an Elephant*	540
	A Hanging	548
James Thurber	*University Days*	626
Eudora Welty	*A Sweet Devouring*	663
Edith Wharton	*Henry James Asks Directions*	676
E. B. White	*Death of a Pig*	680
Tom Wolfe	*The Right Stuff*	701
Virginia Woolf	*The Death of the Moth*	710
Richard Wright	*Innocence*	715

History

Frederick Lewis Allen	*Main Street America–1900*	7
Hannah Arendt	*Denmark and the Jews*	14
Isaac Asimov	*Pure and Impure: The Interplay of Science and Technology*	26
W. E. B. DuBois	*Jacob and Esau*	169
Paul Fussell	*The Boy Scout Handbook*	261
Randall Jarrell	*The Taste of the Age*	354
Pauline Kael	*Movies on Television*	370
Basil Liddell Hart	*William Tecumseh Sherman: The First Modern General*	417

Jack London	*The Carter and the Carpenter*	434
William Manchester	*How I Slew My First Man*	449
Samuel Eliot Morison	*History as a Literary Art*	501
Lewis Mumford	*Sport and the "Bitch-Goddess"*	516
J. H. Plumb	*The Stars in Their Day*	576
Katherine Anne Porter	*The Future Is Now*	581
Barbara Tuchman	*This is the End of the World: The Black Death*	633
H. G. Wells	*Ellis Island*	659
Tom Wolfe	*The Right Stuff*	701

Philosophy

William James	*Habit*	340
H. L. Mencken	*Criminology*	482
José Ortega y Gasset	*Emotional Reality*	535
Katherine Anne Porter	*The Future Is Now*	581
J. B. Priestly	*Block Thinking*	588
Bertrand Russell	*Education and Discipline*	598

Religion

Gwendolyn Brooks	*Dreams of a Black Christmas*	87
Langston Hughes	*Salvation*	324
Elizabeth Janeway	*Water*	348
C. G. Jung	*A Vision of Life After Death*	365
C. S. Lewis	*The Trouble with "X". . . .*	407
Mary McCarthy	*Catholic Education*	455
V. S. Naipaul	*The New Tehran*	527
Evelyn Waugh	*Half in Love with Easeful Death*	650
Richard Wright	*Innocence*	715

Fine Arts and Architecture

Simone de Beauvoir	*Knowing New York*	52
G. K. Chesterton	*On Sightseeing*	114
Aaron Copland	*How We Listen to Music*	131
Joan Didion	*On the Mall*	149
Aldous Huxley	*Selected Snobberies*	328
Ada Louise Huxtable	*Houston*	333
John McPhee	*The Search for Marvin Gardens*	463
Gay Talese	*Punks and Pushers*	614
Evelyn Waugh	*Half in Love with Easeful Death*	650
Paul West	*The VAB Beside the Sea*	670

II. Social Sciences

Psychology

Bruno Bettelheim	*Joey, A Mechanical Boy*	56
Nigel Calder	*The Comet Is Coming*	96
Robert Coles	*Children of Affluence*	119
M. F. K. Fisher	*Young Hunger*	208
Sigmund Freud	*The Relation of the Poet to Day-Dreaming*	218
Erich Fromm	*The Nature of Symbolic Language*	228

William Golding	*Thinking as a Hobby*	277
Stephen Jay Gould	*A Biographical Homage to Mickey Mouse*	286
Graham Greene	*The Revolver in the Corner Cupboard*	298
William James	*Habit*	340
C. G. Jung	*A Vision of Life After Death*	365
C. S. Lewis	*The Trouble with "X"...*	407
Wyndham Lewis	*The Secret of the Success of Charlie Chaplin*	413
William Manchester	*How I Slew My First Man*	449
Vladimir Nabokov	*Colored Hearing*	522
José Ortega y Gasset	*Emotional Reality*	535
S. J. Perelman	*Dental or Mental, I Say It's Spinach*	571
J. B. Priestly	*Block Thinking*	588

Sociology

Michael Arlen	*Ode to Thanksgiving*	21
Gwendolyn Brooks	*Dreams of a Black Christmas*	87
Willa Cather	*Small-Town Life*	110
W. E. B. DuBois	*Jacob and Esau*	169
Paul Fussell	*The Boy Scout Handbook*	261
Aldous Huxley	*Selected Snobberies*	328
Ada Louise Huxtable	*Houston*	333
Helen Lawrenson	*The Bulls of Pamplona vs. the Ivy League*	398
Wyndham Lewis	*The Secret of the Success of Charlie Chaplin*	413
Jack London	*The Carter and the Carpenter*	434
John McPhee	*The Search for Marvin Gardens*	463
H. L. Mencken	*Criminology*	482
Ashley Montague	*Social Change and Human Change*	494
Dorothy Parker	*Mrs. Post Enlarges on Etiquette*	566
Lillian Ross	*The Vinyl Santa*	594
Gay Talese	*Punks and Pushers*	614
Evelyn Waugh	*Half in Love with Easeful Death*	650
H. G. Wells	*Ellis Island*	659

Anthropology

Guy Davenport	*Finding*	138
Margaret Mead	*New Superstitions for Old*	476
Jessica Mitford	*On Embalming*	487
Ashley Montague	*Social Change and Human Change*	494
Lewis Mumford	*Sport and the "Bitch-Goddess"*	516
J. H. Plumb	*The Stars in Their Day*	576
Evelyn Waugh	*Half in Love with Easeful Death*	650

Political Science

Hannah Arendt	*Denmark and the Jews*	14
Daniel Boorstin	*The Rhetoric of Democracy*	66
E. M. Forster	*Racial Exercise*	213
Walter Lippmann	*The Indispensable Opposition*	425

Jack London	*The Carter and the Carpenter*	434
V. S. Naipaul	*The New Tehran*	527
George Orwell	*Shooting an Elephant*	540
	A Hanging	548
	Politics and the English Language	553

Education

Jacques Barzun	*The Wasteland of American Education*	43
Robert Frost	*Education By Poetry*	238
S. I. Hayakawa	*How Dictionaries Are Made*	304
Randall Jarrell	*The Taste of the Age*	354
Pauline Kael	*Movies on Television*	370
Mary McCarthy	*Catholic Education*	455
Marshall McLuhan	*Classroom Without Walls*	459
Ashley Montague	*Social Change and Human Change*	494
Samuel Eliot Morison	*History as a Literary Art*	501
Bertrand Russell	*Education and Discipline*	598
James Thurber	*University Days*	626
Edmund Wilson	*The Problem of English*	693

Business and Economics

Daniel Boorstin	*The Rhetoric of Democracy*	66
Robert Coles	*Children of Affluence*	119
Joan Didion	*On the Mall*	149
W. E. B. DuBois	*Jacob and Esau*	169
Pauline Kael	*Movies on Television*	370
John McPhee	*The Search for Marvin Gardens*	463
Jessica Mitford	*On Embalming*	487
Lewis Mumford	*Sport and the "Bitch-Goddess"*	516

III. SCIENCE

Physical Sciences

Isaac Asimov	*Pure and Impure: The Interplay of Science and Technology*	26
Jacob Bronowski	*Likenesses*	84
Nigel Calder	*The Comet Is Coming*	96
Annie Dillard	*Mirages*	164
Sir James Jeans	*Why the Sky Looks Blue*	362
J. H. Plumb	*The Stars in Their Day*	576

Technology

Isaac Asimov	*Pure and Impure: The Interplay of Science and Technology*	26
Nigel Calder	*The Comet Is Coming*	96
Marshall McLuhan	*Classroom Without Walls*	459
Lewis Mumford	*Sport and the "Bitch-Goddess"*	516
Katherine Anne Porter	*The Future Is Now*	581
Gay Talese	*Punks and Pushers*	614
Paul West	*The VAB Beside the Sea*	670
Tom Wolfe	*The Right Stuff*	701

726   DISCIPLINES AND THEMES

Life Sciences

Rachel Carson	*The Changing Year*	101
René Dubos	*Territoriality and Dominance*	181
Stephen Jay Gould	*A Biographical Homage to Mickey Mouse*	286
Edward Hoagland	*The Courage of Turtles*	316
Elizabeth Janeway	*Water*	348
Rudyard Kipling	*A Snake Farm*	382
Ashley Montague	*Social Change and Human Change*	494
Barbara Tuchman	*This is the End of the World: The Black Death*	635

IV. POPULAR CULTURE

Media

Michael Arlen	*Ode to Thanksgiving*	21
Daniel Boorstin	*The Rhetoric of Democracy*	66
Nora Ephron	*The Boston Photographs*	199
Stephen Jay Gould	*A Biographical Homage to Mickey Mouse*	286
Randall Jarrell	*The Taste of the Age*	354
Pauline Kael	*Movies on Television*	370
Wyndham Lewis	*The Secret of the Success of Charlie Chaplin*	413
Norman Mailer	*Marilyn Monroe*	444
Marshall McLuhan	*Classroom Without Walls*	459
Susan Sontag	*Science Fiction Films: The Imagination of Disaster*	609

Travel

Simone de Beauvoir	*Knowing New York*	52
G. K. Chesterton	*On Sightseeing*	114
Ernest Hemingway	*The Clark's Fork Valley, Wyoming*	312
Rudyard Kipling	*A Snake Farm*	382
Helen Lawrenson	*The Bulls of Pamplona vs. the Ivy League*	398
V. S. Naipaul	*The New Tehran*	527
H. G. Wells	*Ellis Island*	659

Humor

Michael Arlen	*Ode to Thanksgiving*	21
Russell Baker	*Little Red Riding Hood Revisited*	34
Martin Gardner	*The Harvard Man Who Put the Ease in Casey's Manner*	268
Helen Lawrenson	*The Bulls of Pamplona vs. the Ivy League*	398
Dorothy Parker	*Mrs. Post Enlarges on Etiquette*	566
S. J. Perelman	*Dental or Mental, I Say It's Spinach*	571
Lillian Ross	*The Vinyl Santa*	594
Lewis Thomas	*Notes on Punctuation*	621
James Thurber	*University Days*	626
John Updike	*Crush Vs. Whip*	646

DISCIPLINES AND THEMES

| Evelyn Waugh | Half in Love with Easeful Death | 650 |
| Edith Wharton | Henry James Asks Directions | 676 |

Americana

Frederick Lewis Allen	Main Street America–1900	7
Michael Arlen	Ode to Thanksgiving	21
Jorge Luis Borges	The Disinterested Killer Bill Harrigan	78
Gwendolyn Brooks	Dreams of a Black Christmas	87
Willa Cather	Small-Town Life	110
Joan Didion	On the Mall	149
Paul Fussell	The Boy Scout Handbook	261
Martin Gardner	The Harvard Man Who Put the Ease in Casey's Manner	268
Ada Louise Huxtable	Houston	333
Randall Jarrell	The Taste of the Age	354
Pauline Kael	Movies on Television	370
Norman Mailer	Marilyn Monroe	444
John McPhee	The Search for Marvin Gardens	463
Jessica Mitford	On Embalming	487
Dorothy Parker	Mrs. Post Enlarges on Etiquette	566
Lillian Ross	The Vinyl Santa	594
Evelyn Waugh	Half in Love with Easeful Death	650
H. G. Wells	Ellis Island	659
Paul West	The VAB Beside the Sea	670
Tom Wolfe	The Right Stuff	701

Sports

Roger Angell	On the Ball	11
Martin Gardner	The Harvard Man Who Put the Ease in Casey's Manner	268
Ernest Hemingway	The Clark's Fork Valley, Wyoming	312
Helen Lawrenson	The Bulls of Pamplona vs. the Ivy League	398
Lewis Mumford	Sport and the "Bitch-Goddess"	516
John Updike	Crush Vs. Whip	646

ACKNOWLEDGMENTS

(The Acknowledgments are continued from page ii.)

Two drawings in "University Days," reproduced by permission of Mrs. Helen Thurber. Copyright © 1933, 1961 James Thurber. From *My Life and Hard Times*, published by Harper & Row.

James Agee, "Knoxville: Summer 1915," from *A Death in the Family*. by James Agee, copyright © 1957 by The James Agee Trust. Used by permission of Grosset & Dunlap, Inc.

Frederick Lewis Allen, "Main Street America—1900." Section II of Chapter 1, "A New Century Begins," pages 6–8 from *The Big Change America Transforms Itself 1900–1950* by Frederick Lewis Allen. Copyright, 1952, by Frederick Lewis Allen. By permission of Harper & Row, Publishers, Inc.

Roger Angell, "On the Ball." From *Five Seasons, A Baseball Companion*. Copyright © 1972, 1973, 1974, 1975 by Roger Angell. Reprinted by permission of Simon & Schuster, a Division of Gulf & Western Corporation.

Hannah Arendt, "Denmark and the Jews," A selection from *Eichmann in Jerusalem* by Hannah Arendt. Copyright © 1963, 1964 by Hannah Arendt. This selection appeared originally in *The New Yorker* in slightly different form. Reprinted with permission of Viking Penguin Inc.

Michael Arlen, "Ode to Thanksgiving," from *The Camera Age* by Michael J. Arlen. Copyright © 1978, 1981 by Michael J. Arlen. Reprinted by permission of Farrar, Straus, and Giroux.

Isaac Asimov, "Pure and Impure: The Interplay of Science and Technology." Reprinted by permission of the author. © 1979 by Saturday Review Magazine Corp.

Russell Baker, "Little Red Riding Hood Revisited." © 1979 by The New York Times Company. Reprinted by permission.

James Baldwin, "If Black English Isn't a Language, Then Tell Me, What Is?" © 1979 by The New York Times Company. Reprinted by permission.

Jacques Barzun, "The Wasteland of American Education." Reprinted by permission of the author. Appears in slightly different form as preface to *Teacher in*

ACKNOWLEDGMENTS

America, republished by Liberty Press/Library Classics of Indianapolis. © 1980 by Jacques Barzun.

Simone de Beauvoir, "Knowing New York." From *America Day by Day,* Grove Press. Copyright © 1953 by Grove Press. Reprinted by permission of the author and the author's agent.

Bruno Bettelheim, "Joey, A Mechanical Boy." Reprinted with permission. Copyright © 1959 by Scientific American, Inc. All rights reserved.

Daniel Boorstin, "The Rhetoric of Democracy." From *Democracy and Its Discontents* by Daniel Boorstin. Copyright © 1974 by Daniel Boorstin. Reprinted by permission of Random House, Inc.

Jorge Luis Borges, "The Disinterested Killer Bill Harrigan." From *A Universal History of Infamy* by Jorge Luis Borges. Translated by Norman Thomas di Giovanni. Copyright © 1970, 1971, 1972 by Emece Editores, S. A. and Norman Thomas di Giovanni. Reprinted by permission of the publisher, E. P. Dutton, Inc.

Jacob Bronowski, "Likenesses." From *What is Science?* James R. Newman, Editor. Copyright © 1955 by James R. Newman. Reprinted by permission of Simon & Schuster, a Division of Gulf & Western Corporation.

Gwendolyn Brooks, "Dreams of a Black Christmas." Reprinted from *Report From Part One.* Copyright © by Gwendolyn Blakely, 1972. Reprinted by permission of Broadside Press.

Nigel Calder, "The Comet Is Coming." From *The Comet is Coming.* Copyright © 1980 by Nigel Calder. Reprinted with permission of Viking Penguin Inc.

Rachel Carson, "The Changing Year." From *The Sea Around Us* by Rachel Carson. Copyright © 1950, 1951, 1961 by Rachel L. Carson; renewed 1978 by Roger Christie. Reprinted by permission of Oxford University Press, Inc.

Willa Cather, "Small-Town Life." From *The World and the Parish,* Vol. II by Willa Cather, edited by William M. Curtin, published by the University of Nebraska Press.

G. K. Chesterton, "On Sightseeing," from *All is Grist.* Reprinted by permission of Miss D. E. Collins.

Robert Coles, "Children of Affluence," from *Privileged Ones: Volume V of Children of Crisis* by Robert Coles. Copyright © 1977 by Robert Coles. By permission of Little, Brown and Company in association with the Atlantic Monthly Press.

Aaron Copland, "How We Listen to Music," from *What to Listen for in Music,* by Aaron Copland. Reprinted with permission of McGraw-Hill Book Company. Copyright 1957.

Guy Davenport, "Finding," *The Geography of the Imagination.* Reprinted with permission of North Point Press. Copyright 1981 by Guy Davenport.

Joan Didion, "On the Mall." From *The White Album.* Copyright © 1979 by Joan Didon. Reprinted by permission of Simon & Schuster, a Division of Gulf & Western Corporation.

"On Keeping a Notebook" from *Slouching Towards Bethlehem* by Joan Didion. Copyright © 1966, 1968 by Joan Didion. Reprinted by permission of Farrar, Straus and Giroux, Inc.

Annie Dillard, "Mirages," from pages 142–47 of *Teaching a Stone to Talk: Expeditions and Encounters,* by Annie Dillard. Copyright © 1982 by Annie Dillard. By permission of Harper & Row, Publishers, Inc.

ACKNOWLEDGMENTS

W. E. B. DuBois, "Jacob and Esau," from *W. E. B. DuBois Speaks*. Reprinted with permission of Pathfinder Press. © Philip S. Foner and Shirley Graham DuBois.

René Dubos, "Territoriality and Dominance." From "Human Nature: Man and His Environment" in *Britannica Perspectives*, copyright 1968, reprinted by permission of Encyclopaedia Britannica, Inc.

Ralph Ellison, "Hidden Name and Complex Fate." From *Shadow and Act*, by Ralph Ellison. Copyright © 1964 by Ralph Ellison. Reprinted by permission of Random House, Inc.

Nora Ephron, "The Boston Photographs." From *Scribble, Scribble: Notes on the Media*, by Nora Ephron. Copyright © 1978 by Nora Ephron. Reprinted by permission of Alfred A. Knopf, Inc.

M. F. K. Fisher, "Young Hunger." From *As They Were*, by M. F. K. Fisher. Copyright © 1982 by M. F. K. Fisher. Reprinted by permission of Alfred A. Knopf, Inc.

E. M. Forster, "Racial Exercise." Reprinted from his volume *Two Cheers For Democracy*, by permission of Harcourt Brace Jovanovich, Inc.

Sigmund Freud, "The Relation of the Poet to Day-Dreaming." From *Collected Papers*, Vol. IV, by Sigmund Freud, authorized translation under the supervision of Joan Riviere. Published by Basic Books, Inc. by arrangement with The Hogarth Press Ltd. and The Institute of Psycho-Analysis, London. Reprinted by permission of the publisher.

Erich Fromm, "The Nature of Symbolic Language." From *The Forgotten Language* by Erich Fromm. Reprinted by permission of Holt, Rinehart and Winston, Publishers.

Robert Frost, "Education By Poetry." From *Selected Prose of Robert Frost* edited by Hyde Cox and Edward Connery Lathem. Copyright © 1966 by Holt, Rinehart and Winston, Publishers.

Northrup Frye, "The Keys to Dreamland," from *The Educated Imagination*, Indiana University Press, Bloomington. Copyright 1964 by Indiana University Press.

Paul Fussell, "The Boy Scout Handbook." From *The Boy Scout Handbook and Other Observations*, by Paul Fussell. Reprinted by permission of Oxford University Press, Inc.

Martin Gardner, "The Harvard Man Who Put the Ease in Casey's Manner," from *Edge of Awareness, 25 Contemporary Essays*, edited by Ned E. Hoopes and Richard Peck, copyright 1966. Reprinted with permission of the author.

William Golding, "Thinking as a Hobby." Reprinted by permission of Curtis Brown, Ltd. Copyright © 1961 by William Golding. First published in *Holiday Magazine*.

Stephen Jay Gould, "A Biographical Homage to Mickey Mouse." Reprinted from *The Panda's Thumb* by Stephen Jay Gould, by permission of W. W. Norton & Company, Inc. Copyright © 1980 by Stephen Jay Gould.

Graham Greene, "The Revolver in the Corner Cupboard." From *The Lost Childhood and Other Essays*, by Graham Greene. Copyright © 1951 by Graham Greene. Copyright renewed 1979 by Graham Greene. Reprinted by permission of Viking Penguin Inc.

ACKNOWLEDGMENTS

S.I. Hayakawa, "How Dictionaries Are Made." From *Language in Thought and Action*, Fourth Edition by S.I. Hayakawa, copyright © 1978 by Harcourt Brace Jovanovich, Inc. Reprinted by permission of the publisher.

Lillian Hellman, "The Fig Tree," from *An Unfinished Woman*. Copyright © 1969 by Lillian Hellman. By permission of Little, Brown and Company.

Ernest Hemingway, "The Clark's Fork Valley, Wyoming," Copyright © 1939 Ernest Hemingway; Copyright renewed 1967 Mary Hemingway. Reprinted with the permission of Charles Scribner's Sons from *By Line: Ernest Hemingway*. Copyright © 1967 Mary Hemingway.

Edward Hoagland, "The Courage of Turtles," Copyright © 1968 from *The Courage of Turtles*, by Edward Hoagland, by permission of Random House, Inc.

Langston Hughes, "Salvation," from *The Big Sea*, by Langston Hughes. Reprinted by permission of Hill and Wang, a division of Farrar, Strauss and Giroux, Inc. Copyright 1940 by Lanston Hughes. Copyright renewed © 1968 by Arna Bontemps and George Houston Bass.

Aldous Huxley, "Selected Snobberies," (pages 197-202) from *Music at Night and Other Essays*, by Aldous Huxley. Copyright, 1931, 1959, by Aldous Huxley. By permission of Harper & Row, Publishers, Inc.

Ada Louise Huxtable, "Houston," *Kicked a Building Lately?* by Ada Louise Huxtable. © 1976 by The New York Times Company. Reprinted by permission.

William James, "Habit," from the 1890 edition of *The Principles of Psychology*, Vol. 1, Dover Publications, Inc., NY. Published by arrangement with Henry Holt & Co. Dover Publications, Inc.

Elizabeth Janeway, "Water." Copyright 1965 by Elizabeth Janeway. Reprinted with permission of the author. Published by Condé Nast Publications, Inc.

Randall Jarrell, "The Taste of the Age," excerpted from "The Taste of the Age" from *Kipling, Auden & Co.* by Randall Jarrell. Copyright © 1958 by the Curtis Publishing Company. Reprinted by permission of Farrar, Strauss & Giroux.

Sir James Jeans, "Why the Sky Looks Blue," from *The Stars in Their Courses*. Reprinted with the permission of Cambridge University Press.

C. G. Jung, "A Vision of Life After Death." From *Memories, Dreams, Reflections*, by Carl Jung, recorded and edited by Aniela Jaffe, translated by Richard and Clara Winston. Translation copyright © 1961, 1962, 1963 by Random House, Inc. Reprinted by permission of the publisher.

Pauline Kael, "Movies on Television," from *Kiss Kiss Bang Bang*, Copyright © 1967 by Pauline Kael. First appeared in *The New Yorker*. By permission of Little, Brown and Company in association with the Atlantic Monthly Press.

Rudyard Kipling, "A Snake Farm," from *Brazilian Sketches* by Rudyard Kipling. Copyright 1927, by Rudyard Kipling. Reprinted by permission of Doubleday & Company, Inc.

D. H. Lawrence, "Rex," from *Phoenix: The Posthumous Papers of D. H. Lawrence*. Copyright 1936 by Frieda Lawrence, copyright renewed © 1964 by the Estate of the late Frieda Lawrence Revagli. Reprinted with permission of Viking Penguin Inc.

Helen Lawrenson, "The Bulls of Pamplona vs. the Ivy League." Reprinted with permission from *Esquire* (Feb. 1961). Copyright © 1961 by Esquire Publishing Inc.

ACKNOWLEDGMENTS

C.S. Lewis, "The Trouble with 'X'. . ." From *God in the Dock* copyright © 1970 by C. S. Lewis Pte Ltd, reproduced by permission of Curtis Brown Ltd, London.

Wyndham Lewis, "The Secret of the Success of Charlie Chaplin," from *Time and Western Man,* © 1928 Percy Wyndham Lewis and the Estate of the late Mrs. G. A. Wyndham Lewis by permission. The Wyndham Lewis Memorial trust (a registered charity).

Basil Liddell Hart, "William Tecumseh Sherman: The First Modern General," *Sherman: Soldier, Realist, American,* Reprinted by permission of Kathleen Liddell Hart. Published by Dodd, Mead & Co.

Walter Lippman, "The Indispensable Opposition," *The Atlantic Monthly,* Copyright © 1939, ® 1967, by The Atlantic Monthly Company, Boston, Mass. Reprinted with permission of the publisher. Used with the permission of the President and Fellows of Harvard College.

Jack London, "The Carter and the Carpenter," from *People of the Abyss.* Copyright © 1903.

Norman Mailer, "Marilyn Monroe," from the Chapter, "A Novel Biography" from *Marilyn, A Biography.* Reprinted by permission of the author and the author's agents, Scott Meredith Literary Agency, Inc., 845 Third Avenue, New York, New York 10022.

William Manchester, "How I Slew My First Man," from *Goodbye Darkness: A Memoir of the Pacific War,* Copyright © 1979, 1980 by William Manchester. By permission of Little, Brown and Company.

Mary McCarthy, "Catholic Education," From *Memories of a Catholic Girlhood,* © 1957 by Mary McCarthy. Reprinted by permission of Harcourt Brace Jovanovich, Inc.

Marshall McLuhan, "Classroom Without Walls." From *Explorations in Communication* by Edmund Carpenter and Marshall McLuhan. Copyright © 1960 by Beacon Press. Reprinted by permission of Beacon Press.

John McPhee, "The Search for Marvin Gardens," from *Pieces of the Frame* by John McPhee. Copyright © 1972, 1975 by John McPhee. This essay first appeared in *The New Yorker.* Reprinted with permission of Farrar, Strauss & Giroux.

Margaret Mead, "New Superstitions for Old," in *A Way of Seeing,* by Margaret Mead and Rhoda Metraux. Copyright © 1966, 1970 by Margaret Mead and Rhoda Metraux. By permission of William Morrow & Company.

H. L. Mencken, "Criminology," From *Prejudices, Sixth Series,* by H. L. Mencken. Copyright 1927 by Alfred A. Knopf, Inc. and renewed 1955 by H. L. Mencken. Reprinted by permission of the publisher.

Jessica Mitford, "On Embalming." From *The American Way of Death.* Copyright © 1963, 1978 by Jessica Mitford. Reprinted by permission of Simon & Schuster, a Division of Gulf & Western Corporation.

Ashley Montague, "Social Change and Human Change." Reprinted by permission of G. P. Putnam's Sons from *Man Observed* by Ashley Montague.

Samuel Eliot Morison, "History as a Literary Art," from *By Land and By Sea,* copyright 1928, 1929, 1944, 1948, 1951, 1953 by Priscilla B. Morison.

John Muir, "Digging a Well," from *Story of My Boyhood & Youth,* by John Muir. Copyright 1913 by John Muir. Copyright renewed 1940, 1941 by Wanda Muir Hanna. Reprinted by permission of Houghton Mifflin Company.

ACKNOWLEDGMENTS

Lewis Mumford, "Sport and the 'Bitch-Goddess'." From *Technics and Civilization* by Lewis Mumford, copyright 1942 by Harcourt Brace Jovanovich, Inc.; renewed 1962 by Lewis Mumford. Reprinted by permission of the publisher.

Vladimir Nabokov, "Colored Hearing," *Speak, Memory, An Autobiography Revisited* published by G. P. Putnam's Sons. Copyright 1947, 1948, 1949, 1950, 1951, © 1960, 1966 by Vladimir Nabokov. Reprinted by permission of Mrs. Vladimir Nabokov.

V. S. Naipaul, "The New Tehran," *Among the Believers: An Islamic Journey*, by V. S. Naipaul. Reprinted by permission of Alfred A. Knopf, Inc.

José Ortega y Gasset, "Emotional Reality," from *The Dehumanization of Art, Culture, and Literature*, trans. Helen Weyl. Copyright 1948 © 1968 by Princeton University Press. "A Few Drops of Phenomenology," pages 14–19, reprinted by permission of Princeton University Press.

George Orwell, "Shooting an Elephant," "A Hanging." From *Shooting an Elephant and Other Essays* by George Orwell, copyright 1950 by Sonia Brownell Orwell; renewed 1978 by Sonia Pitt-Rivers. Reprinted by permission of Harcourt Brace Jovanovich, Inc. "Politics and the English Language." Copyright 1946 by Sonia Brownell Orwell; renewed 1974 by Sonia Orwell. Reprinted from *Shooting an Elephant and other Essays* by George Orwell by permission of Harcourt Brace Jovanovich, Inc.

Dorothy Parker, "Mrs. Post Enlarges on Etiquette." From *The Portable Dorothy Parker*, Revised and Enlarged Edition, edited by Brendan Gill. Copyright 1927 by *The New Yorker*. Copyright renewed 1955 by *The New Yorker*. Copyright 1970 by The Viking Press, Inc. Reprinted by permission of Viking Penguin Inc.

S. J. Perelman, "Dental or Mental, I Say It's Spinach," *The Most of S. J. Perelman*, Copyright © 1930–1958 by S. J. Perelman. Reprinted by permission of Simon & Schuster, a Division of Gulf & Western Corporation.

J. H. Plumb, "The Stars in Their Day," from *In the Light of History*, by J. H. Plumb. Reprinted by permission of Houghton Mifflin Company.

Katherine Anne Porter, "The Future Is Now," excerpted from the book *The Collected Essays and Occasional Writings of Katherine Anne Porter*. Copyright © 1950 by Katherine Anne Porter. Originally published in *Mademoiselle*. Reprinted by permission of Delacorte Press/Seymour Lawrence.

J. B. Priestly, "Block Thinking," from *Essays of Five Decades*. Reprinted by permission of A D Peters & Co Ltd.

Lillian Ross, "The Vinyl Santa." From *Talk Stories* (Simon & Schuster). Reprinted by permission; © 1962 The New Yorker Magazine, Inc.

Bertrand Russell, "Education and Discipline." From *In Praise of Idleness, and Other Essays*. Reprinted by permission of George Allen & Unwin Ltd. Copyright 1935.

Logan Pearsall Smith, "Words from the Sea." From *English Idioms* pages 16–19, S.P.E. Tract No. XII. Reprinted with permission of Clarendon Press, Oxford University Press.

Susan Sontag, "Science Fiction Films: The Imagination of Disaster," excerpted and retitled from "The Imagination of Disaster," from *Against Interpretation* by Susan Sontag. Copyright © 1965 by Susan Sontag. Reprinted by permission of Farrar, Straus & Giroux.

ACKNOWLEDGMENTS

Gay Talese, "Punks and Pushers." Text of "Punks and Pushers," Chapter IV (pages 47–56) from *The Bridge* by Gay Talese. Copyright © 1964 by Gay Talese. By permission of Harper & Row, Publishers, Inc.

Lewis Thomas, "Notes on Punctuation," *The Medusa and the Snail* by Lewis Thomas. Copyright © 1974, 1975, 1976, 1977, 1978, 1979 by Lewis Thomas. Reprinted by permission of Viking Penguin, Inc.

James Thurber, "University Days." From *My Life and Hard Times*, published by Harper & Row, Publishers, Inc. Copyright © 1933, 1961 James Thurber.

Barbara Tuchman, "This is the End of the World: The Black Death." From *A Distant Mirror: The Calamitous 14th Century*, by Barbara Tuchman. Copyright © 1978 by Barbara Tuchman. Reprinted by permission of Alfred A. Knopf, Inc.

John Updike, "Crush Vs. Whip," Copyright © 1958 by John Updike. Reprinted from *Assorted Prose*, by John Updike, by permission of Alfred A. Knopf, Inc. Originally appeared in *The New Yorker*.

Evelyn Waugh, "Half in Love with Easeful Death," from *A Little Order*, Copyright © 1977 by the Executors of Mrs. Laura Letitia Gwendolyn Evelyn Waugh.

Eudora Welty, "A Sweet Devouring." Copyright 1957 by Eudora Welty. Reprinted from *The Eye of the Story: Selected Essays and Reviews*, by Eudora Welty, by permission of Random House.

Paul West, "The VAB Beside the Sea." Reprinted with permission of Paul West.

Edith Wharton, "Henry James Asks Directions," From *A Backward Glance*. Copyright 1933, 1934 William R. Tyler; copyright renewed 1961, 1962. Reprinted with the permission of Charles Scribner's Sons.

E. B. White, "Death of a Pig," from pages 17–24 of *Essays of E. B. White*. Essay copyright © 1947 by E. B. White. By permission of Harper & Row, Publishers, Inc. "The Essayist," from pages vii–viii of the Foreword to *Essays of E. B. White*. Copyright 1977 by E. B. White. By permission of Harper & Row, Publishers, Inc.

Edmund Wilson, "The Problem of English," from *A Piece of My Mind* by Edmund Wilson. © 1956 by Edmund Wilson. Reprinted with permission of Farrar, Strauss & Giroux.

Tom Wolfe, "The Right Stuff," excerpted and retitled from "Yeager," from *The Right Stuff* by Tom Wolfe. Copyright © 1979 by Tom Wolfe. Reprinted with permission of Farrar, Strauss & Giroux.

Virginia Woolf, "The Death of the Moth." From *The Death of the Moth and Other Essays*, by Virginia Woolf, copyright 1942 by Harcourt Brace Jovanovich, Inc.; renewed 1970 by Marjorie T. Parsons, Executrix. Reprinted by permission of the publisher.

Richard Wright, "Innocence." Excerpt from pages 9–13 of *Black Boy: A Record of Childhood and Youth* by Richard Wright. Copyright, 1937, 1942, 1944, 1945, by Richard Wright. By permission of Harper & Row, Publishers, Inc.